# Understanding Program Design and Data Structures with C++

# Understanding Program Design and Data Structures with C++

Kenneth A. Lambert
WASHINGTON & LEE UNIVERSITY

Thomas L. Naps
LAWRENCE UNIVERSITY

WEST PUBLISHING COMPANY
Minneapolis/St. Paul   New York   Los Angeles   San Francisco

*To Mom, Dad and Lindsay*

*To Joey*

*Copyeditor:* Lorretta Palagi
*Interior design:* Johnston Design Office
*Composition:* Carlisle Communications
*Cover image:* Pamela J. Vermeer

## WEST'S COMMITMENT TO THE ENVIRONMENT

In 1906, West Publishing Company began recycling materials left over from the production of books. This began a tradition of efficient and responsible use of resources. Today, 100% of our legal bound volumes are printed on acid-free, recycled paper consisting of 50% new paper pulp and 50% paper that has undergone a de-inking process. We also use vegetable-based inks to print all of our books. West recycles nearly 27,700,000 pounds of scrap paper annually—the equivalent of 229,300 trees. Since the 1960s, West has devised ways to capture and recycle waste inks, solvents, oils, and vapors created in the printing process. We also recycle plastics of all kinds, wood, glass, corrugated cardboard, and batteries, and have eliminated the use of polystyrene book packaging. We at West are proud of the longevity and the scope of our commitment to the environment.

West pocket parts and advance sheets are printed on recyclable paper and can be collected and recycled with newspapers. Staples do not have to be removed. Bound volumes can be recycled after removing the covers.

Production, Prepress, Printing and Binding by West Publishing Company.

 TEXT IS PRINTED ON 10% POST CONSUMER RECYCLED PAPER

 **Printed with Printwise**
Environmentally Advanced Water Washable Ink

British Library Cataloguing-in-Publication Data. A catalogue record for this book is available from the British Library.

COPYRIGHT © 1996       By WEST PUBLISHING COMPANY
                       610 Opperman Drive
                       P.O. Box 64526
                       St. Paul, MN 55164–0526

Printed in the United States of America
03 02 01 00 99 98 97 96     8 7 6 5 4 3 2 1 0

Library of Congress Cataloging-in-Publication Data

Lambert, Kenneth (Kenneth A.)
    Understanding Program Design and Data Structures with C++ / Kenneth A.
        Lambert,
    Thomas L. Naps.
        p.   cm.
    Includes bibliographical references and index.
    ISBN 0–314–07340–X (pbk. : alk. paper)
    1. (Object-oriented programming Computer science).   2. C++
    (Computer program language)   I.  Naps, Thomas L.   II.  Title.
QA76.L35     1996
005.13'3—dc20                                    95–45571
                                                     CIP

# Table of Contents

## CHAPTER 4◆    Linked Lists and Pointers                                   153

## Appendixes   ◆

◆    ## Glossary

◆    ## Answers to Selected Exercises

◆    ## Index

# Preface

In the Computing Curricula 1991 report, the Association for Computing Machinery (ACM-IEEE-CS) Joint Curriculum Task Force emphasizes the recurring themes of abstraction, theory, and design in all areas of computer science. A student's first two courses in computer science are pivotal in emphasizing these themes. In the first course, students are introduced to top-down design, structured programming techniques, procedural and data abstraction, and a high level programming language as a vehicle for solving problems. Where the programming language has object-oriented features, such as C++, students can also receive exposure to the ways in which object-oriented methods can support effective design and abstraction. In the second course, students can then encounter more rigorous strategies for developing large, effective programs that solve problems frequently encountered by computer scientists.

*Understanding Program Design and Data Structures with* C++ begins with the assumption that the reader has a working knowledge of problem solving with C++. This should include familiarity with control structures, functions (used nonrecursively), parameter passing, strings, files, arrays, and the definition and use of classes. We refer uninitiated readers to *Understanding Programming and Problem Solving with* C++ by Kenneth A. Lambert and Douglas W. Nance. From this starting point the current text is organized around several objectives:

1. To demonstrate the application of software engineering principles in design, coding, and testing of large programs.
2. To introduce students to the essential data structures such as linked lists, stacks, queues, trees, and (to a lesser extent) graphs. This introduction emphasizes the specification of each structure as an abstract data type before discussing implementations and applications of that structure.
3. To make students aware of the importance of object-oriented methods in developing software, particularly in the design and implementation of abstract data types.
4. To provide a systematic approach to the study of algorithms, an approach that focuses first on understanding the action of the algorithm and then on analyzing the algorithm from a space/time perspective. In particular, searching, sorting, and recursive algorithms are covered in detail.
5. To give students an overview of what lies ahead in computer science.

## Overview and Organization

Throughout the text, we have attempted to explain and develop concepts carefully. These are illustrated by frequent examples and diagrams. New concepts are then used in complete programs to show how they aid in solving problems. We place an early and consistent emphasis on good writing habits and neat, readable documentation. We frequently offer communication and style tips where appropriate. The prologue of the text explicitly states and briefly reviews the C++ prerequisites assumed in the rest of the text. The prologue should be skimmed before starting Chapter 1. Students should feel confident of their ability to work with all of the C++ topics discussed in the prologue before proceeding in the text.

Chapters 1 through 3 collectively present a detailed treatment of the software engineering principles. Chapter 1 introduces big-O analysis as the essential tool used by the computer scientist in evaluating alternative strategies from a time/space perspective. Simple sorting and searching algorithms are used as examples for the application of big-O analysis.

Chapter 2 is a critical chapter in that it introduces the formalism used to present abstract data types used throughout the text. This formalism consists of specifying the ADT's attributes and operations as a set of language-independent preconditions and postconditions before moving to a C++ class declaration as an interface for the ADT. Rules for using and implementing ADTs are developed. One-key tables and two-key tables are presented as examples of ADTs. Because these ADTs lend themselves naturally to the use of keys and elements of different data types, the notions of generic ADTs and parameterized types can be introduced in this chapter and can be implemented with C++ class templates. Because students have studied big-O analysis in the preceding chapter, they are well equipped to compare and contrast the efficiencies of various implementations of these ADTs. These two ADTs and the use of class templates recur in the remainder of the text as we explore more advance techniques for implementing other ADTs.

Chapter 3 pulls together and expands on the software engineering issues that have been introduced in earlier chapters. The first three sections present a detailed treatment of the analysis, design, implementation, testing, maintenance, and obsolescence stages of the software system life cycle. The last two sections of the chapter discuss two topics of rising prominence, formal verification and object-oriented software engineering.

Chapters 4 through 7 cover the use of essential data structures and recursion in advanced problem solving techniques. Each data structure is first defined as an abstract data type and then declared as a C++ class. Various implementations are discussed and compared using the big-O terminology of Chapter 1. This provides a convincing demonstration of the utility of big-O analysis. Chapter 4, devoted to dynamic memory management, pointers, and linked lists, discusses how linked lists might be used as an alternative implementation of the ADTs that were introduced in Chapter 2. Chapter 5 covers stacks and queues, discussing parsing and simulation as applications of these ADTs. Chapter 6 explores recursion in depth. A graduated series of examples is presented, culminating with the use of trial-and-error backtracking as a problem-solving technique. Chapter 7 provides examples of the utility of recursion by using it as the primary technique for processing data in binary trees, general trees, and graphs. The importance of binary search trees as an alternative way of representing keyed tables is also discussed, with comparisons drawn to the array and linked list implementations previously covered in Chapters 2 and 4. The material on general trees, graphs, and networks in the final two sections of Chapter 7 can be omitted without affecting a student's understanding of the chapters that follow.

The background in software engineering and data structures found in Chapters 1 through 7 prepares the student for the more complex sorting and searching algorithms of Chapters 8 and 9. In Chapter 8, sorting methods that break the $O(n^2)$ barrier are investigated. These methods include the shell sort, quick sort, heap sort, and merge sort. Chapter 9 scrutinizes search techniques such as hashing, indexing, indexed sequential search, B-trees, and tries.

We have made a large effort to acknowledge the increasing importance of object-oriented methods in the computer science community. However, object-oriented methods must be seen in the larger context of the concern with abstraction, design, and theory that makes up computer science. In this text, objects are used where relevant in developing designs and abstractions that solve interesting problems.

## ◆ Features

This text has a number of noteworthy pedagogical features.

- *Chapter outlines:* Lists of the important topics covered are given at the beginning of each chapter.
- *Objectives:* Each section starts with a concise list of topics and learning objectives in each section.
- *Exercises:* Short-answer questions appear at the end of each section that are intended to build analytical skills.
- *Programming problems and projects:* Lengthy lists of suggestions for complete programs and projects are given at the end of each chapter. These cover different problem areas in computer science, such as data processing and mathematics. Some problems and projects run from chapter to chapter, providing students with a sense of problem solving as a cumulative enterprise that often requires programming in the large. Several assignments focus explicitly on improving students' communication skills in refining designs and writing documentation.
- *Module specifications:* Specifications are given for many program modules.
- *Structure charts:* We provide charts that reflect modular development and include the use of data flow arrows to emphasize transmission of data to and/or from each module. These charts set the stage for understanding the use of value and reference parameters when functions are introduced.
- *Notes of interest:* These are tidbits of information intended to create awareness of and interest in various aspects of computer science, including its historical context. Special attention is paid to issues of computer ethics and security.
- *Suggestions for test programs:* Ideas included in the exercises are intended to encourage students to use the computer to determine answers to questions and to see how to implement concepts in short programs.
- *Focus on program design:* A complete program is listed at the end of the chapter that illustrates utilization of the concepts developed within the chapter. This section includes the complete development of a project, from user requirements to specifications to pseudocode design to implementation and testing.
- In addition to use of *graphic documentation* to help students visualize algorithms, *run-time trace diagrams* are introduced as a means of analyzing recursive algorithms.
- *Running, testing, and debugging hints:* These hints will be useful to students as they work on the programming problems at the end of each chapter.

- *Tables in chapter-end summaries.* These are frequently used to compare and evaluate various C++ features, data structures, and algorithms. Such compact, side-by-side comparisons emphasize the importance of knowing the relative advantages and disadvantages of the various techniques studied.
- *Reading references:* When appropriate, pointers are given to excellent sources for further reading on topics introduced in the text.
- New terms are italicized when introduced.

In the back of the book there is a complete glossary, as well as appendixes on reserved words, useful library functions, syntax diagrams, character sets and a random number generator. The final section of the book provides answers to selected exercises.

This book covers only that portion of C++ necessary for the first two courses in computer science. Students wanting to learn more about the language are referred to the excellent sources given in Appendix 1.

## ◆ Ancillaries

It is our belief that a broad-based teaching support package is essential for an introductory course using C++. Thus, the following ancillary materials are available from West Publishing Company:

1. Laboratory manual: In keeping with our intent to provide a modern approach and to meet the growing need for laboratory experience as put forth by the new ACM curriculum guidelines, there is a laboratory manual closely tied to the text's pedagogy. The manual provides two kinds of exercises. Each lab experience begins with a few exercises relating to a small set of new concepts, such as the use of reference parameters with functions. The lab experience then uses these new concepts to extend several cumulative, semester-long programming projects. Students thus use the lab experience to build their competence incrementally, and to get a sense of how various concepts play a role in programming in the large. The example programs in the lab experiences are written in platform-independent C++.

2. Program disk: To give students direct access to programs from the text, a disk containing most of these programs is bundled with the book. The disk is in DOS format, but the programs are written in platform-independent C++, which can be run immediately on most implementations.

3. Instructor's manual: This manual contains the following for each chapter:
   a. Outline
   b. Teaching Suggestions
   c. Teaching Test Questions
   d. List of Programs
   e. File of Key Source Code
   f. Transparency Master Listing
   g. Two Complete, Well Documented, Programming Problems
   h. Answers to End-of-Section Exercises
   i. Chapter Test Questions with Difficulty Rating
   j. Answers to Test Questions

4. Transparency masters: More than 75 transparency masters are available to adopters of the text. The set of masters includes figures, tables, and selected other material from the text.

**5.** Computerized test bank: Adopters of this edition will receive a computerized test-generation system. This provides a test bank system that allows adopters to edit, add, or delete test questions.

Each program segment in the text and in the lab manual has been compiled and run. Hence, original versions were all working. Unfortunately, the publication process does allow errors in code to occur after a program has been run. Every effort has been made to produce an error-free text, although this cannot be guaranteed with certainty. We assume full responsibility for all errors and omissions. If you detect any, please be tolerant and notify us or West Publishing Company so they can be corrected in subsequent printings and editions.

This text has been designed to mesh with the text by Kenneth A. Lambert and Douglas W. Nance mentioned earlier. This meshing of texts also allows the current text to be used in a class in which other students may be studying from the second half of *Introduction to Computer Science with* C++. The options afforded by the integration of these three texts allow two possible routes for students in a CS1/CS2 sequence. Those students who are initially uncertain about wanting to take CS2 and are using CS1 as an exploratory course for a possible major can use two separate texts for the two courses. Those students who are certain of pursuing a computer science major when enrolling in CS1 can use one text for the entire CS1/CS2 sequence, thereby holding down their book costs. Contact your West representative for details and examination copies of all of these texts.

## ◆ Acknowledgments

We would like to take this opportunity to thank those who in some way contributed to the completion of this text. Several reviewers contributed significant constructive comments during various phases of manuscript development. They include:

Vicki H. Allan
Utah State University

Clark B. Archer
Winthrop University

Kulbir S. Arora
SUNY–Buffalo

Bonnie Bailey
Morehead State University

David E. Boddy
Oakland University

Jeff Buckwalter
University of San Francisco

Debra Calliss
Arizona State University

Ernest Carey
Utah Valley State College

Tom Cheatham
Middle Tennessee State University

Henjin Chi
Indiana State University

John S. Conery
University of Oregon

Behrouz Forouzan
De Anza College

Roy Fuller
University of Arkansas

Peter J. Gingo
University of Akron

Jeff Guan
University of Louisville

R. James Guild
Cal Lutheran University

Jimmie R. Hattemer
Southern Illinois University

Jack Hodges
San Francisco State University

J. Andrew Holey
St. John's University

Mike Holland
North Virginia Community College

Randall L. Hyde
UC–Riverside

Peter Isaacson
University of Northern Colorado

Michael P. Johnson
Oregon State University

Gwen Kaye
University of Maryland—College Park

Joanne Koehler
University of North Carolina–Greensboro

Stephen P. Leach
Florida State University

Mary Lynch
University of Florida

Jerry Marsh
Oakland University

Eugene M. Norris
George Mason University

Mark Parker
Shoreline Community College

Jandelyn Plane
University of Maryland–College Park

Neelima Shrikhande
Central Michigan University

Michael Stinson
Central Michigan University

David Teague
Western Carolina University

Martha J. Tilmann
College of San Mateo

Ron Wallace
Blue Mountain Community College

Richard G. Weinand
Wayne State University

Pam Vermeer and Tom Whaley of Washington and Lee University offered many helpful suggestions on making the minefield of C++ safer for first-year students.

Six other people deserve special mention because, without their expertise, this book would not exist:

Lorretta Palagi, copyeditor. Lorretta has a wonderful sense of where to apply Occam's razor to a sentence or paragraph, and made many useful suggestions for improving not only style, but content as well.

Peter Krall, production editor. Peter has done a great job of coordinating work on several texts simultaneously. He keeps things running smoothly, and it is a pleasure working with him.

Ellen Stanton, promotion manager. Ellen worked hard to highlight the features of the text that will make it known to the computer science community, and has done a fine job.

Betsy Friedman, developmental editor. Betsy lined up great reviewers and provided them with all of the relevant questions. She then digested the reviews into analyses that focused our attention immediately on the improvements that needed to be made at each phase of the development process.

Halee Dinsey, developmental editor. Halee assisted in putting together several of the ancillary materials.

Jerry Westby, executive editor. Jerry initiated our collaboration on this project. His insight into what makes a book useful is uncanny. We are grateful for his high standards, and for pushing us to make needed changes one more time during the revision process. It is a privilege to work with an editor who is right at the top of his field.

Kenneth A. Lambert                                             November, 1995

# Prologue: A Review of C++ Essentials

This is *not* an introductory programming text. Rather, it assumes that you have acquired basic programming skills and now want to use these skills to explore more advanced problems in computer science.

The purpose of this prologue is to review those C++ tools that are prerequisite to the chapters that follow. The tools you will need to be able to use follow:

- Main program and library files
- Program comments
- Reserved words and identifiers
- Simple data types
- Literals
- Variables
- Symbolic constants
- Expressions and assignment
- Type conversion
- Interactive input and output
- Functions (not including recursion)
- Value and reference parameters
- Selection
- Iteration
- `typedef`
- Enumerated data types
- Structured data types (strings, arrays, structs, and files, but not pointers)

If you are confident in your ability to use these tools, feel free to skim the rest of the prologue and begin Chapter 1 in earnest. If you feel you need a quick review of these C++ topics, read the prologue thoroughly. If you are not familiar with some of the topics, read the prologue in conjunction with a more detailed introductory text on C++ programming, such as *Understanding Programming and Problem Solving with C++* by Kenneth A. Lambert and Douglas W. Nance (St. Paul, MN: West Publishing, 1996).

## Main Program and Library Files

A C++ program typically consists of one or more modules. The top-level or main program module appears in a main program file. Other modules, which may consist of data and function definitions, appear in library files. Some library files are standard and come with any C++ implementation, whereas others must be constructed by the programmer.

The form of a typical main program module is

```
<preprocessor directives>
<global data and function declarations>
int main()
{
        <local data declarations>
        <statements>
        return 0;
}
<main program function implementations>
```

All of the items in angle brackets are optional, but are usually present in most C++ programs. Data and function declarations and function implementations are discussed in the following sections. Preprocessor directives are used at compile time to make the contents of library files available to the main program module or to other modules. The use of the most important of these, **#include**, is shown in the following example:

```
#include <iostream.h>
#include <math.h>
#include "mylib.h"
```

The angle brackets should be used to specify the name of a standard library file, and double quotes should enclose the name of a programmer-defined library file.

The main program function begins with the word **int** and ends with the **}** symbol. The area of code within the **{** and **}** symbols is referred to as the *main program block*. The last statement in a main program block should be **return 0;**.

Each of the other modules in a C++ program is specified as a library consisting of two files: a header file (having an **.h** extension) and an implementation file (having a **.cpp** extension). The header file contains data definitions and function declarations that are to be made available to modules wishing to use this code. The form of a typical header file is

```
#ifndef <header name>
<preprocessor directives>
<data and function declarations>
#define <header name>
#endif
```

The preprocessor directives **#ifndef**, **#define**, and **#endif** are used to prevent multiple inclusions of the library file in one application. At compile time, if this library file has already been included by another module, the **<header name>** (which can be any C++ identifier) will be visible and control will branch to the end of this file. Otherwise, the contents of the library file will be included and the **<header name>** will be made visible.

The implementation file contains function implementations. The form of a typical implementation file is

```
<preprocessor directives>
<function implementations>
```

One of the preprocessor directives should include the header file of this library.

## Program Comments

C++ programmers usually document their code with end-of-line comments. The form of such a comment is

//<text of comment>

The compiler ignores the text of the comment until the end of the current line.

Multiline comments are used primarily for debugging. For example, when you want the compiler to ignore a troublesome chunk of code, you can mark it off as follows:

```
/*
<troublesome chunk of code>
*/
```

## Reserved Words and Identifiers

A table of reserved words in C++ appears in Appendix 1. C++ is case sensitive. All reserved words must be spelled in lowercase. Identifiers must begin with a letter or an underscore. This initial character is followed by zero or more letters, digits, or underscores. Remember that the compiler will treat **IF** as an identifier, not a reserved word, and that **number** and **Number** are two different identifiers.

This text adopts a convention of using uppercase letters for constant identifiers, lowercase letters for all other identifiers, and underscores where needed to suggest multiword identifiers.

## Simple Data Types

The simple data types used in this text are **int**, **float**, and **char**. **int** represents integer values, **float** represents real numbers, and **char** represents the ASCII character set. Occasionally, we use **double** to represent real numbers having greater precision than **float**, and prefix **int** with **long** or **unsigned** to represent large or nonnegative integers, respectively. Boolean values in most C++ implementations consist of two integers: 0, meaning false, and a nonzero value, usually 1, meaning true.

## Literals

The values of simple data types are represented in program code as literals. An integer in decimal format is represented as a sequence of one or more digits. A real number is represented either in fixed-point format or in floating-point format. A printing character in the ASCII range from " to '~' is represented by enclosing the character in single quotes. Some other characters are represented by an escape sequence, as in the following table:

| Literal | Name |
|---------|------|
| \n | New line |
| \t | Tab |
| \" | Double quote |
| \\ | Backslash |
| \0 | Null |

String literals are represented by enclosing zero or more characters, including escaped characters, in double quotes.

## Variables

Variables can be declared with or without default initial values. The form for declaring variables without default values is

<data type> <list of identifiers>;

where **<data type>** is any C++ data type and **<list of identifiers>** is one or more identifiers separated by commas. The form for initializing a variable of a simple data type to a default value within a declaration is

<data type> <identifier> = <initial value>;

where **<initial value>** is the value of any expression. Note that the second form permits only one variable per declaration.

In general, a variable can be declared anywhere it is needed in a program. The scope of a variable is either global, if it is declared in a library file or above the main program block, or is restricted to the block within which it is declared.

## Symbolic Constants

A symbolic constant definition looks just like a variable declaration that specifies a default value, except that the definition begins with the word **const**. For example, the following lines of code define $\pi$ to two decimal places, an upper bound for integer input, and a symbol for the blank space character:

```
const float PI = 3.14;
const int UPPER_BOUND = 100;
const char BLANK = ' ';
```

## Expressions and Assignment

Standard operators are provided to construct expressions that perform arithmetic, comparisons, logic, and assignment. The following table lists the most important of these operators:

| Operator | Meaning |
|----------|---------|
| + | Addition (binary or unary) |
| – | Subtraction or negation |
| * | Multiplication |
| / | Division |
| % | Modulus |
| = | Is equal to |
| < | Is less than |
| > | Is greater than |
| <= | Is less than or equal to |
| >= | Is greater than or equal to |
| != | Is not equal to |
| && | Logical and |
| \|\| | Logical or |
| ! | Logical not |
| ( ) | Parentheses |
| = | Assignment |

The precedence of the operators governs the order in which they are executed within a compound expression. The following list shows the operators in decreasing order of precedence:

```
( )
!
*, /, %
+, -
<, <=, >, >=, ==, !=
&&
||
=
```

Most of these operators are left associative, meaning that operators of the same precedence are executed from left to right. The programmer can use parentheses to force earlier execution of operators of lower precedence in an expression. For example, the expression `2 + 3 * 5` evaluates to 17, and the expression `(2 + 3) * 5` evaluates to 25.

The `/` operator is overloaded for integers and real numbers. Thus, when both operands of `/` are integers, the value returned is the integer quotient. Otherwise, the value returned is a real number. The `%` operator should be used only with integers. All of the other operators in the preceding table can be used in mixed-mode operations with any combination of **int**, **float**, and **char** data values (see the discussion of type conversion below).

Compound expressions that produce Boolean values are executed by using short-circuit evaluation. An expression containing `||` (logical or) returns nonzero (true) if the first operand returns nonzero; otherwise, the second operand is evaluated and its value is returned. An expression containing `&&` (logical and) returns zero (false) if the first operand returns zero; otherwise, the second operand is evaluated and its value is returned. Thus, assuming that `b = 0`, the following example would return zero after evaluating just the first operand:

```
(b != 0) && (a / b)
```

An assignment expression has the side effect of storing a value in a variable, called the *target* of the assignment. The value returned by an assignment expression depends on the context. When the assignment expression is being used to compute a value, the value returned is the value stored during the assignment operation. This is sometimes called an *r-value*, to indicate that it can be used on the right side of another assignment expression. In this case, for example, the assignment expression `c = 5` would have the effect of storing the value 5 in the variable `c` and returning the value **5**. The assignment operator is right associative. This means that cascaded assignment expressions are evaluated from right to left. Assuming that `a`, `b`, and `c` are integer variables, the following expression would first store the value 5 in `c`, then store it in `b`, and finally store it in `a`:

```
a = b = c = 5
```

When the assignment operation is being used as the target of another assignment, the value returned is the address or memory location of the variable into which a value can be stored. This is sometimes called an *l-value*. The following cascaded assignment expression uses parentheses to override the right associativity of the assignment operators in the previous example, with very different effects:

```
((a = b) = c) = 5
```

In this example, the innermost enclosed assignment expression is evaluated first, storing the value of **b** in **a**. This expression returns the address of **a** as the target of the next assignment expression, which stores the value of **c** in **a**. This expression also returns the address of **a** as the target of the outermost parenthesized assignment expression, which stores the value **5** in **a**. Thus, **b** and **c** are not modified at all in this expression.

The fact that assignment expressions return values can cause subtle errors in C++ programs. Assuming that variable **a** contains the value **3**, the following two expressions both return zero, but have very different consequences for a program:

```
a == 0
a = 0
```

The first expression just compares the values of **a** and zero and returns zero. The second expression also has the side effect of resetting **a** to zero.

Most assignment expressions occur in assignment statements, which are formed by ending the expression with a semicolon. Thus, the statement

```
a = 5;
```

has the side effect of storing **5** in variable **a**, and the computer discards the value returned.

## Type Conversion

The computer performs implicit type conversion during mixed-mode operations. For example, any arithmetic or comparison operation on a **float** and an **int** first converts the **int** to a **float** before execution. During assignment, if the left operand is a **float** and the right operand is an **int**, the **int** is converted to a **float**. If the target is an **int** and the right operand is a **float**, then the **float** is truncated to an **int**.

The programmer can perform an explicit type conversion by using either of the following two forms:

```
<type name> (<expression>)
```

```
(<type name>) <expression>
```

Thus, **int(3.14)** would return the value 3, and **(float) 3** would return the value 3.0.

## Interactive Input and Output

Input and output for interactive users can be performed by using the standard input and output streams. The standard output stream, **cout**, is by default connected to the terminal screen. The standard output operator or inserter, **<<**, can be used to send data of numeric, character, or string types to the stream. For example, the following output statement would display the message **"Hi, I'm 6 years old."** followed by a carriage return on the screen:

```
cout << "Hi, I'm " << 6 << " years old" << '.' << endl;
```

The new line character is sent by specifying the **endl** manipulator or by specifying the new line character **'/n'**. Each data value is implicitly converted to characters before being sent to the stream.

The standard input stream, **cin**, is connected to the keyboard. The standard input operator or extractor, **>>**, can be used to receive data from the stream. For example, the following statements would prompt the user for an integer, a real number, and a string and input these values into the corresponding variables:

```
cout << "Enter an int, a float, and a string, "
     << "separated by spaces: ";
cin >> int_value >> float_value >> string_value;
```

Whitespace characters (space, tab, or new line) are used to separate data values during input. All whitespace characters are skipped during input. In the above example, digits are taken from the stream and converted to an integer value that is stored in the integer variable. The same process takes place for the real number and the string value, though these data types increase the range of characters accepted. Integer values input into float variables are implicitly converted to real numbers. Nondigit characters typed during input into an integer variable terminate the input operation for that variable. Thus, if the input characters typed at the keyboard in our example are **675.35 dollars**, three values are actually stored and the entire statement completes execution. The integer value will be **675**, the real number will be **.35**, and the string will be **"dollars"**.

## Functions (Not Including Recursion)

Standard library functions are made available by including the desired library header file. A function interface is specified by a function declaration. A declaration consists of the return type of the function, the function's name, and a parenthesized list of zero or more formal parameter declarations. A semicolon must terminate a function declaration. For example, the declaration of the **math** library function **pow** follows:

```
double pow(double base, double exponent);
```

A function can be called either as a complete statement or within an expression. For example, the **pow** function could be used to compute a value for output or to throw away the result:

```
cout << pow(2, 5) << endl;      // Output the result.

pow(2, 5);                                // Throw the result away.
```

Function declarations of programmer-defined functions should appear either in a library header file or directly before the main program heading in the main program file. They may be listed in any order that is convenient.

For each function declaration, a function implementation should exist. It should appear either in a library implementation file or below the main program block. A function implementation consists of a function heading and a block of code enclosed in curly braces. The function heading should be an exact copy of the function declaration, with the trailing semicolon omitted. The block of code can contain data declarations and statements. Functions that return a value should do this by executing a **return** statement at the logical end of the function. For example, the following code might implement a function that returns the square of its argument.:

```
double square(double x)
{
    return x * x;
}
```

Functions that return no value but are executed for their side effects are called **void** functions. The following function displays **"Hello world!"** on the screen:

```
void hello_world()
{
    cout << "Hello world!" << endl;
}
```

Note that this function also declares no parameters. This is the kind of function normally called as a stand-alone statement:

```
hello_world();
```

The parentheses must be included in the call, even though no arguments are expected.

## Value and Reference Parameters

C++ supports two primary parameter passing modes, *pass by value* and *pass by reference*. Pass by value is safe, in that the function works on a local copy of the actual parameter. Pass by reference allows side effects, in that the address of the actual parameter is referenced within the function. For example, the following function declaration is intended to specify an operation that computes the roots of a quadratic equation:

```
void compute_roots(float a, float b, float c,
    float &root1, float &root2);
```

The first three formal parameters are declared as value parameters to specify the input arguments to the function. The last two parameters are declared as reference parameters (using the ampersand) to specify the return values of the function.

In general, the scope of the formal parameters and locally declared data names is the body of the function.

## Selection

C++ has three kinds of selection statements. The **if** statement supports one-way decisions. For example, the following code increments a counter if a number is odd:

```
if (odd(x))
    odd_count = odd_count + 1;
```

The parentheses enclosing the Boolean expression are required.

The `if . . . else` statement supports two-way or multiway decisions. For example, the following code divides one number by another or outputs an error message if the second number is zero:

```
if (second != 0)
    cout << first / second << endl;
else
{
    cout << "ERROR: the program cannot divide" << first << " by ";
    cout << second << endl;
}
```

Note the use of a compound statement in the `else` clause. In general, simple statements in C++ end with a semicolon and compound statements end with a curly brace.

The `switch` statement supports multiway decisions involving comparisons of the value of a selector expression to a series of constants. For example, the following code represents a command interpreter for a simple text editor.

```
switch (command)
{
    case 'E':
    case 'e': edit();
            break;
    case 'P';
    case 'p': print();
            break;
    case 'Q':
    case 'q': quit();
            break;
    default: cout << "ERROR: commands are e, p, or q." << endl;
}
```

The parentheses enclosing the selector expression (the variable command) are required. The `break` statement must be included in each case if the programmer wishes control to branch to the end of the switch statement. Otherwise, the next case is always evaluated. The `default` clause is optional but highly recommended.

## Iteration

C++ has three kinds of loop structures. The `for` loop is normally used to count from one limit to another, either up or down. The following two loops output the numbers between 1 and 5, first in ascending order and then in descending order:

```
for (int i = 1; i <= 5; ++1)
    cout << i << endl

for (int j = 5; j >= 1; --j)
    cout << j << endl;
```

The form of a `for` loop heading is

```
for (<initialization>; <termination>; <update>)
```

The termination condition is tested at loop entry, and causes the loop to exit if it returns zero (false). Otherwise, the body of the loop executes and the update is run before the termination condition is reexamined. Note that the updates for the two loops use the increment and the decrement operators, respectively.

The `while` loop is normally used as an entry-controlled loop with sentinel values or Boolean flags. For example, the following code adds numbers entered by the user until the value –999 is entered:

```
cout << "Enter a number: ";
cin >> number;
while (number != -999)
{
    sum = sum + number;
    cout << "Enter a number: ";
    cin >> number;
}
```

The parentheses enclosing the Boolean expression are required.

The `do . . . while` loop can be used instead of a `while` loop when it is known that a process must be performed at least once. For example, the following code takes input data until it falls within a range of values specified by a lower bound and an upper bound:

```
do
{
    cout << "Enter a value: ";
    cin >> value;
} while ((value < lower_bound) || (value > upper_bound));
```

The parentheses enclosing the Boolean expression are required.

## Typedef

Sometimes it is convenient to create a name for a data type and use it to declare variables, function parameters, and so forth. For example, one might create a type name, `boolean`, to represent Boolean values, as follows:

```
const int TRUE = 1;
const int FALSE = 0;

typedef int boolean;
```

Then one can use these names to define a Boolean function that tests data for validity, as follows:

```
boolean is_valid(int data, int lower_bound, int upper_bound)
{
    if ((data >= lower_bound) && (data <= upper_bound))
        return TRUE;
    else
        return FALSE;
}
```

# Enumerated Types

Occasionally a programmer needs to use mnemonic symbols to represent data values such as the days of the week or the primary colors. Rather than use strings, which require memory space that is a linear function of the number of characters needed in a symbol, the programmer can use enumerated values. An enumerated type in C++ specifies a set of symbolic constants that map to integers at run time. For example, the following code declares types and variables to represent the weekdays and the primary colors:

```
enum weekday {MON, TUE, WED, THUR, FRI};
enum primary_color {RED, YELLOW, BLUE};

weekday day = MON;
primary_color color = RED;
```

Enumerated values of the same type can be compared and assigned. Any enumerated value can be cast to its underlying integer representation, and integers within the range of an enumerated type can be cast to the corresponding enumerated value. Thus, the code

```
cout << int(MON) << endl;
```

would display the value **0** on the screen, and the code

```
color = primary_color(2);
```

would assign the enumerated value **BLUE** to the variable **color**. C++ does not implicitly convert between integers and enumerated values.

# Structured Data Types (Arrays, Strings, Structs, and Files But Not Pointers)

An array variable is declared in C++ by specifying the base type, the name of the variable, and the physical size of the array. For example, the following code declares an array of characters and an array of integers, both capable of storing 10 data values:

```
char char_array[10];
int int_array[10];
```

Alternatively, one could create a name for an array type with a **typedef** and then use the type name to declare a variable. Thus, two arrays of integers could be declared as

```
typedef int int_array_type[10];
int_array_type array1, array2;
```

Arrays can have any base type, including other arrays. The maximum physical size of an array is system dependent.

C++ arrays reflect the underlying memory model in three ways:

1. Array index positions are numbered from 0 to $N-1$, where $N$ is the physical size of the array specified in its declaration. This implies that **a[0]** is the first possible data value in the array **a** and **a[n - 1]** is the last possible value.
2. A reference to an array variable without a subscript is a reference to the base address of the entire array. Thus, assignment of one array variable to another may result in assigning the base address of the source array to the target, resulting in an alias rather than a copy of the original array.

**3.** Arrays are always passed by reference as parameters to C++ functions. Thus, a formal array parameter declaration does not need and should not use the ampersand as a specifier of a reference parameter.

Care should be taken in three areas when programming with arrays in C++. First, there is no range bound error checking, either at compile time or at run time. Loops that process entire arrays should be checked by hand carefully. A **for** loop should usually have the form

```
for (int i = 0; i < MAX; ++ i)
    process(a[i]);
```

where **MAX** represents either the last physical location in the array or the location of the last element currently used by the program in the array. Note that the initial value of **i** is **0** and its last value as an index is **MAX-1**.

Second, array parameters that are intended to be modified in functions can be declared as in the following example, assuming a base type of **element**:

```
void change_array(element the_array[]);
```

Note that the size of the array is not specified. Because the array is passed by reference, arrays of elements of any size can be passed to this function.

Third, array parameters that are not intended to be modified can be passed as constant parameters, as in the following example:

```
void display_array(const element the_array[]);
```

The actual array is passed by reference to this function also, but the compiler will disallow assignments to the constant parameter in the function body.

Strings can be conveniently represented as arrays of characters. This representation is compatible with the representation of strings used by the standard C++ **string** library. Indeed, C++ treats string literals as constant arrays of characters. For example, you could define a string type, declare two variables, input data into them, and output results in the following code:

```
typedef char string[20];

string first_name, last_name;

cout << "Enter your first name:";
cin >> first_name;
cout << "Enter your last name:";
cin >> last_name;
cout << "Hi, " << first_name << " " << last_name << "!" << endl;
```

As with other arrays, assignments of whole strings do not result in copying one string to another. This can be accomplished with the **string** library function **strcpy**, whose form is

```
strcpy(<destination string variable>, <source string>);
```

The first argument to **strcpy** must be a variable (the target of the copy). The second argument can be either a variable or a literal.

The **strlen** function returns the current number of characters stored in its string parameter. C++ relies on a special null character, represented as **'\0'**, as a sentinel that is stored in the array cell immediately following the last character currently in the string. Thus, a character array of physical size 20 has room for a string of up to 19 characters and the null character.

The **strcmp** function returns zero if its string arguments are equal, a negative integer if the first is less than the second, or a positive integer if the first is greater than the second. The arguments to **strcmp** can be any combination of string literals and/or variables.

Data values of different types can be combined into one data structure by using **struct**. This is similar to the record facility in other programming languages. For example, the following code defines a type for representing a person's name, address, phone number, salary, and age and declares two variables of this type:

```
struct person
{
      string name, address, phone_number;
      float salary;
      int age;
};
person manager, clerk;
```

Note the semicolon, which is required, following the right curly brace. The items enclosed in the curly braces are called the members of the **struct**. They can be of any data type (including string, which we assume to be defined by the programmer elsewhere). Members are referenced by using the selector or dot operator, as follows:

```
manager.name = "Sandra Speedup";
manager.address = "300 Park Avenue/nRoanoke, VA/n24018";
manager.phone_number = "703-775-3316";
manager.salary = 60000.00;
manager.age = 25;
```

Unlike a C++ array, a **struct** can be copied by assignment. Thus, the statement

```
clerk = manager;
```

copies the values of all of the members of **manager** into **clerk**. Also unlike a C++ array, a **struct** parameter is passed by value as a parameter to a function, unless the ampersand is used explicitly to specify it as a reference parameter in the formal parameter declaration.

File processing in C++ is accomplished by means of file streams. The program gains access to these by

```
#include <fstream.h>
```

The following code opens a file stream for output to a file named **"myfile"**, prints an integer, a real number, and a string to the file, closes the file, and then performs input on it as well:

```
int int_value;
float float_value;
char string_value[20];
ofstream out_file;
ifstream in_file;
```

```
out_file.open("myfile");
out_file << 45 endl << 3.14 << endl << "Hi!" << endl;
out_file.close();
in_file.open("myfile");
in_file >> int_value >> float_value >> string_value;
in_file.close();
```

File stream input and output operations work in essentially the same way as input and output operations on the standard streams (cin and cout). To control a loop for the input of an arbitrary number of data values from an input file stream one can use a **while** loop with a priming input statement. The following example copies integers from one file stream to another:

```
in_file >> data;
while (! in_file.eof())
{
    out_file << data << endl;
    in_file >> data;
}
```

Note that an attempt to input data must be made before the end-of-file condition can be tested with the **eof** function.

# 1

# Algorithm Analysis: Space and Time Considerations

*Nothing puzzles me more than time and space.*
Charles Lamb, 1775–1834

In this chapter, we introduce a technique for analyzing the efficiency of algorithms. We can then use this technique, known as *big-O analysis,* to categorize algorithms with respect to the length of time and the amount of storage they require for their execution with data sets of different sizes. In Sections 1.2 and 1.3, we will use big-O analysis to examine the time efficiency of some simple sorting algorithms. In Section 1.4, we will use big-O analysis to describe the interplay between the time and storage requirements of an algorithm. In Section 1.5, we will analyze the time efficiency of simple *search algorithms.* Finally, in the Focus on Program Design section, we will discuss a scheme for developing programs to measure empirically the efficiency of an algorithm.

 ## 1.1 Designing Programs: A Look Back and a Look Ahead

### OBJECTIVES

- to develop a perspective on the study of computer science beyond the learning of a particular programming language, such as C++

- to be able to identify criteria by which complex software is evaluated

This chapter marks an important step in your exploration of computer science. Up to this point, it has been difficult to divorce your study of computer science from the learning of C++. You have developed problem-solving skills, but the problems we have encountered have been very focused. That is, the problems were chosen specifically to illustrate a particular feature of C++. This is the way that problem-solving skills must be developed: Start with small problems and work toward large ones.

By now you know many of the features of the C++ programming language. You are ready to direct your attention toward larger, more complex problems that require you to integrate many of the particular skills you have developed. Now our attention will be directed more toward issues of software design and less toward describing C++. If we need a particular feature of C++ that has not yet been discussed, we will introduce it when appropriate. But our primary objective is to study more complex problems and the software design issues that arise out of them. From here on, we view C++ primarily as the vehicle to implement, test, and experiment with our solutions to problems. The techniques of software design we are about to explore will enable us to write programs that have the following characteristics:

- *Large:* Actually our programs could properly be called systems since they typically involve numerous modules that interact to solve one complex problem.
- *Reliable:* The measure of the reliability of a system is that it can anticipate and handle all types of exceptional circumstances.
- *Flexible:* The system should be easily modified to handle circumstances that may change in the future.
- *Expandable and reusable:* If the system is successful, it will frequently spawn new computing needs. We should be able to incorporate solutions to these new needs into the original system with relative ease.
- *Efficient:* The system should make optimal use of time and space resources.
- *Structured:* The system should be divided into compact modules, each of which is responsible for a specific, well-defined task.
- *User-friendly:* The system should be clearly documented so that it is easy to use. Internal documentation helps programmers maintain the software, and external documentation helps users use it.

In designing software to meet these criteria, one of the key skills you must develop is the ability to choose the appropriate tools for the job. You should not have to rediscover algorithms and techniques for information storage and retrieval each time you write a new program. As a computer scientist, you must have a detailed knowledge of algorithms and data storage techniques at your fingertips and be able to apply this knowledge when designing software to solve a variety of problems. You should be able to look into your storehouse of algorithms and data storage strategies, choose the most appropriate methods, and then tailor them to the application at hand.

As you expand your knowledge of computer science, you will find that a given problem frequently lends itself to more than one method of solution. Hence, in addition to knowing the individual principles, you must also be able to evaluate them comparatively. This comparative evaluation must be conducted in as systematic and quantitative a fashion as possible. That is, you must be able to justify your choice of a method by presenting cogent arguments based on facts and figures pertinent to the problem. Given this perspective on computer science, we must turn our attention to a twofold task:

**1.** Stocking our algorithmic toolbox with methods that have become standards in computer science.
**2.** Developing criteria for knowing which tool to choose in a particular situation.

To begin this task, we reach back to the sorting and searching algorithms that you probably encountered in your first computer science course. We also consider some new techniques for sorting and searching. We then evaluate these techniques for their efficiency in terms of execution time and use of space (memory) resources. To conduct such a time/space analysis, we introduce what has come to be known as big-O notation. In effect, big-O notation is the mathematical measuring stick by which computer scientists quantitatively evaluate algorithms. It allows us to place algorithms into categories based on their efficiency. Such categorization helps us determine whether or not a proposed solution is practical in terms of the real-world requirements and constraints dictated by the problem.

# Simple Sorting Algorithms

**1.2**

## OBJECTIVES

- to develop a functional interface that can be used with a variety of sorting algorithms
- to understand the potential difference in efficiency between the computer operations of comparing data items and interchanging them
- to be able to trace in detail the comparisons and interchanges of data items that occur during execution of the bubble sort algorithm
- to be able to trace in detail the comparisons and interchanges of data items that occur during execution of the selection sort algorithm
- to be able to trace in detail the comparisons and interchanges of data items that occur during execution of the insertion sort algorithm

Our discussion in this section will use an array of objects that we want to sort in ascending order according to a given attribute for each object. The attribute on which the sort is based is known as the key attribute. For instance, we may wish to arrange a list of student objects in alphabetical order according to student last name or a list of inventory objects in order according to product identification numbers. To provide a suitable setting for our upcoming discussion of the sorting problem, we will make the following assumptions:

**1.** The objects being sorted are of type **element**. **element** is a synonym for whatever class of object we wish to place in an array.

**2.** If necessary, the **element** class overloads the standard C++ operators **==**, **>**, and **<** that are used by the sort algorithms. Operator **=** is used for copying elements, while **>** and **<** compare two elements with respect to the key attribute.

For example, the following declarations would provide a setting for sorting a simple array of integers:

```
const int MAX_LIST_SIZE = 100;
typedef int element;
typedef element list_type[MAX_LIST_SIZE];
```

We wish to write a sort function that meets the following specifications:

```
// Function: sort
// Sorts a list of elements into ascending order
//
// Inputs: a list of elements in random order and its
// current length
// Output: the list of elements arranged in ascending
// order

void sort(list_type list, int n);
```

Two aspects of these declarations are worth noting. First, the fashion in which we have made our constant and type definitions allows this function to sort an array of any size and base type provided that the definitions are appropriately altered. This method of declaration represents an attempt to make the C++ function abstract: It embodies an algorithm that can sort a variety of data types.

Second, the measure of an algorithm's run-time efficiency is in direct proportion to the number of elementary machine operations that must be performed as the algorithm is executed. With sorting algorithms, these elementary machine operations compare and interchange two data items. Depending on the amount of data in the element type in the preceding declarations, it is entirely possible that interchanging two data items could be considerably more costly in machine time than comparing two items. Why? An interchange of large data items will generate a loop that moves a significant number of bytes at the machine language level.

Our analysis of run-time efficiency should take this into account. It may well be more important to minimize data interchanges at the expense of comparisons. This complication did not enter into our earlier discussion of sorting because, at that stage, we were concerned with sorting arrays of simple, unstructured data items only.

## Bubble Sort

The first algorithm we will scrutinize is the *bubble sort*. Given a list of data objects stored in an array, a bubble sort causes a pass through the array to compare adjacent pairs of keys. Whenever two keys are out of order with respect to each other, the associated objects are interchanged. The effect of such a pass through a list of names is traced in Figure 1.1, where a "snapshot" of the array after each comparison is given. Notice that after such a pass, we are assured that the list will have the name that comes last in alphabetical order in the final array position. That is, the last name will "sink" to the bottom of the array, and preceding names will gradually "percolate" to the top.

If one pass through an array of $n$ objects can guarantee that the object with the key that comes last in order is in the appropriate position, then slicing off the last element and passing through the remaining $n - 1$ entries using the same logic will guarantee that the object with the key second to last in order is in its appropriate position. Repeating the process for a total of $n - 1$ passes eventually

◆ FIGURE 1.1

Trace of bubble sort on an array with four names

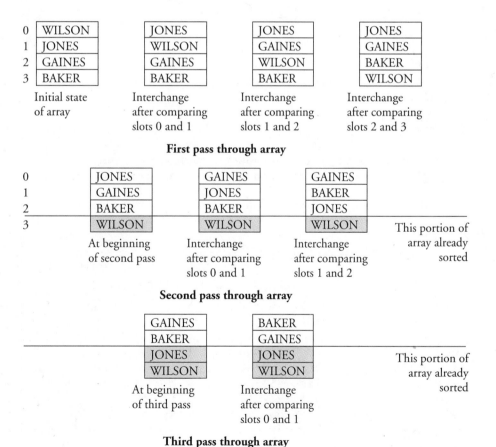

ensures that all objects are in their appropriate positions. In general, on the $k$th pass through the array, $n - k$ comparisons of pairs must be made.

Thus, the bubble sort algorithm involves a nested loop structure. The outer loop controls the number of (successively smaller) passes through the array. The inner loop controls the pairs of adjacent entries being compared.

If we ever make a complete pass through the inner loop without having to make an interchange, we can declare the array sorted and avoid all future passes through the array. A top-level pseudocode development of the algorithm is

1. Initialize counter k to zero
2. Initialize Boolean exchange_made to TRUE
3. While (k < n – 1) and exchange_made
   3.1. Set exchange_made to FALSE
   3.2. Increment counter k
   3.3. For each j from 0 to n – k
      3.3.1. If entry in jth slot > entry in(j + 1)st slot
      3.3.1.1. Exchange these entries
      3.3.1.2. Set exchange_made to TRUE

The complete C++ function to implement this algorithm for an array of objects follows. The function assumes the existence of appropriate data declarations.

```cpp
void bubble_sort(list_type list, int n)
{

    int j, k;
    boolean exchange_made = TRUE;
    element temp;

    k = 0;

    // Make up to n - 1 passes through array, exit
    // early if no exchanges are made on previous pass

    while ((k < n - 1) && exchange_made)
    {

        exchange_made = FALSE;
        ++k;
        // Number of comparisons on kth pass
        for (j = 0; j < n - k; ++j)
            if (list[j] > list[j + 1])
            {
                // Exchange must be made
                temp = list[j];
                list[j] = list[j + 1];
                list[j + 1] = temp;
                exchange_made = TRUE;
            }
    }
}
```

| | | Kth pass |
|---|---|---|
| 0 | BARBER | |
| . | . | |
| . | . | |
| . | . | N – K names |
| J | NEWTON | still require |
| J + 1 | HENDERSON | ordering |
| . | . | |
| . | . | |
| . | . | |
| N – K | MILLER | |
| N – K + 1 | PETERSON | |
| . | . | K – 1 names |
| . | . | are in |
| . | . | appropriate |
| N – 1 | YATES | positions |

Out of order? { J, J + 1

| EXAMPLE 1.1 | Trace the action of the function **bubble_sort** if **n** is 5 and the array **list** initially contains |

### First pass through array

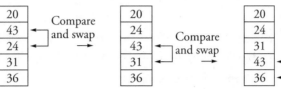

### First pass through array

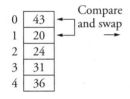

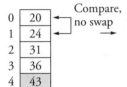

**exchange_made** remained false throughout the inner loop, so the algorithm is done.

In the next section we analyze in detail the run-time efficiency of the bubble sort. But we should first consider two other sorting algorithms to which the efficiency of bubble sort may be compared: *selection sort* and *insertion sort*.

## Selection Sort

The strategy of the bubble sort is to place the (current) largest array value in the (current) last array slot, then seal off that slot from future consideration, and repeat the process. The selection sort algorithm has a similar plan, but it attempts to avoid the multitude of interchanges of adjacent entries. To do this, on the *k*th pass through the array, it determines the position of the smallest entry among

```
list[k], list[k + 1], ..., list[n]
```

Then this smallest entry is swapped with the *k*th entry, **k** is incremented by 1, and the process is repeated. Figure 1.2 illustrates how this algorithm works on repeated passes through an array with six entries. Asterisks are used to indicate the successively smallest (alphabetically) entries as they are being correctly located in the array.

As we see next, the C++ function for selection sort uses, as its inner loop, a simple algorithm to find the minimum entry and store its position in the variable

◆ FIGURE 1.2

Trace of selection sort logic

| Original order of Keys | k = 0 | k = 1 | k = 2 | k = 3 | k = 4 |
|---|---|---|---|---|---|
| DAVE | ARON* | ARON* | ARON* | ARON* | ARON* |
| TOM | TOM | BEV* | BEV* | BEV* | BEV* |
| PAM | PAM | PAM | DAVE* | DAVE* | DAVE* |
| ARON | DAVE | DAVE | PAM | PAM* | PAM* |
| BEV | BEV | TOM | TOM | TOM | SAM* |
| SAM | SAM | SAM | SAM | SAM | TOM* |

min_position. This inner loop avoids the potentially frequent interchange of array elements that is necessary in the inner loop of **bubble_sort**.

```
void selection_sort(list_type list, int n)
{

    int index;
    element temp;

    // Make n - 1 passes through successively smaller segments

    for (int j = 0; j < n - 1; ++j)
    {

        index = j;
        // Find index of the smallest element
        for (int k = j + 1; k < n; ++k)
            if (list[k] < list[index])
                index = k;
        if (index != j)
        {
            // Exchange must be made
            temp = list[index];
            list[index] = list[j];
            list[j] = temp;
        }
    }
}
```

Example 1.2 indicates that the selection sort algorithm swaps no data values until exiting the inner loop. This apparently reduces the number of data interchanges and makes the selection sort more efficient than the bubble sort. Is this a significant improvement? Or have other subtle inefficiencies been introduced to offset this apparent gain? These are difficult questions to answer unless we have a better grasp of how to measure program efficiency. We'll explore efficiency in the next section; but first, let's look at one more sorting algorithm for comparison purposes.

**EXAMPLE 1.2**    Trace the action of the function **selection_sort** if **n** is 5 and the array **list** initially contains

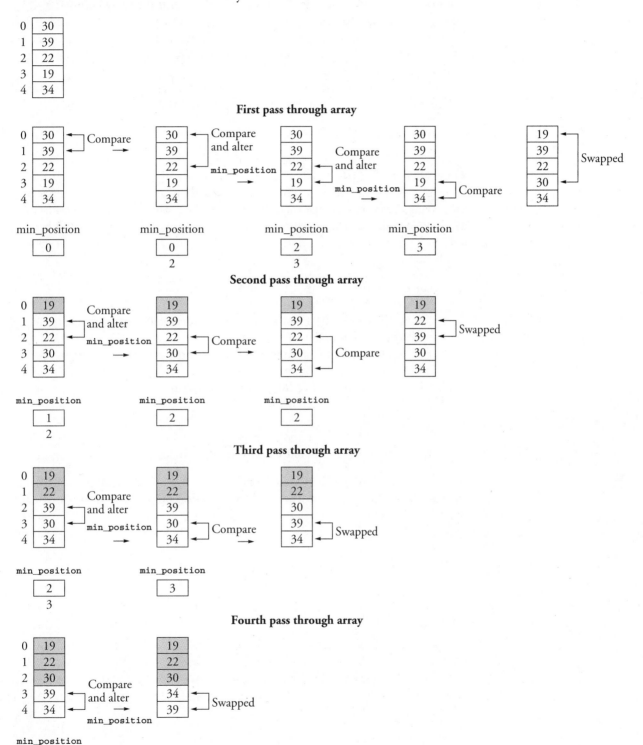

**First pass through array**

**Second pass through array**

**Third pass through array**

**Fourth pass through array**

## Insertion Sort

Although it reduces the number of data interchanges, the selection sort apparently will not allow an effective—and automatic—loop exit if the array becomes ordered during an early pass. In this regard, bubble sort is more efficient than selection sort for an array that is nearly ordered from the beginning. However, even with just one entry out of order, bubble sort's early loop exit can fail to reduce the number of comparisons that are made.

The insertion sort attempts to take greater advantage of an array's partial ordering. The goal is that on the $k$th pass through, the $k$th element among

```
list[0], list[1], ..., list[k]
```

should be inserted into its rightful place among the first $k$ entries in the array. Thus, after the $k$th pass ($k$ starting at 1), the first $k$ elements of the array should be in sorted order. This is analogous to the fashion in which many people pick up playing cards and arrange them in order in their hands. Holding the first ($k$ – 1) cards in order, a person will pick up the $k$th card and compare it with cards already held until its appropriate spot is found. The following steps will achieve this logic:

1. For each k from 1 to n - 1 { k index of array element to insert }
    1.1 Set item_to_insert to list[k]
    1.2 Set j to k – 1 ( j starts at j – 1 and is decremented until insertion position is found )
    1.3 While (insertion position not found) and (not beginning of array)
        1.3.1 If item_to_insert < list[j]
            1.3.1.1 Move list[j] to index position j + 1
            1.3.1.2 Decrement j by 1
        1.3.2 Else
            1.3.2.1 The insertion position has been found
    1.4 item_to_insert should be positioned at index j + 1

In effect, for each pass, the index **j** begins at the ($k$ – 1)st element and moves that element to position $j$ + 1 until we find the insertion point for what was originally the $k$th element.

◆ FIGURE 1.3

Trace of repeated passes from insertion sort

| Original order of Keys | First pass $k = 1$ | Second pass $k = 2$ | Third pass $k = 3$ | Fourth pass $k = 4$ | Fifth pass $k = 5$ |
|---|---|---|---|---|---|
| PAM | PAM | DAVE | ARON | ARON | ARON |
| SAM | SAM* | PAM | DAVE | DAVE | BEV |
| DAVE | DAVE | SAM* | PAM | PAM | DAVE |
| ARON | ARON | ARON | SAM* | SAM | PAM |
| TOM | TOM | TOM | TOM | TOM* | SAM |
| BEV | BEV | BEV | BEV | BEV | TOM* |

Insertion sort for each value of **k** is traced in Figure 1.3. In each column of this diagram the data items are sorted in alphabetical order relative to each other above the item with the asterisk; below this item the data are not affected.

To implement the insertion sort algorithm in C++ we have the following code:

```
void insertion_sort(list_type list, int n)
{
    int j, k;
    element item_to_insert;
    boolean still_looking;

    // On the kth pass, insert item k into its correct position among
    // the first k entries in array.

    for (k = 1; k < n; ++k)
    {
    // Walk backwards through list, looking for slot to insert list[k]
            item_to_insert = list[k];
            j = k - 1;
            still_looking = TRUE;
            while ((j >= 0) && still_looking )
                    if (item_to_insert < list[j])
                    {
                            list[j + 1] = list[j];
                            --j;
                    }
                    else
                    still_looking = FALSE;
        // Upon leaving loop, j + 1 is the index
        // where item_to_insert belongs
        list[j + 1] = item_to_insert;
    }
}
```

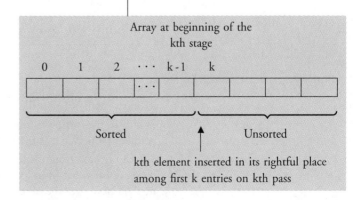

Array at beginning of the
kth stage

0    1    2   · · ·  k-1   k

Sorted          Unsorted

kth element inserted in its rightful place
among first k entries on kth pass

**EXAMPLE 1.3**   Trace the action of the function `insertion_sort` if `n` is 5 and the array `list` initially contains

0 | 80
1 | 40
2 | 32
3 | 54
4 | 61

**First pass (k=2)**

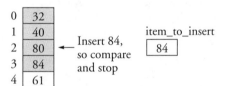

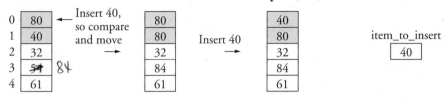

**Second pass (k=3)**

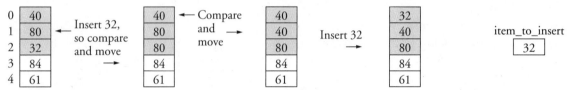

**Third pass (k=4)**

0 | 32
1 | 40
2 | 80
3 | 84
4 | 61

Insert 84, so compare and stop

item_to_insert

84

**Fourth pass (k=5)**

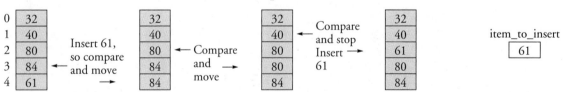

---

**EXERCISES 1.2**

1. Which of the sorting methods studied in this section allows a possible early exit from its inner loop? What is the potential advantage of using this early exit?

2. Which of the sorting methods studied in this section allows a possible early exit from its outer loop? What is the potential advantage of using this early exit?

3. Which of the sorting methods studied in this section does not allow for the possibility of an early exit from its inner or outer loops? What potential advantage does this method have over the other two methods that were presented?

**4.** Suppose that, initially, an array contains seven integer entries arranged in the following order:

```
0  43
1  40
2  18
3  24
4  39
5  60
6  12
```

Trace the order of the array entries after each successive pass of the bubble sort.

**5.** Repeat Exercise 4 for the selection sort.

**6.** Repeat Exercise 4 for the insertion sort.

**7.** Consider the following sort algorithm. Which of the methods studied in this section does this new algorithm most closely resemble? In what ways is it different from that method? Trace the action of this new sort algorithm on the array from Exercise 4.

```
void sort(list_type list, int n)
{
      int j, k;
      boolean exchange_made = TRUE;
      element temp;

      k = 0;
      while ((k < n - 1) && exchange_made)
      {
            exchange_made = FALSE;
            ++k;
            for (j = n - 1; j > k + 1; -j)
                if (list[j] < list[j - 1])
                {
                      temp = list[j];
                      list[j] = list[j - 1];
                      list[j - 1] = temp;
                      exchange_made = TRUE;
                }
      }
}
```

**8.** Consider the following sort algorithm. Which of the methods studied in this section does this new algorithm most closely resemble? In what ways is it different from that method? Trace the action of this new sort algorithm on the array from Exercise 4.

```
void sort(list_type list, int n)
{
      int j, k, position;
      element temp;

      for (k = 0; k < n - 1; ++k)
      {
```

```
                position = 0;
                for (j = 1; j < n - k + 1; ++j)
                        if (list[j] > list[position])
                                position = j;
                temp = list[n - k + 1];
                list[n - k + 1] = list[position];
                list[position] = temp;
        }
    }
```

9. Consider the following sort algorithm. Which of the methods studied in this section does this new algorithm most closely resemble? In what ways is it different from that method? Trace the action of this new sort algorithm on the array from Exercise 4.

```
void sort(list_type list, int n)
{
        int j, k;
        boolean done;
        element temp;

        for (k = n - 1; k > 0; -k)
        {
                j = k;
                done = FALSE;
                while ((j <= n - 1) && ! done)
                    if (list[j] > list[j + 1])
                    {
                            temp = list[j];
                            list[j] = list[j - 1];
                            list[j - 1] = temp;
                            ++j;
                    }
                    else
                            done = TRUE;
        }
    }
```

10. Devise sample data sets to demonstrate the *best case* and *worst case* behavior of the bubble sort, insertion sort, and selection sort. That is, for each sorting algorithm, construct data sets that illustrate the minimum and maximum number of comparisons required for that particular algorithm.

11. Construct a data set in which just one value is out of order and yet the Boolean test of the **exchange_made** variable never allows an early exit from the outer loop of bubble sort. How does the insertion sort perform on this same data set? Better, worse, or the same? Explain why.

12. Modify the sorting algorithms of this section so that they receive an additional argument indicating whether the sort should be in ascending or descending order.

13. The inner loop of an insertion sort can be modified merely to find the appropriate position for the *k*th array entry instead of actually shifting items to make room for this entry. The shifting of items and placement of the original *k*th entry can then be achieved in a separate loop. Write a new insertion sort function that implements this modification. Intuitively, is your new version more or less efficient than the old version? Why?

**14.** Modify all of the sorting algorithms presented in this chapter to include counters for the number of comparisons and data interchanges that are made. Then run those sorting algorithms on a variety of data sets, maintaining a chart of the counters for each algorithm. Prepare a written statement to summarize your conclusions about the relative efficiencies of the algorithms.

---

## 1.3 Which Sort Is Best? A Big-O Analysis

### OBJECTIVES

- to understand the formal definition of big-O notation

- to be able to use big-O notation to classify the time efficiency of algorithms involving nonrecursive, iterative control constructs

- to see the relationship between an algorithm's big-O classification and its expected run time on a computer

- to recognize often-used big-O categories

- to apply big-O notation in analyzing the time efficiencies of the bubble sort, selection sort, and insertion sort algorithms

Computers do their work in terms of certain fundamental operations: comparing two numbers, moving the contents of one memory word to another, and so on. It should come as no surprise to you that a simple instruction in a high-level language such as C++ may be translated (via a compiler) into many of these fundamental machine-level instructions. On most modern computers the speeds of these fundamental operations are measured in microseconds—that is, millionths of a second—although some larger supercomputers are beginning to break the nanosecond (billionth of a second) barrier. Let's assume, for the sake of argument, that we are working with a hypothetical computer that requires one microsecond to perform one of its fundamental operations.

With execution speeds of this kind, it makes little sense to analyze the efficiency of those portions of a program that perform only initializations and final reporting of summary results. The key to analyzing a function's efficiency is to scrutinize its loops and, even more importantly, its nested loops. Consider the following two examples of nested loops intended to sum each of the rows of an $N \times N$ two-dimensional array matrix, storing the row sums in the one-dimensional array **rows** and the overall total in **grand_total**.

---

### EXAMPLE 1.4

```
grand_total:= 0;
for (k = 0; k< n - 1; ++k)
{
        rows[k] = 0;
        for (j = 0; j < n - 1; ++j)
        {
                rows[k] = rows[k] + matrix[k,j];
                grand_total = grand_total+ matrix[k,j];
        }
}
```

### EXAMPLE 1.5

```
grand_total = 0;
for (k = 0; k < n - 1; ++k)
{
        rows[k] = 0;
        for (j = 0; j < n - 1; ++j)
                rows[k] = rows[k] + matrix[k,j];
        grand_total = grand_total+ rows[k];
}
```

---

If we analyze the number of addition operations required by these two examples, it should be immediately obvious that Example 1.5 is better in this respect. Because

Example 1.4 incorporates the accumulating of `grand_total` into its inner loop, it requires $2N^2$ additions. That is, the additions `rows[k] + matrix[k, j]` and `grand_total + matrix[k, j]` are each executed $N^2$ times, for a total of $2N^2$. Example 1.5, on the other hand, accumulates `grand_total` after the inner loop; hence it requires only $N^2 + N$ additions, which is less than $2N^2$ for any $N$ after 1. Example 1.5 is seemingly guaranteed to execute faster than Example 1.4 for any nontrivial value of $N$.

But note that "faster" here may not have much significance in the real world of computing. Assuming that our hypothetical computer allows us to declare an array that is 1000 by 1000. Example 1.4 would require two seconds to perform its additions; Example 1.5 would require just over one second. On a larger 100,000 by 100,000 array, Example 1.4 would crunch numbers for slightly under six hours and Example 1.5 would take about three hours.

Although Example 1.5 is certainly better from an aesthetic perspective, it is not good enough to be appreciably different from a user's perspective. That is, in situations where one version will respond within seconds, so will the other. Conversely, when one is annoyingly slow, the other will be also. In terms of the *order of magnitude* of run time involved, these versions should not be considered significantly different. For the 1000 by 1000 array, both versions would be fast enough to allow their use in an interactive environment. For the 100,000 by 100,000 array, both versions would dictate an overnight run in batch mode since an interactive user is no more willing to wait three hours than six hours for a response.

Thus, because of the phenomenal execution speeds and very large amounts of available memory on modern computers, proportionally small differences between algorithms often have little practical impact. Such considerations have led computer scientists to devise a method of algorithm classification that makes more precise the notion of order of magnitude as it applies to time and space considerations. This method of classification, typically referred to as *big-O notation* (in reference to "on the *o*rder of"), hinges on the following definition:

> **Big-O notation:** Suppose there exists a function $f(n)$ defined on the nonnegative integers such that the number of operations required by an algorithm for an input of size $n$ is less than some constant $C$ times $f(n)$ for all but finitely many $n$. That is, the number of operations is *proportional* to $f(n)$ for all large values of $n$. Such an algorithm is said to be an $O[f(n)]$ algorithm relative to the number of operations it requires to execute. Similarly, we could classify an algorithm as $O[f(n)]$ relative to the number of memory locations it requires to execute.

Figure 1.4 provides a graphical aid to understanding this formal definition of big-O notation. In general, we expect an algorithm's run time to increase as it manipulates an increasing number of data items, that is, as $n$ increases. This increasing run time is depicted by the somewhat irregular, wavy curve in Figure 1.4. Now compare the wavy curve representing actual run time to the smoother curve of $C^*f(n)$. Note that, for some small values of $n$, the actual number of operations for the algorithm may exceed $C^*f(n)$. However, the graph indicates that there is a point on the horizontal axis beyond which $C^*f(n)$ is always greater than the number of operations required for $n$ data items. This is precisely the criterion that defines an algorithm's being $O[f(n)]$.

To say that an algorithm is $O[f(n)]$ thus indicates that the function $f(n)$ may be useful in characterizing how the algorithm is performing for large $n$. For such $n$,

◆ FIGURE 1.4
Graphical representation of
$O(f(n))$

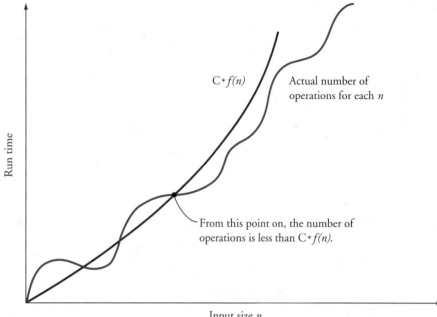

we are assured that the operations required by the algorithm will be bounded by a constant times $f(n)$. The phrasing "for all large values of $n$" in the definition highlights the fact that there is little difference in the choice of an algorithm if $n$ is reasonably small. For example, almost any sorting algorithm would sort 100 integers instantly.

We should also note that a given algorithm may be $O[f(n)]$ for many different functions $f$. As Figure 1.5 depicts, any algorithm that is $O(n^2)$ will also be $O(n^3)$.

Our main interest in classifying an algorithm with big-O notation is to find a relatively simple function $f(n)$ such that $C*f(n)$ parallels the number of operations as closely as possible. Hence, saying that an algorithm is $O(n^2)$ is considered a better characterization of its efficiency than saying it is $O(n^3)$.

The importance of the constant $C$, known as the constant of proportionality, lies in comparing algorithms that share the same function $f(n)$; it makes almost no difference in the comparison of algorithms for which $f(n)$ is of different magnitude. It is therefore appropriate to say that the function $f(n)$ dominates the run-time performance of an algorithm and characterizes it in its big-O analysis. The following example should help clarify this situation.

Consider two algorithms $L_1$ and $L_2$ with run-times equal to $2n^2$ and $n^2$, respectively. The constants of proportionality of $L_1$ and $L_2$ are 2 and 1, respectively. The dominating function $f(n)$ for both of these algorithms is $n^2$, but $L_2$ runs twice as fast as $L_1$ for a data set of $n$ values. The different sizes of the two constants of proportionality indicate that $L_2$ is faster than $L_1$. Now suppose that the function $f(n)$ for $L_2$ is $n^3$. Then, even though its constant of proportionality is half of what it is for $L_1$, $L_2$ will be frustratingly slower than $L_1$ for large $n$. This latter comparison is shown in Figure 1.6.

**EXAMPLE 1.6**

Use big-O analysis to characterize the two code segments from Examples 1.4 and 1.5, respectively.

◆ **FIGURE 1.5**
Any algorithm that is $O(n^2)$
is also $O(n^3)$

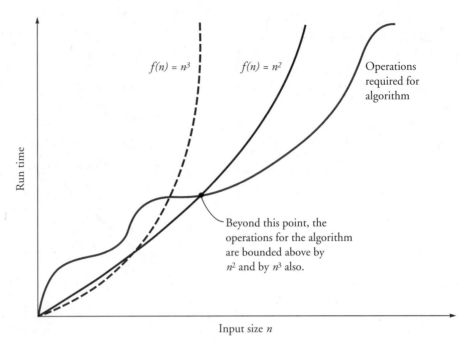

$f(n) = n^3$    $f(n) = n^2$    Operations
required for
algorithm

Beyond this point, the
operations for the algorithm
are bounded above by
$n^2$ and by $n^3$ also.

Run time

Input size $n$

◆ **FIGURE 1.6**
Graphical comparison of
two run times

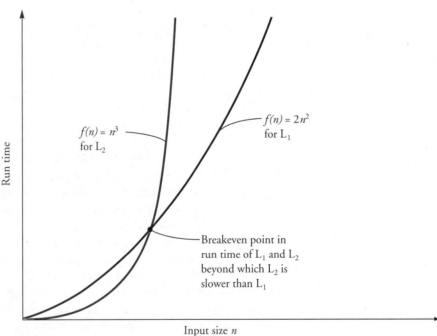

$f(n) = n^3$
for $L_2$

$f(n) = 2n^2$
for $L_1$

Breakeven point in
run time of $L_1$ and $L_2$
beyond which $L_2$ is
slower than $L_1$

Run time

Input size $n$

Because the algorithm of Example 1.4 performs $2N^2$ additions, it is characterized as $O(N^2)$ with 2 as a constant of proportionality. We previously determined that the code of Example 1.5 performs $N^2 + N$ additions. However, $N^2 + N <= 1.1N^2$ for any $N >= 10$. Hence, we can characterize Example 1.5 as an $O(N^2)$ algorithm using 1.1 as a constant of proportionality. These two characterizations demonstrate that, although Example 1.5 is almost twice as fast as Example 1.4, they are in the same big-O category. Coupled with our earlier analysis of these two examples, this is an indication that algorithms in the same big-O category may be expected to have the same orders of magnitude in their run times.

*How well does the big-O notation provide a way of classifying algorithms from a real-world perspective?* To answer this question, consider Table 1.1. This table presents some typical $f(n)$ functions we will use to classify algorithms and their order of magnitude run times for inputs of various sizes on a hypothetical computer. From this table, we can see that an $O(n^2)$ algorithm will take hours to execute for an input of size $10^5$. How many hours is dependent on the constant of proportionality in the definition of the big-O notation.

Regardless of the value of this constant of proportionality, a categorization of an algorithm as an $O(n^2)$ algorithm has thus achieved a very practical goal. We now know that, for an input of size $10^5$, we cannot expect an immediate response for such an algorithm. Moreover, we also know that, for a reasonably small constant of proportionality, we have an algorithm for which submission as an overnight job would not be impractical. That is, unlike an $O(n^3)$ algorithm, we could expect the computer to finish executing our algorithm in a time frame that would be acceptable if it could be scheduled to not interfere with other uses of the machine. On the other hand, an $O(n^3)$ algorithm applied to a data set of this size would be completely impractical.

*How does one determine the function $f(n)$ that categorizes a particular algorithm?* We give an overview of that process here and illustrate it by doing actual analyses for our three sorting algorithms. It is generally the case that, by analyzing the loop structure of an algorithm, we can estimate the number of run-time operations (or amount of memory units) required by the algorithm as a sum of several terms, each dependent on $n$, the number of items being processed by the algorithm. That is, typically we are able to express the number of run-time operations (or amount of memory) as a sum of the form

$$f_1(n) + f_2(n) + \ldots + f_k(n)$$

Moreover, it is also typical for us to identify one of the terms in this expression as the *dominant term*. A dominant term is one that, for bigger values of $n$, becomes so large that it allows us to ignore all the other terms from a big-O perspective. For instance, suppose that we had an expression involving two terms such as

$$n^2 + 50n$$

Here, the $n^2$ term dominates the $50n$ term since, for $n >= 50$, we have

$$n^2 + 50n <= n^2 + n^2 = 2n^2$$

Thus, $n^2 + 50n$ would lead to an $O(n^2)$ categorization because of the dominance of the $n^2$ term.

◇ **TABLE 1.1**

Some typical $f(n)$ functions and associated run times

| Assuming proportionality constant $K = 1$ and one operation per microsecond, approximate run times for input of size | | |
|---|---|---|
| $f(n)$     $10^3$ | $10^5$ | $10^6$ |
| $log_2 n$    0.000010 seconds | 0.000017 seconds | 0.000020 seconds |
| $n$      0.001 seconds | 0.1 seconds | 1 second |
| $n\ log_2 n$    0.01 seconds | 1.7 seconds | 20 seconds |
| $n^2$      1 second | 3 hours | 12 days |
| $n^3$      17 minutes | 32 centuries | $3 \times 10^4$ centuries |
| $2^n$      $10^{285}$ centuries | $10^{10^4}$ years | $10^{10^5}$ years |

In general, the problem of big-O categorization reduces to finding the dominant term in an expression representing the number of operations or amount of memory required by an algorithm.

---

**EXAMPLE 1.7**

Use big-O notation to analyze the time efficiency of the following fragment of C++ code.

```
for (k = 1; k <= n / 2; ++k)
{
    .
    .
    .
        for (j = 1; j <= n * n; ++j)
        {
            .
            .
            .
        }
}
```

Since these loops are nested, the number of times statements within the innermost loop are executed is the product of the number of repetitions of the two individual loops. Hence the efficiency is $n^3/2$, or $O(n^3)$ in big-O terms, with a constant of proportionality equal to 1/2.

---

Note that the important principle illustrated by this example is that, for two loops with $O[f_1(n)]$ and $O[f_2(n)]$ efficiencies, the efficiency of the nesting of these two loops (in any order) is $O[f_1(n) * f_2(n)]$.

---

**EXAMPLE 1.8**

Use big-O notation to analyze the time efficiency of the following fragment of C++ code.

```
for (k = 1; k <= n / 2; ++k)
{
    .
    .
    .
}
for (j = 1; j <= n * n; ++j)
{
    .
    .
    .
}
```

Since one loop follows the other, the number of operations executed by both of them is the sum of the individual loop efficiencies. Hence the efficiency is $n/2 + n^2$, or $O(n^2)$ in big-O terms.

---

The important principle illustrated by Example 1.8 is that, for two loops with $O[f_1(n)]$ and $O[f_2(n)]$ efficiencies, the efficiency of the sequencing of these two loops (in any order) is $O[f_D(n)]$ where $f_D(n)$ is the dominant of the functions $f_1(n)$ and $f_2(n)$.

---

**EXAMPLE 1.9**

Use big-O notation to analyze the time efficiency of the following fragment of C++ code.

```
k = n;
while (k > 1)
{
    .
    .
    .
    k = k / 2;
}
```

Since the loop control variable is cut in half each time through the loop, the number of times that statements inside the loop will be executed is $\log_2 n$. Note that the halving of a loop is central to the binary search algorithm, which will be explored further in Section 1.5. The principle emerging from Example 1.9 is that an algorithm that halves the data remaining to be processed on each iteration of a loop will be an $O(\log_2 n)$ algorithm.

---

Table 1.2, which lists frequently occurring dominant terms, will prove helpful in our future big-O analyses of algorithms.

It is worthwhile to characterize briefly some of the classes of algorithms that arise due to the dominant terms listed in Table 1.2. Algorithms whose efficiency is dominated by a $\log_a n$ term [and hence are categorized as $O(\log_a n)$] are often called *logarithmic algorithms*. Because $\log_a n$ will increase much more slowly than $n$ itself, logarithmic algorithms are generally very efficient. Algorithms whose efficiency can be expressed in terms of a polynomial of the form

$$a_m n^m + a_{m-1} n^{m-1} + \ldots + a_2 n^2 + a_1 n + a_0$$

are called *polynomial algorithms*. Since the highest power of $n$ will dominate such a polynomial, such algorithms are $O(n^m)$. The only polynomial algorithms we will discuss in this book have $m = 1, 2$, or $3$, and they are called *linear, quadratic,* or *cubic algorithms,* respectively.

Algorithms with efficiency dominated by a term of the form $a^n$ are called *exponential algorithms*. Exponential algorithms are of more theoretical rather than

◇ **TABLE 1.2**

Common dominant terms in expressions for algorithmic efficiency, based on the variable $n$

| |
|---|
| $n$ dominates $\log_a n$, $a$ is often 2 |
| $n \log_a n$ dominates $n$, $a$ is often 2 |
| $n^2$ dominates $n \log_a n$ |
| $n^m$ dominates $n^k$ when $m > k$ |
| $a^n$ dominates $n^m$ for any $a > 1$ and $m \geq 0$ |

practical interest because they cannot reasonably be run on typical computers for moderate values of $n$.

## Big-O Analysis of Bubble Sort

We are now ready to carry out some real comparisons between the three sorting methods we have discussed so far—bubble, insertion, and selection. To do so, we must determine functions $f(n)$ that allow us to make statements like "Sorting algorithm X requires $O[f(n)]$ comparisons." If it turns out that all three sorts share the same $f(n)$ function, then we can conclude that the differences between them are not approaching an order of magnitude scale. Rather, they would be more subtle distinctions, which would not appear as dramatic run-time differences.

We also realize that the key to doing a big-O analysis is to focus our attention on the loops in the algorithm. We do that first for the bubble sort. Recall the loop structure of the bubble sort.

```
k = 0;
exchange_made = TRUE;
while ((k < n - 1) && exchange_made)
{
        exchange_made = FALSE;
        ++k;
        for (j = 0; j < n - k; ++j)
              if (list[j] > list[j + 1])
              {
                    temp = list[j];
                    list[j] = list[j + 1];
                    list[j + 1] = temp;
                    exchange_made = TRUE;
              }
}
```

Inner Loop

Outer Loop

Assume that we have a worst case possible for bubble sort, in which the `exchange_made` variable is always set to TRUE so that an early exit is never made from the outer loop. If we then consider the comparison at the top of the inner loop, we note that it will be executed first $n - 1$ times, then $n - 2$ times, and so on down to one time for the final execution of the inner loop. Hence, the number of comparisons will be the sum of the sequence of numbers:

$(n - 1)$ $(n - 2)$

.
.
.

1

A formula from algebra will show this sum to be

$n(n - 1) / 2$

Thus we conclude that the bubble sort is an $O(n^2)$ algorithm in those situations for which the `exchange_made` test does not allow an early loop exit.

## A NOTE OF INTEREST

### Artificial Intelligence and the Complexity of Algorithms

Perhaps no area of computer science demands as much in terms of efficient algorithms as does *artificial intelligence* (AI). Those engaged in research in this field are concerned with writing programs that have the computer mimic intelligent human behavior in limited domains such as natural language understanding, theorem proving, and game playing. Why is efficiency so important in such programs? Typically the strategy behind such a system is to have the computer search an enormous number of possibilities for the solution to the problem it is given. These possibilities comprise what is typically called the *state space* for the problem. For instance, for a computer program that plays a game such as checkers or chess, the state space would be a suitable representation of all game board configurations that could eventually be generated from the current state of the game. The computer's goal is to search through the state space, looking for a state in which it would win the game. The state space determined by the initial configuration of a chess game has been computed to be about $10^{120}$ different possible moves. The time required for a computer to examine each of these different moves, assuming it could examine one every microsecond, would be $10^{95}$ years. Even for a simpler game such as checkers, the time

required for a computer to search all states in the game would require $10^{23}$ years.

The reason for these extraordinarily large and impractical time frames is that a "brute force" strategy of searching all states in such AI applications leads to exponential algorithms. To avoid exponential algorithms, researchers in artificial intelligence have attempted to follow the lead of human reasoning. That is, the human mind seems able to eliminate many of the possibilities in a search space without ever examining them. Similarly AI programmers attempt to weed out large sections of the state space to be searched using what are known as *heuristics*. Heuristics are rules of thumb that enable one to rule out a vast number of possible states by doing some relatively simple computations. For instance, in checkers or chess, a heuristic might involve a mathematical formula that attached a positive or negative weight to a particular state of the game. Those states for which the heuristic value indicates a probable lack of success in future searching are simply eliminated from the state space. Since a heuristic is the computational equivalent of an educated guess, it runs the risk of making an error. However, it is often viewed as a worthwhile risk if it can enhance the efficiency of the search algorithm to a category that is no longer exponential.

## Big-O Analysis of Insertion Sort

Recall that the loop structure of the insertion sort is given by

```
for (k = 1; k < n; ++k)
{
    item_to_insert = list[k];
    j := k - 1;
    still_looking = TRUE;
    while ((j >= 0) && still_looking )
        if (item_to_insert < list[j])
        {
            list[j + 1] = list[j];
            --j;
        }
        else
            still_looking = FALSE;
    list[j + 1] = item_to_insert;
}
```

Outer Loop

Inner Loop

Here, if the inner loop is never short-circuited by **still_looking**, the comparison appearing as its first statement will be executed once for the first execution of the outer loop, then twice, and so on, reaching $n - 1$ executions on the final pass.

We have a situation virtually identical to our preliminary analysis of the bubble sort. That is, the number of comparisons can be bounded by $n^2/2$ and the algorithm is therefore $O(n^2)$. Of course, with the insertion sort, the hope is that setting the Boolean variable **still_looking** in the **else** clause can reduce the number of comparisons made by the inner loop. However, it is clear that we can concoct many data sets for which this will have little or no effect. So, as with bubble sort, we are forced to conclude that insertion sort cannot guarantee better than $O(n^2)$ comparisons.

## Big-O Analysis of Selection Sort

The loop structure of this algorithm was given by

```
for (int j = 0; j < length - 1; ++j)
{
    index = j;
    for (int k = j + 1; k < length; ++k)        Inner
        if (list[k] < list[index])              Loop
            index = k;                                  Outer
    if (index != j)                                     Loop
    {
        temp = list[index];
        list[index] = list[j];
        list[j] = temp;
    }
}
```

A little investigation uncovers a familiar pattern to the nested loops of the selection sort. Observe that the first time the inner loop is executed, the comparison in the **if** statement will be made $n - 1$ times. Then it will be made $n - 2$ times, $n - 3$ times, etc., and, finally, just one time. This is precisely the way the **if** statement in the bubble sort was executed in repeated passes. Thus, like the bubble and insertion sorts, the selection sort is an $O(n^2)$ algorithm in terms of number of comparisons. The area in which the selection sort potentially offers better efficiency is that the number of interchanges of data in array locations is guaranteed to be $O(n)$ because the swap in selection sort occurs in the outer loop. In both of the other sorts, the swap occurs in the inner loop but is subject to a conditional test. This means that, in their worst cases, both of the other algorithms require $O(n^2)$ swaps as well as $O(n^2)$ comparisons.

Despite the fact that selection sort will usually fare better in the number of data interchanges required to sort an array, it has a drawback not found in the other two. It is apparently impossible to short-circuit the nested loop in selection sort when it is given a list in nearly sorted order. So, for such data sets, the selection sort may be an order of magnitude worse than the other two. This is initially rather disheartening news. It seems as if it is impossible to declare any of the sorts a decisive winner. Indeed, our big-O analyses indicate that there is little to choose from the bubble, insertion, and selection algorithms.

The fact that we were able to reach such a conclusion systematically, however, is significant. It reveals the value of a big-O analysis. After all, even knowledge of a negative variety can be valuable in choosing appropriate algorithms under certain circumstances. For instance, if a particular application usually involved adding a small amount of data at the end of an already sorted list and then resorting, we now know we should avoid a selection sort. Moreover, when we study more powerful sorting techniques in the next section (and again in Chapter 8), we will see that it is indeed possible to break the $O(n^2)$ barrier limiting each of our three methods.

**EXERCISES 1.3**

1. Do a big-O analysis for those statements inside each of the following nested loop constructs.

   **a.** 
   ```
   for (k = 1; k <= n; ++k)
        for (j = 6; j <= m; ++j)
             .
             .
             .
   ```

   **b.** 
   ```
   for (k = 1; k <= n; ++k)
     {
          j := n;
          while (j > 0)
          {
               .
               .
               .
               j = j / 2;
          }
     }
   ```

   **c.** 
   ```
   k = 1;
   do
   {
        j = 1;
        do
        {
             .
             .
             .
             j = 2 * j;
        } while j <= n;
        ++k;
   } while k <= n;
   ```

2. Suppose we have an algorithm that requires precisely

   $$6 * \log_2 n + 34 * n^2 + 12$$

   operations for an input of $n$ data items. Indicate which of the following are valid big-O classifications of the algorithm.

   **a.** $O(n^3)$

   **b.** $O(n^2)$

   **c.** $O(n)$

   **d.** $O(n^2 * \log_2 n)$

   **e.** $O(n * \log_2 n)$

   **f.** $O(\log_2 n)$

   **g.** $O(1)$

   Of those that you have indicated are valid, which is the best big-O classification? Why?

3. A certain algorithm always requires 32 operations, regardless of the amount of data input. Provide a big-O classification of the algorithm that reflects the efficiency of the algorithm as accurately as possible.

4. An algorithm has an efficiency $O[n^2 \sin(n)]$. Is it any better than $O(n^2)$ for a large integer $n$?

5. Suppose that each of the following expressions represents the number of logical operations in an algorithm as a function of $n$, the size of the list being manipulated. For each expression, determine the dominant term and then classify the algorithm in big-O terms.
   a. $n^3 + n^2\log_2 n + n^3\log_2 n$
   b. $n + 4n^2 + 4^n$
   c. $48n^4 + 16n^2 + \log_8 n + 2^n$

6. Consider the following nested loop construct. Categorize its efficiency in terms of the variable $n$ using big-O notation. Finally, suppose the statements indicated by the ellipses required four main memory accesses (each requiring one microsecond) and two disk file accesses (each requiring one millisecond). Express in milliseconds the amount of time this construct would require to execute if $n$ were 1000.

```
x = 1;
do
{
        y = n;
        while (y > 0)
        {
                .
                .
                .
                —y;
        }
        x = x + x;
} while x < n * n;
```

7. Look back at the data set you constructed for Exercise 1 in Section 1.2. Evaluate the performance of insertion sort on that data set in terms of a big-O analysis.

8. You and a friend are engaged in an argument. She claims that a certain algorithm is $O(n^2 * \log_2 n)$ in its efficiency. You claim that it is $O(n^2)$. Consider and answer the following questions.
   a. Are there circumstances under which both of you could be correct? If so, explain them.
   b. Are there circumstances under which both of you could be wrong? If so, explain them.
   c. Are there circumstances under which she could be right and you could be wrong? If so, explain them.
   d. Are there circumstances under which she could be wrong and you could be right? If so, explain them.

9. You and your friend are engaged in another argument. She claims that a certain algorithm is $O(n^2 + \log_2 n)$ in its efficiency. You claim that it is $O(n^2)$. Consider and answer the following questions.
   a. Are there circumstances under which both of you could be correct? If so, explain them.
   b. Are there circumstances under which both of you could be wrong? If so, explain them.

**c.** Are there circumstances under which she could be right and you could be wrong? If so, explain them.

**d.** Are there circumstances under which she could be wrong and you could be right? If so, explain them.

**10.** Is an $O(n^2)$ algorithm also an $O(n^3)$ algorithm? Justify your answer in a carefully written paragraph.

## 1.4 The Time/Space Trade-off: Pointer Sort and Radix Sort

### OBJECTIVES

- to understand the concept of a pointer *index*
- to understand the difference between physically sorting and logically sorting
- to be able to apply pointers when logically sorting an array without interchanging data items
- to understand what is meant by the time/space trade-off
- to understand the radix sort algorithm and be able to trace its action on appropriate data sets
- to analyze the time and space efficiency of the radix sort algorithm
- to understand why the radix sort algorithm is not as generally applicable as other sorting algorithms we have studied

Early in our discussion of efficiency considerations, we noted that true run-time efficiency was best measured in fundamental machine operations and that one instruction in a high-level language may actually translate into many such primitive operations. To illustrate this, suppose that the data being sorted by one of our algorithms are records, each of which requires 100 bytes of internal storage. Then, depending on your computer, it is entirely conceivable that one comparison or assignment statement in a high-level language could generate a machine language loop with 100 repetitions of such fundamental operations: one for each of the bytes that must be swapped. Those seemingly innocent portions of code, which swap two records using a temporary storage location, actually lead to the movement of 300 bytes inside the machine.

The first question we address in this section is whether, in such a situation, we can replace this large-scale internal transfer of entire records with the much swifter operation of swapping two integers. Although the solution we discuss does not achieve an order of magnitude speed increase in the big-O sense, it nonetheless reduces the number of actual machine-level swaps by a factor proportional to the record length involved, a factor that could produce a noticeable improvement in the function's run time.

### Bubble Sort Implemented with Pointers

So far our algorithms to sort data have implicitly assumed that the data are to be *physically sorted,* that is, the data are to be arranged in order within the array being sorted. Hence, the data in the first index of our list array are the data that come first in order according to the key field; the data in the second index, second in order; and so on. However, if we are only interested in processing the data of a list in order by key field, is it really necessary that the data be arranged in physically ordered fashion in computer memory? No. It is possible to step logically through the data in order by key without physically arranging it that way in memory. To do so, we must use another array of *pointers.*

> **Pointer:** A pointer is a memory location in which we store the location of a data item as opposed to the data item itself. In the case of an array, a pointer is the index position of a data item in the array.

Pointers can keep track of the *logical order* of the data without requiring it to be physically moved. At the end of our sorting routine, `pointer[0]` tells us the location of the data that should come first in our alphabetical listing; `pointer[1]` contains the location of the data that should come second; and so on. The sorting algorithm itself uses the logic of the bubble sort to interchange pointers instead of interchanging actual data. The actual data never move; they remain precisely where

◆ FIGURE 1.7

"Before" (left) and "After" (right) snapshots of pointer sort

| | Key field of list | pointer | | Key field of list | pointer |
|---|---|---|---|---|---|
| 0 | MAXWELL | 0 | | MAXWELL | 3 |
| 1 | BUCKNER | 1 | | BUCKNER | 1 |
| 2 | LANIER | 2 | | LANIER | 2 |
| 3 | AARON | 3 | | AARON | 0 |

Snapshot of list and pointer immediately after initialization

Snapshot of list and pointer returned by pointer_bubble_sort

they were stored on initial input. Instead of the expensive, time-consuming swapping of potentially large records, we are able to swap integer pointers quickly.

A C++ function to implement this *pointer sort* technique follows. In addition to the declarations we have already been using in this chapter, this function assumes an external declaration of the form

```
typedef int pointer_array[MAX_LIST_SIZE];
```

Besides the list array, the function receives an array pointer of type pointer_array. The function initializes the pointer array to the state pictured in the "Before" snapshot of Figure 1.7. Then, via repeated swaps of integer pointers, the array is returned as shown in the "After" snapshot. As the figure indicates, the list array itself is never altered.

```
void pointer_bubble_sort(list_type list, pointer_array pointer, int n)
{
        int j, k, temp;
        boolean exchange_made = TRUE;

        // Initialize pointer array

        for (k = 0; k < n; ++k)
                pointer[k] = k;

        k = 0;

        // Make up to n - 1 passes through array, exit early if no exchanges are made
        // on previous pass

        while ((k < n - 1) && exchange_made)
        {
            exchange_made = FALSE;
            ++k;
            for (j = 0; j < n - k; ++j)
                    if (list[pointer[j]] > list[pointer[j + 1]])// Compare via pointers
                    {
                            temp = pointer[j]; // Swap pointers
                            pointer[j] = pointer[j + 1];
                            pointer[j + 1] = temp;
                            exchange_made = TRUE;
                    }
        }
}
```

**EXAMPLE 1.10**

Given the physically ordered list of Figure 1.7, trace the action of function `pointer_bubble_sort` on the array of pointers during each pass through the algorithm.

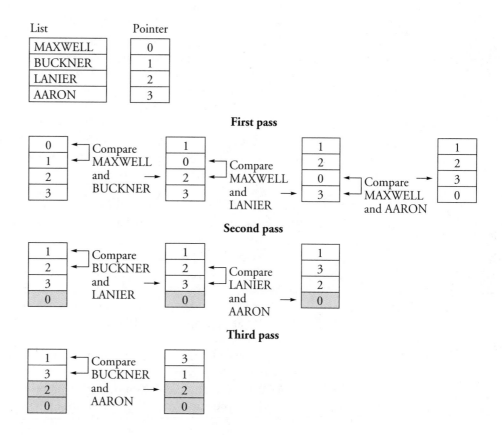

**EXAMPLE 1.11**

Suppose that `pointer_bubble_sort` was invoked from a main program or another function via the call

```
pointer_bubble_sort (student_list, pointer,
    number_of_students);
```

where `number_of_students`, `student_list`, and `pointer` are of appropriate types. If the logical order established by the pointer array is alphabetical by student name, explain how a report that listed students alphabetically could be printed after this invocation. Assume the existence of a function `print_heading` to print column headings for the report and a function `print_student` to receive an individual student object and print it in formatted form as one detail line of the report.

After the call to `pointer_bubble_sort`, `pointer[0]` contains the position of the object that is first in alphabetical order, `pointer[1]` contains the position of the object that is second, and so on. Hence the following loop will step through all of the entries in the desired order:

```
print_heading();
for (k = 0; k < number_of_students; ++k)
      print_student(student_list[pointer[k]]);
```

**Efficiency Analysis for Sorts Implemented with Pointers.** The pointer technique illustrated here for the bubble sort may also be used with the insertion and selection algorithms. In any of these cases, the mere introduction of the pointer strategy will not reduce the big-O categorization of the sort. However, in cases where the data items being sorted use enough internal storage to slow down swapping times substantially, the pointer sort can attain a considerable savings in run time.

Is this run-time savings achieved without any sacrifice? An old saying that has been passed down by computer people since the days of the early vacuum tube machines is "You get nothing for nothing." We have not escaped the consequences of that adage by using pointers to increase run-time efficiency. The pointers store *data about data;* this requires additional memory. If your application is not approaching the limits of memory, this cost may not be crucial. In certain situations, however, it could be the last straw for a program running short of memory. Thus, the pointer sort is essentially a trade-off; by using more memory, we get a program that runs faster.

This *time/space trade-off* continually recurs in the analysis of computer algorithms. Many sophisticated techniques to increase speed will need to store substantial data about data to do so. Those algorithms that solve a problem in a fashion that saves space *and* decreases run time are indeed worthy of special praise. We will be sure to note them.

Finally, the notion of a pointer, as defined and introduced here, plays an important role in our study of data structures beginning in Chapter 4. The time you spend exploring the details of the pointer sort technique will prove very valuable in your understanding of this topic in the future.

## Radix Sort

The *radix sort* algorithm is also called the *bin sort,* a name derived from its origin as a technique used on (now obsolete) machines called card sorters. These machines would sort a deck of keypunched cards by shuffling the cards into small bins, then collecting the cards from the bins into a newly arranged deck, and repeating this shuffling–collection process until the deck was magically sorted. There was, as we shall see, a very clever algorithm behind this rapid shuffling.

For integer data, the repeated passes of a radix sort focus first on the ones digit of each number, then on the tens digit, the hundreds digit, and so on until the highest order digit of the largest number is reached. For string data, the first pass hinges on the rightmost character in each string with successive passes always shifting their attention one character position to the left. To illustrate the algorithm, we will trace it on the following list of nine integers:

459 254 472 534 649 239 432 654 477

On each pass through this data, radix sort will arrange it into ten sublists (bins)—one sublist for each of the digits 0 through 9. Hence, on the first pass, all the numbers with a ones digit equal to zero are grouped in one sublist, all those with a ones digit equal to one are grouped in another sublist, and so on. The resulting sublists follow:

| Digit | Sublist | | |
|---|---|---|---|
| 0 | | | |
| 1 | | | |
| 2 | 472 | 432 | |
| 3 | | | |
| 4 | 254 | 534 | 654 |
| 5 | | | |
| 6 | | | |
| 7 | 477 | | |
| 8 | | | |
| 9 | 459 | 649 | 239 |

The sublists are then collected into one large list with the numbers in the sublist for 0 coming first, then those in the sublist for 1, and so on up to the sublist for 9. Hence we would have a newly arranged list:

```
472 432 254 534 654 477 459 649 239
```

This new list is again partitioned into sublists, this time keying on the tens digit. The result is shown below:

| Digit | Sublist | | |
|---|---|---|---|
| 0 | | | |
| 1 | | | |
| 2 | | | |
| 3 | 432 | 534 | 239 |
| 4 | 649 | | |
| 5 | 654 | 254 | 459 |
| 6 | | | |
| 7 | 472 | 477 | |
| 8 | | | |
| 9 | | | |

Note that in each sublist the data are arranged in order relative to their last two digits. The sublists would now be collected into a new master list:

```
432 534 239 649 654 254 459 472 477
```

Now, focusing on the hundreds digit, the master list would be classified into ten sublists one more time. These final sublists are shown below. When the sublists are collected from this final partitioning, the data are arranged in ascending order.

| Digit | Sublist | | |
|---|---|---|---|
| 0 | | | |
| 1 | | | |
| 2 | 239 | 254 | |
| 3 | | | |
| 4 | 432 | 459 | 472 | 477 |
| 5 | 534 | | |
| 6 | 649 | 654 | |
| 7 | | | |
| 8 | | | |
| 9 | | | |

A pseudocode statement of the radix sort algorithm follows.

1. Begin with the current digit as the ones digit
2. while there is still a digit on which to classify data
   2.1 for each number in the master list
       2.1.1 add that number to appropriate sublist, keying on current digit
   2.2 for each sublist (from 0 through 9)
       2.2.1 append that sublist to a newly arranged master list
   2.3 Advance the current digit one place to the left

If the radix sort is being applied to character strings instead of integers, this algorithm would have to proceed from the rightmost character to the leftmost character instead of from the ones digit to the highest order digit.

**Efficiency of Radix Sort.** An analysis of the loop structure in the preceding pseudocode for radix sort indicates that, for each pass through the outer `while` loop, $O(n)$ operations must be performed. These $O(n)$ operations consist of the arithmetic necessary to isolate a particular digit within a number, appending that number to the proper sublist, and then collecting it again into a new master list. Since the outer `while` loop will only be executed $C$ times—where $C$ is the number of digits (or characters) in the integer (or string)—the radix sort is an $O(n)$ sorting algorithm.

Although the radix sort is significantly faster than the other $O(n^2)$ algorithms we have studied in this chapter, there are again trade-off factors to consider. It is potentially much less space efficient than the other sorting algorithms we have studied. This is due to the need for storing sublists for each of the possible digits in the number or characters in the string. Using arrays to store the sublists and without any prior knowledge about the distribution of the data, we would be forced to allocate an additional $10n$ storage locations when sorting an array of $n$ integers and $27n$ storage locations when sorting $n$ strings of letters and blanks. We shall alleviate this memory crunch somewhat when we study linked lists in Chapter 14, but even then the radix sort will remain a space-inefficient algorithm compared to other sorting algorithms. Other criteria negating the very good time efficiency of the radix sort are its inflexibility for data of varying size and the fact that, although $O(n)$ in time, its constant of proportionality in this regard is often large enough to make it less time efficient than the more sophisticated sorting algorithms we will study in Chapter 8.

EXAMPLE 1.12    Assume the existence of the following declarations and function to perform a radix sort on an array of four-digit numbers.

```
int const MAX_LIST_SIZE = 100;

typedef int list_type[MAX_LIST_SIZE];
typedef list_type bin_structure_type[10];
typedef int bin_counter_type[10];

// Function: digit
// Computes the kth digit in number
//
```

```
// Inputs: integers number and k
// Output: the kth digit in number

int digit(int number, int k);

// Function: initialize_counters
// Initializes all counters to zero
void initialize_counters(bin_counter_type bin_counters);

// Function: add_to_bin
// Insert number in bin_structure indicated by place
//
// Inputs: a bin_structure, a bin_counter a number and a place
// Outputs: a bin_structure and a bin_counter

void add_to_bin(bin_structure_type bins,
        bin_counter_type bin_counters, int number, int place);

void collect_bins(list_type list, bin_structure_type bins,
        bin_counter_type bin_counters);
```

Then the C++ code for this radix sort would be

```
void radix_sort(list_type list, int n)
{
    int j, k;
    bin_structure_type bins;
    bin_counter_type bin_counters;

    initialize_counters(bin_counters);

    // For k loop controls digit used to classify data.
    for (k = 1; k <= 4; ++k)
    {
        // For j loop iterates through all numbers, putting them into
        // bin determined by kth digit.
        for (j = 0; j < n; ++j)
            add_to_bin(bins, bin_counters, list[j], digit(list[j], k));
        collect_bins(list, bins, bin_counters);
        initialize_counters(bin_counters);
    }
}
```

## EXERCISES 1.4

**1.** Suppose that you are given the following list of keys:

| | |
|---|---|
| 0 | 9438 |
| 1 | 3216 |
| 2 | 416 |
| 3 | 9021 |
| 4 | 1142 |
| 5 | 3316 |
| 6 | 94 |

Show what the contents of the pointer array would be after each pass through the outer loop of function `pointer_bubble_sort` discussed in this section.

2. Consider again the data set given in Exercise 1. How many passes would be made through the outer loop of the radix sort algorithm for these data? Trace the contents of the array after each of these passes.

3. Consider the following list of strings:

| 0 | CHOCOLATE |
|---|-----------|
| 1 | VANILLA |
| 2 | CARAMEL |
| 3 | PEACH |
| 4 | STRAWBERRY |
| 5 | CHERRY |

How many passes would be made through the outer loop of the radix sort algorithm for these data? Trace the contents of the list after each of these passes.

4. Explain the difference between physical and logical ordering.

5. Cite an application in which the mere logical ordering of data, as achieved by the pointer sort technique, would not be sufficient; that is, give an application in which physical ordering of data is required.

6. What is the time/space trade-off? Define and discuss various contexts in which it may arise.

7. When the bubble sort was modified with an array of pointers, did it improve its $O(n^2)$ run-time efficiency in a significant sense? Under what circumstances would you call the improvement in efficiency significant? Provide your answer to this question in a short essay in which you define "significant" and then explain why the circumstance you describe would lead to a significant improvement.

8. The bubble, insertion, and selection sort algorithms are all $O(n)$ in their space requirements. That is, each algorithm requires memory proportional to $n$ to sort the items in an array of $n$ items. From a big-O perspective, what are the space requirements of these algorithms when the pointer sort technique is incorporated into their logic?

9. Would you expect the pointer strategy to have the *least* effect on the run-time efficiency of the bubble, selection, or insertion sort? Provide a rationale for your answer in a short essay.

10. Suppose you have 1000 objects to be sorted. Would the run-time efficiency of the pointer sort increase significantly if the 1000 objects were broken into four groups, each group sorted, and then merged together as one large sorted array as compared to sorting the initial unsegmented array? Why or why not?

11. Incorporate the pointer sort technique into the selection sort algorithm.

12. Incorporate the pointer sort technique into the insertion sort algorithm.

13. Write the assumed and any other necessary functions in the version of `radix_sort` given in Example 1.12.

14. Write a radix sort function to sort an arbitrary array of integers. Analyze the space efficiency of your function.

15. Write a radix sort function to sort an array of strings. Analyze the space efficiency of your function. Be sure to state carefully the assumptions you make about strings in performing your analysis of space efficiency.

16. Describe the complications in implementing the radix sort algorithm for an array of real numbers. Discuss a strategy that could be used to overcome these complications.

## A NOTE OF INTEREST

### Computer Graphics, Visualization, and Virtual Reality

In *computer graphics,* the efficiency of algorithms and the speed of the processing hardware are of vital importance. Recent hardware developments now enable scientists to transform numeric data into computer images approaching the quality of photographs in their realism. The essential principle behind such graphics is to develop a numerical model of a physical phenomenon and then, via sophisticated mathematical algorithms, transform the model into a picture on the screen of a high-resolution graphics workstation. With faster computers and algorithms, more considerations of physical laws can be built into such models. The result of being able to incorporate more such laws is to produce images that appear very realistic.

The computational cost of such photorealism remains steep, however, progress is being made. Each year the Association of Computing Machinery's Special Interest Group on Computer Graphics (ACM SIGGRAPH) sponsors an art show at their annual meeting. The best of the digital imagery displayed at these shows is typically highlighted in the July issue of *Communications of the ACM.* For example, "Digital Image—Digital Cinema" [*Communications of the ACM,* 33, No. 7 (July 1990):30–39] and "Art & Design & Computer Graphics Technology" [*Communications of the ACM,* 34, No. 7 (July 1991):30–39] present full-color portfolios that demonstrate the degree to which the computer is influencing art and graphic design.

Who knows? Might we someday achieve the situation described by Robert Heinlein in his science-fiction novel *The Moon Is a Harsh Mistress.* In this story the president of the United States, Adam Selene, appears only on television, never in person. Why? Because he is not a human being, but solely the product of computer-generated graphic images. Such animation may soon be possible as faster hardware merges with the more efficient rendering algorithms that experts in computer graphics are now developing. Such techniques are giving rise to a new area of research known as virtual reality, in which the computer is used to view ideas without having to build a physical model.

Though it's unlikely that virtual reality will create a simulated president such as Adam Selene, it is already having a dramatic effect in design-intensive fields such as architecture. Donald Greenberg of Cornell University described such virtual reality systems in "Computers and Architecture" [*Scientific American,* 264, No. 8 (February 1991)]. According to Greenberg, "advanced modeling and rendering algorithms allow designers and clients to walk visually through buildings long before construction . . . seeing results of their design decisions immediately and revising them interactively."

## 1.5 Simple Search Algorithms

Many programs extensively employ algorithms that find a particular data item in a large collection of such items. Such algorithms, typically called *search algorithms,* are given the value of a key field that identifies the item being sought; they then return either all of the data associated with that particular key or a flag indicating that it could not be found. You saw a search algorithm in Section 10.4 when we described some operations that were frequently required in processing arrays. We now explore search algorithms and subject them to an efficiency analysis using the big-O notation we have developed.

The search operation will look for an object in a list that is associated with a target key value. Thus, rather than comparing two objects of type element, the search algorithm will have to compare a key value and an object of type element. We will assume that the element type has overloaded the standard operators for comparing a key value and an object of the element type. The general setup for the search algorithms we discuss in this chapter is given by the following skeletal declarations:

## OBJECTIVES

- to formalize a context in which search algorithms may be applied
- to understand the logic of the sequential search algorithm
- to analyze the efficiency of the sequential search algorithm
- to understand the logic of the binary search algorithm
- to recognize situations in which a key-to-address transformation may be used as an O(1) search method

```
int const MAX_LIST_SIZE = 100;
typedef int element;
typedef element list_type[MAX_LIST_SIZE];

// Function: search
// Find the object associated with the target key
// value
//
// Inputs: a list of objects, its length, and a
// target key value
// Outputs: if the target key is found, Boolean
// value TRUE and the object
// associated with the target key; otherwise,
// Boolean FALSE

boolean search(list_type list, int n,
        key_type target, element &object,);
```

Figure 1.8 graphically portrays this setup.

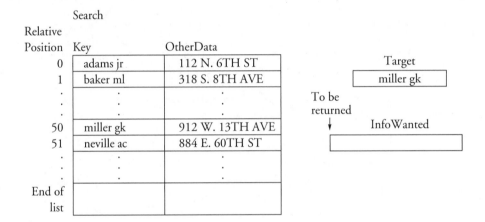

◆ FIGURE 1.8

General setup for search algorithm

## Sequential Search Algorithm

The task of a computer scientist working with search algorithms may be compared to that of a librarian. Just as the librarian must devise a method of storing books on shelves in a fashion that allows patrons to easily find the books they want, so must a computer scientist devise methods of organizing large collections of electronic data so that records within that data can always be quickly found. Imagine the plight of the librarian who just throws books on shelves as they are unpacked from shipping boxes, without any consideration toward organizing the chaos! Unless the library had an artificially small collection, it would take patrons an impractical length of time to find their reading material. Because of the lack of any organizational order imposed on the books, the only search strategy available would be to pull books from the shelves in some arbitrary sequence until the desired book was found.

As a programmer given a completely unordered set of data, this is the same strategy you would have to follow. The logic of such a *sequential search* strategy is extremely simple and appears in the following function `sequential_search`.

```
boolean sequential_search(list_type list, int n,
    key_type target, element &object)
{
    int k = 0;
    boolean found = FALSE;
    while ((k < n) && ! found)
        if (list[k] == target)
            found = TRUE;
        else
            ++k;
    if (found)
        object = list[k];
    return found;
}
```

**Efficiency of Sequential Search.** Unfortunately, the simplicity of the sequential search is offset by its inefficiency as a search strategy. Obviously, the average number of probes into the list before the target key is found will be $n/2$, where $n$ is the number of records in the list. For unsuccessful invocations of the function, all $n$ records must be checked before we can conclude failure. Thus, in terms of a big-O classification, the method is clearly $O(n)$. This may not seem bad when compared to the $O(n^2)$ efficiency of our sorting methods, but searching is conceptually a much simpler operation than sorting: It should be significantly faster. Moreover, though $O(n)$ may seem fast enough at microsecond speeds, there are many applications where an $O(n)$ time factor can be unacceptably slow.

For instance, when a compiler processes your source program in C++, it must continually search a list of identifiers that have been previously declared. (This list is typically called a *symbol table*.) Hence, in such an application, the search operation merely represents the inner loop within a much more complex outer loop that is repeating until it reaches the end of your source file: an inner loop that, repeated at $O(n)$ speeds, would make your compiler intolerably slow.

Another situation in which $O(n)$ is not good enough for searching occurs when the list being searched is stored in a *disk file* instead of a main memory array. Now, because accessing data on disk is a much slower operation than accessing data in main memory, each probe into the list might conceivably require approximately one millisecond (one-thousandth of a second) instead of a microsecond. Searching such a list of one million records at $O(n)$ speed would hence require one thousand seconds instead of just one second, which is too long to wait for one record and is certain to generate angry users. We conclude that, although the sequential search may be fast enough for small and infrequently accessed lists stored in main memory, we need something that is better by an order of magnitude for many practical applications.

## Binary Search Algorithm

By paying what may initially seem like a small price, we can dramatically increase the efficiency of our search effort using a *binary search* algorithm.

1. The list of objects with keys must be maintained in physically sorted order unless we are willing to use an additional list of pointers similar to that used in the **pointer_bubble_sort** algorithm. (See the exercises at the end of this section.)

2. The number of objects in the list must be maintained in a separate variable.

**3.** We must be able to access randomly, by relative position, objects in the list. This is the type of access you have in C++ arrays.

For instance, suppose that the list of integer keys appearing in Figure 1.9 has the access facility of the third point just cited and that we wish to locate the randomly accessible data associated with the target key 1649. The strategy of the binary search is to begin the search in the middle of the list. In the case of Figure 1.9, this would mean beginning the search with the key found at position 4. Since the target we are seeking is greater than the key found at position 4, we are able to conclude that the key we want will be found among positions 5 through 9—if at all.

We will split those positions that remain viable candidates for finding the target by accessing the middle position:

$(5 + 9) / 2 = 7$

Since the key at position 7 is greater than **target**, we are able to conclude that the key being sought will be found in positions 5 or 6—if it is to be found at all. Notice that, after only two accesses into the list, our list of remaining viable candidates for a match has shrunk to 2. (Compare this figure to a sequential search after two accesses into the same list.) We now split the distance between positions 5 and 6, arriving (by integer arithmetic) at position 5. Here we find the key being sought after a mere three probes into the list.

Crucial to the entire binary search algorithm are two pointers, **low** and **high**, to the bottom and top, respectively, of the current list of viable candidates. We must repeatedly compute the middle index of that portion of the list between **low** and **high** and compare the data at that middle index to the target using the following logic.

```
If list[middle] equals the target
        Search is done
        Target has been found in list
Else if list[middle] < target
        Low must be set to middle + 1
Else
        High must be set to middle - 1
```

Should these pointers ever merge, that is, if **high** were to equal to **low**, we would conclude that the target does not appear in the list. The entire algorithm is formalized in the following C++ function:

◆ FIGURE 1.9

Physically ordered random access list of keys for binary search

| Position | Key |
|----------|------|
| 0 | 1119 |
| 1 | 1203 |
| 2 | 1212 |
| 3 | 1519 |
| 4 | 1604 |
| 5 | 1649 |
| 6 | 1821 |
| 7 | 2312 |
| 8 | 2409 |
| 9 | 3612 |

Number of Records $n = 10$
**target** = 1649

```
boolean binary_search(list_type list, int n, key_type target, element &object)
{
        int low, middle, high;
        boolean found = FALSE;

        low = 0;
        high = n;
        while ((low <= high) && ! found)
        {
            middle = (low + high) / 2;
            if (list[middle] == target)
                  found = TRUE;
            else if (list[middle] < target)
                  low = middle + 1;
            else
                  high = middle - 1;
        }
        if (found)
           object = list[middle];
        return found;
}
```

|   | Key |   |
|---|-----|---|
| 0 | 102 | Initial low |
| 1 | 183 | |
| . | 219 | |
| . | 264 | If target > 351, then |
| middle | 351 | low must be reset to |
| . | 499 | point at 499 |
| . | 506 | |
| . | 530 | |
| n − 1 | 642 | Initial high |

//work with high end

work with low end

|   | Key |   |
|---|-----|---|
| 0 | 102 | Initial low |
| 1 | 183 | |
| . | 219 | |
| . | 264 | If target < 351, then |
| middle | 351 | high must be reset to |
| . | 499 | point at 264 |
| . | 506 | |
| . | 530 | |
| n − 1 | 642 | Initial high |

---

**EXAMPLE 1.13**    Trace the action of function **binary_search** as it locates the record associated with target 1519 in the array of Figure 1.9.

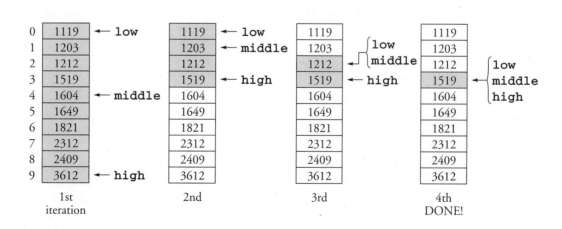

target
| 1519 |

**EXAMPLE 1.14**    Trace the action of function `binary_search` as it reports that target 2392 cannot be found in the array of Figure 1.9.

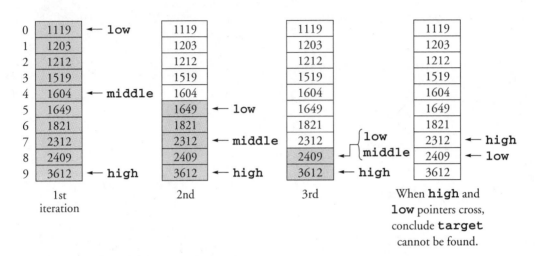

target

2392

| | 1st iteration | 2nd | 3rd | When **high** and **low** pointers cross, conclude **target** cannot be found. |

**Efficiency of Binary Search.** As indicated by the shaded portions of the lists in the preceding examples, the binary search continually halves the size of the list that must still be searched. This continual halving is critical to the effectiveness of the algorithm. When applied to the list of keys in Figure 1.9, the method in the worst case would require four different accesses. For an ordered list of 50,000 keys, the worst case efficiency is a mere 16 different accesses. (In case you do not believe this dramatic increase in efficiency as the list gets larger, try plugging 50,000 into a hand-held calculator and count how many times you must halve the displayed number to reduce it to 1.) The same list of 1,000,000 records stored on disk that would require approximately 1000 seconds to search sequentially will result in a virtually instantaneous response with the binary search strategy.

More formally, for a list of $n$ items, the maximum number of times we would cut the list in half before finding the target item or declaring the search unsuccessful is

$$(\log_2 n) + 1$$

Thus, the binary search is the first $O(\log_2 n)$ algorithm we have studied (see Example 1.10). In terms of the categorizations discussed in Section 1.3, it is a logarithmic algorithm. Expressions involving a $\log_2 n$ factor will arise frequently as we analyze other algorithms. They are extremely fast when compared to $O(n)$ algorithms, particularly for large values of $n$.

The drawback of the binary search lies not in any consideration of its processing speed but rather in a reexamination of the price that must be paid for being able to use it. For a volatile list (that is, one undergoing frequent additions and deletions), the requirement of maintaining the list in physical order can be quite costly. For large lists, it makes the operations of adding and deleting records so inefficient that the very fast search speed is all but negated. We will analyze this problem of list maintenance in more detail in future chapters.

## Key-to-Address Transformations    *Sheet #4 p1 right column*

A search technique so simple that it is often overlooked presents itself in certain situations where a record's key value can be transformed conveniently into a position within a list by applying a function to the key value. For instance, suppose that a school assigns its students five-digit identification numbers in which the first two digits indicate the student's year of matriculation and the last three digits are simply assigned in a sequential fashion among students matriculating in a given year. Hence the fourteenth student admitted in the class of 1992 would have the identification number

$$\underbrace{9\ 2}_{\text{year of matriculation}} \qquad\qquad \underbrace{0\ 1\ 4}_{\text{sequence number within that year}}$$

In such a situation, student records could be stored in a two-dimensional table in which rows were indexed by year of matriculation and columns indexed by sequence number within a given year. Then the integer arithmetic operations

```
key / 1000
```

and

```
key % 1000
```

would yield a given student's row and column index, respectively. The address of a student's record could therefore be obtained from the student's identification number using a mere two operations.

In such situations, the search efficiency to locate a student's record is O(1) in its big-O classification. The apparent restriction that must apply for this technique to work is that the transformation applied to a key to yield an address cannot yield the same address for two different students. As we shall see in Chapter 9, even this restriction can be relaxed somewhat if slightly more sophisticated search techniques are employed. Another drawback of the key-to-address transformation technique is its potentially inefficient use of space. You will perform such a space analysis for this strategy in this section's exercises.

## EXERCISES 1.5

1. Suppose that an array contains key values

   ```
   18 40 46 50 52 58 63 70 77 90
   ```

   in index locations 0 through 9. Trace the index values for the **low**, **high**, and **middle** pointers in the binary search algorithm if the **target** 43 is being sought. Repeat for **target** values 40 and 90.

2. In Exercise 10 of Section 1.2 we defined the notions of best case and worst case behavior of an algorithm. Devise sample data sets to demonstrate the best case and worst case behavior of the binary search algorithm.

3. What is a compiler symbol table? Explain why a sequential search applied to such a table is not a practical strategy.

4. Explain the difference in run-time efficiency considerations for a program that manipulates data in a main memory array versus one that accesses data stored in a disk file.

**5.** How many times would the **while** loop in function **binary_search** be executed if $n = 1,000,000$?

**6.** Consider the following modified version of the binary search algorithm. (Modifications are indicated by a comment highlighted by asterisks.) Will this new version of the binary search algorithm work correctly for all data? If not, specify a situation in which this version will fail.

```
boolean binary_search(list_type list, int n, key_type target, element &object)
{
    int low, middle, high;
    boolean found = FALSE;

    low = 0;
    high = n;
    while ((low < high) && ! found)
    {
        middle = (low + high) / 2;
        if (list[middle] = target)
            found = TRUE;
        else if (list[middle] < target)
            low = middle;          // *** Modification here ***
        else
            high = middle;         // *** Modification here ***
    }
    if (found)
        object = list[middle];
    return found;
}
```

**7.** Consider the following modified version of the binary search algorithm. (Modifications are indicated by a comment highlighted by asterisks.) Will this new version of the binary search algorithm work correctly for all data? If not, specify a situation in which this version will fail.

```
boolean binary_search(list_type list, int n, key_type target, element &object)
{
    int low, middle, high;
    boolean found = FALSE;

    low = 0;
    high = n;
    do                             // *** Use do. . .while instead of while ***
    {
        middle = (low + high) / 2;
        if (list[middle] = target)
            found = TRUE;
        else if (list[middle] < target)
            low = middle + 1;
        else
            high = middle - 1;
    } while ((low < high) && ! found); // *** Loop exit condition
    if (found)
        object = list[middle];
    return found;
}
```

8. Consider the example of a key-to-address transformation for student identification numbers given in this section. Discuss the space efficiency of this strategy. On what factor is the space efficiency dependent?

9. Devise a key-to-address transformation to locate records in a data structure for employees of the East Publishing Company. Departments in the company are identified by a one-letter code A–Z. An employee's payroll identification number consists of a department code followed by another one-letter code representing the employee's pay rate classification, and a two-digit number assigned in sequential fashion to employees within a given department. Hence, the identification number DX40 is assigned to the 40th employee in department D; the X indicates the employee's pay rate category.

10. The requirement for the binary search that the data in an array be physically ordered can actually be circumvented by keeping track of the logical order of the data via a pointer array analogous to that used in the pointer sort. Rewrite the binary search algorithm under such an assumption. Explain why it might be advantageous to use this technique.

11. Implement the following modification to the sequential search algorithm. Temporarily insert the key for which you are searching at the end of the list. Search sequentially until you find this key; then examine the position where you found it to determine whether or not the search was successful. Note that this strategy requires your knowing the number of items in the list rather than a sentinel value stored at the end of the list. Comment on the run-time efficiency of this new strategy versus the sequential search algorithm discussed in this chapter.

12. Modify the insertion sort algorithm of Section 1.2 so that it finds the insertion point for the next array entry using an appropriate modification of the halving strategy employed by the binary search algorithm. Once this insertion point is determined, other array entries must be moved accordingly to make room for the entry being inserted. After completing this modified version of the insertion sort, perform a big-O analysis of its efficiency.

13. Imagine that you have been hired to write an information retrieval program for a company or organization. You must interview people within the organization to determine exactly what their information retrieval needs are. Construct questions that you could ask in such an interview to enable you to determine which search strategy would be most appropriate for the program you must write. Then, in an essay explain how answers to these questions would dictate your choice of search strategy.

## FOCUS ON PROGRAM DESIGN

We will close each chapter with a special section that focuses on the design issues that have arisen in the chapter. In the Focus section of this first chapter we examine how we can augment a program to help us analyze its own efficiency. This technique, known as *profiling*, consists of inserting counters that accumulate the total number of times that certain critical operations are performed as an algorithm executes.

We will illustrate the technique on a program that determines all prime numbers less than or equal to a specified positive integer **number**. For purposes of this program, we will use the mathematical property that a number is prime if it has no divisors other than 1 or itself. For example, 37 is such a number. Also, note that 1 is not prime by definition.

The complete program is given below. Those portions of the program that are shaded represent additions necessary to implement the profiling of the program. We will return to a discussion of these additions after you have had a chance to read the program. Pay particular attention to the **list_all_primes** function, because it is central to analyzing the efficiency of the program.

```cpp
// Program file: primes.cpp
#include <iostream.h>
#include <iomanip.h>
#include <math.h>
#include "boolean.h"

const char SKIP = ' ';

// Global data for profiling only
const boolean PROFILE = TRUE;
int profiled_operations;

int get_a_number();

// Function: print_one_message
// Print a message for 1

void print_one_message();

// Function: print_message
// Print a heading for the output
//
// Input: the integer read

void print_message(int number);

// Function: list_all_primes
// Print list of all primes less than or equal to the integer read
//
// Input: the integer read

void list_all_primes(int number);

// Function: list_all_primes
// If integer read is one,
// then print a message for one
// else
// Print list of all primes less than or equal to the integer read
//
// Input: the integer read

void examine_the_number(int number);

// Function: more_data
// Determines whether number = -999 (the sentinel for end of input)
// Input: the integer read
// Output: TRUE, if the input is not the sentinel, FALSE otherwise

boolean more_data(int number);

// Function: profile_report
// Report a comparison of number of profiled operations to O(number^2)
//
// Inputs: the number being profiled and a global count of operations
void profile_report(int number);
```

```cpp
int main()
{
      int number;

      number = get_a_number ();
      while (more_data(number))
      {
             examine_the_number (number);
             number = get_a_number ();
      }
      return 0;
}


int get_a_number()
{
      int number;
      boolean done;


      do
      {
             cout << endl;
             cout << "Enter a positive integer; <-999> to quit.";
             cin >> number;
             done = (number == -999) || (number >= 0);
      } while (! done); // assumes valid data
      return number;
}


void print_one_message()
{
      cout << endl;
      cout << setw(10) << SKIP
             << "--------------------------"
             << endl;
      cout << endl;
      cout << setw(20) << SKIP << "1 is not prime by definition." << endl;
}


void print_message(int number)
{
      cout << endl;
      cout << setw(10) << SKIP
             << "--------------------------"
             << endl;
      cout << endl;
      cout << setw(20) << SKIP << "The number is " << number << ". "
             << " The prime numbers" << endl;
      cout << setw(20) << SKIP << "less than or equal to "<< number
             << " are:" << endl;
      cout << endl;
```

```
}
void list_all_primes(int number)
{

        boolean prime;
        int candidate, divisor;
        float limit_for_check;

        if (PROFILE)
           profiled_operations = 0;
        for (candidate = 2; candidate <= number; ++candidate)
        {
           prime = TRUE;
           divisor = 2;
           limit_for_check = sqrt(candidate);
           while ((divisor <= limit_for_check) && prime)
           {
                if (candidate % divisor == 0)
                        prime = FALSE; // Candidate has a divisor
                else
                        ++divisor;
                if (PROFILE)
                        ++profiled_operations;
           }
           if (prime)                             //Print in list of primes
              cout << setw(35) << candidate << endl;
        }
}
void examine_the_number(int number)
{
        if (number == 1)
                print_one_message();
        else
        {
                print_message(number);
                list_all_primes (number);
                profile_report (number)
        }
}


boolean more_data(int number)
{
        return number != -999;
}

void profile_report(int number)
{
        cout << endl;
        cout << "   For N: " << setw(3) << number << endl;
        cout << endl;
        cout << "   Number of profiled operations: "
             << profiled_operations << endl;
```

```
        cout << "    Compare to O(number^2): "
             << number * number << endl;
        cout << endl;
}
```

We turn our attention to trying to analyze the time efficiency of the `list_all_primes` function. The nested loop structure of this function is given by the following schematic:

```
for each candidate from 2 to number
    .
    .
    while          Inner while          Outer for loop
        .          loop executed        executed
        .          candidate – 2 or     number – 1 times
                   fewer times
```

Certainly the schematic indicates that we are safe in saying that function `list_all_primes` is $O(number^2)$ in its time efficiency. However, the early exit condition from the inner loop will be reached quite often. This leads us to believe that the algorithm may actually be substantially faster then $O(number^2)$.

Unfortunately, determining how much faster it is than $O(number^2)$ by using a purely mathematical analysis may be impossible or at least require a knowledge of mathematical number theory beyond our present means. We propose instead to use the computer to help us analyze the algorithm from an empirical perspective. An examination of the shaded code in the partial listing given here indicates that profiling the `list_all_primes` algorithm is achieved by:

1. Declaring a global Boolean constant that is set to TRUE to "turn on" profiling. All executable statements related to profiling are conditionally qualified by

   `if PROFILE . . .`

   Thus, to turn off profiling in the program, you would merely set this constant to FALSE.
2. A global variable `profiled_operations` is initialized to zero upon entry to `list_all_primes` and then increased by 1 each time an addition or % operation is performed.
3. A `profile_report` function is called conditionally by the main program to report a comparison between $N^2$ and the actual number of operations performed during execution of the algorithm.

We should justify the use of globally declared data within the function `list_all_primes`. The alternative would be to add extra parameters to the formal parameter list of `list_all_primes`—parameters that are concerned with profiling instead of the actual algorithm implemented by `list_all_primes`. That is, the profiling data items are completely extraneous to the logic of the function; they are there only to measure empirically the performance of the algorithm. As such, adding them to the formal parameter list would make the interface to the function considerably more confusing than necessary.

We emphasize that the use of global data is an exceptional circumstance, occurring in specialized contexts such as profiling. In general, the maxim that functions should only use locally declared data remains true.

Here are a few sample runs, with profiling output only.

```
Enter a positive integer, <-999> to quit. 17
      .
      . (primes listed here)
      .
   For N: 17
   Number of profiled operations: 55
   Compare to O(N^2): 289
Enter a positive integer, <-999> to quit. 45
      .
      . (primes listed here)
      .
   For N: 45
   Number of profiled operations: 296
   Compare to O(N^2): 2025
Enter a positive integer, <-999> to quit. 100
      .
      . (primes listed here)
      .
   For N: 100
   Number of profiled operations: 1133
   Compare to O(N^2): 10000
Enter a positive integer, <-999> to quit. 150
      .
      . (primes listed here)
      .
   For N: 150
   Number of profiled operations: 2414
   Compare to O(N^2): 22500
Enter a positive integer, <-999> to quit. -999
```

What have we learned from the runs of this profiled program? The observed number of operations that are reported by the program offer empirical evidence that we are well within the bounds of an $O(N^2)$ algorithm. They indicate that we can perhaps even place the algorithm into a more efficient big-O category. What category? This could be explored by fine-tuning the **profile_report** function to compare the actual number of performed operations with $n^r$ for values of $r$ less than 2 or with $n * \log_2 n$.

At the time we introduced the **list_all_primes** algorithm in Chapter 6, we commented that it was not necessarily the best way to perform this task. We can now suggest a number of ways to improve the algorithm and evaluate the efficiency of each succeeding version of the algorithm by a combination of formal big-O analysis and empirical profiling. Our series of refinements is illustrative of a process that can often be applied to the first version of an algorithm. That is, reflection on how a given algorithm works can often lead to a new algorithm, which achieves the same end in a much more efficient manner.

**Observation 1** The greatest divisor of a number, other than itself, cannot exceed one-half of the number.

**Observation 2** Divisors of a number come in pairs. For instance, 36 is divided evenly by 4 since 4 * 9 = 36. Here the divisor 4 is paired with the divisor 9. The search for divisors in the inner loop of our algorithm need not consider the larger value in such a divisor pair. Why? Because it cannot find such a larger divisor without first finding the smaller value in the divisor pair.

**Observation 3** The Greek mathematician Eratosthenes devised a "sieve" technique for finding all prime numbers between 2 and **num**. The *sieve of Eratosthenes* can be viewed as a Boolean array indexed from 2 to **num** and initialized to TRUE in all of its locations. Successive array indices are

> *Multiples of 2 greater than 2 are set to FALSE.*
> *Multiples of 3 greater than 3 are set to FALSE.*
> *Multiples of 4 can be ignored. Why?*
> *Multiples of 5 greater than 5 are set to FALSE.*
> *Multiples of 6 can be ignored. Why?*
> *Multiples of 7 greater than 7 are set to FALSE.*

and so on. The prime numbers are those array indices where a true value remains.

You will be asked to continue exploration of such prime number algorithms in the problems. Profiling can be a valuable aid in such exploration. It provides statistical evidence of an algorithm's performance in cases where pure mathematical analysis may be inconclusive.

## RUNNING, DEBUGGING AND TESTING HINTS

1. When profiling an algorithm, use a Boolean constant that can be set to TRUE or FALSE to turn profiling on or off, respectively.
2. When using integer counters in profiling a program, be careful that the number of operations executed by the algorithm does not overflow the capacity of integer storage. Most C++ implementations offer additional integer data types that can accommodate values too large for standard integers. Consult local system reference materials to find out what your version of C++ may offer in this regard.

## SUMMARY

### Key Terms

| | | |
|---|---|---|
| artificial intelligence | exponential algorithm | profile |
| best case | heuristics | proportional |
| big-O analysis | insertion sort | quadratic algorithm |
| big-O notation | linear algorithm | radix sort |
| bin sort | logarithmic algorithm | search algorithm |
| binary search | logical order | selection sort |
| bubble sort | $\log_2 n$ search algorithm | sequential search |
| compiler symbol table | order of magnitude | sieve of Eratosthenes |
| computer graphics | permutation | state space |
| cubic algorithm | physically sorted | symbol table |
| data about data | pointer sort | time/space trade-off |
| disk file | pointers | worst case |
| dominant term | polynomial algorithm | |

### Key Concepts

- ◆ An integral part of designing efficient software is the selection of appropriate algorithms to perform the task at hand.
- ◆ Two of the criteria used in selecting algorithms for a given task are time and space efficiency. An algorithm's time efficiency determines how long it requires to run. An algorithm's space efficiency is a measure of how much primary and secondary memory it consumes.
- ◆ Three simple sorting algorithms are the bubble sort, insertion sort, and selection sort. The latter minimizes the number of data interchanges that must be made at the expense of not being more efficient for data that are already partially ordered.
- ◆ Pointer sort and radix sort are techniques to enhance the time efficiency of a sort at the expense of increased space requirements.
- ◆ Three simple search algorithms are the sequential search, binary search, and key-to-address transformation technique.
- ◆ Profiling is an empirical technique that can be used to measure an algorithm's efficiency when a big-O analysis is inconclusive.
- ◆ Big-O analyses of sort and search algorithms discussed in this chapter are summarized in the following table:

| Algorithms | Time Efficiency | Additional Comments |
|---|---|---|
| Bubble sort | $O(n^2)$ comparisons and interchanges in worst case | Can be faster if input data already almost sorted. |
| Insertion sort | $O(n^2)$ comparisons and interchanges in worst case | Also can be faster if input data already almost sorted. |
| Selection sort | $O(n^2)$ comparisons, $O(n)$ interchanges in worst case | Not significantly faster if input data already almost sorted. |
| Pointer sort | Reflects number of comparisons of method on which it is layered | Though number of interchanges not reduced, amount of data swapped for each interchange is potentially less. Drawback is the additional memory required for pointers. |
| Radix sort | $O(n)$ comparisons and interchanges | Limited in the types of data on which it works, though $O(n)$ may have a large constant of proportionality, which can make the $O(n)$ rating a misleading one. For arrays, it has a large space requirement for storing sublists. |
| Sequential search | $O(n)$ probes into list in worst case | Most inefficient of search algorithms we will study, but still appropriate for small lists stored in main memory. |
| Binary search | $O(\log_2 n)$ probes in worst case | Drawbacks are that we must continually maintain a count of number of records in list and that the list must be maintained in sorted order. |
| Key-to-address transformation | $O(1)$ list probes | Not applicable for many types of keys. Potential space inefficiencies. |

PROGRAMMING
PROBLEMS
AND PROJECTS

1. Incorporate each of the observations cited in the Focus on Program Design section into the **list_all_primes** algorithm. For each successive modification to the algorithm, run a series of tests in which you use profiling to measure the efficiency of the resulting algorithm. Write up the results of your experimentation, addressing these issues:

   **a.** Which technique produces the fastest runs?

   **b.** Does any technique appear to be an order of magnitude better in its time efficiency? Cite results from profiling to back up your claims in this regard.

   **c.** What trade-offs are involved in using these techniques to achieve a faster run time?

2. Suppose that you know the keys in a list are arranged in increasing order. How could the sequential search algorithm presented in this chapter be improved with this knowledge? Rewrite the C++ function to incorporate this improvement and then test your new function in a complete program.

3. Rewrite the binary search algorithm presented in this chapter with a splitting strategy other than halving. One possibility would be to use an interpolation strategy that would examine the target's distance from the current **low** and **high** pointers. This is more analogous to the way in which we look up names in a phone book. That is, for a name beginning with *S,* we do not open the phone book to the middle page but rather to a point approximately two-thirds of the way from the beginning of the book. Test run your program against a pure binary search and, through tracing the performance of each algorithm, determine whether there is any significant difference between the two techniques.

4. Repeat Problem 3, but change your algorithm so that, after the initial interpolative guess as to the location of the target, data locations are examined sequentially in an appropriate direction until the key is found or until it can be determined that the key is not in the list.

5. Consider a list of records for students at a university. The list includes fields for student name, credits taken, credits earned, and total grade points. Write a program that, based on a user's request, will sort the list of records in ascending or descending order keying on one of the four fields within the record. For instance, the user might specify that the sort should proceed in descending order according to credits earned. As much as possible, try to refrain from having to write a separate sort function for each particular ordering and field. Experiment by developing different functions based on each of the five sorting strategies discussed in this chapter.

6. Consider the same list of records as in Problem 5. Now write a function to sort the records in descending order by credits earned. Records having the same number of credits earned should be arranged in descending order by total grade points. Those with the same number of credits earned and total grade points should be arranged alphabetically by name. Incorporate this function into the complete program that you wrote for Problem 5. Experiment by developing different functions based on each of the five sorting strategies discussed in this chapter.

7. Rewrite the pointer sort with the pointer array as a local variable instead of as a global variable. How would this affect a higher level function that calls on the pointer sort? Illustrate by calling your new version of the pointer sort from a sample main program.

8. Merge the segmenting strategy described in Exercise 10 from Section 1.4 with the insertion sort, bubble sort, and selection sort algorithms. Empirically test how this

affects the run time of the sort on a file of 1000 records. Does altering the number of segments affect the run time?

9. Implement the binary search algorithm for a disk file containing approximately 1000 records of the structure described in Problem 5.

10. Design a complete program to load information into the data base for employees of East Publishing Company described in Exercise 9 of Section 1.5. Then repeatedly call on a search function to retrieve the information associated with a given employee's identification key.

11. A *permutation* of the integers from 1 to $N$ is an arrangement of these integers in which no repetition occurs. For example,

  3 1 4 5 2

and

  5 3 2 4 1

are two permutations of the integers from 1 to 5. Write a function to load an array indexed from $0 \ldots N - 1$ with a randomly generated permutation of the integers from 0 to $N - 1$. (If your version of C++ does not have a random number generator, see Appendix 5, in which an algorithm for generating random numbers in standard C++ is discussed.) This function should be an $O(n)$ algorithm. Once you have written this function, use it to load an array repeatedly, which is then passed to a sorting algorithm such as bubble, selection, or insertion sort. Add profiling counters to the sort algorithm to keep track of the number of comparisons and data interchanges performed by the algorithm. Average these profiling counters over repeated invocations of the sort function and describe how these averages fit into the big-O analyses that were done in this chapter. Do you observe any discrepancies between your averages and the predictions of the big-O analyses? If so, attempt to explain them. For any or all of Problems 12 through 16, design a program to answer the question posed. Then analyze the time efficiency of your program by using an appropriate combination of big-O analysis and profiling. Run your program to try to see the relationship between big-O classification and actual run time as measured by a clock. Finally, for each program you implement, attempt to refine its run-time efficiency by making observations similar to those described in the Focus on Program Design section of this chapter.

12. In the first century A.D. the numbers were separated into "abundant" (such as 12, whose divisors have a sum greater than 12), "deficient" (such as 9, whose divisors have a sum less than 9), and "perfect" (such as 6, whose divisors add up to 6). In all cases, you do not include the number itself. For example, the only numbers that divide evenly into 6 are 1, 2, 3, and 6, and $6 = 1 + 2 + 3$. Write a program to list all numbers between 2 and $N$ and classify each as abundant, deficient, or perfect and keep track of the numbers in each class.

13. In the first century A.D., Nicomachus wrote a book entitled *Introduction Arithmetica*. In it, the question "How can the cubes be represented in terms of the natural numbers?" was answered by the statement that "Cubical numbers are always equal to the sum of successive odd numbers and can be represented this way." For example,

$$1^3 = 1 = 1$$
$$2^3 = 8 = 3 + 5$$
$$3^3 = 27 = 7 + 9 + 11$$
$$4^3 = 64 = 13 + 15 + 17 + 19$$

Write a program to find the successive odd numbers whose sum equals $k^3$ for $k$ having the values from 1 to $N$.

14. A conjecture, first made by the mathematician Goldbach, whose proof has defied all attempts, is that "every even number larger than two can be written as the sum of two prime numbers." For example,

$$4 = 2 + 26 = 3 + 38 = 3 + 5$$
$$10 = 3 + 7100 = 89 + 11$$

Write a program that determines for every even integer $N$ with $2 <= N$ two prime numbers $P$ and $Q$ such that $N = P + Q$.

15. A pair of numbers $M$ and $N$ are called "friendly" (or they are referred to as an "amicable pair") if the sum of all the divisors of $M$ (excluding $M$) is equal to the number $N$ and the sum of all the divisors of the number $N$ (excluding $N$) is equal to $M$ ($M \neq N$). For example, the numbers 220 and 284 are an amicable pair because the only numbers that divide evenly into 220 (1, 2, 4, 5, 10, 11, 20, 22, 44, 55, and 110) add up to 284, and the only numbers that divide evenly into 284 (1, 2, 4, 71, and 142) add up to 220. Write a program to find at least one other pair of amicable numbers. Be prepared to let your program search for some time.

16. A consequence of a famous theorem (of the mathematician Fermat) is the fact that

$$2^{(P-1)} \% P = 1$$

for every odd prime number $P$. An odd positive integer $K$ satisfying

$$2^{(K-1)} \% K = 1$$

is called a pseudoprime. Write a program to determine a table of pseudoprimes and primes between 2 and $N$. How many pseudoprimes occur that are not prime numbers?

17. The importance of communication skills in "selling" a program to those who will eventually use it should not be underestimated. Keeping this in mind, write a user's guide for the program you developed in Problem 5. You should assume that the user is able to log onto (or boot) the system, but beyond that has no other knowledge of how to run this or any other program. Remember that unless the user's guide is very, very clear *and* very, very concise, it will probably be thrown in a file drawer—and your program never used.

18. (For the mathematically inclined) consider the claim that exponential algorithms will, *in general,* become practical on parallel processing machines. Provide a carefully constructed argument in which you show that adding more processors to a machine can never result in an exponential algorithm becoming practical for a wide variety of data sets. Your argument should explain the relationship between the number of processors used and the size of the data set that can be accommodated in reasonable time by the exponential algorithm. In essay form, justify the claim that the only real mathematical answer to solving a problem with an exponential algorithm in reasonable time is to discover a nonexponential algorithm that solves the same problem.

19. One of the drawbacks to the bubble sort algorithm is that a data set with just one item out of order can lead to worst-case performance for the algorithm. First, explain how this can happen. Because of this phenomenon, a variation on the bubble sort called a *shaker sort* will, on alternative passes through the array, put the largest entry into the last index and then the smallest entry into the first index. Explain how this idea can eliminate the worst case performance of bubble sort on an array with just one item out of order. Then implement the shaker sort algorithm. Profile the number of comparisons and data interchanges in both the shaker sort and the

bubble sort for a variety of data sets. Keep track of the empirical results you obtain from profiling these two algorithms. Finally, in a written report, compare the performance of these two algorithms based on your empirical data. Be sure that your report addresses situations in which the shaker sort will actually perform worse than the plain bubble sort.

# 2 Data: From Abstraction to Implementation

*Our life is frittered away by detail ... Simplify, simplify.*
Henry David Thoreau, 1817–1862

In your first course in computer science, you learned the control structures typically used in developing algorithms. You were probably introduced to techniques to describe such control structures before you wrote them in C++. For instance, you may have used pseudocode to depict iterative and decisional considerations involved in algorithms. You might have used modular structure charts to model the stepwise refinement process that subdivides a complex problem into smaller, more manageable problems.

Later in your first course, you learned some typical data structures used in conjunction with algorithms to solve problems. Some of these, such as files and arrays, are built in to C++. Other data structures, such as lists and strings, must be constructed by the programmer. You might have learned about the C++ class as the primary means of building new data structures. Classes allow programmers to implement systems that have been specified using object-oriented design. You might even have learned object-oriented design in an informal way. We now wish to consider the problem of designing and implementing data structures from a more abstract, conceptual perspective.

In Section 2.1, we discuss the importance of building abstract models of data and draw analogies to the model building often done by engineers. In Section 2.2, we show how a C++ class can be used to bridge the gap between an object-oriented design of an abstract data type and its implementation. We use a one-key table as an example. We introduce the notion of a *generic type* in Section 2.3, by showing how one can parameterize a one-key table for its component types using a C++ *class template*. In Section 2.4, we use the generic one-key table ADT to implement a two-key table ADT. Each of these abstract data types is presented first as a conceptual object, equipped with formal properties and operations; various implementations of these abstractions are also discussed and evaluated. As we pursue our study of data structures in later chapters, the two abstract data types introduced in this chapter will continue to appear in applications.

## 2.1 The Computer Scientist as a Builder of Models

Recall the goals we set for ourselves in Section 1.1: designing software systems that are large, reliable, flexible, expandable, and efficient. Clearly, these are nontrivial. How can we have a reasonable chance of attaining them? The evolution of the answer to this question is an indication of how far the young discipline of computer science has progressed. In the late 1950s and early 1960s, there was a widely held belief that designing effective software systems was something akin to an occult art. That is, those who succeeded in designing such systems did so for a variety of mysterious reasons that could not be discerned. Their success, as opposed to the high percentage of software designers who failed, was somewhat mystical—similar to the spark of unfathomable inspiration that separates a great painter from a doodler.

## Object-Oriented Software Engineering

This view of successful software designers began to change in the latter part of the 1960s. It became increasingly evident that their methodology is typical of an engineer's approach to problem solving. What characterizes this engineering approach? To answer the question, consider the various phases involved in the successful development of a complex structure such as a bridge. First, the engineer gets together with the (often nontechnical) people who want the bridge built to learn about the function of the bridge: Is it to be part of a heavily traveled urban freeway or a one-lane country road? From such meetings, the engineer develops a conceptual picture of the bridge. This picture exists as an abstract entity in the engineer's mind and perhaps in very rough form as an initial drawing. At this stage the engineer is working with ideas and ignoring most physical construction details; that is, the engineer is working with *abstractions*.

As an object-oriented model, the bridge consists of a set of attributes and behaviors, specifying the relationships among its component parts and to its environment and potential users.

The next steps allow the engineer to come successively closer to the tangible implementation of the bridge as a physical structure. A miniature prototype of the bridge will be built. The prototype will consist of only a few attributes that allow the engineer to study the behavior of the bridge. This model will allow the engineer to come face-to-face with many potential construction problems. It also provides a way to check whether the bridge will serve the needs specified by those who originally wanted the bridge built. This prototype will be followed by the development of detailed plans in blueprint form. Again this represents a step away from the purely abstract view of the bridge toward its actual implementation. These blueprints provide the essential details to the contractor who will eventually build the bridge. This contractor completes the entire process by implementing the engineer's plans in the physical structure of the bridge. One can think of object-oriented design as the building of successively more refined and detailed prototypes, each of which fills in more of the attributes and behavior specified in a model.

As we review the engineering approach, two important points should be made.

1. The entire process that culminates in the building of the bridge is a series of refinements from an abstract view of the bridge to its very tangible implementation. This process parallels very closely the phases in the development of a successful software system, beginning with a purely conceptual view of the problem to be solved and culminating with the implementation of a solution to that problem in (C++) program code.
2. This engineering approach truly places the emphasis on design issues. The design process is a very creative endeavor. Typically, during the design process, engineers will want to try various combinations of possible options and will

frequently change their minds about many significant aspects of the overall design. The time for such experimentation is when the design exists only in abstract form, that is, when such creative considerations are possible—even encouraged—because of the openness of the conceptual model. As the model draws nearer to actual implementation, a myriad of details specific to the chosen implementation make similar "what-if" reasoning expensive and often impossible for all practical purposes.

As early software developers analyzed frequent programming failures, they looked to the already established field of engineering for a paradigm. The engineering methodology of successively refining abstract models toward an eventual implementation made sense as an approach to developing programs also. A system designer who moves too quickly into the detailed coding phase of a programming project is analogous to an engineer who allows construction of a bridge to begin before adequate planning has been done. Both are heading for final results that are inelegant and riddled with serious flaws. However, because of the more rigorous design methodology embedded for years in their profession, engineers did not find themselves in this predicament as often as did programmers.

The solution seemed obvious: Attempt to embed a similarly rigorous methodology into the discipline of computer science. Hence software engineering has developed into an important area of study within computer science. It represents an attempt to apply the structured methods of engineering to software development. At the same time, it fosters creativity by freeing the system designer from the details of program code and allowing work at a higher level of abstraction. Its goal is to assure that software is produced in a way that is cost effective and reliable enough to deserve the increasing trust we are placing in it. We will follow its dictates as we begin our excursion into more advanced programming methodology.

When an object-oriented programming language is available, object-oriented modeling and design help software engineers realize an abstract model directly in an implementation. The attributes and behavior of an abstract class can be implemented directly in the form of classes in an object-oriented programming language like C++. This has two major consequences for the software development process:

1. Prototypes can be developed very rapidly when there is little or no gap between design and implementation.
2. Many design errors still cannot be detected prior to implementation. In an object-oriented implementation, these errors are much easier to locate and correct.

We will examine many examples of this process in the remaining chapters of this book.

**EXERCISES 2.1**

1. What are the characteristics of the software engineering approach to system development?
2. From a software design perspective, explain why it is less costly to consider changes in design when the system is being modeled abstractly instead of when it is being implemented. Be sure to specify what factors enter into your consideration of the term *costly*.
3. You are working on a large software project as part of a development team. Another member of the team maintains that doing a conceptual design for the software will

only result in getting a late start in writing C++ code and will make the project fall behind schedule. Write a tactful memorandum to this team member in which you provide a convincing argument against the team member's position.

## 2.2 The One-Key Table Abstract Data Type

### OBJECTIVES

- to understand what is involved in defining an abstract data type (ADT)

- to understand what is meant by data abstraction

- to see how ADTs facilitate conceptual model building

- to understand what is meant by the implementation of an ADT

- to formally define and be able to use the one-key table ADT

- to compare and contrast several implementations of the one-key table ADT

- to see the motivation for two guidelines that govern the definition and implementation of all ADTs: the ADT use rule and the ADT implementation rule

- to recognize the shortcomings of each of these implementations and recognize the need for more sophisticated implementations to be studied in future chapters.

In Chapter 1, we approached sorting and searching from the perspective of manipulating an array of objects, each of which had a designated key field. So many data processing activities organize information by key fields that it would seem worth our while to view a collection of such objects from an abstract perspective. Doing so may allow us to bring the power of abstraction to bear in a variety of applications. The best way to clarify the conceptual, model-building approach is to provide an example.

### EXAMPLE 2.1

We have been storing a person's age in a database. Each year, we must increment the person's age by one. We also wish to add information about the person's height and weight, and remove any information about the person's waistline. The database (called person) is represented so that we can add, retrieve, or remove information (all integer values) by specifying keys (all string values). The following pseudocode algorithm describes our task:

1. Retrieve the value at the "age" key from person.
2. Add one to this value.
3. Store the sum at the "age" key in person.
4. Store the person's height at the "height" key in person.
5. Store the person's weight at the "weight" key in person.
6. Remove the value at the "waistline" key in person.

The states of a sample table before and after this process are depicted in Figure 2.1.

The high-level solution presented in Example 2.1 is totally independent of considerations regarding how the one-key tables will be represented in C++. Such considerations are details of the eventual implementation of one-key tables and must be completely avoided at this early stage of design. To consider them now would place severe restrictions on the design endeavor.

Instead, the high-level pseudocode takes the perspective that one-key tables are abstract entities that are manipulated by abstract operations such as *retrieve* and *store*. As we begin to refine this pseudocode, it is necessary to pin down exactly what we mean by these abstractions. That is, we must define the notion of a one-key table precisely enough to ensure that our pseudocode algorithm is unambiguous. Yet, our definition must be entirely conceptual: It must be free from

◆ FIGURE 2.1

States of a one-key table before and after operations

| person | |
|---|---|
| key | value |
| age | 43 |
| waistline | 34 |

⟶

| person | |
|---|---|
| key | value |
| age | 44 |
| height | 70 |
| weight | 150 |

specifics about how a one-key table will be implemented in a programming language. Such a definition will allow us to refine our algorithm without worrying about details of how a one-key table will eventually be represented.

To define a one-key table, or any other data type, at such a conceptual level is to define it as an abstract data type (ADT).

---

**Abstract data type (ADT):** An ADT is a collection of data objects that share a defined set of properties and operations for processing the objects.

---

In providing a definition for an ADT such as a one-key table, we must specify both the properties and operations shared by all one-key tables. Typically the properties are specified by describing the individual elements composing an object *and* the relationships among those individual elements. The operations may be specified using preconditions and postconditions. A precondition for an ADT operation must indicate what can be expected to be true before the operation is performed. A postcondition indicates what can be expected to be true after the operation is performed.

Toward that end, we introduce the following definition of the one-key table ADT:

**One-key table:** A one-key table is a collection of objects, each of which belongs to the same class. Each object in the collection is associated with a unique key value. The set of all key values must have a well-defined ordering in the sense that, for two different key values *a* and *b*, we can determine whether *a* < *b* or *a* > *b*. Clearly, data values such as integers, real numbers, symbols of an enumerated type, and strings meet this ordering criterion. Some examples of one-key tables are shown in Figure 2.2. Note that the objects stored in the tables are of relatively simple types; objects with a more complex internal structure may be stored in one-key tables as well.

◆ FIGURE 2.2
Some typical one-key tables

| person | | salaries | | lineup | | class_rank | |
|---|---|---|---|---|---|---|---|
| **key** | **value** | **key** | **value** | **key** | **value** | **key** | **value** |
| age | 44 | ortiz | 55000.00 | C | Berra | 1 | Steinmetz |
| height | 70 | smith | 45000.00 | CF | Mantle | 2 | O'Leary |
| weight | 150 | vaselli | 62000.00 | SS | Kubek | 3 | Rakowski |

The operations for a one-key table follow.

---

**Create operation**
Preconditions:    Receiver is an arbitrary one-key table in an unpredictable state.
Postconditions:   Receiver is initialized to an empty table.
**Empty operation**
Precondition:     Receiver is a one-key table.
Postcondition:    If receiver contains no objects, the Boolean value TRUE is returned; otherwise, the Boolean value FALSE is returned.

---

**Length operation**

Precondition:     Receiver is a one-key table.

Postcondition:    The number of objects currently in the table is returned.

**Store operation**

Preconditions:    Receiver is a one-key table. **target** is a key value. **item** is an object to be inserted in receiver. If target is not a key already in the table, there is memory available to store **item**.

Postconditions:   If an object is already associated with **target** in receiver, it is replaced by **item**. Otherwise, receiver has **item** inserted and associated with **target**.

**Remove operation**

Preconditions:    Receiver is a one-key table. **target** is a key value associated with an object to be removed from the table.

Postconditions:   If the object with the **target** key can be found in the table, it is removed, **item** contains the object associated with **target**, and the operation returns TRUE. Otherwise, the operation returns FALSE, **item**'s contents are undefined, and the table is left unchanged.

**Retrieve operation**

Preconditions:    Receiver is a one-key table, and **target** is a key value to be found in the table.

Postconditions:   If the **target** can be found in the table, then **item** contains the object associated with **target** and the operation returns TRUE. Otherwise, the operation returns FALSE, and **item**'s contents are undefined. In either case, the one-key table is left unchanged.

Several comments are now in order.

**1.** The term *receiver* refers to the object or the instance of the ADT being operated on.

**2.** Some of the operations, such as **length**, **empty**, and **retrieve**, merely reveal information about the internal state of the object. Other operations, such as **store** and **remove**, change information in the internal state of the object.

**3.** Note that a one-key table is described from a completely conceptual perspective: There is no hint of a realization of one-key tables in a particular programming language.

**4.** The **create** operation will be a standard operation for every ADT we discuss. It represents an initialization process which any object must undergo before it can be successfully acted on by other operations. We have tried to emphasize this point in the definition of the ADT by frequently mentioning the need for a "previously created" one-key table in the precondition for an operation. In future ADT definitions we shall frequently leave this unsaid. Remember that the assumption is that no object is ever acted on by any operation until it has been created.

The effect of each operation is highlighted in Figure 2.3 for a one-key table in which the key is a string representing a name and the object is a real number representing a grade point average.

◆ FIGURE 2.3

The effects of the operations on a one-key table

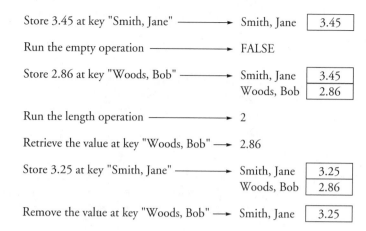

◆ FIGURE 2.4

Hierarchy of levels of abstraction for implementing a one-key table

The separation of an ADT's specification from declarations and instructions that implement the data type in a particular language is called *data abstraction*. It turns out that some abstract data types will have very easy implementations in C++. The C++ implementations of other abstract data types will be much less direct. At early stages of problem analysis, we don't want the considerations of a programming language to influence our solution to the problem. Such considerations should come later, after we have accurately described the problem.

An abstract data type may be viewed as a formal description of data elements and relationships that are envisioned by the software engineer; it is thus a conceptual model. Ultimately, however, this model will be implemented in an appropriate computer language via declarations for the elements and relationships and instructions (often in the form of function calls) for the operations. At an even deeper level, the implementation of the abstract data type in a computer language is translated by the compiler into a physical, electronic representation on a particular computer. This hierarchy of levels of abstraction is illustrated in Figure 2.4.

## A C++ Interface for the One-Key Table ADT

The first step in moving toward an implementation of an ADT in an object-oriented language such as C++ is to restate the operations that act on ADT objects as declarations of public member functions in a class declaration module. We shall call such a collection of function declarations the C++ *interface for an ADT*. A class declaration module that specifies the interface for the one-key table ADT is

```
// Class declaration file: onetable.h

#ifndef ONE_TABLE_H

#include "boolean.h"
#include "element.h"
#include "assoc.h"

// Declaration section

// We assume that constant MAX_TABLE_SIZE
// and types boolean, element, association, and key_type
// are already defined.

class one_key_table
{

        public:

        // Class constructors

        one_key_table();
        one_key_table(const one_key_table &table);

        // Member functions

        int length();
        boolean empty();
        void store(const key_type &target, const element &item);
        boolean retrieve(const key_type &target, element &item);
        boolean remove(const key_type &target, element &item);
        one_key_table& operator = (const one_key_table &table);

        protected:

        // Data members

        int table_length;
        association data[MAX_TABLE_SIZE];

};

#define ONE_TABLE_H
#endif
```

Note several things about this module:

1. There is a declaration of a second class constructor, the copy constructor. This constructor does not appear in the abstract definition of the ADT, but is necessary for the C++ implementation. The computer uses this operation when-

ever an instance of a one-key table is passed as a value parameter to a function or is returned as a function's value.

**2.** The assignment operator is overloaded, so that a one-key table object can be assigned to a variable.

**3.** The remaining public member functions exactly reflect the operations that we listed in the conceptual definition given earlier. This should be true in general for any ADT that we implement as a C++ class.

**4.** The key and element types are abstract, in that we do not really have to know what they are from the perspective of the one-key table class.

**5.** The protected data members in the class declaration section also provide a clue as to how we will be representing a one-key table in C++. We will maintain the current length of a table in a data member called `table_length`. We will use an array, called `data`, of *association* objects to store the data in the table. The association class, declared in the header file `assoc.h`, must therefore be included before the declaration of the one-key table class.

**6.** The use of the association class to implement a one-key table class is completely hidden from users of the one-key table. They have awareness only of using keys, elements, and one-key tables.

The following example presents a short driver module that would use the one-key table class just declared. We assume that the header file `element.h` has defined the `element` type as an `int` and the `key_type` as a `string`.

## EXAMPLE 2.2

```
// Program file: tabdriv.cpp

#include <iostream.h>
#include "strlib.h"
#include "element.h"
#include "onetable.h"

int main()
{
    one_key_table john;                    // Create table

    element item;                          // Auxiliary variable

    john.store("weight", 150);
    john.store("height", 72);
    john.store("age", 40);                 // Store some data

    if (john.retrieve("age", item))        // Retrieve the data
        cout << "Age = " << item << endl;
    else
        cout << "Failure" << endl;
    if (john.retrieve("height", item))     // Retrieve the data
        cout << "Height = " << item << endl;
```

```
          else
              cout << "Failure" << endl;
          if (john.retrieve("weight", item))       // Retrieve the data
              cout << "Weight = " << item << endl;
          return 0;

}
```

## Implementations of the One-Key Table ADT

We will consider two implementations of a one-key table in this section; each will have major shortcomings from an efficiency perspective. In future chapters, we will explore more sophisticated implementations that can improve these inefficiencies. Before we examine the implementations, let us discuss the association ADT. Briefly, an association consists of two attributes, a key and a value. The only purpose of an association is to help us organize the data in a one-key table. We specify the interface for the association ADT as follows.

| | |
|---|---|
| **Create operation** | |
| Preconditions: | Receiver is an association in an unpredictable state. **key** is a key value. **item** is the object to be associated with **key**. |
| Postcondition: | Receiver is initialized to associate **item** with **key**. |
| **Get key operation** | |
| Preconditions: | Receiver is an association. |
| Postconditions: | **key** is returned. |
| **Get value operation** | |
| Preconditions: | Receiver is an association. |
| Postconditions: | **value** is returned. |
| **Set value operation** | |
| Preconditions: | Receiver is an association. **item** is an object to be inserted. |
| Postconditions: | **item** replaces the object currently in the association. |

The C++ class declaration module for association is

```
// Class declaration file: assoc.h

#ifndef ASSOC_H

#include "element.h"

// Declaration section

// We assume that types element and key_type are already
// defined.

class association
{
        public:

        // Class constructors

        association();
        association(const association &a);
        association(const key_type &key,
            const element &item);
```

```
    // Member functions

    key_type get_key();
    element get_value();
    void set_value(const element &item);
    association& operator = (const association &a);

    private:

    // Data members

    key_type the_key;
    element the_value;
};


#define ASSOC_H
#endif
```

**Implementation 1: Physically Ordered Array with Binary Search** The strategy of this implementation is to maintain the array of associations in physical order by key. For example, the association at `data[0]` will have the smallest key, while the association at `data[table_length - 1]` will have the largest key.

---

**EXAMPLE 2.3**

This ordering will support a binary search during the **retrieve** operation. The code for this is modeled after the algorithm we analyzed in Chapter 11:

```
boolean one_key_table::retrieve(const key_type &target,
    element &item)
{
    int first, last, middle;
    key_type key;
    boolean success = FALSE;

    first = 0;
    last = table_length;
    while ((first < last) && ! success)
    {
        middle = (first + last) / 2;
        key = data[middle].get_key();
        if (key == target)
            success = TRUE;
        else if (key > target)
            last = middle - 1;
        else
            first = middle + 1;
    }
    if (success)
        item = data[middle].get_value();
    return success;
}
```

---

◆ FIGURE 2.5

Storing an item at a new
key in a one-key table

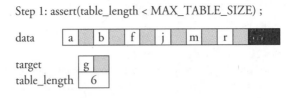

Step 1: assert(table_length < MAX_TABLE_SIZE) ;

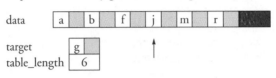

Step 2: search for key greater than or equal to key to be stored

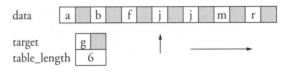

Step 3–4: keys not equal and room exists, so shift data to the right.

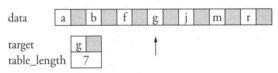

Step 5: insert new association into appropriate slot and increment table_length

To store an object in the table in this implementation, we must do the following:

1. Search for the first association in the array that has a key greater than or equal to that of the item we are adding.
2. If the association's key is equal to our target key, just replace the item in that association with our new item and quit.
3. Otherwise, examine the current length of the table to ensure that there is room to add a new association. In this implementation, use the C++ **assert** function to halt program execution if there is no memory available. Otherwise, beginning with the current association, move all associations down one slot in the array.
4. Finally, create and insert a new association into the array slot that has been vacated and increase by 1 the length of the table.

These actions are highlighted in Figure 2.5. Carefully study Figure 2.5 in conjunction with examining the code in Example 2.4.

EXAMPLE 2.4    Write complete C++ code for the **store** operation. This operation must maintain a correspondence between the physical order of the associations in the array and the logical order of the keys in the associations.

```
void one_key_table::store(const key_type &target, const element &item)
{
        int probe = 0;
        boolean found = FALSE;
        key_type key;

        while ((probe < table_length) && ! found)            // Search for position
        {
                key = data[probe].get_key();
                if (key >= target)
                        found = TRUE;
                else
                        ++probe;
        }
        if (found && (key == target))                        // Key already in table
                data[probe].set_value(item);
        else
        {
                assert(table_length < MAX_TABLE_SIZE); // Room available?
                for (int i = table_length; i > probe; --i) // Yes, move them over
                        data[i] = data[i - 1];
                association a(target, item);
                data[probe] = a;
                ++table_length;
        }
}
```

As you can see, the excellent efficiency of retrievals with this implementation is paid for by potentially expensive insertions and removals. The **create**, **remove**, **empty**, and **length** operations are left as exercises.

**Implementation 2: Unordered Array with Sequential Search** Our second implementation attempts to eliminate the inefficiency involved in moving a potentially large number of objects each time a **store** is performed. The encapsulation of the one-key table ADT still includes an array of associations and a counter. However, now when an association is added, it is merely added after the last item currently stored in the array. Figure 2.6 illustrates this

◆ FIGURE 2.6
A more efficient store operation

Physical order of keys in array does not correspond to logical order in table.

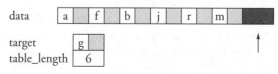

Therefore, new data are always added to the right of the last data in the table.

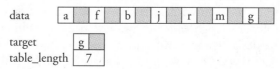

strategy. As you can see, the increase in efficiency of the **store** operation is being bargained for a decrease in efficiency for retrievals. The **retrieve** operation would now require a sequential search. The details of this implementation are left for you as exercises.

These trade-offs in efficiency for various operations are what make the one-key table ADT a particularly interesting one to study. We will return to it often in future chapters.

## Observations on ADTs and Their Implementations

We can now make some observations about the relationship between ADTs and their various implementations. These observations represent general conclusions that may be applied to all of the ADTs we will study. Here, we illustrate them with the one-key table ADT and its two implementations.

First, high-level logic, such as that presented in Example 2.1, cannot distinguish between different implementations of an ADT. We should be able to plug any implementation of an ADT into high-level logic without changing that logic. This shielding of high-level logic from any implementation details is summarized in the following two rules:

> **ADT use rule:** Algorithms that use an abstract data type should only access variables of that ADT through the operations provided in the ADT definition.

> **ADT implementation rule:** An implementation of an abstract data type must provide an interface that is entirely consistent with the operations specified in the ADT's definition.

If users and implementors of ADTs comply fully with these rules, all high-level logic will be plug-compatible with all possible implementations of an ADT. The implementation is said to exhibit *information hiding:* It hides information from higher level logic. This is the ideal. In some situations, the syntax of C++ will force us into compromising the ideal. We will be careful to point those situations out and hold such compromises to a minimum.

Second, if high-level logic cannot tell the difference between two implementations, then why would we ever want more than one implementation of an ADT? Part of the answer lies in the different time and space efficiencies that various implementations provide. For instance, applications that perform frequent retrievals from a one-key table would benefit from the choice of the implementation in which the physical order of the associations in the array mirrors the logical order of the keys in the associations.

Another aspect of the answer to this question is the limitations that an implementation may impose as it attempts to model an abstraction. For instance, an array implementation of the one-key table ADT imposes a maximum length limitation. When we study linked lists in Chapter 4, we will be able to provide an implementation of the one-key table ADT that does not have this maximum length restriction.

The availability of different implementations of an ADT—all compatible from their outward interface—gives rise to some very exciting prospects for the software design endeavor we have been describing in this chapter. At a high level, we design complex software by constructing a model that operates only on abstract data types. Once we have a high-level model with which we are satisfied, we can plug in the best implementation of the ADT for our particular application.

## A NOTE OF INTEREST

### Association Lists and Dictionaries

The idea of associating data objects with key values in tables probably received its first expression in a programming language when LISP was developed more than 30 years ago. LISP, an acronym for List Processing Language, was designed to process lists of symbolic information in AI applications. These applications frequently need to associate information with a symbol. For example, a natural language processing application will have to maintain a dictionary of terms in a language. The keys for a dictionary would be symbols representing the words, and the values would be definitions or other information associated with the words. Every dialect of LISP recognizes a particular kind of list called an *association list*. An association list is a list consisting of key/value pairs. Once an association list has been defined, a LISP programmer can look up the value associated with a given key by using the LISP function **assoc**.

The object-oriented language Smalltalk, which is also used in many symbol processing applications, comes with a built-in hierarchy of collection classes. One subclass of the Smalltalk collection class is called a *dictionary class*. The dictionary class is similar to the association list in LISP. One difference is that the implementation of a dictionary in Smalltalk is geared toward very efficient retrievals, whereas a LISP association list supports only a linear search method.

Our one-key table ADT borrows much from these ideas in LISP and Smalltalk. In particular, the order of the data in the conceptual table is not specified for the user of the table, but it may be important for the efficiency of the implementation. One major difference is that we allow any key values that can be ordered, whereas LISP and Smalltalk usually allow only strings or symbols as keys. Another major difference is that all of the data values in our one-key table must be of the same type; LISP and Smalltalk allow objects of different types to be stored in the same association list or dictionary.

If formalized big-O analysis is inconclusive about which is the best implementation, it is relatively painless to experiment with several implementations. Different implementations can be plugged in, we can empirically profile their performance, and then choose the best. With the ADT approach, all this experimentation can be done without any modification of the high-level model.

**EXERCISES 2.2**

1. Complete the implementation of the one-key table by developing code for the **create**, **length**, **empty**, and **remove** operations. Be sure to obey the ADT implementation rule.

2. Provide a big-O efficiency analysis of the two different implementations of the store operation. You should consider both the number of comparisons and data interchanges in this analysis.

3. Consider the second implementation of the **store** operation. Is there a way to take advantage of the fact that the array is sorted when looking for the target key's appropriate position? If so, write an improved version of the function and provide a big-O analysis.

4. Provide a big-O efficiency analysis of the **remove** operation. You should consider both the number of comparisons and data interchanges in this analysis.

5. Is there a way to improve the efficiency of the **remove** operation for the second implementation? If so, write a new version and provide a big-O analysis.

6. Some applications may need to process all of the objects currently in a one-key table. For example, one might wish to output all of the objects in the order of their keys. It would be useful to provide two new operations, called **keys** and **values. keys** returns a sorted array of the keys currently in the table, and **values** returns an unsorted array of the objects currently in the table. First specify these as ADT operations with preconditions and postconditions, and then write the C++ code for them.

## 2.3 The One-Key Table as a Generic Type

**OBJECTIVES**

- to understand the potential interactions among data types used to define ADTs

- to understand how generic types avoid the limitations imposed by these interactions

- to learn how to recognize where a generic type would be useful, and how to spot types that can be generalized

- to learn how to design, implement, and extend a C++ class template to represent a generic type

The one-key table is a fairly flexible ADT. Objects of any type can be stored in a table, as long as the objects are all of the same type. Objects may be associated with keys of any type, as long as the keys are capable of being ordered. We have used the type names `element` and `key_type` to indicate this generality, both in the abstract specification of the ADT and in the C++ implementations of the one-key table. In fact, both `element` and `key_type` are also ADTs, so we have a good example of how three different ADTs (including `association`) can be used to construct a new ADT.

Nevertheless, our one-key table ADT has a serious limitation. We have said that `element` and `key_type` can be any types we wish, but all tables in an individual application must have the same `element` type and the same `key_type`. The reason for this is that there can be only one definition of `element` and one definition of `key_type` in an application. This means that clients who wish to use a table of integers keyed by strings and a table of strings keyed by integers cannot use our ADT. A client may object that a table is a table, no matter what the key type and element type are. The client is right: if the table, key, and element types are truly abstract, then they should not interact in this restrictive way.

A similar problem arises in the case of algorithms. If an algorithm for computing the square root of a number only functioned for one particular number, users would object that the algorithm should work for any number in the problem domain. We write an algorithm to solve a general class of problem instances, and typically represent the algorithm as a function and the class of problem instances as a formal parameter to the function.

In the case of data types, we would like to generalize ADTs to accommodate a class of different component types. When an ADT is defined, its component types would be specified as formal parameters. When an object of that type is created, the application would fill in the formal type parameters with the particular component types desired. In the case of the one-key table, an application could use several different key and element types, and still be using the same ADT for one-key tables. This kind of ADT is known as a generic type.

### Class Templates

Not all programming languages support the definition of generic types. In C++, a class template is used to represent generic ADTs. In the case of one-key tables, a C++ class template allows the pseudocode

Create a table of integers keyed by strings
Create a table of real numbers keyed by strings
Create a table of persons keyed by strings
Create a table of strings keyed by integers

to be represented in C++ as

```
one_key table<string, int> ints_by_strings;
one_key table<string, float> floats_by_strings;
one_key table<string, person> persons_by_strings;
one_key table<int, string> strings_by_ints;
```

in one application, where the identifiers listed in angle brackets are the names of types or classes in C++. These statements would create new, empty tables capable of storing elements of the specified types at keys of the specified types. Once they are created, each of these tables is manipulated by using the standard operations described in our ADT definition.

We will first consider how to define a class template to allow users to specify the element type of a one-key table, and then show how to extend the definition to support the parameterization of key types. We start with the class declaration module of the one-key table from Section 2.2, and replace every instance of the type name `element` with the shorter notation `E`. `E` will serve as the formal parameter name for the element type. For example, the member function declaration

```
void store(const key_type &target, const element &item);
```

becomes

```
void store(const key_type &target, const E &item);
```

Because associations contain elements, the association class must also be generalized to take the element type as a parameter. We pass the type parameter `E` to the association class when we define the data member for the array, using the notation <E>, as follows:

```
association<E> data[MAX_TABLE_SIZE];
```

Finally, we specify that `E` is a type parameter for a one-key table class template by changing the heading of the class declaration to be

```
template <class E> class one_key_table
```

The rest of the code for the data members and declarations of member functions remains the same:

```
// Class declaration file: onetable.h

#ifndef ONE_TABLE_H

#include "boolean.h"
#include "element.h"
#include "assoc.h"

// Declaration section

// Generic class for element type E.

// We assume that constant MAX_TABLE_SIZE
// and the key type are already defined in element.h.

template <class E> class one_key_table
{

    public:

    // Class constructors

    one_key_table();
    one_key_table(const one_key_table<E> &table);

    // Member functions
```

```
                        int length();
                        boolean empty();
                        void store(const key_type &target, const E &item);
                        boolean retrieve(const key_type &target, E &item);
                        boolean remove(const key_type &target, E &item);
                        one_key_table<E>& operator = (const one_key_table<E> &table);

                        protected:

                        // Data members

                        int table_length;
                        association<E> data[MAX_TABLE_SIZE];

                    };

                    #define ONE_TABLE_H
                    #endif
```

Before we can use the new template class, we must make changes in the class implementation module for the one-key table and in the modules that implement the association ADT. For example, the implementation of the **store** function would now be

```
template <class E>
void one_key_table<E>::store(const key_type &target, const E &item)
{
      int probe = 0;
      boolean found = FALSE;
      key_type key;

      while ((probe < table_length) && ! found)          // Search for position
      {
            key = data[probe].get_key();
            if (key >= target)
                    found = TRUE;
            else
                    ++probe;
      }
      if (found && (key == target))                       // Key already in table
            data[probe].set_value(item);
      else
      {
            assert(table_length < MAX_TABLE_SIZE);        // Room available?
            for (int i = table_length; i > probe; --i)    // Yes, move them over
                    data[i] = data[i - 1];
            association<E> a(target, item);
            data[probe] = a;
            ++table_length;
      }
}
```

Note four things about the changes that have been made to this function:

1. The notation **template <class E>** appears above the function heading. The same prefix should appear above the function heading of every member function in the implementation module.
2. The notation **<E>** appears after the class name in the function heading. This notation should also be the same in the heading of every member function.
3. The symbol **E** appears where the element type is specified in the formal parameter list in the function heading. Here we are using the template parameter to refer to the type of a formal parameter to the function.
4. The notation **<E>** appears once more, when a new association is created. Here, we are passing a template parameter to another type.

If the use of **E** and **<E>** in the preceding example still seems confusing, here is a rule of thumb for distinguishing them: We use the angle bracket notation when we wish to specify an object as a parameter of a type; we omit the angle brackets when we wish to refer to a type directly (as the type of a variable or parameter of a function).

The remaining changes to the one-key table class are left as exercises. The following example is a driver program that tests the revised classes. We assume that the key type is defined as **string**.

## EXAMPLE 2.5

```cpp
// Program file: testgen1.cpp

#include <iostream.h>
#include <iomanip.h>
#include "boolean.h"
#include "strlib.h"
#include "onetable.h"

int main()
{
    one_key_table<int> ints;              // Create tables
    one_key_table<string> strings;
    one_key_table<float> floats;

    int i; // Auxiliary variables
    float f;
    string s;

    ints.store("age", 40);                // Store some data
    strings.store("hair color", "brown");
    floats.store("salary", 50540.00);

    if (ints.retrieve("age", i))       // Retrieve the data
            cout << "Age = " << i << endl;
    if (floats.retrieve("salary", f))
            cout << fixed << setprecision(2) << showpoint
                 << "Salary = " << f << endl;
```

```
        if (strings.retrieve("hair color", s))
                cout << "Hair color = " << s << endl;
        return 0;
    }
```

To remove the remaining restriction that all tables in an application have the same key type, we can extend the template class by adding a formal parameter for the key type. As before, we start by replacing each instance of the word **key_type** in the current class declaration module by a shortened form, in this case, **K**. Because the association class uses the key type, we pass **K** as a parameter to **association** in the data member declaration, as follows:

```
    association<K, E> data[MAX_TABLE_SIZE];
```

Finally, we change the heading of the class declaration to be

```
    template <class K, class E> class one_key_table
```

Once again, the rest of the code for the data structures and function declarations remains the same:

```
// Class declaration file: onetable.h

#ifndef ONE_TABLE_H

#include "boolean.h"
#include "element.h"
#include "assoc.h"

// Declaration section

// Generic class for key type K and element type E.

// We assume that constant MAX_TABLE_SIZE is already defined.

template <class K, class E> class one_key_table
{

        public:

        // Class constructors

        one_key_table();
        one_key_table(const one_key_table<K, E> &table);

        // Member functions

        int length();
        boolean empty();

        void store(const K &target, const E &item);
        boolean retrieve(const K &target, E &item);
        boolean remove(const K &target, E &item);
        one_key_table<K, E>& operator =
                (const one_key_table<K, E> &table);
```

```
         protected:

             // Data members

             int table_length;
             association<K, E> data[MAX_TABLE_SIZE];

     };

#define ONE_TABLE_H
#endif
```

The implementation of the default class constructor specifies a list of two type parameters for the class template above the function heading:

```
template<class K, class E>
one_key_table<K, E>::one_key_table()
{
        table_length = 0;
}
```

When the rest of the class implementation module for the one-key table and the modules for the association class have been suitably modified, we can run the test driver in the next example.

## EXAMPLE 2.6

```
// Program file: testgen2.cpp

#include <iostream.h>
#include "strlib.h"
#include "onetable.h"

int main()
{
        one_key_table<string, int> ints_by_strings;          // Create tables
        one_key_table<int, string> strings_by_ints;

        int i_element; // Auxiliary variables
        string s_element;

        ints_by_strings.store("age", 40);                    // Store some data
        strings_by_ints.store(911, "emergency");

        if (ints_by_strings.retrieve("age", i_element))      // Retrieve the data
              cout << "Age = " << i_element << endl;
        if (strings_by_ints.retrieve(911, s_element))
              cout << "911 = " << s_element << endl;
        return 0;
}
```

The process of recognizing the need for generalizing a type is a bit like the process of spotting patterns of instructions that can be generalized as functions. In the case of functions, we see a general pattern that is shared by several chunks of code. We place this pattern in a function block, and parameterize the function for whatever variations occur in the original patterns. In the case of data types, we have a general pattern in a class definition that would have to be repeated in new class definitions if we were to use other component types (tables of integers, tables of strings, etc.). We preserve this pattern in a generic type, and parameterize the type for the component types that might vary for different applications of the type. We now formalize these ideas in another principle for the design of abstract data types:

> **ADT Generality Rule:** An abstract data type should not be limited by the types of its components. Wherever possible, users should be able to specify the component types of a generic abstract data type.

Generic types provide an extremely powerful way of modeling data, and C++ class templates are an excellent way of representing generic types in a programming language. Many of the abstract data types that we discuss in the following chapters are good candidates for generalization. Therefore, we will make frequent use of class templates in our implementations.

## EXERCISES 2.3

1. Complete the implementation of the one-key table ADT that is parameterized for the element type only.
2. Complete the implementation of the one-key table ADT that is parameterized for the element type and the key type.
3. Write the specifications for a generic *ordered collection* ADT. An ordered collection is like an array, in that data can be stored or examined by specifying an integer index position. However, unlike an array, an ordered collection maintains a count of the number of data values currently stored in it. This count is used to restrict the range of allowable index values (from zero to count - 1). Data can be added to or removed from either end of the collection, subject to the preconditions that the collection is not full or not empty, respectively.
4. Declare and implement the ordered collection class that you specified in Exercise 3.
5. Use the ordered collection class to implement the **keys** and **values** operations for generic one-key tables.

## 2.4 The Two-Key Table Abstract Data Type

Consider the problem of maintaining statistics for a baseball league. The statistics might be printed in a newspaper as follows:

|  | AB | HITS | 2B | 3B | HR | AVE |
|---|---|---|---|---|---|---|
| Alomar | 521 | 192 | 25 | 6 | 29 | .369 |
| Brett | 493 | 180 | 16 | 3 | 41 | .365 |
| Canseco | 451 | 160 | 30 | 1 | 50 | .354 |
| Dribble | 590 | 205 | 41 | 10 | 20 | .347 |
| Hubble | 501 | 167 | 21 | 2 | 17 | .333 |
| Marachino | 485 | 156 | 32 | 4 | 24 | .321 |
| Noguchi | 562 | 180 | 24 | 2 | 32 | .320 |
| Perez | 499 | 159 | 21 | 4 | 21 | .318 |
| Sokoloski | 480 | 149 | 16 | 10 | 15 | .310 |
| Tanenbaum | 490 | 150 | 14 | 0 | 23 | .306 |

A database for storing this information should be organized so that we could quickly obtain answers to queries such as "How many hits does Alomar have?" One way to conceptualize this organization is to imagine a table in which the desired data object is retrieved by specifying two keys, the name of the player and the category of the statistic. In the case of our example query, the answer might be obtained by running the abstract operation

```
retrieve the data at keys "Alomar" and "HITS"
```

This manner of conceptualizing and using a database is so common that we will develop a new abstract data type, the two-key table, that can be used by any application. As with the one-key table, we first specify the attributes and behavior of the two-key table conceptually. Then we choose an implementation in C++. Finally, we do a big-O analysis of the behavior of our implementation and discuss the trade-offs of alternative implementations.

**Two-key table:** A two-key table is a collection of objects, each of which belongs to the same class. Each object in the collection is associated with two key values, called *key1* and *key2*. Each key1 value, called a *primary key*, is unique. Each key2 value, called a *secondary key*, may be used with more than one primary key, but must indicate a unique data element when associated with a primary key. The set of all key1 values must have a well-defined ordering in the sense that, for two different key1 values *a* and *b*, we can determine whether *a* < *b* or *a* > *b*. The same property holds for the set of all key2 values.

The operations for a two-key table follow.

---

**Create operation**
Preconditions:     Receiver is an arbitrary two-key table in an unpredictable state.
Postconditions:    Receiver is initialized to an empty table.

**Empty operation**
Precondition:      Receiver is a two-key table.
Postcondition:     If receiver contains no objects, the Boolean value TRUE is returned; otherwise, the Boolean value FALSE is returned.

**Store operation**
Preconditions:     Receiver is a two-key table. **key1** is the key1 value. **key2** is the key2 value. **item** is an object to be inserted in **receiver.** If **key1** and **key2** do not specify an item already in the table, there is memory available to store **item.**
Postconditions:    If an object is already associated with **key1** and **key2** in the table, it is replaced by **item**. Otherwise, the table has **item** inserted and associated with the key1 and key2 values.

**Remove operation**
Preconditions:     Receiver is a two-key table. **key1** and **key2** are the key values associated with an object to be removed from the table.
Postconditions:    If the object with the key values **key2** and **key2** can be found in the table, it is removed from the table, **item** contains the object associated with the key values **key2** and **key2**, and the operation returns TRUE. Otherwise, the operation returns FALSE, **item**'s contents are undefined, and the table is left unchanged.

---

**Retrieve
operation**

Preconditions:     Receiver is a two-key table. **key1** and **key2** are the key
values associated with an object to be found in the table.

Postconditions:    If the pairing of **key1** and **key2** can be found in table,
then **item** contains the object associated with **key1** and
**key2** and the operation returns TRUE. Otherwise, the
operation returns FALSE, and **item**'s contents are undefined.
In either case, the table is left unchanged.

As you can see from these definitions, a two-key table is really an extension of
a one-key table with an extra key. Note that we do not specify a **length** operation,
however, because a two-key table is not a linear data structure.

## A Class Template for the Two-Key Table Abstract Data Type

In the spirit of our policy of making ADTs as general and flexible as possible, we
will represent our conceptual definition of the two-key table ADT as a C++ class
template. This will allow an application to specify the type of each key and the item
type when a two-key table is created. For example, the table of baseball statistics
discussed earlier could be declared as

```
two_key_table<string, string, int> statistics;
```

where the last parameter is the type of data to be stored in the table, and the other
parameters are the types of keys (first and second, respectively).

The C++ class declaration module for a two-key table class template is

```
// Class declaration file: twotable.h

#ifndef TWO_TABLE_H

#include "boolean.h"

// Declaration section

// Generic class for key1 type K1, key2 type K2, and element type E.

template <class K1, class K2, class E> class two_key_table
{

    public:

    // Class constructors

    two_key_table();
    two_key_table(const two_key_table<K1, K2, E> &table);

    // Member functions

    boolean empty();
    void store(const K1 &key1, const K2 &key2, const E &item);
    boolean retrieve(const K1 &key1, const K2 &key2, E &item);
```

```
    boolean remove(const K1 &key1, const K2 &key2, E &item);
    two_key_table<K1, K2, E>& operator = (const two_key_table<K1, K2, E> &table);

protected:

// Data members

// To go here when we consider alternative implementations

};


#define TWO_TABLE_H
#endif
```

Note that the interface to the class template, the function declarations, and component type parameters, exactly mirrors our conceptual definition.

## A Two-Dimensional Array Implementation

Since a two-key table is a two-dimensional data structure at the conceptual level, we might try to represent it as a two-dimensional array in C++. After all, we represented a one-key table as a one-dimensional array. Each row of the array would represent a **key1**, while each column would represent a **key2**. We could then choose between a direct mapping of keys to index positions along each dimension of the array (supporting efficient retrievals) or a random mapping (supporting efficient insertions).

Because there are now two keys to map to two index positions in the array, the association class must be extended to represent the association of a value with two keys. We do this by defining a derived class of association, **two_key_association**, that contains the extra key. This approach has the effect of preserving the original association class for the use of one-key tables:

```
// Class declaration file: twoassoc.h

#ifndef TWO_ASSOC_H

// Declaration section

template <class K1, class K2, class E> class two_key_association : public
    association
{
    public:

    // Class constructors

    two_key_association();
    two_key_association(const two_key_association<K1, K2, E> &a);
    two_key_association(const K1 &key1, const K2 &key2,
        const E &new_item);

    // Member functions
```

```
        K2 get_key2();
        two_key_association<K1, K2, E>& operator =
                (const two_key_association<K1, K2, E> &a);


        private:


        // Data members
        K2 the_key2;


};


#define TWO_ASSOC_H
#endif
```

Two other questions must be answered before we can write the definitions of the data members for the two-key table. First, what will be the maximum size of a two-key table? The answer to this question for one-key tables was specified by a constant, **MAX_TABLE_SIZE**, used to define the maximum size of the array representing the table, and defined in the header file **element.h**. For a two-dimensional array, we will need two constants, **MAX_ROW_SIZE** and **MAX_COL_SIZE**, to define the maximum sizes of the two dimensions. Application modules will again specify these values, with the understanding that **MAX_ROW_SIZE** represents the maximum number of possible **key1** values in a two-key table, and **MAX_COL_SIZE** represents the maximum number of possible **key2** values.

Second, how will we maintain the current number of objects stored in a two-key table? A one-key table used an integer data member, **table_length**, representing the next available location in the array for storing data. The situation in a two-dimensional array is more complicated. We need to know both the position of the next available row (for a new **key1**) and the next available column in each row (for a new **key2**). Therefore, we will define two data members, an integer variable and an array of integers, to represent these attributes.

The data members for the two-dimensional array can now be added to the class declaration module of the two-key table:

```
// Data members

two_key_association<K1, K2, E> data[MAX_ROW_SIZE][MAX_COL_SIZE];
int row_length;
int col_lengths[MAX_ROW_SIZE];
```

The next example shows how we would implement the **store** operation, assuming that we simply pick the next available row and column for a new object at **key1** and **key2**.

**EXAMPLE 2.7**    Write the implementation of the member function that stores an object in a two-key table. We assume that if the **key1** is new, we enter at a new row, and if **key2** is new, we enter at a new column.

```
template <class K1, class K2, class E>
void two_key_table<K1, K2, E>::store(const K1 &key1, const K2 &key2, const E &item)
{
    int row, col;
    boolean found = FALSE;
    key_type row_key, col_key;

    row = 0;
    col = 0;
    while ((row < row_length) && ! found)                    // Search key1 in rows
    {
        data[row][col].get_key(row_key);
        if (key1 == row_key)
            found = TRUE;
        else
            ++row;
    }
    if (found)                                               // key1 already in table
    {
        found = FALSE;                                       // Search for key2 in column
         while ((col < column_lengths[row]) && ! found)
        {
            col_key = data[row][col].get_key2();
            if (key2 == col_key)
                    found = TRUE;
            else
                    ++col;
        }
        if (found)                                           // key2 also already in table
            data[row][col].set_value(item);
        else
        {
            assert(column_lengths[row] < MAX_COL_SIZE);   // Room available
            two_key_association<E><K1><K2> a(key1, key2, item);  // for column?
            data[row][col] = a;                         // Add a new key2
            ++column_lengths[row];
        }
    }
    else
    {
        assert(row_length < MAX_ROW_SIZE);   // Room available for row?
        association a<K1, K2, E>(target, item);
        data[row][0] = a;                // Add a new key1
        column_lengths[row] = 1;
        ++row_length;
    }
}
```

By now, you will probably have surmised that there are some serious drawbacks to this implementation. The most obvious one is the length and complexity of the **store** operation presented above. With so many alternative cases to consider and data to maintain, this code will be very difficult to read, understand, and get correct. Moreover, the **retrieve** and **remove** operations will be almost as complicated.

As far as efficiency is concerned, the current implementation introduces a new data structure, the array for maintaining the current lengths of the columns, that results in a linear growth of memory for the maximum number of secondary keys that an application needs in a table. The current version also forces us to add a data member to the association class to represent a second key. The only advantage is that binary searches for a target object might be very fast, assuming that one can get the code correct!

The choice of this implementation seems so unreasonable that we will not even leave its completion as an exercise, but rather look for a simpler one.

## Using One-Key Tables to Implement Two-Key Tables

Another way to think of a two-key table is as a one-key table. Each key in this table will represent a **key1** in the two-key table. At each of these keys, we store another one-key table. Each key in each of these tables will represent a **key2** in the two-key table. Thus, the data elements stored at the keys in the nested one-key tables will be the data elements stored in the two-key table.

The advantage of this representation is that it allows us to use higher level components to construct our two-key table ADT. This will allow us to use higher level operations as well. For example, the operation for retrieving a data element at **key1** and **key2** in a two-key table can now be conceptualized as follows:

1. Retrieve the element at key1 of the top-level one-key table
2. If the retrieval is successful then
    3. From this element (also a one-key table), retrieve the element at key2

The advantage of this implementation over the two-dimensional array implementation is that in this one, the code for the search operations has already been written, so we just invoke them by name. In the two-dimensional array implementation, we are forced to reinvent the wheel by rewriting this code.

Here is a class declaration module for a two-key table that uses one-key tables to support high-level implementations of two-key operations:

```
// Class declaration file: twotable.h

#ifndef TWO_TABLE_H

#include "boolean.h"
#include "onetable.h"

template <class K1, class K2, class E> class two_key_table
{

    public:

    // Class constructors

    two_key_table();

    two_key_table(const two_key_table<K1, K2, E> &table);
```

```
// Member functions

boolean empty();
void store(const K1 &key1, const K2 &key2, const E &item);
boolean retrieve(const K1 &key1, const K2 &key2, E &item);
boolean remove(const K1 &key1, const K2 &key2, E &item);
two_key_table<K1, K2, E>& operator = (const two_key_table<K1, K2, E> &table);

protected:

// Data members

one_key_table<K1, one_key_table<K2, E>> data;

};


#define TWO_TABLE_H
#endif
```

The interface of the two-key table class stays the same, but the new implementation has just one data member. This is a one-key table whose key type is **K1** and whose element type is another one-key table. The key type of this second one-key table is **K2** and its element type is **E**. Carefully examine the line of code that defines this data member, especially the ordering of the angle brackets, so that you understand how the type parameters are passed to set up the data structure.

The next example shows how we can take advantage of the new data member definitions to implement the **retrieve** operation for two-key tables.

---

**EXAMPLE 2.8**

Write the implementation of the **retrieve** operation for the two-key table class specified in the class declaration module given earlier.

```
template <class K1, class K2, class E>
boolean two_key_table<K1, K2, E>::retrieve(const K1 &key1, const K2 &key2, E &item)
{
      one_key_table<K2, E> table;

      if (data.retrieve(key1, table))            // Retrieve nested table
            return table.retrieve(key2, item);   // Retrieve data item
      else
            return FALSE;
}
```

---

After working through the code for the two-dimensional array implementation, this code must seem almost magically simple. However, this code represents a straightforward use of the one-key tables in the new data representation. Using the data member **data**, we attempt to retrieve a table at **key1**. If we are successful, we use this table to attempt to retrieve an item at **key2**. If we are successful here, the item is returned and the function returns TRUE. If either of the retrievals fails, the function returns FALSE.

Not only is this version easy to read, understand, and get correct, but we no longer need to consider the alternatives of linear search or binary search to implement a retrieval. These considerations have been resolved at a lower level, during the implementation of the one-key table. The next example shows how to implement a **store** operation for this version. Be sure to compare it to the other version in Example 2.7.

---

**EXAMPLE 2.9**    Write the implementation of the **store** operation for the one-key table implementation of the two-key table ADT.

```
template <class K1, class K2, class E>
void two_key_table<K1, K2, E>::store (const K1 &key1, const K2 &key2, const E &item)
{
        one_key_table<K2, E> table;

        data.retrieve(key1, table);     // Access nested table, if any
        table.store(key2, item);        // Store data in table
        data.store(key1, table);        // Place nested table in top-level table
}
```

---

## Comparing the Two Implementations

Our intuition in choosing a two-dimensional array implementation for a two-key table seemed natural: One can think of each structure as consisting of a grid in which a data item is located by specifying a row and column. Moreover, since we were able to map a key in a one-key table to an index position in a one-dimensional array, it seemed logical to try to map two keys to the two indices of a two-dimensional array. However, when we turned to the actual data structures and algorithms for implementing this version, we quickly became lost in a welter of complexity. We found it necessary to introduce complex auxiliary data structures, like an array of column lengths and a two-key association class, and to write pages of code for each individual operation.

By reconceiving a two-key table as a one-key table whose data items are other one-key tables, we were able to simplify both the data structures used in the implementation and the code used in the operations. The one-key table ADT handles most of the work of representing the data and implementing the operations. We no longer have to think about using auxiliary ADTs such as the association, much less about subclassing it to represent a second key. We no longer have to decide between an implementation that supports binary search (fast retrievals) or linear search (fast insertions).

On the other hand, the one-key table implementation gives us less control over the way that a two-key table behaves than we might wish. If a client of the two-key table desires fast retrievals and the one-key table implements a linear search, the client is stuck with that. Moreover, clients can no longer specify separate maximum row and column sizes for two-key tables. This last factor can lead to a serious inefficiency in the use of memory, where storage would be allocated for rows or columns in the table that are not really needed by the application. We will see a way to remedy this last problem in later chapters.

The contrast between the two implementations can be viewed as a contrast between a *layered system* and an *unlayered system*. The one-key table implementation places a layer of high-level types and operations between the two-key table ADT and the underlying C++ data structures and operations. The two-dimensional array implementation represents the two-key table ADT directly in terms of the underlying C++ data structures and operations. Layered systems are generally easy to design and maintain; unlayered systems may be more efficient but are usually much more difficult to design and maintain.

These considerations lead us to formulate one more principle for the design of abstract data types:

> **ADT layering rule:** Existing abstract data types should be used to implement new abstract data types, unless direct control over the underlying data structures and operations of the programming language is a critical factor. A well-designed implementation consists of layers of ADTs.

## EXERCISES 2.4

1. Complete the one-key table implementation of the two-key table ADT.
2. Write a program that uses a two-key table to store and retrieve the baseball statistics described earlier in this section. Explain how you handle the data in the last column, which appear to be real numbers rather than integers.
3. A data item is located in a three-key table by specifying three keys. Write an abstract definition and an appropriate C++ class declaration module for this ADT. Remember to adhere to the ADT reuse and layering rules.

## FOCUS ON PROGRAM DESIGN

Suppose that you are computer operations manager for Wing-and-a-Prayer Airlines. In that role, you receive the following important memorandum:

```
                        MEMORANDUM
               Wing-and-a-Prayer Airlines


     TO: Computer Operations Manager
   FROM: Vice President in Charge of Scheduling
   DATE: August 28, 1995
     RE: Matching flights and pilots

As you know, we presently have 1500 flights (with
identification numbers 3000 to 4499) and employ 1400
pilots (with identification numbers 1000-2399) to fly
them. However, because of factors such as type of
airplane, amount of pilot experience, pilot geographic
locations, and FAA regulations, each of our pilots
qualifies to fly on only a relatively small percentage of
flights. To help our schedulers, we frequently need to
answer questions such as the following:

1. Given a flight, what are the identification numbers of
   the pilots qualified to fly it?
2. Given a pilot number, what are the flight numbers that
   pilot is qualified to fly?
3. Given a flight number and a pilot number, do we have a
   match? In other words, is the specified pilot
   qualified for the particular flight?

Right now our schedulers attempt to answer such questions
by time-consuming manual methods. I'm sure that you can
easily computerize this task for them. Thanks in advance
for your help in this matter.
```

◆ FIGURE 2.7
Flight/pilot data base for
Wing-and-a-Prayer Airlines

| Pilot Number | Flight Number | | | | | |
|---|---|---|---|---|---|---|
| | 3000 | 3001 | 3002 | ... | 4498 | 4499 |
| 1000 | TRUE | FALSE | FALSE | ... | TRUE | FALSE |
| 1001 | FALSE | FALSE | FALSE | ... | TRUE | TRUE |
| 1002 | TRUE | TRUE | FALSE | ... | FALSE | FALSE |
| . | . | . | . | ... | . | . |
| . | . | . | . | ... | . | . |
| . | . | . | . | ... | . | . |
| 2398 | FALSE | TRUE | FALSE | ... | FALSE | FALSE |
| 2399 | FALSE | FALSE | TRUE | ... | FALSE | TRUE |

Faced with this charge, one abstract conceptualization you might consider is that of the table pictured in Figure 2.7. Here a TRUE entry in a particular row and column indicates the pilot is qualified for the corresponding flight; FALSE indicates the pilot is not qualified. Given the two-dimensional table of Figure 2.7 as a model of the pilot/flight data for Wing-and-a-Prayer, we choose a two-key table ADT to represent the data. The first key will be the pilot number, and the second key will be the flight number, both represented as integers. The data will be Boolean values.

We define the following constants in **element.h** to represent the dimensions of the table:

```
const MIN_PILOT = 1000;
const MAX_PILOT = 2399;
const MIN_FLIGHT = 3000;
const MAX_FLIGHT = 4999;

const MAX_TABLE_SIZE = MAX_FLIGHT - MIN_FLIGHT + 1;
```

We begin the design of the algorithms by writing the pseudocode for the top-level query loop:

1. Initialize all of the items in the table to FALSE
2. Load the table by reading pairs of numbers representing a pilot and a flight for which the pilot is qualified. Assign TRUE to these locations.
3. Do
   3.1 Read a Query
   3.2 If Query is a flight number then
       3.2.1 Travel along corresponding column, writing out number of each qualified pilot
   3.3 Else if Query is a pilot number
       3.3.1 Travel along corresponding row, writing out each flight for which the pilot is qualified
   3.4 Else if Query is flight and pilot number
       3.4.1 Access information at that row and column
       3.4.2 If TRUE
           Write ('QUALIFIED') Else
           Write ('NOT QUALIFIED')
   While the user wishes to continue with queries

The first two steps set up the two-key table with data values. The third step handles the interaction with the users of the system. Each of these steps can be implemented as a C++ function that passes the table as a parameter. Assuming function names `init_table`, `get_data`, and `take_queries` for these steps, we have a main program

```
#include <iostream.h>
#include "boolean.h"
#include "element.h"
#include "twotable.h"

int main()

{
        two_key_table<int, int, boolean> is_qualified;

        init_table(is_qualified);
        get_data(is_qualified);
        take_queries(is_qualified);
        return 0;
}
```

The process of associating the initial value FALSE with each pair of pilots and flights in the table can be described by a nested loop. The outer loop runs through consecutive pilot numbers from 1000 to 2399. The inner loop runs through consecutive flight numbers from 3000 to 4999. On each pass through the inner loop, we invoke the `store` operation with the two loop control variables to insert the value FALSE into the appropriate place in the table:

```
void init_table(two_key_table<int, int, boolean> &table)
{
      boolean can_fly = FALSE;

      for (int pilot = MIN_PILOT; pilot <= MAX_PILOT; ++pilot)
            for (int flight = MIN_FLIGHT; flight <= MAX_FLIGHT; ++flight)
                  table.store(pilot, flight, can_fly);
}
```

Setting the flags of the pilots who are qualified for certain flights is a process of prompting the user for the relevant pilot/flight pairs. The function uses two auxiliary functions, `get_integer` and `more_input_desired`. `get_integer` prints a message and recovers from any input errors. `more_input_desired` returns the Boolean result of asking the user whether to continue the process.

```
void get_data(two_key_table<int, int, boolean> &table)
{
    int pilot, flight;
    boolean can_fly = TRUE;

    do
    {
        cout << "Enter pilot number from " << MIN_PILOT << " to "
            << MAX_PILOT << ": ";
```

```
                pilot = get_integer(MIN_PILOT, MAX_PILOT);
                cout << "Enter flight number from " << MIN_FLIGHT << " to "
                    << MAX_FLIGHT << ": ";
                flight = get_integer(MIN_FLIGHT, MAX_FLIGHT);
                table.store(pilot, flight, can_fly);
            } while (more_input_desired());
    }
```

Alternatively, we could qualify every third pilot automatically for every fourth flight, just so we would have some test data to run:

```
void get_data(two_key_table<int, int, boolean> &table)
{
        boolean can_fly = TRUE;
        for (int pilot = MIN_PILOT; pilot <= MAX_PILOT; ++pilot)
            if (pilot % 3 == 0)
                for (int flight = MIN_FLIGHT; flight <= MAX_FLIGHT;
                    ++flight)
                if (flight % 4 == 0)
                    table.store(pilot, flight, can_fly);
}
```

The main query loop displays a menu of four commands: display all of the flights for a given pilot, display all of the pilots for a given flight, answer yes or no for a given pilot/flight pair, and quit the program. Depending on the user's choice, the system runs any of three different functions to carry out the commands.

```
void take_queries(two_key_table<int, int, boolean> &table)
    {
        char query;
        do
        {
                display_menu();
                query = get_char('1', '4');
                switch (query)
                {
                        case '1':   find_flights(table);
                                    break;
                        case '2':   find_pilots(table);
                                    break;
                        case '3':   find_pilot_and_flight(table);
                                    break;
                        default:    cout << "Program terminated." << endl;
                }
        } while (query != '4');
    }
```

To find all of the flights for which a given pilot is qualified, we get the pilot number from the user and run a retrieval on each flight number in the table. The successful retrievals lead to output:

```
void find_flights(two_key_table<int, int, boolean> &table)
    {
        int pilot;
```

```
        cout << "Enter a pilot number, from " << MIN_PILOT << " to "
             << MAX_PILOT << ": ";
        pilot = get_integer(MIN_PILOT, MAX_PILOT);
        cout << "Eligible flights." << endl;
        for (int flight = MIN_FLIGHT; flight <= MAX_FLIGHT; ++flight)
              if (table.retrieve(pilot, flight, can_fly) && can_fly)
                    cout << flight << endl;
}
```

Note that the Boolean value of **retrieve** specifies whether or not there is an entry in the table at a given pilot and flight, whereas the Boolean value **can_fly** specifies the information stored at these keys.

To find all of the pilots who are qualified for a given flight, we get the flight number from the user and run a retrieval on each pilot number in the table. The successful retrievals lead to output:

```
void find_pilots(two_key_table<int, int, boolean> &table)
{
        int flight;

        cout << "Enter a flight number, from " << MIN_FLIGHT << " to "
             << MAX_FLIGHT << ": ";
        flight = get_integer(MIN_FLIGHT , MAX_FLIGHT );
        cout << "Eligible pilots." << endl;
        for (int pilot = MIN_PILOT; pilot <= MAX_PILOT; ++pilot)
              if (table.retrieve(pilot, flight, can_fly) && can_fly)
                    cout << pilot << endl;
}
```

To find whether or not a given pilot is eligible for a given flight, we get both values from the user and run one retrieval:

```
void find_pilot_and_flight(two_key_table<int, int, boolean> &table)
{
        int pilot, flight;
        boolean can_fly;

        cout << "Enter a pilot number, from " << MIN_PILOT << " to "
             << MAX_PILOT << ": ";
        pilot = get_integer(MIN_PILOT, MAX_PILOT);
        cout << "Enter a flight number, from " << MIN_FLIGHT << " to "
             << MAX_FLIGHT << ": ";
        flight = get_integer(MIN_FLIGHT, MAX_FLIGHT);
        if (table.retrieve(pilot, flight, can_fly) && can_fly)
              cout << "The pilot is eligible for this flight" << endl;
        else
              cout << "The pilot is not eligible for this flight" << endl;
}
```

The auxiliary functions **more_input_desired**, **display_menu**, **get_integer**, and **get_char** are

```
void display_menu()
{
        cout << "1 Find the flights for a given pilot" << endl;
        cout << "2 Find the pilots for a given flight" << endl;
        cout << "3 Find whether or not a given pilot is qualified for a given
                << "flight"
                << endl;
        cout << "4 Terminate program" << endl;
        cout << endl << "Enter a number: ";
}

int get_integer(int min, int max)
{
        int data;
        cin >> data;
        while ((data < min) || (data > max))
        {
                cout << "Error: number must be >= " << min << " and <= "
                        << max << endl;
                cout << "Try again: ";
                cin >> data;
        }
        return data;
}

char get_char(char min, char max)
{
        char data;

        cin >> data
        while ((data < min) || (data > max))
        {
                cout << "Error: character must be >= " << min << " and <= "
                        << max << endl;
                cout << "Try again: ";
                cin >> data;
        }
        return data;
}

boolean more_input_desired()

{
        char query;

cout << "Do you wish to continue? [Y/N] " ;
        cin >> query;
        return (query == 'Y') || (query == 'y');
}
```

RUNNING, DEBUGGING AND TESTING HINTS

1. When accessing an ADT, be sure that you only use those operations specified in the ADT definition. This is the ADT use rule. For instance, it would be wrong to access an object in a one-key table by referring to its array index. This would be assuming that the implementor of the ADT is storing data in an array. Such an assumption is not warranted according to the definition of this ADT.

2. When writing the implementation of an ADT, be sure that the functions you develop obey the interface established by the ADT's definition. This is the ADT implementation rule. For instance, if you, as implementor, need a counter to keep track of the number of objects in a one-key table, don't add the counter as an extra parameter in function calls. Instead, encapsulate it as a private or protected data member of the implementation.

3. When providing the implementation of an ADT, be sure that each individual operation is thoroughly tested and debugged before it is used by higher level logic. Then if errors occur when higher level modules execute, you can be assured that these errors are the result of the algorithms that use the ADT and are not in the implementation of the ADT.

4. The importance of the `create` operation for an ADT should not be underestimated. From the implementor's perspective, here is where crucial initializations occur that will ensure the smooth functioning of other operations. From the perspective of the user of the ADT, you must be sure to call the create operation for each instance of a variable of that type. Failing to do so will usually lead to very bizarre program behavior.

## SUMMARY

### Key Terms

abstract data type
abstraction
ADT generality rule
ADT implementation rule
ADT layering rule
ADT use rule
data abstraction

implementation
information hiding
interface for an ADT
one-key table
ordered collection
physically ordered array
   implementation

primary key
secondary key
two-dimensional array
   implementation
two-key table
unordered array
   implementation

### Key Concepts

◆ Computer scientists engage in a modeling process as they develop software to satisfy users' needs. In this respect, the way in which a computer scientist works parallels the engineering profession. Consequently, this systematic approach toward the development of successful software is often called software engineering.

◆ Abstract data types are defined apart from considerations of their implementation in a particular programming language. A complete definition for an abstract data type must include a description of the individual elements, the relationship between these individual elements, and the operations that can be performed on them. These operations are conveniently specified as function and function declarations.

◆ The ADT use rule, the ADT implementation rule, the ADT generality rule, and the ADT layering rule are guidelines governing the relationship between implementations of an ADT and higher level algorithms using that implementation.

◆ We must often determine which of a variety of implementations is best in terms of time and space efficiency for a particular application.

◆ The one-key table is an ADT characterized by operations that store, retrieve, or remove data. All of these operations are performed relative to a particular key value.

◆ A physically ordered array with binary search and an unordered array with pointer sort are two ways of implementing a one-key table.

◆ The two-key table is an ADT characterized by operations that store, retrieve, or remove data. All of these operations are performed relative to two particular key values.

◆ A two-dimensional array and a one-key table of one-key tables are two ways of implementing a two-key table.

## PROGRAMMING PROBLEMS AND PROJECTS

Many of the problems in this chapter require that you write the implementation for an ADT and then use that ADT in a program. It is often interesting to work on such a problem with a classmate. One of you provides the implementation of the ADT; the other writes the higher level algorithm that uses the ADT. If you both obey the ADT use implementation rules, you should be able to work independently of each other and develop an elegant solution to the problem.

In other problems you are asked to write an ADT definition as part of your answer to the problem. Your definition should be presented first in formal precondition and postcondition form and then translated into an appropriate C++ interface. Be sure you are not ambiguous in your presentation of the definition and interface. This aspect of these problems will serve to test the precision with which you write and document.

1. Complete the program in the Focus on Program Design section and test it.

2. Write a small-scale text editor system by loading lines of text from a file into an array of strings.

   a. Allow the user of your program to modify appropriately the text in this array of strings. These modifications should be performed by accessing the strings in the array only through string ADT operations.

   b. Once the text has been modified, write the array of strings out to a new text file.

   c. Test your text editor by using it to create and then modify a modest C++ program, which you then provide as input to your compiler.

3. Write a simple database manager for a bank that uses a one-key table class to store bank accounts, where a bank account is a class.

4. If you are familiar with the notion of a set from your previous work in mathematics, formalize the definition of a set as an abstract data type. Be sure to minimally include the following operations in your definition:

   Given a value $V$ and a set $S$, determine whether or not $V$ is in $S$.

   Given two sets $S1$ and $S2$, determine whether or not $S1$ is equal to $S2$. Given two sets $S1$ and $S2$, determine whether or not $S1$ is a subset of $S2$.

   Given a value $V$ and a set $S$, add the value $V$ to the set $S$.

   Given a value $V$ and a set $S$, remove the value $V$ from the set $S$.

   Given two sets $S1$ and $S2$, return their set intersection.

   Given two sets $S1$ and $S2$, return their set difference.

   Given two sets $S1$ and $S2$, return their union.

5. Invented by mathematician John H. Conway (*Scientific American,* October 1970, p. 120), The Game of Life models the growth and changes in a complex collection of

living organisms. The model can be interpreted as applying to a collection of micro-organisms, an ecologically closed system of animals or plants, or an urban development. Start with a checkerboard of size $N \times N$ on which "markers" are to be placed. Each location that is not on a border has eight neighbors. The markers are born, survive, or die during a "generation" according to the following rules:

*Survival:* Markers with two or three neighboring markers survive to the next generation.

*Death:* Markers with four or more neighbors die from overcrowding and are removed for the next generation. Markers with zero or one neighbors die from isolation and are removed for the next generation.

*Birth:* Each empty location that has exactly three markers in the eight neighboring locations is a birth location. A marker is placed in the location for the next generation.

For example, on a 6 × 6 space the following pattern

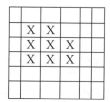

would look as follows in the next generation:

Certain patterns are stable; for example,

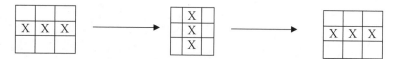

Other patterns repeat a sequence:

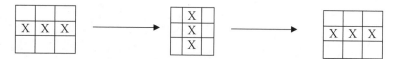

Because, conceptually, two $N \times N$ matrices are required to implement The Game of Life, it is clear that memory limitations could easily become a problem for a large $N$. After initializing the first generation, print it. Then calculate the next generation in another array and print this too. Repeat for a specified number of generations. Your output should be an "X" for live cells and a blank otherwise.

Develop the high-level logic of your program by employing the fundamental assign/retrieve operations for matrices.

6. The radix sort algorithm, presented in Section 1.4, uses the notion of bins: data repositories that contain numbers or strings in a particular category as the algorithm progresses. Formalize the concept of a bin for the radix sort algorithm by providing an ADT definition for it. Then provide an implementation for your bin ADT and use the operations provided by the bin ADT to write a high-level version of the radix sort.

**7.** The definition of the one-key table ADT in Section 2.4 specifies that each object in the list must have a unique key value, that is, a key value shared by no other value in the list. Consider a variation on this ADT in which we allow multiple records to share the same key value (for example, several people may have identical names). Call this ADT a one-key table with duplicate keys.

**a.** Provide a complete definition for this ADT. Be very precise about what happens for each of the **store**, **remove**, and **retrieve** operations. Do you need to add any new operations because of the possibility of duplicate keys?

**b.** Translate your definition from part **a** into a C++ interface for a one-key table with duplicate keys.

**c.** Develop an implementation for this ADT. Discuss in a written statement any limitations of your implementation relative to the definition and interface of parts **a** and **b.**

**d.** Test your implementation by plugging it into a program like that of this chapter's Focus on Program Design section. In a program such as this one, how can you distinguish between employees who have the same name?

# 3 Software Engineering and the System Life Cycle

*I believe in Michelangelo, Velazquez, and Rembrandt; in the might of design.*
George Bernard Shaw
(1856–1950)

In Chapter 2 we discussed a philosophy of software design called software engineering. This philosophy emphasizes an evolutionary progression from the building of a conceptual model of the system to the eventual implementation of that model in a programming language such as C++. At the heart of this progression lies the abstract data type as a means of conceptualizing the data needs of the system before considering how those needs are to be implemented.

In Chapter 1, we described some relatively simple algorithms to perform operations on arrays and illustrated how to evaluate such algorithms using big-O notation. The purpose of this description was twofold. First, as software designers, we need to be aware of the variety of algorithms available to perform a particular task such as sorting or searching. Chapter 1 began to equip us with this knowledge in a systematic, organized fashion. Second, along with an understanding of various algorithms, we must be able to evaluate and select the best of all possible algorithms for a particular application. Big-O analysis provides us with a guide for such evaluation and selection.

It is now time to put the methods described in the preceding chapters into the context of large-scale systems development. In so doing, we will describe a series of phases known as the software system life cycle. As we walk through these phases, we hope you begin to appreciate the enormous complexity involved in the development of successful software systems. It is not uncommon for a problem that appears to be simple to spawn a variety of complications. Handling such complications in a graceful and efficient fashion is an essential ingredient to succeeding in computer science.

In Section 3.1, we examine the initial analysis phase of the system life cycle. This phase is followed by the design and implementation phases, as described in Section 3.2. Section 3.3 treats the testing, maintenance, and obsolescence stages.

Sections 3.4 and 3.5 provide a brief glimpse of some future directions in software engineering. In Section 3.4, we discuss formal verification as an alternative to testing. In Section 3.5, we investigate a design paradigm called *object-oriented design*.

## 3.1 The Analysis Phase of the System Life Cycle

### OBJECTIVES

- to understand what is done during the analysis phase of systems development
- to be able to define the responsibilities of a systems analyst
- to gain additional familiarity with the use of data flow diagrams as a tool for modeling user needs
- to recognize the importance of oral and written communication skills in the analysis phase

It has been said that the only simple problems in computing are those defined in textbooks. Perhaps a key to the truth of this statement is its use of the word *defined*. Once a problem has been specifically defined, the most difficult obstacle to solving that problem may well have been surmounted. In the analysis phase you must define in detail the problem that you are charged with solving.

It is important to remember that in trying to provide such a definition, you are typically working with a problem originally posed by someone other than yourself. We have tried to emphasize this fact in the preceding chapter by introducing problems in the form of memoranda from computer users. This is done to emphasize that programs are written not for computer scientists but for computer users, users who often know virtually nothing about the computer other than a vague (and often inaccurate) notion that it can magically take care of all of their record-keeping and computational needs. Bridging the gap between potentially naive users and the computer-oriented people who eventually are responsible for implementing the software system constitutes the first phase of the system life cycle.

Though many people are aware that *systems analysts* work with computers in some way, few know specifically what a systems analyst does. More than anything else, the systems analyst is responsible for the *analysis* phase of the system life cycle. A systems analyst talks to the users who initally request the system to learn exactly what these users need. This is done not only by talking to users, but also by studying in detail what these users do. For instance, a systems analyst working for a bank on an automated teller system would have to become an expert on the various duties and responsibilities of a teller. Having learned what the automated system is supposed to do, the systems analyst must then develop formal specifications describing the system and its requirements. The technical people who design and code the software will work from these specifications.

### Using Data Flow Diagrams

A *data flow diagram* is a graphic specification technique often used by systems analysts to provide a clear picture of a user's requirements. On the surface, a data flow diagram could be viewed as a collection of circular "bubbles" joined by strings. (In fact, data flow diagrams are sometimes referred to as bubble diagrams.) The strings connecting the bubbles are officially called data flows and are named in a way that reflects the information they carry. The circular bubbles represent processes that transform incoming data flows into outgoing data flows, which may in turn be acted on by another process.

Figure 3.1 depicts a portion of a data flow diagram that describes how a payroll department might operate. Rectangular boxes in a data flow diagram indicate initial sources and final destinations of data flows. In Figure 3.1, the EMPLOYEE is both an initial source (of hours worked and ID number) and a final destination (of a formatted paycheck). Parallel lines highlight a database that must be accessed to do the required processing. For instance, in Figure 3.1, the hourly rate must be retrieved from the EMPLOYEE INFORMATION FILE by the COMPUTE PAY process.

◆ FIGURE 3.1
Data flow diagram for payroll department

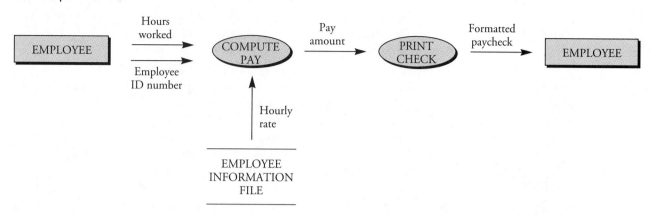

EXAMPLE 3.1

You receive the following memorandum from the registrar at the University of Hard Knocks. In it she requests you to automate the university's record-keeping on its students. Provide a data flow diagram to depict the information processing done by the registrar.

```
                        MEMORANDUM
                 University of Hard Knocks


   TO: Director of Data Processing
 FROM: Head Registrar
 DATE: July 29, 1995
   RE: Automation of record-keeping on students

As you know, we presently maintain our student records by
manual methods. We believe the time has come to
computerize this operation and request that you do so
for us.

Here is what we need. Each student's record consists of
his or her name, the number of credits that student has
taken, the number of credits earned, and the total grade
points for that student. We maintain these records by a
student's last name. Of course, at numerous times, we
must add new students to our records and remove those who
have graduated or withdrawn from school. Students often
come into our office and request to see their current
record, so we must be able to find that information
quickly. At the end of each semester we print a grade
report for each student. This report consists of the four
items cited plus the student's GPA. At the end of the
year, the Dean of Students requests two lists of
graduating seniors. One of these lists is to be printed
in alphabetical order by student name. The other is
printed in order by student grade point average.
```

Certainly the situation described in this memo is an oversimplification of any real college registrar's office. However, even this relatively unsophisticated situation can offer us some interesting food for thought. For one thing, the memo demonstrates the fact that your first contact with a user requesting the system will often leave gaps in your knowledge about the system that is actually needed. The head registrar's memo leaves unanswered the following questions:

1. What is the university's definition of grade points?
2. When grade reports are printed for each student, is it important that they be printed in any particular order?
3. Since grade reports are printed at the end of each semester, do you need some means of updating a student's record at the end of a semester?
4. What is the method used to compute a student's GPA?
5. What separates seniors who graduate from those seniors who don't graduate?
6. Is the list printed in order by student GPA arranged from best student to worst student or vice versa?

You would have to communicate those questions to the registrar before the specifics of the system could be modeled in a data flow diagram. Suppose that you do that and receive the following reply.

```
                         MEMORANDUM
                   University of Hard Knocks


    TO: Director of Data Processing
  FROM: Head Registrar
  DATE: August 2, 1995
    RE: Responses to your questions


Question 1: Four grade points are assigned for a
one-credit A grade, three for a B, two for a C, one for a
D, and zero for an F. Courses worth more than one credit
have their corresponding grade points multiplied
accordingly.

Question 2: Grade reports should be printed in
alphabetical order by student last name.

Question 3: At the end of each semester, faculty members
turn in grades for each class they teach. We use the
grades on these class rosters to update a student's
academic information before printing a grade report.

Question 4: GPA is computed as the quotient of total
grade points divided by credits taken.

Question 5: A graduating senior must have earned at least
120 credits.

Question 6: The list is to be printed from best student
to worst student.
```

◆ FIGURE 3.2
Data flow diagram of information to be processed in
registrar's system

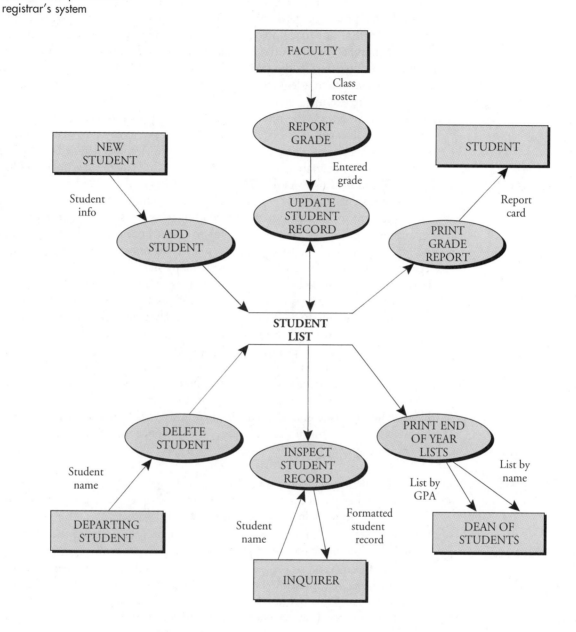

This sort of diaglogue with the registrar allows you, a systems analyst, to
generate the data flow diagram in Figure 3.2. In this figure, the process Print Grade
Report transforms a student academic record into an appropriately formatted
report card. Similarly, the process Update Student Record transforms newly
reported grades for a student into an appropriately updated student record in the
Student List database.

## Perfecting the Model

The role of the data flow diagram in the various phases of modeling that occur in the development of a system is to provide an initial overview of the fashion in which a user processes information. Data flow diagrams for a system would be developed before any decisions are made regarding the modular structure and abstract data types on which the eventual program will be based. In this sense, they represent the first step in the progression of structured techniques used to ensure that a software system adequately meets the needs of its end users.

For more complex systems, data flow diagrams such as that appearing in Figure 3.2 may have to be refined into a collection of more detailed subordinate diagrams. Additionally, the systems analyst may have to provide written specifications for each process represented in the diagram. A more detailed discussion of these aspects of the analysis phase may be found in *Modern Structured Analysis* by Edward Yourdon (Englewood Cliffs, N.J.: Prentice-Hall, 1989).

The systems analyst serves as a liaison and translator between the users and the implementors of the system. Depending on the size and structure of the organization, the systems analyst may or may not become involved in the design and coding of the system. Typically, such involvement will occur in smaller organizations where the analyst may wear many hats, but not in larger organizations where staff sizes allow for a greater degree of specialization.

Because an exact assessment of the end user's needs is vital for the most satisfactory design of the system, the systems analyst must have excellent interpersonal communication skills as well as a strong computer background.

It is beyond the scope of this text to present any detailed treatment of systems analysis strategies. Instead, we will occasionally present specifications for programs in the form of memoranda from hypothetical users. These memoranda will serve as realistic reminders of the role of the user in the software development process. Yet they will be simplistic enough to avoid the massive headaches often connected with the analysis phase of a project. Instead, we will concentrate on the next phases of the software system life cycle.

## EXERCISES 3.1

1. Consider the memorandum from Wing-and-a-Prayer's vice president in charge of scheduling (see the Focus on Program Design of Chapter 2). Draw a data flow diagram to model the information processing that it describes.

2. Draw a data flow diagram to model the information processing activities that you do each month to maintain your checking account at a local bank.

3. BugFree Incorporated sells software for personal computers. Most orders that BugFree receives come from subscribers to computer magazines who respond to BugFree's advertisement by filling out forms in the ads and then mailing them to the company. BugFree also uses a toll-free phone number to accept orders, answer inquiries, and handle payments and cancellations of orders. Software ordered from BugFree is either sent directly to the customer or to local computer stores, which then distribute the product to the customer. This rapidly expanding business must keep records on its customers, product inventory, and billing information. Draw a data flow diagram to depict the flow of information at BugFree.

4. For this task, you'll work with another student. Each of you should develop a memorandum to specify what you view as the information-processing needs of an administrative office at your school (or any other office environment with which you may be familiar). Your memorandum should provide information similar to that provided by the registrar at the University of Hard Knocks (see Example 3.1). Exchange your

memoranda and draw a data flow diagram to model the activity described in the other person's memo. Then get together with the other person to resolve any questions you might have and to critique the accuracy and completeness of the other's data flow diagram.

5. Consider the following memorandum from the registrar at the renowned American Basket Weaving University—one of the main competitors of the University of Hard Knocks.

---

```
                        MEMORANDUM
            American Basket Weaving University

    TO: Director of Data Processing
  FROM: Head Registrar
  DATE: July 29, 1996
    RE: Automation of record-keeping on students

Records for students at our school consist of a
university identification number, a last name, a first
name, a middle initial, a Social Security number, a list
of courses the student has taken along with the grade
received in each course, and a list of extracurricular
activities in which the student has indicated an
interest. A university identification number for a
student consists of a six-digit number; the first two
digits represent the year a student entered the
university. The remaining four digits are simply assigned
on a sequential basis as students are admitted to the
school. For instance, the student with ID number 930023
is the 23rd student admitted in the class that entered
A.B.W.U. in 1993.

Given this database, we frequently need to work with it
in the following ways:
■ Find and display all data for a particular student, as
  identified by university ID number.
■ Add and delete student records from the database.
■ Print records for all students in Social Security
  number order, starting with the most recent class and
  working backwards.
■ Add, change, or delete the information on a course for
  a particular student. For instance, change the grade
  received by student 930023 in CompSci2 from C to B.
■ Find all students with an extracurricular interest that
  matches a particular target interest. Students'
  extracurricular interests are viewed as arbitrarily
  long strings. These strings are entered into our
  records directly from information provided by students
  on their registration forms. For instance, a given
  student may have indicated PLAYING BASKETBALL and GOING
  TO PLAYS as her two interests. We would want to be able
  to find this student (as well as students who indicated
  an interest such as WATCHING BASKETBALL or SHOOTING
  BASKETBALLS) if we were to search our database for
  students who had an interest matching BASKETBALL.
```

Develop a data flow diagram to model the information processing that occurs in the registrar's office at A.B.W.U.

6. Write an essay in which you defend or attack the following position: To prepare for a career as a systems analyst, it is more important to develop interpersonal communication skills than it is to acquire a mass of technical knowledge about specific computer systems.

## 3.2 The Design and Implementation Phases of the System Life Cycle

Given specifications for the user's requirements, the next phase in the system's development is the construction of a relatively detailed design plan. This will guide future work on the implementation of the system. Note that, during the design phase, emphasis switches from understanding and specifying user needs to specifying how we will develop a software system to meet those needs. As such, we begin to consider, from a technical perspective, the data structures that will be needed to process information in the system. This processing of information must be achieved in a fashion consistent with the data flow diagrams and other documents produced during the analysis phase.

### Design

The key feature of a design plan is that it must effectively divide the overall problem into a collection of smaller, more manageable problems. Each of these smaller units will be handled by a separate program module in the implementation phase. These modules should be tested, verified, and debugged individually before being integrated into the entire system.

We can draw certain analogies between this modular structuring of a program and the boss–worker relationships that typically exist in any large corporation. Just as any effective boss must be able to delegate responsibilities, program modules that control the major logical decisions in a software system must be able to rely on lower level modules to perform subordinate tasks reliably.

Modular structure charts, which we have been using throughout this text, represent one of the most important graphic tools used by software designers to reflect the relationships between the modules comprising the entire software system. Given a comprehensive data flow diagram from the analysis phase, the software designer can transform this into an initial structure chart by roughly equating each process in the data flow diagram with a module in the structure chart (see Figure 3.3). This initial structure chart can then be refined into a more detailed design by establishing hierarchical relationships between modules and by adding lower level modules.

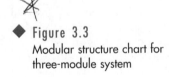

◆ Figure 3.3
Modular structure chart for three-module system

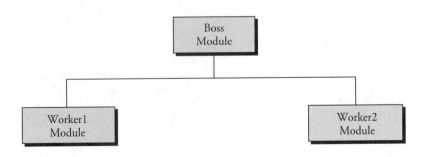

What distinguishes a good modular structure from a poor one? To answer this question we may again draw some apt comparisons between software structure and corporate boss–worker relationships. First, we note that such a structure should be developed in a *top-down* fashion. The overriding principle of top-down design is that we make decisions about the responsibilities of top-level bosses before deciding what the lower level workers are to do. If such decisions are made in a way that progresses downward on a level-by-level basis in the structure chart, we find that boss modules truly will control the major logic of a program, just as corporate bosses should be in control of the most important aspects of their company's policy.

To proceed in an opposite, bottom-up fashion is to court organizational disaster. That is, if we decide what worker modules are to do before considering the responsibilities of boss modules, we frequently run into situations where a boss module is forced into some very clumsy program logic. By proceeding bottom-up, we are not able to see the full range of subordinate tasks that a boss may require. The end result is that the boss will have to take care of minor details—a situation comparable to a corporate executive's having to momentarily leave his or her desk to go out on the assembly line and fasten a bolt that everyone else had forgotten. Such distraction can only result in the boss's doing a poorer job in more important areas of responsibility.

A second criterion to be used in judging the modular structure of a system is the degree to which individual modules are *functionally cohesive*. That is, each module should focus on achieving one particular predefined task without having unexpected side effects on the performance of other modules in the same system. For instance, a module responsible for formatting an output line in a report should not also be updating a field within a customer's record. This could potentially cause great confusion for the module whose assigned task was to guarantee updating of the entire customer record. Thus, as a system designer, you must ensure that you break down the system into its component modules following the "natural" lines of decomposition. The case studies presented in our Focus on Program Design sections will help you develop a feel for what such natural lines are. This talent will be further honed as you take more advanced courses in software engineering.

A third criterion used to evaluate the modular structure of a system is the way in which the modules within the system interact with each other. This interface between a pair of modules is often referred to as *coupling*. In drawing modular structure charts, we have used unlabeled arrows to indicate whether a given module receives data from its calling module, returns information to its calling module, or both. These data flow arrows have thus given some sense of the coupling between two modules.

Ideally, a given module in a system works independently of the others. Yet we can never attain this ideal because modules must interact with each other in any meaningful system. Hence the goal is to hold this interaction to a minimum. That is, there should be no more coupling between modules than necessary to allow them to perform their respective tasks within the framework of the overall system.

Consider the following example of a situation in which an excess of coupling could exist between two modules. Suppose we have a module to update a customer record for a business. One of the tasks subordinate to updating this record is to read new transactions in which the customer has taken part and to update the balance owed field within the customer record. Schematically, the relationship between these two modules is given in Figure 3.4.

◆ FIGURE 3.4

Portion of modular structure
chart for coupling example

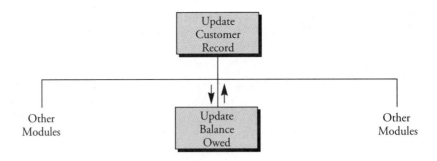

The coupling question that arises from this figure is: How do the data flow arrows between the modules Update Customer Record and Update Balance Owed eventually resolve themselves as parameters? One possibility would be for Update Customer Record to pass the entire customer record to Update Balance Owed as a reference parameter. A second possibility is for Update Customer Record merely to pass the balance owed field within the customer record to Update Balance Owed. From a data coupling perspective, the second alternative is much better. In the first alternative, more coupling than necessary exists between the modules because Update Balance Owed is given access to more than it requires to do its specific task. A careless error in Update Balance Owed could inadvertently alter another field such as an address or name within the customer record. Hence, the Update Balance Owed module could have erroneous side effects that might corrupt the entire system. The second alternative, on the other hand, completely eliminates the chance of this happening by simply not allowing Update Balance Owed to access fields it does not specifically need. Thus, minimizing coupling has guarded the system against any inadvertent side effects of a low-level module.

Having generated a structure chart in which modules are functionally cohesive and minimally coupled, the designer must then describe the general data structures to be manipulated by the system and the logic to be followed by each module. In an ideal world, the former could be done simply by specifying the abstract data types that the system will need. This ideal situation occurred in the Focus on Program Design section of Chapter 2. There we had a flight scheduling application for which the two-key table ADT provided a perfect fit.

In more complex situations, an ADT may provide only a starting point in describing the data structures required by the system. For example, we may need the operations provided by a one-key table ADT plus a few more operations that are not included in the ADT's definition. This situation occurs in the registrar's system we analyzed in Example 3.1. This application requires everything offered by a one-key table ADT plus the ability to traverse the table in decreasing GPA order as well as alphabetically by name.

Fortunately, because we have designed our ADT as a class to be used in an object-oriented system, we can easily add new features by means of derived classes and inheritance.

Because applications frequently require variations on off-the-shelf ADTs, it is not inappropriate for the designer to give some indication of how such variations might be accomplished. This is illustrated in the following example.

EXAMPLE 3.2    Design a modular structure chart along with the data structures for the registrar's system analyzed in Example 3.1.

As a designer presented with a data flow diagram from the analysis phase (Figure 3.2), your task is to transform it into an appropriate modular structure chart for the system. To a certain extent, the processes specified in the data flow diagram have already provided an initial breakdown of the problem facing the registrar. This initial breakdown can be represented in what is frequently called a first-cut (or first-level) structure chart, an early, relatively rough modular structure for a system. It's called "first-cut" because we intend to modify and expand on its structure as we go through a stepwise refinement of the system's design.

The first-cut structure chart for the registrar's system is presented in Figure 3.5. Transforming this first-cut structure chart into a final modular structure that completely specifies the system's design will require careful consideration of such issues as the user interface presented by our program and the implementation of data structures needed by the system. First, we want our top-level program to interact with users through a menu of choices. We want the user to be able to select a particular operation; the program should then dispatch processing to the appropriate subordinate module. Hence, we will need a Get Selection module that is assigned the task of handling this interface between the user and the menu of choices. Second, we must begin to consider the pertinent data structures, their implementation, and the subordinate modules necessary to access these data structures.

◆ FIGURE 3.5

First-cut structure chart for registrar's system

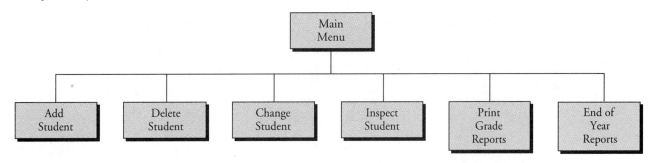

For the registrar's system, the crucial data structure is the one-key table of student records. As we have already indicated, the one-key table used in this system must be extended to allow for traversing in name and in GPA order. In this design of the registrar's system, we will use a derived class of the one-key table called a traversal table. A traversal table inherits the behavior of a one-key table for storing and fast retrievals on a student key name. It extends this behavior to support traversals of the data in the table according to a specified attribute of the data.

Therefore, we will need the new subclass and new modules to produce formatted lists in name order and GPA order. With these considerations taken into account, a refined structure chart emerges. This final structure chart (Figure 3.6) now provides us with a detailed blueprint of the system's design.

After determining the modular structure chart and major data structures for a system, the final step in the design process is to develop specifications for each module in the system. A variety of techniques are available for doing this; our preference is to follow the three-step approach we have used consistently throughout the text:

1. *Specify the task to be performed by the module.* This should be a brief description of what the module does, with minimal reference to how it does it or who is using it.
2. *Specify the input data for the module.* This serves to specify the preconditions for the module; that is, what we know to be true upon entry to the module.
3. *Specify the output data for the module.* This serves to specify the postconditions for the module; that is, what we know to be true upon leaving the module.

◆ FIGURE 3.6
Modular structure for registrar's system

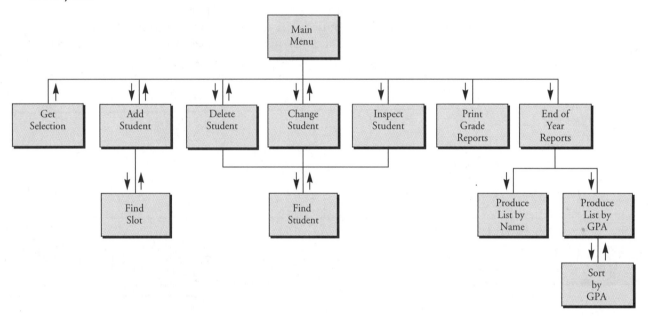

---

### EXAMPLE 3.3

Provide a modular specification for the Add Student module in the design of the registrar's system from Example 3.2.

Because that design specified a physically ordered array as an implementation technique for the student list, our modular specification should take this into account.

**Module:** Add Student
**Task:** Adds student record to table of students
**Inputs:** A table of students
**Output:** A table of students with length increased by 1

---

**EXAMPLE 3.4**

Provide a modular logic specification for the Find Student module in the design of the registrar's system from Example 3.2.

> **Module:** Find Student
> **Task:** Attempts to locate record for student in table of students
> **Inputs:** Table of students and target name
> **Outputs:** A Boolean value TRUE if found, and the record for the student, or the Boolean value FALSE if not found

In summary, the design phase of the system life cycle includes developing specifications for

1. The modular structure of the program
2. The major data structures to be used by the program
3. The logic needed by individual modules.

The system designer thus produces a set of documents that is then used by programmers who begin the actual coding of the system in an appropriate computer language. As we shall see, an effective design will facilitate this coding effort and will lead to a rather natural way of testing and verifying the correctness of the software that is written.

## Implementation

In the implementation phase, you must churn out the code in C++ (or another appropriate language) necessary to put into effect the blueprint developed in the design phase. Although the terminology "churn out" may seem a bit degrading considering the amount of effort that must go into the writing of a program, we use it to stress the importance of the design phase. Given an appropriate set of formal specifications from the design phase, coding the programs really can be an easy task. The completeness of the design phase is the key to determining how easy coding is. Time spent in the design phase will be more than repaid by time gained in coding. This point cannot be overemphasized! The most common mistake made by most beginning programmers is jumping almost immediately into the *coding phase,* thereby digging themselves into holes they could have avoided by more thorough consideration of design issues.

A side issue of the coding phase is *documentation,* the insertion of explanatory remarks into your program so that it makes sense when read by someone else (or by yourself at some time in the distant future). Few computer scientists like to write documentation. However, that does not eliminate the absolute need to write it.

In the real world, programs are worked on by teams of programmers, not just one individual. In such an environment, you must explain to other people who will have to work with it what your code is doing. Moreover, should your code have to undergo revisions in the future (often termed *program maintenance*), your documentation will be vitally important. Without it, those programmers doing the revisions could waste days or even weeks trying to decipher logic that the passage of time has made cryptic. Computer lore is filled with horror stories of programmers who were assigned the unenviable task of maintaining poorly documented code. Edward Yourdon has presented this problem by saying,

> *Virtually every major organization that began computerizing 20 years ago is now faced with 20-year-old systems whose implementation is a mystery, and, far worse,*

*whose user requirements are a mystery. The only solution to this crisis in the future is to maintain accurate, up-to-date documentation for as long as the system itself survives* [*Modern Structured Analysis* (Englewood Cliffs, N.J.: Prentice-Hall, 1989), p. 448].

At a minimum, each module you write should include documentation stating its general purpose, identifying all parameters and major local variables, and clarifying any obscure code segments. So, get into the habit of documenting all functions via the "Function; Inputs; Outputs" style that we have been using throughout the text. When combined with other written specifications from the analysis and design phases, well-documented code will help ensure that your software system has a long and productive lifetime.

**EXERCISES 3.2**

1. What is meant by the term *functionally cohesive* in reference to modular structure charts?

2. What is meant by the term *coupling* in reference to modular structure charts?

3. Explain why the following portion of a modular structure chart for a payroll system is not functionally cohesive. Correct the modular structure to make it more functionally cohesive.

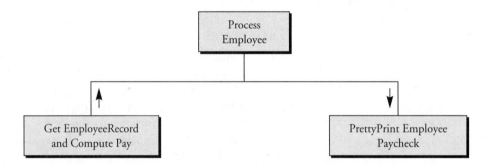

4. Suppose that we have a search module that receives a customer identification key and then searches for that customer's record in a table of records, returning it to the calling module. Suppose also that this search module prints a `"CANNOT FIND CUSTOMER"` message if the record associated with this key cannot be located. From the perspective of functional cohesion, why is the printing of this message a poor strategy?

5. Explain why using global variables is a poor strategy from a data coupling perspective.

6. Suppose that a student record at the University of Hard Knocks contains information about the student's grades in courses the student has taken and about the tuition that the student owes the university. Why should a module that computes a student's grade point average not be passed the entire student record as a parameter?

7. Data flow diagrams and modular structure charts are graphic modeling tools related to the development cycle of a software system. Discuss the similarities and differences between these two tools.

8. In Exercise 6 of Section 3.1 you analyzed a system requested by the registrar at American Basket Weaving University. Now follow up this analysis by doing a design for the system. Include a complete set of module specifications in your design.

## 3.3 Testing, Maintenance, and Obsolescence Phases of the System Life Cycle

### OBJECTIVES

- to realize that we must develop well-conceived strategies for testing software if we are to ensure its reliability
- to understand the differences between modular, system, and acceptance testing
- to understand the difference between white box and black box testing
- to know what is meant by the robustness of a module
- to be able to use the finite state machine paradigm as a means of guarding against invalid input
- to gain insight into developing test cases for modules
- to realize the importance of being able to maintain a software system over its lifetime of use

A program's usefulness is ultimately demonstrated in the final three phases—testing, maintenance, and obsolescence—of the system life cycle.

### Testing

An endeavor far more creative than coding and documentation is the testing that must be coordinated with a system's implementation. This chapter's Notes of Interest will attest to the importance of software reliability; it has become a moral and ethical issue as well as a technical one. Given this importance, how do we systematically verify the correctness of the software we develop?

First, we must realize that the testing and verification phase is a critical and full-fledged phase of the system life cycle. As such, time must be allocated for it. A common mistake made by beginning programmers is to assume the correctness of their program after one or two successful test runs. Though you should feel confident that your software will be error-free if it has been carefully designed, even well-designed systems must be thoroughly tested and verified before being released to users.

As an example, consider the following statistics, which summarize the percentages of total project time (not including maintenance) devoted to testing in several computerized systems developed for Air Force space missions.

| Mission | Percent |
| --- | --- |
| SAGE | 47 |
| NAVAL TACTICAL DATA SYSTEM | 50 |
| GEMINI | 47 |
| SATURN V | 49 |

[See R. W. Jensen and C. C. Tonies, *Software Engineering* (Englewood Cliffs, N.J.: Prentice-Hall, 1979), p. 330.] Such statistics are amazingly consistent across a wide variety of large system development projects. "In examining conventionally scheduled projects," Frederick P. Brooks "found few that allowed one-half of the projected schedule for testing, but that most did indeed spend half of the actual schedule for that purpose. Many of these were on schedule until and except in system testing" [*The Mythical Man-Month* (Reading, Mass.: Addison-Wesley, 1982)].

The general rule of thumb is that the *testing phase* of a large project can (and should) consume roughly half of the time scheduled for the project. Of course, assignments in a programming course may not be of the same magnitude as an Air Force space mission, but the message is clear. If you fail to schedule a considerable amount of time to verify the correctness of your program, your users (or instructor) will inevitably find bugs in it.

How exactly does one verify the correctness of a large program? One way is to construct formal mathematical proofs of your algorithm's correctness. Though progress is being made in applying this type of formal mathematical approach (see Section 3.4), the complex problems of most real-world systems do not allow this method to be used efficiently. Consequently, the most often employed method of verifying a program's correctness is to test it thoroughly.

**Modular Testing.** If testing is important enough to take 50% of your time, it must clearly require more than a haphazard approach. Hence, we counsel against strategies such as creating your test data "on the fly" or creating test data by random techniques. Testing must be planned to be convincing. The plan that we shall briefly describe here begins with *modular testing*. Modular testing is the natural outgrowth of the principles of modular design.

The key to modular testing is to test each individual module as it is developed. Do not wait until the entire system has been coded to begin your testing. Thus, testing on the modular level involves the following steps:

1. Develop short *driver modules* that artificially call the modules you have written and report the values returned by these modules.
2. Develop short *stub modules* that (again, artificially) are called by the modules you have written. Such stubs should report the intermediate values they are sent and return appropriate values so that the module being tested can continue execution.
3. Design *test cases* that exercise all the logical possibilities the module may encounter. Be aware that such test cases consist of more than just strategically chosen input data. Each set of input data must also include its expected result (sometimes called the *test oracle*) if it is truly to convince anyone of the module's correctness.

Normally, techniques for writing drivers and stubs are covered in an introductory programming course, and so we assume you are familiar with them. It is the third point about testing on the modular level to which we must turn our attention.

In designing test cases, programmers begin to mix methods of science and art. Every mathematician knows that we can never actually prove anything by testing examples (that is, input data). So, how can we verify a module's correctness by merely concocting examples? One proposed answer is to classify input data according to possible testing conditions. Hence, a finite set of well-chosen equivalence classes of test cases can be sufficient to cover an infinite number of possible inputs. Deciding what such equivalence classes should be is the point at which the process becomes more of an art than a science.

---

**EXAMPLE 3.5**

To illustrate these principles, consider the fee structure at the E-Z Park parking lot. Parking fees for vehicles are based on the following rules:

> *The module is given two data items: a character, which may be 'C' or 'T' indicating whether the vehicle is a car or truck; and an integer number indicating the number of hours the vehicle spent in the parking lot. Cars are charged $1.00 for each of the first three hours they are in the lot and $0.50 for each hour after that. Trucks are charged $2.00 for each of the first four hours they are in the lot and $0.75 per hour thereafter.*

After computing the appropriate charge, a new module (`compute_parking_fee`) is to call on another new module (`pretty_print_ticket`), which appropriately formats a parking fee ticket showing the vehicle type, hours parked, and resulting fee. The `compute_parking_fee` module is given here:

```
// Function: compute_parking_fee
//
// Task: computes charge for parking and calls pretty_print_ticket to output ticket
// Inputs: vehicle type in vehicle category and time spent in hours

void compute_parking_fee (char vehicle_category, int hours)
{
      float charge;

      switch (vehicle_category)
      {
          case 'C':      if (hours <= 3)
                              charge = hours;
                         else
                              charge = 3 + (hours - 3) * .5;
                         break;
          case 'T':      if (hours <= 4)
                              charge = hours * 2;
                         else
                              charge = 8 + (hours - 4) * .75;
      }
      pretty_print_ticket(vehicle_category, hours, charge);
}
```

An appropriate driver main program would simply allow us to repeatedly send data to the `compute_parking_fee` module to check its behavior in a variety of situations. An appropriate stub for the call to `pretty_print_ticket` would merely inform us that we reached this subordinate module and print the values received so that we could be sure they had been transmitted correctly. At this stage, the stub need not concern itself with detailed, formatted output; we are at the moment interested only in testing `compute_parking_fee`.

In testing this module, we can begin by identifying the following six *equivalence classes:*

1. A car in the lot less than three hours
2. A car in the lot exactly three hours
3. A car in the lot more than three hours
4. A truck in the lot less than four hours
5. A truck in the lot exactly four hours
6. A truck in the lot more than four hours.

Choosing one test case for each equivalence class, we arrive at the following set of test cases.

| Vehicle Category | Hours | Expected Results |
| --- | --- | --- |
| 'C' | 2 | Charge = 2.00 |
| 'C' | 3 | Charge = 3.00 |
| 'C' | 5 | Charge = 4.00 |
| 'T' | 3 | Charge = 6.00 |
| 'T' | 4 | Charge = 8.00 |
| 'T' | 8 | Charge = 11.00 |

The test cases for exactly three hours for a car and exactly four hours for a truck are particularly important since they represent *boundary conditions* at which a carelessly constructed conditional check could easily produce a wrong result.

This parking lot example, though illustrative of the method we wish to employ, is artificially simple. The next example presents a more complex testing situation.

<table>
<tr><td>EXAMPLE 3.6</td></tr>
</table>

Consider developing a strategy to test the sorting algorithms we discussed in Chapter 1. Recall that each of these algorithms—bubble sort, insertion sort, and selection sort—received an array of physical size **MAX_LIST_SIZE** and an integer **n** to indicate the logical size of the array, that is, the number of items currently stored in the array.

Our criterion for choosing equivalence classes of test data for such a sorting algorithm is based on two factors:

**1.** The size of *n,* the number of items to be sorted
**2.** The ordering of the original data.

The following table presents a partitioning of test data into equivalence classes for this example.

| Size of *n* | Order of Original Data | Expected Results |
|---|---|---|
| *n* = 1 | Not applicable | Array to be arranged in |
| *n* = 2 | Ascending | ascending order |
| *n* = 2 | Descending | for all cases. |
| *n* midsize and even | Descending | |
| *n* midsize and even | Ascending | |
| *n* midsize and even | Randomized | |
| *n* midsize and odd | Ascending | |
| *n* midsize and odd | Descending | |
| *n* midsize and odd | Randomized | |
| *n* = physical array size | Ascending | |
| *n* = physical array size | Descending | |
| *n* = physical array size | Randomized | |

The module should be run for a minimum of 12 cases, one for each of the classes dictated by our table. Ideally, a few subcases should be run for each of the randomized cases. We cannot overemphasize the importance of testing seemingly trivial cases such as **n = 1** and **n = 2**. These lower boundary conditions are typical examples of data that may cause an otherwise perfectly functioning loop to be incorrectly skipped. Similarly, it is important to test the upper boundary condition in which **n** reaches the physical array size.

**Testing for Robustness.** Yet another issue in modular testing is the question of how a module will react when it receives invalid data. For instance, in our current version of the **compute_parking_fee** module in Example 3.5, there is a potentially disastrous side effect that occurs when the module receives a vehicle type other than 'C' or 'T' . (What is it?)

Similar reasoning dictates that the sort test data of Example 3.6 should perhaps contain test cases for **n = 0** and **n** greater than the physical array size even though such cases should not arise in normal use of the sort module. A *robust* module is one that guards against harmful side effects when it receives invalid or unexpected data.

It is particularly critical that any modules with which the user is to interact be robust. Inadvertent wrong keystrokes by a user can crash a program or, even worse, result in a program performing its computations with incorrect data. Robustness may be so critical in some systems that you may have to improve on the interaction capabilities provided by your programming language. Consider, for instance, what your version of C++ will do when a user enters

**1.l5** (first character is a lowercase L)

instead of

**1.15**

in response to **cin >> x** where **x** is a real number. The accidentally typed lowercase "l" can crash the **>>** operator offered by many versions of C++.

One way to avoid these problems is to write your own function to read a real number. In this function, read the input a character at a time and convert the incoming stream of characters to its corresponding real value. Because you are reading characters instead of reals, nothing the user types can crash your function. If a character that is not expected as part of a real is read, your function can take corrective action and warn the user of the problem.

A paradigm known as a *finite state machine* is often used by software engineers to perform such robustness checks on user input. A finite state machine is best described by a diagram referred to as a *state-transition diagram.* A state-transition diagram for the problem of reading a real number entered in decimal form appears in Figure 3.7.

Interpret the circles in this diagram as the states of the machine. Hence the machine of Figure 3.7 can be in a **LEADING_SPACES** state, a **LEFT** state, a **RIGHT** state, a **DONE** state, or an **ERROR** state. In a particular state, the machine is expecting certain characters as valid input for that state.

◆ **FIGURE 3.7**
State-transition diagram for reading a real number in decimal form

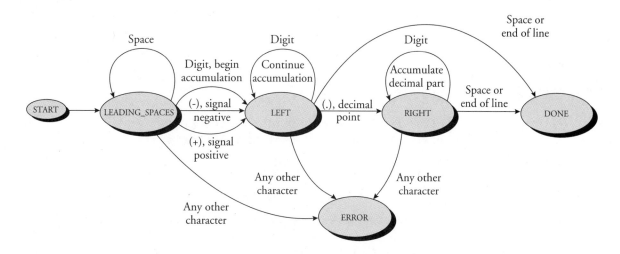

The arrows leading from the states are called *transitions*. Transitions indicate what the machine will do when it encounters a particular character in its current state. Each transition is labeled with one or more characters and, potentially, an action to take upon reading such a character. For instance, when the machine of Figure 3.7 is in the **LEADING_SPACES** state and it reads a space, it remains in the **LEADING_SPACES** state. Consistent with C++ syntax for entering a real number in decimal form, the machine must read a '+', '−', or digit before it can begin the accumulation of a real number value and switch to the **LEFT** state. Any other character read in the **LEADING_SPACES** state results in an error.

While in the **LEFT** state, the machine reads digits on a character-by-character basis. As each digit is read, its value must be added to a running total that will be returned from the function. The only valid transitions from the **LEFT** state occur when a space, end of line, or decimal point is encountered. In a similar fashion, the **RIGHT** state must read characters until the machine reaches the **DONE** or **ERROR** state. You should trace the action of the machine in Figure 3.7 on a variety of input sequences to convince yourself that it correctly handles all possibilities.

The following example illustrates that using C++'s enumerated type makes it relatively easy to translate a finite state machine into a C++ function.

---

**EXAMPLE 3.7**

Write a robust C++ function to read a real number employing the logic of the finite state machine in Figure 3.7.

The strategy of the function is to repeatedly read a character, which is then analyzed in a **switch** statement driven by the current state of the machine.

```
// Function: read_real
// Task: reads a real number in decimal form from current line of input
// characters. If current line of input characters does not constitute a valid
// real number, force user to retype the characters.
//
// Output: a real number

float read_real()
{

// This enumerated type captures the states of Figure 3.7

        enum possibilities {LEADING_SPACES, LEFT, RIGHT, ERROR, DONE};

        char ch;
        possibilities state;
        boolean negative;
        float value, multiplier;

        // Stay in the outer do loop until read a valid real
        // The inner loop embodies the logic of the finite state machine
           in Figure 13.7
        do
        {
                negative = FALSE;
                // Initially assume positive, toggle to signal negative
                multiplier = 0.1;
```

```
value = 0.0;
state = LEADING_SPACES;
do
{
        cin.get(ch);
        if (ch == '\n')
                // Have read an end of line
                state = DONE;
        switch (state)
        {
                case LEADING_SPACES:
                        if (('0' <= ch) && (ch <= '9'))
                        // Have read a digit
                        {
                                state = LEFT;
                                value = 10 * value
                                        + (ch - '0');
                        // convert
                        }
                        else if (ch == '-')
                        // Signal negative number
                        {
                                negative = TRUE;
                                state = LEFT;
                        }
                        else if (ch == '+')
                        // Leading positive sign
                                state = LEFT;
                        else if (ch != ' ')
                                state = ERROR;
                        break;
                case LEFT:
                        if (('0' <= ch) && (ch <= '9'))
                                // Have read a digit
                                        value = 10 * value
                                                + (ch - '0');
                                else if (ch == '.')
                                // Decimal point
                                        state = RIGHT;
                                else if (ch == ' ')
                                // End of current number
                                        state = DONE;
                                else
                                        state = ERROR;
                        break;
                case RIGHT:
                        if (('0' <= ch) && (ch <= '9'))
                                // Have read a digit
                                {
                                        value = value
                                                + multiplier
                                                * (ch - '0');
                                        multiplier = multiplier * .1;
```

```
                                    }
                                    else if (ch == ' ')
                                    // End of current number
                                            state = DONE;
                                    else
                                            state = ERROR;
                            }
                    } while ((state != ERROR) && (state != DONE));
// If there was bad input, force the user to reenter until get valid real
        if (state = ERROR)
                cout << "Bad Number - Please reenter this number";
        if (negative)
                value = - value;
} while(state != DONE);
return value;

}
```

To illustrate the use of the function **read_real**, consider the following driver program and the results of the sample run.

```
#include <iostream.h>
#include <iomanip.h>

int main()
(
        float number;

        cout << fixed << showpoint << setprecision(2);
        do
        {
                number = read_real();
                cout << setw(10) << number << endl;
        } while (number != 0.0);
        return 0;
}
```

A sample run is as follows:

```
45.61
        45.61
11.2
34.8
        11.20
        34.80
19.6 (Note that lowercase L typed instead of digit 1)
Bad Number - Please reenter this number
19.6
        19.60
0.0
        0.00
```

It is probably safe to say that no module of reasonable complexity can be guaranteed to be 100% robust. For each safeguard against invalid data, a user will no doubt find some way of inadvertently bypassing that safeguard. How robust an individual module must be is a reflection of how it fits into the overall modular structure of the system. It is not reasonable to expect every module in a system to guard itself against every potential kind of invalid data. Such a strategy would have the vast majority of modules more preoccupied with this issue than with their assigned responsibility within the system. A better strategy is to have a few modules whose only responsibility is to screen incoming data against invalid values. In this way we can assure that other modules will be called only when we have valid data to give them. The degree to which an individual module should be robust is thus intimately tied to the overall system design and should be stated as part of the specifications for that module.

**White Box/Black Box Testing.** One factor that can influence the design of test cases is the knowledge you have of the design and implementation of the module being tested. If you have detailed knowledge of the design and implementation, you can engage in *white box testing*. That is, the module represents a "white box" because you are aware of the internal logic and data structure implementations in the module. In white box testing, test cases can be partitioned into equivalence classes that specifically exercise each logical path through a module. In *black box testing*, the module is approached without knowledge of its internal structure. You know what the module is supposed to do, but not how it does it.

For instance, in Examples 3.2 and 3.4, we made the design decision to implement the list of students in the registrar's system with a one-key table keyed by student name. This decision allowed us to use fast retrievals in the specifications for the Find Student module. We'll work with this module again in the next example.

| EXAMPLE 3.8 |

To design a complete set of test cases for function **find_student**, we use Table 3.1. The seven cases presented in the table exercise all logical paths through the binary search algorithm.

◇ TABLE 3.1
Test cases

| Test Case | Number of Students | List | Target | Expected Results | Rationale |
|---|---|---|---|---|---|
| I | 10 | ALLEN BAKER DAVIS GREEN HUFF MILLER NOLAN PAYTON SMITH TAYLOR | Try each name in the Students list | Found TRUE. info_wanted contains associated record.  Mid contains associated position | Can we find everything in the full list? |

◇ **TABLE 3.1 (CONTINUED)**

Test cases

| Test Case | Number of Students | List | Target | Expected Results | Rationale |
|---|---|---|---|---|---|
| II | 10 | Same as test case I | Try AARON, NATHAN, ZEBRA | Found FALSE. | Is Found correctly returned as FALSE for Target data items that precede all list elements, follow all list elements, and are interspersed in the middle of the list? This case tests the full list. |
| III | 5 | ALLEN DAVIS HUFF NOLAN SMITH | Same as test case I | Same as test case I | Can we find everything in a mid-sized list? |
| IV | 5 | Same as test case III | Same as test case II | Same as test case II | Same as test case II but for mid-sized list. |
| V | 1 | HUFF | HUFF | Same as test case I | Can we handle successful search in a one-element list? |
| VI | 1 | HUFF | Same as test case II | Same as test case II | Can we handle unsuccessful searches in a one-element list? |
| VII | 0 | | HUFF | Same as test case II | Robustness check. What if we call on find_student with the empty list? |

Note that, in Example 3.8, our test cases are sure to exercise the situation in which the table is completely full. This represents a boundary condition for the algorithm; we are aware of this condition because we are testing from a white box perspective. If we were testing from a black box perspective instead, it might not be possible to exercise all such boundary conditions.

**System and Acceptance Testing.** In practice, testing at the modular level tends to be white box testing since a well-designed module will be compact and focused. Hence it is relatively easy to explore the internal structure of a module and create test cases geared toward that internal structure. As modules merge into a full-fledged software system, the testing of the entire system takes on more of a black box perspective.

In *system testing*, you exercise the interfaces between modules instead of the logic of a particular module. System testing should not occur until each module has been individually tested by white box methods. In larger systems you may find it advantageous to test related subcollections of modules before jumping to a test of the entire system. This will allow you more easily to localize the location of any errors that are found.

Ultimately, the system is tested not only by technical people but by the end users who must work with the system on a regular basis. This final phase of *acceptance testing* carried out by end users is totally black box in nature. Typically end users neither want nor need detailed knowledge of *how* a system is implemented; instead, they have a very substantial interest in *what* the system does. Does it successfully meet the specifications that were described very early in the analysis phase of the project? Consequently, end users will test and ultimately accept or reject the system based on how it meets these specifications.

**Debugging Errors Found During Testing.** The main goal of all testing we have discussed is to find errors. Though at first glance this statement may seem counterproductive, remember that it is better for errors to be detected at the testing stage than when the software is in use (or when your instructor is assigning a grade). Given this negative premise of testing, you must also know how to debug your programs when testing achieves its goal of finding errors. If testing can be categorized as an art, debugging could facetiously be described as bordering on the occult.

The following general guidelines apply to the debugging of all programs:

1. Typing is no substitute for thinking. Don't be too quick to make changes in your source program. Instead, when an error occurs, take your test cases and trace them by hand through the logic currently present in your module. Here the advantage of modular testing becomes apparent. Such hand tracing is nearly impossible if you are working with an entire system; with merely one module it is quite manageable.
2. Make use of the various debugging tools provided with most compilers. These tools allow you to scatter tracer output (to display the value of key variables at various stages of an algorithm) and breakpoints (to halt program execution at a key step so that you can examine the values contained in variables) throughout your program in a conveniently interactive fashion. The time you spend learning how to use such tools will be repaid many times over.
3. Don't assume that, once you've repaired your program for the test case that generated the error, all previous tests cases will still work correctly. You now have a new program, and all of your carefully designed test cases need to be applied again.
4. Leave time to debug so you can avoid "bandage-type" corrections (often called patches). Debugging encourages alternatives that may actually improve the design of your program. There is nothing wrong with completely scrapping an approach that has been shown, by testing, to be ill-conceived. Indeed, to try to make such an approach work by installing repeated and intricate fixes can only lead to a system doomed to a very short life.
5. Keep your test cases in a file so that as you make future modifications you can use them again conveniently.

## Maintenance

What follows acceptance testing of your system? Once your program has been thoroughly tested, it is ready to be released to the users who originally requested it. In theory, you are done; these users will live happily ever after using the program

## A NOTE OF INTEREST

### Software Reliability and Defense Systems

The issue of software testing takes on great importance as we begin to rely increasingly on the computer as an aid in the decision-making process.

In "Computer system reliability and nuclear war" [*Communications of the ACM*, Volume 30, No. 2 (February 1987): 112–131], Alan Borning of the University of Washington evaluated the problems of software testing for the Strategic Defense Initiative, popularly known as Star Wars:

*The SDI envisions a multilayer defense against nuclear ballistic missiles. The computer software to run such a defense would be the most complex ever built. A report by the Defensive Technologies Study Team, commissioned by the Department of Defense to study the feasibility of such a system, estimates a system with 6–10 million lines of code. Enemy missiles would first be attacked in their boost phase, requiring action within 90 seconds or so of a detected launch. This time interval is so short that the human role in the system could be minimal at best, with virtually no possibility of decision making by national leaders. Although pieces of the system could be tested and simulation tests performed, it would be impossible to test the entire system under actual battle conditions short of fighting a nuclear war. It has been the universal experience in large computer systems that there is no substitute for testing under actual conditions of use. The SDI is the most extreme example so far of an untestable system.*

Such systems are somewhat unique in that (we hope) many of them will never actually be used. If they ever are used, it may be too late to engage in the repair of minor flaws that normally arise in the maintenance phase of the system life cycle. It is not an understatement to say that the future of the human race may be riding on the thoroughness with which the systems have been tested. Is there any testing strategy that can be convincing enough under these circumstances? The apparent success of American Patriot missiles in destroying Iraqi Scud missiles in the Persian Gulf War has refueled speculation about the role of computer-controlled defense systems. Of the 43 Scud missiles launched against coalition forces in Saudi Arabia and Kuwait, Patriot systems intercepted 29, while 11 others were allowed to land in the ocean or remote areas of the desert. However, mere numbers can be somewhat deceiving. In his article "Lessons from the Patriot missile software effort" [*IEEE Software*, Volume 8, No. 3 (May 1991): 105–108], Galen Gruman points out:

*In one case, an Iraqi missile intercepted by a Patriot system stationed in Israel was merely knocked off target. In several other cases, debris from the intercepted Scuds damaged homes and injured people. Tougher for any interceptor are missiles that fall apart in flight, since the Patriot at best will hit only one piece, which may not be the warhead. For example, of the Scuds launched against Saudi Arabia and Kuwait, seven (including some that were allowed to fall) broke up during flight and could not be targeted—including one missile whose debris fell on a military barracks near Dhahran, Saudi Arabia, killing 28 soldiers. The Scuds fell apart because they were apparently old and poorly maintained, but both the U.S. and Soviet Union have multiple-warhead missiles designed just to avoid total destruction by antimissile systems.*

that you so painstakingly developed. In practice, unfortunately, it rarely works out this way. Instead, users begin to find flaws with your program. (Nobody is perfect!) These flaws typically are due to such factors as the following:

- Your misunderstanding the users' exact needs during the analysis phase
- Your system's slow performance when it encounters large volumes of user data
- User needs that have changed since you initially did your analysis
- Changes in computer hardware and operating system software.

When flaws like these arise, you must maintain your system. That is, you must make the necessary changes to correct the flaws. Here is where good program design and documentation pay off again. It is absolutely essential that you (or someone else assigned to *maintenance*) be able to understand your code after months or perhaps years away from it. Moreover, if your modules are functionally cohesive and minimally coupled, then you should be able to make the appropriate changes in them without causing problems in other modules of the system. That a program must be maintained is not an indication of poor design; it is rather a fact of the software life cycle. That a program can be easily maintained is actually an indication that it was soundly designed from its conception.

## Obsolescence

As we saw in Chapter 1, despite all your best efforts, your program may become obsolete in time. At that point, the system life cycle must begin anew. You may then be asked to develop a new program to meet the changed needs of the user and to make use of any expanded software capabilities.

## Dynamic Nature of the System Life Cycle

Let us recap the phases of the system life cycle: analysis, design, implementation (coding), testing and verification, maintenance, and obsolescence. Though we have discussed each as a separate entity, they are all interwoven into a dynamic, iterative process. The process is dynamic because the dividing lines between the phases are always changing. That is, as you are doing analysis, you are probably already beginning to consider many design and coding issues. The process is iterative in that, from one phase, you may frequently have to return to an earlier phase. For instance, though you may be designing your system, if a question arises about what the user wants, you will have to return temporarily to analysis before completing the design. Similarly, during implementation, you may find it necessary to alter certain design considerations. The fact that many people are usually involved in the system life cycle—users, analysts, designers, and programmers—also contributes to the volatile nature of systems development.

One way to deal with the dynamic nature of the software life cycle is to engage in a process of *iterative prototyping*. Using this method, analysts construct a simplified model of a system that performs just a few essential functions. Implementors then get this model up and running very quickly as a *prototype* of the entire system. Because the model and implementation are fairly simple at this point, mistakes and design flaws are easy to discover and correct. The system can then be extended and refined as a series of prototyes, which successively approximate the full functionality of the complete system. Object-oriented design, which we discuss more fully in Section 3.5, makes extensive use of iterative prototyping.

Perhaps one of the worst misconceptions about those of us who work in the computer field is that we deal with problems that have very rigid, well-defined solutions. We hope our discussion of the system life cycle has convinced you that nothing could be further from the truth. To truly contribute over the span of the entire life cycle, you must be skilled at communicating with people, thinking abstractly, and then following through on the details of a plan. The effective computer scientist must truly be a person for all seasons.

**EXERCISES 3.3**

1. Summarize what is involved in each of the phases of the system life cycle. If you were to specialize your career in one of these phases, which one would it be? Why? Provide your answer in essay form.

2. What is meant by the term *boundary conditions* for an algorithm?

3. What is a robust module? Should every module in a system be completely robust? Justify your answer in a written essay.

4. Consider the `compute_parking_fee` function discussed in this section (Example 3.5). Is it robust? What does it do if it does not receive a `'C'` or `'T'` for its `vehicle_category` parameter? Rewrite this module to make it more robust.

5. Employees at the University of Hard Knocks are paid by the following rules:

   ■ Employees who sign a contract for a total annual wage are paid 1/52 of that amount each week.

   ■ Hourly employees receive a paycheck based on the number of hours they work in a given week and their hourly rate. They are paid this hourly rate for each of the first 40 hours they work. After 40 hours, they are paid time-and-a-half for each additional hour of work. Moreover, work on a holiday is a special case for hourly employees. They get paid double-time for all holiday work.

   Write a function to compute the pay for an employee of the University of Hard Knocks and then dispatch the appropriate information to a check printing module. Completely test the function you write by integrating it with appropriate driver and stub modules and by designing a complete set of test data for the module.

6. Develop test data for the Add Student module of Example 3.3.

7. Design test data for function `read_real` of Example 3.7. Remember that robustness is a high priority for this module, so your test data should be designed with that in mind. If your test data detect any flaws in the algorithm, fix them.

8. Extend the finite state machine of Figure 3.7 to accept reals entered with C++'s "E" exponential notation. Then incorporate this extended finite state machine into the function `read_real` of Example 3.7. Finally, design test data for the extended function.

9. Extend the function `read_real` of Example 3.7 so that it rejects any number outside of a certain range (to be specified by additional parameters). Illustrate the use of your new function in a driver program.

10. Each type of computer has its own particular syntax for what it allows as a valid file name. Often such a file name may include an optional disk and directory specifier. Along the lines of Figure 3.7, develop a finite state machine to validate an input stream of characters intended to represent a file name on the computer system you use. Then translate your finite state machine into a robust function which returns in a string a file name entered by a user. Design test data for this function and create a driver program to test it.

11. This section has presented modular testing as the design of equivalence classes of test cases that exercise all the logical possibilities a module may encounter. You are working on a software system with a friend who claims that such comprehensive testing is impossible. As evidence, the friend cites a module she has written with 20 `if` statements in it. Your friend points out that there are approximately $2^{20}$ logical paths through this module, and that comprehensive modular testing is therefore impossible. In a written essay, refute your friend's claim. (*Hint:* Consider the cohesion of the module used as an example by your friend.)

---

**3.4 Formal Verification (Optional)**

The approach we have taken in Section 3.3 to ensure software reliability is to emphasize the construction of thorough and convincing test data as a means of verifying program/module correctness. However, this strategy of verification cannot be construed as a formal proof of the algorithm's correctness. We have attempted to show that an algorithm is correct by showing that it works for a comprehensive set of examples. But, from a mathematical perspective, a theorem cannot be proven by

## A NOTE OF INTEREST

### The (Lack of) Responsibility of Software Developers

If you have ever purchased software such as a word processor or spreadsheet for a microcomputer you have probably signed a license agreement in which you agree not to copy the software except for your own backup protection. The fineprint in such software licenses also typically contains disclaimers about the responsibility of the software developer should you eventually do something such as underpay your income tax because of a bug in the spreadsheet you used to keep your tax records.

For instance, the second page of the user's guide of a popular spreadsheet program provides the following disclaimer of warranties. The actual company name (designated here as *X*) is not given. This disclaimer is typical of that used by virtually all software companies.

*The software and user manuals are provided "as is" and without express or limited warranty of any kind by either X or anyone who has been involved in the creation, production, or distribution of the software, including, but not limited to, the implied warranties of merchantability and fitness for a particular purpose.*

*The entire risk as to the quality and performance of the software and user manuals is with you. Should the software and user manuals prove defective, you (and not X or anyone else who has been involved in the creation, production, or distribution of the software) assume the entire cost of all necessary servicing, repair or correction.*

Compare such a disclaimer to the claims that appear in the software ads that adorn all popular computing magazines and you will see a real contradiction. Products that profess to do virtually everything guarantee absolutely nothing.

Perhaps the reservations that software developers have about guaranteeing the reliability of their products should not be surprising given what we have learned about the software system life cycle. The complexity of software design and testing makes it virtually impossible to develop software that is 100% free of bugs. To customers in the software marketplace, the message is clear: *Caveat emptor* (Let the buyer beware)!

example. This is because there are infinitely many possibilities for such examples, hence making it impossible to test every one. Instead of testing, a formal approach to algorithm verification demands an airtight proof using the basic axioms and principles of logic.

## Formal Algorithm Verification by the Method of Inductive Assertions

Some work has been done in this area of formal algorithm verification. We shall attempt to summarize one of the more frequently used techniques, known as the *method of inductive assertions,* by formally proving the correctness of the following algorithm. The algorithm is to compute $N^M$ for $N$, a real, and $M$, a nonnegative integer. Our correctness proof will use the principle of mathematical induction. (This principle is covered extensively in most discrete mathematics texts; be sure to review it before proceeding if you are not familiar with it.)

```
float power(float n, int m)
{
    float r = 1.0;

    while (m > 0)
    {
        r = r * n;
        --m;
    }
    return r;
}
```

A formal proof of such an algorithm involves appropriately identifying the input assertions, output assertions, and loop invariants of the algorithm. All three of these are statements about the algorithm expressed in formal mathematical terms. The input assertions represent all necessary input conditions to the algorithm. For our example, the input assertions would be

$$N \in reals \qquad M \in integers \qquad M >= 0$$

The output assertions represent in formal terms the desired result. Here we would have $R = N^M$ as the lone output assertion for our algorithm.

Finally, we must identify the loop invariants of our algorithm. A *loop invariant* may be thought of as a special type of assertion that expresses a relationship between variables and remains constant through all iterations of a loop. Note that it is not the variables that remain fixed but rather the relationship between them. This is a key distinction to make. As we shall see, correctly identifying loop invariants is often the most crucial and difficult step in setting the stage for a proof (by induction) of an algorithm's correctness.

For the power algorithm under consideration, let $R_k$ and $M_k$ be the respective values of $R$ and $M$ after $k$ times through the **while** loop. Both $R$ and $M$ change each time the loop is executed, while $N$ remains fixed throughout the algorithm. The loop invariant relationship we wish to prove is then given by

$$R_k \times M_k$$

If we can prove this loop invariant, then it follows immediately that the algorithm is correct. Why? If the looping ends after $j$ times through the loop, $M_j$ will be zero because of the conditional test in the **while**. Hence, because of the loop invariant relationship, we will have

$$R_j \times N^{M_j} = N^M$$
$$\downarrow$$
$$R_j \times N^0 = N^M$$
$$\downarrow$$
$$R_j = N^M$$

Therefore, when the loop terminates after $j$ iterations, $R$ will contain the value $N^M$ and thereby satisfy the output assertion. The entire problem of proving the algorithm's correctness has thus been reduced to achieving an inductive proof of the loop invariant relationship.

## Inductive Proof

Now we will work through the inductive proof of

$$R_k \times N^{M_k} = N^M$$

**Basis Step with k = 0.** Before looping begins, $R_0 = 1$ and $M_0 = M$ since these are the values of the variable established by the input assertions. Hence the loop invariant relationship for $k = 0$ becomes

$$1 \times N^M = N^M$$

which is trivially true.

**Inductive Step.** By the standard inductive assumption, we assume

$$R_k \times N^{M_k} = N^M$$

and attempt to show

$$R_{k+1} \times N^{M_{k+1}} = N^M$$

In going from the $k$th pass through the **while** loop to the $(k + 1)$st pass through the loop we have

$$R_{k+1} = R_k \times N \qquad \text{and} \qquad M_{k+1} = M_{k-1}$$

Hence

$$R_{k+1} \times N^{M_{k+1}}$$
$$= (R_k \times N) \times N^{(M_k - 1)}$$
$$= R_k \times N^{M_k}$$
$$= N^M$$

by the inductive assumption.

The inductive step thus completes the formal proof of the algorithm's correctness. Note how the pivotal point in the entire proof was the determination of the loop invariant. This determination drives the rest of the proof. We can summarize the steps involved in the overall proof as follows:

**1.** Specification of input assertions
**2.** Specification of output assertions
**3.** Specification of loop invariants, from which the output assertions follow
**4.** Proof (via induction) of the loop invariants.

## What Do Proofs Really Prove?

One of the valid criticisms of our proof is that it proves correct an algorithm that is obviously correct to start with. This criticism can often be made of formal correctness proofs as they presently stand. That is, the present state of the art in *formal verification* methods has not advanced to the point where they are of value in most realistically complex situations. Other criticisms of the method include the following:

**1.** The proof method assumes the correctness of the input and output assertions. If they are wrong, a proof of the program could be done but the program could still contain errors.
**2.** The proof method says nothing about how the program will act when exceptional conditions occur that deviate from the input assertions.
**3.** The proof method focuses only on the logic within an individual module. It verifies nothing with respect to how the modules of a system will interact.
**4.** The proof method relies on a completely accurate interpretation of the action dictated by a given algorithmic statement. This action is often called the *semantics* of the statement. If our interpretation of a statement's semantics does not match what actually happens when the program runs, the program may result in an error even though it has been proved correct.

## A NOTE OF INTEREST

### Program Verification: Is It Possible?

According to mathematical logician Jon Barwise, an article by University of Minnesota–Duluth, philosopher James Fetzer has touched off a debate that could be "just as exciting and just as acrimonious" as the debates about the nature of mathematics that raged in the early twentieth century. Fetzer's article, entitled "Program verification: The very idea" appears in the September 1988 issue of the *Communications of the ACM* (Volume 31, No. 8: 1048–1063). In it, Fetzer argues that computer programs, as "encodings of algorithms that can be compiled and executed by a machine," defy formal proofs of correctness in the sense discussed in Section 13.4 of this text. Arguing from the premise that "the function of a program is to satisfy the constraints imposed by an abstract machine for which there is an intended interpretation with respect to a physical system," Fetzer argues that "the behavior of that system cannot be subject to conclusive absolute verification but requires instead empirical inductive investigation to support inconclusive relative verifications."

To a degree, Fetzer's article can be viewed as an attack on much of the research being done in formally proving the correctness of programs. As such, it has been the subject of heated criticism from many computer scientists. For instance, one letter of response signed by 10 computer scientists from institutions including the University of Maryland, Cornell University, and Stanford University blasted the *Communications* for even publishing Fetzer's article:

However, by publishing the ill-informed, irresponsible, and dangerous article by Fetzer, the editors of *Communications* have abrogated their responsibility, to both the ACM membership and to the public at large, to engage in serious enquiry into techniques that may justify the practice of computer science as a socially responsible engineering endeavor. The article is ill-informed and irresponsible because it attacks a parody of both the intent and the practice of formal verification. It is dangerous because its pretentious and ponderous style may lead the uninformed to take it seriously [*Communications of the ACM*, Volume 32, No. 3 (March 1989): 287–288).

The war of letters and responses over Fetzer's article raged on in the April 1989 *Communications of the ACM*. At issue appears to be the role of abstract reasoning about algorithms in ensuring the correctness of software that runs on real-world machines. Like many philosophical questions, those raised by Fetzer will probably never be answered to the satisfaction of everyone involved in the debate. Nonetheless, as pointed out by Michael Evangelist, a senior researcher in software technology at MCC in Austin, Texas, "Fetzer has helped to draw the distinction better between reasoning about physical objects and about abstractions of those objects."

5. Practical machine limitations such as round-off and overflow are usually not considered in formal correctness proofs.
6. Proof techniques ignore the problem of unwanted side effects caused by an algorithm. Such side effects may result in an error in the overall system even though each module has been proved correct.
7. Proofs of nonnumerical algorithms such as searching and sorting are much more difficult than proofs of numerical algorithms. [These criticisms are set forth in more expanded form in Glenford Myer, *Software Reliability* (New York: Wiley & Sons, 1976), pp. 319–320.]

Formal correctness proofs must currently be considered as a technique that is mostly of theoretical importance. They simply are not sophisticated enough to find practical application in programs that solve realistically complex problems. However, a technique should not be rejected because it currently has little practical value. Many useful methods in computer science had their roots in pure theory. Perhaps the ultimate hope for the formal correctness methods we have discussed is that they can be automated. That is, in the future we may have software that receives input/output assertions as its input, generates the code to satisfy these assertions, and then proves the correctness of the code. Though it is obviously a long way from happening, such automatic program synthesis does not seem to be impossible in principle. (The potential of formal methods in algorithm verification is the feature topic in the September 1990 issues of *IEEE Computer* and *IEEE Software*.)

**1.** Use the method of inductive assertions to prove the correctness of the following algorithm:

```
// Function: difference
// Computes the difference of two integers
//
// Inputs: two integers
// Output: an integer representing the difference of
// the two input values

int difference (int x, int y)
{
    int result = x;
    int w = y;

    while (w > 0)
    {
        result--;
        w--;
    }
    return result;
}
```

**2.** Use the method of inductive assertions to prove the correctness of the following algorithm:

```
// Function: cube
// Computes the cube of an integer
//
// Inputs: an integer
// Output: an integer representing the cube of the input value

int cube(int x)
{
    int a, b, c, result;

    a = 1;
    b = 0;
    c = x;
    result = 0;
    while (c > 0)
    {
        result = result + a + b;
        b = b + 2 * a + 1;
        a = a + 3;
        c--;
    }
    return result;
}
```

**3.** Could an algorithm that has been proven correct by formal verification methods still produce a "wrong answer" when it is implemented in a particular programming language on a particular machine? Provide a written rationale for your answer.

---

## 3.5 Object-Oriented Design

In Chapter 2 we introduced object-oriented design as a way of building new data types. We saw that thinking of a new data type as a set of objects possessing encapsulated attributes and behavior and representing the new type as a C++ class is an excellent way to build a safe, maintainable, and reusable data type. Thus far in this text, however, we have not said anything about applying the principles of object-oriented design beyond the construction of individual data types. We will first discuss the use of object-oriented design to supplement the methods of software engineering introduced in this chapter. Then we will mention some methods that have been proposed to design entire systems along object-oriented lines.

### The Place of Object-Oriented Design in the Software Life Cycle

Most of the currently existing software systems have not been designed with object-oriented methods. Many of them have been designed using the methods of analysis we have discussed so far in this chapter. Most systems have not been implemented in a purely object-oriented language, either; most are implemented in languages that support few, if any, object-oriented features. Even systems written in a hybrid language like C++ (with many object-oriented features) may consist of many modules that are not object oriented. For all of these reasons, it is important to consider how object-oriented design methods might be used in the context of more conventional methods such as the ones we have discussed so far.

The most obvious candidates for object-oriented design in a system are the modules that implement data structures. We first conceive these as abstract data types possessing attributes and behavior, which the servers or implementors provide to the clients or users. The benefits of designing or retooling existing ADTs along object-oriented lines are obvious: We gain flexibility in maintenance and reuse. For example, the one-key table class can be reused to implement a two-key table class, or it can be extended as a new subclass that supports traversal operations on its elements. As we saw in Chapter 2, good object-oriented design provides generic types that can be specialized for different applications, and it provides layered systems of types and abstract module interfaces throughout a system.

In the context of a conventional design, we might think of some of the modules in a data flow diagram or structure chart as consisting of classes or subsystems of classes. Each module is responsible for providing services to its clients; each module is responsible for properly using the servers on which it depends. In a hybrid language like C++, modules that are represented as classes can be coupled very nicely with parts of a system that are not strictly represented as classes, reflecting all of the specifications provided by data flow and structure charts. For example, the student table module that is at the center of the data flow diagram in Figure 3.2 is a class that provides attributes and behavior to the rest of the system. Supplementing a traditional structured design with object-oriented methods can reduce the amount of time spent in the implementation and testing phases, leaving more time for careful analysis and design.

## Pure Object-Oriented Design

Recent research in software engineering has pointed to the desirability of designing entire software systems along object-oriented lines. According to this view, an entire system should consist of objects that interact as specified by their abstract attributes and behavior. The classes of objects in most systems of this kind fall into three major categories:

**1.** *Interface classes.* These classes are responsible for handling interaction between the system and its end users. A good example of this kind of class is the standard C++ **iostream** class for handling input and output of text. More sophisticated classes would be required for managing interactions among a mouse, windows, pull-down menus, and graphical icons. In the analysis and design phases, the end users are also considered to be objects with their own attributes and behavior. The end users are thus integrated into a model of the software system as clients of the interface classes.

**2.** *Entity classes.* These classes model real objects in a domain, such as bank accounts, personnel records, and lists of these. The classes that we have been using in applications that are not entirely object oriented are of this kind. Entity classes are also considered to be clients of the interface classes, insofar as the interface classes represent or display models of the entities to end users.

**3.** *Control classes.* These classes capture patterns of behavior that control the flow of data within an application. A good example is a menu-driven command interpreter. The input to the interpreter may come from an interface object that handles the display of a menu and the input of a command from an end user. The interpreter would then decode the command and dispatch a message to an entity object, such as a database, to perform some action. The entity object might then send a return message to the interpreter concerning the success of the action performed, so that the controller object could take the appropriate action.

Once analysts have decided which classes are necessary to model a system, an initial prototype can be constructed immediately from existing interface, entity, and control classes. This prototype is then iteratively extended and refined by adding new classes or derived classes to the system.

The design of large systems using object-oriented methods is a subject that you will explore in software engineering courses. In the rest of this text, we will use a combination of conventional and object-oriented analysis and design techniques that should prepare you for further work in software construction.

**EXERCISES 13.5**

**1.** Study the data flow diagram in Figure 3.2 and list which modules can be represented as classes, and which modules are simply operations.

**2.** Redesign the system depicted in Figure 3.2 so that it is entirely object oriented. Begin by classifying the modules into interface, entity, and control modules. This may require you to merge some of the modules that denote simple operations into one module denoting a class. As you go, be sure to base your classifications on the roles and responsibilities each module has to the others as client or server. At the end of the process, you should have a simplified diagram.

**3.** Define your interface and control modules from the previous exercise as C++ classes.

**FOCUS ON PROGRAM DESIGN**

In this section, we complete an important part of the design of the registrar's system as begun in Example 3.2. In particular, we must develop the modules for representing the data structures used by the system. In object-oriented terms, these are the entity classes of the system. There are really just two kinds of entity in the system, a student and a table of students. We first specify the attributes and behavior of the student class, and then represent it as a C++ class definition. Then we do the same for the table class.

In the registrar's system, a student has five attributes, a name, total credits taken, total credits earned, total grade points, and a grade-point average. A name is a string of characters. Total credits taken and earned are integers. Total grade points and grade-point average are real numbers. The registrar must be able to create new student records with appropriately initialized attributes, be able to view these attributes, and be able to modify every attribute except for the student's name and grade-point average. The student object itself will be responsible for computing the grade-point average as a function of the other data in the record.

In addition, other clients of the student class, such as the table of students, must be able to compare two student objects by grade-point average (GPA), for purposes of ordering them for a traversal. All that the client needs to know in order to detect the ordering is whether or not two student's GPAs are in descending order. This operation is specified as a Boolean function. The complete behavior of the student class is specified in the following set of abstract operations:

---

**Create operation**

Preconditions:   Receiver is a student in an unreliable state. **name** is the student's name. **gpa** is the student's grade point average.

Postcondition:   Receiver is initialized with **name** and **gpa**.

**get_name operation**

Preconditions:   Receiver is a student.

Postconditions:  **name** returned.

**get_gpa operation**

Preconditions:   Receiver is a student.

Postconditions:  **gpa** is returned.

**get_credits_earned operation**

Preconditions:   Receiver is a student.

Postconditions:  **credits_earned** is returned.

**get_credits_taken operation**

Preconditions:   Receiver is a student.

Postconditions:  **credits_taken** is returned.

**get_grade_points operation**

Preconditions:   Receiver is a student.

Postconditions:  **grade_points** is returned.

**set_credits_earned operation**

Preconditions:   Receiver is a student. **value** is the new total credits to be inserted.

Postconditions:  **value** replaces **credits_earned** currently in the receiver.

**set_credits_taken operation**

Preconditions:   Receiver is a student. **value** is the new total credits to be inserted.

Postconditions:  **value** replaces **credits_taken** currently in the receiver.

**set_grade_points operation**

Preconditions:   Receiver is a student. **value** is the new total credits to be inserted.

Postconditions:  **value** replaces **grade_points** currently in the receiver.

**Print operation**

Preconditions:   Receiver is a student.

| Postconditions: | **name, credits_taken, credits_earned, grade_points,** and **gpa** have been printed on the terminal screen. |

**gpa_order operation**
Preconditions: Receiver and **s** are students.
Postconditions: Returns TRUE if receiver's **gpa >= s**'s **gpa**, or FALSE otherwise

The C++ class declaration module for **student** is

```
// Class declaration file: student.h

#ifndef STUDENT_H

#include "boolean.h"
#include "strlib.h"

// Declaration section

// We assume that types boolean and string are already defined.

class student
{
        public:
        // Class constructors

        student(string new_name, float new_gpa);
        student(const student &s);

        // Member functions

        string get_name();
        float get_gpa();
        int get_credits_taken();
        int get_credits_earned();
        float get_grade_points();
        void set_credits_taken(int value);
        void set_credits_earned(int value);
        void set_grade_points(float value);
        void print();
        boolean gpa_order(const student &s);
        student & operator = (const student &s);

        private:

        // Data members

        string name;
        float gpa, grade_points;
        int credits_earned, credits_taken;

};

#define STUDENT_H
#endif
```

The implementation module for the student class is left as an exercise.

Now we must decide how to define the list of students for the registar's system. We defined an ordered collection class in Chapter 1. This class supports ordered traversals but does not support retrievals by key value. We defined a one-key table class in Chapter 2 that does support keyed retrievals but no ordered traversals. We could start from scratch and make a new ADT to order for our application, but that would be wasting time and effort in reinventing a wheel that may already be available in one of our two ADTs. By reusing one of them to solve our problem, we will illustrate an important point about object-oriented design.

We would like to use the fast, keyed retrieval operation of a one-key table, but also be able to traverse the data in the table in a specified order. We accomplish these two goals by extending the behavior of a one-key table as a new derived class. We call this derived class a *traversal table*. A traversal table has all of the attributes and behavior of a one-key table. In addition, it has a specialized traversal operation. This operation visits every data value in the table in the order specified by the client, and applies a client's operation to each data value. Thus, the traversal operation will expect two parameters:

**1.** A specification of the way in which the data values should be ordered for traversal
**2.** A specification of the operation to be applied during the traversal.

Both of these parameters will be operations. Here is a specification of the abstract traversal operation:

---

**Traverse operation**

Preconditions:    Receiver is a traversal table. **compare**, which takes two data values as arguments, is the operation to be used to order the data values for traversal. **process**, which takes a single data value as an argument, is the operation to be applied to each data value during the traversal.

Postconditions:   **process** has been applied to each data value in the receiver, according to the order specified by **compare**.

---

Note that a traversal table is just a one-key table that is traversable by some ordering mechanism within the data values. Storing, retrieving, and deleting data from this table still assume an ordering by a primary key value.

To represent a traversal table as a C++ class template, we define it as a derived class of the one-key table class template. The **traverse** operation must be specified as a member function declaration having two parameters of type *pointer to function*. We first present the declaration and then discuss it:

```
// Class declaration file: travtab.h

#ifndef TRAV_TAB_H

#include "onetable.h"

// Declaration section

template <class K, class E> class traversal_table :
    public one_key_table<K, E>
{
```

```
    public:

    // Class constructors

    traversal_table();
    traversal_table(const traversal_table<K, E> &table);

    // Member functions

    traversal_table& operator = (const traversal_table<K, E> &table);

    void traverse(boolean (*compare) (const E &item1, const E &item2),
            void (*process) (E &item));

    protected:

    // Data members

    int pointers[MAX_TABLE_SIZE];

    // Function members

    void prepare_to_traverse(boolean (*compare) (const E &item1,
            const E &item2));

};

#define TRAV_TAB_H
#endif
```

Note that the formal parameter list of the member function **traverse** has two parameters of type pointer to function. Be careful to enclose the **\*<function name>** notation within parentheses so that C++ evaluates the operators in the right order. Note also that the base class is extended by adding a new data member, an array of integers. This array will be used to save the results of a pointer sort whenever the table is prepared for traversal.

The implementation of the **traverse** operation consists of two steps:

1. Call the protected member function **prepare_to_traverse** with the ordering function as a parameter. **prepare_to_traverse** performs a pointer sort on the table, leaving the pointers appropriately arranged in the protected data member **pointers.**
2. Loop through the data member for the table itself, using as index positions the pointers in the **pointers** data member, and apply the **process** function to the value at each position.

Here is the code for the top-level member function **traverse:**

```
template <class K, class E>
void traversal_table<K, E>::traverse(boolean (*compare) (const E &item1,
        const E &item2), void (*process) (E &item))
{
```

```
        E value;

        prepare_to_traverse(compare);
        for (int i = 0; i < table_length; ++i)
        {
              value = data[pointers[i]].get_value();
              process(value);
        }
}
```

Note that the argument passed to **prepare_to_traverse** in this function is the name of the function, **compare**, to be used to order the data values for traversal.

The implementation of **prepare_to_traverse** uses **compare** to perform a pointer sort:

```
template <class K, class E>
void traversal_table<K, E>::prepare_to_traverse(boolean (*compare)
    (const E &item1, const E &item2))
{
    int j, k, temp;
    boolean exchange_made;
    E value1, value2;

    // Initialize pointer array

    for (k = 0; k < table_length; ++k)
          pointers[k] = k;

    k = 0;
    exchange_made = TRUE;

    // Make up to n - 1 passes through array, exit early if no exchanges are made
    // on previous pass

    while ((k < table_length - 1) && exchange_made)
    {
        exchange_made = FALSE;
        ++k;
        for (j = 0; j < table_length - k; ++j)
        {
              value1 = data[pointers[j]].get_value();
              value2 = data[pointers[j + 1]].get_value();
              if (compare(value1, value2))
              {
                    temp = pointers[j];        // Swap pointers
                    pointers[j] = pointers[j + 1];
                    pointers[j + 1] = temp;
                    exchange_made = TRUE;
              }
        }
    }
}
```

## A NOTE OF INTEREST

### IBM and Apple = Pinstripes and T-Shirts

After signing the Treaty of Amiens in 1802, Napoleon said, "What a beautiful fix we are in now; peace has been declared." In July 1991, representatives of IBM and Apple announced an alliance that similarly shocked many industry analysts. IBM has long been positioned in the mainstream of the computer industry, gaining its reputation more from selling the reliability of its corporate image than from technological innovation. Apple, on the other hand, has based its claim to fame on bold new technologies developed by computer enthusiasts with a distinct bent toward "hacking." For instance, the window-based environment of the first Apple Macintosh in 1983 established a new and exciting mode of human–computer interaction. When IBM and Microsoft later "copied" the "look and feel" of the Mac environment to an IBM-compatible operating system, Apple promptly took them to court in a case whose effects on the software industry are still being debated.

Small wonder that eyebrows have been raised by the agreement between these two corporate antagonists. What are the underlying reasons for the move? According to joint press releases, the companies will cooperate on four fronts:

1. IBM will take steps to better integrate the Mac into IBM-based computer networks.
2. Apple will build future machines using IBM's RISC architecture chip technology.
3. The companies will work together on developing data standards for multimedia.
4. There will be a joint endeavor to produce a new, object-oriented operating system that will eventually be marketed for both IBM and Apple computers.

The last of these ventures is the one that seems to be generating the most excitement on an industry-wide basis. The two companies had been working individually on object-oriented operating systems. Apple had been calling their exploratory system Pink; IBM had called theirs Metaphor. It now appears that the Pink and Metaphor research groups will combine their efforts, with the long-range goal that users and third-party software developers will only have to deal with one common interface for a variety of different machines from the two companies. By taking advantage of the abstraction emphasized by the object-oriented approach, the details of the particular machine will be completely hidden.

It all sounds good in theory, but can researchers from two such historically different companies really define a common set of goals? If they can, will it destroy their own individual initiatives? Only time will tell.

---

**RUNNING, DEBUGGING AND TESTING HINTS**

1. When testing a large program, always test modules individually before testing the entire system.
2. When developing test cases, keep them in a file so that they can be used again easily after fixing errors.
3. The finite state machine paradigm is a systematic way of ensuring that users enter valid input to your program.
4. Be sure to design test data that exercise the boundary conditions of a module, which is is where an error is most likely to occur.

## SUMMARY

### Key Terms

| | | |
|---|---|---|
| acceptance testing | finite state machine | stub module |
| analysis | functionally cohesive | systems analyst |
| black box testing | iterative prototyping | system testing |
| boundary conditions | maintenance | test cases |
| coding phase | modular testing | test oracle |
| coupling | pointer to function | testing phase |
| data flow diagram | prototype | transitions |
| documentation | robust | traversal table |
| driver module | state-transition diagram | white box testing |
| equivalence classes | | |

### Key Terms (Optional)

| | | |
|---|---|---|
| formal verification | loop invariant | method of inductive assertions |

### Key Concepts

◆ During the analysis phase of the software system life cycle you must determine the user's requirements. Typically, this involves considerable interaction between the systems analyst and end user. A data flow diagram is one example of a document that would be developed during this phase. Ultimately, the user's requirements must be described in a form suitable to pass on to the design phase.

◆ During the design phase, the user's requirements are examined, and the system that will ultimately meet these requirements begins to take shape. Software designers must turn out a blueprint of the eventual software system that can then be translated into program code. Typical of the documents produced during the design phase are modular structure charts, layout of data structures, and modular logic specifications.

◆ A good design is developed in a top-down fashion. Individual modules within the design should be functionally cohesive: They should focus on one particular task. Modules within the design should be minimally coupled; they should not transfer more information than necessary between themselves. This avoids the possibility of one module inadvertently affecting data being used by another.

◆ Testing and verification can consume up to 50% of the time spent in developing a software system. Each module should be tested as it is finished. Use drivers to feed inputs into the module and stubs to check the module's interactions with subordinate modules.

◆ System and acceptance testing follows modular testing.

◆ The maintenance phase of a system follows its release to users. During this phase, adjustments must be made to the system in response to bugs and changes in user requirements.

◆ Obsolescence is the sixth, and ultimately inevitable, phase of the software system life cycle.

### Key Concepts (Optional)

◆ Formal algorithm verification by such methods as inductive assertions is of theoretical interest now and offers promise of more reliable software in the future.

1. Design a complete set of modular test cases for the system in the Focus on Program Design section. Be as thorough as possible in your testing; pay particular attention to robustness issues. Wherever your testing locates an error, modify the code to fix it. (An interesting class experiment for this program is to turn it into a contest. The student who finds and fixes the most errors wins.)

2. Invite the registrar of your university to your class to discuss the type of data processing operations in which the registrar's office is typically engaged. After this discussion (which should no doubt include time for questions), describe the data involved in the operations of your registrar's office in terms of abstract data types. Develop a data flow diagram to picture the way in which the registrar's office processes information.

3. Consider the following data declaration and function declaration.

```
enum kind_of_triangle {SCALENE, ISOSCELES, EQUILATERAL, IMPOSSIBLE};...


// Function: triangle_type
// Task: determines the type of triangle, given the lengths of the three sides
//
// Inputs: three integers representing the lengths of the three sides of a triangle
// Output:
//    EQUILATERAL, if all sides are equal
//     ISOSCELES, if two sides are equal
//     SCALENE, if all sides are different lengths
//     IMPOSSIBLE, if the integers do not constitute valid triangle sides


kind_of_triangle triangle_type (int side1, int side2, int side3);
```

For this problem, work with another student. Each of you should develop independently, first, a robust version of the function just described and, second, a complete set of test data (including robustness checks) for the function. Next, jointly develop a driver program and test your functions. Have your partner use his or her test data on the function you developed. Then use your test data on your partner's function. The winner is the one whose function fails for the fewer number of test cases.

4. In Exercise 8 of Section 3.2 you designed a system for the registrar at American Basket Weaving University. Implement and fully test that system.

5. In Exercise 10 of Section 3.3 you developed and tested a module to read strings that are valid file names on your particular computer system. Incorporate this module into a larger program that could be used to back up text files. The user should enter two file names: a source file and a destination file. Your program should then copy from the source to the destination. If your file name module does its job correctly, your program should never crash because it tries to access an "invalid file name."

6. In Chapter 8, you developed a program that allowed its user to enter rational numbers and then perform operations on them. Now make your program more user-friendly and robust by reading all rational numbers entered by the user in a module **read_rational**. The logic of this module should be driven by a finite state machine that filters out erroneous input. Submit a diagram of the finite state machine as part of the documentation accompanying your program.

7. Assume that someone has developed a program that allowed its user to enter complex numbers and then perform operations on them. Now make the program more user-friendly and robust by reading all complex numbers entered by the user in a

module **read_complex**. The logic of this module should be driven by a finite state machine that filters out erroneous input. Submit a diagram of the finite state machine as part of the documentation accompanying your program.

8. Assume that you would like to make some extra cash by writing a program to facilitate some activity for a particular business, organization, or school. Write a proposal that clearly explains what your program will do, how much it would cost, why the purchase of this program would be beneficial to the institution, and how soon you could complete this project. Be sure to limit your project so that it does not exceed your ability as a programmer.

9. Research the topic of formal methods in algorithm verification, using the September 1990 issues of *IEEE Computer* and *IEEE Software* as initial references. Then write a paper in which you discuss the role that formal algorithm verification may play in future software development. Your paper should address such issues as how formal verification can reduce the amount of time spent in testing software and how it can be used to ensure a degree of software reliability exceeding what can be achieved by testing alone. Be sure to respond to the criticisms of formal verification summarized in Section 3.4.

10. Interview a systems analyst at a local company or organization. Then, write a paper or prepare a presentation in which you describe the techniques used by that systems analyst to determine user needs and to document these user needs in written or diagrammatic form.

11. The September 1990 issue of *Communications of the ACM* was dedicated to the topic of object-oriented programming. Using the articles in this issue as a starting point, write a research paper in which you describe how software development will be affected by the object-oriented paradigm. Your paper should discuss such issues as building software libraries that are usable in a variety of contexts and building software systems that are easily extended when the need to do so arises.

# 4 Linked Lists and Pointers

*These are the ties which, though light as air, are strong as links of iron.*
Edmund Burke
(1729–1797)

In the previous chapters we discovered that an array implementation (with binary search) of a one-key table requires $O(n)$ data interchanges for the add and delete operations. Attempting to maintain such an array-implemented list in order parallels the dynamics of waiting in a long line. When someone cuts into the middle of the line, there is a domino-like effect that forces everyone behind that person to move back. When someone in the middle of the line decides to leave the line, the reverse effect occurs; everyone behind the departed person is able to move ahead one slot. It is possible to draw an analogy between people waiting in a line and data items stored next to each other in computer memory. If the data items are arranged in some type of order and it becomes necessary to insert into or delete from the middle of the line, a considerable amount of data movement is involved. This data movement requires computer time and decreases program efficiency. The central motivation behind the linked list data structure is to eliminate the data movement associated with insertions into and deletions from the middle of the list. Of course, by now we might suspect that efficiency in eliminating such data movement can only come by trading off other efficiency factors. One of the crucial questions to ask yourself as we study linked lists is "What price are we paying to handle additions and deletions effectively?"

One way of conceptually picturing a linked list is to think of a game some parents use to make the opening of holiday gifts particularly exciting for their children. One feature of the game that helps to build children's anticipation ensures that minor gifts are opened first, gradually building up to the most substantial gift. (Recall from your own childhood experience the partial letdown that occurred when you opened a gift package containing a mere pair of socks after having already unwrapped something significantly more exciting such as a box of candy.) Thus, the premises of this gift-giving game are that gifts may be ranked according to their desirability and that the game is more fun when the most desirable gifts are opened last.

To achieve this end, parents will hide their child's wrapped gifts at various locations throughout the home. For instance, let us suppose a scenario in which parents have bought the following four gifts for their child, which are ranked and hidden as indicated:

| Ranking | Gift | Hiding Place |
|---------|------|--------------|
| Least desirable | Pair of socks | Under bed |
| ↓ | Box of candy | Kitchen drawer |
| | Video game | Basement cabinet |
| Most desirable | Bicycle | Garage |

The parents will then tell the child *only* the location of the least desirable gift; here, for instance, they would give instructions to look under a bed for the first gift. Upon opening that gift, the child will find the uninspiring pair of socks *plus* a more intriguing note with the information that the child's next gift will be in a kitchen drawer. The pattern should now be obvious. From the box of candy, the child follows an informational pointer to a basement cabinet, where the video game is discovered along with a similar informational link to the garage as a location where something bigger and better may be found. Here the now-eager child will uncover a bike along with a final (and no doubt disappointing) note indicating that the end of the chain of gifts has been reached.

A conceptual picture of this chain of gifts is presented in Figure 4.1. This same conceptual picture applies to the *linked list* abstract data structure we are about to study. In this figure, the arrows connecting packages represent the informational note in each package that tells us the location of the next package. Conceptually, the form taken by this informational pointer is not important. However, it is crucial that we have a reliable *pointer* to the leading gift (often called a *head pointer*) and, thereafter, a reliable *pointer* in each package (often called a *node*) to the next package. Should any pointer be flawed, the remaining gifts on the chain become essentially inaccessible (much to the dismay of the child who wanted that bike so desperately).

◆ FIGURE 4.1
A linked chain of gifts

In addition to introducing us to much of the vernacular that comes with linked lists, this review of a simple childhood game can also give us a hint of the ease with which such a linked chain of nodes can handle additions and deletions. For instance, suppose that a sudden windfall allows the parents of the child in our example to buy a baseball glove in addition to the four gifts they had already purchased. Assuming that this new gift is ranked between the video game and the bicycle in desirability, consider what must be done to link it into the gift chain. We must do the following:

1. Find a place to hide it, for example, the attic.
2. Take the informational linking note from the video game package and put it in the baseball glove package. (Why?)

◆ FIGURE 4.2
Adding a baseball glove to
the chain of Figure 4.1

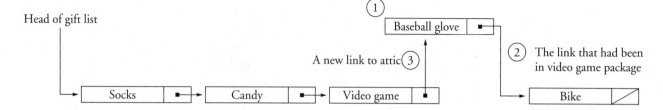

**3.** Insert a new informational pointer in the video game package, indicating the attic as the location of the next node. (Why?)

Figure 4.2 portrays such an addition with circled numbers corresponding to the three steps just described. The important aspect to note in this series of moves is that no gift that was already in place had to be moved to accommodate adding the new gift. From a conceptual perspective, this is why linked lists will be able to avoid the movement of data that was associated with an insertion into an array-implemented list.

Along the same lines, let us now suppose that our shameless parents devour all of their child's candy before the holiday arrives. Clearly they must remove this package from the chain to hide this disgusting behavior from their child. Using Figure 4.3, convince yourself that the following steps will accomplish this deletion:

**1.** Remove the now-empty candy package from the kitchen drawer.
**2.** Before throwing away the empty package, remove the linking note from it and put this note in the package containing the socks.
**3.** Dispose of the incriminating candy container and the linking note that originally was in the package with the socks.

◆ FIGURE 4.3
Removing candy from the
chain of Figure 4.2

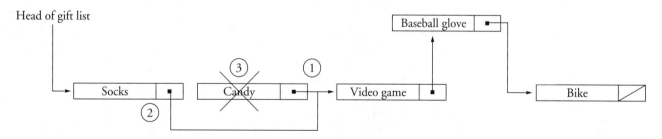

It is important to note again that no package remaining on the chain had to be physically moved to a new location—a situation much different from what happened when we removed a name from an array-implemented list in the last chapter.

Have we strayed too far from computer science in using such a nontechnical, elementary example to introduce our chapter on linked lists? Not at all! In fact, we've achieved two very important goals. First, if you understand all the details of the gift-giving game, then you essentially understand the important concepts involved in the linked list data structure. Second, this is just another illustration of the fact that computer techniques are often just formalizations in a logic machine of the way we, as human beings, have been doing things for many years. Consequently, you should never feel intimidated by such a computer technique; merely try to relate it to an analogous—and familiar—manual method. Doing this will help give substance to the more formal computer science method.

## 4.1 The Linked List as an Abstract Data Type

### OBJECTIVES

- to formalize the notion of a linked list as an ADT
- to understand, at an abstract level, why a linked list allows additions and deletions of nodes with minimal data movement
- to realize, at an abstract level, the price paid in search efficiency for the efficiency gained in adding and deleting nodes
- to realize that, although a linked list may be viewed as an ADT, it is also a data structure that can be used to implement other ADTs, such as one-key tables

Recall from Chapter 2 that to specify an abstract data type (ADT) formally, we must describe the individual elements of the structure, the relationship(s) between these elements, and the logical operations to be performed on the structure.

A formalization for the intuitive notion of a linked list follows. This formalization uses the terminology *linear ordering*. By linear ordering, we mean any ordering of data in which there is an identifiable first element, second element, and so forth. For instance, a string could be viewed as a linear ordering of characters. Also, a one-key table has a linear ordering determined by key values. It is important to realize that linear ordering is a logical concept; it need not coincide with physical ordering of data.

> **Linked list:** A linked list is a collection of elements called nodes. Each node contains a data portion and a pointer. The data portions in all nodes are of the same type. The pointer in a given node contains the location of the node that follows the given node in the linear ordering of the list. The entire list is referenced by a separate head pointer to the first node in the linear ordering. The head pointer is simply the location of this first node. It is not a linked list node and hence has no data associated with it. A special value designated as **NULL** is assigned to a pointer that references an empty linked list. The last node in the ordering contains a null pointer, indicating that there is no node following it. To facilitate movement through a linked list and access to nodes, a linked list also contains two special pointers, called **previous** and **current**. When the list is empty, these pointers each have the value **null**. When the list contains at least one node, **head** always points to the first node. Following an insertion operation, **current** points to the most recently inserted node. Following a removal operation, **current** points to the node after the most recently deleted node (or **NULL** if this was the last node in the list). Following a **next** operation, **current** points to the next node after the previous current one (or **NULL** if this was the last node in the list). **previous** either points to the node before the current node, or is **null** when the list is empty or when **current** points to the first node in the list. A linked list also has a **length** attribute, which records the current number of nodes in the list.

The operations that can be performed on a linked list are:

> **Create operation**
> Preconditions:    Receiver is a linked list in an unpredictable state.
> Postconditions:   **head**, **previous**, and **current** are all set to **NULL**, and **length** is set to zero, so the list is considered empty.
>
> **Destroy operation**
> Preconditions:    Receiver is a linked list.
> Postconditions:   Any existing nodes in the list are returned to the heap. **head**, **previous**, and **current** are all set to **NULL**, and **length** is set to zero, so the list is considered empty.

**Empty operation**

Preconditions: Receiver is a linked list

Postconditions: **empty** returns TRUE if receiver contains no nodes and FALSE otherwise.

**At_end operation**

Preconditions: Receiver is a linked list.

Postconditions: **at_end** returns TRUE if **current** points to the last node in the list and FALSE otherwise.

**Length operation**

Preconditions: Receiver is a linked list

Postconditions: **length** returns the number of nodes currently in the list.

**Next operation**

Preconditions: Receiver is a linked list.

Postconditions: If **current** is not **NULL**, **previous** is set to **current** and **current** is set to point to the next node or to **NULL** if there is no next node. Otherwise, no action.

**First operation**

Preconditions: Receiver is a linked list.

Postconditions: If **head** is not **NULL**, **current** is set to **head** and **previous** is set to **NULL**. Otherwise, no action.

**Retrieve operation**

Preconditions: Receiver is a linked list and **item** is a variable that will return the data in the current node.

Postconditions: If **current** is not **NULL**, the data in the node pointed to by **current** is returned in **item** and the operation returns TRUE. Otherwise, the operation returns FALSE and **item** is undefined.

**Insert operation**

Preconditions: Receiver is a linked list and **item** is the value to be inserted.

Postconditions: If there is enough memory for a new node, **item** is placed in a new node, the new node is inserted before the node that **current** points to, **current** is set to point to the new node, and **length** is incremented. If **current** originally pointed to **head, head** is also set to point to the new node.

**Remove operation**

Preconditions: Receiver is a linked list and **item** is a variable that will return the removed data.

Postconditions: If **current** is not **NULL**, then the current node is removed from the list, **previous** is set to **current**, **current** is set to the next node (or **NULL** if the removed node was the last one in the list), **item** is set to the removed node's data field, and **length** is decremented. If the removed node is the first node in the list, then **head** is set to the next node also. If **current** is **NULL**, no action. If the item is removed, the operation returns TRUE. Otherwise, the operation returns FALSE and item is undefined.

**Traverse operation**

Preconditions: Receiver is a linked list, **compare** is a function of two element arguments that specifies the desired ordering for the traversal. **process** is a function of one element argument to be applied to each element during the traversal.

Postconditions: **process** is applied to the data in each node in the list, in the order specified by **compare**.

◆ FIGURE 4.4
Actions of some linked list operations

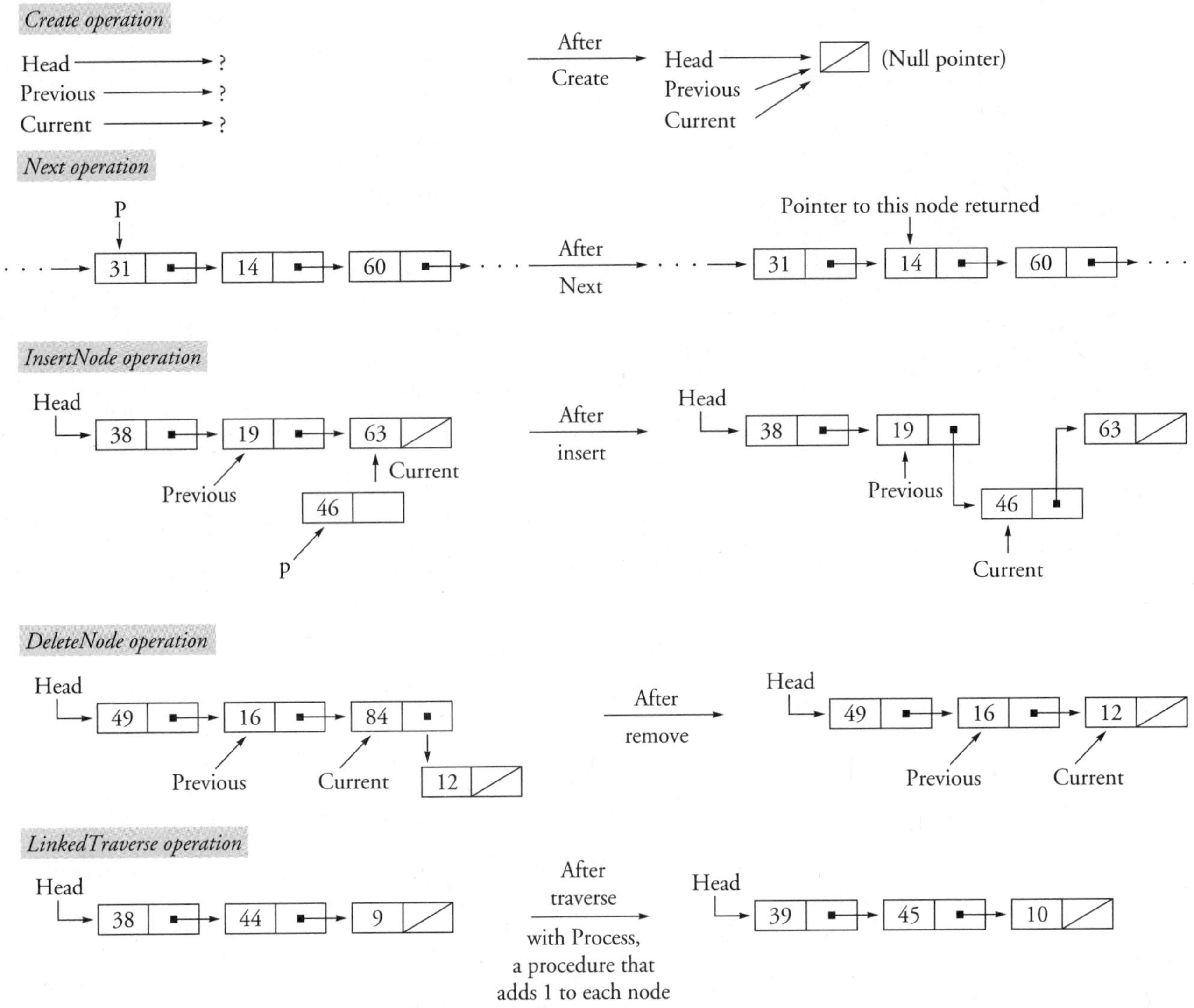

*Create operation*

*Next operation*

*InsertNode operation*

*DeleteNode operation*

*LinkedTraverse operation*

Figure 4.4 depicts the action of the **create, next, insert, first, last, retrieve, remove,** and **traverse** operations on a linked list of integers. Study this figure carefully and observe that every linked list will have three pointers associated with it. After the **create** operation, the pointers for the resulting empty list are **NULL**. For a list that is not empty, the pointer in the final node on the list is **NULL**. Note the distinction between a pointer that is **NULL** and a pointer that is undefined. The former reliably indicates a reference to an empty structure through a specific flagging value. The latter is completely unreliable in terms of what it references.

The figure also indicates that insertion into and deletion from a linked list require a pointer to the node to be acted on and a pointer to the node that precedes this node in the linear ordering of the list. For both of these operations, the pointer to the preceding node is necessary since the pointer within that node must be

◆ FIGURE 4.5
Alphabetically ordered
linked list with four nodes

altered as part of the operation. For example, in Figure 4.4, when we insert 46 after the node containing 19, the node containing 19 is altered by having its pointer reference the node containing 46 instead of the node containing 63. This alteration of the node containing 19 requires that we have a pointer (**previous**) that references it. In the event that the insertion or deletion occurs at the front of the list, the **previous** pointer is set to **NULL** to signal this special condition.

Finally, Figure 4.4 illustrates that the linear ordering of the linked list may not necessarily coincide with the natural ordering of data in the list. In this figure, the linear ordering of the list is not in correspondence with either ascending or descending order by integer value. What defines the linear ordering will vary from application to application.

One application we can immediately envision is to use a linked list as an implementation technique for the one-key table ADT. The linear ordering established by the links would mirror the order determined by the key fields in the nodes. For instance, Figure 4.5 depicts a linked list in which the links establish an alphabetical ordering according to key field.

The operations of adding a node and deleting a node from such a list may also be conveniently represented in such a schematic form. In fact, you will soon discover that the best way to conceive algorithms that manipulate linked lists is to draw what you want to happen via such logical pictures. Such a picture of a linked list is completely at the abstract level; it implies nothing about how the linked list will finally be implemented. Once you understand the concept from such a graphic representation, it is usually a straightforward matter to implement it.

For instance, we now wish to add a node containing PRIM to the list shown in Figure 4.5; all we need to do is to store PRIM in an available memory location outside of the list, such as the one pointed to by **p** in Figure 4.6. We then reset the pointer link of the node containing MARTHA to point to the node containing PRIM, and the pointer link of the node containing PRIM to point to the node containing SAM. This logically maintains the alphabetical order of the data in the nodes without physically moving any of the existing nodes.

Similarly, should you then wish to delete an existing node from the linked list, a graphic representation of the list can again indicate how the pointers should be altered to reflect such a change. For example, given the list of Figure 4.6, the diagram of Figure 4.7 pictorially outlines what must be done if we want to delete the node containing MARTHA. Notice in this figure that, as was the case for insertion, only pointers must be changed to delete a node. Again, no movement of data occurs.

The **destroy** operation is a special function used with classes that rely on dynamic memory, and is discussed in Section 4.3.

## Efficiency Considerations for Linked Lists

These addition/deletion considerations may make a linked list an attractive alternative to an array implementation of a one-key table. The diagrams of Figures

◆ **FIGURE 4.6**
Insertion of node containing
PRIM into linked list of
Figure 4.5

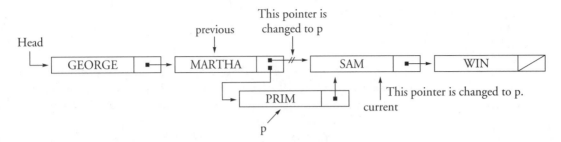

◆ **FIGURE 4.7**
Deletion of node containing
MARTHA from linked list of
Figure 4.6

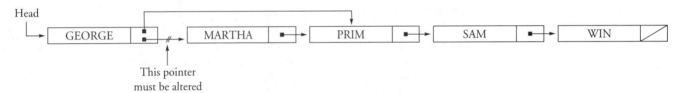

4.6 and 4.7 indicate that insertions and removals merely require the exchange of two pointers. Since pointers are merely locations of other nodes, this means that we are usually manipulating mere integers or similarly simple data in doing such pointer operations. Hence, both additions and deletions would appear to be $O(1)$ operations in terms of data movement for linked lists. This compares very favorably to the massive movement of entire records that was forced by an addition or deletion on an array implementation of a list. In general, such insertion and removal operations will be $O(n)$ in terms of data movement in an array implementation of a list.

Despite this substantive advantage, you should proceed cautiously and not be too quick to adopt the linked list as a cure for all the ills involved with list-oriented systems. The experience you have already gained should make you suspicious that there has to be a trade-off involved to get this superior efficiency for insertion and removal operations. Here the price we pay is to give up random access to the nodes in the list. For example, to access the fourth node, we must follow the head pointer to the first node, the first node's pointer to the second, and so on, until we reach the fourth node. Hence, any operation that requires finding a particular node on the list will essentially have to invoke a sequential search algorithm.

The superb $O(\log_2 n)$ search efficiency that was possible with an array implementation of a list cannot be approached with a linked implementation of the same list because the binary search algorithm we used to achieve this efficiency requires random access into the list. Instead we must settle for the $O(n)$ efficiency of the sequential search. Note that this is even a deterring factor in insertion and removal operations because, typically, an appropriate spot in the list must be found before the addition or deletion can occur. Although the addition or deletion itself may require only $O(1)$ data movements, an $O(n)$ search must usually precede it. At best, if we order the data in the nodes randomly, all insertions could be at the beginning of the list, causing an $O(1)$ amount of work.

Despite this search inefficiency, linked lists can be used to tremendous advantage when implementing lists that are highly *volatile,* that is, lists that frequently undergo insertions and deletions. If the percentage of these operations is sufficiently high in relation to requests for finding and inspecting nodes, then the linked implementation will probably pay off.

Before proceeding, we should clarify one point regarding linked lists as an ADT. That is, although a linked list may be viewed from this abstract perspective, it also represents an implementation strategy for more general linear structures such as the one-key table ADT. In that sense, we can compare the linked list to the array implementation of a one-key table, which we have already studied, and to several other list implementation schemes, which we will present in future chapters.

Thus, a linked list is, from one perspective, an implementation strategy; from another, it's an abstract structure. This is entirely consistent with what we have said regarding the progression from abstraction to implementation that you go through as a designer of layered software systems. The linked list provides another implementation option for the representation of more general linear structures. But it remains an abstraction because we have not yet described how we shall implement a linked list. We turn our attention to these implementation considerations in the next section.

## C++ Interface for the Linked List ADT

To develop an implementation of the linked list ADT, we provide a class declaration module. We will define a generic linked list class, parameterized for the type of data to be stored in the nodes:

```
// Class declaration file: linklist.h

#ifndef LINK_LIST_H

// Declaration section

#include "boolean.h"

template <class E> class linked_list
{

    public:

    // Class constructors

    linked_list();
    linked_list(const linked_list<E> &list);

    // Class destructor

    ~linked list();

    // Member functions
```

```
    boolean empty();
    boolean at_end();
    int length();
    void first();
    void next();
    boolean retrieve(E &item);
    void insert(const E &item);
    boolean remove(E &item);
    void traverse(boolean (*compare) (const E &item1,
          const E &item2), void (*process) (E &item));
    linked_list<E>& operator = (const linked_list<E> &list);

    // Protected data and member functions pertaining to
    // the implementation would go here.

};


#define LINK_LIST_H
#endif
```

**EXERCISES 14.1**

1. In what way is the data structure involved with the pointer sort in Chapters 1 and 2 not a linked list?

2. What are the advantages and the disadvantages of a linked list implementation of a one-key table compared to a physically ordered array implementation?

3. What are the advantages and disadvantages of a linked list implementation of a one-key table compared to an implementation that uses an unordered array with sequential search?

4. What are the advantages and the disadvantages of a linked list implementation of a one-key table when we use it to implement a two-key table?
   For Exercises 5 through 13, use *only* the C++ interface to the linked list ADT to write appropriate program segments.

5. Given that the element type is **int**, write a process function parameter for the traverse operation that will print the square root of each number in a linked list.

6. Given that the element type is **int**, write a process function parameter for the traverse operation that will print the value of each positive number in a linked list. Numbers in the list that are not positive should not be printed.

7. Given that the element type is **int**, write a loop that starts at the beginning of a linked list and returns the position of the first list node with the value zero in its data field. If no such node exists in the list, a zero should be returned.

8. Write a loop that applies a process function to each data value in a linked list, from the first to the last.

9. Write a function **sum** to sum the integers in a linked list of integers.

10. Write a function to remove all of the nodes in a linked list.

11. Write a function called **append** that takes two lists as parameters. The function should tack the contents of the second parameter onto the end of the first parameter. When the function returns, the first parameter should contain the contents of both lists, and the second parameter should be an empty list. Be sure that the operation handles the limiting cases of empty list parameters correctly (appending an empty list with a nonempty list should yield a list containing the data of the nonempty list).

**12.** Write a function called **merge** that receives two linked lists of integers arranged in ascending order. Your function should merge these two lists into a single list, also arranged in ascending order. The merged list should be returned as a third parameter.

**13.** Suppose you sort a list of input values by reading them in one at a time and inserting them into a linked list arranged in ascending order. Clearly, after you have read all of the input values you will have a sorted list. Let's call this algorithm the *linked list sort*. Analyze the time efficiency of this algorithm in terms of number of comparisons and number of data interchanges. Compare its efficiency to that of the other sort algorithms we have studied—insertion, bubble, selection, and radix sort.

---

## ◆ 4.2 Pointer Variables and Dynamic Memory Management in C++

Perhaps the biggest drawback of implementing linear data structures as arrays is the static nature of the memory storage associated with an array. Suppose, for example, we declare an array data of size 100. Then the storage in the array is static in the sense that it is allocated at the time the program is compiled, before it actually runs. Because of this, we are charged for 100 locations whether or not they are all used at run time. When we have only 50 objects to process in the array, 50% of the memory allocation is being wasted. Even more serious is the limitation that, if we have more than 100 objects to process, we must edit and recompile the program using a larger array size.

*C++ pointer variables,* on the other hand, are an example of a technique known as *dynamic memory management.* A feature that is not available in many older languages such as FORTRAN, COBOL, and BASIC, dynamic memory management is used by C++ to allow the programmer to claim only that amount of memory which is actually needed at that point during run time.

To understand dynamic memory management, we must first understand the configuration of memory when your program is loaded into it from an external file. As indicated in Figure 4.8, there are memory costs that must be paid in addition to the storage space required for the object code of your program. In particular, memory must have room to accommodate:

- Various operating system requirements
- A stack used by the operating system for function processing (to be explained in Chapter 5)
- The object code of your program; that is, the machine-language version of your program's instructions.

Notice that the three memory components listed generally will not consume all of the available computer memory. What remains is called the *heap.* Unless you have already used the dynamic memory allocation scheme of a language like C++, your programs have never been able to get at the heap and take advantage of it. With C++'s pointer variables, all this changes.

### Working with Pointer Types and Variables

If we focus on a type definition for a moment, we see that a pointer type is defined in terms of a *base type.* The base type is the type of value pointed to by the pointer value. A pointer type to an integer could be defined as

```
typedef int *int_ptr_type;
```

◆ FIGURE 4.8

Computer memory configuration for typical program

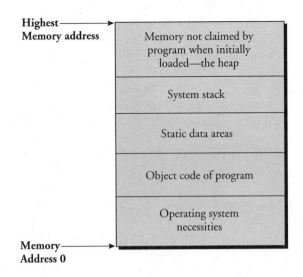

The general form for defining pointer types is

> typedef <base type name> *<pointer type name>;

where **<base type name>** is the name of any C++ data type and **<pointer type name>** is any legitimate C++ identifier.

The declaration

```
int_ptr_type int_ptr;
```

declares **int_ptr** as a pointer variable. **int_ptr** cannot be assigned values of type **int**; **int_ptr** can only contain addresses of locations whose values are of type **int**. The code

```
typedef float *float_ptr_type;

float_ptr_type float_ptr;
```

defines a pointer type to a real number and declares a pointer variable that can hold the address of a real number.

The pointer variables **int_ptr** and **float_ptr** can also be declared without defining pointer types, as follows:

```
int *int_ptr;

float *float_ptr;
```

## Initializing Pointer Variables

A null pointer is represented in C++ as the value 0. By convention, we use the symbolic constant **NULL** in this text to refer to the null pointer. You can define this constant with

```
const int NULL = 0;
```

or by including either the C++ library **stdlib.h** or the C++ library **stddef.h**:

```
#include <stdlib.h>
```

A pointer variable can be initialized in several ways:

**1.** Any pointer variable can be set to the **NULL** value. For example,

```
ptr = NULL;
```

will accomplish this.

**2.** Any pointer variable can be assigned the value of another pointer variable, as long as the two variables are of the same pointer type. Two pointer types are the same if they have the same base type. Thus, if **ptr1** and **ptr2** are variables of the same pointer type, the assignment

```
ptr2 = ptr1;
```

will copy the pointer value stored in **ptr1** into **ptr2**.

**3.** Any pointer variable can be initialized to point to a value of its base type. This is accomplished by using the operator **new**. For example,

```
ptr = new int;
```

has the effect of storing a pointer to an integer value in **ptr**. The state of the computer's memory can be depicted as

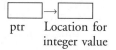

ptr    Location for
       integer value

Actually, **ptr** contains an address of a place where an integer value can be stored. We will see how to store an integer value in this place shortly. The general form for using **new** to initialize a pointer variable is

<pointer variable> = new <base type>;

where the pointer variable's type has the same base type as **<base type>**. When we use **new**, we essentially ask the system to allocate memory for storing a value of the pointer's base type. This memory is *dynamic,* because it was not reserved when the pointer variable was declared. In other words, **new** is a run-time request for memory. You are not charged for the memory requested until you ask for it, and you are not charged for an excess of memory that you may not even need for this particular run of the program.

After a call to **new** for a suitably declared pointer variable **ptr, ptr** is a memory address. As such, its actual value is of little concern to you. Suffice it to say that it is an address somewhere in the heap. How the heap manager was able to arrive at such an address involves a system-dependent process.

## Verifying Memory Allocation

When the system processes a call to **new** from a program, it goes to the heap to allocate an area of the appropriate size for storing a new data value. The heap might be a large area of memory in most systems, but its size is finite. Therefore, after repeated calls to **new**, the memory available for dynamic allocation will be used up. To avoid errors, a program can check to see whether this is the case and take the appropriate action. When heap memory is still available, **new** returns a pointer to a chunk of this memory. If there is no more heap memory, **new** returns the **NULL** value. In programs that use a large amount of dynamic memory, the following kind of code is recommended:

```
ptr = new base_type;
if (ptr != NULL)
      process(ptr);
else
      cout << "Error: no dynamic memory available." << endl;
```

where **process** indicates operations that access the area of memory pointed to by **ptr**. Alternatively, you might use the following code to halt program execution if the heap has no memory:

```
ptr = new base_type;
assert(ptr != NULL);
```

We will see shortly how to return unused dynamic memory from a program to the heap in order to mitigate this problem.

## Defining Pointer Types and Declaring Pointer Variables

The previous definitions and declarations of pointer types and pointer variables are relatively uncomplicated; however, in actual practice, pointer types and variables are a bit more complex. For example, in the next section we will define a pointer to a data structure where one of the members in the data structure is a pointer to a data structure of the same type. These data structures are called *nodes,* and represent a very common use of pointers in programming. To define a node, we can use a C++ *structure definition.* An example is

*declaration*

```
struct node;          // Empty structure definition introduces
                      // identifier for node.
typedef node *node_ptr;   // Type definition of type pointer to a node.

struct node           // Completion of structure definition of a node type.
{
      int data;
      node_ptr next;
};

node_ptr ptr;         // Declaration of a variable that can point
                      // to a node.
```

Notice that the completed structure definition specifies two *members* or pieces of data: an integer named **data** and a pointer to another node named **next**. You will frequently want each structure to point to another structure. Using a structure definition with one member for a pointer permits this. The use of a structure definition with pointers is so common in programming that we will specify its conventional form:

```
struct <node type name>;
typedef <node type name> *<node pointer type name>;
struct <node type name>
{
      <member declaration 1 for data stored in node>
      .
      .
      .
      <member declaration N for data stored in node>
      <node pointer type name> next;
};
```

Several things call for comment:

1. **struct** is a reserved word.
2. The components within the curly braces are called the *members* of the structure or node. They are similar to the data members of a class, except that they are treated as public here.
3. There may be several members of the node that contain the data stored there, such as names, phone numbers, and so forth. In this text, however, we will always store a single, perhaps complex, data object in a node.
4. There should be a member of the node that points to another node of the same type. Its name conventionally is **next**. In more complex structures, such as a *doubly linked list,* we would have a member called **previous** that points to the previous node in the list.
5. The structure definition ends with a semicolon (;) following the curly bracket (}).
6. A new type should always be defined to point to the node type. This is the purpose of the **typedef** immediately following the empty structure definition.

After a pointer to a node structure has been declared, it can be initialized. First, we use **new** to allocate dynamic memory for the structure:

```
ptr = new node;
```

Then we have to initialize the data and next members within the node. We use the *arrow operator,* **->**, for this with a node. This operation is also called a *dereference operation.* For example, we might input the integer value from the keyboard, and set the next pointer to **NULL** with an assignment:

```
cin >> ptr->data;
ptr->next = NULL;
```

Alternatively, we could use the *dereference operator,* **\***, to accomplish the same things:

```
cin >> *ptr.data;
(*ptr).next = NULL;
```

In this text, we will generally use the arrow operator to access the contents of nodes.

The state of the computer's memory after a node has been created and initialized is

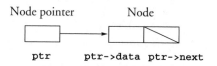

The general form for using the **->** operator is

You should be careful to assign **NULL** to the **next** member when initializing structures of this sort. If you are forming a list of dynamic variables where each dynamic variable contains a pointer variable for pointing to the next one, you can use **NULL** as a way to know when you are at the end of a list.

## `get_node`: A Useful Function

Because it is so important to initialize nodes properly and this is done so often in working with linked lists, we should design a function that makes this task simple and consistent. Whenever we need a new node for a linked list, we will call this function. The function takes as its parameter the data to be placed into the new node. It returns as its value a pointer to the new node. There are two postconditions that the caller of this function can count on:

**1.** The data sent to the function will be stored in the **data** member of the node.
**2.** The **next** member of the node will be set to **NULL**.

Assuming that the node should contain data of type **element**, our function would be called as follows:

```
ptr = get_node(data);
```

Assuming that it returns a pointer of type **node_ptr**, the function's declaration would be

```
// Function: get_node
// Gets a new node containing data
//
// Input: data to be stored in the node
// Output: a pointer to the node containing the data

node_ptr get_node(element data);
```

Assuming that **element** is the name of the type of data to be stored in the node, the function's implementation would be

```
node_ptr get_node(element data)
{
    node_ptr temp = new node;

    temp->data = data;
    temp->next = NULL;
    return temp;
}
```

As you can see, the **get_node** function hides a fair amount of low-level code that would have to be written every time a programmer needs a new node for a list. This is a good example of a function that can make programs more readable and safe.

For applications that use a large amount of dynamic memory, a "safer" **get_node** function would check the success of the **new** operation and halt execution if no more memory is available in the heap:

```
node_ptr get_node(element data)
{
    node_ptr temp = new node;

    assert(temp != NULL);
    temp->data = data;
    temp->next = NULL;
    return temp;
}
```

Some additional examples will serve to clarify the logic involving pointer variables.

**EXAMPLE 4.1**

Suppose we have a pointer type and two pointer variables, **p** and **q**, established by the following declarations:

```
struct node;
typedef node *node_ptr;

struct node
{
        int data;
        node_ptr next;
};

node_ptr p, q;
```

and that a **get_node** function has been defined for nodes containing integer data. Describe the effect of the following sequence of instructions:

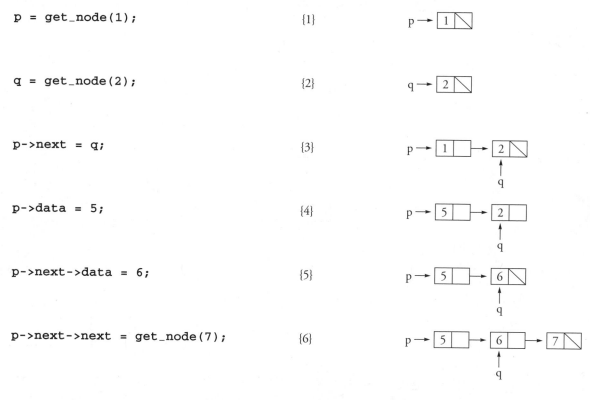

| | | |
|---|---|---|
| `p = get_node(1);` | {1} | |
| `q = get_node(2);` | {2} | |
| `p->next = q;` | {3} | |
| `p->data = 5;` | {4} | |
| `p->next->data = 6;` | {5} | |
| `p->next->next = get_node(7);` | {6} | |

The easiest way to describe such code is to visualize its effect. Consequently, we provide an answer in the form of a series of snapshots, identified by the bracketed number that marks each line of code.

**EXAMPLE 4.2**

Given the declarations in the previous example, write the code that will create 10 nodes, containing integer values 1 through 10, and link them together in ascending order of data.

Obviously, we will need a loop that cycles through the specified range of integer values. On each pass through the loop, we get a new node with the current loop control value as data and link it into its proper place in the list. Our strategy for linking is to place each new node at the beginning of the list. Before we start the loop, we assume that the list (pointed to by **p**) contains one node whose data value is 10. Therefore, we must use a **for** loop that counts down from 9 to 1. We use **q** as a temporary pointer to each new node while we rearrange pointers to link it into the list:

```
p = get_node(10);
for (int i = 9; i <= 1; --i)
{
        q = get_node(i);
        q->next = p;
        p = q;
}
```

The effects of the three statements within the loop when **i** equals 9 are visualized below. Note the importance of the order in which the pointers are rearranged. We do not assign a new value to **p**, the head pointer to the entire list, until the next pointer of the new node has been aimed at the node currently at the beginning of the list.

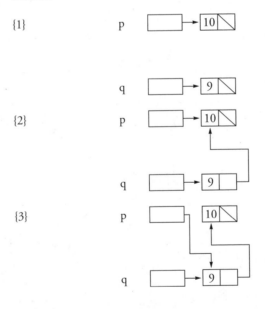

Clearly, programming with C++ pointer variables requires you to have an accurate mental image of the effects of each instruction. Faced with a bug, you must carefully draw linked list pictures and manually execute your code against those pictures until you find the instruction that is going awry.

## Other Operations on Pointer Variables

When you use the operator **new** to initialize a pointer variable, you are asking for dynamic memory to hold a value. This memory should be used as needed, and then returned to the system for other use when not needed. To return a piece of dynamic memory to the system, you use the operator **delete**, as follows:

```
delete ptr;
```

The states of the computer's memory before and after this statement can be depicted as

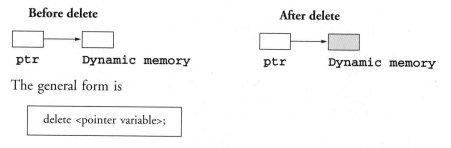

**Before delete**

ptr    Dynamic memory

**After delete**

ptr    Dynamic memory

The general form is

> delete <pointer variable>;

After you have returned a piece of dynamic memory to the system, you should not attempt to access a value in it with a pointer variable. It is possible to do so, but you will not be able to tell that you are now looking into deallocated space. Other parts of a program may now use this dynamic memory for their purposes. The pointer variable's value should be treated as unpredictable after a **delete**. The pointer should be reinitialized with either **NULL** or **new** before it can be used further.

Once they have been initialized, pointer variables can be compared for equality and inequality. For example, suppose pointer variables **p** and **q** have both been initialized to the **NULL** value. Then the comparison **(p == q)** will be TRUE, while the comparison **(p != q)** will be FALSE. The comparisons **(p == NULL)** and **(q == NULL)** will both be TRUE. Let's assume now that **q** is reset to point to an area of dynamic memory, with **q = new int**. Then the comparison **(p == q)** will be FALSE.

In general, you should remember that pointer variables contain the addresses of other areas of memory. Although C++ supports arithmetic and output operations for pointer variables, for our purposes, the only useful operations will be assignment, comparison, dereference, and return of dynamic memory to the system.

**EXERCISES 4.2**

Exercises 1 through 6 refer to the following data declarations:

```
struct node;
typedef node *node_ptr;

struct node
{
        int data;
        node_ptr next;
};


node_ptr a, b, c;
```

1. Specify which of the following statements are syntactically correct. For those that are wrong, explain why they are wrong.
   a. a = b;
   b. a = a->data;
   c. a = a->node_ptr;
   d. delete a;
   e. delete b->data;
   f. delete b;

**2.** Show how the schematic would be changed by each of the following:

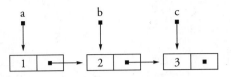

   **a.** `a = a->next;`
   **b.** `b = a;`
   **c.** `c = a->next;`
   **d.** `b->data = c->data;`
   **e.** `a->data = b->next->data;`
   **f.** `c->next = a;`

**3.** Write one statement to change

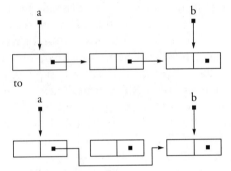

to

**4.** Consider the following list:

A ■──────→ │ 1 │ ■ │──────→ │ 8 │╱│

Write code to create a new linked list element with value 12 and insert it at the beginning of the list headed by **a**.

**5.** Consider the following list:

A ■──────→ │ 1 │ ■ │────→ │ 2 │ ■ │────→ │ 3 │ ■ │────→ │ 4 │╱│

Write code to remove the element at the head of the list and then add this element at the end of the list.

**6.** Indicate the output for each of the following:

```
a. a = new node;
   b = new node;
   a->data = 10;
   b->data = 20;
   b = a;
   a->data = 5;
   cout << a->data << " " << b->data << endl;
b. c = new node;
   c->data = 100;
   b = new node;
   b->data = c->data % 8;
   a = new node;
   a->data = b->data + c->data;
```

```
        cout << a->data << " " << b->data << " " << c->data
            << endl;
    c. a = new node;
       b = new node;
       a->data = 10;
       a->next = b;
       a->next->data = 100;
       cout << a->data << " " << b->data << endl;
```

---

## 4.3 Implementing the Linked List ADT with C++ Pointer Variables

Now that we have covered the syntax and use of C++ pointer variables, we are ready to use them to provide an implementation for the linked list ADT. We begin by specifying the data members and protected utility functions in the linked list class definition module presented in Section 4.1:

```
// Class definition file: linklist.h

#ifndef LINK_LIST_H

// Declaration section

#include "boolean.h"

template <class E> class linked_list
{

    public:

    // Class constructors

    linked_list();
    linked_list(const linked_list<E> &list);

    // Class destructor

    ~linked_list();

    // Member functions

    boolean empty();
    boolean at_end();
    int length();
    void first();
    void next();
    boolean retrieve(E &item);
    void insert(const E &item);
    boolean remove(E &item);
    void traverse(boolean (*compare) (const E &item1,
        const E &item2), void (*process) (E &item));
    linked_list<E>& operator = (const linked_list<E> &list);

    protected:
```

```
                        // Data members

                        struct node;
                        typedef node *node_ptr;

                        struct node
                        {
                             E data;
                             node_ptr next;
                        };

                        int list_length;
                        node_ptr head, current, previous;

                        // Member functions

                        node_ptr get_node(E item);

            };


#define LINK_LIST_H
#endif
```

Note that we define the new type names, **node** and **node_ptr**, which we discussed earlier. They are defined only for the use of the linked list class and its derived classes. Like the protected variable and function names, they are encapsulated within the class definition. The next few examples illustrate how the linked list operations are implemented by using the types **node** and **node_ptr**.

---

**EXAMPLE 4.3**

According to the abstract definition, creating a new linked list object requires setting the three pointers, **head**, **current**, and **previous**, to **NULL**, and setting **list_length** to zero:

```
template <class E>
linked_list<E>::linked_list()
{
    head = NULL;
    current = NULL;
    previous = NULL;
    list_length = 0;
}
```

Note that no new memory is allocated for nodes at this time, since the linked list should be empty. The state of a new linked list in the computer's memory is depicted as

list_length    $\boxed{0}$

head    $\boxed{\diagdown}$

previous    $\boxed{\diagdown}$

current    $\boxed{\diagdown}$

**EXAMPLE 4.4**

Three linked list operations, **empty**, **at_end**, and **length**, simply examine attributes of the list and return the appropriate information:

```
template <class E>
boolean linked_list<E>::empty()
{
    return list_length == 0;
}

template <class E>
int linked_list<E>::length()
{
    return list_length;
}

template <class E>
boolean linked_list<E>::at_end()
{
    return (current != NULL) && (current->next == NULL);
}
```

Note that the function **at_end** returns TRUE just when **current** points to a node and the **next** pointer of that node is **NULL** (this will be the last node in the list). The use of short-circuit evaluation in the Boolean expression in the **if** statement prevents the system from accessing a node's contents when **current** is NULL.

**EXAMPLE 4.5**

The linked list operation **next** should have the effect of moving both the **current** and **previous** pointers ahead in the list, if possible:

```
template <class E>
void linked_list<E>::next()
{
    if (current != NULL)
    {
        previous = current;
        current = current->next;
    }
}
```

The state of the computer's memory before and after this operation on a list containing two nodes is depicted as

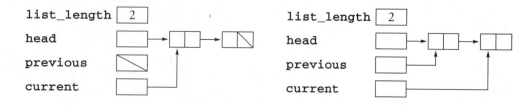

Note these two important things about this example:

1. We should always check to see whether a pointer really points to a node before attempting to access that node's contents with a dereference operation.
2. The order in which **previous** and **current** are reset is critical. If we moved **current** before moving **previous**, they would both point to the same node.

---

**EXAMPLE 4.6**

The abstract definition of the **insert** operation says that if there is enough memory for a new node, **item** is placed in a new node, the new node is inserted before the node that **current** points to, **current** is set to point to the new node, and **list_length** is incremented. If **current** originally pointed to **head**, **head** is also set to point to the new node. Because there are so many postconditions in this definition, we start with a pseudocode algorithm:

Get a new node with item as data
Set the next pointer of the new node to current
If current points to the first node (is equal to head)
        Set head to point to the new node
Else
        Set the next pointer of the previous node to point to the new node
Set current to point to the new node
Increment the length of the list

Because the new node will be placed before the node that **current** points to, the **next** pointer of the new node should first be aimed at this node. If **current** is **NULL** at this point, the node is being placed at the end of the list and the **next** pointer of the new node will remain **NULL**. Then we ask if we are inserting at the beginning of the list or somewhere else. If we are at the beginning, we redirect the **head** pointer to the new node. If we are somewhere else, then the **previous** pointer will point to the node after which our new node will be placed. Therefore, we aim the **next** pointer of the previous node at the new node. After we have considered these alternatives, we update the **current** pointer and the length of the list appropriately. The C++ code for this algorithm follows:

```
template <class E>
void linked_list<E>::insert(const E &item)
{
        node_ptr new_node = get_node(item);

        new_node->next = current;
        if (current == head)
                head = new_node;
        else
                previous->next = new_node;
        current = new_node;
        ++list_length;

}
```

The process of inserting a node in the middle of a linked list is depicted as follows:

Step 1: new_node = get_node(item);

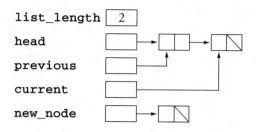

Step 2: new_node ->next = current;

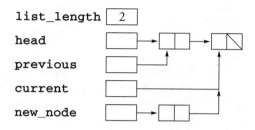

Step 3: previous->next = new_node;

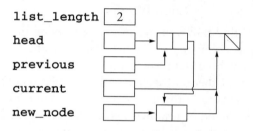

Step 4: current = new_node;

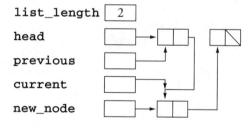

Step 5: ++list_length;

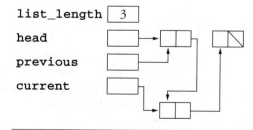

**EXAMPLE 4.7**

The abstract definition of the **remove** operation says that if **current** is not **NULL**, then the current node is removed from the list, **current** is set to the next node, **item** is set to the removed node's data field, and **list_length** is decremented. If the removed node is the first node in the list, then **head** is set to the next node also. If **current** is **NULL**, then there is no action. If the item is not removed, **item** is undefined.

Once again, the number of postconditions for the operation forces us to develop a pseudocode algorithm before coding in C++:

> If current is not NULL
> > Set item to the data in the current node
> > Set a temporary pointer to current
> > If current points to the first node
> > > Set head pointer to next pointer in current node
> > Else
> > > Set next pointer in previous node to next pointer in current node
> > > Set current to next pointer in current node
> > > Return removed node to system heap with temporary pointer
> > > Decrement length of list
> > Return TRUE
> Else
> > > Return FALSE

The critical moves in this process are saving the data in the return parameter and keeping a temporary pointer to the node about to be removed. Recall that once a node has been returned to the system heap, we should not attempt to access its contents, either for the data or for the next pointer value. However, once the node is unlinked from the list, we need to locate it to return it to the heap. In general, a node should be returned to the heap only after its contents have been processed. Note also that we do not have to update the **previous** pointer, because the deleted node was located between the new current node and the previous node, if there was one. The C++ code is

```
template <class E>
boolean linked_list<E>::remove(E &item)
{
        node_ptr old_node = current;

        if (current != NULL)
        {
                item = current->data;
                if (current == head)
                        // Node at beginning of list
                        head = current->next;
                else
                        // Node in middle or at end of list
                        previous->next = current->next;
                current = current->next;
                delete old_node;
                --list_length;
                return TRUE;
        }
```

```
        else
                return FALSE;
}
```

The process of removing a node from the middle of a linked list is depicted as follows:

Step 1: old_node = current;

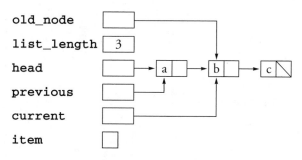

Step 2: item = current->data;

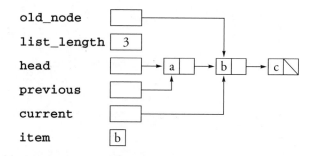

Step 3: previous->next = current->next;

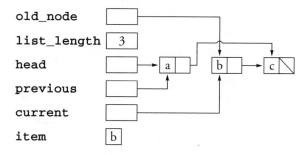

Step 4: current = current->next;

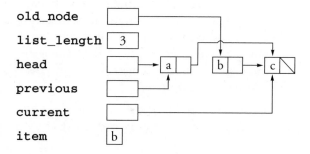

Step 5: delete old_node;

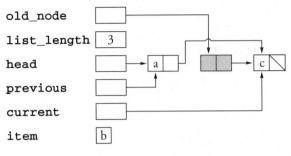

Step 6: --list_length;

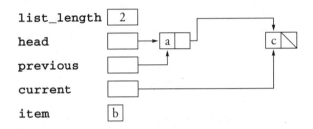

**EXAMPLE 4.8**    The implementation of the **get_node** function should closely resemble the one we constructed in Section 4.2. The only complication is that **node_ptr** is not globally defined, but rather is defined within the **linked_list** class. Therefore, we prefix it with the class name so that the compiler can recognize it:

```
template <class E>
linked_list<E>::node_ptr linked_list<E>::get_node(const E &item)
{
        node_ptr temp = new node;

        assert(temp != NULL);
        temp->data = item;
        temp->next = NULL;
        return temp;
}
```

We consider the implementation of the **traverse** operation in Section 4.4.

## The Copy Constructor for Linked Lists

The copy constructor for linked lists should create new nodes for the receiver object and insert elements from the parameter object into them so that the order of the elements in the two lists is the same. These requirements are accomplished by iterating through the nodes of the parameter object and advancing the current pointer of the receiver object after each insertion of a data element from the parameter's current node:

```
template <class E>
linked_list<E>::linked_list(const linked_list<E> &list)
{
```

```
            node_ptr probe = list.head;
            node_ptr new_node, last;
            list_length = 0;
            head = NULL;
            current = NULL;
            previous = NULL;
            while (probe != NULL)
            {
                    new_node = get_node (probe->data);
                    if (head == NULL)
                        head = new_node;
                    else
                        last->next = new_node;
                    last = new_node;
                    if (probe == list.previous)
                        previous = last;
                    else if (probe == list.current)
                        current = last;
                    probe = probe->next;
                    ++list_length;
            }
    }
```

Note that the copy constructor copies the relative positions of the **current** and **previous** pointers of the parameter **list** to the receiver object.

## Class Destructors and Memory Leakage

Consider the following function definition:

```
void leak_memory()
{
        linked_list<int> list;

        for (int i = 1; i < 10; ++i)
            list.insert(i);
}
```

This function appears to do nothing more than create a new linked list, store 10 integers in it, and return. However, because the implementation of the linked list class uses dynamic memory, an important side effect occurs: For each insertion operation that the client invokes, a piece of dynamic memory is obtained from the heap and used to insert a data element into the list. Thus, when this function returns, 10 pieces of dynamic memory have been taken from the heap and are no longer available for other clients. This phenomenon is called memory leakage, and is a common cause of errors in programs that use dynamic memory. If this function were called frequently enough, the computer would eventually run out of heap memory.

The best way to guard against memory leakage is to provide a class destructor for each class that uses dynamic memory. A class destructor declaration looks just like a default class constructor declaration, except that a tilde ($\sim$) precedes the declaration. The implementation of the destructor should contain code for returning any dynamic memory used by an instance to the heap. In the case of linked lists, the destructor would traverse the nodes and return each one to the heap with **delete**:

```
linked_list::~linked_list()
{
        node_ptr garbage;
        node_ptr probe = head;
        while (probe != NULL)
        {
                garbage = probe;
                probe = probe->next;
                delete garbage;
        }
        list_length = 0;
        head = NULL;
        current = NULL;
        previous = NULL;
}
```

If a destructor is defined for a class, the computer will automatically invoke it when the scope of a linked list variable or value parameter is exited. Thus, the function **leak_memory** returns after the computer has run the destructor function to deallocate the memory used for the **list** variable.

## A NOTE OF INTEREST

### Garbage Collection

Programs that make frequent use of dynamic memory can be error-prone. One kind of error that can occur is the failure to return pieces of dynamic memory to the heap when they are no longer needed. If this failure occurs often enough, the program will run out of memory, perhaps at a critical point in its task.

To avoid the problem of memory leakage, some programming languages have been designed so that the programmer does not have to worry about returning unused memory to the heap at all. The run-time system for these languages has a special module called a garbage collector that automatically recovers unused dynamic memory when it is needed.

Two such languages, Smalltalk and LISP, rely on dynamic memory for all of their data structures, so an automatic garbage collector is an essential part of their design. In Smalltalk, a pure object-oriented language, dynamic memory is used to create new objects. In LISP, which supports a linked list as a standard data structure, dynamic memory is used to add data elements to a list. When an application in either of these languages asks for a new piece of dynamic memory, the computer checks the heap to see whether the request can be satisfied. If not, the garbage collector is invoked, and all of the unused memory locations are returned to the heap. Then the request is granted, if enough dynamic memory is now available.

The garbage collection mechanism works roughly as follows. Every memory location is marked as either referenced by the application or not. A memory location is referenced if it is named by a variable or is part of a linked structure pointed to by such a variable. When memory is allocated for variables, it is marked as referenced. When memory becomes completely unlinked from any variable references in a program, it is marked as unreferenced. Thus, only unreferenced memory locations will be candidates for being returned to the heap.

Garbage collection in early versions of LISP and Smalltalk sometimes degraded the performance of a program. During a collection, an application would appear to pause for a moment while the mechanism did its work. This is one reason why Smalltalk and LISP applications have not received much play in industry, where efficiency in time-critical tasks is a priority. However, much research and devlopment has produced very efficient garbage collection algorithms, so that LISP and Smalltalk programs now perform as well as programs written in languages without any garbage collector.

EXERCISES 4.3

1. Implement the **retrieve** operation for the linked list class.

2. Test the linked list class with a C++ driver program that inserts five integer input values into the list (in random order) and then prints the contents of the list.

3. Test the list processing functions that you wrote in Exercises 5 through 12 of Section 4.1.

4. In Exercise 12 of Section 4.1, you wrote a function that merges the sorted contents of two linked lists into a third list. This function uses new memory, in that new nodes are generated for the result list. Implement and add a more efficient merge function to the linked list interface that uses no new memory. The receiver should be the first list, and the parameter should be the second list. After the process is completed, the receiver should contain the merged list, and the parameter should be returned as an empty list.

5. In Exercise 11 of Section 4.1, you wrote a function that appends the contents of one linked list to the end of another linked list. This function uses new memory, in that the contents of the two input parameters are copied over into a result list. Implement and add a more efficient append function to the list interface that uses no new memory. The receiver should be the first list, and the parameter should be the second list. After the process is completed, the receiver should contain the contents of the two lists, and the parameter should be returned as an empty list. (*Hint:* An implementation requiring the fewest pointer rearrangements would aim the next pointer of the last node in the first list at the first node in the second list).

6. The **append** operation in the previous exercise still takes linear time to locate the last node in the first list. Maintaining a pointer to the last node in a linked list would allow the append operation to be performed in constant time. Add a new attribute to the linked list ADT called **last** (this will be a new data member in the C++ class definition module). Then update the **create, insert, remove**, and **append** operations so that **last** always points to the last node in a linked list, if there is one.

7. A **last** operation would take advantage of the **last** pointer to move the current pointer to the last node in a linked list in constant time. Discuss whether our current implementation of a linked list ADT would support this new operation.

---

## 4.4 Traversing a Linked List

In Chapter 3, we discussed the problem of traversing the data elements in a one-key table in an order specified by alternative key values within the data. We solved the problem by designing and implementing a derived class of the one-key table called a traversal table. This derived class supports a traversal operation that takes two functions as parameters. One function specifies the ordering principle for the traversal, and the other function specifies the operation to be applied to each data element during the traversal. The traversal process consists of two steps: First, order the table, and then, visit each data value according to the new ordering. By using a pointer sort with an extra array, we were able to perform the ordering and traversal steps without altering the ordering by the key values by which the table was originally set up.

Rather than reinventing the wheel to solve the problem of traversing a linked list, we fit the strategy developed in Chapter 3 into the new context of pointers and linked lists. The original strategy in Chapter 3 maintains an array of indices that specifies the desired ordering of elements in a data array. In the context of array processing, these indices are actually used as pointers to locate data. If we could think of a way of maintaining a list of pointers (not integers, but real pointers) in the new context of pointers and linked lists, then we could reuse our pointer sort algorithm to order a linked list for traversal.

If we choose an array of **node_ptr** for our list, we run into an immediate problem. What should be the maximum size of this array? There is no maximum size of a one-key table now that we are using a linked list to implement it. We are faced with the problem that motivated the use of linked lists to begin with: In many cases, either we will waste memory with this new array or we will not have enough memory.

We can solve this new problem by representing the list of pointers as a dynamic data structure. With this representation, there will be just enough memory to store the pointers for a given linked list, and no more. However, we will not have to go to the trouble of implementing this structure as another linked list.

## Dynamic Arrays in C++

Many programming languages present the programmer with only two alternatives for representing linear data structures: arrays of fixed size or linked lists implemented with pointers. C++ provides a third alternative that represents a hybrid of arrays and dynamic data structures. We call it a *dynamic array*. In C++, a dynamic array starts out as a pointer variable. For example, the following data declarations would set up a new dynamic array of integers:

```
typedef int *int_array;

int_array ints = NULL;
```

Note that the variable **ints** is of type pointer to integer and has been initialized to the **NULL** pointer. Thus, we have created a new, empty dynamic array of integers requiring almost no memory.

When we wish to store data in a dynamic array, we must ask for new memory cells from the heap. The only constraint is that we must know how many cells to ask for. This integer value is passed as a parameter to the **new** operator, and a new block of cells is returned to represent the array. In our example, if we needed an array of 10 integers, we would write

```
ints = new int[10];
```

The integer value within the square brackets can be any C++ integer-valued expression. The important thing to note is that this value can be computed at run time, so we have the kind of dynamic memory that fits our application. For example, a linked list implementation might use the statement

```
pointers = new node_ptr[list_length];
```

to create a dynamic array capable of maintaining the results of a pointer sort of the data in the linked list.

A robust program will ask whether or not the **new** operation successfully allocated storage for a dynamic array by comparing the returned result to **NULL**:

```
pointers = new node_ptr [list_length];
if (pointers == NULL)
        <take corrective action>
else
        <process pointers>
```

This error checking is perhaps more important in the case of dynamic arrays than in the case of individual nodes in a linked list, because of the large chunks of memory requested.

When **new** is passed a parameter specifying the number of new cells desired, we receive a *contiguous block* of new cells from the heap. This means that the cells of dynamic memory map directly to consecutive physical memory locations in the heap. Therefore, C++ allows us to use standard array indexing to locate individual cells within this data area. For example, we might initialize the **ints** dynamic array with zeros in the following loop:

```
for (int i = 0; i < 10; ++i)
    ints[i] = 0;
```

When we are finished with the use of a dynamic array for a given problem, we can return its storage to the heap by invoking the **delete** operator. For example, the storage for the **ints** array could be recycled with

```
delete ints;
```

This will have the effect of returning the entire contiguous block of storage to the system heap.

The important thing to remember about a dynamic array in C++ is that it is declared like a pointer but processed like an array. In the case where the array contains pointers to the nodes in a linked list, we could traverse the list by iterating through the array:

```
for (int i = 0; i < list_length; ++i)
    process(pointers[i]->data);
```

The dynamic array appears to be the perfect data structure for solving the problem of modifying the traversal table class to work with linked lists. This is a good example of the way in which choosing the appropriate data structure can ease the solution of a problem.

## Implementing the Traversal

The first step in realizing our new design is to add a data member for the dynamic array of pointers to the linked list class declaration module:

```
// Class declaration file: linklist.h

#ifndef LINK_LIST_H

// Declaration section

#include "boolean.h"

template <class E> class linked_list
{

    public:

    // Class constructors

    linked_list();
    linked_list(const linked_list<E> &list);
```

```
                    // Class destructor

                    ~linked_list();

                    // Member functions

                    boolean empty();
                    boolean at_end();
                    int length();
                    void first();
                    void next();
                    boolean retrieve(E &item);
                    void insert(const E &item);
                    boolean remove(E &item);
                    void traverse(boolean (*compare) (const E &item1,
                            const E &item2), void (*process) (E &item));
                    linked_list <E>& operator = (const linked_list<E> &list);

                protected:

                    // Data members

                    struct node;
                    typedef node *node_ptr;

                    struct node
                    {
                            int data;
                            node_ptr next;
                    };

                    int list_length;
                    node_ptr head, current, previous;
                    node-_ptr *pointers:                    // New data member

                    // Member functions

                    node_ptr get_node(E item);
                    void prepare_to_traverse(boolean (*compare)
                            (const E &item1, const E &item2));

            };

    #define LINK_LIST_H
    #endif
```

Note that we do not bother to define a new type name with **typedef** for our new data member. We simply specify the type of data pointed to, **node_ptr**, and use the * symbol to indicate that the data member **pointers** will be a pointer to a data value of type **node_ptr**. We do not define a separate type name to go with **pointers** because no values of this type will ever be passed as parameters or returned as the values of functions.

Let us now work through several examples to show how we use the dynamic array of pointers in our new implementation.

---

EXAMPLE 4.9

Recall that the design of the member function **traverse** in Chapter 3 consists of two steps: Prepare the array of indices by performing a pointer sort on the data array, and then traverse the data array using the indices in the pointers array. In the new version, we use a similar, top-down strategy. We assume that another member function, **prepare_to_traverse**, performs the first step. Then we accomplish the traversal of the linked list by looping through the pointers in the array. In addition to these two steps, the new implementation is responsible for allocating storage for the array before it is used, and deallocating the storage when its usage is finished:

```
template <class E>
void linked_list<E>::traverse(boolean (*compare) (const E &item1, const E &item2),
        void (*process) (E &item))
{

    if (list_length > 0)                            // Go ahead if list not empty
    {
        pointers = new node_ptr[list_length];       // Allocate new
                                                    // dynamic array
        prepare_to_traverse(compare);               // Do pointer sort
        for (int i = 0; i < list_length; ++i)       // Traverse linked list
            process(pointers[i]->data);             // via pointers in array
        delete pointers;                            // Deallocate dynamic array
    }
}
```

A more robust version of this function would verify that storage has been allocated for the dynamic array before continuing with the processing.

---

EXAMPLE 4.10

The **prepare_to_traverse** operation was described in the Focus on Program Design section of Chapter 3. It essentially performs a pointer sort on the data array. In the new version, it performs a pointer sort on a linked list. We lift the pointer sort algorithm from Chapter 3, place it under a new function heading for traversing linked lists, and make some minor changes to the body of the function:

```
template <class E>
void linked_list<E>::prepare_to_traverse
    (boolean (*compare) (E item1, E item2))
{
    int j, k;
    boolean exchange_made;
    node_ptr probe, temp;

    // Initialize pointer array

    probe = head;
    for (k = 0; k < list_length; ++k)
```

```
        {
                pointers[k] = probe;
                probe = probe->next;
        }

        k = 0;
        exchange_made = TRUE;

        // Make up to n - 1 passes through array, exit early if no
        // exchanges are made on previous pass

        while ((k < list_length - 1) && exchange_made)
        {
                exchange_made = FALSE;
                ++k;
                for (j = 0; j < list_length - k; ++j)
                        if (compare(pointers[j]->data, pointers[j + 1]->data))
                        {
                                temp = pointers[j];       // Swap pointers
                                pointers[j] = pointers[j + 1];
                                pointers[j + 1] = temp;
                                exchange_made = TRUE;
                        }
        }
}
```

The first change occurs in the initialization of the array. We initialize the array by setting a temporary pointer, **probe**, to point to the first node in the linked list. Then we iterate through the array and the list, storing pointers and advancing the **probe** pointer to the next node on each pass.

The second change occurs in the comparison step during the sort. We test two data values for ordering with the **compare** function, using the **->** operator. If **compare** returns TRUE, then the data are out of order and an exchange must be made.

---

**EXERCISES 4.4**

1. Perform a big-O analysis of the time and memory requirements of the traverse operation on linked lists.

2. Propose a reasonable solution to the problem of failure to allocate storage for the dynamic array used during a traverse operation. (*Hint:* You might inform the application about the success of the traversal.)

3. Write a compare function that, when passed as a parameter to traverse, would cause the nodes of a linked list to be visited in reverse order, from the last node to the first node.

---

## 4.5  Using a Linked List to Implement a One-Key Table

In Chapter 2, we analyzed the efficiency of an array-based implementation of a one-key table ADT. We discovered that the principal trade-off is that this implementation supports fast retrievals (with binary search) but slow insertions and removals. The latter operations require a linear number of copy operations, which can be very expensive for large data elements. When the data are particularly volatile, requiring frequent insertions or removals, it might be best to choose the trade-off associated with a linked list implementation. Here we would get linear search times but constant insertion and removal times (in the number of copies required). An additional factor in favor of a linked implementation has gone unnoticed until now. The array implementation of a one-key table forces an application to settle for a fixed upper bound on the number of data elements that can be inserted. This constraint may cause a program to waste memory or not have enough memory to solve a problem. A linked list implementation, which provides memory for a table on an as-needed basis, would use only enough physical memory to accommodate the logical size of the table, and no more.

## Redeclaring the One-Key Table Class

We begin our new implementation of a one-key table by modifying the class declaration module from Chapter 2. We include the header file for the linked list class. The declarations of all of the public member functions (the interface to the class) remain the same. The only change in this module comes in the protected data members section. There we replace the array and the integer data members with a single data member that is a linked list:

```
// Class declaration file: onetable.h

#ifndef ONE_TABLE_H

#include "boolean.h"
#include "assoc.h"
#include "linklist.h"

// Declaration section

// Generic class for key type K and element type E.

template <class K, class E> class one_key_table
{

    public:

    // Class constructors

    one_key_table();
    one_key_table(const one_key_table &table);

    // Member functions

    int length();
    boolean empty();
    void store(const K &target, const E &item);
    boolean retrieve(const K &target, E &item);
    boolean remove(const K &target, E &item);
    one_key_table& operator = (const one_key_table &table);

    protected:
```

```
// Data members

linked_list<association<K, E>> list;

};

#define ONE_TABLE_H
#endif
```

Note that the type of data in each node in the underlying linked list will be **association**. This is specified by passing that type name to **linked_list** as a parameter when the data member for the list is declared. Also, the **table_length** data member is no longer needed, because the length of the table is just the length of the linked list.

## Reimplementing the One-Key Table Class

Another benefit that we gain from representing a one-key table as a linked list rather than an array is that our implementation becomes more abstract. You will recall our discussion of the two-key table and the layering principle in Section 2.4. There we found that it is easier to work with high-level ADT operations than with low-level data structures like arrays that are built in to C++. The same ease of use occurs in the present case. We do not have to deal with array indices or with C++ pointer manipulations; instead we use high-level operations such as **first, next, insert**, and **remove**. A few examples will make this point clear.

---

**EXAMPLE 4.11**

The simplest member functions are those that examine attributes of the one-key table. **empty** and **length** return the answers to the same questions asked of the linked list:

```
template <class K, E>
boolean one_key_table<K, E>::empty()
{
    return list.empty();
}

template <class K, E>
int one_key_table<K, E>::length()
{
    return list.length();
}
```

---

**EXAMPLE 4.12**

For retrievals, a linked list operation must do a linear search for a data value stored by key value in the list. We begin by resetting the current pointer to the head of the list by invoking the **first** operation. Then there are two cases to consider:

1. The list is empty. Then we return FALSE.
2. The list has at least one node. Then we retrieve data from each node, compare the key in the data with the target key, and if the keys match, we return the data and TRUE. If we assume that the logical ordering of the

keys maps directly to the ordering of the nodes in the list, then we can stop an unsuccessful search when a node's key value is greater than the target or when we have just examined the last node in the list.

Since there are several cases to consider, we begin with a pseudocode algorithm:

```
Set success to FALSE
If list not empty
      Set done to FALSE
      Move current pointer to first position
      While not done do
            Retrieve data from the list
            If key associated with data equals target key
                  Set item to data
                  Set success to TRUE
                  Set done to TRUE
            else if current pointer is at the end of the list or key > target
                  Set done to TRUE
            else
                  Move current pointer to the next node in the list
```

The C++ code is slightly more complex than the algorithm, because we must extract the key and the data from an association object:

```cpp
template <class K, E>
boolean one_key_table<K, E>::retrieve(K target, E &item)
{
      boolean done, success;
      K key;
      association<K, E> a;
      success = FALSE;
      if (! list.empty())                        // Are there nodes to examine?
      {
            done = FALSE;
            list.first();                        // Reset current pointer to
                                                 // head of list

            while (! done)
            {
                  list.retrieve(a);
                  key = a.get_key();
                  if (key == target)             // Have we found a match?
                  {
                        item = a.get_value();
                        success = TRUE;
                        done = TRUE;
                  }
                  else if (list.at_end() || (key > target))    // Not in list?
                        done = TRUE;
                  else
                        list.next();             // Keep advancing
            }
      }
      return success;
}
```

| EXAMPLE 4.13 | To store a data value in a table, we create a new association with the key and item. Then if the list is empty, we just insert the new association into the list. Otherwise, we search for the first node in the list whose key is greater than or equal to the new item's key, and insert the node at that position. Once again, a pseudocode algorithm will clarify our strategy: |

> Create a new association with the key and item
> If list is empty
>> Insert the association into the list
> else
>> Set done to FALSE
>> Move current pointer to first position
>> While not done do
>>> Retrieve data from the list
>>> If key associated with data >= target key
>>>> Insert the association into the list
>>>> Set done to TRUE
>>> else if current pointer is at the end of the list
>>>> Move the current pointer to the next node in the list
>>>> Insert the association into the list
>>>> Set done to TRUE
>>> else
>>>> Move current pointer to the next node in the list

Note that there is a special case in the search loop where we must insert the new node after the last node in the list. In that case, we advance the current pointer beyond this node and perform the insertion, which has the effect of appending the new data to the end of the list. The C++ code is

```
template <class K, E>
void one_key_table<K, E>::store(const K &target, const E &item)
    {
    association<K, E> new_data(target, item);
    association<K, E> data;
    K list_key;
    boolean done;

    if(list.empty)
        list.insert(new_data);                      // Insert as first node
    else
    {
        done = FALSE;
        list.first();                               // Reset current to head
        while (! done)                              // of list
        {
            list.retrieve(data);
            list_key = data.get_key();
            if (list_key >= key)                    // Insert before a node?
            {
                list.insert(new_data);
                done = TRUE;
            }
```

```
        else if (list.at_end())              // Insert after last node?
        {
                list.next();
                list.insert(new_data);
                done = TRUE;
        }
        else
                list.next();                  // Advance the search
    }
  }
}
```

As you can see, we have a linear amount of work to do in searching for the position of the data to be inserted in the table, but the linked implementation gives us a constant amount of work to be done in moving data around in the table at that point.

## A NOTE OF INTEREST

### Computer Viruses

Many computer installations are now confronted with a threat akin to germ warfare, which could disable their largest machines. A computer "virus" attacks a computer system in essentially the same way a biological virus attacks the human body.

A computer virus is actually a small undetected program that, over time, infects other programs and eventually disables the entire system. A typical virus in a host program might contain the following instructions:

1. Temporarily suspend execution of host program.
2. Search the computer's memory for other likely uninfected programs.
3. If found, insert a copy of these instructions.
4. Return control of computer back to host program.

This virus would take less than a second to execute, would be virtually undetected, and could attack indefinitely. It can even spread to other computers, when an infected program is swapped or copied for another user.

Adding to the problem is the fact that the saboteur can add instructions to delay the signal for the virus to attack. As researcher Fred Cohen explains, in one company a disgruntled employee instructed the program to remain dormant until his personal password was removed from the system. Once the employee was fired, and his password removed, the virus shut down the entire system.

The Pentagon addresses this problem by isolating its top-secret computers. The military's most sensitive computers are kept in electronically shielded rooms and, when necessary, connected with wire that runs through pipes filled with gas under pressure. The gas pressure would drop if someone attempted to penetrate the pipes to tap into the wires. Marvin Shaefer, chief scientist at the Pentagon computer security center, admits that computers without good access controls are vulnerable to virus attacks.

Computer scientists differ as to whether or not public discussion of computer viruses should even be encouraged. Jerry Lobel, manager of computer security at Honeywell International in Phoenix, expresses concern because "it only takes a halfway decent programmer about half a day of thinking to figure out how to do it. If you tell enough people about it there's going to be one crazy out there who's going to try."

Cohen disagrees, insisting that ignorance is always more dangerous than knowledge. "It's better to have somebody friendly do the experiments, tell you how bad it is, show you how it works, and help you counteract it, than to have somebody vicious come along and do it." If you wait, it might be too late.

If your curiosity is aroused, you can find more detailed accounts of the evolution of the computer virus problem in "Attack of the computer virus" by Lee Dembart (*Discover*, November 1984), "Is your computer infected?" by William D. Marbach (*Newsweek*, February 1, 1988), and *Computer Viruses, Worms, Data Diddlers, Killer Programs, and Other Threats to Your System* by John McAfee and Colin Haynes (New York: St. Martin's Press, 1989).

**EXERCISES 4.5**

1. Use the new implementation of a one-key table to run the program in the Focus on Program Design section of Chapter 2. (Note that you won't have to change any code in the two-key table modules.)

2. Draw a diagram of the different layers of ADTs used in Exercise 1, and discuss the costs and benefits of the layering.

3. Add **merge** and **append** operations to the interface of the one-key table, and implement the operations. (Rely on the corresponding list operations developed in Exercises 4.3.)

4. The traversal table implementation must be updated to reflect the implementation of a one-key table as a linked list. Why can't the new implementation just invoke the traverse operation for linked lists? (Try it and see what happens.) Propose a new implementation of the traversal table, and discuss the maintenance issues that arise during this process.

## FOCUS ON PROGRAM DESIGN

Although we can define the linked list as an ADT, a key theme of this chapter has been that the linked list is of great value when viewed as an implementation technique for other higher level ADTs and their logic. We have seen linked lists used to implement the one-key table and, indirectly, the traversal table and the two-key table ADTs.

Now, in this section, we will use the linked list to implement a very space-efficient version of the radix sort algorithm (see Section 11.4). Moreover, this will be one of those rare instances in which a space-efficient version is also more time efficient. To achieve this, we will specify that the sort algorithm receive a linked list of integers to be sorted, rather than an array. A top-level pseudocode description of radix sort is then given by

Set number_of_digits to the number of digits in largest number in the list
For each k from 1 to number_of_digits
    While the list to sort is not empty
        Transfer the first number in the sort list to the appropriate bin, keying on the kth digit
        (1 corresponding to ones digit, 2 to tens digit, and so forth).
    For each j from 0 to 9
    Append the numbers in jth bin to the list to sort

In our discussion of the radix sort in Section 1.4, we were somewhat shackled by approaches that employed static allocation of the bins used to classify numbers. For instance, we determined that sorting $n$ numbers by this algorithm would require $11n$ storage locations—$n$ for the numbers being sorted and an additional $10n$ locations for the bins associated with the 10 possible digits.

C++ pointer variables provide a new implementation strategy for the bins needed by radix sort. The dynamic allocation associated with these pointer variables will allow each bin to claim only the storage that it needs as the algorithm runs. We propose the following implementation for bins:

```
typedef linked_list bin_structure[9];


bin_structure bins;
```

We assume that the linked list class provides an **append** operation that uses constant time and memory (see Exercises 4.3). This assumption will enable us to

◆ FIGURE 4.9

Appending one bin to another

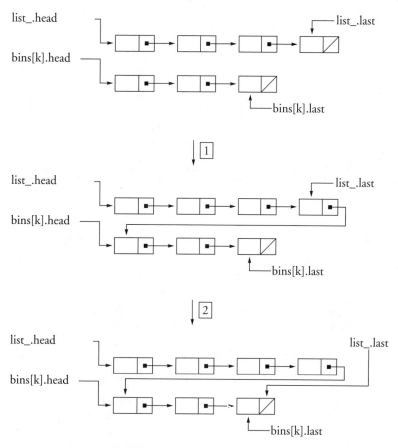

be particularly efficient during that phase of the algorithm that collects the bins associated with particular digits into a new master bin. Figure 4.9 depicts how this efficiency can be achieved. The process of appending bins from the bin structure to the **list_to_sort** requires rearrangement of two pointers in the linked list implementation for each bin.

Compare this to our implementation of bins by arrays in Section 1.4. There the process of appending a bin required physically moving each item in the bin to the array being sorted.

We can now refine our high-level pseudocode for this new version of radix sort. It will require the subordinate modules indicated in the structure chart shown in Figure 4.10. The specifications for each subordinate module are

**Module:** max_number_digits
**Task:** Make one pass through list to determine largest
**Input:** List of integers (assumed to be nonnegative)
**Output:** The number of digits in the largest integer in list

**Module:** digit
**Task:** Use modular arithmetic functions of C++
**Inputs:** Nonnegative integer number
　　　　　k representing a digit position in number,
　　　　　with k = 1 corresponding to ones digit, 2 to tens digit, and so on
**Output:** digit in position k of number

**Module:** transfer_list_to_bin
**Inputs:** List to sort
　　　　　A bin

◆ FIGURE 4.10

Structure chart for RadixSort

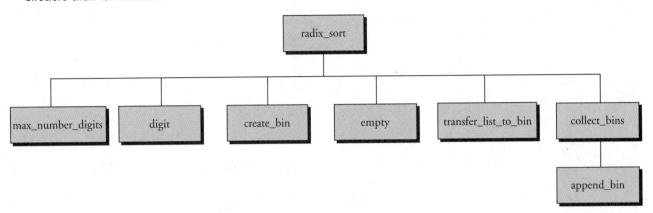

**Outputs:** First number in list to sort has been removed and added to bin
**Module:** collect_bins
**Inputs:** A bin_structure
    List to sort (empty when received)
**Output:** Sublists in bin_structure have been successively appended to sort list
    Order of appending runs from bin 0 to bin 9

These module specifications give rise to the following C++ function for the radix sort algorithm. We present only the top-level sort function; the subordinate modules are left for you to implement in the problems. You will also formally analyze the time and space efficiency of this new implementation of radix sort in the problems.

```cpp
typedef linked_list<int> bin_structure[9];   // Global definition for
                                             // other modules.


void radix_sort(linked_list<int> &list)
{
        bin_structure bins;
        int data, number_of_digits, which_bin;
        boolean success;

        number_of_digits = max_number_digits (list);
        for (int k = 1; k <= number_of_digits; ++k)
        {
                for (int j = 0; j <= 9; ++j)
                        while (! list.empty())
                        {
                                list.first();
                                success = list.retrieve(data);
                                which_bin = digit(data, k);
                                transfer_list_to_bin(list, bins[which_bin]);
                        }
        }
        collect_bins(list, bins);
}
```

1. You must be very careful when programming with pointers; one misplaced pointer can "lose" an entire data structure. Consequently, modular testing is more important than ever. Test the reliability of each module before releasing it for use in a large program.
2. Be sure that you consider the boundary conditions when developing linked list algorithms. Are you sure that your logic covers the empty list, the first node on the list, the last node on the list? For instance, if your insertion algorithm works for all lists but the empty list, it might as well not work at all since you'll never be able to get any data on the list.
3. Never reference the contents of the memory pointed to by `ptr` when `ptr` is a `NULL` pointer. The following loop control structure

```
while ((ptr->data != target) && (ptr != NULL))
```

is asking for trouble. When `ptr` is `NULL`, the reference to `ptr->data` may cause a run-time error before the loop is exited. The positions of the two tests should be reversed to take advantage of short-circuit evaluation in C++.
4. Programming with pointers is programming with logical pictures of linked lists. Draw a picture of what you want to do with a pointer and then write the code to make it happen. When debugging, verify and trace your code by drawing pictures of what it does with your data. For instance, an assignment to a pointer in your code corresponds to aiming an arrow somewhere in your corresponding snapshot of the data structure.

## SUMMARY

### Key Terms

| | | |
|---|---|---|
| append | dynamic memory | linked list |
| arrow operator | management | list traversal |
| C++ pointer variables | dynamic data structure | merge |
| concatenation | head pointer | node |
| data movement | heap | pointer |
| dereference operation | linear ordering | structure definition |
| dynamic array | link | volatile list |

### Keywords

`delete new struct`

### Key Concepts

◆ The linked list structure is especially convenient for implementing a variety of higher level list ADTs in situations where add and delete operations dominate search operations.
◆ The linked list allows insertions and removals to occur by mere pointer manipulation instead of large-scale data movement. The price paid for this gain is the inefficiency of a sequential search strategy.
◆ An overview of the advantages and disadvantages of a linked list versus an array implementation of a one-key table is given in the following table:

| | Implementation of One-Key Table Using Array Maintained in Physical Order So That Binary Search May Be Used | Implementation of One-Key Table Using Linked List |
|---|---|---|
| Insert | $O(\log_2 n)$ comparisons to find location where insertion should occur. $O(n)$ data interchanges to rearrange list. | $O(n)$ comparisons to find location where insertion should occur. $O(1)$ pointer interchanges to rearrange list. |
| Retrieve | $O(\log_2 n)$ comparisons to find data item. | $O(n)$ comparisons to find data item. |
| Remove | $O(\log_2 n)$ comparisons to find data item to remove. $O(n)$ data interchanges to rearrange list. | $O(n)$ comparisons to find data item to delete. $O(1)$ pointer interchanges to rearrange list. |
| Other considerations | Size of list is bounded by physical size of array. | If C++ pointers are used to implement, size of list is bounded only by available space in heap. |

**PROGRAMMING PROBLEMS AND PROJECTS**

1. Complete the development of a linked list radix sort (see the Focus on Program Design section) in stages.
   a. Write the necessary subordinate modules.
   b. Write a main program so that you can thoroughly test the algorithm.
   c. Design test data that are sure to exercise the various boundary conditions of the subordinate modules.
   d. Do a big-O analysis of the time and space requirements of this version of radix sort. If you also implemented an array version of radix sort in Chapter 1, profile both versions by counting the number of operations that each must perform (see the Focus on Program Design section in Chapter 1). Prepare a written report in which you compare the empirical performance of both versions.

2. Wing-and-a-Prayer Airlines maintains four scheduled flights per day, which they identify by the numbers 1, 2, 3, and 4. For each of these flights, they keep an alphabetized list of passengers. The database for the entire airline could hence be viewed as four linked lists. Write a program that sets up and maintains this database by handling commands of the following form:

   Command → Add
   Flight number → 3
   Passenger name → BROWN
   Command → Delete
   From flight number → 1
   Passenger name → JONES
   Command → List
   Flight number → 2
   (List alphabetically all passengers for the specified flight.)
   Use an appropriate string storage strategy for the passenger names.

3. In order to take care of their growing business, the Fly-by-Night Credit Card Company would like to update their customer data file. Write a program in a high-level language that sets up a doubly linked list that can support the following actions on a record:

    **a.** Insert a record into the list in the correct place, sorted according to the social security number of the customer.

    **b.** Update a record if the customer record exists.

    **c.** Delete a record if the customer no longer wishes to patronize the company.

    In the preceding data manipulation activities, the list should always remain in order sorted by the social security number.

**4.** As a struggling professional football team, the Bay Area Brawlers have a highly volatile player roster. Write a program that allows the team to maintain its roster as a linked list in alphabetical order by player last name. Other data items stored for each player are

Height

Weight

Age

University affiliation

As an added option, allow your program to access players in descending order of weight and age.

**5.** Develop a line-oriented text editor that assigns a number to each line of text and then maintains the lines in a linked list by line number order (similar to the fashion in which BASIC programs are maintained on many systems). Your program should be able to process the following commands:

I-line number 'text' (instruction to insert text at specified line number)

L-line1-line2 (instruction to list line1 through line2)

D-line1-line2 (instruction to delete line1 through line2)

If you feel really ambitious, incorporate into your program a string storage strategy that will allow the user to perform editing operations such as inserting and deleting characters within a given line.

**6.** Write a program that, given a file of text, will add to an index those words in the text that are marked by special delimiting brackets []. The words in the index will be printed after the text itself has been formatted and printed. Words in this index should be listed in alphabetical order with a page number reference for each page of text on which they are delimited by the special brackets. Note that this program would be part of a word processing system an author could use when developing a book with an index of terms.

**7.** Write a program that allows input of an arbitrary number of polynomials as coefficient and exponent pairs. Store each polynomial as a linked list of coefficient–exponent pairs arranged in descending order by exponent. Note that the coefficient–exponent pairs need not be input in descending order; it is the responsibility of your program to put them in that order. Your program should then be able to evaluate each of the polynomials for an arbitrary argument X and be able to output each of the polynomials in the appropriate descending exponent order. Be sure that your program works for all "unusual" polynomials such as the zero polynomial, polynomials of degree one, and constant polynomials.

**8.** Redo the Game of Life program that you developed for Problem 5 in Chapter 2, except now use linked lists to implement the two-dimensional table ADT.

**9.** Redo Problem 4 of Chapter 3, for the registrar of American Basket Weaving University, except now use linked lists to implement the ADTs that you designed for that program.

**10.** Consider the following problem, often referred to as the Josephus problem. Imagine that $N$ people have decided to commit mass suicide by arranging themselves in a circle and killing the $M$th person around the circle, with the size of the circle being reduced by one each time a person is killed. The problem is to find out which person is the last to die, or more generally, to find the order in which the people are executed. For example, if $N = 9$ and $M = 5$, then the people are killed in the order 5, 1, 7, 4, 3, 6, 9, 2, and 8. To solve the Josephus problem, write a program that inserts people 1 through $N$ into a list and then appropriately deletes people from the list until only one is left.

11. Computers can store and do arithmetic only with integers of limited size. When integers surpass that limiting value, overflow occurs and the results will either be unreliable or cause your program to die with a run-time error. However, by altering the implementation of an integer, you can develop algorithms to do virtually limitless integer arithmetic. The basis of such an implementation is to store each digit of an integer in a list. That is, represent an integer as a list of digits. Then develop algorithms to do integer arithmetic operations on a digit-by-digit basis, taking carries, borrows, and so forth into account as you do when performing these operations by hand. After carefully considering which list implementation best suits the problem, develop functions to perform extended integer addition, subtraction, multiplication, and division (quotient and remainder). As one test case, add the following integers and print the sum:

$$5643127821$$
$$+\ 9276577159$$

12. By consulting reference manuals for your version of C++ and by writing a variety of experimental programs, attempt to discover the details of how your C++ compiler manages the allocation of memory in the heap. Prepare a written report in which you describe your findings.

13. Your friend offers the following criticism of linked lists: "The problem with linked lists is that they cannot be used with large databases stored in files since pointers represent locations in main memory." Explain the fallacy in your friend's criticism. Then, in a detailed statement, discuss how linked lists could be implemented for data stored in random access files.

# CHAPTER

# 5 Stacks and Queues

*Achilles: What would happen if you took some popping-tonic without having previously pushed yourself into a picture? Tortoise: I don't precisely know, Achilles, but I would be rather wary of horsing around with these strange pushing and popping liquids.*

Douglas Hofstadter

*The other line always moves faster.*

Barbara Ettore

In the last chapter we introduced the linked list as a data structure designed to handle conveniently the insertion and deletion of entries in a linearly ordered list. In this chapter we study two special types of linearly ordered lists: the stack and the queue. These lists are special because of the restrictions imposed on the way in which entries may be inserted and removed. Both structures may be implemented by arrays or dynamically allocated linked lists.

The restriction placed on a stack is often described as *last-in/first-out* (*LIFO*). Consider, for example, the order in which a smart traveler will pack a suitcase. To minimize shuffling, the last item packed should be the first worn. Another familiar example of such a storage strategy is that of the pop-up mechanism used to store trays for a cafeteria line. The first trays loaded into the mechanism may well have a long wait before they escape to a passing diner.

A list of data items processed via a LIFO scheduling strategy is called a *stack*. As we shall see in this and later chapters, stacks are an extremely useful data structure. They find extensive applications in the processing of subroutine calls, the syntactical checking and translation of programming languages by compilers, and the powerful programming technique of recursion (see Chapter 6).

In contrast to the linear order of a stack, a *queue* is a *first-in/first-out* (*FIFO*) list. This latter name comes close to completely characterizing the restricted types of adds and deletes that can be performed on a queue. Insertions are limited to one end of the list, whereas deletions may occur only at the other end. The conceptual picture that emerges from the notion of a queue is that of a waiting line; for example, jobs waiting to be serviced by a computer, or cars forming a long line at a busy toll booth.

## 5.1 The Stack Abstract Data Type and its Implementation

The last-in/first-out nature of the stack implies that all additions and deletions occur at one designated end of the stack. That designated end is called the top, and the operations of adding to or deleting from the stack are referred to as *pushing* and *popping,* respectively. More formally, we define the stack ADT as follows.

**Stack.** A stack is a restricted list in which entries are added to and removed from one designated end called the top.

The operations to be performed on a stack are specified by the following preconditions and postconditions.

**Create operation**
Preconditions:     Receiver is an arbitrary stack in an unpredictable state.
Postconditions:    Receiver is initialized to the empty stack.
**Empty operation**
Preconditions:     Receiver is a previously created stack.
Postconditions:    Returns TRUE if receiver is empty, FALSE otherwise.
**Push operation**
Preconditions:     Receiver is a previously created stack. **item** is a value to be added to the top of the stack. There is memory available to store the new item in the stack.
Postconditions:    Receiver is returned with **item** added to the top of the stack.
**Pop operation**
Preconditions:     Receiver is a previously created stack. The stack is not empty.
Postconditions:    The stack has its top value removed, and this value is returned.
**on_top operation**
Preconditions:     Receiver is a previously created stack. The stack is not empty.
Postconditions:    Returns the value on the top of the stack. Unlike **pop**, the stack is left unchanged.

Figure 5.1 depicts the critical push and pop operations for the stack ADT. Conceptually, it is easiest to develop a mental image of the **push** and **pop** operations if you picture a stack as a vertical list with the first entry at the bottom and the last at the top. Then, as indicated in Figure 5.1, adding to the stack—that is, pushing—essentially makes this stack become taller, and removing from the stack—that is, popping—results in a shorter stack.

◆ FIGURE 5.1
Pushing onto and popping from the stack

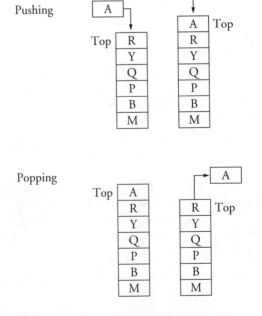

## Stacks and Function Calls

Before we discuss methods of implementing a stack, we shall give some hint of their importance in the processing of function calls. Of key importance to the processing of functions in any language is that the return from a function must be to the instruction immediately following the call that originally transferred control to the function. For example, in the partial coding that follows:

```
int main()
{
      int q;
      .
      q = sub1(q);                 // Call sub1
      cout << q;
      .
}

void sub3()
{
      .
      .
      .
      .
}

void sub2(int q)
{
      .
      sub3();                      // Call Sub3
      p = p - q;
      .
}

void sub1(int b)
{
      .
      b = sub2(a);                 // Call sub2
      a = a + b;
      .
}
```

the order of operations would be

1. Leave **main** and transfer to **sub1**.
2. Leave **sub1** and transfer to **sub2**.
3. Leave **sub2** and transfer to **sub3**.
4. Return from **sub3** to the instruction p = p - q in sub2.
5. Return from **sub2** to the instruction a = a + b in sub1.
6. Return from **sub1** to the instruction cout << q in main.
7. End of **main**.

Each time a call is made, the machine must remember where to return upon completion of that function.

A stack is precisely the structure capable of storing the data necessary to handle calls and returns in this sequence. The data for each call of a function is stored in a data structure called an *activation record*. This record contains space for

◆ FIGURE 5.2

Memory stack generated by
previous partial coding

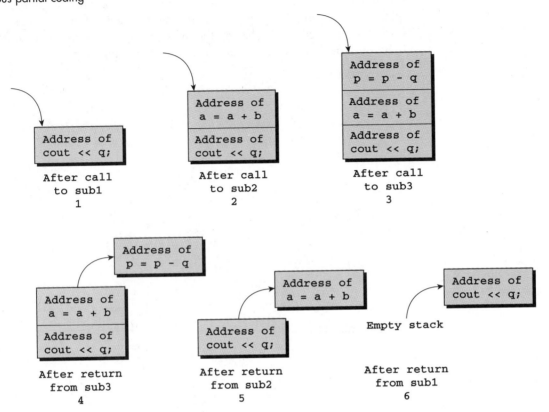

C++ Interface for the Stack Abstract Data Type

the return address (the address of the instruction following the call of the function) and any values or addresses of actual parameters for that call of the function. Hence the preceding partial coding would generate a stack that develops as illustrated in Figure 5.2. (The numbers in the figure correspond to the order of operations just shown on the preceding list.) Each time a call to a function is made, a return address is placed in an activation record and this is pushed on top of the stack. Each time a function is completed, the top record on the stack is popped to determine the memory address to which the return operation should be made. The nature of the leave–return sequence for functions makes it crucial that the first return address accessed be the last one that was remembered by the computer. Because there is only one point, the top, at which data may enter or exit a stack, it is the ideal data structure to be used for this "last-stored, first-recalled" type of operation.

This description of the method by which a compiler actually implements function calls is just one illustration of the utility of stacks. In Chapter 6, we'll discuss a different type of function usage called recursion, and examine in detail the role of the stack in handling such a recursive call.

## C++ Interface for the Stack Abstract Data Type

The transition from defining a stack as an ADT to implementing this structure in a computer language requires, as usual, an interface to the ADT's operations. A C++ class declaration module for the stack ADT follows:

```
// Class declaration file: stack.h

#ifndef STACK_H

#include "boolean.h"
#include "element.h"

// We assume that constant MAX_STACK_SIZE
// is already defined in element.h

// Declaration section

template <class E> class stack
{

    public:

    // Class constructors

    stack();
    stack(const stack &s);

    // Member functions

    boolean empty();
    void push(const E &item);
    E pop();
    E on_top();
    stack<E>& operator = (const stack &s);

    // Protected data pertaining to
    // the implementation would go here.

};

#define STACK_H
#endif
```

We will discuss two implementations of the stack class in C++. The first uses an array and, consequently, limits the size to which a stack may grow. The second employs a linked list with pointer variables, thereby allowing the stack to become as large as the free space in the C++ heap.

## Array Implementation of a Stack

Using an array to implement a stack is relatively straightforward. Because insertions and deletions occur at the same end of a stack, only one pointer will be needed. We call that pointer **top**. The array of elements will be called **data**, and its size is specified by the constant **MAX_STACK_SIZE**, defined in the application. Thus, the C++ protected data members for the stack class are

```
int top;
E data[MAX_STACK_SIZE];
```

In Figure 5.3, we trace it through the function example from Figure 5.2. As in Figure 5.2, the numbers below each array correspond to the operations performed in our previous sequence of function calls and returns. The empty stack is signaled

◆ FIGURE 5.3
Array implementation of
stack from Figure 5.2

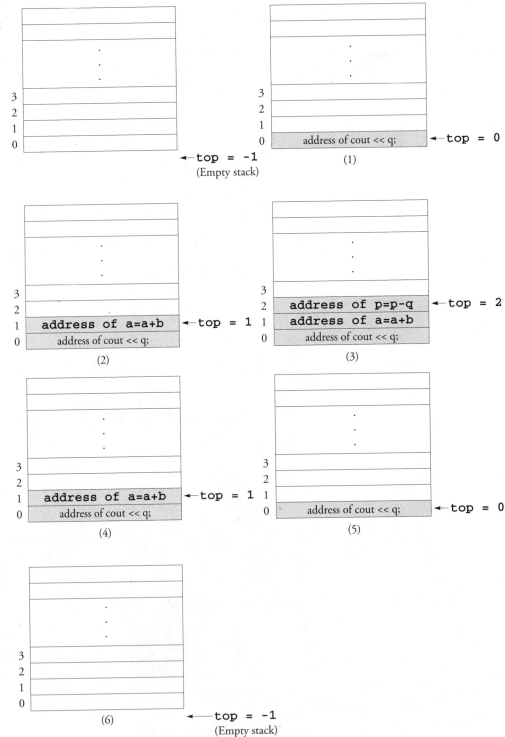

by the condition **top = -1**. If we think of **top** as pointing to the last entry pushed, then the two instructions

```
++top;
data[top] = item;
```

will push the contents of **item** onto the stack. Popping an entry from the stack into item requires

```
item = data[top];
--top;
```

Complete functions for the push and pop operations follow in Example 5.1.

**EXAMPLE 5.1**    Implement the **push** and **pop** operations for an array implementation of a stack.

```
template <class E>
void stack<E>::push(E item)
{
        assert(top < MAX_STACK_SIZE - 1);
        ++top;
        data[top] = item;
}


template <class E>
E stack<E>::pop()
{
        E item;

        assert(! empty());
        item = data[top];
        --top;
        return item;
}
```

Note that the **assert** function is invoked to enforce the preconditions on each member function.

## Linked List Implementation of a Stack

When we choose a linked list implementation of a stack, we are paying the price of a relatively small amount of memory space needed to maintain linking pointers for the dynamic allocation of stack space. A stack with the three integer entries 18, 40, and 31 would appear as follows:

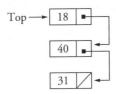

We also have the benefit of reusing a class already developed. The easiest way to use the linked list class to implement a stack class is to make the stack class a derived class of the linked list class. The derived class adds functions for inserting, removing, and examining data at the beginning of a linked list. However, we must prevent clients of the stack class from using any of the operations on linked lists, such as **first** or **next**. Defining the mode of inheritance as **protected** rather than **public** will allow the stack class to inherit all of the public and protected operations from the linked list class, but prevent clients of the stack class from using them:

```
// Class declaration file: stack.h

#ifndef STACK_H

#include "boolean.h"
#include "linklist.h"

// Declaration section

template <class E> stack : protected linked_list<E>
{

    public:

    // Class constructors

    stack();
    stack(const stack &s);

    // Class destructor

    ~stack();

    // Member functions

    boolean empty();
    void push(const E &item);
    E pop();
    E on_top();
    stack<E>& operator = (const stack &s);
```

```
        };

        #define STACK_H
        #endif
```

Note that there are no data members in this definition. They are maintained in the parent class, `linked_list`. Note also that the module specifies a class destructor (`~stack()`). This kind of operation, introduced in Chapter 4, is used by the computer to return dynamic memory to the heap when objects using it go out of scope.

Functions to push and pop the stack now become nothing more than insertions to and deletions from the beginning of a linked list. As such, they use high-level linked list operations already developed in Chapter 4. You will write them as exercises at the end of this section.

---

**EXAMPLE 5.2**

To illustrate the use of stack operations in a program, let's consider a program that will check an arithmetic expression to make sure that parentheses are correctly matched (nested). Our program considers

$$(3 + 4 * (5 \% 3))$$

to make sure that each left parenthesis is paired with a following right parenthesis in the expression.

A first-level pseudocode for this problem is

Get a character from the keyboard
While the character does not equal end of line
     If it is a '('
        push it onto the stack
     Else if it is a ')'
        Check for empty stack before popping previous '('
     Get a character from the keyboard
Check for empty stack

The growing and shrinking of the stack is illustrated in Figure 5.4. Assuming the existence of the basic stack operations, a program that examines an expression for correct use of parentheses is

```cpp
// Program file: parens.cpp

#include <iostream.h>

#include "boolean.h"
#include "stack.h"

int main()
{
        stack<char> s;
        char symbol;

        cin.get(symbol);
        while (symbol != '\n')
        {
```

```
        if (symbol == '(')
            s.push(symbol);
        else if (symbol == ')')
            if (s.empty())
                cout << "The parentheses are not correct. " << endl;
            else
                symbol = s.pop();
        cin.get(symbol);
    }
    if (! s.empty())
        cout << "The parentheses are not correct. " << endl;
    return 0;
}
```

◆ FIGURE 5.4
Using a stack to check for balanced parentheses

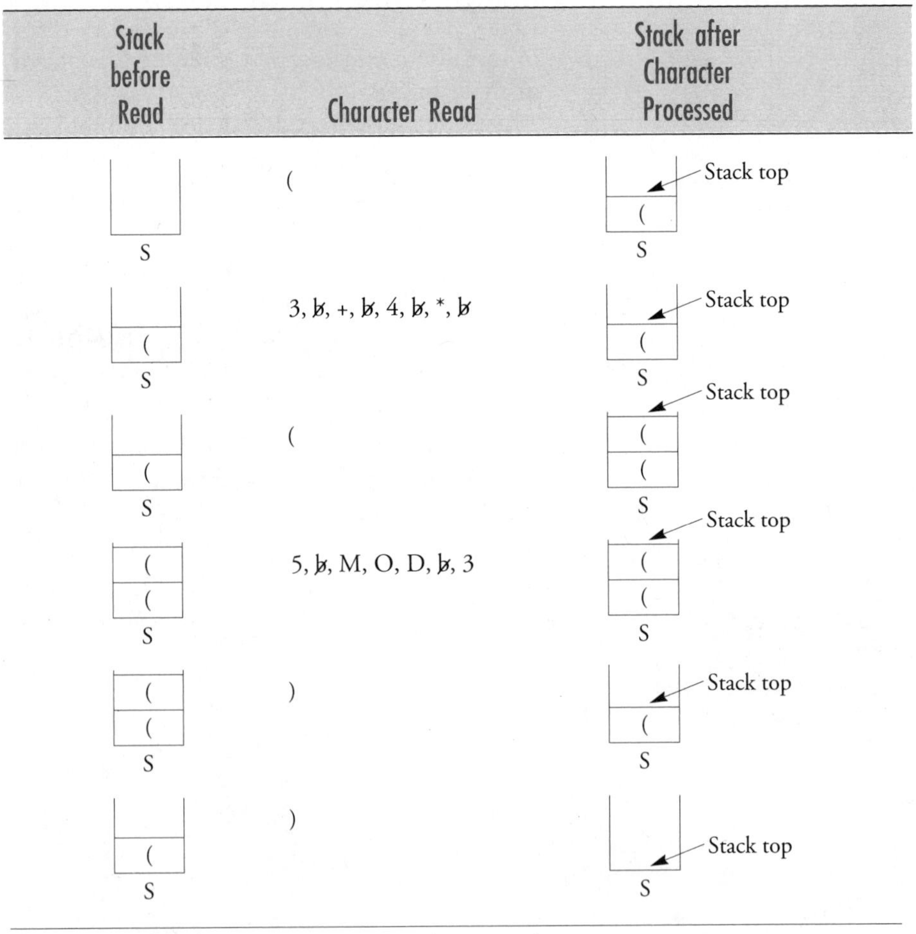

*b̸ represents a blank space

This program will print an error message for an invalid expression and nothing for a valid expression. Several modifications of this short program are available and are suggested in the following exercises.

---

**EXERCISES 5.1**

1. Draw a picture of the stack of integers **s** after each one of the following operations is performed:

```
stack<int> s;
s.push(4);
s.push(10);
s.push(12);
item = s.pop();
s.push(3 * item);
item = s.on_top();
s.push (3 * item);
```

2. The **on_top** operation described in the definition of the stack as an abstract data type is actually unnecessary since it can be defined in terms of other stack operations. Provide such a definition of the **on_top** operation.

3. Write functions to implement each of the following operations for an array implementation of a stack. Be consistent with the operations already implemented in Example 5.1.
   **a. create** (do both the default constructor and the copy constructor)
   **b. empty**
   **c. on_top**

4. Write functions to implement each of the following stack operations for a linked list implementation of a stack.
   **a. create** (do both the default constructor and the copy constructor)
   **b. destroy**
   **c. empty**
   **d. push**
   **e. pop**
   **f. on_top**

5. Using the program for checking parentheses (Example 5.2), illustrate how the stack grows and shrinks when the following expression is examined:

   (5 / (3 – 2 * (4 + 3) – (8 / 2)))

6. Modify the program in Example 5.2 so that several expressions may be examined. Also provide more descriptive error messages.

7. Write a program that utilizes a stack to print a line of text in reverse order.

8. It is not necessary to use a stack to check expressions for matching parentheses. Write an algorithm that describes this task using a simple integer counter.

9. An alternative definition of the stack class in C++ does not derive the stack class from the linked list class. Instead, it maintains a linked list as a data member. Compare this implementation to the one that derives the stack class from the linked list class (*hint*: how will the copy constructor, the destructor, and the assignment operation be different?).

## 5.2 An Application of Stacks: Parsing and Evaluating Arithmetic Expressions

### OBJECTIVES

- to understand the differences between the infix, postfix, and prefix forms of algebraic expressions
- to see why the postfix and prefix forms of expressions never need parentheses to override operator hierarchy
- to be able to convert infix expressions to their postfix and prefix equivalents using manual methods
- to understand the computer algorithm that relies on a stack to convert infix expressions to their postfix equivalents
- to be aware of the role of infix and in-stack priority functions in driving the algorithm to convert infix expressions to postfix
- to understand the algorithm that uses a stack to evaluate a postfix expression

Often the logic of problems for which stacks are a suitable data structure involves the need to backtrack, to return to a previous state. For instance, consider the problem of finding your way out of a maze. One approach to take would be to probe a given path in the maze as deeply as possible. Upon finding a dead end, you would need to backtrack to previously visited maze locations in order to try other paths. Such backtracking would require recalling these previous locations in the reverse order from which you visited them.

Not many of us need to find our way out of a maze. However, the designers of compilers are faced with an analogous backtracking situation in the evaluation of arithmetic expressions. As you scan the expression

$$A + B / C + D$$

in left-to-right order, it is impossible to tell upon initially encountering the plus sign whether or not you should apply the indicated addition operation to A and the immediately following operand. Instead, you must probe further into the expression to determine whether an operation with a higher priority occurs. While you undertake this probing of the expression, you must stack previously encountered operation symbols until you are certain of the operands to which they can be applied.

Further compounding the backtracking problem just described are the many different ways of representing the same algebraic expression. For example, the assignment statements

$$Z = A * B / C + D;$$
$$Z = (A * B) / C + D;$$
$$Z = ((A * B) / C) + D;$$

should all result in the same order of arithmetic operations even though the expressions involved are written in distinctly different forms. The process of checking the syntax of such an expression and representing it in one unique form is called *parsing* the expression. One frequently used method of parsing relies heavily on stacks.

### Infix, Postfix, and Prefix Notation

Conventional algebraic notation is often termed *infix* notation; the arithmetic operator appears between the two operands to which it is being applied. Infix notation may require parentheses to specify a desired order of operations. For example, in the expression $a/b + c$, the division will occur first. If we want the addition to occur first, the expression must be parenthesized as $a/(b + c)$.

Using *postfix* notation (also called reverse Polish notation after the nationality of its originator, the Polish logician Jan Lukasiewicz), the need for parentheses is eliminated because the operator is placed directly after the two operands to which it applies. Hence, $A / B + C$ would be written as $A\ B / C +$ in postfix form. This says:

**1.** Apply the division operator to $A$ and B.
**2.** To that result, add $C$.

The infix expression $A / (B + C)$ would be written as $A\ B\ C + /$ in postfix notation. Reading this postfix expression from left to right, we are told to

**1.** Apply the addition operator to $B$ and $C$.
**2.** Then divide that result into $A$.

Although relatively short expressions such as the preceding ones can be converted from infix to postfix via an intuitive process, a more systematic method is required for complicated expressions. We propose the following algorithm for humans (and will soon consider a different one for computers):

**1.** Completely parenthesize the infix expression to specify the order of all operations.
**2.** Move each operator to the space held by its corresponding right parenthesis.
**3.** Remove all parentheses.

Consider this three-step method as it applies to the following expression in which $\wedge$ is used to indicate exponentiation:

$$A \,/\, B \wedge C + D * E - A * C$$

Completely parenthesizing this expression yields

$$(((A \,/\, (B \wedge C)) + (D * E)) - (A * C))$$

Moving each operator to its corresponding right parenthesis, we obtain

$$(((A/(B\wedge C)\,) + (D*E)) - (A*C))$$

Removing all parentheses, we are left with

$$A \; B \; C \wedge \,/\, D \; E * + A \; C * -$$

Had we started out with

$$A \,/\, B \wedge C - (D * E - A * C)$$

our three-step procedure would have resulted in

$$((A/(B\wedge C)) - ((D*E) - (A*C)))$$

Removing the parentheses would then yield

$$A \; B \; C \wedge \,/\, D \; E * A \; C * --$$

In a similar way, an expression can be converted into *prefix* form, in which an operator immediately precedes its two operands. The conversion algorithm for infix to prefix specifies that, after completely parenthesizing the infix expression according to order of priority, we move each operator to its corresponding left parenthesis. Applying the method to

$$A \,/\, B \wedge C + D * E - A * C$$

gives us

$$((A/(B\wedge C)) + ((D*E) - (A*C)))$$

and finally the prefix form

$$+ \,/\, A \wedge B \; C - * D \; E * A \; C$$

The importance of postfix and prefix notation in parsing arithmetic expressions is that these notations are completely free of parentheses. Consequently, an expression in postfix (or prefix) form is in unique form. In the design of compilers, this parsing of an expression into postfix form is crucial because having a unique form for an expression greatly simplifies its eventual evaluation. Thus, in handling an expression, a compiler must

**1.** Parse into postfix form.
**2.** Apply an evaluation algorithm to the postfix form.

We limit our discussion here to postfix notation. The techniques we cover are easily adaptable to the functionally equivalent prefix form.

## Converting Infix Expressions to Postfix

First consider the problem of parsing an expression from infix to postfix form. Our three-step function is not easily adaptable to machine coding. Instead, we will use an algorithm that has the following as its essential data structures:

**1.** A stream of characters containing the infix expression and terminated by the special delimiter #
**2.** A stack named **op_stack**, which may contain
   **a.** Arithmetic operators: +, −, *, and /
   **b.** The left parenthesis, (. The right parenthesis, ), is processed by the algorithm but never stored in the stack
   **c.** The special delimiter #
**3.** A string named **postfix** containing the final postfix expression.

To eliminate details that would only clutter the main logic of the algorithm, we will assume that the string representing the infix expression contains *tokens* (that is, incoming symbols) consisting only of the arithmetic operators +, −, *, and /; parentheses; the delimiting character #; and operands that each consist of a single uppercase alphabetic character. We will also assume that these tokens may be read from a line without any intervening spaces. Later, we will consider some of the complications introduced by tokens of varying size and type and by the exponentiation operator ^. Thus, for the present, the algorithm we discuss will convert infix expressions of the form

$$A * B + (C - D / E)$$

into their corresponding postfix notation.

The description of the algorithm is as follows:

**1.** Define a function **infix_priority**, which takes an operator, parenthesis, or # as its argument and returns an integer as

| Character | * | / | + | − | ( | ) | # |
|---|---|---|---|---|---|---|---|
| Returned Value | 2 | 2 | 1 | 1 | 3 | 0 | 0 |

This function reflects the relative position of an operator in the arithmetic hierarchy and is used with the function **stack_priority** (defined in step 2) to determine how long an operator waits in the stack before being appended to the postfix string.

**2.** Define another function `stack_priority`, which takes the same possibilities for an argument and returns an integer as

| Character | * | / | + | – | ( | ) | # |
|---|---|---|---|---|---|---|---|
| Returned Value | 2 | 2 | 1 | 1 | 0 | Undefined | 0 |

This function applies to operators in the operator stack as their priority in the arithmetic hierarchy is compared to that of incoming operators from the infix string. The result of this comparison determines whether or not an operator waits in the stack or is appended to the postfix string.

**3.** Initialize `op_stack` by pushing #.

**4.** Read the next character `ch` from the infix expression.

**5.** Test `ch` and

    5.1 If `ch` is an operand, append it to the postfix string.

    5.2 If `ch` is a right parenthesis, then pop entries from stack and append them to postfix until a left parenthesis is popped. Doing this ensures that operators within a parenthesized portion of an infix expression will be applied first, regardless of their priority in the usual arithmetic hierarchy. Discard both left and right parentheses.

    5.3 If `ch` is a #, pop all entries that remain on the stack and append them to the **postfix string**.

    5.4 Otherwise, pop from the stack and append to the postfix string operators whose `stack_priority` is greater than or equal to the `infix_priority` of `ch`. Stop this series of popping operations when you reach a stack element whose `stack_priority` is less than the `infix_priority` of `ch`. This comparison, keying on the priority of `ch` from the infix string and operators that have previously been pushed onto the operator stack, ensures that operators are applied in the right order in the resulting postfix string. After popping these operators, push `ch`.

**6.** Repeat steps 4 and 5 until `ch` is the delimiter #.

The key to the algorithm is the use of the stack to hold operators from the infix expression that appear to the left of another given operator even though that latter operator must be applied first. The defined functions `infix_priority` and `stack_priority` are used to specify this priority of operators and the associated pushing and popping operations. This entire process is best understood by carefully tracing through an example.

---

**EXAMPLE 5.3**

Parse the infix expression

$$A * B + (C - D / E) \#$$

into its equivalent postfix form. Trace the contents of the operator stack and the postfix string as each character is read.

The solution to this problem is presented in Table 5.1. In this table, the parenthesized numbers in the Commentary column refer to subcases of step 5 in the preceding algorithm.

---

◇ **TABLE 5.1**
Parsing of infix expression
*A * B + (C – D/E)*#

| ch | op_stack | postfix | Commentary |
|----|----------|---------|------------|
|    | #        |         | Push **#** |
| A  |          |         | Read **ch** |
|    |          | A       | Append **ch to postfix (5.1)** |
| *  |          |         | Read **ch** |
|    | *<br>#   |         | Push **ch (5.4)** |
| B  |          |         | Read **ch** |
|    |          | AB      | Append **ch to postfix (5.1)** |
| +  |          |         | Read **ch** |
|    | +<br>#   | AB*     | Pop *, append * to **postfix, push ch (5.4)** |
| (  |          |         | Read **ch** |
|    | (<br>+<br># |      | Push **ch (5.4)** |
| C  |          |         | Read **ch** |
|    |          | AB*C    | Append **ch to postfix (5.1)** |
| –  |          |         | Read **ch** |
|    | –<br>(<br>+<br># |  | Push **ch (5.4)** |
| D  |          |         | Read **ch** |
|    |          | AB*CD   | Append **ch to postfix (5.1)** |
| /  |          |         | Read **ch** |
|    | /<br>–<br>(<br>+<br># |  | Push **ch (5.4)** |
| E  |          |         | Read **ch** |
|    |          | AB*CDE  | Append **ch to postfix (5.1)** |
| )  |          |         | Read **ch** |
|    | +<br>#   | AB*CDE/– | Pop and append to **postfix until ( reached** (5.2) |
| #  |          |         | Read **ch** |
|    |          | AB*CDE/– + # | Pop and append rest of stack to **postfix (5.3)** |

The following C++ function implements our algorithm for converting infix expressions of the form we have specified. You should study and thoroughly understand this algorithm before moving on to this chapter's Focus on Program Design section. There, the infix-to-postfix algorithm will be the focal point for an entire program that works with expressions of a slightly more complicated form.

```cpp
void infix_to_postfix(string &postfix)
{
    char item, ch;
    stack<char> op_stack;
    op_stack.push('#');
    do
    {
        cin.get(ch);
        if (('A' <= ch) && (ch <= 'Z'))
            postfix.append_char(ch);
        else if (ch == ')')
        {
            item = op_stack.pop();
            while (item != '(')
            {
                postfix.append_char(item);
                item = op_stack.pop();
            }
        }
        else if (ch == '#')
        {
            while (! op_stack.empty())
            {
                item = op_stack.pop();
                postfix.append_char(item);
            }
        }
    }
```

"A" < = ch AND ch < = "Z"

postfix    .    Input ch    Q

op_stack

In this case, transfer ch to postfix.

ch = ")"

postfix    Input ch

op_stack

In this case, pop stack until encounter matching left parenthesis.

ch = "#"

postfix    Input ch

op_stack

In this case, pop rest of stack to postfix.

```
    else
    {
        item = op_stack.pop();
        while (stack_priority(item) >= infix_priority(ch))
            {
                postfix.append_char(item);
                item = op_stack.pop();
            }
            op_stack.push(item);
            op_stack.push(ch);
        }
    } while (ch != '#');
}
```

In this case, pop stack until encounter item of lower priority (+). Then push incoming ch.

## Evaluating Postfix Expressions

Once an expression has been parsed and represented in postfix form, another stack plays an essential role in its final evaluation. To evaluate a postfix expression, we repeatedly read characters from the postfix expression. If the character read is an operand, push the value associated with it onto the stack. If it is an operator, pop two values from the stack, apply the operator to them, and push the result back onto the stack. After the last operand in the postfix expression has been processed, the value of the expression is the one entry on the stack. The technique is illustrated in the following example.

---

**EXAMPLE 5.4**

Consider the postfix expression from Example 5.3.

$A B * C D E / - + #$

Let us suppose that the symbols $A$, $B$, $C$, $D$, and $E$ had associated with them the following values:

| Symbol | Value |
|--------|-------|
| $A$ | 5 |
| $B$ | 3 |
| $C$ | 6 |
| $D$ | 8 |
| $E$ | 2 |

The evaluation of the expression under this assignment of values proceeds as indicated in Figure 5.5.

◆ FIGURE 5.5
Evaluation of
*AB*CDE/−+#*

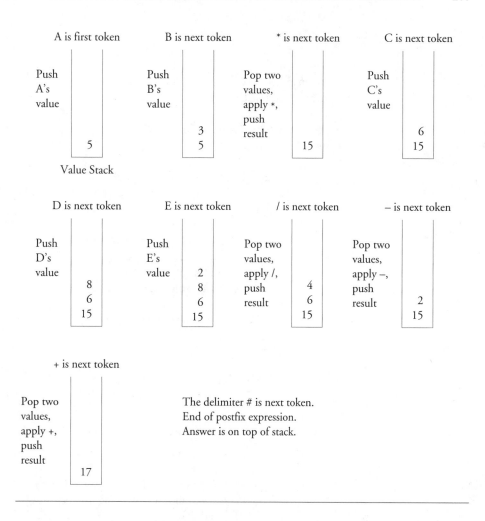

If we assume functions **value_of**, which will return the value associated with a particular symbol; **eval**, which will return the result of applying an operator to two values; and **next_token**, which will return the next token to be read from the postfix expression, the C++ function to evaluate a postfix expression is given by

```
// Assume a suitable implementation of the string ADT,
// augmented by a next_token operation.  next_token(s) is
// a function which returns successive characters from a
// string s.  That is, the first time it is called it returns the
// first character in s, then the second character in s, and so forth.

// Also we assume the existence of a function value_of which
// associates a character with its real value—similar to the
// fashion in which each variable in a program is associated with
// a value. Since our tokens are only single characters, an easy way
// of implementing value_of would be to use an array of reals
// indexed by the subrange 0 .. 25. In effect, this would create a
// mini, 26-location "memory." Finally, we assume the existence of
// an eval function which receives two real operands and the
// operator to apply to them. eval returns the result of applying
// that operator to the operands.
```

```
float evaluate(const string &postfix)
{
        char ch;
        float result, v1, v2;
        stack<float> value_stack;

        ch = next_token(postfix);
        while (ch != '#')
        {
                if (('A' <= ch) && (ch <= 'Z'))
                        value_stack.push(value_of(ch));
                else
                {
                    v2 = value_stack.pop();
                    v1 = value_stack.pop();
                    result = eval(v1, v2, ch);
                    value_stack.push(result);
                }
                ch = next_token(postfix);
        }
        return value_stack.on_top();
}
```

### EXERCISES 5.2

1. What are the infix, postfix, and prefix forms of the following expression?:

   $A + B * (C - D) / (P - R)$

2. Trace the contents of the stack as the postfix form of the expression in Exercise 1 is evaluated. Assume the following assignment of values: $A = 6$, $B = 4$, $C = 3$, $D = 1$, $P = 12$, and $R = 11$.

3. Consider the expression with the infix notation

   $P + (Q - F) / Y$

   Using the algorithm discussed in this section to transform this into a postfix expression, trace the state of both the operator stack and postfix string as each character of the infix expression is processed. Conduct your trace following the style of Table 5.1.

4. Using the postfix expression you obtained in Exercise 3, trace the stack of real values that would develop as the postfix expression is evaluated. You should indicate the numeric values on the stack as each character in the postfix expression is processed. Assume the values $F = 4$, $P = 10$, $Q = 18$, and $Y = 2$.

5. Parse the infix expression

   $P * (Q / Y) + A - B + D * Y \#$

   using the following definitions of **infix_priority** and **stack_priority**:

| Priority | * | / | + | − | ( | ) | # |
|----------|---|---|---|---|---|-----------|---|
| Infix    | 2 | 2 | 4 | 4 | 5 | 0 | 0 |
| Stack    | 1 | 1 | 3 | 3 | 0 | Undefined | 0 |

## A NOTE OF INTEREST

### Logic Programming and Backtracking

In the 1960s, J. Robinson, a mathematical logician, discovered an algorithm for automating the process of proving theorems in first-order predicate logic. This discovery made the discipline of logic programming possible. A logic program consists of a set of assertions. Some of these describe particular facts, such as "Ken is over 40 years old." Other assertions describe general facts or rules, such as "All people over 40 years old have gray hair." A program consisting of these two facts can be used to prove other facts, such as "Ken has gray hair." The proof can be executed on a computer after one enters the known facts, expressed in the syntax of a logic programming language, into a database and inputs a request for the proof of the unknown fact to the computer.

PROLOG is a logic programming language that provides a syntax for describing assertions and queries and an interpreter for user interaction and theorem proving. To return to our example, the known facts, expressed in the syntax of PROLOG, might be entered interactively at the `->` prompt into the database as follows:

```
-> assert(over_40(ken)).
OK

-> assert(gray_hair(X) :- over_40(X)).
OK
```

Queries for proofs of unknown facts might be entered as follows:

```
-> gray_hair(ken).
Yes

-> over_50(ken).
No
```

The PROLOG interpreter uses Robinson's algorithm to derive the unknown fact that Ken has gray hair from the fact that Ken is over 40 and the rule that if any individual is over 40, then it has gray hair. In our example, the algorithm starts with a goal of proving `gray_hair(ken)`. It finds a rule,

`gray_hair(X) :- over_40(X)`, whose consequent, `gray_hair(X)` matches the goal. The algorithm then tries to prove the rule's antecedent, `over_40(X)`, with `X = ken`. A fact that matches this goal, `over_40(ken)`, is found in the database, so the query or unknown fact, `gray_hair(ken)` has been proved.

Theorem proving is complicated by the fact that there may be rules that seem relevant but lead to dead ends. For example, suppose that the rules "All individuals with 4 children have gray hair" and "All individuals with weak backs have 4 children" are the other facts in the database. These rules might be expressed in PROLOG as follows:

1. `gray_hair(X) :-`
   `has_4_children(X)`
2. `has_4_children(X) :-`
   `has_weak_back(X)`

If the algorithm happens to try rule (1) before the one discussed earlier, it will not be able to prove that Ken has gray hair. It will try to prove that Ken as 4 children, and fail when it discovers no assertion that Ken has a weak back.

To solve this problem, the algorithm must backtrack, when a subgoal fails, to an earlier point in the process and try an alternative rule in the database. To support backtracking, the PROLOG interpreter maintains a stack of subgoals that are waiting to be proved. When a subgoal fails, the interpreter pops it off the stack and tries to prove the subgoal now at the top. In our example, the subgoals `has_weak_back(ken)` and `has_4_children(ken)` would both be popped off the stack, and the interpreter would then try our other rule for `gray_hair`. If the stack of subgoals becomes empty, then no proof of the given query can be found.

The use of a stack to implement the execution of a logic program is another example of the abstraction/implementation duality that we have emphasized throughout this book. At the abstract level, the logic programmer thinks in terms of first-order predicate logic, and does not worry about how the computer proves theorems. At the implementation level, a backtracking algorithm supported by stack operations handles the real work of finding proofs.

Trace this parsing operation following the style of Table 5.1.

**6.** Using the postfix string you obtained in Exercise 5, trace the stack of real numeric values that would develop as the postfix expression is evaluated. You should indicate the values on the stack as each character in the postfix expression is processed. Assume the values $A = 4$, $B = 3$, $D = 2$, $P = 1$, $Q = 4$, and $Y = 2$.

**7.** Write an implementation of the **append** operation that is suitable for use with postfix strings in this section's **infix_to_postfix** function.

8. Write implementations of the **next_token**, **value_of**, and **eval** operations that are suitable for this section's evaluate function.

9. Explain how the relationship between the stack priorities and infix priorities of **(**, **)**, **∗**, **/**, **+**, **−**, and **#** controls the parsing of the infix expression. Then explain how you would extend the definition of the stack and infix priority functions of this section to include an exponentiation operator **^**. The exponentiation operator should be right associative; that is, in an expression such as A **^** B **^** C, the exponentiations should occur in right-to-left order.

10. How would the functions **infix_priority** and **stack_priority** be extended to include the Boolean operators **<**, **>**, **<=**, **>=**, **==**, **!=**, **&&**, **||**, and **!**? Justify your choices of priority values for these Boolean operators.

---

## 5.3 The Queue Abstract Data Type: Its Use and Implementations

### OBJECTIVES

- to understand the definition of the queue ADT
- to understand what is meant by a computer simulation
- to be able to use the queue ADT in a simulation program
- to examine three implementations of the queue ADT: array, circular array, and linked list

The stack ADT that we have studied in the first two sections of this chapter is a last-in/first-out list. The next type of restricted list that we will examine, the queue, is a first-in/first-out list. All additions to a queue occur at one end, which we will designate as the rear of the queue. Items that enter the queue at the rear must move up to the front of the queue before they can be removed. **enqueue** is the name of the operation that adds an item to the rear of a queue, and **dequeue** is the name of the operation that removes an item from the front of a queue.

The operations on a queue thus parallel the dynamics of a waiting line. The linear order underlying a queue is determined by the length of time an item has been in the queue. This concept is depicted in Figure 5.6. The analogy of a waiting line makes a queue the obvious ADT to use in many applications concerned with scheduling. Before we explore such applications, however, we must formally define a queue as an ADT.

**Queue.** A queue is merely a restricted form of a list. In particular, the restrictions on a queue are that all additions to the queue occur at one end, the rear, and all removals from the queue occur at the other end, the front. The effect of these restrictions is to ensure that the earlier an item enters a queue, the earlier it will leave the queue. That is, items are processed on a first-in/first-out basis.

The five basic operations on a queue are specified by the following preconditions and postconditions.

◆ FIGURE 5.6

Abstract data type queue as computer embodiment of waiting line

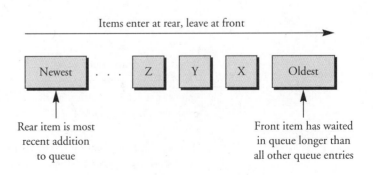

Items enter at rear, leave at front

| Newest | . . . | Z | Y | X | Oldest |

Rear item is most recent addition to queue

Front item has waited in queue longer than all other queue entries

**Create operation**
Preconditions:              Receiver is an arbitrary queue in unknown state.
Postconditions:             Receiver is initialized to the empty queue.
**Empty operation**
Preconditions:              Receiver is a previously created queue.
Postconditions:             Returns TRUE if queue is empty, FALSE otherwise.
**Enqueue operation**
Preconditions:              Receiver is a previously created queue. **item** is a value to be
                            added to the rear of the queue. There is memory available to
                            store the new item in the queue.
Postconditions:             **item** is added to the rear of the queue.
**Dequeue operation**
Preconditions:              Receiver is a previously created queue. The queue is not empty.
Postconditions:             Receiver has its front value removed, and **dequeue** returns
                            this value.

**at_front operation**
Preconditions:              Receiver is a previously created queue. The queue is not empty.
Postconditions:             **at_front** returns the value at the front of the queue.
                            Unlike **dequeue**, the queue is left unchanged.

---

**EXAMPLE 5.5**

To help conceptualize queue operations, consider the following sequence of actions
on a queue of integers.

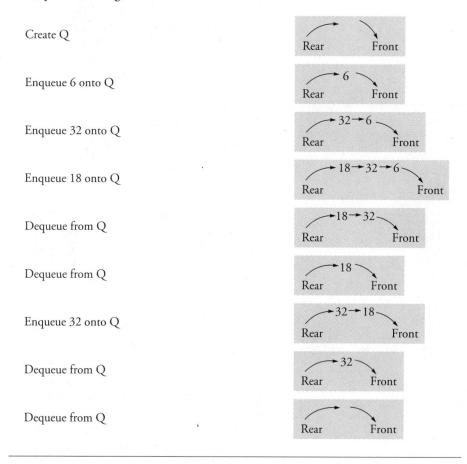

Create Q

Enqueue 6 onto Q

Enqueue 32 onto Q

Enqueue 18 onto Q

Dequeue from Q

Dequeue from Q

Enqueue 32 onto Q

Dequeue from Q

Dequeue from Q

## Application of a Queue in Computer Simulation

Before discussing implementations of a queue, we will examine how this ADT can be used in an application known as computer *simulation*. To introduce the notion of a simulation, consider the following question.

> *The star car washing team at Octopus Car Wash requires precisely four minutes to wash a car. A car arrives on the average at Octopus every four minutes. In a typical 10-hour day at Octopus, how long does a car have to wait between its arrival and beginning its wash?*

It's tempting to answer this question by reasoning that the combination of four minutes to wash a car and four minutes between arrivals implies that no car should wait at all. However, such reasoning would not reflect the reality that cars arrive sporadically. Such sporadic arrival patterns are what can cause dreadful waiting lines.

That cars arrive, on the average, every four minutes really means that, in any given minute, there is a 25% chance that a car will arrive. We wish to reflect the notion of "chance" in a program that models the operation of Octopus Car Wash during a typical day. A computer simulation is a program that models a real-life event. To incorporate chance into simulations, a special function known as a *random number generator* is used.

A random number generator is a function that returns an unpredictable numerical value each time it is called. For our purposes, the value returned from a random number generator will be a real value greater than or equal to zero but less than 1. We will approach a random number generator as a "black box" function. That is, we will not worry about the internal logic of how such numbers are generated. Many versions of C++ supply a random number generator; if yours doesn't, you might use the one given by the **random_generator** class in Appendix 6. Our only concern in using a random number generator is that if we call on the function **random** in a loop such as the following

```
For each k from 1 to 100
      output random()
```

then we should see 100 values that obey statistical properties of randomness. Essentially these properties require that no pattern of values tends to recur and that values are evenly spread over the interval from 0 to 1. How will a random number generator be used to reflect the "reality" of cars arriving at Octopus Car Wash? We will view each iteration through a loop as one minute in the daily operation of Octopus. On each iteration, we will call on **random** to generate a random number. If it is less than or equal to 0.25 (corresponding to the 25% chance of an arrival), our program will interpret that as a car arriving during that minute. If the random number is greater than 0.25, the program decides that no car arrived during that minute.

When a car does arrive, it will be added to the waiting queue of cars. So that we may accumulate some statistical results, the car will be time-stamped with the time that it entered the queue. This time stamp will allow us to determine how long a car has been in the queue before it finally reaches the front. Conceptually, the queue at the core of this simulation is depicted in Figure 5.7. Pseudocode for the Octopus Car Wash simulation is

◆ **FIGURE 5.7**
Cars waiting at Octopus Car
Wash, time-stamped with
the minute of their arrival

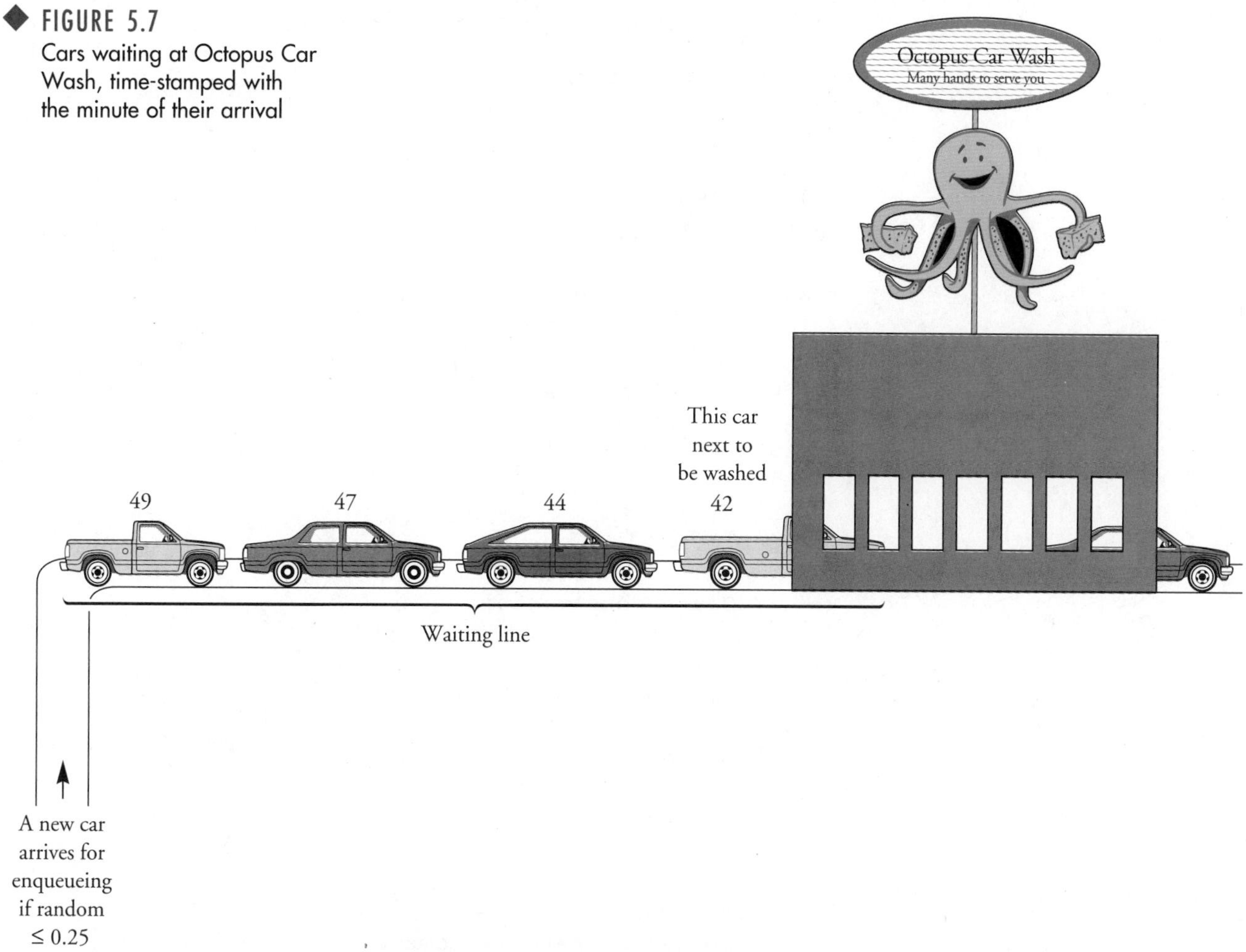

This car
next to
be washed

49        47        44        42

Waiting line

A new car
arrives for
enqueueing
if random
≤ 0.25

Initialize statistical counters
Create the queue of time-stamped cars
For each minute in the day's operation
        Call on the random number generator to determine if a new car
            arrived
        If a new car arrived
            Time-stamp and enqueue in onto the queue of cars
        If no car is currently being washed and the queue of waiting cars is
            not empty
            Dequeue a car from the queue for washing
            Use the time stamp for the car just dequeued to
                determine
                how long it waited
            Add that wait time to the accumulating total wait time
            Record that we have just begun to wash a car
    If a car is being washed
        Reduce by one minute the time left before we are done washing it

To refine this pseudocode into a C++ main program, we must establish a formal
C++ interface for the queue ADT.

# C++ Interface for the Queue Abstract Data Type

```cpp
// Class declaration file: queue.h

#ifndef QUEUE_H

#include "boolean.h"
#include "element.h"

// We assume that constant MAX_QUEUE_SIZE
// is already defined in element.h

// Declaration section

template <class E> class queue
{

    public:

    // Class constructors

    queue();
    queue(const queue<E> &q);

    // Member functions

    boolean empty();
    void enqueue(const E &item);
    E dequeue();
    E at_front();
    queue<E>& operator = (const queue<E> &q);

    // Protected data and member functions pertaining to
    // the implementation would go here.

};

#define QUEUE_H
#endif
```

---

**EXAMPLE 5.6**   Use the preceding C++ interface to write a main program for the Octopus Car Wash simulation. Assume the existence of a **random_generator** class.

```cpp
// Program file: octopus.cpp
// A program to simulate the operation of the Octopus Car Wash over
// 10 hours (600 minutes) of operation.  The variables time_for_wash
// and prob_of_arrival represent the time it takes to run one car through
// Octopus's star car wash team and the probability that a car
// arrives for a wash in any given minute.  This program assumes the
// existence of a queue data type and a random number generator invoked
// by a call to the parameterless function random.
```

```cpp
#include <iostream.h>
#include <iomanip.h>

#include "boolean.h"
#include "queue.h"
#include "random.h"

random_generator generator;

float random();

int main()
{
        int time_for_wash,
        minute,
        time_entered_queue,
        cars_washed,
        total_queue_min,
        time_left_on_car;
        float prob_of_arrival;
        queue<int> car_queue;

        cout << "Enter time to wash one car: ";
        cin >> time_for_wash;
        cout << "Enter probability of arrival in any minute: ";
        cin >> prob_of_arrival;
        cars_washed = 0;
        total_queue_min = 0;
        time_left_on_car = 0;
        for (minute = 1; minute <= 600; ++minute)
        {
                if (random() < prob_of_arrival)
                        car_queue.enqueue(minute);
                if ((time_left_on_car == 0) && ! car_queue.empty())
                {
                        time_entered_queue = car_queue.dequeue();
                        total_queue_min = total_queue_min +
                                (minute - time_entered_queue);
                        ++cars_washed;
                        time_left_on_car = time_for_wash;
                }
                if (time_left_on_car != 0)
                        --time_left_on_car;
        }
        cout << setw(4) << cars_washed << " cars were washed" << endl;
        cout << "Average wait in queue " << setw(8) << setprecision(2)
                << float(total_queue_min) / cars_washed << endl;
        return 0;
}

float random()
{
        return generator.next_number(1,10)/10.0;
}
```

A sample run would appear as follows:

```
Enter time to wash one car 4
Enter probability of arrival in any minute 0.25
150 cars were washed
Average wait in queue 15.53
```

The sample run of the program in Example 5.6 provides an indication of how the sporadic arrival of cars can cause a backlog of work at Octopus Car Wash. One of the great values of simulation programs is that they allow cost-free experimentation with various scenarios to see if a situation might improve or worsen. For instance, the program we have written for Octopus could be used to explore how adding help to the car wash team (and correspondingly reducing the amount of time it takes to wash a car) could affect the build-up of cars waiting for service. You will get a chance to explore further the use of queues for computer simulations in the exercises and problems in the remainder of this chapter.

Another noteworthy point about Example 5.6 is that it works with a queue even though we have no idea of how the queue of cars is actually implemented. Of course, this should not be surprising; this is the value of designing programs and data structures from an ADT perspective. However, given the high-level logic in our example, we should now turn our attention to ways in which the scheduling queue might be implemented.

## A NOTE OF INTEREST

### Computer Simulations: Blessing or Curse?

The computer's ability to condense a large span of time (such as 600 minutes in Example 5.6) into the very short time frame required for a run of a simulation program is the blessing and the curse of computer simulations. It makes the computer a very valuable experimental tool. In addition to providing a much faster means of experimentation, simulation programs allow researchers and decisionmakers to set up initial conditions that would be far too risky if allowed in real life.

For example, consider the area of environmental studies. Here researchers can use simulation programs to create scenarios that would be far too time-consuming and dangerous if they were carried out in the environment. Researchers could use simulation software to see what might happen if pollution of a river were allowed to continue in an uncontrolled manner. If the results of the simulation indicate that all fish in the river would be gone within 10 years, nothing has really been lost. Moreover, some valuable information has been gained; decisionmakers in the environmental arena would know that some sort of pollution controls are necessary. Further experimentation with the simulation could be done to determine exactly what type and degree of controls should be imposed.

What can go wrong with decisions based on the result of computer simulation? Clearly, if the model on which the program is based is not an accurate reflection of the situation being simulated, results could be produced that would disastrously mislead decisionmakers. Additionally, we saw in Example 5.6, building the complex mathematical models used in simulation programs is a very sensitive process. Even models that seem to be relatively comprehensive can produce surprisingly inaccurate output. Hence, the real issue in using simulation results to support the decision-making process is the accuracy of the model on which the program is based. The authors of such a program must combine expertise in programming techniques with high levels of sophisticated knowledge in the relevant discipline(s). This is a situation in which computer science must truly become interdisciplinary.

The importance of simulation as an area of application within computer science is reflected in two issues of the *Communications of the ACM* that have been dedicated to this topic. The November 1985 issue (Volume 28, No. 11) reported on simulation models in such diverse areas as molecular genetics, aviation, and seismology. The October 1990 issue (Volume 33, No. 10) explored simulation in the context of parallel events, on-line scheduling, and semiconductor manufacturing.

## Array Implementation of a Queue

From the definition of a queue, it is evident that two pointers will suffice to keep track of the data in a queue: one pointer to the front of the queue and one to the rear. This premise underlies all of the queue implementations we discuss in this section.

Let us consider computer jobs being scheduled in a batch processing environment, a good example of a queue in use. Suppose further that all job names are strings and that jobs are scheduled strictly in the order in which they arrive. Then an array and two pointers can be used to implement the scheduling queue. We will encapsulate the array and pointers in the class declaration module:

```
// Class declaration file: queue.h

#ifndef QUEUE_H

#include "boolean.h"
#include "element.h"

// We assume that constant MAX_QUEUE_SIZE
// is already defined in element.h

template <class E> class queue
{

    public:

    // Class constructors

    queue();
    queue(const queue<E> &q);

    // Member functions

    boolean empty();
    void enqueue(const E &item);
    E dequeue();
    E at_front();
    queue<E>& operator = (const queue<E> &q);

    protected:

    // Data members

    int front, rear;
    E data[MAX_QUEUE_SIZE];

    // Member function

    boolean full();

};

#define QUEUE_H
#endif
```

If the **front** and **rear** pointers are initially set to 0 and –1, respectively, the state of the queue before any insertions or deletions appears as shown in Figure 5.8. Recalling that insertions may be made only at the rear of the queue, suppose that job NEWTON now arrives to be processed. The queue then changes to the state pictured in Figure 5.9. If job NEWTON is followed by PAYROLL, the queue's status must change to that of Figure 5.10, which shows that the addition of any item to the queue requires two steps:

```
++rear;
data[rear] = item;
```

If the system is now ready to process NEWTON, the front entry must be removed from the queue to an appropriate location designated by **item** in Figure 5.11. Here the instructions

```
item = data[front];
++front;
```

achieve the desired effect.

It should be clear that the conditions in Table 5.2 signal the associated boundary conditions for an array implementation of a queue.

The conditions allow us to develop our brief two-line sequences for adding to and removing from a queue into full-fledged functions. These in turn assume the existence of the Boolean-valued functions **empty** and **full** to check whether or not the **enqueue** and **dequeue** operations are possible. In the exercises, you will be asked to write the **create**, **empty**, and **full** operations.

◆ FIGURE 5.8
Empty queue

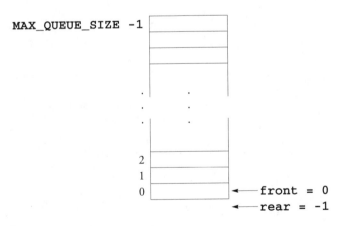

◆ FIGURE 5.9
NEWTON added to the rear
of the queue

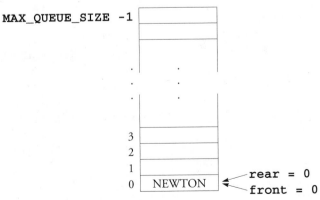

◆ FIGURE 5.10
PAYROLL added after
NEWTON

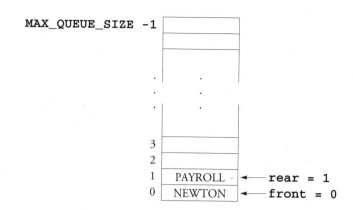

◆ FIGURE 5.11
NEWTON removed from the
queue

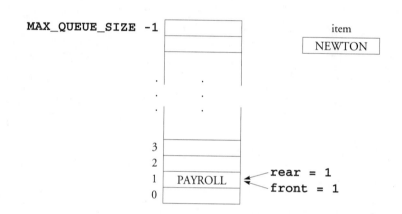

◇ TABLE 5.2
Boundary condition checks
for array implementation of
queue

| Condition | Special Situation |
|---|---|
| `rear < front` | Empty queue |
| `front = rear` | One-entry queue |
| `rear = MAX_QUEUE_SIZE` | No more entries may be added to queue |

EXAMPLE 5.7      Write the **enqueue** and **dequeue** operations for an array implementation of the
queue ADT.

```
void enqueue(E item)
{
        assert(! full());
        ++rear;
        data[rear] = item;
}
```

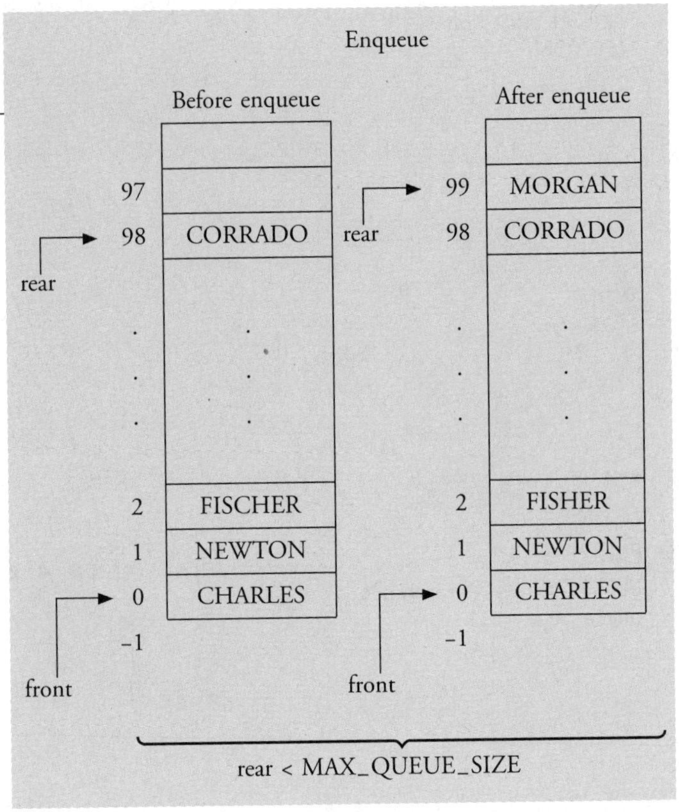

Enqueue

Before enqueue | After enqueue

| | |
|---|---|
| 97 | 99 MORGAN |
| 98 CORRADO (rear) | 98 CORRADO |
| . | . |
| . | . |
| . | . |
| 2 FISCHER | 2 FISHER |
| 1 NEWTON | 1 NEWTON |
| 0 CHARLES | 0 CHARLES |
| -1 | -1 |

rear < MAX_QUEUE_SIZE

```
E dequeue()
{
        E item;

        assert(! empty());
        item = data[front];
        ++front;
        return item;
}
```

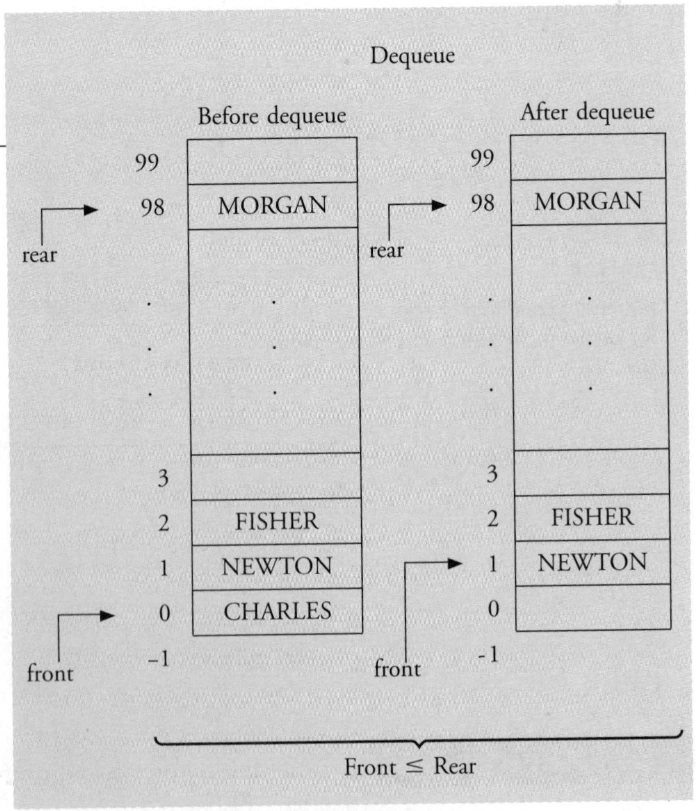

Dequeue

Before dequeue | After dequeue

| | |
|---|---|
| 99 | 99 |
| 98 MORGAN (rear) | 98 MORGAN (rear) |
| . | . |
| . | . |
| . | . |
| 3 | 3 |
| 2 FISHER | 2 FISHER |
| 1 NEWTON | 1 NEWTON |
| 0 CHARLES (front) | 0 |
| -1 | -1 |

Front ≤ Rear

◆ FIGURE 5.12
A full queue

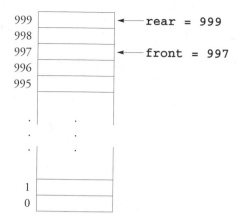

◆ FIGURE 5.13
Active queue moved down

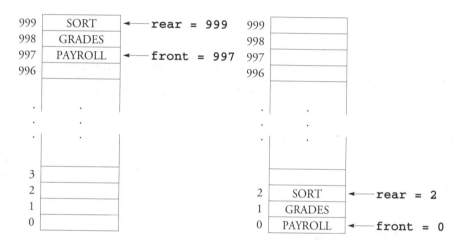

As it now stands, our implementation of a queue as a scheduling structure for jobs in a batch environment functions effectively until **rear** matches **MAX_QUEUE_SIZE - 1**. Then a call to **enqueue** fails even though only a small percentage of slots in the array may actually contain data items currently in the queue structure. In fact, given the queue pictured in Figure 5.12, we should be able to use slots 0—996 again.

This is not necessarily undesirable. For example, it may be that the mode of operation in a given batch environment is to process 1000 jobs, then print a statistical report on these 1000 jobs, and finally clear the queue to start another group of 1000 jobs. In this case, the queue in Figure 5.12 is the ideal structure because data about jobs are not lost even after they have left the queue.

However, if the goal of a computer installation were to provide continuous scheduling of batch jobs, without interruption after 1000 jobs, then the queue of Figure 5.12 would not be effective. One strategy that could be employed to correct this situation is to move the active queue down the array upon reaching the condition **rear** equals **MAX_QUEUE_SIZE - 1**, as illustrated in Figure 5.13. If the queue contains a large number of items, however, this strategy would not be satisfactory because it would require moving all of the individual data items. We will discuss two other strategies that allow the queue to operate in a continuous and efficient fashion: a circular implementation and a linked list implementation.

## Circular Implementation of a Queue

Circular implementation of a queue essentially allows the queue to wrap around upon reaching the end of the array. This transformation is illustrated by the addition of the item UPDATE to the queue in Figure 5.14. To handle the pointer arithmetic necessary for this implementation of a queue, we must make the front and rear pointers behave in a fashion analogous to an odometer in a car that has exceeded its mileage capacity. A convenient way of doing this is to use C++'s % operator. For instance, if we replace

```
++front;
```

in Example 5.7 with

```
front = front % MAX_QUEUE_SIZE;
```

and

```
++rear;
```

with

```
rear = rear % MAX_QUEUE_SIZE;
```

we will achieve the wraparound effect depicted in Figure 5.14. Unfortunately, it is clear from Figure 5.14 that **rear < front** will no longer suffice as a condition to signal an empty queue. To derive this condition, consider what remains after we remove an item from a queue that has only a single item in it. There are two possible situations, as illustrated in Figure 5.15. An inspection of both cases reveals that after the lone entry has been removed, the relationship

```
(rear % MAX_QUEUE_SIZE ) == front
```

holds between the pointers. There is a problem, however, with immediately adopting this as a check for an empty queue. This same relationship between pointers also exists when the queue is full.

◆ FIGURE 5.14

Queue wraps around when
UPDATE is added

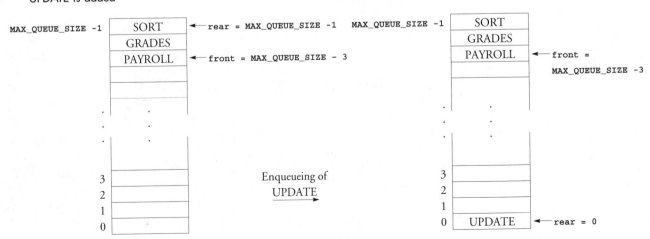

◆ FIGURE 5.15

Removing from one-entry queue

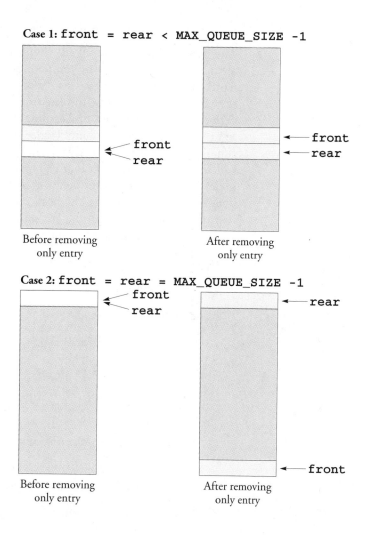

**Case 1:** `front = rear < MAX_QUEUE_SIZE -1`

front
rear

front
rear

Before removing
only entry

After removing
only entry

**Case 2:** `front = rear = MAX_QUEUE_SIZE -1`

front
rear

rear

front

Before removing
only entry

After removing
only entry

◇ TABLE 5.3

Boundary condition checks for circular queue with encapsulated counter

| Condition | Special Situation |
| --- | --- |
| Counter is 1 | One-entry queue |
| Counter is 0 | Empty queue |
| Counter is **MAX_QUEUE_SIZE** | Full queue |

This apparent contradiction can be avoided easily if we add a counter to our encapsulation of the queue to keep track of the number of items currently in the queue. Then, as Table 5.3 indicates, tests for empty and full conditions need merely check this counter.

The actual implementation of queue operations using a circular array strategy is left for you to do in the exercises.

## Linked List Implementation of a Queue

The linked list method allows a queue to be completely dynamic with size restrictions imposed only by the pool of available nodes. Essentially, the queue is represented as a linked list with an additional rear pointer to the last node in the list so that the list need not be traversed to find this node. We define a queue as a new derived class of linked list, and assume that the linked list class maintains a pointer to the last node as an attribute. Hence the linked list implementation of the queue containing PAYROLL, GRADES, and SORT would appear as in Figure 5.16. We will follow the convention that the front pointer for the queue points at the first node, while the rear pointer points at the last node. Hence we access the first actual item in the queue through the head pointer of the linked list, and the last actual item in the queue through the last pointer of the linked list.

The class declaration module for a queue as a derived class of linked list is

```
// Class declaration file: queue.h

#ifndef QUEUE_H

#include "boolean.h"

// Declaration section

template class <class E> queue : protected linked_list<E>
{

    public:

    // Class constructors

    queue();
    queue(const queue<E> &q);

    // Class destructor

    ~queue();

    // Member functions

    boolean empty();
    void enqueue(const E &item);
    E dequeue();
    E at_front();
    queue<E>& operator = (const queue<E> &q);

};

#define QUEUE_H
#endif
```

Note that the specifications of the data members for a queue disappear, in that they are inherited from the parent linked list class.

Appropriate functions for handling additions to and removals from the queue follow. Notice that from a calling module's perspective, it would make little difference whether these low-level functions used an array or a linked list to

◆ **FIGURE 5.16**
Queue with three data
nodes

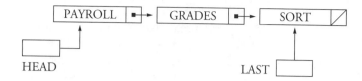

implement the queue. For each implementation, we have bundled all the information involved with the queue into a single object of class queue. Hence the calling protocol for these modules is the same regardless of the implementation being used. Remember that is the essence of data abstraction: The details of how a data structure is actually implemented are hidden as deeply as possible in the overall program structure.

**EXAMPLE 5.8**

Code the **enqueue** and **dequeue** operations for a linked list implementation of a queue.

**enqueue** will insert data at the end of the linked list. Therefore, we move the **previous** pointer to the last node, set the **current** pointer to NULL, and call **insert** with the data:

```
template <class E>
void queue<E>::enqueue(E item)
{
    previous = last;
    current = NULL;
    insert(item);
}
```

**dequeue** will remove data from the beginning of the linked list. Therefore, we call **first** to position the pointers, and call **remove** to delete the data from the linked list:

```
template <class E>
E queue<E>::dequeue()
{
    E item;
    boolean success;

    assert(! empty());
    first();
    success = remove(item);
    return item;
}
```

Note that the second function implementation is more abstract and high level than the first, in that the second consists just of calls of public member functions, while the first accesses the underlying representation of the linked list. If this representation in the parent class were changed, we would have to update the first two lines of code in the **enqueue** function.

## Priority Queues

So far we have used a batch scheduling application as an example of how a queue might be used in an operating system. Typically, such batch scheduling might also give higher priorities to certain types of jobs. For instance, at a university computer center, students in introductory computer science courses may receive the highest priority for their jobs to encourage a quick turnaround. Students in upper division courses may have the next highest priority, whereas jobs related to faculty research, which require a great deal of computation, get the lowest possible priority. These jobs could be classified as types A, B, and C, respectively. Any A job is serviced before any B or C job, regardless of the time it enters the service queue. Similarly, any B job is serviced before any C job. A data structure capable of representing such a queue requires just one *front pointer* but three *rear pointers,* one for each of the A, B, and C priorities.

A queue with eight jobs waiting to be serviced might appear as shown in Figure 5.17, which tells us that STATS, PRINT, and BANK are the A jobs awaiting service; COPY and CHECK, the B jobs; and UPDATE, AVERAGE, and TEST, the C jobs. If a new A job, PROB1, were to arrive for service, it would be inserted at the end of the A queue, between BANK and COPY. Because jobs can be serviced only by leaving the front of the queue, PROB1 would be processed before any of the B or C jobs.

Because insertions in such a *priority queue* need not occur at the absolute rear of the queue, it is clear that an array implementation may require moving a substantial amount of data when an item is inserted at the rear of one of the higher priority queues. To avoid this, you can use a linked list to great advantage when implementing a priority queue. Whenever an item arrives to be inserted into a given priority level, the rear pointer for that priority gives us an immediately accessible pointer to the node after which the item is to be inserted. This avoids a costly sequential search for the insertion point. If a dummy leader is included at the beginning of the list, the empty conditions for any given priority are as shown in Table 5.4. The specifics of writing a formal ADT definition of a priority queue

◆ **FIGURE 5.17**

Priority queue with eight jobs at three priority levels

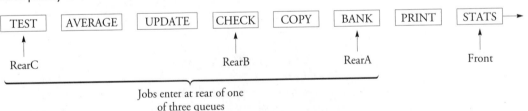

Jobs enter at rear of one of three queues

◇ **TABLE 5.4**

Empty conditions for a priority queue

| Condition | Priority |
|---|---|
| `front = rear1` | For priority 1, the highest priority |
| `rear1 = rear2` | For priority 2 |
| `rear(n - 1) = rearn` | For priority $n$ |

and providing an implementation for it are included as exercises at the end of this section. In Chapter 7, we will see that priority queues may also be implemented using the special type of tree structure known as a heap (not to be confused with the heap maintained in C++ as described in chapter 4). Unlike the implementation we have just discussed, the heap will conveniently allow an unrestricted number of different priorities.

**EXERCISES 5.3**

1. Suppose you are given a queue that is known to contain only positive integers. Use only the fundamental queue operations to write a function

   ```
   void replace(queue<int> &q, int old_int, int new_int);
   ```

   which replaces all occurrences of the positive integer **old_int** in the queue with the positive integer **new_int**. Other than doing this, the queue is to remain unchanged. Avoid passing through the queue more than once.

2. Suppose that you are given a queue of real numbers. Using only the fundamental queue operations, write a function that returns the average value of an entry in the queue.

3. Augment the simulation program of Example 5.6 by
   a. Counting the number of minutes during the day when the Octopus Car Wash team is idle; that is, there are no cars in the queue waiting to be washed.
   b. Counting how many cars are left waiting in the queue at the end of the day.
   Make no assumptions about how the **car_queue** might be implemented.

4. Consider a circular array implementation of a queue in which the array is declared to have an index range 0..4. Trace the status of the array and the **front** and **rear** pointers after each of the following successive operations.

   ```
   enqueue SMITH
   enqueue JONES
   enqueue GREER
   dequeue
   enqueue CARSON
   dequeue
   enqueue BAKER
   enqueue CHARLES
   enqueue BENSON
   dequeue
   enqueue MILLER
   ```

5. Implement the **create** and **empty** operations for a (noncircular) array implementation of a queue. Be sure that your answers are consistent with the implementation of enqueue and dequeue in Example 5.7.

6. Provide data member declarations for a circular array implementation of a queue. Then use these declarations to implement each of the four basic queue operations.

7. Suppose that we adopt the following conventions for the **front** and **rear** pointers associated with a queue. **front** is to point at the next item to be removed from the queue. **rear** is to point at the first available location, that is, the next location to be filled. Following these conventions, implement all four queue operations for a noncircular array representation of the ADT.

8. Repeat Exercise 7 for a circular array representation.

9. In a queue used to schedule batch jobs on a computer system, it is often convenient to allow users to remove a job from the queue after submitting it. (They may, for example, realize that they accidentally submitted a job with an infinite loop.) Develop a function header for this removal operation. Be sure that you document it appropriately. Then implement it for a circular array representation of a queue.

10. Repeat Exercise 9 for a linked list representation of a queue.

11. Provide a formal ADT definition for the priority queue. Then implement the ADT under the assumption that possible priority values are drawn from a set that could be used to index an array. See if you can make your implementation of each operation $O(1)$ in its efficiency.

12. Discuss ways in which the Octopus Car Wash simulation of Example 5.6 does not reflect the way in which a car wash really operates. Then discuss ways in which the pseudocode logic behind this example should be modified to overcome these shortcomings.

---

## A NOTE OF INTEREST

### Operating Systems and Scheduling Resource Use in a Time-Sharing Environment

One of the primary problems facing designers of operating systems is the allocation and scheduling of resources that must be shared by a number of users. For instance, consider a simple time-sharing system that allows multiple users, each on a video terminal, and also has one shared printer. Suppose that the currently running process, called process A, makes a request to use the printer. Then, before this process completes its task on the printer, its allotted time (often called a time burst) expires, and it is replaced by process B as the currently running process. If process B requests the printer while it is running, we have a clear problem. If process B is granted the printer, its output will be interspersed with that from Process A, which did not complete its printing before its time burst expired. Obviously, we cannot let process B continue to run.

The solution developed by operating systems designers to honor both of these requests is to use multiple queues—one containing those processes that have cleared access to all resources they require to run, and one for processes that have requested a resource currently owned by another process. The former of these queues is often called the

ready queue; the latter is termed the blocked queue. Hence the solution to the scenario described in the first paragraph involves two steps.

1. Move process A from its currently running state to the ready queue when its time burst expires (because it has all the necessary resources to start running again).

2. Move process B to the blocked queue when it requests the printer already owned by process A. Here it would remain until process A is done with the printer, at which time the front entry in the blocked queue for the printer (B in this case) would be moved to the ready queue.

In practice, the addition and removal of processes to and from these queues is controlled by special flags called semaphores. For a thorough exposition on operating system queues and semaphores, see Abraham Silberschatz and Peter B. Galvin, *Operating System Concepts*, 4th ed. (Reading, Mass.: Addison-Wesley, 1994).

---

## FOCUS ON PROGRAM DESIGN

The application of the parsing algorithm described in Section 5.2 is not limited to compilers. Many of the programs typically used by scientists, engineers, and mathematicians can be greatly enhanced by allowing the user to interactively enter an algebraic expression as opposed to embedding the expression inside the program. Consider, for instance, the situation described in the following memorandum from the head of the physics department at the University of Hard Knocks.

MEMORANDUM
University of Hard Knocks

   TO: Director of Computer Center
 FROM: Head of Physics Department
 DATE: November 22, 1996
   RE: Making integration program more versatile

In physics, we find frequent application to take the integral of a function `f(x)` over the interval from `a` to `b` on the real number line. As you are aware, this essentially means that we wish to find the area under the graph of the function between endpoints `a` and `b`, as indicated in the following diagram:

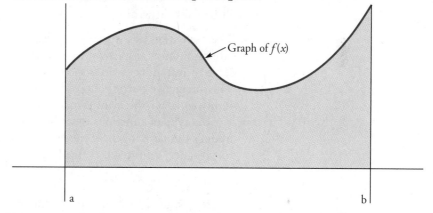

We presently have a program that obtains a good approximation of this area by adding up the areas of a large number of small rectangles, each with base along the interval from `a` to `b` and top passing through the graph of `f(x)`. This concept is highlighted in the next diagram.

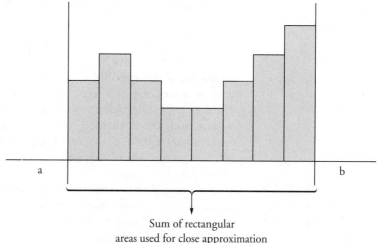

Sum of rectangular
areas used for close approximation

The user of our program can interactively enter the
endpoints *a* and *b* and the number of rectangles. The
result is a very good approximation when enough
rectangles are used.

Our problem is not with the accuracy of the approximation
but with the fact that to change the function *f*(x), the
user must edit the definition of the function in the
source program and then recompile. Can you help us by
writing a program which will allow the user to enter the
function *f*(x) interactively? The functions we integrate
in this fashion can be defined in terms of the standard
arithmetic operations of addition, subtraction,
multiplication, division, and exponentiation. Thanks in
advance for your prompt assistance.

The physics department head has presented us with a substantial task in the
preceding memorandum. Consider some of the subordinate problems with which
we will be faced in writing this program:

- The evaluation of integrals; that is, areas under graphs of functions. Obtaining numerical answers to mathematical problems of this variety will serve to introduce us to a subject known as *numerical analysis*.
- The interactive *parsing* and evaluation of a function will give us an opportunity to adapt the algorithms introduced earlier.
- For the type of functions described in the memorandum, the problem of finding the next token in the expression can become complicated. Consider, for instance, a function defined by the expression

$$3.14 * X \wedge 3 + X \wedge 2$$

where $\wedge$ is used to denote exponentiation. Here, from a stream of incoming characters, we must be prepared to select a token that may be a real number, the variable *X*, or an arithmetic operator. The problem of recognizing tokens in an incoming stream of characters is called *lexical analysis*. To keep our situation relatively simple, we will assume that all tokens must be separated by a space and no other operations such as trigonometric functions may be used in defining the function *f*.

## Modular Structure Chart for the Integral Evaluation System

With these comments in mind, we turn our attention toward designing a solution to the integration problem. Recall that the first step in this design process is to develop a modular structure chart reflecting the way in which we will partition the problem into subproblems (see Figure 5.18). Since both conversion from infix to postfix and the evaluation of a postfix expression require fundamental stack operations, we have located our stack processing modules at the deepest level of the structure chart. Here they will be accessible by both the parsing and evaluation algorithms.

Interestingly, our system will also make use of a queue. Because the tokens in the postfix expression are now more complicated objects than single characters, we need a data structure to append tokens to as they are processed by the infix-to-postfix algorithm. A queue emerges as a very nice ADT for this purpose. Hence the structure chart also indicates the presence of fundamental queue operations at a level accessible by both the parsing and evaluation algorithms.

◆ FIGURE 5.18
Modular structure chart for
integration problem

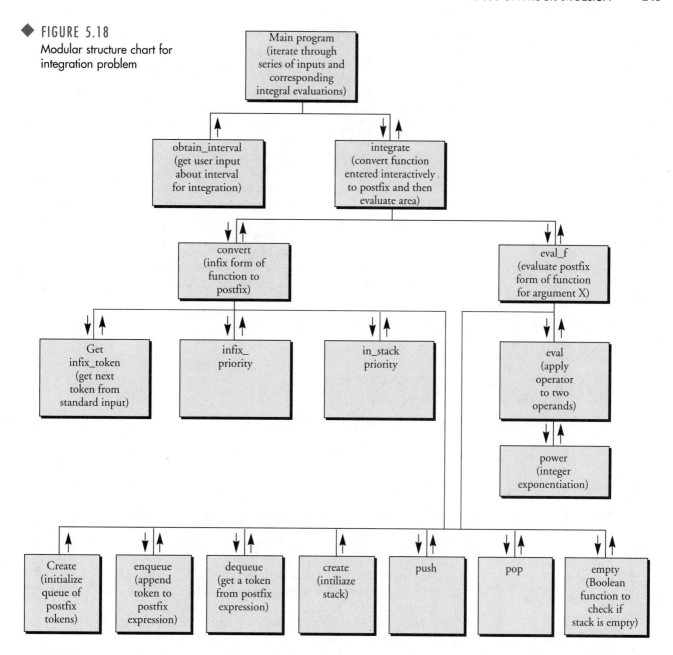

## Data Structures for the Integral Evaluation System

We will need a queue to store the postfix expression that is built as the infix expression goes through our conversion algorithm. The data in this queue are more complex than characters, however. This is because the tokens needed from the infix string being entered by the user are not necessarily individual characters. Rather, such tokens will fall into one of the three following categories:

1. *A real number:* If the token is a real number, the lexical analysis phase of our algorithm must convert it from the appropriate stream of digits and decimal point as typed by the user.
2. *The variable X:* The infix expression defines the function in terms of this general variable. When the function is evaluated, a particular value is then substituted for *X.*

**3.** *An operator:* We broadly include +, −, *, /, ^, (, ), and the special delimiter # in this category.

The problem with a token that may be either a real number or a character is that we essentially need a data type that can assume one of several identities, depending on the current token. In the abstract, we can think of each token as having two attributes: a *code* telling us which class of token it is (real number, operator, or variable) and a *value* that the particular token assumes (a particular real number, operator, or variable name). To represent this information, we place the code attribute in a new class called *token.* Because the codes are of the same type, the code attribute will be treated as the *fixed part* of a C++ structure. Because the values can be of different types (**float** or **char**), the value attribute will be treated as the *variant part* of a C++ structure. Structure variants can be represented in C++ as *unions.* A union allows several data members of different types to be declared in a structure, but only one of them may be used at any given time. The currently used member is identified by examining the value of the fixed part of the structure. The structure definition that we will use for tokens follows:

```
enum token_code {REAL_VALUE, VAR_X, OPERATOR};

struct token_record
{
     token_code code;
     union
     {
          float real_value;
          char operator;
          char var_x;
     };
};
```

The following points concerning variant parts or unions should now be made:

**1.** Each variant part or union should have associated with it a *tag member* in the fixed part of the structure.
**2.** The tag member should be an ordinal type, such as **int**, **char**, or an enumeration. This will allow examination of the tag member's value in a **switch** statement.
**3.** Only one member in a union can store a value at any given time.
**4.** Before storing a value in a member of a union, the programmer should set the corresponding tag member to the appropriate value. In our example, the tag member should be set to **REAL_VALUE** before storing a real number in the variant part, or to **OPERATOR** or to **VAR_X** before storing a character there.
**5.** Before using the value in a member of a union, the programmer should check to see that the corresponding tag member has the appropriate value. This is typically done with a **switch** statement. In our example, the programmer should use the value of the **real_value** member only if the tag member has the value **REAL_VALUE**.
**6.** Failure to adhere to the rules specified above can cause program errors. In our example, an attempt to access the **real_value** member of the variant part if the tag member contains the value **OPERATOR** may cause an error.

Variant parts or unions are defined by a form as follows:

```
union
{
      <type 1> <member 1>;
      <type 2> <member 2>;
      .
      .
      .
      <type n> <member n>;
};
```

**union** is a reserved word. The members of a union are indented for readability. The member names in a union lie in the same scope as the enclosing structure member names.

Here is the class declaration module for the token class:

```
// Class declaration file: token.h

#ifndef TOKEN_H

enum token_code {REAL_VALUE, VAR_X, OPERATOR};

// Declaration section

class token
{

      public:

      // Class constructors:

      token();
      token(token_code code);
      token(const token &t);

      // Member functions

      token_code code();
      float real_value();
      char op();
      char var_x();
      void set_code(token_code code);
      void set_real_value(float value);
      void set_op(char op);
      void set_var_x(char var_x);
      token& operator = (const token &t);

      protected:

      // Data members
```

```
struct token_record
{
      token_code code;
      union
      {
            float real_value;
            char op;
            char var_x;
      };
};

token_record the_token;
```

```
};
```

In processing any given token object, we first examine the code and then use the value appropriately. Moreover, we can use the token class as an element type in other data structures like stacks and queues. For example, the three kinds of token used in parsing can be created, pushed onto a stack of tokens, and then popped off and output:

```
token number(REAL_VALUE);
token operator(OPERATOR);
token variable(VAR_X);
stack<token> tokens;
token to_output;
number.set_real_value(3.14);
operator.set_operator('+');
variable.set_var_x('X');
tokens.push(number);
tokens.push(operator);
tokens.push(variable);

while (! tokens.empty())
{
      to_output = tokens.pop();
      switch (to_output.code())
      {
            case REAL_VALUE:    cout << to_output.real_value();
                                break;
            case OPERATOR:      cout << to_output.operator();
                                break;
            case VAR_X:         cout << to_output.var_x();
      }
      cout << endl;
}
```

Given this specification of a token type, an appropriate data structure for the postfix expression is a queue whose elements are of type **token**.

The final data structure needed by our program is a stack. Actually, two conceptual stacks are needed: one for operator symbols during the parsing phase and one for values during the evaluation phase. However, by making **token** the class of items in the stack, we can use just one stack structure for both of the conceptual stacks that are needed.

The module specifications for the integral evaluation problem posed by the head of the physics department follow.

1. **Module:** main program
   **Task:** Repeatedly call on modules to obtain input specifications and then evaluate integral.

2. **Module:** obtain_interval
   **Task:** Issue appropriate prompts and read user input. Terminate when $a >= b$.
   **Outputs:** Interval endpoints $a$ and $b$, number_of_rectangles to use in approximating area

3. **Module:** integrate
   **Task:** Compute width of each rectangle as $(b - a)$/number_of_rectangles. Call on module convert to convert infix expression read from standard input to postfix notation. Initialize area to zero. Repeatedly evaluate $f$ at the midpoint of the base of the current rectangle, multiply this by the width of the base, add resulting product to area accumulation.
   **Inputs:** Endpoints $a$ and $b$, and number-of-rectangles for which area is to be accumulated
   **Outputs:** Approximation to area under graph of function entered interactively by user

4. **Module:** infix_to_postfix
   **Task:** Follow algorithm described in Section 5.2 of text.
   **Outputs:** Postfix queue of tokens, delimited by #, corresponding to what user enters from standard input

5. **Module:** get_infix_token {*Note:* This module is responsible for lexical analysis.}
   **Task:** Gets the next token from the standard input stream
   **Inputs:** Infix expression being read from standard input
   **Outputs:** from_infix, a token containing the next token read from standard input
   **Logic:** {*Note:* We assume all tokens separated by one space.}
   Initialize value field of from_infix to zero. {In case token is a real number.}
   Do
      Let ch be next character read from standard input
      switch ch
         1. case ' ' : We are done.
         2. case 'X' : Set from_infix to ch
         3. case '+', '–', '*', '/', '^', '(', ')', '#' : Set from_infix to ch
         4. case '.' : Set a Multiplier to 0.1 for future accumulation.
         5. case '0', '1', '2', .. '9':   if left of decimal
                                   Set value to 10 * value plus ch
                      else
                                   Set value to value + multiplier * ch
         Divide multiplier by 10 for next iteration.
     While ch is not ' '

6. **Module:** infix_priority
   **Task:** See Section 5.2 of text.
   **Inputs:** $t$, a token
   **Outputs:** Infix priority rank of $t$

7. **Module:** in_stack_priority
   **Task:** See Section 5.2 of text.
   **Inputs:** *t,* a token
   **Outputs:** In-stack priority rank of *t*

8. **Module:** eval_f
   **Task:** See evaluation algorithm in Section 5.2 of text.
   **Inputs:** Postfix queue representation of function *f, x,* the real number at
   which *f is to be evaluated*
   **Outputs:** The real number *f*(*x*)

9. **Module:** eval
   **Task:** Select the appropriate C++ operation based on op.
   **Inputs:** v1, v2: the values of two operands and op: character containing
   operator +, −, *, /, ^
   **Outputs:** Numeric result of applying op to v1 and v2.

The complete C++ program for the integral evaluation system follows, with
reference to the module specifications. Also included are graphic documentation
and sample runs to give you a more detailed grasp of how the program functions
in its interaction with a user.

```cpp
// Program file: focus.cpp

// Program to compute area under curve of function entered
// interactively.  A stack is used to convert function
// expression to postfix notation (which is stored in a queue)
// and then to evaluate.
// Valid function expressions can contain the variable X,
// numeric constants, operators +, -, *, /, ^ (for
// exponentiation) and appropriate parentheses.

#include <iostream.h>
#include <iomanip.h>
#include <math.h>
#include <ctype.h>

#include "token.h"
#include "strlib.h"
#include "stack.h"
#include "queue.h"

const char END_TOKEN = '#';

void obtain_interval(float &a, float &b,
     int &number_of_rectangles);

void integrate(float a, float b, int number_of_rectangles,
     float &area);

void infix_to_postfix(queue<token> &postfix);

void get_infix_token(token &from_infix);
```

```cpp
int infix_priority(token t);

int instack_priority(token t);

float eval_f(queue<token> postfix, float x);

float eval(float v1, float v2, char op);

boolean is_op(char ch);

int main()
{
    float a, b, area;
    int number_of_rectangles;

    obtain_interval(a, b, number_of_rectangles);
    cout << fixed << showpoint << setprecision(3);
    while (a < b)
    {
        integrate(a, b, number_of_rectangles, area);
        cout << "Approximation to area is " << setw(10)
            << area << endl;
        cout << endl;
        obtain_interval(a, b, number_of_rectangles);
    }
    return 0;
}
void obtain_interval(float &a, float &b,
    int &number_of_rectangles)
{

    cout << "Enter left and right endpoints "
        << "(left >= right to quit)--> ";
    cin >> a >> b;
    if (a < b)
    {
        cout << "Enter number of rectangles for "
            << "computing area--> ";
        cin >> number_of_rectangles;
    }
}

void integrate(float a, float b, int number_of_rectangles,
    float &area)
{
    stack<token> token_stack;
    queue<token> postfix;
    int count;
    float width, x;

    width = (b - a) / number_of_rectangles;
    count = 0;
```

```
        x = a;
        infix_to_postfix(postfix);

        while (count < number_of_rectangles)
        {
                area = area + eval_f(postfix, x + width / 2.0) * width;
                x = x + width;
                ++count;
        }
}

void infix_to_postfix(queue<token> &postfix)
{
        token bottom_stack(OPERATOR);
        token from_stack, from_infix;
        stack<token> token_stack;
        char ch;

        // Must push END_TOKEN to correspond with
        // algorithm in Section 14.2

        bottom_stack.set_op(END_TOKEN);
        token_stack.push(bottom_stack);
        cout << "Enter function with spaces between tokens, "
             << then <ENTER>";
        cin.get(ch);
        do
        {
                get_infix_token(from_infix);
                if ((from_infix.code() == REAL_VALUE)||
                    (from_infix.code() == VAR_X))
                    //We have an operand -- variable or number.
                    postfix.enqueue (from_infix);
                else if (from_infix.op() == ')')
                {
                    from_stack = token_stack.pop();
                    while (from_stack.op() != '(')
                    {
                            postfix.enqueue (from_stack);
                            from_stack = token_stack.pop();
                    }
                }
                else if (from_infix.op() == END_TOKEN)
                    while (! token_stack.empty())
                    {
                            from_stack = token_stack.pop();
                            postfix.enqueue(from_stack);
                    }
                else
        // We have one of arithmetic operators +, -, *, /, ^ or )
                {
                        from_stack = token_stack.pop();
                        while (instack_priority(from_stack) >=
```

```
                            infix_priority(from_infix))
                {
                        postfix.enqueue(from_stack);
                        from_stack = token_stack.pop();
                }
                token_stack.push(from_stack);
                token_stack.push(from_infix);
        }
    } while (! ((from_infix.code() !== OPERATOR) &&
        (from_infix.op() == END_TOKEN)));
}
void get_infix_token(token &from_infix)
{
        const char SPACE = ' ';
        char ch = ' ';
        float multiplier = 0.1;
        boolean left_of_decimal = TRUE;
        int column = 0;

        do
        {
            ++column
            cin.get(ch);
            if (is_op(ch))
            {
                    from_infix.set_code(OPERATOR);
                    from_infix.set_op(ch);
            }
            else if (isdigit(ch))
            {
                if (column == 1)
                {
                        from_infix.set_code(REAL_VALUE);
                        from_infix.set_real_value(0);
                }
                if (left_of_decimal)
                from_infix.set_real_value
                        (from_infix.real_value() * 10.0 + (ch - '0'));
                else
                {
                        from_infix.set_real_value
                            (from_infix.real_value() * multiplier
                                    + (ch - '0'));
                        multiplier = multiplier / 10.0;
                }
            }
            else if (ch == '.')
            {
                    left_of_decimal = FALSE;
                    multiplier = 0.1;
            }
            else if (ch == 'X')
            {
```

```
                        from_infix.set_code(VAR_X);
                        from_infix.set_var_x(ch);
                }
        } while ((ch != '\n') && (ch != SPACE) && (ch != END_TOKEN));
}

int infix_priority(token t)
{
        int priority = 0;

        switch (t.op())
        {
                case '^':                priority = 3;
                                         break;
                case '*':
                case '/':                priority = 2;
                                         break;
                case '+':
                case '-':                priority = 1;
                                         break;
                case '(':                priority = 4;
                                         break;
                case ')':
                case END_TOKEN:          priority = 0;
        }
        return priority;
}

int instack_priority(token t)
{
        int priority = 0;

        switch (t.op())
        {
                case '^':                priority = 3;
                                         break;
                case '*':
                case '/':                priority = 2;
                                         break;
                case '+':
                case '-':                priority = 1;
                                         break;
                case '(':
                case END_TOKEN:          priority = 0;
        }
        return priority;
}

float eval_f(queue<token> postfix, float x)
{
        token result(REAL_VALUE);
        token t1, t2, t3;
        stack<token> token_stack;
```

```
    // Will push END_TOKEN
    t1 = postfix.dequeue();

    // Put token back into queue for next call to eval_f
    postfix.enqueue(t1);

    // We're done when encounter operator that is
    // END_TOKEN.

    while (! ((t1.code() == OPERATOR) && (t1.op() == END_TOKEN)))
    {
        if (t1.code() != OPERATOR)
            if (t1.code() == REAL_VALUE)
                token_stack.push(t1);
            else
            {
                t1.set_code(REAL_VALUE);
                t1.set_real_value(x);
                token_stack.push(t1);
            }
        else
        {
            t2 = token_stack.pop();
            t3 = token_stack.pop();
            result.set_real_value(eval(t3.real_value(),
                t2.real_value(),
                t1.op()));
            token_stack.push(result);
        }
        t1 = postfix.dequeue();
        postfix.enqueue(t1);
    }
    result = token_stack.pop();
    return result.real_value();
}

float eval(float v1, float v2, char op)
{
    float result = 1;

    switch (op)
    {
        case '+':   result = v1 + v2;
                    break;
        case '-':   result = v1 - v2;
                    break;
        case '*':   result = v1 * v2;
                    break;
        case '/':   result = v1 / v2;
                    break;
        case '^':   result = pow(v1, v2);
                    break;
    }
```

```
    return result;
}

boolean is_op(char ch)
{
    return (ch == '+') || (ch == '-') || (ch == '*')
           || (ch == '/') ||(ch == '^') || (ch == '(')
           || (ch == ')') || (ch == END_TOKEN);
}
```

Sample runs:

```
Enter left and right endpoints (left >= right to quit)-> 0 3
Enter number of rectangles for computing area-> 10
Enter function with spaces between tokens, then <ENTER>
3
Approximation to area is 9.000

Enter left and right endpoints (left >= right to quit)-> 0 3
Enter number of rectangles for computing area-> 10
Enter function with spaces between tokens, then <ENTER>
X ^ 2
Approximation to area is 8.978

Enter left and right endpoints (left >= right to quit)-> 0 3
Enter number of rectangles for computing area-> 100
Enter function with spaces between tokens, then <ENTER>
X ^ 2
Approximation to area is 9.000

Enter left and right endpoints (left >= right to quit)-> 0 1
Enter number of rectangles for computing area-> 100
Enter function with spaces between tokens, then <ENTER>
( X + 2 ) ^ 3 / ( X + 1 )
Approximation to area is 10.526

Enter left and right endpoints (left >= right to quit)-> 0 0
```

## RUNNING, DEBUGGING AND TESTING HINTS

1. In applications in which the size to which a stack or queue may grow is hard to predict, use a linked list to implement the ADT. That way, you can take advantage of C++'s dynamic memory management to avoid having to worry about a full data structure.
2. Many scientific and mathematical application programs can be enhanced by allowing users to enter function definitions at run time. This chapter's Focus on Program Design section provides an example of how such run-time definitions of a function can be done.
3. When debugging simulations, use a random number sequence that remains the same over different runs of the program. Without such a sequence, your program will behave differently on separate runs even though you provide it with identical inputs. This is because you are getting a different pattern of random numbers. Appendix 6 indicates how you can ensure a fixed sequence of random numbers from one run of the program to the next.

# SUMMARY

## Key Terms

| | | |
|---|---|---|
| activation record | numerical analysis | ready queue |
| blocked queue | parsing | rear pointer |
| first-in/first-out (FIFO) | pop | semaphores |
| fixed part | postfix | simulation |
| front pointer | prefix | stack |
| infix | priority queue | stack priority |
| infix priority | push | token |
| last-in/first-out (LIFO) | queue | union |
| lexical analysis | random number generator | variant part |

## Key Concepts

◆ Conceptually, a stack is simpler than a queue since all additions and deletions are limited to one end of the structure, the top. For this reason, a stack is also known as a last-in/first-out (LIFO) list. Like a queue, a stack may be implemented using either an array or a linked list.

◆ The simplicity of the stack as an abstract structure belies the importance of its application. Stacks play a crucial role in the parsing done by language compilers.

◆ Parsing, as we have studied it in this chapter, involves the conversion of an expression from infix to postfix notation. In infix notation, an algebraic operator is located between its two operands. In postfix notation, the operator follows its two operands.

◆ Expressions in postfix notation do not require parentheses to override the standard hierarchy of algebraic operations.

◆ Stacks process function calls when a program executes.

◆ A queue is a first-in/first-out (FIFO) data structure used in processing of data such as job scheduling in a large university computer environment. There are two basic pointers, front and rear, associated with this structure. New data items are added to the rear of the queue, and the data item that is about to be processed is removed from the front of the queue.

◆ The relative advantages and disadvantages of three implementations of queues—array, circular array, and linked list—are summarized in the following table:

| Implementation | Advantages | Disadvantages |
|---|---|---|
| Array | A record of queue entries remains even after they have been removed. | Static allocation of storage limits overall queue size. Array locations cannot be reused once entries are removed from queue. |
| Circular array | Array locations can be reused once entries are removed from the queue. | Static allocation of storage limits overall queue size. |
| Linked list | With C++ pointer variables, the queue can grow dynamically to take full advantage of all space available in C++'s heap. | Could be less space efficient than array implementations since each node in queue must include a pointer field as well as data fields. |

◆ Primary applications of queues are in the areas of operating systems and computer simulation of events.

**PROGRAMMING PROBLEMS AND PROJECTS**

1. Write a program that will parse infix expressions into prefix form.

2. Write a program to call for input of a decimal number and convert it to its binary equivalent using the method described in the following flowchart. Note that this method produces the binary digits for the given number in reverse order. Use a stack to get them printed in the correct order.

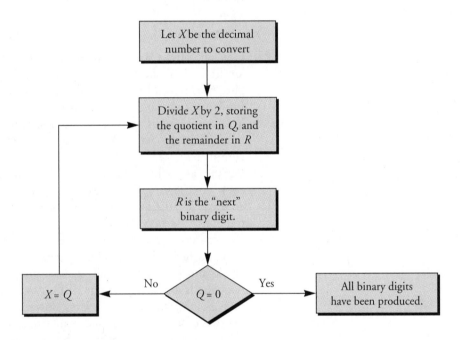

3. Programming Problem 2 for Chapter 4, you developed a passenger list processing system for the various flights of Wing-and-a-Prayer Airlines. Wing-and-a-Prayer management would now like you to extend this system so that it processes logical combinations of flight numbers. For example, the command

`LIST 1 OR 2`

should list all passengers whose name appears on the flight 1 list or the flight 2 list. Your program should also accept the logical operators **AND** and **NOT** and allow parenthesized logical expressions obeying the standard logical hierarchy

NOT
AND
OR

4. A tax form may be thought of as a sequence of items, each of which is either a number or defined by an arbitrary mathematical formula involving other items in the sequence. To assist them in their tax-planning strategy, top management at the Fly-by-Night credit card company desires a program that would allow them to enter interactively numbers or formulas associated with given lines of a tax form. Once all

such lines have been defined, users of the program may redefine the number or formula associated with a particular line, and all other lines dependent on that one should be appropriately updated. Note that, since formulas may be entered interactively, your program will have to use a stack to evaluate them. You will in effect have written a small-scale spreadsheet program.

5. Write a program that will accept commands of the following form:

- `INPUT <variable name>`
- `<variable name> = infix expression involving variables names and arithmetic operators +, -, *, /`
- `PRINT <variable name>`
- `GO`

These commands are to be stored in an array of strings until the **GO** command is entered. Once the **GO** command is entered, your program should execute the previously stored commands. "Execute" here means the following:

- **For an INPUT command**: Send a question mark to the terminal and allow the user to enter a real number; this real number is then stored in the variable name.

- **For an assignment statement**: Parse the expression into postfix form and then evaluate it, storing the results in the variable name on the left of the equality sign.

- **For a PRINT instruction**: Write to the terminal the numerical contents of the specified variable name.

- To make things relatively easy you may assume a syntax that
  Allows variable names consisting of one uppercase alphabetical character.
- Allows only one variable name following the commands for **INPUT** or **PRINT**.
- Allows one blank space after the commands for **INPUT** and **PRINT** and no blank spaces anywhere else.

For an additional challenge, enable your program to handle successfully the exponentiation operator ^ within assignment statement expressions. The following example should illustrate the need for care in handling this exponentiation operator:

$3^{2^3} = 3^8$, not $9^3$

6. This problem is an extension of Problem 5 for a "compiler" for a primitive programming language. Write a program that will accept commands of the following form:

- `INPUT <variable name>`
- `PRINT <variable name>`
- `<variable name> = infix arithmetic expression involving variable names and arithmetic operators +, -, *, /, ^`
- `GOTO <line>` { `ALWAYS, or`

  `IF infix logical expression involving variable names and operators +, -, *, /, ^, & (for AND),| (for OR), !(for NOT), <, >, =` }
- `STOP`
- `RUN`

These commands are to be stored in an array of strings until the **RUN** command is entered. Upon encountering the **RUN** command, your program should execute the previously stored commands. "Execute" here means the following:

- **For an INPUT command**: Send a question mark to the terminal and allow the user to enter a real number, which is stored in the variable name.
- **For a PRINT command**: Write to the terminal the numerical contents of the specified variable name.
- **For an assignment command**: Parse the expression into postfix form and then evaluate it. Store the result in the variable name on the left of the equality sign.
- **For a GOTO command**: Branch to the line number specified when the **ALWAYS** condition follows the line number or when the infix expression that follows the **if** evaluates to true. Here "line number" refers to the relative position of the line in the sequence of lines that were entered prior to the **Run** command. The first line number in this sequence is "00".
- **For a STOP command**: Halt execution.

To make things relatively easy, you may assume a syntax that

- Specifies that one and only one blank space follows **INPUT**, **PRINT**, **GOTO**, and line number. No other blanks appear anywhere.
- Allows only one variable name to follow **INPUT** or **PRINT**.
- Only allows variable names consisting of one uppercase alphabetical character.
- Only allows line numbers consisting of two digits: 00 through 99.

The usual hierarchy for operators is assumed.

7. Modify the program in the Focus on Program Design section so that it also integrates expressions involving the functions sin, cos, tan, exp, and ln. Test your modified program by having it evaluate the following integrals:

   **a.** $\sin(X * 2) + \cos X / 2$ between 0 and 1
   **b.** $3 * (X + 4) \wedge 2 + \tan(X / 2)$ between 0 and 1
   **c.** $3 * (X + 4) \wedge 2 + \tan X / 2$ between 0 and 1
   **d.** $\exp \ln X \wedge 3$ between 1 and 3
   **e.** $\exp \ln(X \wedge 3)$ between 1 and 3

8. If you have access to a graphics library in your version of C++, write a program that allows a user to define interactively a function and then displays a graph of the function between two specified endpoints.

9. Develop a program to simulate the processing of batch jobs by a computer system. The scheduling of these jobs should be handled via a queue (or priority queue for more of a challenge). Examples of commands that your program should be able to process are

| Command | Purpose |
|---------|---------|
| **ADD** | To add an entry to queue. |
| **DELETE** | To take an item out of the queue. |
| **STATUS** | To report on items currently in queue. |

10. In Chapter 8 you developed a program to keep track of a bank's records. Now the bank has asked you to develop a program to simulate the arrival of customers in a waiting line at the bank. Factors to consider are the average time it takes to service one customer, the average number of customers that arrive in a given time period, and the number of service windows maintained by the bank. These factors should be provided as input to your program. Statistics such as the length of time the average customer has to spend in the waiting line could be very helpful in the bank's future planning.

11. Here is a problem typically encountered in text formatting applications.

    *Given a file of text, that text delimited by special bracketing symbols [ and ] is to be considered a footnote. Footnotes, when encountered, are not to be printed as normal text but are instead stored in a footnote queue. Then, when the special symbol # is encountered, all footnotes currently in the queue are printed and the queue should be returned to an empty state.*

    What you learn in solving this problem will allow you to make good use of string storage techniques discussed in earlier chapters.

12. To improve their services, the Fly-by-Night credit card company (Problem 3, Chapter 4) has decided to give incentives to their customers for prompt payment. Customers who pay their bills two weeks before the due date receive top priority and a 5% discount. Customers who pay their bills within one week of the due date receive next priority and a 1% discount. Third priority is given to customers who pay their bills on or within two days after the due date. The customers who pay their bills thereafter are assigned the lowest priority. Write a program to set up a priority queue to access customer records accordingly.

13. The Bay Area Brawlers professional football team (Problem 4, Chapter 4) has been so successful in recent weeks that the team management is considering the addition of several new ticket windows at the team's stadium. However, before investing a sizable amount of money in such an improvement, they would like to simulate the operation of ticket sales with a variety of ticket window configurations. Develop a computer program that allows input of such data as number of ticket windows, average number of fans arriving each hour as game time approaches, and average length of time to process a ticket sale. Output from your program should include statistics such as the average waiting-line length each hour as game time approaches and the amount of time the average fan had to wait in line before having his or her ticket request processed. Use queues to represent each of the waiting lines.

14. Consider the design for an implementation of the radix sort algorithm and its associated bin (sublist) structure that was discussed in Chapter 4's Focus on Program Design section. Note that queues could provide an alternative implementation for the bin structure needed by radix sort. What queue implementation would provide the most space-efficient bin structure for radix sort? Why? Develop a complete radix sort program that uses queues to implement the bins needed by the algorithm and then accesses these bins *only* through the defined ADT operations for a queue. Is this implementation of radix sort more or less time efficient than that described in Chapter 4's Focus on Program Design section? Justify your answer in a written memorandum.

15. As Director of Computer Operations for Wing-and-a-Prayer Airlines, you receive the following memorandum. Design and write a simulation program according to the specifications in the memorandum.

```
┌─────────────────────────────────────────────────────────────┐
│                       MEMORANDUM                            │
│                 Wing-and-a-Prayer Airlines                  │
│                                                             │
│     TO: Director of Computer Operations                     │
│   FROM: President, Wing-and-a-Prayer Airlines               │
│   DATE: September 30, 1996                                  │
│     RE: Wasted Fuel and Time                                │
│                                                             │
│   Wing-and-a-Prayer Airlines is becoming increasingly       │
│   concerned about the amount of fuel being wasted as its    │
│   planes wait to land at and take off from world-famous     │
│   O'Hair Airport. Could you please help us write a program  │
│   to simulate the operation of one day's activity at O'Hair │
│   and report on the times spent waiting to land and take    │
│   off for each Wing-and-a-Prayer flight? Input data to the  │
│   program should include                                    │
│                                                             │
│   ■ Average number of Wing-and-a-Prayer arrivals each hour  │
│   ■ Average number of other airline arrivals each hour      │
│   ■ Average number of Wing-and-a-Prayer departures each     │
│     hour                                                     │
│   ■ Average number of other airline departures each hour    │
│   ■ Number of available runways                             │
│   ■ Average time a runway is in use for an arrival          │
│   ■ Average time a runway is in use for a departure         │
│                                                             │
│   By appropriately adjusting these parameters, we hope to   │
│   do some valuable ''what-if'' analyses regarding the time  │
│   spent waiting for a runway by our arrivals and            │
│   departures.                                               │
└─────────────────────────────────────────────────────────────┘
```

16. If an arithmetic expression is written in prefix notation, then there is no need to use parentheses to specify the order of operators. For this reason, some compilers translate infix expressions (such as 2 + 8) to prefix notation (+ 2 8) first and then evaluate the prefix string. Write a program that will read prefix expressions and then compute and display the value of the indicated arithmetic expression. Assume that the operands are single-digit positive integers separated by blanks. The operators can be +, −, *, and /, also separated by blanks and having their usual meanings of add, subtract, multiply, and divide.

17. Implement the following robustness enhancements for the program in this chapter's Focus on Program Design section.

    a. Make the **get_infix_token** module more robust by allowing the user to separate individual tokens with an arbitrary number of zero or more spaces.

    b. Make the **get_infix_token** module more robust by guarding against input of an invalid arithmetic operator.

    c. Make the **get_infix_token** module more robust by guarding against an invalid character in a stream of characters intended to be a real number. When such an invalid character is detected, allow the user to recover from the point of error rather than forcing the user to retype the entire line.

18. This chapter's Note of Interest on "Computer Simulations: Blessing or Curse?" cites two issues of the *Communications of the ACM* that have been dedicated to the topic of simulation. Using these two issues as a starting point, research and prepare a written report on computer simulation. Your report could discuss any or all of the following:

a. Examples of disciplines and industries in which simulation has been used to great advantage.

b. Limitations and inaccuracies that arise in modeling a system by computer simulation. Techniques that can be used to measure and monitor such inaccuracies.

c. The reliance of many simulation programs on the effective generation of random numbers.

d. The potential danger in relying on the results of simulation programs without examining the validity of their underlying models.

19. This chapter's Focus on Program Design section demonstrated how a computer program can be used to solve a mathematical problem in interactive fashion. In particular, the type of problem solved by this program is the evaluation of integrals. Explore other types of mathematical problems that can be solved interactively by software systems available at your school. (The *Mathematica* program from Wolfram Research is one example of such a system available at many universities.) Prepare a report on the results of your explorations. In keeping with the theme of this chapter's Focus on Program Design section, be sure that your report includes a discussion of the types of mathematical expressions that can be parsed and evaluated by such systems.

# 6 Recursion

*It's deja vu all over again.*
  Lawrence Peter (Yogi) Berra

*Research is the process of going
up alleys to see if they are
blind.*

  Marston Bates

Many problems are suited to iterative control by methods such as **while**, **do**, and **for** loops. Some of these problems can more easily be solved by designing functions that call themselves. In computer science this form of self-reference is called *recursion*. We are now ready to embark on a detailed study of recursive problem solving.

In this chapter, we first examine the essentials of recursive functions. Now that we are familiar with stack operations, we will also be able to explain how recursion is implemented. The "invisible" data structure underlying *recursive functions* is a stack used by the system to process the call-and-return pattern of functions in a program (Section 5.1). By examining the role of this system stack more closely, you will build confidence in your ability to express algorithms recursively. In time, you will use this technique without hesitation in your problem solving.

Then we will begin to use recursion to explore problems for which nonrecursive solutions would be exceedingly difficult to fathom. We hope that you will be amazed at the ease with which recursion handles such problems. We will demonstrate that recursion is a natural and elegant way to solve many complex problems. We will also begin to explore the price paid for this elegance: the compactness of a recursive solution to a complex problem is not necessarily an accurate statement of its time or space efficiency.

Finally, we will use recursion to develop a problem-solving methodology known as *trial-and-error*, or nondeterministic, *backtracking*. In theory this technique can solve a large variety of problems. Unfortunately, in practice, the technique is so computationally expensive that it can only be used to solve small instances of such problems in a reasonable amount of time.

## 6.1 Controlling Simple Iteration with Recursion

Any recursive algorithm must have a well-defined stopping state, or *termination condition*. Without careful logical control by means of such conditions, recursive functions can fall prey to looping in endless circles. To illustrate this, let us suppose that we have access to an output device known as a pen plotter. Such a device is equipped with a pen held by a mechanical hand that is under control of the computer.

Typical functions to manipulate the pen could include

| Function | Action |
|----------|--------|
| `line(n)` | Draw a line of length $n$ in the current direction. |
| `right_turn(d)` | Alter current direction by rotating $d$ degrees in clockwise direction. |

Such functions are not unlike those found in the Logo programming language or the "turtle" graphics toolkits that accompany many popular C++ compilers. If you have access to such a compiler, you may wish to explore developing some recursive graphic figures.

If we assume that the pen is initially set to draw a line toward the north—the top of the plotting page—then the following sequence of instructions

```
line(10);
right_turn(90);
line(10);
right_turn(90);
line(10);
right_turn(90);
line(10);
```

will clearly draw a square with sides of length 10.

Let us now try to predict what will happen when the following recursive function draw is invoked by the initial call **draw(1)**.

```
void draw(int side)
{
        line(side);
        right_turn(90);
        draw(side + 3)        // Recursive call
};
```

The initial call **draw(1)** will result in a line of length 1 in a northerly direction. We then rotate the pen toward the east and, via a recursive call, generate a line of length 4. This is followed by a rotation to the south and a new invocation for a line of length 7. The emerging pattern should now be clear; the resulting right-angled spiral is shown in Figure 6.1.

Unfortunately, our spiral-producing function has tumbled into a vicious circle loop of self-reference. There is currently no way to turn off the *recursive calls* made to draw. Consider what happens, however, if we provide ourselves with a *recursive termination condition* (or recursive out) as in the following new version of **draw**:

```
void draw(int side)
{
    if (side <= 34)           // Recursive termination condition
    {
        line(side);
        right_turn(90);
        draw(side + 3)        // Recursive call
    }
}
```

◆ FiGURE 6.1

Runaway recursive spiral

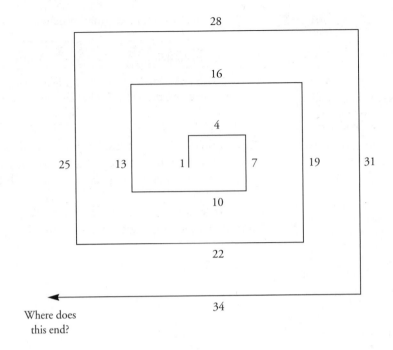

Where does
this end?

Now after drawing the line of length 34 in Figure 6.1, our **draw** function invokes itself once more, passing 37 for the parameter **side**. Since the recursive termination condition is now FALSE, no line of length 37 will be drawn. More importantly, no further recursive invocation of **draw** will be made. Hence, we return immediately from the call to **draw** with **side** being 37. Moreover, that return triggers returns (in reverse order) from all the previous invocations of **draw**, eventually ending up at the instruction following our initial call; that is, **draw(1)**.

The important point to stress here is that, to use recursion appropriately, we must use a recursive termination condition to avoid an infinite series of recursive calls. If we were to view each recursive call as a descent one level deeper into an algorithm's logic, we in effect must use a recursive termination condition to allow a corresponding ascent back to the level of the first call to the function. This concept is highlighted in Figure 6.2.

## Linked Lists as Recursive Data Structures

In Section 6.1 we defined the linked list ADT. We can now reformulate that definition from a recursive perspective. The key to such a perspective is the realization that the pointer leading from each linked list node references another linked list. More formally:

> **Linked list:** A linked list is a pointer that is either NULL (the recursive termination condition signaling an empty list) or references a node designated as the head node. The head node contains a data field and a pointer that satisfies the criteria for being a linked list.

Though an English composition teacher may find fault with our defining a linked list in terms of itself, our new definition is nonetheless completely free of ambiguity. For instance, to verify that the list in Figure 6.3 is a linked list, we note the following:

◆ **FIGURE 6.2**

Unwinding from descent
through recursive calls

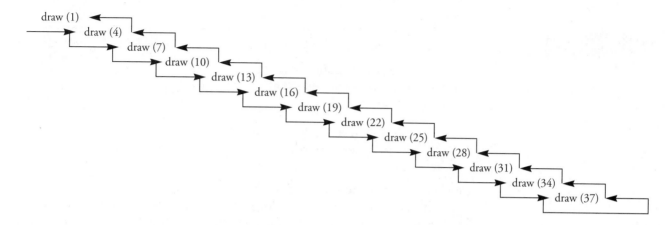

◆ **FIGURE 6.3**

Recursive view of a linked
list

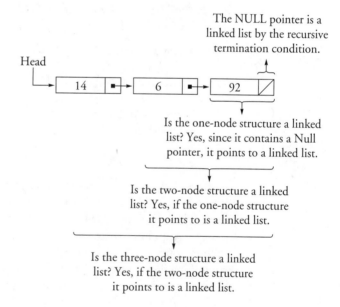

The NULL pointer is a
linked list by the recursive
termination condition.

Is the one-node structure a linked
list? Yes, since it contains a Null
pointer, it points to a linked list.

Is the two-node structure a linked
list? Yes, if the one-node structure
it points to is a linked list.

Is the three-node structure a linked
list? Yes, if the two-node structure
it points to is a linked list.

**1.** The head node in the three-item structure contains a pointer to an embedded two-item structure, which we must verify as a linked list.

**2.** The head node in the two-item structure contains a pointer to an embedded one-item structure.

**3.** The head node in the one-node structure contains a NULL pointer.

**4.** By the recursive termination condition, a NULL pointer meets the criteria for being a linked list.

**5.** Hence the one-node structure in step 3 contains a pointer to a linked list and meets the criteria for being a linked list.

**6.** Similarly, we climb up the recursive ladder to verify that the two-node and, consequently, the three-node structures in steps 1 and 2 meet the criteria for being linked lists.

Not only does our recursive definition unambiguously specify the linked list ADT, but it also provides a natural way to implement linked list operations by recursive functions. Consider the following example.

---

EXAMPLE 6.1

A linked list is implemented by C++ pointer variables in the following declarations:

```
typedef struct node;
typedef node *linked_list;
struct node
{
    element data;
    linked_list next;
};
```

Develop a recursive implementation of the traverse operation.

The implementation literally flows from our recursive definition of the linked list structure. That is, if the list we are traversing is empty there is nothing to do; otherwise we must process the data in the head node and recursively traverse the linked list referenced by the **next** field in the head node. This logic is embodied in the following C++ function:

```
void traverse(linked_list list, void (*process (element &data))
{
    if (list != NULL)
    {
        process(list->data);
        traverse(list->next, process);
    }
}
```

A trace of the recursive function **traverse** for the list of Figure 6.3 is given in Figure 6.4. This trace shows that the function is initially called with a list pointer to the node containing 14. The data are processed, and the first recursive call then passes in a pointer to the node containing 6. The data item 6 is processed, and a pointer to the node containing 92 is recursively passed to the function. The node containing 92 is processed, and a NULL pointer is recursively passed to the function. Since the recursive termination condition (**list == NULL**) is now met, we unwind

◆ FIGURE 6.4
Trace of recursive function **traverse** on the linked list of Figure 6.3

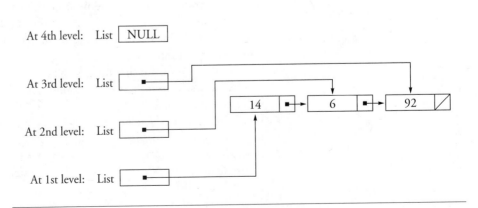

from the series of recursive calls. As we return to each prior recursive level, there is nothing left to do since the recursive call is the last operation at that level.

A recursive function is called *tail recursive* if only one recursive call appears in the function and that recursive call is the last operation performed at that procedural level. (That is, nothing else must be done after returning from a deeper recursive level.) The `traverse` function of Example 6.1 is clearly tail recursive. Typically, such a tail-recursive function can be easily recast in the form of a nonrecursive function using a `while` or `do` control structure. We have already seen how to do this for `traverse` in Chapter 4.

## How Is Recursion Implemented?

As we begin to examine recursive algorithms that are not tail recursive, we will also need to understand in detail *how* a computer language implements recursion. Here again we encounter the abstraction/implementation duality we have emphasized throughout the book. Recursion is a powerful conceptual tool. But unless you understand details of how recursion is implemented, your use of it will be limited to an intuitive approach that often employs a trial-and-error strategy to reach a solution.

In Section 5.1, we indicated that the stack is an essential data structure in a compiler's implementation of function calls. The role of a system stack being manipulated by the function calls in your program becomes even more crucial as we use recursion. To illustrate this, let us consider a problem more computationally oriented than our previous graphics and linked list examples. $N$ factorial, denoted $N!$, is defined by

$$N! = N \times (N - 1) \times (N - 2) \times \ldots \times 2 \times 1$$

That is, $N!$ is the product of the first $N$ integers. We note that an alternate way of defining $N!$ is by means of using $(N - 1)!$

$$N! = \begin{array}{l} 1 \text{ if } N = 1 \text{ or } N = 0 \\ N * (N - 1)! \text{ otherwise} \end{array}$$

Notice that this alternative definition is a *recursive definition* because it uses the notion of factorial to define factorial. Despite this circularity, we have a perfectly valid definition because of the recursive termination condition in the special definition of 1!.

To see how recursion works for factorial computation, think of the preceding definition as a series of clues that will eventually allow us to unravel the mystery of how to compute $N!$. That is, to compute $N!$, the recursive definition really tells us to

**1.** Remember what $N$ is.
**2.** Go compute $(N - 1)!$.
**3.** Once we've computed $(N - 1)!$, multiply that by $N$ to get our final answer.

Of course, when we use the definition to determine how to compute $(N - 1)!$, we find out that we must, in turn, compute $(N - 2)!$. Computing $(N - 2)!$ will involve finding $(N - 3)!$. This downward spiral will eventually end with 1!, allowing us to begin the actual series of multiplications that will bring us to the appropriate answer. Figure 6.5 illustrates the logic of the recursive method for computing $N$ factorial. In particular, if $N$ were 4, the sequence of recursive invocations of the definition and resulting computations would be as shown in Figure 6.6.

The program in Example 6.2 calls a recursively defined `factorial` function. The associated run indicates the behavior of the program for an input of 4.

◆ FIGURE 6.5
Recursive computation of N!

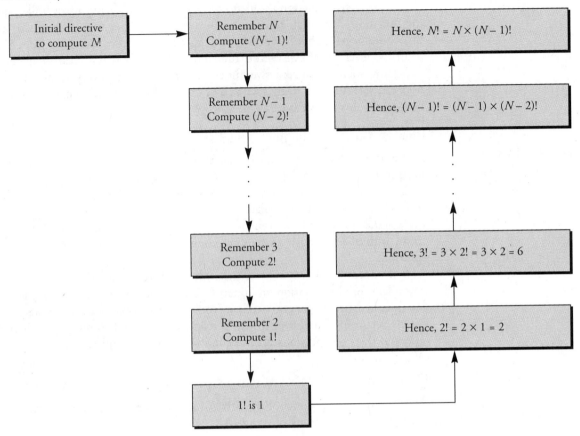

◆ FIGURE 6.6
Recursive computation of 4!

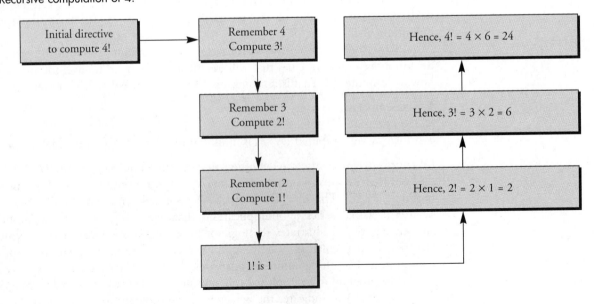

## EXAMPLE 6.2

```cpp
// Program file: factor.cpp

#include <iostream.h>
#include <iomanip.h>

int indent = 0;

int factorial(int n);

int main()
{
    int m;

    cout << "ENTER NUMBER for FACTORIAL COMPUTATION-> ";
    cin >> m;
    cout << factorial(m) << endl;
    return 0;
}

int factorial(int n)
{
    int result;

    cout << setw(indent) << "" << "ENTERING FACTORIAL WITH N = " << n << endl;
    if ((n == 1) || (n == 0))
    {
        cout << setw(indent) << "" << "LEAVING FACTORIAL WITH N = " << n;
        cout << ", FACTORIAL(N) = " << 1 << endl;
        --indent;
        return 1;
    }
    else
    {
        ++indent;
        result = n * factorial(n - 1);
        cout << setw(indent) << "" << "LEAVING FACTORIAL WITH N = " << n;
        cout << ", FACTORIAL(N) = " << result << endl;
        --indent;
        return result;
    }
}
```

A sample run for the preceding code follows.

```
ENTER NUMBER for FACTORIAL COMPUTATION->4
  ENTERING FACTORIAL WITH N = 4
   ENTERING FACTORIAL WITH N = 3
    ENTERING FACTORIAL WITH N = 2
     ENTERING FACTORIAL WITH N = 1
     LEAVING FACTORIAL WITH N = 1, FACTORIAL(N) = 1
    LEAVING FACTORIAL WITH N = 2, FACTORIAL(N) = 2
```

```
LEAVING FACTORIAL WITH N = 3, FACTORIAL(N) = 6
LEAVING FACTORIAL WITH N = 4, FACTORIAL(N) = 24
24
```

The output statements used on entry to and exit from function **factorial** in Example 6.2 are not necessary but have been included to demonstrate the precise call and return sequence triggered by the initial call of **factorial(4)** in the main program. It is crucial to note that the output from output statements implies that we must in some sense have multiple copies of the variable $N$, one copy for each descent to a recursively deeper level. As we shall see, a stack keeps track of these multiple copies of $N$ in the appropriate fashion.

It is also important to emphasize that function **factorial** would not be tail recursive even if the output statements were removed. This is because the recursive call to factorial is not the last operation performed by the algorithm. After a return from the call to factorial $(N - 1)$, we must multiply by $N$. It is this multiplication that is the final operation performed. The fact that we multiply by $N$ after returning from a recursive call indicates that, for algorithms that are not tail recursive, we must have some means of preserving the values of parameters and local variables at each level of the recursive execution of the algorithm.

The comments **// Return Point 1** and **// Return Point 2** in Example 6.2 will allow us to trace the role played by a stack as this program is run. We have already alluded to the existence of a general system stack onto which return addresses are pushed each time a function or function call is made. Let us now explain it more fully. Each time a function or function call is made, an item called a *stack frame* or activation record will be pushed onto the system stack. The data in this stack frame consist of the return address and a copy of each local variable and parameter for the function. Figure 6.7 illustrates how stack frames are pushed and popped from the system stack when **factorial(4)** is invoked. Return addresses have been indicated by referring to the appropriate comments in the C++ code.

Although function **factorial** of Example 6.2 provides an illustration of an algorithm that is not tail recursive, you could still validly argue that the computation of $N!$ could be achieved more easily by a nonrecursive, iterative loop structure. To sense the real power and elegance of recursion, we must begin to explore algorithms that more subtly manipulate the stack frames hidden below the surface of recursive processing. These stack frames provide us with a "free" stack data structure; that is, a structure that we need not declare formally and that we control completely by the recursive calling pattern of our algorithm.

◆ FIGURE 6.7
Sequence of pushes and
pops in computing 4!

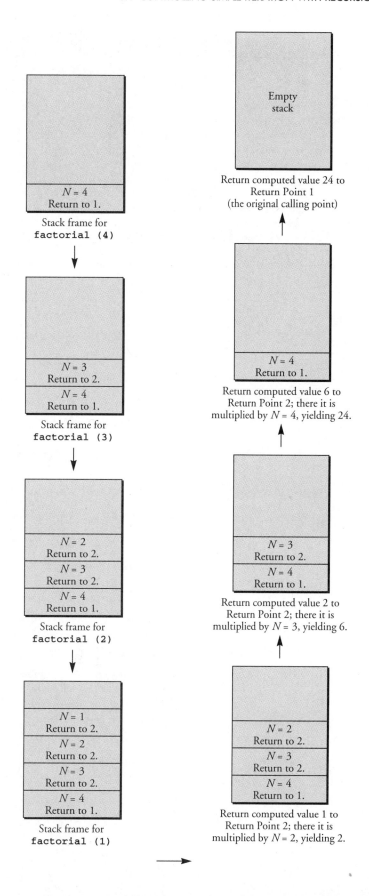

$N = 4$
Return to 1.

Stack frame for
**factorial (4)**

$N = 3$
Return to 2.
$N = 4$
Return to 1.

Stack frame for
**factorial (3)**

$N = 2$
Return to 2.
$N = 3$
Return to 2.
$N = 4$
Return to 1.

Stack frame for
**factorial (2)**

$N = 1$
Return to 2.
$N = 2$
Return to 2.
$N = 3$
Return to 2.
$N = 4$
Return to 1.

Stack frame for
**factorial (1)**

Empty
stack

Return computed value 24 to
Return Point 1
(the original calling point)

$N = 4$
Return to 1.

Return computed value 6 to
Return Point 2; there it is
multiplied by $N = 4$, yielding 24.

$N = 3$
Return to 2.
$N = 4$
Return to 1.

Return computed value 2 to
Return Point 2; there it is
multiplied by $N = 3$, yielding 6.

$N = 2$
Return to 2.
$N = 3$
Return to 2.
$N = 4$
Return to 1.

Return computed value 1 to
Return Point 2; there it is
multiplied by $N = 2$, yielding 2.

## A NOTE OF INTEREST

### Language Definition

The syntax of most computer languages can be recursively defined. This is of tremendous importance in the writing of compilers, most of which rely heavily on stacks and recursion to parse source programs.

A broader question than the definition and parsing of programming languages is the ability of the computer to process natural languages such as English. Researchers in the field of artificial intelligence are attempting to use more general recursive techniques to define the syntax of natural languages and, consequently, program the computer to cope with this more complex type of language. To date, their work has met with success only in highly restricted domains of natural language such as that used to express word problems in algebra or interact with databases in a structured query language. Despite these present limitations, research in language definition and the consequent processing of that language by a computer should be one of the most intensely explored fields within computer science in the future.

**EXERCISES 6.1**

1. Stand between two parallel mirrors and see how recursion works for you.

2. Consider the following pair of functions to compute $N!$

```
int factorial(int n)
{
     return fact_helper(n, 1);
}

int fact_helper(int n, int result)
{

     if ((n ==0) || (n == 1))
          return result;
     else
          return fact_helper(n - 1, n * result);
}
```

Is `fact_helper` tail recursive? Will it work? Explain why or why not.

3. Each of the following functions offers a slight variation on the traverse function developed in Example 6.1. For each function, indicate what output would be produced if the function were called initially with the linked list of Figure 6.3 and the process function merely printed the data field of each node. If the function would crash with a run-time error for the data of Figure 6.3 or any other test case, explain why.

```
a. void traverse(linked_list list, void (*process) (element &data))
   {
        if (list != NULL)
        {
             traverse(list->next, process);
             process(list->data);
        }
   }
```

**b.** 
```
void traverse(linked_list list, void (*process) (element &data))
{
        process(list->data);
        if (list->next != NULL)
            traverse(list->next, process);
}
```
**c.** 
```
void traverse(linked_list list, void (*process) (element &data))
{
        if (list->next != NULL)
        {
            process(list->data);
            traverse(list->next, process);
        }
}
```

**4.** Which of the functions in Exercise 3 are tail recursive?

**5.** The following programs are intended to read a string character by character, put each character on the system stack, and then print the string of characters in reverse order. Which one(s) actually achieve the intent? Which one(s) don't? Why not? What will be the output of each program for input of 'MADAM'?

**a.** 
```
// Print out a string in reverse order to check if palindrome
#include <iostream.h>
void reverse();
int main()
{
        reverse;
        return 0;
}
// Keep recursively stacking characters until end of string.
// Then print it out in reverse by unstacking.

void reverse()
{
        char ch;        // Here ch is locally declared
        cin.get(ch);
        if (ch != '\n')
        {
                reverse();
                cout.put(ch);
        }
        else
                cout.put('\n');
}
```
**b.** 
```
// Print out a string in reverse order to check if palindrome
#include <iostream.h>
char ch;                  // Here ch is globally declared
void reverse();
int main()
{
        reverse;
        return 0;
}
```

```
// Keep recursively stacking characters until end of string.
// Then print it out in reverse by unstacking.

void reverse()
{
        cin.get(ch);
        if (ch != '\n')
        {
                reverse();
                cout.put(ch);
        }
        else
                cout.put('\n');
}
```

6. Given the declarations for the linked list structure in Example 6.1, write a recursive function to search the list for a particular item and return a pointer to the item in the list if it is found. If the item is not found in the list, a NULL pointer should be returned.

7. Suppose that **number_array** is declared as follows:

```
typedef int number_array[100];
```

Study the following function and determine what it computes. (*Hint:* Try to trace it for several small instances of the array and $N$ values.)

```
int compute(number_array a, int n)
{
        if (n == 0)
                return a[n];
        else if (a[n] < compute(a, n - 1))
                return a[n];
        else
                return compute(a, n - 1);
}
```

8. Write a recursive function of two integer arguments $M$ and $N$, both greater than or equal to zero. The function should return $M^N$.

9. Write a recursive function of two integer arguments $M$ and $N$, $M > 1$ and $N > 0$. The function should return the integer log of $N$ to the base $M$. This is defined to be the least integer $L$ such that $M^{L+1} > N$. (*Hint:* Though your function only receives two arguments, embed within it an auxiliary function of three arguments—$M$, $N$, and $L$. Call on the auxiliary function initially with $L = 0$; the auxiliary function is then called recursively.)

10. Given the declaration of **number_array** in Exercise 7, write a function **product** that receives two arguments, one of type **number_array** and another argument **N** that indicates the logical size of **number_array**. Remember that the logical size of an array is the number of indices that store well-defined data items. Function **product** should return the product of the entries in the array from indices 1 through $N$.

11. Insert tracer output instructions at strategic points and use them to debug the following version of a function, which attempts to compute factorials recursively. After

you've debugged the function, write a statement in which you explain the behavior of the function as originally coded and also why the function did not work in this original form.

```
int factorial(int n)
{
        if ((n == 0) || (n == 1))
                return 1;
        else
        {
                --n;
                return n * factorial(n);
        }
}
```

## 6.2 Weaving More Complex Recursive Patterns

### OBJECTIVES

- to recognize problems particularly suited to recursive solutions

- to be able to state the solutions to such problems as a simpler instance of the same problem

- to be able to trace the performance of a recursive algorithm using a run-time trace diagram

- to use an algorithm's run-time trace diagram to estimate the time and space efficiency of the algorithm

- to see how recursive algorithms that potentially involve more than one recursive call at each level may lead to an exponential time efficiency

- to develop an intuitive approach for developing recursive solutions to problems

The recursive algorithms we have examined so far share the property that, at each level of recursive execution of the algorithm, at most one recursive call will be made. The pattern of operations on the system stack for such algorithms is that a series of stack frames is pushed, a recursive termination condition is reached, and then all stack frames are successively popped until we return to the execution level of the main program. More complex recursive algorithms involve multiple recursive calls at each level of execution. Correspondingly, the pattern of operations on the system stack will not be a series of uninterrupted pushes followed by a series of uninterrupted pops. Instead, the system stack will initially grow a bit, then shrink, then grow again, then shrink, and so forth.

### Towers of Hanoi Problem

An old legend has it that monks were given the painstaking task of moving a collection of $n$ stone disks from one pillar, designated as pillar A, to another, designated as pillar C. Moreover, the relative ordering of the disks on pillar A had to be maintained as they were moved to pillar C. That is, as illustrated in Figure 6.8, the disks, all of different sizes, were to be stacked from largest to smallest, beginning from the bottom. Additionally, the monks were to observe the following rules in moving disks:

- Only one disk could be moved at a time.
- No larger disk could ever be placed on top of a smaller disk on any pillar.
- A third pillar B could be used as an intermediate to store one or more disks while they were being moved from their original source A to their destination C.

Consider the following recursive solution to this problem:

1. If $n = 1$, merely move the disk from A to C.
2. If $n = 2$, move the first disk from A to B. Then move the second disk from A to C. Then move the first disk from B to C.
3. If $n = 3$, call on the technique already established in step 2 to move the first two disks from A to B using C as intermediate. Then move the third

◆ FIGURE 6.8
Towers of Hanoi problem

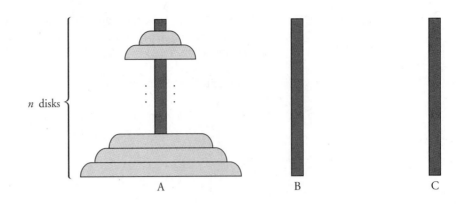

*n* disks

A                    B                    C

disk from A to C. Then use the technique in step 2 to move the first two disks from B to C using A as an intermediate

.
.
.

*n.* For general *n,* use the technique in the previous step to move *n* – 1 disks from A to B using C as an intermediate. Then move one disk from A to C. Then use the technique in the previous step to move *n* – 1 disks from B to C using A as an intermediate.

Notice that this technique for solving the Towers of Hanoi describes itself in terms of a simpler version of itself. That is, it describes how to solve the problem for *n* disks in terms of a solution for *n* – 1 disks. In general, any problem you hope to solve recursively must be approached in this fashion. This strategy is important enough to state as a principle.

> **Principle of recursive problem solving:** When trying to solve a problem by recursion, always ask yourself "What could I do if I had a solution to a simpler version of the same problem?"

If you can see how to use the solution to a smaller version of the problem in solving the original problem, you have hurdled your toughest obstacle. All that remains is to determine the recursive termination conditions. This can be done by answering the question "Under what circumstances is this problem so simple that a solution is trivial?" Your answer to this question will define parameter values that trigger an immediate return from the recursive algorithm.

**EXAMPLE 6.3**

Implement a C++ solution to the Towers of Hanoi problem. Our earlier discussion has indicated that the problem for *n* disks can be defined in terms of *n* – 1 if we switch the roles played by certain pillars. This switching can be achieved by altering the order in which parameters are passed when recursive calls are made. When a value of 1 is passed in for *n,* we have reached the recursive termination condition. The comments **// Return Point 1** and **// Return Point 2** in the following C++ code will be used in a later trace of function **hanoi.**

```
void hanoi(int n, char source, char destination, char intermediate)
{
        if (n == 1)
                cout << "Move disk from " << source << " to " << destination;
        else
        {
                // In every recursive call hanoi works with n - 1
```

```
                hanoi(n - 1, source, intermediate, destination);    // Return Point 1
```

diagram x

The first recursive call transfers $n-1$ disks from **source** to **intermediate**, using **destination** for temporary storage.

source    intermediate    destination

```
                cout << "Move disk from " << source << " to " << destination;
```

diagram y

The single remaining disk is then transferred from **source** to **destination**.

source    intermediate    destination

```
        hanoi(n - 1, intermediate, destination, source);    // Return Point 2
```

diagram z

The second recursive call transfers $n-1$ disks from **intermediate** to **destination**, using **source** for temporary storage.

source    intermediate    destination

```
        }
}
```

Unlike previously studied recursive algorithms in which only one recursive call was made each time the function was invoked, function **hanoi** will reinvoke itself twice each time it is called with *n* > 1. The result is a more complicated algorithm that could not be implemented easily by using mere iterative control structures. Implicitly, through its recursive calls, function **hanoi** is weaving an intricate pattern of push and pop operations on the system stack.

**EXAMPLE 6.4**

To illustrate, we trace through the actions affecting the system stack when a call of the form

```
hanoi(3, 'A', 'C', 'B')
```

is initiated. The values in the return address portion of the stack are the documentary // **Return Point** labels in our **hanoi** function.

1. We enter **hanoi** with the following stack frame. **n** is not 1, so the condition in the **if** statement is FALSE.

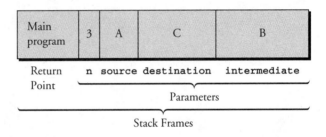

2. We encounter **hanoi(n - 1, source, intermediate, destination)** with A, B, C as first, second, and third arguments. Because this represents a (recursive) function call, some stacking must be done.

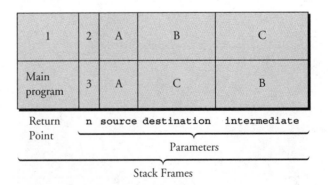

3. We reenter **hanoi**. Notice that as we enter this time, the function's view of the parameters is **n** = 2, **source** = A, **destination** = B, and **intermediate** = C. Because **n** is not 1, the condition in the **if** statement is FALSE.

**4.** We encounter `hanoi(n - 1, source, intermediate, destination)`. Because this is a recursive call, stacking occurs.

| Return Point | n | source | destination | intermediate |
|---|---|---|---|---|
| 1 | 1 | A | C | B |
| 1 | 2 | A | B | C |
| Main program | 3 | A | C | B |

Return Point ⎬ n source destination intermediate

Parameters

Stack Frames

**5.** We reenter `hanoi` with **n** = 1, **source** = A, **destination** = C, and **intermediate** = B. Because **n** = 1, the condition in the **if** statement is TRUE. ,
**6.** Hence

**`Move disk from A to C`**

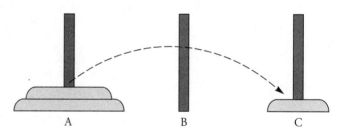

is printed and a return triggers a popping of a return address (1) and four parameters, leaving the system stack as follows:

| Return Point | n | source | destination | intermediate |
|---|---|---|---|---|
| 1 | 2 | A | B | C |
| Main program | 3 | A | C | B |

Return Point ⎬ n source destination intermediate

Parameters

Stack Frames

**7.** Because the return address popped was 1

`Move disk from A to B`

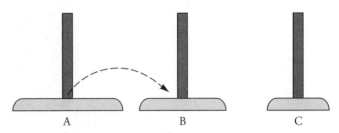

is printed and

`hanoi(n - 1, intermediate, destination, source)`

is encountered with **n** = 2, **source** = A, **destination** = B, and **intermediate** = C.

**8.** The call pushes a return address and four parameters onto the system stack.

| Return Point | n | source | destination | intermediate |
|---|---|---|---|---|
| 2 | 1 | C | B | A |
| 1 | 2 | A | B | C |
| Main program | 3 | A | C | B |

Parameters

Stack Frames

**9.** We reenter **hanoi**, this time with **n** = 1, **source** = C, **destination** = B, and **intermediate** = A.

**10.** Because **n** = 1, the **if** statement generates the output

`Move disk from C to B`

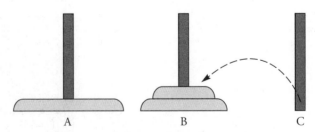

and a return.

**11.** The return pops a frame from the system stack and we return to the statement labeled by 2 with **n** = 2, **source** = A, **destination** = B, and **intermediate** = C.

**12.** But statement 2 triggers a return itself, so a stack frame is popped again and we return to the statement labeled 1 with **n** = 3, **source** = A, **destination** = C, and **intermediate** = B.

**13.** Statement 1 triggers the output

**Move disk from A to C**

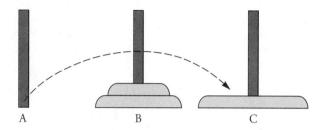

and we are immediately at another call

```
hanoi(n - 1, intermediate, destination, source)
```

Hence the status of the system stack is changed to

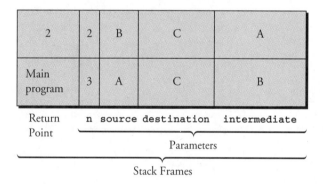

| 2 | 2 | B | C | A |
|---|---|---|---|---|
| Main program | 3 | A | C | B |

| Return Point | n | source | destination | intermediate |
|---|---|---|---|---|

Parameters

Stack Frames

**14.** We reenter **hanoi** with **n** = 2, **source** = B, **destination** = C, and **intermediate** = A. Because **n** is not 1, another call is executed and more values are stacked.

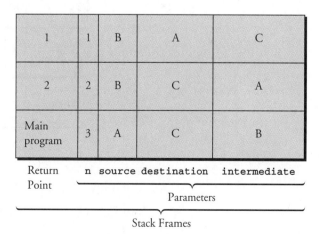

| 1 | 1 | B | A | C |
|---|---|---|---|---|
| 2 | 2 | B | C | A |
| Main program | 3 | A | C | B |

| Return Point | n | source | destination | intermediate |
|---|---|---|---|---|

Parameters

Stack Frames

**15.** We reenter **hanoi**, with **n** = 1, **source** = B, **destination** = A, and **intermediate** = C. Because **n** = 1, we print

**Move disk from B to A**

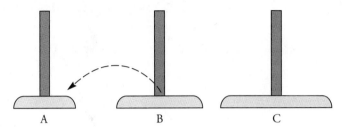

and return.

**16.** The return prompts the popping of the system stack. The return address popped is the statement labeled 1. Statement 1 causes output

**Move disk from B to C**

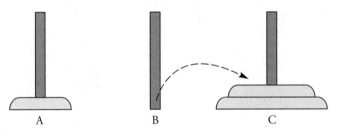

with the stack frames left at

| Return Point | n | source | destination | intermediate |
|---|---|---|---|---|
| 2 | 2 | B | C | A |
| Main program | 3 | A | C | B |

Parameters

Stack Frames

**17.** The output from statement 1 is followed by a recursive call

```
hanoi(n - 1, intermediate, destination, source)
```

| 2 | 1 | A | C | B |
|---|---|---|---|---|
| 2 | 2 | B | C | A |
| Main program | 3 | A | C | B |
| Return Point | n | source | destination | intermediate |

Parameters

Stack Frames

Hence another frame is pushed onto the stack.

**18.** We reenter **hanoi** (for the last time), with **n** = 1, **source** = A, **destination** = C, and **intermediate** = B. Because **n** = 1, we output

**Move disk from A to C**

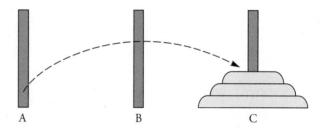

and return.

**19.** But now the return pops return address 2 from the stack, so return to statement 2 with the system stack given by

| 2 | 2 | B | C | A |
|---|---|---|---|---|
| Main program | 3 | A | C | B |
| Return Point | n | source | destination | intermediate |

Parameters

Stack Frames

**20.** Statement 2 is another return, so pop the stack again. The return address popped is 2, the same return point. But this time the return will transfer control back to the original calling location—and we are done!

As long-winded as this example is, it is essential that you understand it. Recursive functions are crucial to many of the algorithms used in computer science, and you can acquire the necessary familiarity with recursion only by convincing yourself that it really works. If you have some doubt or are not sure you understand, we recommend that you trace through the **hanoi** function with **n** = 4 (be prepared to go through a lot of paper).

### Efficiency Analysis of the Recursive Towers of Hanoi Algorithm

An analysis of the time and space efficiency of a recursive algorithm is dependent on two factors. The first of these is the depth, that is, number of levels, to which recursive calls are made before reaching the recursive termination condition. Clearly, the greater the depth, the greater the number of stack frames that must be allocated and the less space efficient the algorithm becomes. It is also clear that recursive calls to a greater depth will consume more computer time and hence make the algorithm less time efficient. The second factor affecting efficiency analyses (particularly time efficiency) of recursive algorithms is the amount of resource (time or space) consumed at any given recursive level.

Figure 6.9 portrays this leveled view of a recursive algorithm as a hierarchy of the recursive calls that are (potentially) made as the algorithm executes. Such a

◆ **FIGURE 6.9**
Generalized hierarchy of
calls by recursive algorithm

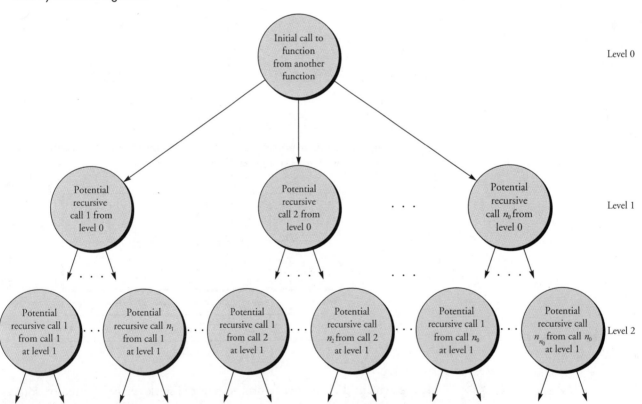

Descent continues from each potential call until recursive
termination condition is reached.

Total time is sum of times spent processing at each level.

hierarchy can be used as a diagrammatic model of the run-time behavior of a recursive algorithm. Consequently, we will call the hierarchy associated with the execution of a particular recursive program a *run-time trace diagram* for that algorithm. Figure 6.10 presents a run-time trace diagram for the Towers of Hanoi algorithm with **n** = 4 disks.

A run-time trace diagram can often be used in analyzing the time and space efficiency of an algorithm. We will provide two general principles for carrying out such analyses and then illustrate them in the context of the Towers of Hanoi algorithm.

**Space efficiency of a recursive algorithm:** Because a stack frame must be allocated at each level of recursive execution, the space efficiency of a recursive algorithm will be proportional to the deepest level at which a recursive call is made for a particular set of values, that is, the deepest level in its run-time trace diagram.

**Time efficiency of a recursive algorithm:** Because processing time is associated with each recursive call, the time efficiency of a recursive algorithm will be proportional to the sum, over all levels, of the times spent processing at each level.

◆ **FIGURE 6.10**
Run-time trace of function Hanoi with *n* originally 4. (Numbers next to circles indicate order of recursive calls.)

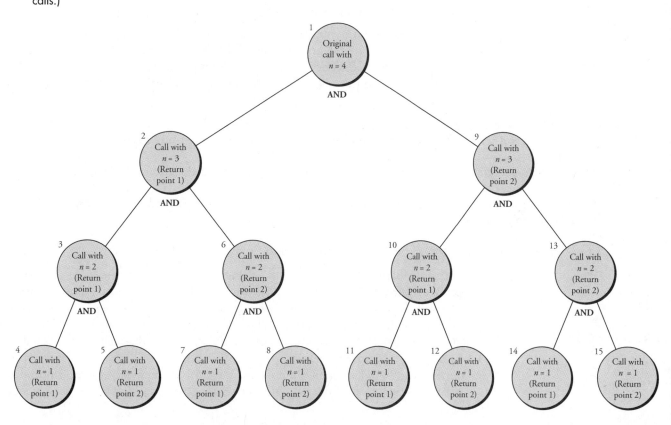

EXAMPLE 6.5

Use the run-time trace diagram of function **hanoi** to analyze the time and space efficiency of the algorithm.

A graphic representation of this diagram for four disks is given in Figure 6.10. Note that the two calls descending from each call are linked by **AND**. This is to emphasize that, when **n** is not 1, both potential recursive calls in the function **hanoi** will be made. The fact that both potential calls are made has a rather dramatic effect on the time efficiency of the algorithm. In particular, calling **hanoi** initially with **n** = 4 results in a total of 15 calls in the run-time trace. The numbers outside the circles in Figure 6.10 indicate the order in which these 15 calls are made. Increasing **n** to 5 in this figure would add an additional level with 16 calls to the run-time trace. In general, adding one disk adds only one level to the run-time trace diagram but doubles (plus 1) the number of calls in the diagram. This implies that the space efficiency of hanoi relative to the system stack is $O(n)$, but, since every call in the run-time trace diagram will be made, the time efficiency is $O(2^n)$.

---

The analysis carried out in the preceding example demonstrates that the **hanoi** algorithm falls into the class of exponential algorithms as defined in Section 1.3. This is the first exponential algorithm we have encountered. Recall from our discussion of algorithm efficiency in Section 1.3 that such algorithms are impractical to run for even moderate values of **n**. We shall at this point complete the Hanoi legend by noting that, if the monks of Hanoi use the recursive algorithm that we have described here, the exponential efficiency of the algorithm insures that the world will exist for many more centuries.

### Recursive Implementation of the Binary Search Algorithm

Do not let our solution to the Towers of Hanoi problem mislead you into thinking that every recursive algorithm having more than one recursive call will be exponential in its efficiency. Consider, for example, a recursive formulation of the binary search algorithm. Recall the interface to this algorithm that we developed in Section 1.5:

```
// Function: binary_search
// If data is found in list, return position of data, otherwise, return -1
//
// Inputs: A sorted list of data elements, the length of the list, and a
// target key
// Outputs: Function returns target's position if target is found in
// list, and -1 otherwise

int binary_search(list_type list, int n, key_type target);
```

The principle of recursive problem solving (stated in our discussion of the Hanoi problem) directs us to solve the binary search problem in terms of a simpler version of itself. Toward this end, we employ a perspective often used in recursive algorithms that act on an array: We view the algorithm as occurring between a certain subrange of array indices. For the binary search, that subrange is specified by **low ... high** where **low** is initially 0 and **high** is initially **n**. The "simpler version" of the binary search needed for a recursive statement of the algorithm is then a version that works on a smaller subrange of array indices. This subrange ultimately may become so small that it triggers the recursive termination condition for an unsuccessful search.

An intuitive recursive statement of the binary search logic then becomes:

If (recursive termination for unsuccessful search)
    Return –1 (and recursion terminated)
else
    Compute middle index between low and high
    If (target is found at middle index)
        Search is successful
        (and recursion terminated by returning middle index)
    Else if (target is less than data at middle index)
        Recursively call with same low and middle – 1 as high
    else
        Recursively call with middle + 1 as low and same high

According to this logic, the recursive calls result in a continual narrowing of the range to be searched until either the target is found or a recursive termination condition for an unsuccessful search is reached.

To determine what this unsuccessful recursive termination condition is, consider Figure 6.11. It portrays successive recursive calls on an array in which the target does not exist. The shaded regions of these array snapshots indicate the index subrange in which **target = 152** could possibly be found on successive recursive calls. Note that, on the fourth recursive call, no portion of the array is shaded; the condition **low = high** exists. This condition is therefore the recursive termination

◆ FIGURE 6.11
Unsuccessful search for array with 15 key values

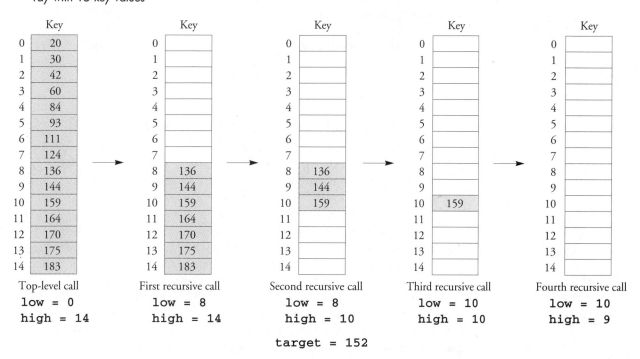

| | | | | |
|---|---|---|---|---|
| Top-level call | First recursive call | Second recursive call | Third recursive call | Fourth recursive call |
| **low = 0** | **low = 8** | **low = 8** | **low = 10** | **low = 10** |
| **high = 14** | **high = 14** | **high = 10** | **high = 10** | **high = 9** |

**target = 152**

check for an unsuccessful search. The following example presents the code for the recursive binary search in its entirety.

EXAMPLE 6.6

Developing a recursive version of the binary search requires that we use an auxiliary function to work with the index subrange **low ... high**. Using this auxiliary function will allow us to preserve the interface to function **binary_search.** This interface should not require its user to pass in an initial low value of 0. Instead, the user need only pass in the **n**, the number of objects in list. From there, the front-end portion of function **binary_search** need only call on its auxiliary function, passing in 0 for **low** and **n** for **high**.

```
int binary_search(list_type list, int n, key_type target)
{
return binary_search_aux(list, 0, n, target);
}

int binary_search_aux(list_type list, int low, int high, key_type target)

{
    int middle;

    if (low == high)
        return -1;
    else
    {
        middle = (low + high) / 2;
        if (list[middle] == target)
            return middle;
        else if (list[middle] < target)
            return binary_search_aux(list, low, middle - 1, target);
        else
            return binary_search_aux(list, middle + 1, high, target);
    }
}
```

## Efficiency Analysis of the Recursive Binary Search

As we did for the Towers of Hanoi problem, we will use a run-time trace diagram of potential recursive calls to analyze the efficiency of the recursive implementation of the binary search algorithm. This diagram appears in Figure 6.12. For the specific case of an array with 15 data items, the run-time trace stops at level 3, as indicated in Figure 6.13. The **OR**s that appear in these two figures are indicative of the fact that, at any given level, we will make, at most, one recursive call or the other, but not both. This is important and, as we have seen, different from the **AND** pattern of recursive calls in the Hanoi problem. It implies that the work done at any given level is simply the work done at one node along that level.

In the binary search, the work done at any node is $O(1)$ since we are merely comparing the **target** item to the data at the **mid** position. Hence the time efficiency of the recursive version of this algorithm will merely be proportional to the number of levels in the run-time trace for an array with **n** items. In Figures

◆ **FIGURE 6.12**
Run-time trace diagram of
potential calls for recursive
binary search algorithm

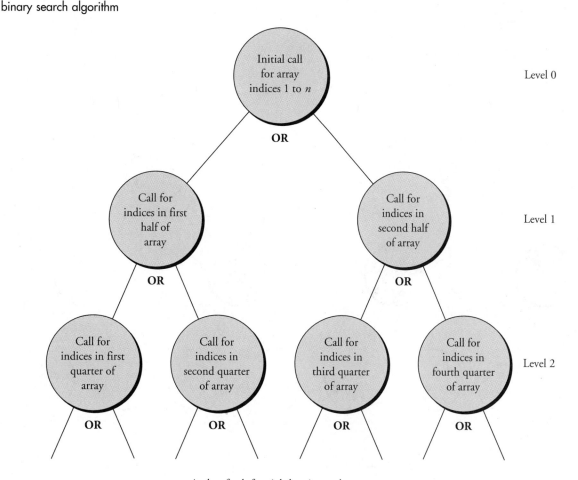

And so forth for eighths, sixteenths . . .

6.12 and 6.13, we can see that doubling the number of items in the array will merely add one level to the run-time trace diagram. That is, the number of levels in the diagram is $\log_2 n + 1$ (truncated). With the $O(1)$ work done at each level, we can thus conclude that the time efficiency of a recursive binary search is $O(\log_2 n)$. Similarly, since a stack frame will be allocated for each recursive level, the additional space requirements of the algorithm (beyond the array itself) are $O(\log_2 n)$. Note that our earlier nonrecursive implementation of the binary search algorithm did not carry with it this additional cost in space efficiency.

## Recursive Computation of "*N* Choose *K*"

The preceding discussion of the binary search algorithm has honed our ability to use the run-time trace diagram to measure the efficiency of a recursive algorithm.

Trace of Figure 6.12 for
specific case of array with
15 data items

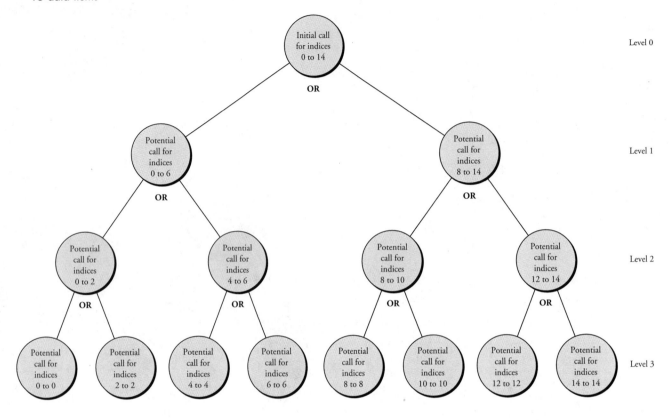

It did not, however, represent a solution to a problem that would be difficult to conceptualize without recursion. We close this section with an example in the latter category.

The phrase "*N* choose *K*" is often used in the combinatorics branch of mathematics to refer to the number of ways that we could choose *K* objects from among *N* different objects. For instance, "52 choose 13" represents the number of ways that you could be dealt a bridge hand (that is, 13 cards out of 52). We seek a recursive function to compute *N* choose *K* for arbitrary *N* and *K*, *K* <= *N*.

Our principle of recursive problem solving asks us to consider how we could use a solution to a simpler version of the same problem. For *N* choose *K*, a simpler version of the same problem could mean a solution for a smaller value of *N* or *K*. Let us designate our *N* objects as object #1, object #2, . . . , object #(*N* − 1), object #*N*. Figure 6.14 indicates that we can partition selections of *K* objects from these *N* as those groups of *K* objects that come strictly from objects #1, #2, . . . , #*N* − 1 and those groups of *K* objects that include object #*N* in addition to *K* − 1 chosen among objects #1, #2, . . . , #*N* − 1. In other words,

## A NOTE OF INTEREST

### Recursion Need Not Be Expensive

We have seen that the use of recursion has two costs: extra time and extra memory are required to manage recursive function calls. These costs have led some to argue that recursion should never be used in programs. However, as Guy Steele has shown (in "Debunking the 'expensive procedure call' myth," *Proceedings of the National Conference of the ACM,* 1977), some systems can run recursive algorithms as if they were iterative ones, with no additional overhead. The key condition is to write a special kind of recursive function called a *tail-recursive function.* A function is tail recursive if no work is done in the function after a recursive call. For example, according to this criterion, the factorial function that we presented earlier is not tail recursive, because a multiplication is performed after each recursive call. We can convert this version of the factorial function to a tail-recursive version by performing the multiplication before each recursive call. To do this, we will need an additional parameter that passes the accumulated value of the factorial down on each recursive call. In the last call of the function, this value is returned as the result:

```
int fact_iter(int n, int result)
{
        if (n == 1)
                return result;
        else
                return fact_iter(n - 1,
                n * result);
}
```

Note that the multiplication is performed before the recursive call of the function, when its parameters are evaluated. When the function is initially called, the value of `result` should be 1:

```
int factorial(int n)
{
        return fact_iter(n, 1);
}
```

Steele showed that a smart compiler can translate tail-recursive code in a high-level language to a loop in machine language. The machine code treats the function parameters as variables associated with a loop, and generates an iterative process rather than a recursive one. Thus, there is no linear growth of function calls and extra stack memory is not required to run tail-recursive functions on these systems.

The catch is that a programmer must be able to convert a recursive function to a tail-recursive function and find a compiler that generates iterative machine code from tail-recursive functions. Unfortunately, some functions, like the one used to solve the Towers of Hanoi problem, are difficult or impossible to convert to tail-recursive versions, and the compiler optimizations are not part of the standard definitions of many languages, among them, C++. If you find that your C++ compiler supports this optimization, you should try converting some functions to tail-recursive versions and see if they run faster than the original versions.

◆ **FIGURE 6.14**

Formulating `choose (N, K)` in terms of `choose (N - 1, K)` and `choose (N - 1, K - 1)`

Any selection of $K-1$ objects from among these $N-1$ objects generates a selection of $K$ objects by adding object #$N$ to the $K-1$ selected.

| Object #1 | Object #2 | Object #3 | . . . | Object #$(N-2)$ | Object #$(N-1)$ | Object #$N$ |
|---|---|---|---|---|---|---|

Any selection of $K$ objects from among these $N-1$ objects is also a selection of $K$ objects from among object #1 $\cdots$ object #$N$.

```
choose(N, K) =

choose(N - 1, K)              Ways of selecting K objects from among the first N-1
+ choose (N - 1, K - 1)       Ways of selecting K - 1 objects from among the first
                              N - 1 and then including object #N
```

The preceding equation appears to be the recursive key we need to write our function. We need only develop recursive termination conditions to complete the puzzle. Note from the preceding equation that one of the terms being summed, **choose (N – 1, K)**, will recursively reduce $N$ until it eventually equals $K$. But, in such a case, we are merely asking for the number of combinations of $N$ objects selected $N$ at a time—and there is trivially only one such combination. Hence, our first recursive termination condition is when $N = K$, for which we immediately return the value 1.

To develop the second recursive termination condition, we examine the second term, **choose(N – 1, K – 1)**, in the sum. Since both $N$ and $K$ will be reduced by this recursion, $K$ will eventually reach 0. But the number of ways of choosing 0 objects from among $N$ is again trivially 1. Consequently, the second recursive termination condition is when $K = 0$; this condition flags the immediate return of the value of 1.

---

**EXAMPLE 6.7**  Implement a recursive $N$ choose $K$ function based on the preceding discussion.

```
// Function: choose
// Computes N choose K, that is, the number of ways of selecting K objects from N
//
// Inputs: N, the number of objects being selected from
// and K, the number of objects being selected
// Outputs: The value of N choose K

int choose(int n, int k)
{
        if ((k == 0) || (n == k))
                return 1;
        else
                return choose(n - 1, k) + choose(n - 1, k - 1);

}
```

---

**EXAMPLE 6.8**  Trace the **choose(n, k)** function by developing the run-time trace diagram for choose(4, 2).

This diagram is provided in Figure 6.15. The numbers next to the circles indicate the order in which calls are made.

---

**EXERCISES 6.2**

1. Trace the stack frames that are pushed and popped from the system stack as the Towers of Hanoi algorithm executes for $n = 4$ disks.

2. Is the recursive binary search algorithm presented in this section tail recursive? Provide a written rationale for your response.

3. Construct run-time trace diagrams in the style of Example 6.8 for a variety of values of **n** and **k** in the function **choose(n, k)**. Judging from the run-time trace diagrams you construct, make conjectures about the time and space efficiency of this algorithm. Support these conjectures in a written statement.

4. Consider the following version of the function **binary_search_aux** from Example 6.6 to which a tracer output statement has been added. What output would

◆ FIGURE 6.15
Run-time trace diagram for
`choose(4, 2)`

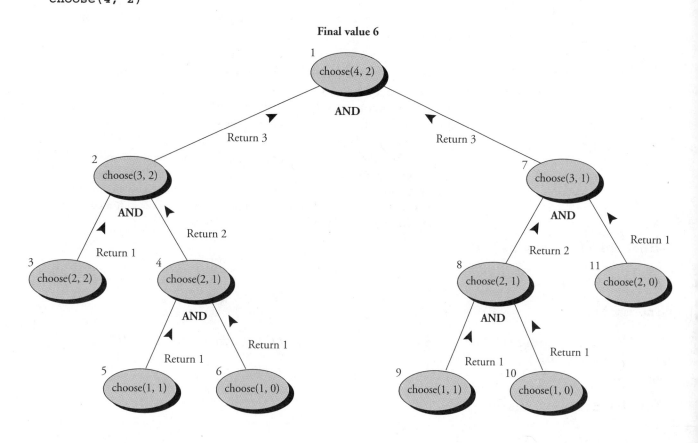

be produced from this tracer output if we were to call on function
**binary_search** from Example 6.6 with a list of 16 integers containing these
key values

12 34 67 89 113 125 169 180 191 201 225 237 256 270 299 304

and a **target** of 191?

```
int binary_search_aux(list_type list, int low, int high,
     key_type target)
{
     int middle;

     cout << low << " " << high << endl;              // Tracer output added here
     if (low > high)
          return -1;
     else
     {
          middle = (low + high) / 2;
          if (list[middle] == target)
               return middle;
```

```
            else if (list[middle] < target)
                    return binary_search_aux(list, low, middle - 1, target);
            else
                    return binary_search_aux(list, middle + 1, high, target);

    }
}
```

5. Repeat Exercise 4 but this time with a **target** of 6.

6. We chose not to include **list** as a formal value parameter to the function **binary_search_aux** in Example 6.6. Analyze what would be the cost in space and time efficiency if **list** were to be included as a value parameter to this function.

7. Consider the following recursive function and associated top-level call. Comments of the form // **Return Point N** label possible return points from recursive calls. What would a stack frame for this function contain? Show by a series of stack "snapshots" how the stack would be manipulated for the calls indicated. Finally, provide the output that would be produced by these calls.

```
#include <iostream.h>

int weird(int m, int n);

int main()
{
        cout << weird(1, 3) << endl;                    // Return Point 1
        return 0;
}

int weird(int m, int n)
{
        cout << m << "" << n << endl;
        if (m == 0)
                return n + 1;
        else if (n == 0)
                return weird(m - 1, 1);                 // Return Point 2
        else
                return weird(m - 1, weird(m, n - 1));   // Return Points 3 and 4
}
```

8. Function **hanoi** developed in this section specified the sequence of disk moves that would have to be performed to complete the Towers of Hanoi problem for *n* disks. Now write a recursive function that computes the exact number of disk moves needed to solve the Towers of Hanoi problem for *n* disks. (*Hint:* Express the number of individual moves necessary to transfer *n* disks in terms of the number of moves necessary to transfer *n* – 1 disks.)

9. Write a recursive function to determine the minimum entry in an array of *n* integers.

10. Write a recursive implementation of the insertion sort algorithm.

11. Suppose we have an amount of money *M* that is divisible evenly by 10 cents. Write a recursive function that computes the number of ways that *M* can be broken down into half dollars, quarters, and dimes.

12. In essay form, discuss some of the trade-offs in terms of time and space efficiency that are made when recursion is used.

13. Both a modular structure chart and a run-time trace diagram reflect a hierarchical pattern of how functions are called in a program. In a carefully written statement, explain the differences between these two diagrammatic techniques.

---

## A NOTE OF INTEREST

### Fractal Geometry and Recursive Patterns

Fractal geometry as a serious mathematical endeavor began with the pioneering work of Benoit Mandelbrot, a Fellow of the Thomas J. Watson Research Center, IBM Corporation. Fractal geometry is a theory of geometric forms so complex that they defy analysis and classification by traditional Euclidean means. Yet fractal shapes occur universally in the natural world. Mandelbrot has recognized them not only in coastlines, landscapes, lungs, and turbulent water flow but also in the chaotic fluctuation of prices on the Chicago commodity exchange.

The c-curve that appears on the cover of this book is an instance of a fractal shape. It represents a series of recursive patterns of increasing levels of complexity. When the level is zero, the c-curve is a simple line, specified by the endpoints <x1, y1> and <x2, y2>. A level $N$ c-curve is composed of two level $N - 1$ c-curves connected at right angles. Thus, a level 1 c-curve is composed of two perpendicular lines, and a level 2 c-curve is three quarters of a square, which begins to resemble the letter C.

Our level 12 c-curve was generated on a graphics workstation by running a recursive function written in C++:

```
void c_curve(int x1, int y1, int x2,
    int y2, int level)
{
    int xm, ym;

    if ( level == 0)
        draw_line (x1, y1, x2, y2);
    else
    {
        xm = (x1 + x2 + y1 - y2)/2;
        ym = (x2 + y1 + y2 - x1)/2;
        c_curve(x1, y1, xm, ym,
            level - 1);
        c_curve(xm, ym, x2, y2,
            level - 1);
    }
}
```

---

## 6.3 Recursion, Trial-and-Error Backtracking, and Generalized Nested Loops

In the previous section, we have seen examples of recursive algorithms in which the number of recursive calls at each recursive level is (potentially) more than one. In this section we shall consider what happens when the number of recursive calls made on any given level is under the control of an iterative control structure such as a **for**, **while**, or **do** loop.

As an example of the class of problems we will study in this section, consider the notion of a permutation.

> **Permutation:** A permutation of the integers 1, 2, . . ., $N$ is an ordered arrangement of these integers in which each integer appears exactly once.

For instance, two possible permutations of the integers 1, 2, 3, 4 are 3 2 1 4 and 2 4 3 1.

### The Permutation Problem

We now pose the following problem: For input of $N$, devise a program that outputs all permutations of the integers 1, 2, . . ., $N$.

EXAMPLE 6.9
The following program solves this problem, but only for the special case where $N = 4$.

```cpp
#include <iostream.h>

int main()
{
    for (int k1 = 1; k1 <= 4, k1++)
        for (int k2 = 1; k2 <= 4; k2++)
            if (k1 != k2)
                for (int k3 = 1; k3 <= 4; k3++)
                    if ((k2 != k3) && (k1 != k3))
                        for (int k4 = 1; k4 <= 4; k4++)
                            if ((k3 != k4) && (k2 != k4)
                                && (k1 != k4))
                                cout << setw(2) << k1 << " "
                                    << setw(2) << k2 << " "
                                    << setw(2) << k3 << " "
                                    << setw(2) << k4 << " "
                                    << endl;

    return 0;
}
```

The strategy of this program is to use a **for** loop to control a variable that runs through the four possibilities for each of the four permutation positions. Hence four loops emerge, nested within each other. When an inner loop generates a number that matches one at a previously generated position, the **if** statement is used to reject that number.

---

The program in Example 6.9 constitutes a simple and straightforward approach to the permutation problem. But it falls far short of solving the general problem as originally posed because it works only for the number 4, not for a general $N$ to be input when the program runs. Note that the requirement that $N$ be entered at run time is what causes the major complication. Certainly, the strategy of using nested loops would allow us to write one program that works for $N = 2$, another that works for $N = 3$, another for $N = 4$, and so on. However, in addition to having a ridiculous number of nested **for** loops for reasonably large $N$, the decision as to which permutations to generate would instead be made at the time the appropriate program is compiled and not when it runs. Computer scientists typically call this a *binding time problem*. Here we would prefer to bind a value to $N$ when our program runs instead of when it compiles. Clearly, the later the binding time, the more versatile the program. To do this, we need some means of simulating arbitrarily deep nested loops when the program runs.

To see how we can use recursion to achieve such a simulation, consider the diagram of permutation possibilities in Figure 6.16. This diagram bears a resemblance to what we called a run-time trace of recursive calls in the preceding section. Interpret the diagram by viewing any given path from the node labeled Start down to the base level of the diagram as a potential candidate for a permutation of 1, 2, . . . , $N$. As we progress from one level to the next along a path, we encounter the next digit in this potential permutation.

◆ FIGURE 6.16
Candidates for permutations

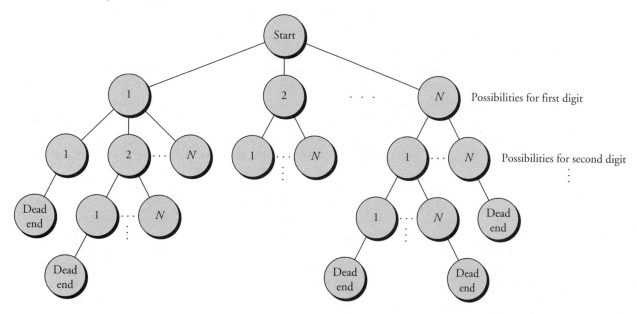

Conceptually we must use recursion to generate all the paths that appear in the figure. As soon as we generate a path with two equal numbers on it, we abandon that dead-end path and backtrack one level to continue the path along a potentially more fruitful route. If we ever complete one entire permutation along a path, we will output it, backtrack a level, and continue looking for more permutations that share the beginning of this path. At a given point in our search for a permutation, we need only store the current path. For this, a simple global array will do. Thus, the array **current_permutation** of Figure 6.17 will store in its *j*th subscript the number in the *j*th position of the permutation currently being generated. The limiting factor on the size of permutations generated by our program will be the dimension of this array.

A complete program to solve our permutation problem follows. The heart of the program is the recursive function **attempt**. This function receives three parameters:

| Parameter | Explanation |
|---|---|
| **n** | The number of numbers to be permuted in the current run. |
| **level** | The level in the tree of Figure 6.16; that is, the position in **current_permutation** at which **attempt** is to attempt placement of a new value. |
| **possibility** | The new value to be placed at this level. |

◆ FIGURE 6.17
Current exploration of permutations beginning with
2 1 4

current_permutation                                                                 max_permutation

| 1 | 2 | 3 | 4 | 5 | · · · | Size |
|---|---|---|---|---|---|---|
| 2 | 1 | 4 | Undefined | Undefined | · · · | Undefined |

**attempt** initially calls on a function **add_to_current_path** to actually place **possibility** at the appropriate level. Once this placement is made, there are three states in which the **current_permutation** array could be.

1. The placement of the value **possibility** at the designated level could have completed a successful permutation. In this case, call on a function to print the permutation and then remove **possibility** from **current_permutation** at the given **level** so that we may continue seeking additional permutations.

2. The placement of the value **possibility** at the designated level did not complete a permutation but does represent a valid beginning of length **level** for a potential permutation. For instance, this case would occur if **n**, **level**, and **possibility** were 6, 4, and 5, respectively, and we called **attempt** with **current_permutation** as pictured in Figure 6.17. The **current_permutation** array would be extended to contain 2 1 4 5. Here what we must do is to test the possible candidates for a value at the next position; that is, at depth **(level + 1)**. This is done by an iterative series of recursive calls to **attempt**, passing a variety of values for **possibility** at **(level + 1)**. This iterative series of recursive calls is what achieves the desired simulation of nested looping. After all of these deeper level possibilities (that is, those below the beginning of the current permutation in Figure 6.16) have been explored, we return and can remove **possibility** from **current_permutation** at position **level** since (recursively) all permutations with this beginning arrangement will have been generated.

3. The placement of the value **possibility** at **level** destroys the viability of the current path by adding a number that appeared earlier in the permutation. For instance, calling on **attempt** with **n** = 6, **level** = 4, and **possibility** = 1 would cause an invalid path for the state of **current_permutation** given in Figure 6.17. In this case we do nothing

◆ **FIGURE 6.18**
Modular structure chart for permutations program

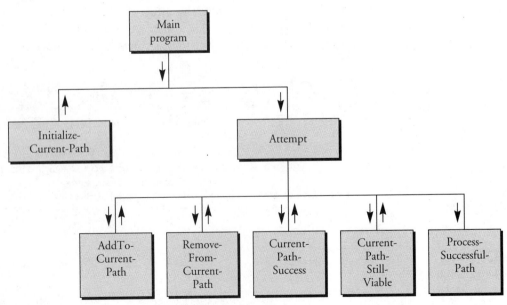

but retract from the placement of this invalid possibility before attempting to place other possible values.

You should carefully study how these three potential cases are handled in our recursive function attempt in the example program. The modular structure chart presented in Figure 6.18 indicates how **attempt** invokes other functions. In the Focus on Program Design section, we adapt the technique illustrated here to a broader class of problems.

```cpp
// Program file: permute.cpp

// Use recursion to find all permutations of 1,2, ..., N.

#include <iostream.h>
#include <iomanip.h>
#include <limits.h>

#include "boolean.h"

const int MAX_PERMUTATION_SIZE = 100;
const int UNDEFINED = INT_MAX;

int current_permutation[MAX_PERMUTATION_SIZE + 1];

// Function: initialize_current_path
// Initializes all indices in array to the UNDEFINED flag.
//
// Inputs: The current_permutation array in an unreliable state
// Outputs: The initialized array

void initialize_current_path();

// Function: attempt
// After locating possibility at specified level, check if we have a permutation.
// If so, print it. If not, check whether or not a permutation is still possible
// for this placement of possibility.  If so, attempt placement at deeper level
// by recursive call.
//
// Inputs: n, the number of numbers we are attempting to permute;
//            level, the current depth of the solution path as portrayed in
//            Figure 6.6
//            possibility, the number we wish to place at that level
// Outputs: Relative to this level, the array is returned unaltered.  However,
//            if permutation was found, contents of this array are printed.

void attempt(int n, int level, int possibility);

// Function: add_to_current_path
// Assign possibility to this level.
//
// Inputs: level, the current depth of the solution path
//            possibility, the number we wish to place at that level

void add_to_current_path(int level, int possibility);
```

```
// Function: remove_from_current_path
// Remove value at that level.
//
// Inputs:  the deepest level to which solution path has grown
// Outputs: Suitably altered array

void remove_from_current_path(int level);


// Function: current_path_success
// Check if contents of array through index level constitute a complete
// permutation of the first n numbers.
//
// Inputs:  The array, level, the depth to which the solution path has grown,
//                n, the number of numbers we are attempting to permute.
// Outputs: TRUE if permutation, FALSE otherwise.


boolean current_path_success(int n, int level);


// Function: current_path_still_viable
// Check if contents of array through index level constitute a viable
// beginning for the permutation of the first n numbers.
//
// Inputs:  The array, level, the depth to which the solution path has grown,
//                n, the number of numbers we are attempting to permute.
// Outputs: TRUE if viable, FALSE otherwise.
boolean current_path_still_viable(int level);


// Function: process_successful_path
// Write out first n indices of the array
//
// Inputs:  The array and n, the number of numbers we are attempting to permute.

void process_successful_path(int n);

int main()
{
      int n;
      initialize_current_path();
      cout << "Permutation  of integers from 1 to ? ";
      cin >> n;
      for (int k = 1; k <= n; ++k)
            attempt(n, 1, k);
      return 0;
}


void initialize_current_path()
{
      for (int k = 1; k < MAX_PERMUTATION_SIZE; ++k)
            current_permutation[k] = UNDEFINED;
}
void attempt(int n, int level, int possibility)
```

```
{
        add_to_current_path(level, possibility);
        if (current_path_success(n, level))
                process_successful_path(n);
        else if (current_path_still_viable(level))
                for (int k = 1; k <= n; ++k)
                        attempt(n, level + 1, k);
        remove_from_current_path(level);
}

void add_to_current_path(int level, int possibility)
{
        current_permutation[level] = possibility;
}

void remove_from_current_path(int level)
{
        current_permutation[level] = UNDEFINED;
}

boolean current_path_success(int n, int level)
{
        boolean success = TRUE;
        int k = 1;

        if (n > level)
                success = FALSE;
        else
                while ((k <= level - 1) && success)
                {
                        success = current_permutation[k] != current_permutation[level];
                        ++k;
                }
        return success;
}

boolean current_path_still_viable(int level)
{

        boolean viable = TRUE;
        int k = 1;

        while ((k <= level - 1) && viable)
                {
                        viable = current_permutation[k] != current_permutation[level];
                        ++k;
                }
        return viable;
}

void process_successful_path(int n)
{
```

```
for (int k = 1; k <= n; ++k)
        cout << setw(3) << current_permutation[k];
cout << endl;
}
```

You may have noticed that certain efficiency considerations have not been taken into account in writing the previous program. For example, the initialization of the `current_permutation` array actually is unnecessary in this particular implementation. Also, the call to `remove_from_current_path` could have been eliminated since the undefined flag that this function assigns is quickly replaced without ever being explicitly used. Finally, additional global data could be used to keep track of information that would eliminate the necessity of using loops in the `current_path_success` and `current_path_still_viable` functions. You will be asked to rewrite the program taking these economies into account in the exercises.

Our purpose in this section has not been to present the most compact version of a permutations program, but rather to illustrate how recursion can be used to simulate *generalized nested loops* whose nesting depth can be established at run time. Such generalized nested loops can then be used in situations where trial-and-error backtracking is an appropriate strategy in searching for a problem's solution. In this context, we have intended the permutations program to be illustrative of a general problem-solving approach rather than a solution to a particular problem.

Consider what we must abstract from the permutations program to view it as a general template for trial-and-error backtracking instead of a mere permutation printer. Figure 6.16 presents the problem of finding permutations as a problem in finding certain types of paths through a maze. We probe deeper and deeper along a given path (that is, add new numbers to the current permutation) until we reach a predefined goal or reach a dead end. As we take a new step along the current path, we must analyze the state in which it has placed us:

**1.** Have we reached a goal state?
**2.** Have we reached a state that, though not itself a goal, is still a viable start toward that goal?
**3.** Have we reached a dead end?

For each of the three cases we take appropriate action such as

**1.** Processing a goal state; for example, printing it out, tallying a counter, or setting a flag signaling that we are done.
**2.** Probing further along a viable path by recursively taking another step.
**3.** No action in the case of a dead end.

After taking the appropriate action, we then retract from the step that led us to the current state, possibly returning to a higher recursive level where we may find ourselves in the midst of a similar three-state analysis. The essence of this trial-and-error backtracking logic is illustrated in Figure 6.19. Upon reaching a dead end for path A, you must retrace steps $9 \rightarrow 8 \rightarrow 7 \rightarrow 6 \rightarrow 5$ before you can attempt new path B. The retracing of states that have been visited previously is conveniently done by unwinding from recursive calls.

In this chapter's Focus on Program Design section and the programming problems, you will see how this type of logic can be used to solve a wide variety of problems.

◆ FIGURE 6.19
Backtracking problem illustrated by maze solution

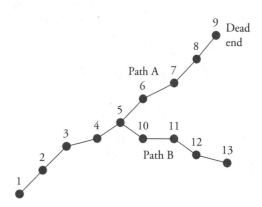

EXERCISES 6.3

1. Consider the permutations program discussed in Section 6.3. Suppose that $N = 3$ in a particular run of this program and that we printed out the contents of the **current_permutation** array each time the attempt function was invoked in this run. How many times would the array be printed? What would be the overall output?

2. Suppose you used the permutations function of this section to compute all permutations of 1, 2, 3, and 4. What would the complete run-time trace diagram of recursive function calls look like for such a run? Can you generalize from this diagram of function calls the efficiency of the permutations function? State your answer in big-O terms with respect to both stack size and number of stack operations. Provide justification for your answer in a written statement.

3. Rewrite the example program for permutations in a fashion that takes into account the efficiency considerations discussed in Section 6.3. These considerations are discussed in the paragraph that follows the program.

4. What is the output from the following program?:

```
#include <iostream.h>

void y(int a, int b, int c);

int main()
{
        y(16, 1, 4);
        return 0;
}

void y(int a, int b, int c)
{
        int k;

        if (b <= c)
        {
                cout << a << endl;
                for (k = b; k <= c; ++k)
                        y(k, b + 1, c);
        }
}
```

**5.** What is the output from the following program?:

```cpp
#include <iostream.h>

void tough(int b, int c, int d);

int main()
{
        tough(1, 4, 12);
        return 0;
}

void tough(int b, int c, int d)
{
        int k;

        if (b <= c)
        {
                cout << d << endl;
                for (k = b; k <= c; ++k)
                        tough(b + 1, c, k);
        }
}
```

**6.** A car's odometer may be viewed as a physical implementation of a nested loop. Each loop cycles through the digits 0...9, with the one's digit cycling the fastest, then the ten's digit, and so forth. Write a function to simulate an $N$-digit odometer ($N$ determined at run time) by creating a generalized nested loop structure that will run through, in sequence, all possible settings for the odometer.

We have emphasized throughout this text that computer scientists must work at varying levels of abstraction. With this in mind, consider the program of the last section not merely as a permutation printer but rather as illustrative of a more abstract problem-solving technique. In fact, a careful examination of the function **attempt** in the permutations program will show that it is nearly independent of the particular problem of searching for permutations. That is, the algorithm behind **attempt** could be used in any analogous search for a solution in which there were $N$ additional possibilities at the current level. We shall now indicate the power of this abstract approach to trial-and-error backtracking by sketching a solution to another problem that could be solved with the same methodology. You will then complete the solution in the programming problems.

### The Eight Queens Problem

Consider what has come to be known as the Eight Queens problem. This problem has long intrigued chess fanatics. It requires determining the various ways in which eight queens could be configured on a chessboard so that none of them could capture any other queen. (The rules of chess allow a queen to move an arbitrary number of squares in a horizontal, vertical, or diagonal fashion.) Figure 6.20 illustrates one such configuration.

Applying backtracking logic to this problem we could attempt to find a path to a configuration by successively attempting to place a queen in each column of a

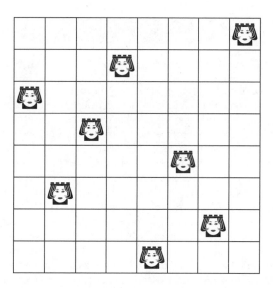

◆ **FIGURE 6.20**
One successful eight queens
configuration

chessboard until we reach a dead end: a column in which the placement of queens in prior columns makes it impossible to place the queen being moved. This situation is pictured in Figure 6.21. Here, the sixth queen cannot be placed due to the placement of the first five queens.

When we reach such a dead end, we must backtrack one column (to column 5 in Figure 6.21), and attempt to find a new placement for the queen in that column. If placement in the previous column is impossible, we must backtrack yet another column to attempt the new placement. This backtracking through previous columns continues until we finally are able to reposition a queen. At that point, we can begin a new path by again attempting to position queens on a column-by-column basis until another dead end is reached or until a fully successful configuration is developed.

◆ **FIGURE 6.21**
Dead end in queen placement

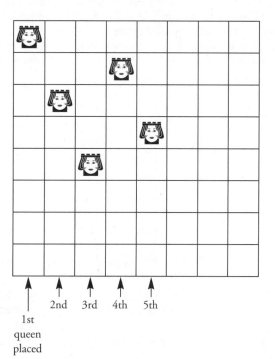

## A NOTE OF INTEREST

### Recursion, LISP, and the Practicality of Artificial Intelligence

Artificial intelligence, the science of implementing on computers the problem-solving methods used by human beings, is one of the most rapidly expanding fields within computer science. Research in this field includes enabling computers to play games of strategy, to understand natural languages, to prove theorems in logic and mathematics, and to mimic the reasoning of human experts in fields such as medical diagnosis. Only recently has artificial intelligence become a commercially viable area of application, capable of solving some real-life problems apart from the idealized setting of a pure research environment. More and more, we are seeing artificial intelligence systems that perform such practical functions as aiding business executives in their decision-making processes and providing a "near-English" user-interface language for database management software.

What has sparked the sudden emergence of artificial intelligence? Why wasn't it possible to produce commercially feasible programs in this field until recently? One of the primary answers to these questions is tied to the language in which most artificial intelligence programming is done. This language is called *LISP* (for LISt Processor). Interestingly, the control structures of LISP are based almost entirely on recursion. What a C++ programmer would view as normal iterative control structures (for example, `while`, `do`, and `for` loops) appear in various versions of LISP only as infrequently used, nonstandard extensions to the language.

One of the reasons that a recursively based language such as LISP is so ideally suited to this field is that most problem-solving methods in artificial intelligence involve searching for a particular goal state; that is, searching for a path leading to a complete problem solution. This is similar to the approaches we have taken in the permutation problem and the Eight Queens problem in this chapter.

The complexity of problems studied in artificial intelligence leads to run-time trace diagrams of enormous size. Interestingly, LISP has been available as a recursive language ideally suited to such problems for a long time. It is one of the oldest high-level programming languages, having been first developed by John McCarthy in the late 1950s.

Researchers who work in artificial intelligence have realized since LISP's introduction that its ability to process general data structures recursively was, on a theoretical basis, exactly what they needed. The problem through the years has been that, because of the very high overhead associated with recursion (and some other features built into LISP), computer hardware has not been fast enough to run LISP programs in practical applications. Thus, researchers were restricted not by LISP itself but rather by the ability of computer hardware to execute LISP programs in reasonable times. One of the major reasons for the recent emergence of artificial intelligence has been the increase in speed of computing hardware and the decrease in cost of this same hardware. This has made it possible for users to have dedicated computer resources capable of meeting the demands of LISP's recursive style. As hardware continues to improve, applications in LISP and artificial intelligence will become increasingly sophisticated.

If you are curious about LISP and the important role that it plays at some of the frontiers of research in programming languages, consult the September 1991 issue of the *Communications of the ACM* (Volume 34, no. 9). This entire issue was devoted to LISP and described its ability to adapt to many computing environments.

The key to a program that finds all possible configurations for the eight queens is a function that attempts to place a queen in a given square and, if successful, recursively calls itself to attempt the placement of another queen in the next column. Such a function in skeletal pseudocode form follows:

```
void try_queen (K, J)

// Place a queen in row K, column J.
// Analyze state reached by this placement.
// If appropriate, recurse to place queen in next column.

Actually put queen at position K, J
If this results in successful configuration
        Tally this configuration
Else if no queen in immediate danger
```

```
       For each L from 1 to 8
              try_queen(L, J + 1)
  Retract from position K, J
```

The similarities between this sketch of a solution to the Eight Queens problem and our complete solution to the permutation problem should convince you that, from an abstract perspective, both problems are really the same. We have intentionally left the Eight Queens problem unfinished. Still to be resolved are such issues as:

- The initial call(s) to **try_queen**.
- How to represent the chessboard.
- How to check whether placing a queen at position **K, J** puts it in immediate danger. That is, how to determine whether there is currently another queen sharing the same row, column, or diagonal.

The resolution of these issues is left for your enjoyment in the programming problems at the end of the chapter. Additional problems given there further illustrate the far-reaching applicability of the trial-and-error backtracking method.

## RUNNING, DEBUGGING AND TESTING HINTS

1. Recursion is an elegant and powerful tool. It combines iterative control with a built-in data structure, the system stack. To properly control that iteration, be sure that you provide an appropriate recursive termination condition for your algorithms.
2. Be sure that, when you invoke a function recursively, you are in some sense passing in a smaller, simpler version of the problem being solved. Otherwise, your algorithm will infinitely recur.
3. The use of tracer output can be valuable in debugging recursive algorithms. However, you must be careful not to insert so many tracer output statements that you become lost in the copious output they produce. Remember that recursive algorithms are often exponential in efficiency and, consequently, may be exponential in the amount of output produced by tracers also. You must be careful to insert tracer output statements judiciously. Where appropriate, use a Boolean constant that can be toggled to TRUE or FALSE to control whether or not the tracer output is produced.

## SUMMARY

### Key Terms

| | | |
|---|---|---|
| binding time problem | recursive definition | stack frame |
| generalized nested loops | recursive function | tail-recursion |
| LISP | recursive termination | termination condition |
| recursion | condition | trial-and-error backtracking |
| recursive call | run-time trace diagram | |

### Key Concepts

◆ Stacks process function calls when a program executes. Understanding the role of the stack in this application is essential to effective use of the programming technique known as recursion.

◆ A recursive function invokes itself with a simpler version of the same problem it was originally given. Ultimately there must be a recursive termination condition to break a series of recursive function calls.

◆ In tail recursion, no further processing occurs at any level of recursion after a return from a recursive call is made.

◆ A function's stack frame contains memory locations for all parameters and local variables and the machine address of the point to return to after the function completes execution at the current level.

◆ A run-time trace diagram can often be used to help analyze the efficiency of a recursive algorithm. If the diagram indicates that multiple recursive calls are made at each level, there is a good chance that the algorithm is in the class of exponential algorithms.

◆ Recursion can be used to solve a complex class of search problems by using a trial-and-error backtracking strategy. However, often such solutions can consume a tremendous amount of resources, particularly in terms of run-time efficiency.

◆ Do not be misled into thinking that recursion is necessarily the most efficient programming technique because the code that expresses it is often compact and lacking in any explicit loop control statements such as **while** or **do**. The very nature of a recursive call generates iteration without any need for **while** or **do**. The iteration control mechanism in recursion is the recursive termination condition that triggers a series of returns before another recursive call is made. Hence, from a time-efficiency perspective, a recursive algorithm's measure of effectiveness is closely tied to the number of times it must iterate its recursive call-and-return pattern. Moreover, with recursion, we pay a price in memory efficiency that is not present in other iterative control structures. This price is system stack space.

◆ The value of recursion lies in the way in which it enables us to express algorithms compactly and elegantly for a certain class of problems. Since we use recursion frequently throughout the rest of this text, you will learn to acquire a feel for the type of problems particularly suitable to this powerful technique. In the next chapter, we will see that recursion is an indispensable strategy for manipulating a data structure known as a tree. In later chapters, recursion will be explored as a means of sorting and searching.

**PROGRAMMING PROBLEMS AND PROJECTS**

1. Write a program to call for input of a decimal number and convert it to its binary equivalent using the method described in the following flowchart:

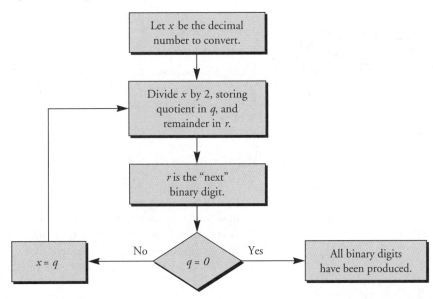

Note that this method produces the binary digits for the given number in reverse order. One strategy for printing the digits in the correct order would be to store them in an array as they are produced and then print the array. However, this strategy would have the drawbacks of allocating unnecessary storage for an array and then limiting the size of the binary number to the size of the array. Your program is not to employ this strategy. Rather call for input of the decimal number in your main program and then immediately transfer control to a function that in turn is called recursively, stacking the binary digits as they are produced. Once division by 2 yields 0, the succession of returns can be used to print the digits one by one as they are popped from this stack.

**2.** The $N$th Fibonacci number is defined by

1 if $N$ is 1.

1 if $N$ is 2.

The sum of the previous two Fibonacci numbers otherwise.

Write a recursive function to compute the $N$th Fibonacci number. Then, using a run-time trace diagram, analyze the efficiency of your function.

**3.** Euclid devised a clever algorithm for computing the greatest common divisor (GCD) of two integers. According to Euclid's algorithm,

$$GCD(M, N) = \begin{cases} GCD(N, M) \text{ if } N > M \\ M \text{ if } N = 0 \\ GCD(N, M \% N) \text{ if } N > 0 \end{cases}$$

Write a recursive function to compute GCDs via Euclid's method.

**4.** Suppose that you have $N$ thousand dollars and can use it to buy a combination of Orange computers (which cost \$1000 each), HAL computers (which cost \$2000 each), or MAX computers (which cost \$4000 each). How many different combinations of Orange, HAL, and MAX computers could be bought with your $N$ thousand dollars? Write a program that receives $N$ as input and responds with the number of possible combinations.

*Hint:* If $N$ were 100, then the number of combinations is

*The number of combinations totaling \$100,000 and involving Orange and HAL computers only*

*PLUS*

*The number of combinations totaling \$96,000 and involving potentially all three brands*

Think about this hint for a while and extend it to a recursive function that answers this question.

**5.** Ackermann's function is defined recursively for two nonnegative integers $m$ and $n$ as follows:

$$Ackermann(m,n) = \begin{cases} n + 1 \text{ if } m = 0 \\ Ackermann(m - 1, 1) \text{ if } n = 0 \\ Ackermann(m - 1, Ackermann\ (m,n - 1)) \text{ otherwise} \end{cases}$$

Write a recursive version of this function. Develop a run-time trace diagram for the function when $m = 2$ and $n = 3$. Attempt to deduce the big-O efficiency of the recursive version with respect to stack size and stack operations. Justify your answer in a written statement.

**6.** If you have access to an appropriate graphics device, write the functions `line` and `right_turn` described in Section 6.1. Then experiment by writing recursive functions that call on these functions (and others you may develop) to produce a variety of interesting figures.

7. Write a function that receives a set of $N$ integers and then prints all subsets of this set.

8. Write a program that completes the solution of the Eight Queens problem as sketched in the Focus on Program Design section.

9. A $K$-permutation of the first $N$ positive integers, $K <= N$, is a permutation of a $K$-element subset of $\{1, 2, \ldots, N\}$. Write a function to generate all possible $K$-permutations of the first $N$ positive integers.

10. A continued fraction is a number of the form that follows (where each $a_i$ is an integer):

$$a_1 + \cfrac{1}{a_2 + \cfrac{1}{a_3 + \cfrac{1}{a_4 + }}}$$

$$\cfrac{1}{a_n}$$

Though a continued fraction is composed of integers $a_i$, it has a real value. For example, consider the following continued fraction and its indicated real value.

$$1 + \cfrac{1}{2 + \cfrac{1}{6 + \cfrac{1}{5}}} = 1 + \cfrac{1}{2 + \cfrac{1}{\frac{31}{5}}} = 1 + \cfrac{1}{2 + \frac{5}{31}} = 1 + \cfrac{1}{\frac{67}{31}} = \frac{98}{67} = 1.46$$

Provide a type definition of your implementation of a continued fraction. Then, write a recursive function that receives a continued fraction and returns its associated real value.

11. There are five other teams in the same league as the Bay Area Brawlers (Problem 4, Chapter 4, and Problem 13, Chapter 5). Over a given five-week period, the Brawlers must play each of the other teams exactly once. Using recursion, write a program to determine the ways in which such a five-week schedule could be accomplished. For an added challenge, introduce more realistic scheduling considerations into this problem. For instance, have your program determine the ways in which a 15-game schedule could be constructed such that each of the six teams in the league plays each of the other teams exactly three times, but never consecutively.

12. Write a function that uses a random number generator to produce mazes. One way of viewing a maze is as a two-dimensional array of structures:

```
struct location
{
        boolean
        north_blocked,
        east_blocked,
        south_blocked,
        west_blocked;
};
```

At each square in the array, the Boolean attributes are set to indicate whether or not we can proceed in the indicated direction. After your maze-generating function is working, develop a function that uses trial-and-error backtracking to solve the maze.

13. A transportation network such as the following can be represented as a two-dimensional integer array with rows and columns indexed by the cities in the network. The number stored at position (**K**, **J**) of such an array represents the distance of the link between two cities. Zero indicates that two cities are not directly linked.

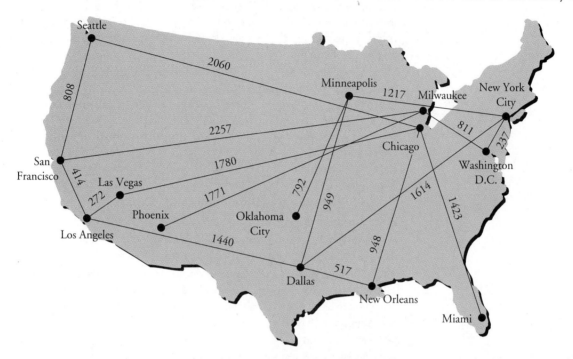

Write a program which, for input of two cities, outputs all possible paths connecting the two cities. Then modify the program so that it outputs only the shortest path linking the two cities. Use a trial-and-error backtracking strategy to do this. We will discuss a more efficient algorithm for solving this problem in the next chapter.

14. Another classic chess problem that can be solved by trial-and-error backtracking is known as the Knight's Tour. Given a chessboard with a knight initially placed at coordinates $x_0$, $y_0$ the problem is to specify a series of moves for the knight that will result in each board location being visited exactly once. From a given square on the chessboard, a knight may move to any of the eight numbered squares in the following diagram:

|   | 3 |   | 2 |   |
|---|---|---|---|---|
| 4 |   |   |   | 1 |
|   |   |   |   |   |
| 5 |   |   |   | 8 |
|   | 6 |   | 7 |   |

Write a program to find a valid Knight's Tour.

**15.** A famous theorem in mathematics states that four colors are enough to color any map in a fashion that allows each region on the map to be a different color from any of its adjacent neighbors. Write a program that initially allows input of a map. One way of doing this is to input each region followed by a list of its adjacent neighbors. This information can then be stored in a two-dimensional Boolean array with rows and columns indexed by region names. Store TRUE at row **K**, column **J**, if region **K** and region **J** are neighbors; otherwise store FALSE. Once your program has appropriately stored the information associated with the input map, it should use trial-and-error backtracking to find a pattern for coloring the map with four colors. Note that the Four-Color Theorem from mathematics guarantees that such a pattern can be found.

**16.** Write a program to find a solution to the following stable marriage problem (or indicate that no solution exists for the input data). According to this problem, we have $N$ men and $N$ women, each of whom has stated distinct preferences for their possible partners. The data regarding these preferences is the input for this problem. It can be stored in two two-dimensional arrays: one in which each woman has rated each of the men as 1st choice, 2nd choice, . . . , $N$th choice and another in which each man has similarly rated each of the women. Given this input, a solution to the stable marriage problem is to find $N$ couples (marriages) such that

1. Each man is part of exactly one couple (marriage).

2. Each woman is part of exactly one couple (marriage).

3. There does not exist a man and a woman who are not married to each other but who would prefer each other to their current spouses.

If a pair as specified in requirement 3 does exist, then the assignment of $N$ couples is said to be unstable and should be avoided. Note that the stable marriage problem is representative of many real-life problems in which assignments have to be made according to preferences.

**17.** Write a program to analyze football team scores by computing the point spread for any team A playing any team B. Your program should compute the point spreads as follows:

*Level I analysis: Team A played B in past*
*Level II analysis: Average point spreads for situations such as*

> A played C—point spread 3
> C played B—point spread 7

> *Total point spread 10*

*Level III analysis: Average point spread for situations such as*

> A played C—point spread 3
> C played D—point spread –14 (C lost)
> D played B—point spread 7

> *Total point spread –4*

*Level IV analysis: Average point spreads for situations such as*

> A played C—point spread 3
> C played D—point spread –14
> D played E—point spread 21
> E played B—point spread 4

*Total point spread 14*

All level II point spreads are then averaged for a final level II point spread figure. Point spreads are similarly averaged for levels III and IV. Items that potentially need to be stacked (via recursion) in this program include

- Accumulated point spread at current position
- Number of scores reflected in the accumulated point spread at current position
- Current position; that is, team A playing team B
- Path to the current position; that is, teams played to get to the current position.

**18.** Write a solution to the Towers of Hanoi problem in which you use a nonrecursive iterative control structure and a stack. In effect, your stack will simulate the role played by the system stack in the recursive version of the algorithm. In a written statement, compare the time and space efficiency of your nonrecursive solution to the recursive solution presented in this chapter. Is your solution faster than the exponential recursive solution? If so, explain why it is. Otherwise, explain why it is still exponential in its run time.

**19.** If you have had a course in discrete mathematics, then you may be familiar with recurrence relations and methods for explicitly solving them. Use your knowledge of recurrence relations to analyze the time and space efficiencies of the Towers of Hanoi and recursive binary search algorithms. Your analysis should be presented as a precise mathematical argument, citing any results that you use but do not prove.

# 7 Binary Trees, General Trees, and Graphs

*Except during the nine months before he draws his first breath, no man manages his affairs as well as a tree does.*
George Bernard Shaw, 1856–1950

Human beings organize much of the world around them into *hierarchies.* For instance, an industrial body functions effectively only by defining a collection of client–server relationships among its participants. We have emphasized throughout the text that computer scientists design a software system by breaking it down into modules and defining hierarchical client–server relationships among those modules. In Chapter 6, we used hierarchical run-time trace diagrams to analyze the efficiency of recursive algorithms. To continue this discussion, we now introduce the idea of trees.

The familial parent-child relationship allows a natural breakdown of a family's history into a genealogical tree. In computer science, a *tree* is a data structure that represents such hierarchical relationships between data items.

To introduce some of the terminology of tree structures, consider the record of a student at a typical university. In addition to the usual statistical background information such as social security number, name, and address, a typical student record contains listings for a number of courses, exams and final grades in each course, overall grade-point average, and other data relating to the student's performance at the college. Figure 7.1 is a tree structure representing such a student record. As in genealogical trees, at the highest *level* (0) of a tree is its *root* (also called the *root node*). Here STUDENT is the root node. The nodes NAME, ADDRESS, SSN, COURSE, and GPA, which are directly connected to the root node, are the *child nodes* of the *parent node* STUDENT. The child nodes of a given parent constitute a set of *siblings.* Thus NAME, ADDRESS, SSN, COURSE, and GPA are siblings. In the hierarchy represented by a tree, the child nodes of a parent are one level lower than the parent node. Thus NAME, ADDRESS, SSN, COURSE, and GPA are at level 1 in Figure 7.1.

A link between a parent and its child is called a *branch* in a tree structure. Each node in a tree except the root must descend from a parent node via a branch. Thus LAST NAME, FIRST NAME, and MIDDLE NAME descend from the parent node NAME. The root of the tree is the *ancestor* of all the nodes in the tree.

◆ **FIGURE 7.1**
Tree structure representing a
student record

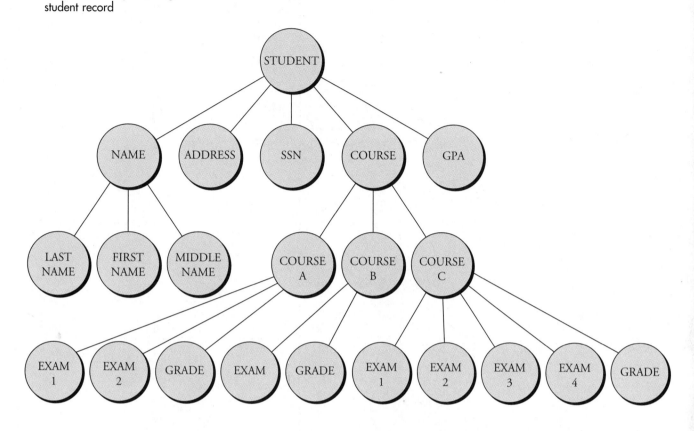

A node with no children is called a *leaf node*. In Figure 7.1, GPA is a leaf
node. LAST NAME, FIRST NAME, MIDDLE NAME, EXAM 1, and EXAM 2,
for instance, also are leaf nodes.

A *subtree* is a subset of a tree that is itself a tree; the tree in Figure 7.2 is a
subtree of the tree in Figure 7.1. This subtree has the root node NAME. Similarly,
the tree in Figure 7.3 is another subtree of the tree in Figure 7.1. Notice that the
tree in Figure 7.3 is a subtree of the tree in Figure 7.1 and the tree in Figure 7.4.

◆ **FIGURE 7.2**
Subtree of Figure 7.1

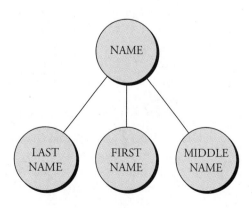

◆ **FIGURE 7.3**
Another subtree of Figure
7.1

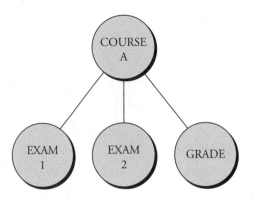

◆ **FIGURE 7.4**
Another subtree of Figure
7.1

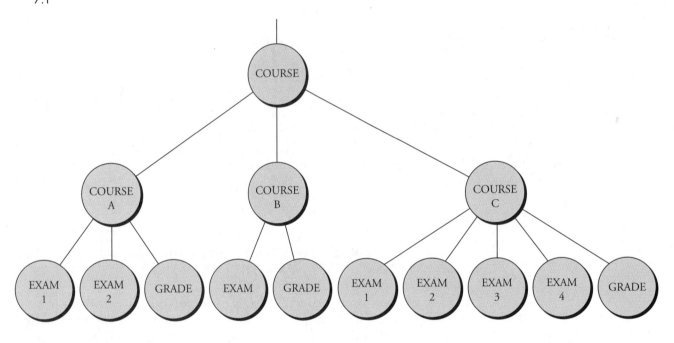

## 7.1 General Trees and Binary Trees as Abstract Data Types

It is evident from the preceding discussion that a tree has the following interesting property: Any given node within a tree is itself the root node of a completely analogous tree structure. That is, a tree is composed of a collection of substructures, each of which also meets the criteria for being a tree. This sounds dangerously circular, and, to formally describe a tree in this fashion, we must be sure to give ourselves an escape from the recursion. This is done via the following definition of a tree as an abstract data type:

> **Tree:** A general tree is a set of nodes that is either empty (the recursive termination condition), or has a designated node called the root from which descend zero or more subtrees. Each node is not an ancestor of itself, and each subtree itself satisfies the definition of a tree.

## OBJECTIVES

- to define partially the general tree ADT
- to define completely the binary tree ADT
- to understand conceptually the effect of each of the binary tree operations
- to become familiar with some examples of binary trees such as heaps, arithmetic expression trees, and binary search trees

We defer completing the definition of a general tree to Section 7.5, where we will more formally discuss the operations associated with this ADT.

Two points about this partial definition should be emphasized. First, the recursive fashion in which a tree is defined should provide a strong hint that most tree-processing algorithms will also be recursive. Second, most operations on the tree data structure are closely linked to the hierarchical relationship among nodes for that particular tree. This hierarchical relationship may vary greatly from tree to tree. To consider some examples of such relationships, which are found quite often in computer science applications, let us restrict our attention for the moment to an abstract data type called a *binary tree*.

> **Binary tree:** A binary tree is a tree in which each node has exactly two subtrees. These two subtrees are designated as the left and right subtrees, respectively. Note that either or both of these subtrees could be empty.

We specify the following operations on a binary tree in terms of preconditions and postconditions.

---

**Create operation**
Preconditions:     Receiver is a binary tree in an unpredictable state.
Postconditions:    Receiver is initialized to the empty binary tree.

**Empty operation**
Preconditions:     Receiver is a previously created binary tree.
Postconditions:    Returns TRUE if the tree is empty, FALSE otherwise.

**Insert operation**
Preconditions:     Receiver is a previously created binary tree based on a particular hierarchical property. `item` is a value to be inserted in the tree. There is memory available in the tree for the new item.
Postconditions:    `item` is added to the tree in a way that maintains the tree's hierarchical property.

**preorder_traverse operation**
Preconditions:     Receiver is a previously created binary tree, and `process` is an algorithmic process that can be applied to each node in the tree.
Postconditions:    Each node of the tree is visited in the following order: root of the tree first, then recursively all nodes in left subtree, then recursively all nodes in right subtree. As each node is visited, `process` is applied to it.

**inorder_traverse operation**
Preconditions:     Receiver is a previously created binary tree, and `process` is an algorithmic process that can be applied to each node in the tree.
Postconditions:    Each node of the tree is visited in the following order: First visit recursively all nodes in left subtree of the tree, then visit the root of the tree, then recursively all nodes in right subtree. As each node is visited, `process` is applied to it.

**postorder_traverse operation**
Preconditions:     Receiver is a previously created binary tree, and `process` is an algorithmic process that can be applied to each node in the tree.
Postconditions:    Each node of the tree is visited in the following order: First visit recursively all nodes in left subtree of the tree, then visit recursively all nodes in right subtree, then visit the root of the tree. As each node is visited, `process` is applied to it.

---

Several remarks are in order concerning this definition. First, the three traversal procedures require some clarification. With a linked list, there is only one obvious traversal because there was only one node that could be reached from any given node. However, with a binary tree, at any node, some choices need to be made:

- Should we apply **process** to the data field of the root before proceeding to the left and right subtrees?
- Should we apply **process** to the nodes in the left subtree and right subtree before processing the data in the root?
- Should we apply **process** to all the nodes in one of the subtrees, then to the root, and finally to all the nodes in the other subtree?

The answers to these questions determine the type of traversal. Figure 7.5 demonstrates the different orders in which nodes are visited under the three traversals.

◆ **FIGURE 7.5**

Differences between preorder, inorder, and postorder traversals

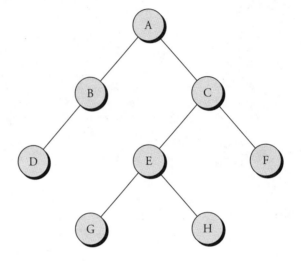

Order in which nodes are processed:

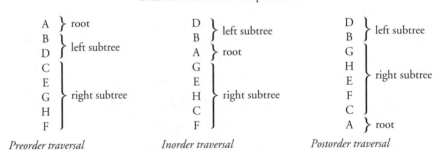

| A } root | D } left subtree | D } left subtree |
| B | B | B |
| D } left subtree | A } root | G |
| C | G | H |
| E | E | E } right subtree |
| G } right subtree | H } right subtree | F |
| H | C | C |
| F | F | A } root |
| *Preorder traversal* | *Inorder traversal* | *Postorder traversal* |

Second, the **insert** operation specified in our ADT definition for a binary tree provides a generic tree-building operation. That is, repeated applications of the **insert** operation on an initially empty binary tree typically lead to the construction of a binary tree. However, it is virtually impossible to define or implement the **insert** operation in a way that is general enough for all applications that will use a binary tree. Each instance of a binary tree is highly dependent on the hierarchical relationship between nodes that defines that particular binary tree. Therefore, we have linked our specification of the **insert** operation to the hierarchical relationship underlying a particular binary tree.

The following three examples provide illustrations of hierarchical relationships that can be used in defining binary trees. We will often use trees based on these hierarchical properties as examples in the remainder of the chapter. However, these three properties should by no means be considered exhaustive—virtually every application that uses a binary tree will have its own essential property. The point to be emphasized now is that the **insert** operation must, in its implementation, always be tailored to the property that defines a tree.

---

**EXAMPLE 7.1**

The tree of Figure 7.6 is a binary tree. Each node of this tree has two subtrees (null or non-null) designated as the left subtree and the right subtree. The particular hierarchical relationship underlying this tree is that the data in any given node of the tree are greater than or equal to the data in its left *and* right subtrees. A tree with this property is said to be a *heap* and to have the *heap property*. (This notion is not to be confused with the heap maintained by C++ for allocating space to pointer variables as described in Chapter 4.) We will discuss heaps in more detail in the next section. Also, they will prove particularly important in our discussion of more powerful sorting methods in Chapter 8. The programming problems at the end of this chapter also indicate how a heap may be used to implement the priority queue abstract data type introduced in Chapter 5. The heap property is one example of a hierarchical relationship that can underlie a tree and hence must be preserved when various operations are performed on the tree.

◆ **FIGURE 7.6**

Binary tree with the heap property

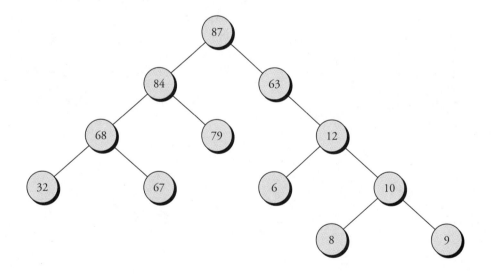

---

**EXAMPLE 7.2**

A second example of a hierarchical relationship underlying a binary tree structure is shown in Figure 7.7. This binary tree exhibits the property known as the *ordering property;* the data in each node of the tree are greater than all of the data in that node's left subtree and less than or equal to all the data in the right subtree. A binary tree with the ordering property is often called a *binary search tree.* We shall see the importance of trees possessing this property when we explore binary trees as a means of implementing a one-key table in Section 7.3.

◆ **FIGURE 7.7**
Binary search tree with the
ordering property

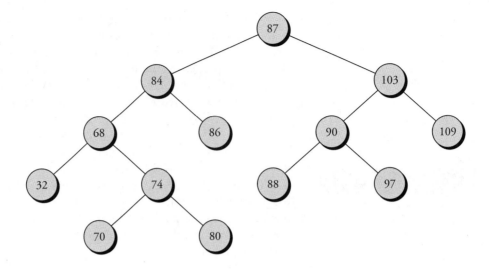

<table>
<tr><td></td></tr>
</table>

| EXAMPLE 7.3 |

As a final example of a hierarchical relationship that can determine the arrangement of data in a binary tree, consider Figure 7.8, in which we have a binary tree representation of the infix algebraic expression

```
(A - B) + C * (E / F)
```

Take a moment to make particular note of Figure 7.8. Since we will be referring back to it frequently throughout this chapter, you may want to clip the page or mark it with a bookmark.

◆ **FIGURE 7.8**
Binary expression tree for
`(A - B) + C *`
`(E/F)`

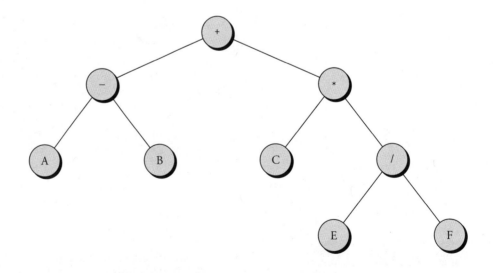

The hierarchical relationship of a parent to its children in this tree is that of algebraic operator to its two operands. Note that an operand may itself be an expression (that is, a subtree) which must be evaluated before the operator in the parent node can be applied. Note also that, if the order of evaluation in the expression changes as in

◆ FIGURE 7.9

Binary expression tree for
`(A - B) + C * E/F`

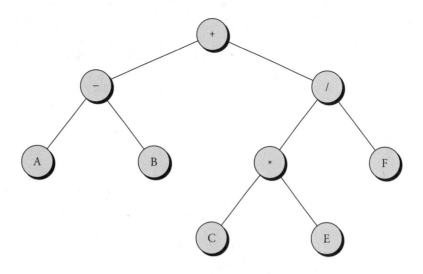

```
(A - B) + C * E / F
```

then the corresponding binary expression tree must also change as reflected in Figure 7.9.

Contemporary compilers make use of tree structures in obtaining forms of an arithmetic expression for efficient evaluation. As we've seen, there are basically three forms for an arithmetic expression such as that corresponding to Figure 7.8: infix, prefix, and postfix.

| Expression | Form |
|---|---|
| `(A - B) + C * (E / F)` | infix |
| `+ - A B * C / E F` | prefix |
| `A B - C E F / * +` | postfix |

All three of these forms are immediately available to us if we know exactly how the corresponding tree should be traversed. The *inorder traversal* of the binary tree for an arithmetic expression gives us the expression in unparenthesized infix form. The *preorder traversal* of the same tree leads us to the prefix form of the expression, whereas the *postorder traversal* of the tree yields the postfix form of the expression. We shall study procedures for these three traversals in Section 7.2, when we discuss a method of implementing a binary tree.

---

We close this section with a C++ interface for the binary tree ADT. In the sections that follow, we will analyze two implementations that adhere to this interface.

### C++ Interface for the Binary Tree ADT

```
// Class declaration file: bintree.h

#ifndef BINARY_TREE_H

#include "boolean.h"
```

```
// Definition section

// We assume that type boolean is already defined

template <class E> class binary_tree
{

        public:

        // Class constructors

        binary_tree();
        binary_tree(const binary_tree<E> &bt);

        // Class destructor

        ~binary_tree();

        // Member functions

        boolean empty();
        void insert(const E &item);
        void preorder_traverse(void (*process) (E &item));
        void inorder_traverse(void (*process) (E &item));
        void postorder_traverse(void (*process) (E &item));
        binary_tree<E>& operator = (const binary_tree &bt);

        // Protected data and member functions pertaining to
        // the implementation would go here.

};

#define BINARY_TREE_H
#endif
```

**EXERCISES 7.1**

1. Draw a binary tree for the following expression:

   `A * B - (C + D) * (P / Q)`

2. Represent the following information as a binary tree:

   ```
   struct name
   {
           string first_name, last_name;
   };

   struct year
   {
           string first_sem, second_sem;
   };

   struct student
   ```

```
    {
            name student_name;
            year year_of_study;
    };
```

**3.** What, in an abstract sense, does a tree structure represent?

**4.** Indicate which of the following are binary search trees with the ordering property. Carefully explain what is wrong with those that are not.

**a.**

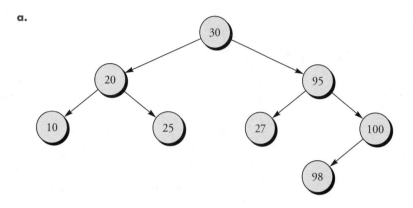

**b.**

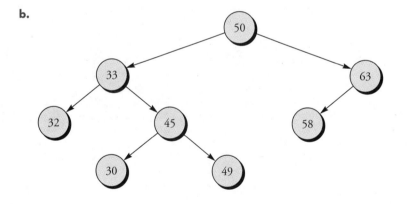

**c.**

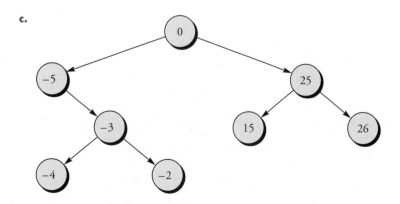

**d.**

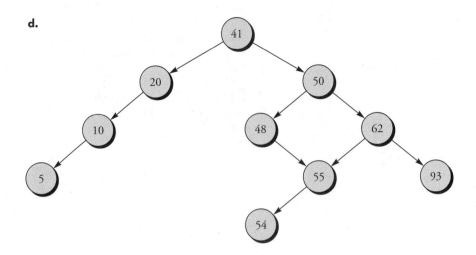

**5.** Indicate which of the following are binary trees with the heap property. Carefully explain what is wrong with those that are not.

**a.**

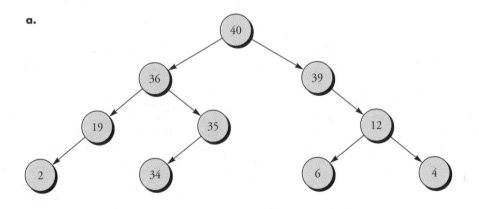

**b.**

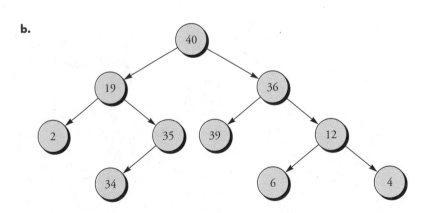

**c.**

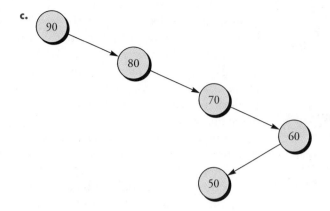

6. Given the following binary tree, indicate the order in which nodes would be processed for each of the preorder, postorder, and inorder traversals.

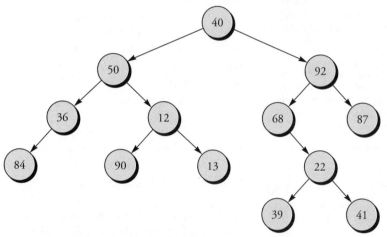

7. Construct some binary search trees with the ordering property. Then do some inorder traversals of these trees. What do you observe about the order in which nodes are processed? Be as specific as possible in stating your answer.

8. Given the following postorder and inorder traversals of a binary tree, draw the tree

   Postorder: ABCDEFIKJGH
   Inorder: CBAEDFHIGKJ

   Attempt to deduce your answer in a systematic (and recursive) fashion, not by trial-and-error methods. After you have solved this problem, write a statement in which you describe the method you used to solve it and explain how this method could be applied to similar problems.

9. Draw binary expression trees corresponding to the algebraic expression whose:
   **a.** infix representation is `P / (Q + R) * X - Y`.
   **b.** postfix representation is `X Y Z P Q R * + /- *`.
   **c.** prefix representation is `+ * - M N P / R S`.

10. In a written statement, explain how the arrangement of data in a binary expression tree reflects the order of operations in the corresponding expression.

# 7.2 Linked Implementation of a Binary Tree

## OBJECTIVES

- to become familiar with the linked implementation of the binary tree ADT
- to be able to implement the **insert** operation for a binary search tree with the ordering property
- to see how the shape of a binary search tree is dependent on the order in which data arrive for insertion into the tree
- to develop algorithms for the three traversal operations on the linked implementation of a binary tree

Consistent with the way in which we have studied other data structures, we now have a very good idea of *what* a tree is without any consideration of *how* we will implement it. We now explore this latter issue.

Two common methods are available for implementing binary trees. One method, known as *linked implementation,* uses dynamic allocation of nodes and pointers to these nodes. The other, which does not require the overhead of maintaining pointers, is called a *linear implementation* or *array implementation.* In this section and the next, we focus on the linked implementation. We will see how this implementation is particularly well suited for binary search trees and binary expression trees.

Because each node in a binary tree may have two child nodes, a node in a linked implementation has two pointer members, one for each child, and one or more members for storing data. When a node has no children, the corresponding pointer members are NULL. Figure 7.10 is a linked representation of the binary expression tree of Figure 7.8. The left and right members are pointers to (that is, memory addresses of) the left child node and the right child node of the current node.

For the moment, let us give a detailed description of the linked representation of the binary tree of Figure 7.8. Once the concept is thoroughly understood, we will return to using C++ pointer variables for the actual implementation of binary trees. For example, we can implement the tree of Figure 7.10 as shown in Table 7.1 by building the left subtree for each node before considering the right subtree. The numbers on top of the cells in Figure 7.10 represent the addresses given in the left and right members.

In the linked representation, insertions and deletions involve no data movement except the rearrangement of pointers. Suppose we wish to modify the tree in Figure 7.8 to that in Figure 7.11. (This change might be needed due to some recent modification in the expression represented by Figure 7.8.) The insertion of the nodes containing – and P into the tree structure can be achieved easily by simply adding the nodes - and P in the next available spaces in the array and adjusting the corresponding pointers.

For the implementation of the tree shown in Figure 7.10, the effect of this insertion is given by Table 7.2. The adjusted pointers and data fields have been circled. Notice that the change in row 1 of the Right column and the additional rows 10 and 11 are all that is necessary. No data were moved.

◆ **FIGURE 7.10**
Linked representation of the binary expression tree of Figure 7.8

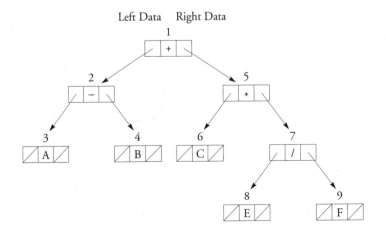

◇ TABLE 7.1
Implementation of Figure
7.10 using array of
records

| Node | Data | Left | Right |
|------|------|------|-------|
| 1 | + | 2 | 5 |
| 2 | – | 3 | 4 |
| 3 | A | NULL | NULL |
| 4 | B | NULL | NULL |
| 5 | * | 6 | 7 |
| 6 | C | NULL | NULL |
| 7 | / | 8 | 9 |
| 8 | E | NULL | NULL |
| 9 | F | NULL | NULL |

◆ FIGURE 7.11
Desired modification of Figure 7.8

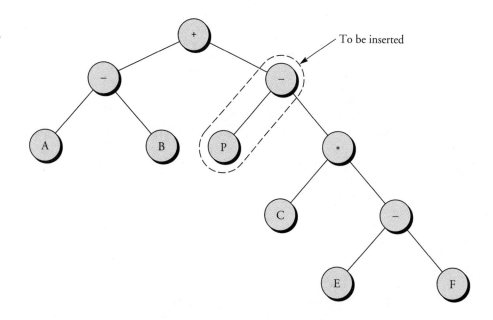

To be inserted

◇ TABLE 7.2
Modification of Table 7.1
by insertions into the tree of
Figure 7.8

| Row | Data | Left | Right |
|-----|------|------|-------|
| 1 | + | 2 | 10 |
| 2 | – | 3 | 4 |
| 3 | A | NULL | NULL |
| 4 | B | NULL | NULL |
| 5 | * | 6 | 7 |
| 6 | C | NULL | NULL |
| 7 | / | 8 | 9 |
| 8 | E | NULL | NULL |
| 9 | F | NULL | NULL |
| 10 | – | 11 | 5 |
| 11 | P | NULL | NULL |

Similarly, if we wish to shorten the tree in Figure 7.8 by deleting the nodes
* and C, then all we must do is rearrange the pointers to obtain the altered tree,
as shown in Figure 7.12. The effect of this deletion is given in Table 7.3. As
before, the adjusted pointers and data fields have been circled.

A more formal statement of the algorithm underlying such insertions and
deletions is dependent on the hierarchical property that forms the basis for the tree

◆ **FIGURE 7.12**
Another modification of Figure 7.8

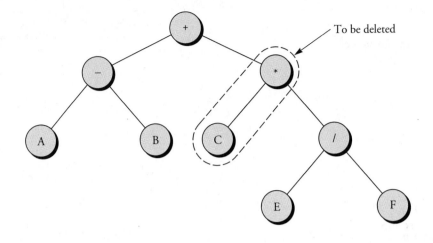

◇ **TABLE 7.3**
Modification of tree of
Figure 7.8

| Row | Data | Left | Right | Modified tree |
|---|---|---|---|---|
| 1 | + | 2 | 7 | |
| 2 | – | 3 | 4 | |
| 3 | A | NULL | NULL | |
| 4 | B | NULL | NULL | |
| 5 | * | | | Unused space after deletion of '*' and 'C' |
| 6 | C | | | |
| 7 | / | 8 | 9 | |
| 8 | E | NULL | NULL | |
| 9 | F | NULL | NULL | |

structure. We will soon examine in detail insertion and deletion algorithms for binary search trees.

Now that we have explained the linked representation of a binary tree by using pointer values that can be explicitly traced, we will use the following general structure description with C++ pointer variables to implement this structure in the remainder of this and the next sections:

```
struct node;
typedef node *node_ptr;

struct node
{
        element data;
        node_ptr left;
        node_ptr right;
};
```

As we did for the pointer implementation of a linked list in Chapter 4, we embed this set of data definitions in the class definition for a binary tree, along with a data member for the root pointer:

```
// Class declaration file: bintree.h

#ifndef BINARY_TREE_H

#include "boolean.h"

// Declaration section

// We assume that type boolean is already defined

template <class E> class binary_tree
{

    public:

    // Class constructors

    binary_tree();
    binary_tree(const binary_tree<E> &bt);

    // Class destructor

    ~binary_tree();

    // Member functions

    boolean empty();
    void insert(const E &item);
    void preorder_traverse(void (*process) (E &item));
    void inorder_traverse(void (*process) (E &item));
    void postorder_traverse(void (*process) (E &item));
    binary_tree<E>& operator = (const binary_tree<E> &bt);

    protected:

    // Data members

    struct node;
    typedef node *node_ptr;
    struct node
    {
        E data;
        node_ptr left;
        node_ptr right;
    };

    node_ptr tree;
```

```
        // Helper member functions would go here

};

#define BINARY_TREE_H
#endif
```

Note the comment about helper member functions. Because we will use recursion to implement many of the tree processing algorithms, we need a way of passing the tree data member as a parameter to each recursive function. Since this data member is protected, it cannot be a parameter of the public functions. Therefore, each of the operations in question will consist of a public function calling a protected helper function that carries out the recursive algorithm on the tree. We will need one such function for **insert** and for each of the traversal operations.

Recall that we also defined a utility function, **get_node**, in Chapter 14 to take care of the details of creating and initializing a new node for a linked list. We can write a similar function for binary trees as well:

```
template <class E>
binary_tree<E>::node_ptr binary_tree<E>::get_node(const E &data)
{
        node_ptr temp = new node;

        assert(temp != NULL);
        temp->data = data;
        temp->left = NULL;
        temp->right = NULL;
        return temp;
}
```

Note that **get_node** asks for new memory from the system heap and then checks for successful allocation before initializing the contents of a node. Now we have two pointers in a node to set to NULL. Therefore, if a pointer to a node is returned, the node is a leaf node.

---

**EXAMPLE 7.4**

Using the linked representation of a binary tree, implement the **insert** operation for a binary search tree with the ordering property. The **insert** operation passes the new element and the protected data member **tree** to a helper function, **insert_aux**:

```
template <class E>
void binary_tree<E>::insert(const E &data)
{
        insert_aux(tree, data);
}
```

The helper function **insert_aux** then performs the insertion:

```
template <class E>
void binary_tree<E>::insert_aux(node_ptr &tree, const E &data)
{
    if (tree == NULL)
        tree = get_node(data);
```

```
    else if (data < tree->data)
          insert_aux(tree->left, data);
    else
          insert_aux(tree->right, data);
}
```

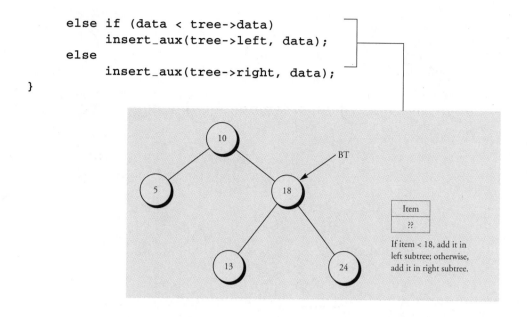

If item < 18, add it in left subtree; otherwise, add it in right subtree.

The **insert_aux** function of Example 7.4 implies that insertion of new nodes will always occur at the leaf nodes of a tree. As with insertion into a linked list, no data are moved; only pointers are manipulated. However, unlike the steps required by a linked list, we do not have to traverse the list sequentially to determine where the new node belongs. Instead, we use the *insertion rule*—if less than, go left; otherwise, go right—so that we traverse by subdividing the tree to determine the position for a new node. For example, if the **insert** function of Example 7.4 is successively fed numerical items in the following order:

```
16  8  -5  20  30  101  0  10  18
```

the binary search tree that results can be traced by the sequence in Figure 7.13. Note that the shape of the binary search tree is dependent on the order in which data items are given to the **insert** operation. This dependency of the shape of the tree on the order in which data arrive for insertion complicates any attempt to analyze the efficiency of the insert function in Example 7.4. We will provide a more detailed analysis of binary search trees with the ordering property in Section 7.3.

## Implementing Traversal Operations on a Binary Tree

In Section 7.1 we described conceptually three different traversal operations on a binary tree: preorder, inorder, and postorder. In Example 7.3, we established correspondences between these three traversals and the prefix, infix, and postfix forms of the algebraic formula represented by a binary expression tree. However, it is important to reiterate that the three traversals apply broadly to all binary trees, regardless of the hierarchical relationship underlying their structure.

Recall from Section 7.1 the threefold dilemma facing us at each node we visit in a traversal of a binary tree:

**1.** Do we process the data contained in the node at which we are currently located?

◆ FIGURE 7.13
Growth of search tree when
data arrive in order 16 8 -5
20 30 101 0 10 18

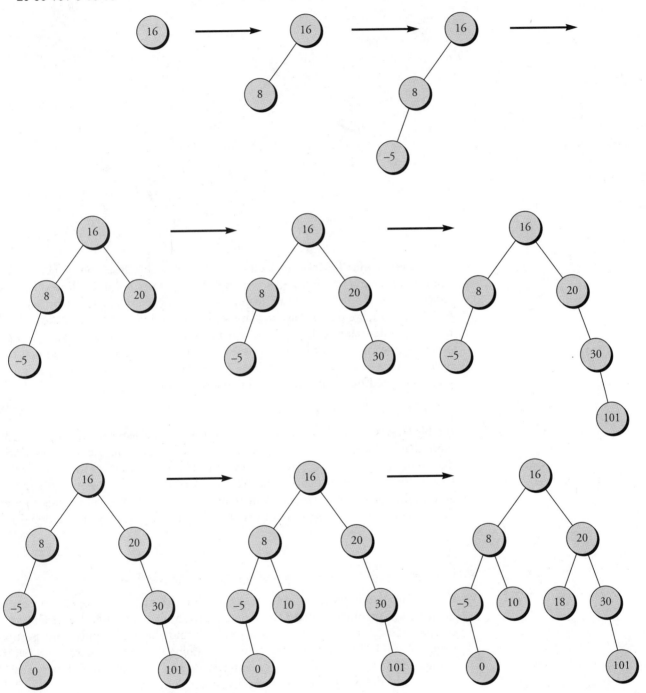

**2.** Do we remember the location of the current node (so that we can return to process it) and visit (and process) all nodes in its left subtree?

**3.** Do we remember the location of the current node (so that we can return to process it) and visit (and process) all nodes in its right subtree?

Each of the three choices represents a valid choice. The route chosen out of the three-way dilemma dictates the order in which the nodes are visited and processed.

## Preorder Traversal of a Binary Tree

In a preorder traversal, the three options are combined in the following order:

**1.** First, process the root node.
**2.** Then, recursively visit all nodes in the left subtree.
**3.** Finally, recursively visit all nodes in the right subtree.

These three ordered steps are recursive. Once the root of the tree is processed, we go to the root of the left subtree, and then to the root of the left subtree of the left subtree, and so on until we can go no farther. Following these three steps, the preorder traversal of the tree of Figure 7.8 would process nodes in the order

```
+ - A B * C / E F
```

which is the prefix form of the expression

```
(A - B) + C * (E / F)
```

Hence we conclude that if to process a node means to print it, then a preorder traversal of a binary expression tree will output the prefix form of the expression.

The preorder traversal of an existing binary tree implemented via the linked representation can be accomplished recursively using the following pair of functions, where **preorder_aux** is the helper function for the public member function **preorder_traverse:**

```cpp
template <class E>
void binary_tree<E>::preorder_traverse(void (* process) (E &item))
{
    preorder_aux(tree, process);
}


template <class E>
void binary_tree<E>::preorder_aux(node_ptr tree, void (* process) (E &item))
{
    if (tree != NULL)
    {
        process(tree->data);
        preorder_aux(tree->left, process);
        preorder_aux(tree->right, process);
    }
}
```

First, process root node.

Second, traverse left subtree.

Third, traverse right subtree.

## Inorder Traversal of a Binary Tree

The inorder traversal of a binary tree proceeds as outlined in the following three ordered steps:

**1.** First, recursively visit all nodes in the left subtree.
**2.** Then, process the root node.
**3.** Finally, recursively visit all nodes in the right subtree.

By carefully following these steps for the tree of Figure 7.8 and assuming "process" means "print," we obtain the readily recognizable infix expression

```
A - B + C * E / F
```

Unless we add parentheses, this infix expression is not equivalent to the order of operations reflected in the tree of Figure 7.8. The fact that prefix and postfix notations do not require parentheses to avoid such ambiguities makes them distinctly superior to infix notation for evaluation purposes.

An implementation of the recursive algorithm for an inorder traversal is given in the following pair of functions for a linked representation of a binary tree:

```
template <class E>
void binary_tree<E>::inorder_traverse(void (* process) (E &item))
{
    inorder_aux(tree, process);
}


template <class E>
void binary_tree<E>::inorder_aux(node_ptr tree, void (* process) (E &item))
{
    if (tree != NULL)
    {
        inorder_aux(tree->left, process);
        process(tree->data);
        inorder_aux(tree->right, process);
    }
}
```

Second, process root node.

First, traverse left subtree.

Third, traverse right subtree.

## Postorder Traversal of a Binary Tree

The third standard traversal of a binary tree, the postorder traversal, entails an arrangement of options that postpones processing the root node until last.

**1.** First, recursively visit all nodes in the left subtree of the root node.
**2.** Then, recursively visit all nodes in the right subtree of the root node.
**3.** Finally, process the root node.

Applying these three steps to the binary expression tree of Figure 7.8 yields the postfix form of the underlying expression:

```
A B - C E F / * +
```

The actual implementation of the postorder traversal operation is completely analogous to the inorder and preorder operations. Consequently, we will leave it as an exercise.

Although we have illustrated the three traversal algorithms using binary expression trees, we emphasize that the traversals apply in general to *any* binary tree. Indeed, as we shall see in the next section, the inorder traversal when used in combination with a tree exhibiting the hierarchical ordering property of a binary search tree will neatly allow us to implement a one-key table using a binary tree.

## Copying and Destroying a Binary Tree

Two of the binary tree class operations that require traversals are the copy constructor and the destructor. The copy constructor should copy all of the data elements in the original (parameter) tree to the new (receiver) tree. Not only should this operation preserve the ordering of the data in the new binary tree, but the structure of the nodes should be exactly the same as in the original tree. Thus, the root node of the new tree should contain the same data element as the root node of the original tree, and so on for each subtree. To guarantee both ordering and structure, we perform a preorder traversal of the original tree. When a node in the original tree is visited, its data element is inserted into the new tree with **insert**. Then the left and right subtrees are copied in the same manner. Unfortunately, we cannot use the **preorder_traverse** operation for copying the original tree, because the **process** function would have no access to the new tree. Therefore, a new helper function must be written that performs the preorder traversal directly. The code for the copy constructor and the helper function is

```
template <class E>
binary_tree<E>::binary_tree(const binary_tree<E> &bt)
{
// Pass the original tree's data member to the traversal function.
    copy_aux(bt.tree);
}


template <class E>
void binary_tree<E>::copy_aux(node_ptr tree)
{
    if (tree != NULL)
    {
// Copy from original to new (receiver) tree.
        insert(tree->data);
        copy_aux(tree->left);
        copy_aux(tree->right);
    }
}
```

Note that the identifier **tree** in the helper function refers to the data member of the original tree, not to the receiver tree's data member. The receiver tree's data member is accessed with the same identifier within the implementation of **insert**.

Recall from Chapter 4 that any class that uses dynamic memory in its implementation should have a class destructor operation. This function returns any memory used for nodes to the system heap. The class destructor is run automatically by the computer when a variable or parameter bound to an instance of the class goes out of scope. Given these requirements, we need a traversal algorithm that visits the leaf nodes of a tree first, deletes them from the tree, and then visits the leaf nodes at the next level up. Clearly, a preorder traversal will not work, because that would delete root nodes first. An inorder traversal would delete the left subtree before the root node, but the root node would be lost before we could visit the leaves of the right subtree. A postorder traversal would be just right because it would first delete the left subtree, and then the right subtree, before deleting a root node. The recursive process guarantees that the leaf nodes at any level in the tree are deleted first. Once again, we cannot use an established traversal operation, because of scope problems. So we present the code for the class destructor and a new helper operation that carries out a mass deletion in postorder:

```
template <class E>
binary_tree<E>::~binary_tree()
{
    destroy_aux(tree);
    tree = NULL;
}


template <class E>
void binary_tree<E>::destroy_aux(node_ptr tree)
{
    if (tree != NULL)
    {
        destroy_aux(tree->left);
        destroy_aux(tree->right);
        delete tree;        // Return leaf node to system heap.
    }
}
```

Note that the identifier **tree** refers in both of these functions to the receiver's data member. After **destroy_aux** has returned any nodes to the system heap, the top-level destructor operation sets the data member to NULL to indicate an empty binary tree.

**EXERCISES 7.2**

1. Using a preorder traversal of the tree you derived in Exercise 1 from Section 7.1, obtain the prefix form of the expression in that exercise.

2. Sketch the binary search tree that would result when the **insert** function of Example 7.4 is used for data that arrive in the following orders:
   **a.** 100 90 80 70 60 50 40 32 20 10
   **b.** 60 80 30 90 70 100 40 20 50 10
   **c.** 60 50 70 40 80 30 90 20 100 10
   Provide a brief written statement in which you describe how the shape of the binary search tree is related to the order in which data arrive for insertion into the tree.

3. Consider the following search trees with the ordering property. For each, specify an order of arrival of data items that would result in that particular tree if the insert function of Example 7.4 is used.

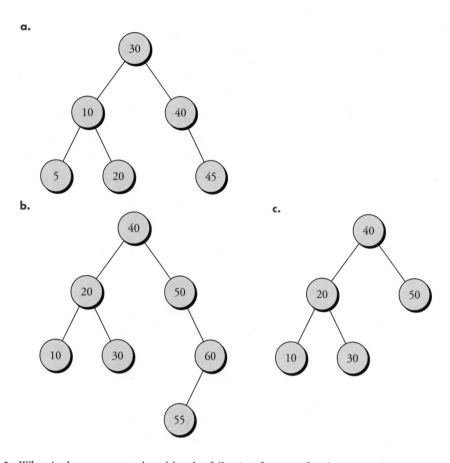

**4.** What is the output produced by the following function for the pictured tree?

```
void tree_walk(node_ptr tree)
{
    if (tree == NULL)
        cout << "OOPS" << endl;
    else
    {
        tree_walk(tree->right);
        tree_walk(tree->left);
        cout << tree->data << endl;
    }
}
```

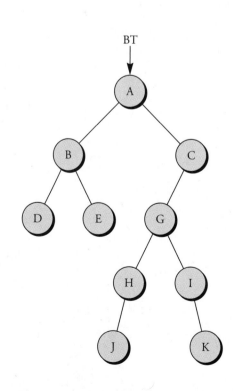

**5.** How does the output from Exercise 4 change if the statement

```
cout << tree->data << endl;
```

is moved ahead of the recursive calls to **tree_walk**?

**6.** How does the output from Exercise 4 change if the statement

```
cout << tree->data << endl;
```

is located between the recursive calls to **tree_walk**?

**7.** Repeat Exercises 4, 5, and 6 for the following tree:

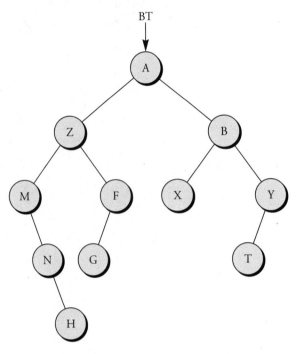

**8.** A *ternary tree* is a tree in which each node may have at most three children. A pointer/record structure for a linked implementation of such a tree could thus be given by the following declarations:

```
struct node;
typedef node *node_ptr;
struct node
{
    element data;
    node_ptr left;
    node_ptr middle;
    node_ptr right;
};
```

What would be the output produced by the following **tree_walk** function

```
void tree_walk(node_ptr tree)
{

    if (tree != NULL)
    {
        cout << tree->data << endl;
```

```
        tree_walk(tree->right);
        tree_walk(tree->middle);
        tree_walk(tree->left);
    }
}
```

if it were initially called with the root pointer to the tree in the following diagram?

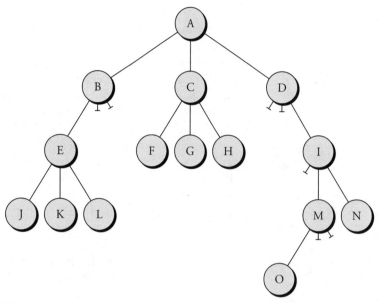

9. Write implementations of the **create** and **empty** operations for a binary search tree with the ordering property using the linked representation method.

10. Write an implementation of the postorder traversal operation for a linked representation of a binary tree.

11. Write a function that reads an algebraic expression in prefix notation and builds the binary tree corresponding to the expression (see Example 7.3). Assume that all tokens in the expression are individual characters.

12. Write a function that reads an algebraic expression in postfix notation and builds the binary tree corresponding to the expression (see Example 7.3). Assume that all tokens in the expression are individual characters.

13. Implement one of the traversal algorithms in a nonrecursive fashion by using a stack to keep track of pointers to nodes that must be visited when you finish processing the current subtree. Your stack will approximate the role played by the system stack in the recursive version of the algorithm.

14. Suppose that you have a binary tree representation of an algebraic expression consisting of the operators +, −, *, / and operands that are uppercase letters. Suppose also that you have a function value that, given an operand, will return the numeric value associated with that operand. Write a recursive function to evaluate the expression tree.

15. Write a function to solve the following puzzle. Assume that the element type is **char**. Your function receives two strings of the same length. The first represents the order in which the nodes of a tree would be visited by a preorder traversal. The second represents the order in which nodes from the same tree would be visited by an inorder traversal. Your function is to construct the tree from these two traversals.

16. Write a Boolean-valued function that receives two binary trees composed of the same type of data. The function should return TRUE if the two trees are identical,

that is, if they have precisely the same shape and have the same values in each node. Otherwise, it should return FALSE.

**17.** How could the inorder traversal of a binary tree be used to sort data logically? Provide your answer in the form of a precise written statement.

---

## 7.3 Binary Search Tree Implementation of a One-Key Table

### OBJECTIVES

- to realize how a binary search tree with the ordering property can be used to provide an effective implementation of the one-key table ADT introduced in Chapter 12

- to develop an algorithm for deleting a node from a binary search tree

- to analyze the efficiency of this new implementation of the one-key table ADT

- in particular, to compare the efficiency of this new one-key table implementation with the efficiencies of other implementations we have previously studied

The implementations we have considered for the one-key table have been found lacking in certain respects. The physically ordered array implementation of Chapter 2 allowed for the fast inspection of objects via the binary search algorithm but necessitated excessive data movement when objects were added to or deleted from the list. The linked list implementation suggested in Chapter 4 handled insertions and removals nicely but presented us with an undesirable $O(n)$ search efficiency due to the lack of random access.

In this section, we shall see that by implementing a one-key table using a binary tree with the ordering property, we can achieve efficiency in both searching and adding or deleting while at the same time keeping the list in order. Moreover, we do not have to pay too great a price in other trade-offs to achieve this best of both worlds. Indeed, binary trees with the ordering property are called binary search trees precisely because of their frequent application in efficiently implementing one-key tables.

A binary search tree is organized via the hierarchical ordering property discussed in Example 7.2 in Section 7.1. Recall that this ordering property stipulates the following:

*For any given data item X in the tree, every node in the left subtree of X contains only items that are less than X with respect to a particular type of ordering. Every node in the right subtree of X contains only items that are greater than or equal to X with respect to the same ordering.*

For instance, the tree of Figure 7.14 illustrates this property with respect to alphabetical ordering. You can quickly verify that an inorder traversal of this tree (in which the processing of each node consists merely of printing its contents) leads to the following alphabetized list:

| | |
|---|---|
| ARPS | NATHAN |
| DIETZ | PERKINS |
| EGOFSKE | SELIGER |
| FAIRCHILD | TALBOT |
| GARTH | UNDERWOOD |
| HUSTON | VERKINS |
| KEITH | ZARDA |
| MAGILLICUDDY | |

This allows us to reach the following important conclusion. That is, an inorder traversal of a binary search tree will visit nodes in ascending order. Hence such a tree may be viewed as an ordered table. The first table element is the first item visited by the inorder traversal. More generally, the $n$th element visited by the inorder traversal corresponds precisely to the $n$th element in the table. Given this view of a binary search tree as an implementation of a one-key table, let us now consider the operations of adding, deleting, and finding (retrieving) nodes in the table.

◆ FIGURE 7.14
Ordering property with respect
to alphabetical ordering

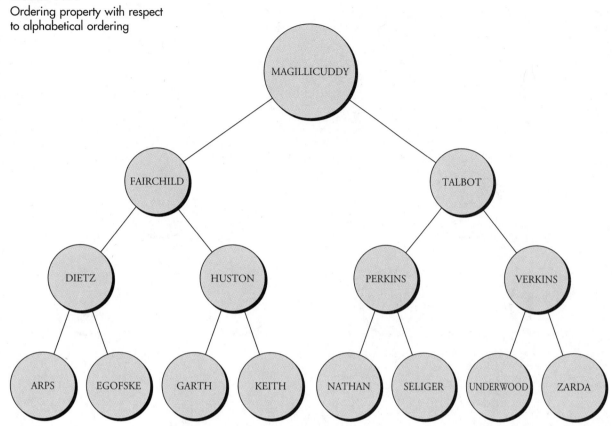

## Adding Nodes to the Binary Search Tree Implementation of a One-Key Table

Insertion of a new key into such a tree is a fairly easy process that may well require significantly fewer comparisons than insertion into a linked list. The specifics of the insert operation were developed in Example 7.4. Consider, for example, the steps necessary to insert the key 'SEFTON' into the tree of Figure 7.14 in such a fashion as to maintain the ordering property. We must

1. Compare SEFTON to MAGILLICUDDY. Because SEFTON is greater than MAGILLICUDDY, follow the right child pointer to TALBOT.
2. Compare SEFTON to TALBOT. Because SEFTON is less than TALBOT, follow the left child pointer to PERKINS.
3. SEFTON is greater than PERKINS. Hence follow the right child pointer to SELIGER.
4. SELIGER is a leaf node, so SEFTON may be added as one of its children. The left child is chosen because SEFTON is less than SELIGER.

The resulting tree for the sample insertion is given in Figure 7.15.

Provided that the tree maintains a full shape, the number of nodes on a given branch will be at most

$$\log_2 n + 1$$

◆ FIGURE 7.15
Tree in Figure 7.14 with the
insertion SEFTON

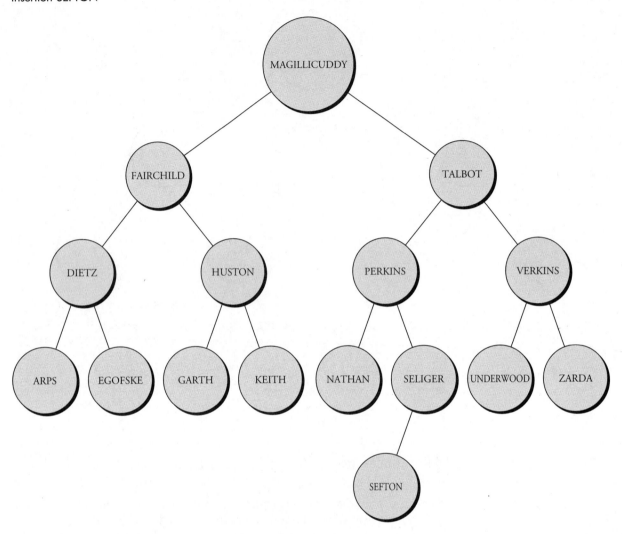

where *n* is the total number of nodes in the tree. By *full* we mean that all nodes
with fewer than two children must occur at level *m* or *m* – 1 where *m* is the deepest
level in the tree. In other words, all nodes above level *m* – 1 must have exactly two
children. Hence, adding ROBERTS to the tree of Figure 7.15 by the insertion rule
would destroy its fullness.

Given this definition of full, the ($\log_2 n$ + 1) figure for the maximum number
of nodes on a branch emerges immediately upon inspection or, more formally,
using a proof by mathematical induction. Our purpose here, however, is not to give
the details of such a proof but rather to emphasize that a binary search tree presents
an alternative to a linked list structure for the type of processing involved in
maintaining ordered lists. Moreover, it is a particularly attractive alternative when
the tree is full, because substantially fewer comparisons are needed to locate where
in the structure an insertion is to be made. For instance, if *n* is 1024, the linked list
may require as many as 1024 comparisons to make an insertion. Because $\log_2 1024$

is 10, the full binary search tree method will require at most 11 comparisons. This difference becomes even more dramatic as *n* gets larger. For an ordered list with 1,000,000 entries, a linked list may require that many comparisons, but the full binary search tree requires a mere 21 comparisons.

What happens when the tree is not full? We will comment on that situation at the end of this section, when we discuss the overall efficiency considerations for this implementation of a one-key table. Before that, however, consider the operations of finding and deleting data in a binary search tree.

## Searching for Data in a Binary Search Tree Implementation of a One-Key Table

The insertion rule also dictates the search path followed through a binary search tree when we are attempting to find a given data item. Interestingly, if we trace the nodes visited on such a search path for a full tree, we will probe exactly the same items that we would in conducting a binary search on a physically ordered array containing the same data. For instance, if we are searching for SMITH in the tree of Figure 7.14, we will have to probe MAGILLICUDDY, TALBOT, and PERKINS. These are precisely the items that would be probed if the binary search algorithm were applied to the physically ordered list associated with Figure 7.14. Our analysis of such a tree has allowed us to conclude that, as long as the binary search tree remains full, the search efficiency for this method of implementing a one-key table matches that of the physically ordered array implementation. That is, the search efficiency is $O(\log_2 n)$.

## Deleting Data in a Binary Search Tree Implementation of a One-Key Table

The deletion algorithm for a binary search tree is conceptually more complex than that for a linked list. Suppose, for instance, that we wish to remove TALBOT from the list represented by the tree of Figure 7.14. Two questions arise:

**1.** Can such a deletion be achieved merely by manipulating pointers?
**2.** If so, what does the resulting tree look like?

To answer these questions, begin by recalling that all that is necessary to represent a one-key table with a binary search tree is that, for each node in the tree

**1.** The left subtree must contain only items less than it.
**2.** The right subtree must contain only items greater than or equal to it.

With the preservation of this ordering property as the primary goal in processing a deletion, one acceptable way of restructuring the tree of Figure 7.14 after deleting TALBOT appears in Figure 7.16; essentially, SELIGER moves up to replace TALBOT in the tree. The choice of SELIGER to replace TALBOT is made because SELIGER represents the greatest data item in the left subtree of the node containing TALBOT. As long as we choose this greatest item in the left subtree to replace the item being deleted, we guarantee preservation of the crucial ordering property that enables the tree to represent the list accurately.

Given this general motivation for choosing a node to replace the one being deleted, let us now outline a case-by-case analysis of the deletion algorithm. Throughout this analysis, we assume that we have a pointer P to the item that we wish to delete. The pointer P may be one of the following:

◆ **FIGURE 7.16**
Restructuring the tree in Figure 7.14 after deleting TALBOT

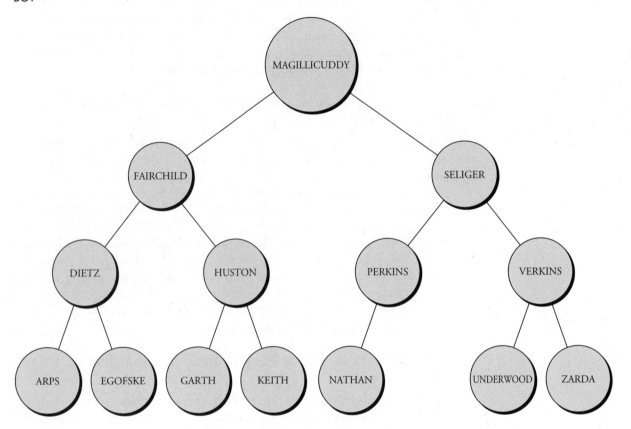

1. The root pointer for the entire tree.
2. The left child pointer of the parent of the node to be deleted.
3. The right child pointer of the parent of the node to be deleted.

Figure 7.17 highlights these three possibilities; the algorithm applies whether 1, 2, or 3 holds.

◆ **FIGURE 7.17**
Three possibilities for the pointer P

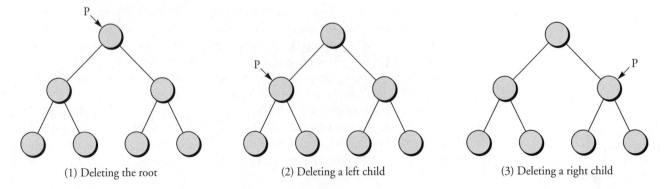

We now examine three cases of node deletion on a binary search tree:

**1.** The node to be deleted has no children.
**2.** The node to be deleted has a right child but no left child.
**3.** The node to be deleted has a left child.

**Case 1.** The node pointed to by P, that is, the node to be deleted, has no children. This is the easiest of all the cases. It can be compactly handled

```
X = P;
P = NULL;
delete X;
```

**Case 2.** The node pointed to by P, that is, the node to be deleted, has a right child but no left child. This case poses no more problems than case 1 and is described in Figure 7.18. The node to be deleted is merely replaced by its right child. The necessary C++ coding is

```
X = P;
P = X->right;
delete X;
```

◆ **FIGURE 7.18**

In case 2 the node pointed to by P has a right but no left child

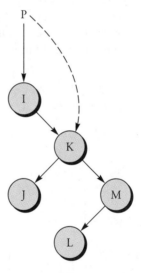

**Case 3.** The node pointed to by P, that is, the node to be deleted, has a left child. In Figure 7.19, node M is to be deleted, and it has left child K. In this case, because we have a non-null left subtree of the node to be deleted, our previous discussion indicates that we must find the greatest node in that left subtree. If the node pointed to by **P->left** (node K in the figure) has no right child, then the greatest node in the left subtree of P is **P->left** itself. Figure 7.19 pictorially describes this situation; the dotted lines indicate new pointer values.

The partial coding to achieve this pointer manipulation is given by:

```
X = P;
P = X->left;
P->right = X->right;
delete X;
```

If the node pointed to by **P->left** does have a right child, then to find the greatest node in the left subtree of P we must follow the right branch leading from

◆ FIGURE 7.19
Case 3 with `P->left`
(node K) having no right
children

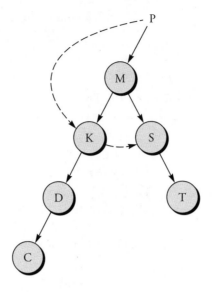

`P->left` as deeply as possible into the tree. In Figure 7.20, node R is the one chosen to replace the deleted node. This figure gives the schematic representation, with the pointer changes necessary to complete the deletion. The coding necessary for this slightly more complicated version of case 3 is

```
X = P;
Q = X->left->right;
QParent = X->left;
```

◆ FIGURE 7.20
Case 3 with `P->left`
having a right child

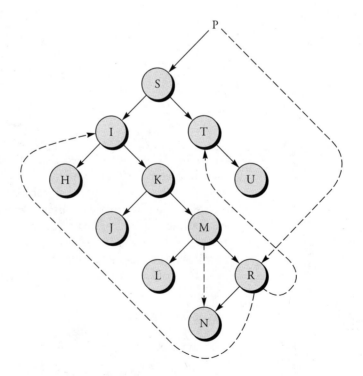

```
// Q will eventually point to node which will replace P.
// QParent will point to Q's parent.
// The following loop forces Q as deep as possible
// along the right branch from P->left.

while (Q->left != NULL)
{
        Q = Q->right;
        QParent = QParent->right;
}

// Having found node Q to replace P, adjust pointers
// to appropriately link it into the tree.

Q->right = X->right;
P = Q;
QParent->right = Q->left;
Q->left = X->left;
delete X;
```

## Efficiency Considerations for Binary Search Tree Implementation of a One-Key Table

It is important to note that, in all three cases, the deletion of a node from the tree involved only pointer manipulation and no actual data movement. Hence, in a one-key table maintained with a binary search tree, we are able to process both insertions and deletions by the same pure pointer manipulation that makes linked lists so desirable. Moreover, the binary search tree approach apparently allows us to locate data for retrieval, insertion, or deletion much faster than a linked list representation would. However, there are aspects of the binary tree method that tarnish its performance in comparison to a linked list. These aspects are discussed next.

The binary search tree implementation requires more memory in two respects. First, each node has two pointers instead of the one required in a singly linked list. This proliferation of pointers is particularly wasteful because many of the pointers may be NULL. Second, we currently can traverse the tree in order only by using recursive techniques. Even in a language that allows recursion, a substantial amount of overhead is needed to maintain the stack used by recursive calls.

The $O(\log_2 n)$ efficiency of the binary search tree method is only an optimal, not a guaranteed, efficiency. It is contingent on the tree remaining nearly full. The tree remaining full is in turn contingent on the order in which the data are added and deleted. In the worst possible case, data entering the tree structure in the wrong order can cause the tree to degenerate into a glorified linked list with a corresponding $O(n)$ efficiency. (The exercises at the end of this section have you explore this relationship between the order in which data arrive for insertion and the resulting search efficiency of the binary search tree.)

Both of these drawbacks can be overcome. We can avoid the overhead associated with recursion if we use a technique (known as *threading*) that puts to good use the pointers that are otherwise wasted as NULL.

Moreover, by using a technique known as *height balancing*, the binary search tree can be maintained in a fashion that approaches fullness at all times, regardless of the order in which data arrive for entry. This nearly full form is enough to completely guarantee the $O(\log_2 n)$ search efficiency. Originally devised by G. M. Adelson-Velskii and Y. M. Landis, the height-balancing algorithm is sufficiently complex to be beyond the scope of this book. In-depth treatments of it and the threading technique cited above are given in *Data Structures in C++* by Ellis Horowitz and Sartaj Sahni (New York: Computer Science Press, 1990) and in *Introduction to Data Structures and Algorithm Analysis with C++* by George J. Pothering and Thomas L. Naps (St. Paul, Minn.: West Publishing, 1995).

Overall, the binary search tree implementation of a one-key table would seem to be the best of the three implementations we have studied for situations in which additions, deletions, and searches must all be processed efficiently. Even when steps are not taken to correct the two disadvantages we have cited, it offers the addition/deletion advantages of a linked list with a search efficiency that is bounded between $O(\log_2 n)$ and $O(n)$.

**EXERCISES 7.3**

1. Which of the following binary search trees are full?

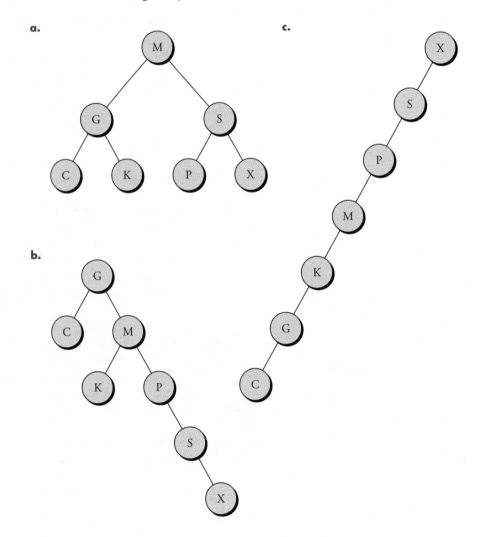

a.

b.

c.

**2.** The key values 1 through 10 are to be inserted in a binary search tree. Specify orders of arrival for these values to create trees that correspond with each of the following shapes.

**a.**

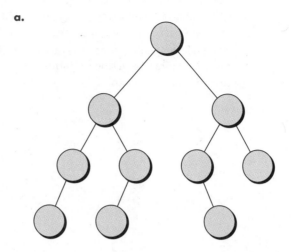

**b.**                                    **c.**

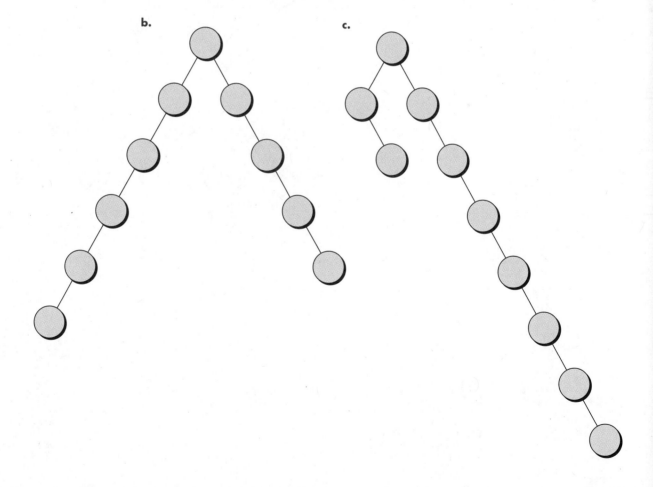

**3.** In an essay, discuss the relative merits of maintaining a one-key table by a binary search tree, a singly linked list, and a doubly linked list.

**4.** In an essay, discuss how the order in which data are entered into a binary search tree affects the fullness of the tree. Be sure to identify the best and worst possible cases. Analyze the efficiency of tree operations to add, delete, and find data for each of these cases.

**5.** The node containing 46 is to be deleted from each of the following binary search trees. Assuming the deletion algorithm described in this section is used, draw the tree after the deletion of 46.

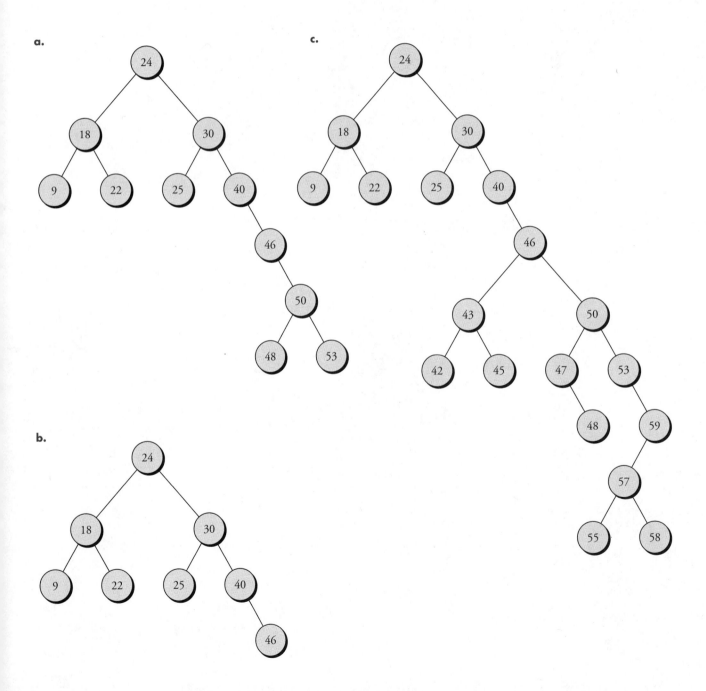

**6.** In Example 7.4 we provided an implementation of the **insert** operation for a binary search tree. What does the function in that example do when we try to insert a key value that already exists in the tree? Modify the function so that, when we try to insert such a key value, the tree is left unaltered.

**7.** The implementation of the **insert** operation for a binary search tree in Example 7.4 is recursive. Write a nonrecursive implementation of this operation.

**8.** Develop recursive and nonrecursive implementations of the algorithm to search for a particular data item in a binary search tree.

**9.** Develop a complete implementation of the algorithm to delete an item from a binary search tree. This will essentially require that you combine into one module the three cases discussed in this section. For an added challenge, try writing the function so that it handles deletion by using the "mirror image" of these three cases.

**10.** Look back to the definition of the one-key table ADT in Chapter 2. Provide a complete implementation of the table operations using a binary search tree as the underlying data structure. (*Hint:* You should provide comparison operations for the association class, so that associations can be the objects stored in binary trees.)

**11.** Suppose you are given a list of data in increasing order of keys. Develop a C++ algorithm that will load this list into an optimal binary search tree.

**12.** A binary search tree could itself be considered an ADT that is derived from the more generic binary tree ADT defined in Section 7.1. Write a complete definition and a C++ interface for the binary search tree as an ADT. Be sure that the set of operations you describe will allow your binary search tree ADT to be used as an implementation strategy for the one-key table ADT.

---

## 7.4 Linear Implementation of the Binary Tree Abstract Data Type

### OBJECTIVES

- to become familiar with the linear implementation of the binary tree ADT

- to recognize the advantages and disadvantages of the linear implementation versus the linked implementation

- to see why the linear implementation is particularly well suited to representing a binary tree with the heap property

- to analyze the efficiency of the **insert** operation for a linear implementation of a binary tree with the heap property

The linear implementation of a binary tree uses a one-dimensional array of size $[2^{(d+1)} - 1]$ where $d$ is the depth of the tree, that is, the maximum level of any node in the tree. In the tree of Figure 7.8, the root + is at the level 0, the nodes – and * are at level 1, and so on. The deepest level in this tree is the level of E and F, level 3. Therefore, $d = 3$ and this tree will require an array of size $2^{(3+1)} - 1 = 15$.

Once the size of the array has been determined, the following method is used to represent the tree:

**1.** Store the root in the first location of the array.
**2.** If a node is in location $n$ of the array, store its left child at location $2n$, and its right child at location $(2n + 1)$.

With the aid of this scheme, the tree of Figure 7.8 is stored in the array tree of size 15 shown in Figure 7.21. Locations `tree[7]` through `tree[12]` are not used.

An encapsulated definition of the binary tree ADT for this linear representation is given by:

```
    protected:

    // Protected data members

    struct node                        // Either NULL or a node
    {
        boolean null;
        E data;
    };

    node tree[MAX_TREE_NODES];         // Array of nodes
    int number_nodes;                  // Number of nodes in tree
```

◆ FIGURE 7.21

Tree of Figure 7.8 stored in a linear representation using an array

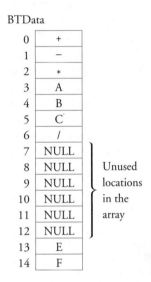

The **create** operation simply sets the **number_nodes** data member to zero and initializes the **null** member of all nodes in the array locations to TRUE. The **null** flags are necessary to detect whether or not a given tree node has children. A tree node at location $n$ has a left subtree if and only if the node at location $2n$ contains a **null** flag of FALSE. A similar consideration applies to the right subtree of the tree node at location $n$.

## Efficiency Considerations for the Linear Representation

The main advantages of this method lie in its simplicity and the fact that, given a child node, its parent node can be determined immediately. If a child node is at location $n$ in the array, then its parent node is at location $n/2$.

In spite of its simplicity and ease of implementation, the linear representation method has all the costs that come with physically ordering items. Insertion or deletion of a node in a fashion that maintains the hierarchical relationships within the tree may cause considerable data movement up and down the array and hence use an excessive amount of processing time. Also, depending on the application, memory locations (such as locations 7 through 12 in Figure 7.21) may be wasted due to partially filled trees.

## Using the Linear Implementation for a Heap

One type of binary tree for which the linear implementation of a binary tree proves to be ideal is the heap, as defined in Example 7.1. The data in a heap can be embedded in an array without ever wasting any locations. To prove this claim, we will show that, given a heap with $N - 1$ nodes embedded in an array with no gaps, we can add an $N$th node and maintain the dense packing of data in the array.

To illustrate the algorithm for doing this, consider the heap with eight nodes pictured in Figure 7.22. The numbers outside the circular nodes in this figure indicate the array indices where data would be stored in the linear representation of a binary tree.

◆ FIGURE 7.22
A heap with eight nodes

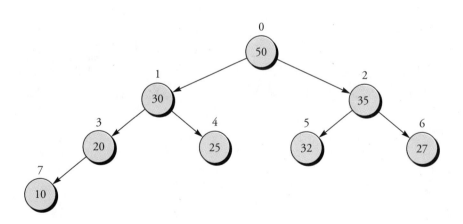

Now suppose we want to add 40 to the heap of Figure 7.22. We will begin by comparing 40 to the data in the least index, which does not yet have two children: 20 at index 3 in Figure 7.22. Figure 7.23 shows a series of data interchanges that "walk 40 up" a path until the tree is transformed into a heap. The algorithm to achieve this "walking up" is given in the following example.

◆ FIGURE 7.23

Transforming heap to accommodate insertion of 40 (numbers outside circles indicate array index positions)

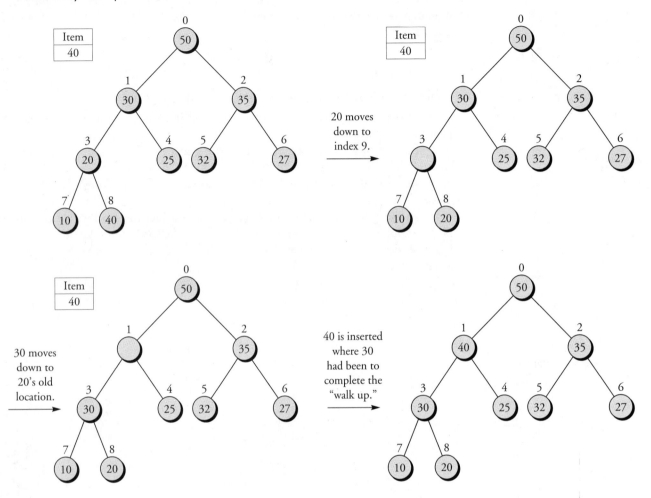

20 moves down to index 9.

30 moves down to 20's old location.

40 is inserted where 30 had been to complete the "walk up."

---

**EXAMPLE 7.5**    Implement the **insert** operation for a linear representation of a binary tree with the heap property.

```
template <class E>
void binary_tree<E>::insert(const E &item)
{
    int location, parent;

    assert(number_nodes < MAX_TREE_NODES);
    ++number_nodes;

    // Now walk the new item up the tree, starting at location
```

```
location = number_nodes;
parent = location / 2;
while ((parent >= 1) &&
       (tree[parent - 1].data < item))
{
     tree[location - 1] = tree[parent - 1];
     location = parent;
     parent = location / 2;
}
tree[location - 1].data = item;
tree[location - 1].null = FALSE;
}
```

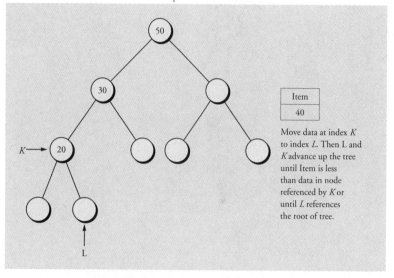

Item
40

Move data at index $K$ to index $L$. Then L and $K$ advance up the tree until Item is less than data in node referenced by $K$ or until $L$ references the root of tree.

Note that the logic of the algorithm is simplified if we pretend that the array representing the heap is indexed from 1 to **number_nodes,** rather than from 0 to **number_nodes** - 1. We map these logical indices to actual positions in the C++ array by subtracting one during each array reference.

### Efficiency Analysis of `insert` for Linear Representation of Heap

Clearly the time efficiency of adding an item to the heap is directly proportional to the length of the path that the item must "walk up" as its appropriate position is determined. Because the linear representation of a heap leaves no unused gaps between values stored in the array, doubling the number of items in the heap will add only one level to the resulting binary tree. Thus, a heap with $n$ nodes will have $\log_2 n$ levels using the linear representation. In other words, the length of the path that a new item will follow, and hence the efficiency of the **insert** operation, is $O(\log_2 n)$.

In the exercises at the end of this section, you will explore an algorithm to delete a node from a heap. That exploration will show how a heap could be used to implement the priority queue ADT defined in Chapter 5.

## A NOTE OF INTEREST

### Computer Security and Tree-Structured File Systems

One of the prime concerns in developing operating systems for multiuser computers is to ensure that a user cannot, in an unauthorized fashion, access system files or the files of other users. A convenient data structure to implement such a file directory system is a tree such as that pictured here:

every node in his or her subtree. That is, the user is viewed as the owner of every node in the subtree. To jump outside of this subtree of naturally owned files and directories requires that special permissions be given the user by other users or by the operating system itself. Hence the tree

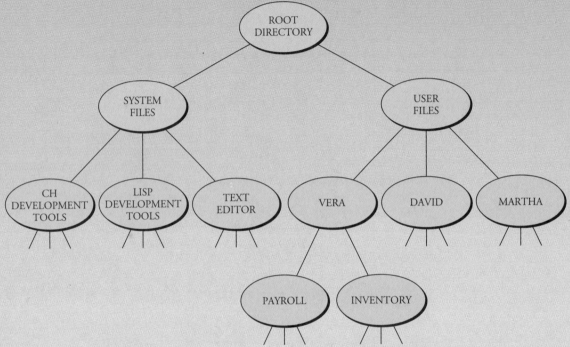

Each interior node of the tree can be viewed as a directory containing various system information about those files or subdirectories that are its descendants. Leaf nodes in the tree are the actual files. Hence, in the diagram, files can be broken down into system files and user files. System files consist of the C++ DEVELOPMENT TOOLS, the LISP DEVELOPMENT TOOLS, and the TEXT EDITOR. User directories are called VERA, DAVID, and MARTHA. One of the very convenient features of such a system is that it allows the user to extend this tree structure as deeply as desired. For instance, in the given tree directory structure, we see that user VERA has created subdirectories for files related to PAYROLL and INVENTORY. DAVID and MARTHA could have similarly partitioned subdirectories to organize their work.

In addition to offering users the convenience of being able to group their files into appropriate subdirectories, such a file system offers a very natural solution to the problem of file security. Since each individual user is, in effect, the root of a miniature subordinate file system within the overall system, a user is given, by default, free access to

structure offers convenience as well as a means of carefully monitoring the integrity of the file system.

AT&T's UNIX operating system, developed at Bell Laboratories in the early 1970s, was one of the first to use such a tree-structured directory system. The widespread popularity of UNIX today and the adoption of this scheme by a significant number of other operating systems is evidence of the attractive way in which it combines user convenience with system security. However, this is not to say that such systems are completely free of security problems. Once the security of such a system is slightly compromised, the tree structure lends itself to a cascade of far-reaching security breaks. Brian Reid's article "Reflections on Some Recent Widespread Computer Break-ins" in the February 1987 issue of *Communications of the ACM* (Volume 30, No. 2) provides an interesting account of how such security problems surfaced at Stanford University and spread to an entire network of computers. An entertaining narrative of another security incident is presented by Clifford Stoll in *The Cuckoo's Egg* (New York: Doubleday, 1989).

| EXAMPLE 7.6 | In this example, we illustrate how the postorder traversal algorithm may be implemented for a linear array implementation of a binary tree. The algorithm is slightly more difficult for this representation since the tree is the encapsulation of an array and a count of the number of nodes. Unlike the linked implementation, there is not an explicit root pointer for the tree; instead, the root of the entire tree is understood to be at index 0. The following function, **postorder_traverse**, compensates for this by acting as a mere "front-end" for a local auxiliary function, which is where the actual recursion takes place. Our front-end function **postorder_traverse** simply passes a root pointer value of 0 to the auxiliary function to start the recursion. We must also assume that a flagging null value of TRUE occupies array locations that are not currently storing data in the tree. This allows the auxiliary function to detect when the equivalent of a NULL pointer is passed. Finally, an offset of 1 is added to the values $2n$ and $2n + 1$ to obtain the locations of the left and right children, respectively, of a node in a C++ array where the first index position is zero. |
|---|---|

```
template <class E>
void binary_tree<E>::postorder_traverse(void (*process) (E &item))
{
     if (number_nodes > 0)
          postorder_aux(1, process);
}


template <class E>
void binary_tree<E>::postorder_aux(int location,
     void (*process) (E &item))
{
     if (location < MAX_TREE_NODES)
          if (! tree[location].null)
          {
               postorder_aux(2 * location, process);
               postorder_aux(2 * location + 1, process);
               process(tree[location].data);
          }
}
```

Third, process
root node.

First, traverse
left subtree.

Second, traverse
right subtree.

---

| EXERCISES 7.4 | **1.** Suppose that items arrive for insertion into a heap in the following order:

10  20  30  40  50  60  70  80  90  100 |
|---|---|

Using the algorithm of Example 7.5, trace the contents of the tree array after each item is added to the heap.

2. Write implementations of the **create** and **empty** operations for a binary tree with the heap property using the linear array implementation. Be sure that your **create** operation is consistent with the postorder traversal algorithm of Example 7.6.

3. Write implementations of the preorder and inorder traversal operations for a linear array implementation of a binary tree.

4. Implement the following operation for a linear representation of a binary tree with the heap property.

```
void remove(E &item);
```

(*Hint:* When the root is removed, temporarily replace it with the tree node in the last active index of the array. Then develop an algorithm to walk this new root down a branch of the tree until the tree becomes a heap again.) In a written statement, indicate how the **insert** function of Example 7.5 and the **remove** function that you have written for this exercise could be used to implement a priority queue (Chapter 15) using a heap.

5. In a written statement discuss the relative advantages and disadvantages of the linear array implementation of a binary tree versus the linked implementation described in Section 7.2.

---

## 7.5 General Trees

### OBJECTIVES

- to understand how a general tree may be implemented using a linked representation of a binary tree
- given the implementation of a general tree by a binary tree, to examine which traversal operations for the underlying binary tree make sense when it is interpreted as a general tree

We began this chapter with a discussion of the many ways in which hierarchical structures are used to organize information around us. We then quickly dictated that at most two children could be used, which focused all of our attention on the seemingly restricted case of the binary tree. What about all of those applications requiring a hierarchical relationship where a parent may have an unrestricted number of children? You may have become suspicious that we are avoiding such considerations because they are too difficult.

Fortunately, we have a much more educationally sound reason. That is, we may use a binary tree to implement a general tree. The nice implication of this rather surprising statement is that we will not have to spend a significant amount of time discussing general trees because we have unknowingly studied them in our thorough analysis of binary trees. Moreover, the formal operations on a general tree may be viewed as operations derived from those associated with a binary tree.

The real key to using a restricted type of tree such as a binary tree to implement a more general type of tree is to adjust our perspective. For example, consider the general genealogical tree of Figure 7.24. Here BILL is the first child of the JONES family, with KATY, MIKE, and TOM as BILL's siblings. Similarly, LARRY is the first child of MARY, with PAUL and PENNY as siblings. Now, in a linked representation of binary tree, we have two pointer fields associated with each node. We have called these pointer fields left and right because it suited our perspective at the time. However, we shall now switch that perspective in the following way. One of the pointer fields is to be viewed as a pointer to the leftmost child of a node in a general tree. The second pointer identifies the next sibling to the right of the node under consideration in the general tree. Since the children of a node taken in this context form an ordered set of nodes, we can regard the leftmost child of a node as first and the sibling to the right of this node as sibling. We will henceforth adopt this terminology for the two link fields involved with the

◆ FIGURE 7.24
Genealogical tree

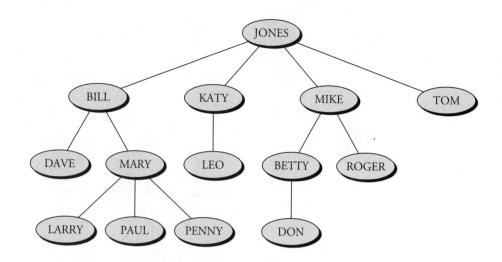

binary tree representation of a general tree. Figure 7.25 gives the binary representation of the general genealogical tree shown in Figure 7.24.

◆ FIGURE 7.25
Binary tree representation of genealogical tree in Figure 7.24

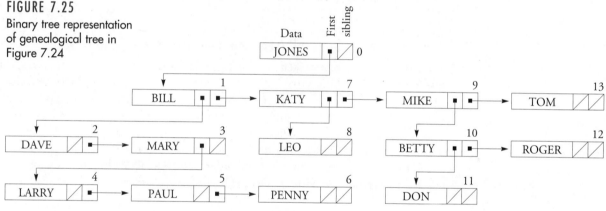

Note that we number the pointers in the tree of Figure 7.24. This numbering is reflected in Table 7.4. You should carefully check all first and sibling

◇ TABLE 7.4
Tree in Figure 7.24 stored in array of records for data and pointers

| Location | Data | FirstChild | Sibling |
|---|---|---|---|
| 0 | JONES | 1 | 0 |
| 1 | BILL | 2 | 7 |
| 2 | DAVE | 0 | 3 |
| 3 | MARY | 4 | 0 |
| 4 | LARRY | 0 | 5 |
| 5 | PAUL | 0 | 6 |
| 6 | PENNY | 0 | 0 |
| 7 | KATY | 9 | 9 |
| 8 | LEO | 0 | 0 |
| 9 | MIKE | 10 | 13 |
| 10 | BETTY | 11 | 12 |
| 11 | DON | 0 | 0 |
| 12 | ROGER | 0 | 0 |
| 13 | TOM | 0 | 0 |

values to convince yourself that the scheme used to fill this array was to store a node before any of its children, and then recursively store the leftmost child.

The representation in terms of C++ pointer variables (and the representation we shall henceforth use) requires the following type declarations:

```
protected:

// Protected data members

struct node;
typedef node *node_ptr;
struct node
{
        E data;
        node_ptr first;
        node_ptr sibling;
};

node_ptr tree;
```

## Traversals of a General Tree Implemented Via a Binary Tree

Since this implementation scheme for a general tree is nothing more than a special interpretation of a binary tree, all of the traversals defined for a binary tree clearly exist for the general tree. A more relevant question than the mere existence of a traversal, however, is the significance of the order in which the nodes of a general tree are visited when its corresponding binary tree is traversed. Of particular interest in this regard are the preorder and postorder traversals.

You should verify that the preorder traversal algorithm for a binary tree applied to Figure 7.24 visits nodes in the following order:

```
JONES
    BILL
        DAVE
        MARY
            LARRY
            PAUL
            PENNY
    KATY
        LEO
    MIKE
        BETTY
            DON
        ROGER
TOM
```

The indentation here has been added to highlight the fact that the preorder traversal will recursively process a parent node, and then process the child nodes from left to right.

Relative to the general tree pictured in Figure 7.24, we see that the effect of the preorder traversal is to fix on a node at one level of the tree and then run through all of that node's children before progressing to the next node at the same level (the sibling). There is a hint here of a generalized nested loop situation which, as you will see, has some interesting applications in the programming problems at the end of this chapter.

The other traversal of interest in a binary tree representation of a general tree is the postorder traversal. In this regard, it should first be verified that the postorder traversal applied to Figure 7.24 (and its binary tree implementation in Figure 7.25) yields the following listing:

PENNY
PAUL
LARRY
MARY
DAVE
LEO
DON
ROGER
BETTY
TOM
MIKE
KATY
BILL
JONES

In general, the postorder traversal works its way up from the leaf nodes of a tree, ensuring that no given node is processed until all nodes in the subtree below it have been processed.

**EXERCISES 7.5**

**1.** How would you implement a preorder traversal to print nodes in a fashion that has children indented under their parents?

**2.** Consider the following abstract graphical representation of a general tree:

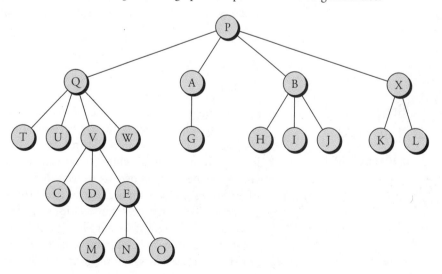

Provide a specific C++ record description for a node in this tree as you would represent it. (Do not make any assumption about maximum possible number of children.) Then draw a specific picture of how this tree would actually be stored using the record description you have chosen.

3. Given the tree from Exercise 2, in what order would nodes be visited by a preorder traversal? A postorder traversal?

4. For this exercise you are to assume a linked binary tree representation of a general tree. Write a function that meets the following specification:

```
// Function: add_child
// Insert a tree as the kth subtree of another tree.
// If the root node of the tree already has k or more subtrees, the new
// tree becomes the kth subtree and the former Kth subtree becomes
// the (K+1)st subtree.
// If the root node of the tree has fewer than K subtrees,
// then the new tree is inserted as the last subtree of the root node.

template <class E>
void general_tree<E>::add_child(node_ptr &gt, node_ptr st, int k)
```

5. Use the function you developed for Exercise 4 in another function to generate the following tree. Verify that you have generated the correct tree with a traversal function that outputs the tree in appropriate fashion.

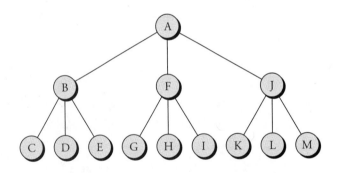

6. Is a binary tree a special case of a general tree? Provide a written rationale to justify your answer.

---

## 7.6 Graphs and Networks: Bidirectional Trees

The key defining characteristic of a tree is the hierarchical relationship between parent and child nodes. In a tree, this hierarchical relationship is a one-way relationship. That is, within the tree there is pointer information that allows us to descend from parent to child. However, there is generally no pointer information within the tree that allows us to ascend from a child node to its parent. In many information storage applications such a one-way relationship is not sufficient. Consider, for instance, the relationship between students and courses at a university. Each student is enrolled in several courses and could thus be viewed as a parent node with children consisting of the courses he or she is taking. Conversely, each course enrolls many students and could thus be viewed as a parent

- to understand the definition and operations for the graph ADT
- to understand the definition and operations for the network ADT
- to understand how a two-dimensional table may be used to implement the graph and network ADTs
- to realize why the two-dimensional table representation of a graph or network often results in a sparse matrix
- to understand traversal algorithms for graphs and networks
- to understand Dijkstra's algorithm for finding the shortest path between two nodes in a network

node with children consisting of the students enrolled in that particular course. The data structure that emerges from this type of bidirectional relationship is pictured in Figure 7.26.

In terms of an abstract data-type, the representation of such a bidirectional relationship between nodes is called a *graph*.

**Graph:** A graph consists of two sets. One set is a fixed set of objects called *nodes*. The other is a set of *edges,* the contents of which vary depending on the operations that have been performed on the graph. A node is a data element of the graph, and an edge is a direct connection between two nodes. A node may also be called a *vertex* of the graph. If an edge exists between two nodes, we say that the second node is adjacent to the first node.

The operations associated with the graph ADT are specified in terms of the following preconditions and postconditions:

**Create operation**
Preconditions:     Receiver is graph in an unpredictable state.
Postconditions:     Graph is initialized to a state with no edges. That is, no nodes are connected to any other nodes, including themselves.

**add_edge operation**
Preconditions:     Receiver is an arbitrary graph that has been initialized by **create** and, potentially, affected by other operations. **node1** and **node2** are two nodes in the graph.
Postconditions:     Receiver is returned with an edge from **node1** to **node2**. If an edge already existed from **node1** to **node2**, the graph is not affected.

**remove_edge operation**
Preconditions:     Receiver is an arbitrary graph that has been initialized by **create** and, potentially, affected by other operations. **node1** and **node2** are two nodes in the graph.
Postconditions:     If there is an edge from **node1** to **node2**, it is removed. Otherwise the graph is not affected.

**Edge operation**
Preconditions:     Receiver is an arbitrary graph that has been initialized by **create** and, potentially, affected by other operations. **node1** and **node2** are two nodes in the graph.
Postconditions:     **edge** returns TRUE if there is an edge from **node1** to **node2**, FALSE otherwise.

**Traverse operation**
Preconditions:     Receiver is an arbitrary graph that has been initialized by **create** and, potentially, affected by other operations. **start** is a node at which the traversal is to start. **process** is an algorithmic process that can be applied to each graph node.
Postconditions:     Receiver is returned with each node that can be reached from **start** affected by **process**. A given node can be reached from **start** if the given node is the start node or if there is a sequence of edges $E_0, E_1, \ldots, E_n$ such that $E_0$ begins at the **start** node, the node at which $E_i - 1$ ends is the node at which $E_i$ begins, and $n$ is the given node. In effect, the sequence of edges determines a path from **start** to the given node. The path is composed of edges between adjacent nodes. **process** is not applied to any node more than once.

◆ **FIGURE 7.26**

Bidirectional relationship
between students and
courses

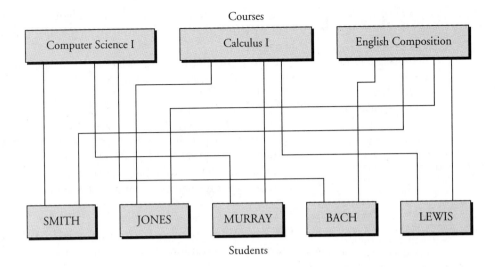

Notice that, as it relates to Figure 7.26, the formal definition of a graph does not
rule out the possibility of an edge connecting two courses or connecting two
students. It is merely the nature of this course–student relationship that makes the
existence of such a course-to-course edge or student-to-student edge impractical. In
other applications, such as the transportation network pictured in Figure 7.27, it
may be entirely feasible for any node in the graph to have an edge connecting it to
any other node.

To illustrate how a graph grows from an initial state with no edges, suppose
that we start with a set of nodes labeled A, B, C, D. Figure 7.28 traces the effect

◆ **FIGURE 7.27**

Transportation network as
graph in which edges represent flights between cities

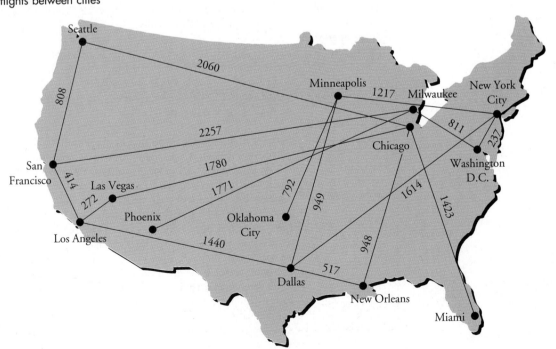

◆ FIGURE 7.28

Graph affected by sequence of **add_edge** and **remove_edge** operations

**create** G
(1)

**add_edge** A → B
(2)

**add_edge** B → C
(3)

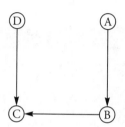

**add_edge** D → C
(4)

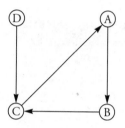

**add_edge** C → A
(5)

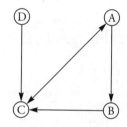

**add_edge** A → C
(6)

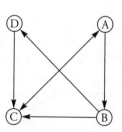

**add_edge** B → D
(7)

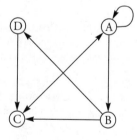

**add_edge** A → A
(8)

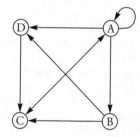

**add_edge** A → D
(9)

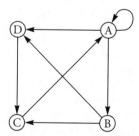

**remove_edge** A → C
(10)

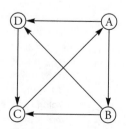

**remove_edge** A → A
(11)

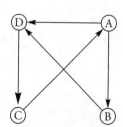

**remove_edge** B → C
(12)

of a sequence of `add_edge` and `remove_edge` operations on a graph with these nodes. Note from this figure that the concept of an edge carries with it the notion of a direction. That is, it is possible to have an edge from `node1` to `node2` in a graph G without there being a corresponding connection in the opposite direction. Figure 7.28, picture (8), also illustrates that it is possible to have an edge from a node to itself.

By convention, when we draw a graph without arrows on the edges, it is implicit that all edges run in both directions. Thus, in Figure 7.27, the line connecting San Francisco and Los Angeles implicitly represents two edges—the one from San Francisco to Los Angeles and the one from Los Angeles to San Francisco.

We will sometimes use the terminology *directional graph*, or *digraph*, to emphasize that a particular graph has some edges that exist only in one direction. Figure 7.29 illustrates a digraph. In a digraph, we use arrows on edges to specify the direction of an edge between nodes.

## A NOTE OF INTEREST

### Hypertext

Hypertext is a new technology that allows users to browse through any kind of information that can be stored electronically (text, images, sound, and video). Users experience hypertext associatively, as a set of one-key tables. Each entry in a table is a chunk of information presented to the user by some output device. Where the output device is a visual display, the keys for locating other entries in the tables are embedded as hotspots in the currently visible chunk of information. The user retrieves a desired entry by targeting a hotspot with a mouse or cursor device. This entry in turn may have other embedded keys. Each entry also has a hotspot for returning to the entry from which its key was triggered. More structured queries for entries can be executed by entering key terms into a search engine, which returns a list of all the entries that satisfy a query. Hypertext also has the feel of a graph, in that users can freely move back and forth in a nonlinear fashion among the entries or nodes.

As an example, one might begin with a query for Beethoven's Ninth Symphony. From the answer list one might then select a biography of the composer (text and images). After reading a couple of pages, one might next point at a hotspot referencing the last movement of the Ninth Symphony to listen to a few bars (sound). Returning to the biography, one might finally hit another hotspot to play a bit of *Immortal Beloved*, a film about Beethoven's life (video).

According to John B. Smith and Stephen F. Weiss (in "Hypertext," *Communications of the ACM* Volume 31, No. 7 (July 1988)), this unrestricted associativity among hypertext nodes parallels the flexibility of human memory. Smith and Weiss cite the following quotation from Vannevar Bush, a well-known electrical engineer who speculated as early as the 1940s about the way in which humans think:

*The human mind . . . operates by association. With one item in its grasp, it snaps instantly to the next that is suggested by the association of thoughts, in accordance with some intricate web of trails carried by the cells of the brain.*

*Selection by association, rather than indexing may yet be mechanized. One cannot hope . . . to equal the speed and flexibility with which the mind follows an associative trail, but it should be possible to beat the mind decisively in regard to the permanence and clarity of the items resurrected from storage.*

Early hypertext systems were implemented as a set of files residing on a single disk in the user's personal computer. With the growth of the INTERNET and networking technology, most hypertext systems are now distributed among many different physical sites. The World Wide Web, the most well known of these systems, supports public browsing by INTERNET users from thousands of sites around the world. The nodes of information in the Beethoven example mentioned earlier might each be located at different sites in different parts of the world, though from the user's perspective the information seems connected in a seamless way.

If the notion of electronic hypertext intrigues you, begin by consulting the *Communications of the ACM* issue cited above. More recently, *Communications of the ACM* Volume 33, No. 3 (March 1990), *Communications of the ACM* Volume 35, No. 1 (January 1992), and *Communications of the ACM* Volume 38, No. 8 (August 1995) have all been dedicated to this revolutionary and rapidly growing field.

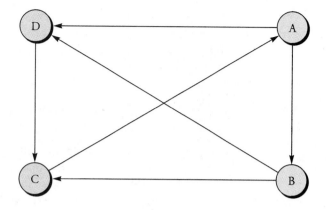

◆ FIGURE 7.29
A four-node digraph

Before providing a C++ interface for the graph ADT, we should clarify a point of ambiguity in the definition of the traversal operation. In particular, this operation does not establish a unique order of visiting nodes that can be reached from the start node. The following examples illustrate two potential orders in which nodes can be visited starting at A in the graph of Figure 7.29.

---

**EXAMPLE 7.7**

Consider a traversal from start node A in the digraph of Figure 7.29 guided by the following strategy: a given path starting at A should be explored as deeply as possible before another path is probed. If we assume that B is the first node adjacent to A, then the traversal will proceed from A to B. If we then assume that C is the first node adjacent to B, the traversal will continue from B to C. From C, it is not possible to visit any nodes that have not already been visited. Hence, we will backtrack to B and, from there, continue the traversal to D since D is adjacent to B. Hence the overall order in which nodes would be visited by a traversal under the strategy and assumptions of this example is

        A, B, C, D

The strategy exemplified here is often called a *depth-first traversal* since a given path is probed as deeply as possible before we backtrack and explore another path.

---

**EXAMPLE 7.8**

Indicate the order in which nodes would be visited in a traversal starting at node A in the digraph of Figure 7.29 following a strategy that does not probe one path as deeply as possible but rather "fans out" to all nodes adjacent to a given node. Hence we would proceed from A to B and then to D, since both B and D are adjacent to A. Since all nodes adjacent to A have been exhausted, we would fan out from B, the first node we visited from A. This takes us to C by the edge B → A C, completing the traversal in the overall order

        A, B, D, C

The fan-out strategy exemplified here is often termed a *breadth-first traversal.*

Examples 7.7 and 7.8 just begin to scratch the surface of the variety of graph traversal strategies that exist. We shall soon examine the implementation of these traversal strategies more closely. At this time the point to emphasize is that the graph traversal operation is open to a variety of implementation techniques.

## C++ Interface for the Graph ADT

Before we can develop graph algorithms in detail, we must provide a C++ interface for this ADT. This is done in the following class declaration module. The interface makes the assumption that the data in graph nodes are drawn from a range of values that can serve both as keys for tables and as values over which a **for** loop can iterate, such as **int, char,** or an enumerated type. Our reasons for making this assumption will become apparent when we discuss ways of implementing graphs.

```
// Class declaration file: graph.h

#ifndef GRAPH_H

#include "boolean.h"

// Definition section

// We assume that type boolean is already defined

template <class Node> class graph
{

      public:

      // Class constructors

      graph();
      graph(const graph<Node> &g);

      // Member functions

      boolean add_edge(const Node &node1, const Node &node2);
      void remove_edge(const Node &node1, const Node &node2);
      boolean edge(const Node &node1, const Node& node2);
      void traverse(Node &start, void (*process) (Node &item));
      graph <Node>& operator = (const graph<Node> &g);

      // Protected data and member functions pertaining to
      // the implementation would go here.

};

#define GRAPH_H
#endif
```

### The Network ADT

Graphs such as that shown in Figure 7.27 are somewhat special in that the edges have weights associated with them, here representing distances between nodes (cities). Such a graph is an example of the *network* abstract data type.

> **Network:** A network is a graph in which each edge has a positive numerical *weight*. The operations associated with the network ADT are the same as those for the graph ADT with the exceptions that the `add_edge` operation must now specify the weight of the edge being added and we must add an operation which, given two nodes, returns the weight of the edge that may exist between them.

These two new operations are specified by the following preconditions and postconditions.

---

**add_edge operation**

Preconditions:    Receiver is an arbitrary network that has been initialized by create and, potentially, affected by other operations. `node1` and `node2` are two nodes in network. `weight` is a positive number representing the weight of an edge to be added from `node1` to `node2`.

Postconditions:    Receiver has an edge of weight `weight` from `node1` to `node2`. If an edge already existed from `node1` to `node2`, the weight of that edge is now `weight`.

**edge_weight operation**

Preconditions:    Receiver is an arbitrary network that has been initialized by `create` and, potentially, affected by other operations. `node1` and `node2` are two nodes in the network.

Postconditions:    `edge_weight` returns zero if there is no edge from `node1` to `node2` and the numerical value of the edge if it exists.

---

Graphs and networks provide excellent examples of how a theoretical area of mathematics has found very relevant application in computer science. It is beyond the scope of this text to provide a comprehensive treatment of graphs and networks. Rather, our purpose in the rest of this section is to provide you with an overview of a data structure that you will no doubt encounter again as you continue your study of computer science. More in-depth treatments of graphs and networks can be found in numerous advanced texts on data structures such as *Data Structures in C++* by Ellis Horowitz and Sartaj Sahni (New York: Computer Science Press, 1990) and *Introduction to Data Structures and Algorithm Analysis with C++* by George J. Pothering and Thomas L. Naps (St. Paul, Minn.: West Publishing, 1995).

### Implementation of Graphs and Networks

A graph may be conveniently implemented using a two-dimensional table of Boolean values. For instance, the information in Figure 7.26 is contained in Table 7.5, a two-dimensional table. In this table, the value TRUE indicates the presence of an edge between two nodes and the value FALSE indicates the absence of such an edge. In the case of a network, the two-dimensional table implementation still applies. Now, however, the data stored in the table is of a type compatible with edge weights. Such a two-dimensional table implementation of the transportation

◇ **TABLE 7.5**

Two-dimensional table
implementation of graph
from Figure 7.26

| Course | SMITH | JONES | MURRAY | BACH | LEWIS |
|---|---|---|---|---|---|
| Computer Science | TRUE | FALSE | TRUE | TRUE | FALSE |
| Calculus I | FALSE | TRUE | TRUE | FALSE | TRUE |
| English Comp. | TRUE | TRUE | FALSE | TRUE | TRUE |

network from Figure 7.27 is given in Table 7.6. Note that the data are mirrored across the diagonal of the table because all edges are bidirectional.

Table 7.6 illustrates a quality typically found in two-dimensional table implementations of large graphs and networks: the sparseness of nontrivial data. Hence, the methods we have discussed for implementing sparse tables actually provide alternative implementation strategies for graphs and networks. In fact, the pilot/flight database problem of Wing-and-a-Prayer Airlines, with which we introduced the two-key table ADT in Chapter 2, may now be viewed as a graph problem. This problem presented us with a bidirectional tree in which each pilot could have multiple flights as child nodes and, conversely, each flight could have multiple pilots as child nodes.

In the discussion of the two graph/network algorithms that follow, we do not tie ourselves to a particular implementation strategy for representing the underlying data structure. Rather, we discuss the algorithms in terms of the operations associated with the abstract data type involved and leave implementation considerations for the exercises at the end of this section and the programming problems at the end of the chapter.

◇ **TABLE 7.6**

Two-dimensional table
implementation of network
from Figure 7.27

| | NY | Wash | Miam | Milw | Chi | NOrl | Mpls | OklC | Dals | LVeg | Phex | Stl | SFra | LA |
|---|---|---|---|---|---|---|---|---|---|---|---|---|---|---|
| NY | | 237 | | 811 | | | 1217 | | 1614 | | | | | |
| Wash | | | | | | | | | | | | | | |
| Miam | | | | 1423 | | | | | | | | | | |
| Milw | 811 | | | | | | | | | | 1771 | | 2257 | |
| Chi | | 1423 | | | | 948 | | | | 1780 | | 2060 | | |
| NOrl | | | | | 948 | | | | 517 | | | | | |
| Mpls | 1217 | | | | | | | 792 | 949 | | | | | |
| OklC | | | | | | | 792 | | | | | | | |
| Dals | 1614 | | | | | 517 | 949 | | | | | | | 1440 |
| LVeg | | | | | 1780 | | | | | | | | | 272 |
| Phex | | | | 1771 | | | | | | | | | | |
| Stl | | | | | 2060 | | | | | | | | | 808 |
| SFra | | | | 2257 | | | | | | | | 808 | | 414 |
| LA | | | | | | | | | 1440 | 272 | | | 414 | |

### Examples of Graph Algorithms: Depth-First and Breadth-First Traversals

In many practical applications of graphs, there is frequently a need to visit systematically all the nodes on a graph from a designated starting node. One such application occurs in a political campaign when the organizers of the campaign are interested in having their candidate visit all important political centers. The presence or absence of direct transportation routes (that is, edges) between such centers will determine the possible ways in which all the centers could be visited. At the moment, our only concern is the development of an algorithm that ensures that all possible nodes are visited. Such an algorithm will provide an implementation for the graph traversal operation. Later in the chapter we investigate how to determine the shortest possible distances from one node to all others.

**Depth-First Traversal.** This technique was illustrated in Example 7.7. The main logic of the depth-first algorithm is analogous to the preorder traversal of a tree. It is accomplished recursively as follows:

1. Designate the starting node as the search node and mark it as visited.
2. Find a node adjacent to the search node (that is, connected by an edge from the search node) that has not yet been visited. Designate this as the new search node (but remember the previous one) and mark it as visited.
3. Repeat step 2 using the new search node. If no nodes satisfying step 2 can be found, return to the previous search node and continue from there.
4. When a return to the previous search node in step 3 is impossible, the search from the originally chosen search node is complete.

This algorithm is called a depth-first traversal because the search continues progressively deeper into the graph in a recursive manner.

To illustrate this function more clearly, consider Figure 7.30; its table implementation is shown in Table 7.7. Suppose we have a function called `search_from`, which is invoked to begin a depth-first traversal from a given node on the graph. The steps followed by the algorithm are as follows:

1. We begin by marking node 1 visited and invoke `search_from(1)`.
2. Both nodes 2 and 3 are adjacent to node 1 according to the matrix implementation of the graph, but node 2 is encountered first on a left-to-right scan of the row for 1; so the search goes to node 2. We invoke `search_from(2)`, and node 2 is marked as visited.

◆ FIGURE 7.30

Graph to illustrate depth-first search

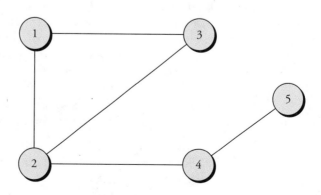

◇ **TABLE 7.7**
Table implementation of
Figure 7.30

|   | 1 | 2 | 3 | 4 | 5 |
|---|---|---|---|---|---|
| 1 | FALSE | TRUE | TRUE | FALSE | FALSE |
| 2 | TRUE | FALSE | TRUE | TRUE | FALSE |
| 3 | TRUE | TRUE | FALSE | FALSE | FALSE |
| 4 | FALSE | TRUE | FALSE | FALSE | TRUE |
| 5 | FALSE | FALSE | FALSE | TRUE | FALSE |

3. Since node 3 is the first unvisited node adjacent to node 2, the search now goes to node 3, `search_from(3)` is invoked, and node 3 is marked as visited.
4. Since there is no unvisited node adjacent to node 3, we say that this node has exhausted the search; the search goes back to its predecessor, that is, to node 2.
5. From node 2, we visit node 4.
6. From node 4, we proceed to node 5. All nodes have now been visited, and the depth-first traversal is complete.

Use Table 7.7 to verify these steps.

We note that the order in which nodes are visited in a depth-first traversal is not unique. This is because the order is dependent on the manner in which "adjacent" nodes are chosen. That is, given two unvisited nodes adjacent to another node, which one should be chosen to invoke the **search_from** function? In practice, this will usually be determined by the ordering of the data type used to implement the nodes in the graph.

**EXAMPLE 7.9**

Implement the depth-first traversal algorithm under the assumption that the node data type is a key value type.

As with our implementation of the postorder traversal operation for a binary tree in Example 7.6, we use an auxiliary function as the real recursive workhorse. The traverse function is itself merely a front-end, which appropriately sets the stage for the auxiliary function **search_from**.

We can now see the reason for the restriction placed on the node type in our C++ interface for the graph ADT. It must be a type capable of keying a table and controlling an iterative loop structure. Both of these properties are assumed in the code of Example 7.9.

**Breadth-First Traversal.** An alternate graph traversal to the depth-first strategy is the breadth-first traversal. Instead of proceeding as deeply as possible along one path from the current node in the graph, the breadth-first traversal examines all nodes adjacent to the current node before proceeding more deeply along any given path. Hence, for the graph of Figure 7.31, implemented by Table 7.8, a breadth-first traversal starting at node 1 would visit nodes in the order 1, 2, 3, 4, 5 (as opposed to the order 1, 2, 4, 5, 3 dictated by a depth-first traversal).

A breadth-first traversal of a graph involves the following steps:

1. Begin with the start node, and mark it as visited.
2. Proceed to the next node having an edge connection to the node in step 1. Mark it as visited.

◆ FIGURE 7.31

Graph to illustrate breadth-
first traversal

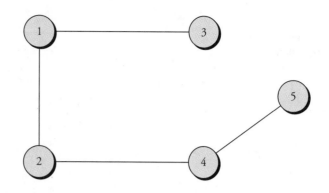

◇ TABLE 7.8

Table implementation of
Figure 7.31

|   | 1 | 2 | 3 | 4 | 5 |
|---|---|---|---|---|---|
| 1 | FALSE | TRUE  | TRUE  | FALSE | FALSE |
| 2 | TRUE  | FALSE | FALSE | TRUE  | FALSE |
| 3 | TRUE  | FALSE | FALSE | FALSE | FALSE |
| 4 | FALSE | TRUE  | FALSE | FALSE | TRUE  |
| 5 | FALSE | FALSE | FALSE | TRUE  | FALSE |

**3.** Come back to the node in step 1, descend along an edge toward an unvisited node, and mark the new node as visited.

**4.** Repeat step 3 until all nodes adjacent to the node in step 1 have been marked as visited.

**5.** Repeat steps 1 through 4 starting from the node visited in 2, then starting from the nodes visited in step 3 in the order visited. Keep this up as long as possible before starting a new scan.

You will be asked to explore this strategy in the programming problems at the end of the chapter.

## Example of a Network Algorithm: Finding Shortest Paths

If the graph under consideration is a network in which edge weights represent distances, then an appropriate question is: From a given node called the **source**, what is the shortest distance to all other nodes in the network?

For instance, the network of Figure 7.32 could be thought of as showing airline routes between cities. An airline would be interested in finding the most economical route between any two given cities in the network. The numbers listed on the edges would, in this case, represent distances between cities. Thus, the airline wishes to find the shortest path that can be flown from node 3 in order to reach nodes 1, 2, 4, and 5.

Suppose we want to find the shortest path from node 1 to node 3. From Figure 7.32, we note that this path would be $1 \rightarrow 2 \rightarrow 3$, yielding a total weight of $800 + 410 = 1210$. An algorithm to find such a path was discovered by E. W. Dijkstra. For convenience in discussing Dijkstra's algorithm, often called the shortest path algorithm, let us assume that the nodes in the network under consideration are numbered 1, 2, . . ., **number_of_nodes**. That is, the node type is the subrange of the integers given by 1 . . . **number_of_nodes**.

◆ FIGURE 7.32

Network with edge weights representing distances

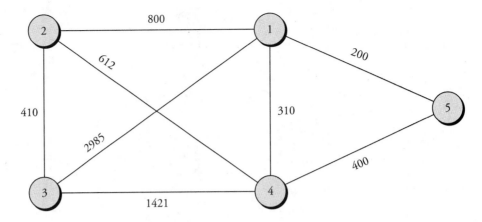

Given such a collection of nodes, Dijkstra's algorithm requires three arrays in addition to a suitable implementation of the network M. These three arrays are identified as follows:

```
int distance[MAX_DISTANCE_SIZE];
int path[MAX_PATH_SIZE];
boolean included[MAX_INCLUDED_SIZE];
```

Identifying one node as the source, the algorithm proceeds to find the shortest distance from source to all other nodes in the network. At the conclusion of the algorithm, the shortest distance from **source** to node **j** is stored in **distance[j]**, whereas **path[j]** contains the immediate predecessor of node **j** on the path determining this shortest distance. While the algorithm is in progress, **distance[j]** and **path[j]** are being continually updated until **included[j]** is switched from FALSE to TRUE. Once this switch occurs, it is known definitely that **distance[j]** contains the shortest distance from **source** to **j**. The algorithm progresses until all nodes have been so included. Hence it actually gives us the shortest distance from **source** to every other node in the network.

Given the source node in the network M, the algorithm may be divided into two phases: an initialization phase followed by an iteration phase, in which nodes are included one by one in the set of nodes for which the shortest distance from **source** is known definitely.

During the initialization phase, we must

1. Initialize included[source] to TRUE and included [j] to FALSE for all other j.
2. Initialize the distance array via the rule
   if j = source
      distance[j] = 0
   else if edge_weight(m, source, j) <>0
      distance[j] = edge_weight(m, source, j)
   else if j is not connected to source by a direct edge
   (that is, if edge_weight(m, source, j) = 0)
      distance[j] = Infinity
3. Initialize the path array via the rule
   if edge_weight (M, source, J) <> 0
      path[j] = source
   else
      path[j] = Undefined

Given this initialization, the iteration phase may be expressed in a generalized pseudocode form as follows:

Do

Find the node J that has the minimal distance among those nodes not yet included
Mark J as now included
For each R not yet included
    If there is an edge from J to R
        If distance[j] + edge_weight (M, J, R) < distance[R]
        distance[R] = distance[J] + edge_weight (M, J, R)
          path[R] = J
While all nodes are not included

The crucial part of the algorithm occurs within the innermost **if** of the **for** loop. Figure 7.33 provides a pictorial representation of the logic involved here. The nodes included with the circle represent those nodes already included prior to a given iteration of the **do** loop. Node J in Figure 7.33 represents the node found in the first step of the **do** loop; R represents another arbitrary node, which has not yet been included. The lines emanating from source represent the paths corresponding to the current entries in the distance array. For nodes within the circle—that is, those already included—these paths are guaranteed to be the shortest distance paths. If J is the node having the minimal entry in distance among those not yet **included**, we will add J to the circle of included nodes and then check to see if J's connections to other nodes in the network which are not yet **included** may result in a newly found shorter path to such nodes.

Referring to Figure 7.33 again, the sum of two sides of a triangle

```
distance [j] + edge_weight(m, j, r)
```

may in fact be shorter than the third side,

```
distance[r]
```

This geometric contradiction is possible because these are not true straight-sided triangles, but "triangles" whose sides may be very complicated paths through a network.

◆ FIGURE 7.33
**do . . . while** loop logic in shortest-path (Dijkstra's) algorithm

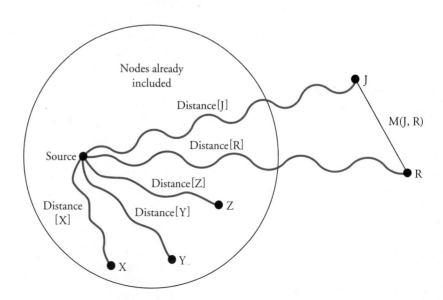

◆ FIGURE 7.34

Guaranteeing the minimality of distance to J once it is included

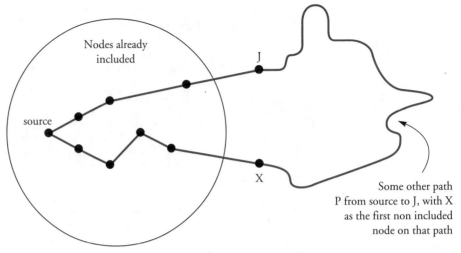

Criterion for Including J insures
Distance [J] ≤ Distance [X] ≤ Length of path P

It is also apparent from Figure 7.33 why Dijkstra's algorithm works. As the node J in this figure is found to have the minimal distance entry from among all those nodes not yet included, we may now include it among the nodes whose minimal distance from the source node is absolutely known. Why? Consider any other path P to J containing nodes that are not yet included at the time J is included. Let X be the first such nonincluded node on path P. Then clearly, as the first nonincluded node on the path P, X must be adjacent to an included node. However, as Figure 7.34 indicates, the criterion that dictated the choice of J as an included node ensures that

```
distance[J]    ≤ The total edge weight through node X on the path P
               ≤ Total edge weight of path P
```

This inequality demonstrates that, once J is included, there exists no other path P to J through a nonincluded node that can yield a shorter overall distance. Hence we have verified our claim that including a node guarantees our having found a path of shortest possible distance to that node.

---

EXAMPLE 7.10

To be sure you understand Dijkstra's algorithm before you attempt to implement it, trace it through on the network of Figure 7.32 with **source = 1**.

Initially, we would have

> distance[2] = 800    path[2] = 1
> distance[3] = 2985    path[3] = 1
> distance[4] = 310    path[4] = 1
> distance[5] = 200    path[5] = 1

in accordance with steps 2 and 3 of the initialization phase. According to the iteration phase of the algorithm, we would then, in order, perform these steps:

**1.** Include node 5; no change in `distance` and `path` needed.

| | |
|---|---|
| distance[2] = 800 | path[2] = 1 |
| distance[3] = 2985 | path[3] = 1 |
| distance[4] = 310 | path[4] = 1 |
| distance[5] = 200 | path[5] = 1 |

**2.** Include node 4; update `distance` and `path` to

| | |
|---|---|
| distance[2] = 800 | path[2] = 1 |
| distance[3] = 1731 | path[3] = 4 |
| distance[4] = 310 | path[4] = 1 |
| distance[5] = 200 | path[5] = 1 |

(Note that it is shorter to go from node 1 to node 4 to node 3 than to follow the edge directly connecting node 1 to node 3.)

**3.** Include node 2; update `distance` and `path` to

| | |
|---|---|
| distance[2] = 800 | path[2] = 1 |
| distance[3] = 1210 | path[3] = 2 |
| distance[4] = 310 | path[4] = 1 |
| distance[5] = 200 | path[5] = 1 |

(Now we find that traveling from node 1 to node 2 to node 3 is even better than the path determined in step 2.)

4. Finally node 3 is included with (obviously) no changes made in **distance** or **path**.

---

EXERCISES 7.6

1. Indicate the order in which nodes would be visited if a depth-first traversal of the network in Figure 7.27 were initiated from SEATTLE. Use the adjacency relationships from Table 7.6.

2. Repeat Exercise 1 but initiate the traversal from MIAMI.

3. Repeat Exercise 1 for a breadth-first traversal.

4. Repeat Exercise 2 for a breadth-first traversal.

5. Trace the contents of the **distance, path,** and **included** arrays as Dijkstra's shortest path algorithm is applied to the transportation network of Figure 7.27. Use PHOENIX as the **source** node.

6. Repeat Exercise 5 with MILWAUKEE as the **source** node.

7. Using a two-dimensional table, write functions to implement each of the basic operations for the graph abstract data type. Then provide a big-O time efficiency analysis of each of the operations. How is this analysis affected by a particular sparse matrix technique that may be underlying the two-dimensional table? Be as specific as possible in stating your answer.

8. Using a two-dimensional table, write functions to implement each of the basic operations for the network abstract data type.

9. In a written statement, discuss the implications of eliminating the requirement that type **node** be a subrange of an ordinal type in the C++ interface for the graph ADT. Your statement should identify problems that this would cause and outline strategies for solving such problems.

---

FOCUS ON
PROGRAM DESIGN

Throughout this text we have emphasized the importance of big-O algorithm analysis as a means of predicting beforehand the practicality of an algorithm in a given application. In this regard, big-O notation and analysis serve a vital purpose—the estimation of the time and space requirements of an algorithm in order of magnitude terms. However, when designing software systems in the very competitive and demanding real world, we often require a more detailed measurement of an algorithm's performance than that which can be achieved simply with a big-O analysis. One reason for this is the variety of complications that cannot be conveniently plugged into a big-O formula. Included among these complications are the following:

■ The variety of hardware on which an algorithm must ultimately be executed. There will be vast differences in both the time and space limitations of such hardware. Moreover, the details of such limitations are often buried deep in system reference manuals and can be exceedingly hard to find.

■ Discrepancies that frequently arise between a user's projection of his or her computer needs and the unforeseen demands that materialize once the software system is put into use. A good systems analyst can hold those discrepancies to a minimum but not totally eliminate them.

■ The elements of chance and probability that are inherent in many algorithms.

An example of this final point is the order of arrivals for insertion into a binary search tree. We can guarantee that search efficiency in a binary search tree will be between $O(n)$ and $O(\log_2 n)$. We can specify best and worst cases. But what happens in between? When do we cross over from response times that are acceptable to those that are not? Real-life data are rarely best case or worst case. Hence the "in-between" question is often of vital importance. Yet it is also the one that a pure big-O analysis leaves relatively unanswered.

In this section, we present a program that can serve as a start toward further exploration of the questions just posed. The program reads a list of unordered integers from a file, creates a binary search tree containing those integers, and then prints the binary search tree using indentation to reflect the level at which various nodes occur in the tree. In its present form, the program will allow you to test hypotheses about the relationship of the order of arrivals for insertion into a binary search tree and the resulting shape of the tree. In the first programming problem, you will extend the exploratory capabilities of the program, making it a substantive experimental tool.

A modular structure chart for the program is given in Figure 7.35. The program essentially brings together tree processing modules that we have already discussed on an individual basis; therefore, we do not provide the module specifications here. Pseudocode for the main program is

Create the tree
While not end of file
      Get a number from the file
      Insert the number into the tree
Print the tree

One twist is needed in the preorder traversal algorithm. To achieve indentation reflecting the depth of a node in the tree, we must keep track of our current level as we recursively call and then return from function **preorder_traverse**. The ideal solution would be to declare a local counter in the function that would retain its value from one invocation of the function to the next. Unfortunately, this is impossible with local variables in C++.

We are left with two alternatives: Tag the level counter along as an additional reference parameter for the **preorder_traverse** function or use a global level counter. The former alternative will alter the procedural interface to the **preorder_traverse** operation and hence violate the ADT implementation rule (formulated in Chapter 2). Hence we choose the latter alternative—use of a global variable—as the lesser of two evils. You should be aware that the need to

◆ FIGURE 7.35
Modular structure chart for **testtree.cpp** program

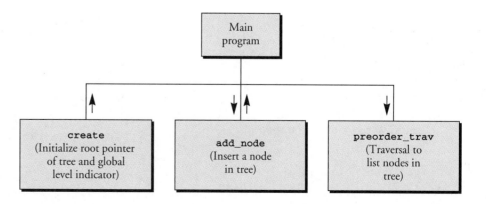

preserve the value of a variable between invocations of a function is one instance in which the use of a global variable in a function can be justified, provided that you carefully document its use.

Here is the change required in the implementation of the helper function **preorder_aux** for running the tests:

```
template <class E>
void binary_tree<E>::preorder_aux(node_ptr tree, void (*process) (E &item))
{
        if (tree != NULL)
        {
                process(tree->data);
                ++level;
        // Increase before recursing
                preorder_aux(tree->left, process);
                preorder_aux(tree->right, process);
                --level;
        // Decrease after recursing
        }
}
```

The complete program and a sample run follow. You will have the chance to explore the program more thoroughly in the end-of-chapter programming problems.

```
// Program file: testtree.cpp

// This program illustrates working with a binary tree.
// Input is an unordered list of integers from a file.
// Output is a character-based representation of the binary search
// tree that is constructed from the input integers.

#include <iostream.h>
#include <fstream.h>

int level = 0;                  // Global variable to maintain current level in tree.
                                // Must be declared for access by tree module.

#include tree.h

const char SPACE = ' ';

void print(int &number);

int main()
{
    int number;
    ifstream input_file;
    binary_tree<int> tree;
```

```
        input_file.open("numbers");
        input_file >> number;
        while (! input_file.eof())
        {
                tree.insert(number);
                input_file >> number;
        }
        input_file.close();
        tree.preorder_traverse(print);
        return 0;
}

void print(int &number)
{
        if (level == 0)
                cout << setw(4) << number << endl;
        else
                cout << setw(level * 4) << SPACE << setw(4) << number << endl;
}
```

A sample run with the input file

results in the following output. Graphic lines have been added to highlight how the indentation reflects the tree structure.

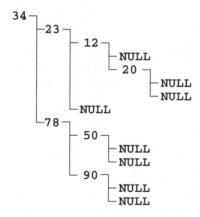

1. Trees are inherently recursive data structures, so learn to think recursively when devising algorithms that process trees.
2. When using the linear array representation of a binary tree, remember that all array locations must be initialized to a flagging Null value if the implementations of other operations are to work correctly.
3. The use of a preorder traversal to print a tree with indentation to reflect the depth of a node is a handy tracing tool to use when debugging a tree program that has gone awry. Keep such a function in your library, so it is readily available when the need arises. For more information, see this chapter's Focus on Program Design section.
4. When using a binary search tree to implement a one-key table, some experimentation may be necessary to determine the efficiency of this technique for the particular data of your application.

## SUMMARY

### Key Terms

| | | |
|---|---|---|
| ancestor | graph | parent node |
| binary search tree | heap | postorder traversal |
| binary tree | heap property | preorder traversal |
| binary implementation of a one-key table | height balancing | root |
| | hierarchy | root node |
| binary tree implementation of general tree | inorder traversal | siblings |
| | insertion rule | subtree |
| branch | leaf node | ternary tree |
| breadth-first traversal | level | threading |
| child node | linear implementation | tree |
| depth-first traversal | linked implementation | tree traversal |
| digraph | network | vertex |
| directional graph | ordering property | weight |
| edge | | |
| general tree | | |

### Key Concepts

◆ Trees are a data structure used to reflect a hierarchical relationship among data items. Indicative of this hierarchy is the parent–child terminology used to express the relationship between items on successive levels of the tree. Trees are by nature recursive structures, with each node of a tree being itself the root of a smaller, embedded subtree.

◆ Binary trees are trees in which each parent may have at most two child nodes. Although this seems like a major restriction, binary trees find a wide range of applications. Three such applications are the representation of algebraic expressions, one-key tables, and priority queues.

◆ Two ways of implementing a binary tree are the linear representation and the linked representation. The former method uses an array and requires no pointers but is prone to wasting a large number of array locations. The latter uses pointers and consequently is able to take advantage of C++'s dynamic memory allocation.

◆ There are three standard ways of traversing a binary tree: that is, three ways of visiting all nodes exactly once. These are the preorder, postorder, and inorder traversals.

◆ In a preorder traversal, the current root node is processed, followed recursively by the nodes in its left subtree and then its right subtree.

◆ In a postorder traversal, all nodes in the left subtree of the current root are recursively processed. Then all nodes in the right subtree are processed, and the root itself is processed last.

◆ In an inorder traversal, the nodes in the left subtree are processed first, followed by the root node, and finally the nodes in the right subtree of the root. The inorder traversal is critical in the binary tree implementation of a one-key table because the order in which it visits nodes corresponds precisely to the ordering of items as first, second, third, . . . , within the list represented by the tree.

◆ The binary search tree implementation of a one-key table is the third such table implementation we have studied. The other two were the array implementation (Chapter 12) and the linked list implementation (Chapter 14). The following table summarizes the relative advantages and disadvantages of the three methods.

| Method | Search | Additions/Deletions | Other Comments |
|---|---|---|---|
| Physically ordered array | $O(\log_2 n)$ with binary search | Excessive data movement | Data must be physically ordered |
| Linked list | Requires sequential search, hence $O(n)$ | Only pointer manipulation required | |
| Binary search tree | Bounded between $O(\log_2 n)$ and $O(n)$ though advanced methods can guarantee the former | Only pointer manipulation required | May necessitate the overhead associated with recursive traversals |

◆ The binary tree may be used to implement the general tree structure. The preorder and postorder traversals emerge as the most important for this particular application.

◆ Graphs and networks are abstract data structures that are more complex than trees because they reflect bidirectional rather than hierarchical relationships. Depth-first and breadth-first traversals and finding the shortest path are examples of algorithms that manipulate graphs and networks.

## PROGRAMMING PROBLEMS AND PROJECTS

1. Extend and experiment with the program from this chapter's Focus on Program Design section in the following ways:

   a. Use the program as it currently appears to acquire a feel for the relationship between the order of input data and the shape of the binary search tree that results.

   b. Instead of reading data from a file, randomly generate the data being inserted in the tree. Use the random number generator available in your version of C++ or, if none is available, the random number generator that appears in Appendix 6.

**c.** After a tree has been generated, add the capability to selectively delete nodes from the tree. Reprint the tree after deleting a node as verification that it has retained the critical ordering property.

**d.** Use the random generation capability from part b to build some very large trees. Instead of printing out these trees after they have been generated, compute the length of the average path that must be followed to find a node in the tree.

Do the results of your experiment indicate that, for random data, binary search trees yield a search efficiency that is $O(\log_2 n)$ or $O(n)$? Justify your conclusion with a written statement that is backed up by empirical data provided from your experimental runs.

**e.** Extend part d by computing the maximal path length in each randomly generated tree. What percentage of randomly generated trees has a maximal path length that is $O(n)$?

**f.** Depending on the availability of graphics functions in your version of C++, change the present character-based tree printout into a more appealing graphical representation.

**2.** Use a binary tree to implement the one-key table in the registrar's system from Example 3.1.

**3.** Modify the airline reservation system you developed for Wing-and-a-Prayer Airlines in Problem 2, Chapter 4, so that the alphabetized lists are maintained with binary trees instead of linked lists.

**4.** Write a program that sorts the records of the Fly-by-Night credit card company file (Problem 3, Chapter 4) in alphabetical order by the last name and then the first name of the customer. Use a binary tree and its inorder traversal to accomplish the sort.

**5.** Recall the roster maintenance system that you wrote for the Bay Area Brawlers in Problem 4 from Chapter 4. The system has been so successful that the league office would like to expand the system to include all the players in the league. Again the goal is to maintain the list of players in alphabetical order, allowing for frequent insertions and deletions as players are cut, picked up, and traded among teams. In addition to storing each player's height, weight, age, and university affiliation, the record for each player should be expanded to include team affiliation, years in league, and annual salary. Because the database for the entire league is many times larger than that for just one team, maintain this list as a binary search tree to increase efficiency.

**6.** Write a program that reads an expression in its prefix form and builds the binary tree corresponding to that expression. Then write functions to print the infix and postfix forms of the expression using inorder and postorder traversals of this tree. Then see if you can extend the program to evaluate the expression represented by the tree.

**7.** Given a file containing some arbitrary text, determine how many times each word appears in the file. Your program should print out in alphabetical order the words that appear in the file, with their frequency counts. For an added challenge, do not assume any maximum word length; this will enable you to combine trees with the string handling methods you have already learned.

**8.** Here is a problem you will encounter if you write statistical analysis software. Given an arbitrarily long list of unordered numbers with an arbitrary number of different values appearing in it, determine and print the marginal distribution for this list of numbers. That is, count how many times each different value appears in the list and then print each value along with its count (frequency). The final output should be arranged from smallest to largest value. This problem can be solved in elegant fashion using trees. An example of such output as produced by COSAP (Conversationally Oriented Statistical Analysis Package) of Lawrence University follows:

```
Command? Marginals Judge
                    Pine County Criminal Cases
```

M A R G I N A L F R E Q U E N C I E S

| Variable Judge | JUDGE BEFORE WHOM CASE BROUGHT (2) | | |
|---|---|---|---|
| Value label | Value | Absolute Frequency | Relative Frequency |
| ALLEN | 1 | 677 | 80.8% |
| JONES | 2 | 88 | 10.5% |
| KELLY | 3 | 26 | 3.1% |
| MURCK | 5 | 47 | 5.6% |

**838 Valid 0 Missing 838 Total Observations**

Here the data file contained 838 occurrences of the values 1, 2, 3, and 5. Each value was a code number assigned to a particular judge.

9. Many compilers offer the services of a cross-referencing program to aid in debugging. Such a program will list in alphabetical order all the identifiers that appear in a program and the various lines of the program that reference them. Write such a cross-reference for your favorite language using a binary tree to maintain the list of identifiers that are encountered.

10. A relatively easy game to implement with a binary tree is to have the computer try to guess an animal about which the user is thinking by asking the user a series of questions that can be answered by yes or no. A node in the binary tree to play this game could be viewed as

Yes/No pointers leading to

1. *Another question.*
2. *The name of the animal.*
3. *NULL.*

If NULL, have your program surrender and then ask the user for a new question that uniquely defines the animal being thought of. Then add this new question and animal to the growing binary tree database.

11. For this problem, you are to write a program that will differentiate expressions in the variable X. The input to this program will be a series of strings, each representing an infix expression to be differentiated. Each such expression is to be viewed as a stream of tokens. Valid tokens are integers, the variable X, the binary operators (+, -, *, /, ^), and parentheses. To make scanning for tokens easy, you may assume that each token is followed by exactly one space, with the exception of the final token, which is followed by the end-of-line character.

First your program will have to scan the infix expression, building up an appropriate binary tree representation of it. For this you should be able to borrow significantly on the work you did in parsing expressions in Chapter 5. The major difference here is that the end result of this parse is to be a binary tree instead of a postfix string.

Once the binary expression tree is built, traverse it, building up another binary expression tree, which represents the derivative of the original expression. The following differentiation rules should be used in this process:

Suppose C is a constant, and S and T are expressions in X:

```
Diff(C) = 0
Diff(X) = 1
Diff(S + T) = Diff(S) + Diff(T)
Diff(S - T) = Diff(S) - Diff(T)
Diff(S * T) = S * Diff(T) + T * Diff(S)
Diff(S / T) = ((T * Diff(S)) - (S * Diff(T))) / (T ^ 2)
Diff(S ^ C) = (C * S ^ (C - 1)) * Diff(S)    // the infamous chain rule
```

Finally, once the binary expression tree for the derivative has been built, print the expression. Print it in completely parenthesized infix notation to avoid ambiguity.

Note that there are three distinct phases to this problem:

- Parsing of the original infix expression into a binary tree representation
- Building a binary tree representation of the derivative
- Printing the derivative in completely parenthesized infix notation.

For an added challenge on this problem, simplify the derivative before printing it. Simplify the expression for the derivative according to the following rules:

```
S + 0 = S
0 + S = S
S - 0 = S
S * 0 = 0
0 * S = 0
S * 1 = S
1 * S = S
0 / S = 0
S ^ 0 = 1
S ^ 1 = S
S - S = 0
0 / S = 0
S / S = 1
S / 0 = 'DIVISION BY ZERO'
0 / 0 = 'UNDEFINED'
```

12. Wing-and-a-Prayer Airlines (Problem 3) is expanding their record-keeping database. This database may now be pictured hierarchically as

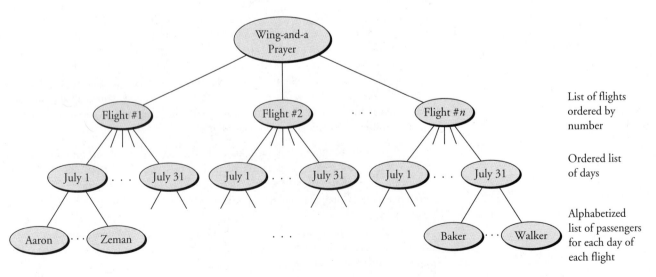

List of flights ordered by number

Ordered list of days

Alphabetized list of passengers for each day of each flight

Write a program to maintain this database. Your program should process requests to add, delete, or list the following:

- Specified flight number
- Specified day of the month (for a given flight number)
- Specified passenger or all passengers (for a given flight number and day of the month).

**13.** Many statistical analysis packages support a "cross-tabulation" command designed to explore the relationship between statistical variables. A cross-tabulation between two variables produces a two-dimensional table containing a frequency count for each possible ordered pair of values of the two variables. However, these statistical packages typically allow this type of analysis to proceed even further than merely exploring two variables. For instance, in a legal-system database, we might be interested in cross-tabulating a defendant's age with the judge before whom the defendant stood trial. We may then wish to cross-tabulate this result with the sex of the defendant. Sex in this case is called the control variable. We would output one such cross-tabulation table for each possible value of sex. Note that this type of output is not limited to just one control variable. There may be an arbitrary number of control variables and tables to cycle through. Moreover, the variables have an arbitrary number of observations and are all in arbitrary order. Yet for each variable the list of possible values is always printed in smallest to largest order. The general tree structure that emerges for handling cross-tabulation is

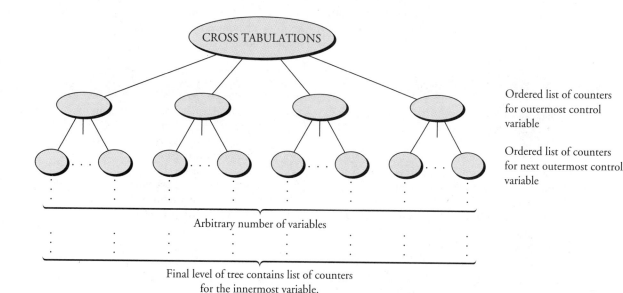

Write a program to handle the task of producing statistical cross-tabulations.

**14.** Write a program to print the nodes of a tree level by level; that is, all level 0 nodes, followed by all level 1 nodes, followed by all level 2 nodes, and so on. (*Hint:* This program will afford an excellent opportunity to practice using a queue in addition to a tree.)

**15.** Operating systems often use general trees as the data structure on which their file directory system is based. Leaf nodes in such a system represent actual files or empty directories. Interior nodes represent nonempty directories. For instance, consider the following situation:

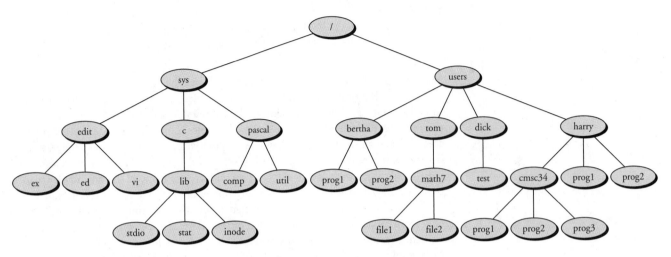

A directory entry is specified by its pathname. A pathname consists of tree node names separated by slashes. Such a pathname is absolute if it starts at the root; that is, if it starts with a slash (/). It is relative to the current directory if it does not start with a slash.

In this assignment, you are to write a command processor that will allow a user to manipulate files within such a directory structure. The commands accepted by your processor will be in the form of numbers associated with particular operations and pathnames, as shown in the following table:

| Number | Operation | Pathname |
|--------|-----------|----------|
| 1 | Change directory | Absolute pathname, relative pathname, or ". ." for parent |
| 2 | Make a new directory | Absolute or relative pathname |
| 3 | Make a new file | Absolute or relative pathname |
| 4 | Remove a file | Absolute or relative pathname |
| 5 | Remove a directory, but only if it is empty | Absolute or relative pathname |
| 6 | Remove a directory and, recursively, everything below it | Absolute or relative pathname |
| 7 | Print directory entries in alphabetical order | Absolute or relative pathname |
| 8 | Recursively print directory entries in alphabetical order | Absolute or relative pathname |
| 9 | Print current directory name | |
| 10 | Quit processing commands | |

Since even intelligent tree-walking users can easily get lost, your command processor should be prepared to trap errors of the following variety:

- Specifying a nonexistent pathname
- Specifying a pathname that is a file when it should be a directory
- Specifying a pathname that is a directory when it should be a file

Upon detecting such an error, have your command processor print an appropriate error message and then return to accept the next user command.

16. Trees have significant applications in the area of artificial intelligence and game playing. Consider, for instance, the game of FIFTEEN. In this game, two players take turns selecting digits between 1 and 9 with the goal of selecting a combination of digits that add up to 15. Once a digit is chosen, it may not be chosen again by

either player. Rather than immediately considering a tree for the game of FIFTEEN, let us first consider a tree for the simpler game of SEVEN with digits chosen in the range 1 to 6. A tree that partially represents the states that may be reached in this game follows:

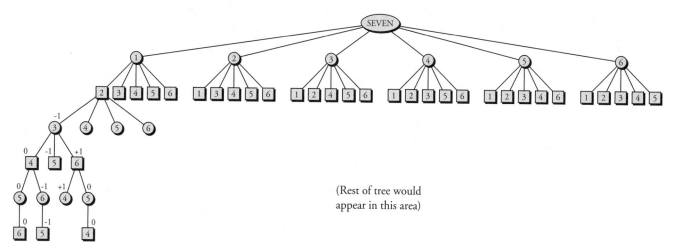

(Rest of tree would
appear in this area)

In this tree, circular nodes represent the states that may be reached by the player who moves first (the computer), and square nodes represent the states that may be reached by the player who moves second (a human opponent). The +1, 0, or –1 attached to each node represents weighting factors designed to help the computer choose the most advantageous move at any given stage of the game. The rules used to compute these weighting factors follow:

- If the node is a leaf node, its weight is determined by some static weighting function. In this case, the static weighting function used was to assign +1 to a leaf node representing a computer win, 0 to a leaf node representing a draw, and –1 to a leaf node representing a human win.
- If the node is a node in which the computer will move next (that is, a state occupied by the human opponent), then the weighting factor of the node is the maximum of the weighting factors of its children.
- If the node is a node in which the human opponent will move next, then the weighting factor of the node is the minimum of the weighting factors of its children.

In its turn, the computer should always choose to move to the node having the maximum possible weighting factor. The rationale behind this technique, called the minimax technique, is that the computer will move in such a way as to always maximize its chances of winning. The human opponent, if playing intelligently, will always move to a node having a minimum weighting factor. Thus in the partial game shown, the computer would choose 4 if the human had been naive enough to select the 6 node with the weighting factor of +1.

Write a program to build a weighted game tree for the game of FIFTEEN and then have the computer play against a human opponent. Note that this game is really the game of tic-tac-toe if one considers the following matrix:

| 4 | 9 | 2 |
| 3 | 5 | 7 |
| 8 | 1 | 6 |

All winning tic-tac-toe paths add up to 15.

Give some consideration as to the time and efficiency of your algorithm. Many games simply cannot be completely represented via a general tree because of space limitations. Consequently, a partial game tree is built in which the leaf nodes may not actually be the final moves made in the game. In such situations, the static weighting function applied to the leaf nodes in the game tree requires a bit more insight to develop.

**17.** Consider a priority queue (see Chapter 5, Section 5.3) in which each item is assigned a different priority. Discuss how a binary tree with the heap property could be used to maintain such a priority queue. Write functions for a heap implementation of the basic priority queue operations:

```
create
empty
insert(item, success)
remove(item, success)
```

Categorize the run-time efficiency of the **insert** and **remove** operations in big-O terms. Would a linear implementation or a linked implementation of the binary tree be most advantageous for this application? Explain why.

Finally, use your priority queue implementation to solve a problem such as Problem 12 in Chapter 5 or to simulate the servicing of priority-rated jobs on a time-sharing computing system.

**18.** Implement Dijkstra's shortest path algorithm using a suitable two-key table representation scheme to store the network data. Test your program with the transportation network pictured in Figure 7.27. Note that this same problem appeared in Chapter 6 as Problem 13. There you used a different algorithm for solving it. In a written statement, compare the efficiencies of the two algorithms.

**19.** A breadth-first traversal of a graph was discussed in Section 7.6. Implement this algorithm as a C++ function. (*Hint:* Use a queue.)

**20.** You are given a binary tree of integers implemented by a linked representation. Such a tree is said to be *weight balanced* if the sum of all the entries in the left subtree of the root equals the sum of all the entries in the right subtree of the root. Write a Boolean-valued function that receives a root pointer to such a tree and returns TRUE if the tree is weight balanced and FALSE otherwise. Then write a complete program to test your function. Finally, adjust your function so that it returns TRUE only when *every* subtree of the original tree is weight balanced.

**21.** Explore some additional graph and network algorithms in one of the advanced texts cited earlier in this chapter, such as Horowitz and Sahni, *Data Structures in C++* (New York: Computer Science Press, 1990) or Pothering and Naps, *Introduction to Data Structures and Algorithm Analysis with C++* (St. Paul, Minn.: West Publishing, 1995). Then prepare a written or oral report in which you explain the logic behind one of the algorithms you explore.

CHAPTER  **8** More Powerful Sorting Methods

CHAPTER OUTLINE

8.1 The Shell Sort Algorithm

*Efficiency of the Shell Sort*

8.2 The Quick Sort Algorithm

*Efficiency of the Quick Sort*

*A Note of Interest: Privacy Issues Kill Lotus Database*

8.3 The Heap Sort Algorithm

*Efficiency of the Heap Sort*

8.4 The Merge Sort Algorithm

*Analysis of the Merge Sort*

*A Note of Interest: Public-Key Cryptography*

*Never mistake motion for action.*
Ernest Hemingway,
1889–1961

In Chapter 1 we analyzed three simple sorting algorithms: bubble sort, insertion sort, and selection sort. We also discussed a technique, called a pointer sort, which can be combined with any of these three algorithms to minimize data movement when large records are being sorted by a particular key field. The essence of the pointer sort is to maintain an array of pointers that dictates the logical order of the records in an array of records. When the sorting algorithm dictates a swap, only the pointers must be interchanged, not the actual records.

With all three of our sorting algorithms, however, we ran into a barrier. This barrier was a run-time efficiency of $O(n^2)$ comparisons. Since the pointer sort technique reduces data movement but not the number of comparisons, this barrier exists whether or not we incorporate the pointer sort idea into the sorting algorithm. Our goal in this chapter is to study sorting algorithms that break the $O(n^2)$ comparisons barrier. These new algorithms will make use of what we have learned since Chapter 1. In particular, both recursion and a conceptual understanding of trees are essential prerequisites to analyzing these more powerful methods.

The general setup for the sort algorithms of this chapter is the same as the one we used in Chapter 1:

```
const int MAX_LIST_SIZE = 100;
typedef int element;
typedef element list_type[MAX_LIST_SIZE];
```

We wish to write a sort function that meets the following specifications:

```
// Function: sort
// Sorts a list of elements into ascending order
//
// Inputs: a list of elements in random order and its current length
// Output: the list of elements arranged in ascending order

void sort(list_type list, int n);
```

Although our algorithms for this chapter are presented in the context of sorting arrays in ascending order, they apply more generally to any list whose elements can be directly accessed (for example, one-key tables) and they can be easily modified to sort in descending order. Moreover, one of the methods we discuss (merge sort) actually does not require direct access into the list. Hence it could be applied to lists that are just sequentially accessible such as sequential files and linked lists.

## 8.1 The Shell Sort Algorithm

The *shell sort,* named after its inventor D. L. Shell, incorporates the logic of the insertion sort to a certain extent. However, instead of sorting the entire array at once, it first divides the array into smaller, noncontiguous segments, which are then separately sorted using the insertion sort. The advantage of doing this is twofold. First, where a comparison dictates a swap of two data items in a segment, this swap within a noncontiguous segment of the array moves an item a greater distance within the overall array than the swap of adjacent array entries in the usual insertion sort. This means that one swap is more likely to place an element closer to its final location in the array when using shell sort than when using the simple insertion sort. For instance, a large-valued entry that appears near the front of the array will more quickly move to the tail end of the array because each swap moves it a greater distance in the array. The second advantage of dividing the array into segments is tied to the first; that is, because early passes tend to move elements closer to their final destination than early passes would in a straight insertion sort, the array becomes partially sorted quite fast. The fact that the array is likely to become partially sorted relatively early then allows the embedded insertion sort logic to make more frequent use of its check for an early exit from its inner loop. (Recall that this check is what makes the insertion sort particularly efficient for arrays that are partially sorted.) An example will help clarify this shell sort rationale.

---

**EXAMPLE 8.1**

Suppose we have an array containing the following integers:

*80 93 60 12 42 30 68 85 10*

We first divide this into three segments of three elements each.

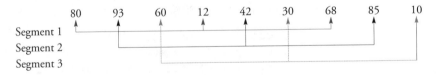

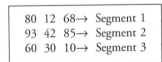

```
80  12  68→  Segment 1
93  42  85→  Segment 2
60  30  10→  Segment 3
```

and sort each of the segments:

```
12  68  80
42  85  93
10  30  60
```

The original array, partially sorted, now appears as

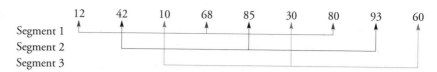

Segment 1
Segment 2
Segment 3

We divide this partially sorted array as

| | |
|---|---|
| 12  10  85  80  60 | → Segment 1 |
| 42  68  30  93 | → Segment 2 |

These segments are then sorted and the array takes the form

Segment 1
Segment 2

Finally, this array is sorted as one segment; 12 and 30, and 93 and 85 are swapped to give us the sorted array

*10 12 30 42 60 68 80 85 93*

---

The key to the shell sort algorithm is that the whole array is first fragmented into $K$ segments for some number $K$, where $K$ is preferably a prime number. These $K$ segments are given by

$$a[0], a[K + 1], a[2 * K + 1], ..., a[2], a[K + 2], a[2 * K + 2], ...$$

.

.

.

$$a[K], a[2 * K], a[3 * K], ...$$

Because each segment is sorted, the whole array is partially sorted after the first pass. For the next pass, the value of $K$ is reduced, which increases the size of each segment, hence reducing the number of segments. Preferably, the next value of $K$ is also chosen so that it is prime relative to its previous value, or *relatively prime*. (Two integers are said to be relatively prime to each other if they have no common factor greater than 1.) The process is repeated until $K = 1$, at which point the array is sorted. The insertion sort is applied to each segment, so each successive segment is partially sorted. Consequently, the later applications of the insertion sort become very efficient, dramatically increasing the overall efficiency of the shell sort.

To emphasize the fashion in which the shell sort algorithm relies on the logic of insertion sort, we present a **segmented_insertion_sort function**, which arranges each of $k$ segments in an $n$-element array into ascending order. Compare this function with the function for insertion sort that was given in Chapter 1. You will see that **segmented_insertion_sort** moves an item from position $j$ to position $j + k$. When $k = 1$, this is precisely the original insertion sort algorithm.

```
void segmented_insertion_sort(list_type list, int n, int k)
{
    int j;
    element item_to_insert;
    boolean still_looking;

    for (int i = k; i < n; ++i)
    {
        item_to_insert = list[i];
        j = i - k;
        still_looking = TRUE;
        while ((j >= 0) && still_looking)
            if (item_to_insert < list[j])
            {
                list[j + k] = list[j];
                j = j - k;
            }
            else
                still_looking = FALSE;
        list[j + k] = item_to_insert;
    }
}
```

With $n = 6$ and $k = 3$, the array is divided into three segments of two elements each.

```
80 12 --> Segment 1
93 42 --> Segment 2
60 30 --> Segment 3
```

Sort each of the segments:
```
12    80
42    93
30    60
```

Given the `segmented_insertion_sort` function, we now merely call on this with values of $k$ that become successively smaller. Eventually, `segmented_insertion_sort` must be called with $K = 1$ to guarantee that the array, viewed as one segment, is completely sorted.

The function `shell_sort` that follows illustrates these successive calls to `segmented_insertion_sort` for values of $k$ that are repeatedly halved.

```
void shell_sort(list_type list, int n)
{
    int k = n / 2;

    while (k > 0)
    {
        segmented_insertion_sort(list, n, k);
        k = k / 2;
    }
}
```

## Efficiency of the Shell Sort

The shell sort is also called the *diminishing increment sort* because the value of $k$ (the number of segments) continually decreases. The method is more efficient if the successive values of $k$ are kept relatively prime to each other, thereby helping to ensure that a pair of values previously compared to each other are not compared again. D. E. Knuth has mathematically estimated that, with relatively prime values of $k$, the shell sort will execute in an average time proportional to $O[n(\log_2 n)^2]$ (see Donald E. Knuth, *Searching and Sorting*, Volume 3 of *The Art of Computer Programming* Menlo Park, Calif.: Addison-Wesley, 1973). However, the sort will work for any values of $k$, as long as the last value of $k$ is 1. For instance, note that in the version of **shell_sort** we have given, the successive values of $k$ will not often be relatively prime. When the values of $k$ are not relatively prime, then the efficiency of the shell sort is of the order $O(n^r)$, where $1 < r < 2$. The particular value of $r$ makes the sort less efficient than $O[n(\log_2 n)^2]$ for large values of $n$, but better than the $O(n^2)$ methods of Chapter 1.

The shell sort is most efficient on arrays that are nearly sorted. In fact, the first chosen value of $k$ is large to ensure that the whole array is fragmented into small individual arrays, for which the insertion sort is highly effective. Each subsequent sort causes the entire array to be more nearly sorted, so that the efficiency of the insertion sort as applied to larger partially sorted arrays is increased. Trace through a few examples to convince yourself that the partially ordered status of the array for one value of $k$ is not affected by subsequent partial sorts for a different value of $k$.

It is not known with what value of $k$ the shell sort should start, but Knuth suggests a sequence of values such as 1, 3, 7, 15, . . . , for reverse values of $k$; that is, the $(j + \text{one})$th value is two times the $j$th value plus 1. Knuth suggests other possible values of $k$, but generally the initial guess at the first value of $k$ is all that you need. The initial guess will depend on the size of the array and, to some extent, on the type of data being sorted.

## EXERCISES 8.1

1. Consider the **shell_sort** function given in this section. Suppose we were to trace the contents of the array being sorted after each call to the function **segmented_insertion_sort**. What would we see as output if we called **shell_sort** with the following key array?

   60 12 90 30 64 8 6

2. Repeat Exercise 1 for a six-element array that initially contains

   1 8 2 7 3 6

3. Where did the shell sort get its name?

4. Why is the shell sort most efficient when the original data are in almost sorted order?

5. What advantage do the relatively prime values of the increments have over other values in a shell sort? Formulate your answer in a precise written statement that explains why relatively prime values are better.

6. What property must the sequence of diminishing increments in the shell sort have to ensure that the method will work?

7. Provide examples of best case and worst case data sets for the shell sort algorithm presented in this section. Justify your data sets by explaining why they generate best case and worst case performance.

8. In Chapter 1, **pointer_sort** used an index of pointers to sort data logically without rearranging it. Identify the sort algorithm that was behind the C++ **pointer_sort** function. Adapt the pointer sort function to the shell sort algorithm.

9. The version of shell sort presented in this section uses the following sequence of diminishing increments:

   $n/2, n/4, \ldots, 8, 4, 2, 1$

Rewrite the shell sort so that the following sequence of diminishing increments is used:

$k, \ldots, 121, 40, 13, 4, 1$

Here $k$ represents the largest member of this sequence, which is $<= n$ where $n$ is the logical size of the array being sorted.

## The Quick Sort Algorithm

### 8.2

**OBJECTIVES**

- to understand the logic behind the Quick Sort algorithm
- to understand the role played by the partitioning subalgorithm in Quick Sort
- to develop a C++ function to perform Quick Sort
- to analyze the efficiency of the Quick Sort algorithm; in particular, to see the relationship between the efficiency of the QUICK SORT algorithm and the way in which the subordinate partitioning subalgorithm splits the array.

Even though the shell sort provides a significant advantage in run time over its $O(n^2)$ predecessors, its average efficiency of $O[n(\log_2 n)^2]$ may still not be good enough for large arrays. The next group of methods, including the *quick sort,* has an average execution time of $O(n \log_2 n)$, which is the best that can be achieved. Compared to $O[n(\log_2 n)^2]$ or $O(n^r)$ for $1 < r < 2$, an $O(n \log_2 n)$ sort is often a good choice as the main vehicle for large sorting jobs.

The essence of the quick sort algorithm, originally devised in 1961 by C. A. R. Hoare, is to rely on a subordinate algorithm to partition the array. The process of partitioning involves moving a data item, called the *pivot,* in the correct direction just enough for it to reach its final place in the array. The partitioning process, therefore, reduces unnecessary interchanges and potentially moves the pivot a great distance in the array without forcing it to be swapped into intermediate locations. Once the pivot item is chosen, moves are made so that data items to the left of the pivot are less than (or equal to) it, whereas those to the right are greater (or equal). The pivot item is thus in its correct position. The quick sort algorithm then recursively applies the partitioning process to the two parts of the array on either side of the pivot until the entire array is sorted.

In the next example, we illustrate the mechanics of this partitioning logic by applying it to an array of numbers.

---

**EXAMPLE 8.2**

Suppose the array contains integers initially arranged as

15 20 5 8 95 12 80 17 9 55

Table 8.1 shows a partitioning pass applied to this array. The following steps are involved:

1. Remove the first data item, 15, as the pivot, mark its position, and scan the array from right to left, comparing data item values with 15. When you find the first smaller value, remove it from its current position and put it in position **a[0]**. (This is shown in line 2.)
2. Scan line 2 from left to right beginning with position **a[1]**, comparing data item values with 15. When you find the first value greater than 15, extract it and store it in the position marked by parentheses in line 2. (This is shown in line 3.)
3. Begin the right-to-left scan of line 3 with position **a[7]** looking for a value smaller than 15. When you find it, extract it and store it in the position marked by the parentheses in line 3. (This is shown in line 4.)

◇ TABLE 8.1

Each call to `quick_sort` partitions an array segment. The asterisk (*) indicates the pivot value (here 15).

| Line Number | a[0] | a[1] | a[2] | a[3] | a[4] | a[5] | a[6] | a[7] | a[8] | a[9] |
|---|---|---|---|---|---|---|---|---|---|---|
| 1 | 15* | 20 → | 5 | 8 | 95 | 12 | 80 | 17 | 9 | ← 55 |
| 2 | 9 | 20 | 5 | 8 | 95 | 12 | 80 | 17 ← | ( ) | 55 |
| 3 | 9 | ( ) | 5 → | 8 | 95 | 12 | 80 | 17 | 20 | 55 |
| 4 | 9 | 12 | 5 | 8 | 95 ← | ( ) | 80 | 17 | 20 | 55 |
| 5 | 9 | 12 | 5 | 8 | ( ) | 95 | 80 | 17 | 20 | 55 |
| 6 | 9 | 12 | 5 | 8 | 15 | 95 | 80 | 17 | 20 | 55 |

4. Begin scanning line 4 from left to right at position `a[2]`. Find a value greater than 15, remove it, mark its position, and store it inside the parentheses in line 4. (This is shown in line 5.)

5. Now, when you attempt to scan line 5 from right to left beginning at position `a[4]`, you are immediately at a parenthesized position determined by the previous left-to-right scan. This is the location to put the pivot data item, 15. (This is shown in line 6.) At this stage, 15 is in its correct place relative to the final sorted array.

Notice that all values to the left of 15 are less than 15, and all values to the right of 15 are greater than 15. The method will still work if two values are the same. The process can now be applied recursively to the two segments of the array on the left and right of 15. Notice that these recursive calls eventually sort the entire array. The result of any one call to function `quick_sort` is merely to partition a segment of the array so that the pivotal item is positioned with everything to its left being less than or equal to it and everything to its right being greater than or equal.

---

The function **partition** that follows achieves one partitioning pass in the overall `quick_sort` algorithm as described in Example 8.2. The indices `lo` and `hi` represent the pointers that move from the left and right, respectively, until they meet at the appropriate location for the pivot. The pivotal value is initially chosen to be `a[lo]`. We will discuss later the possible implications of choosing a different pivotal value. Note that it is crucial for **partition** to return in **pivot_point** the position where the pivotal value was finally inserted. This information will allow the `quick_sort` function that calls on **partition** to determine whether or not a recursive termination condition has been reached.

```
// Partition array between indices lo and hi.
// That is, using list[lo] as pivotal value, arrange
// entries between lo and hi indices so that all
```

```
// values to left of pivot are less than or equal
// to it and all values to right of pivot are
// greater than or equal to it.
//
// Input: array and lo and hi
// Output: Partitioned array, and pivot_point
// containing final location of pivot.

void partition(list_type list, int lo, int hi, int &pivot_point)
{
        element pivot = list[lo];

        while (lo < hi)
        {

                while ((pivot < list[hi]) && (lo < hi))
                        --hi;
                if (hi != lo)
                {
                        list[lo] = list[hi];
                        ++lo;
                }

                while ((pivot > list[lo]) && (lo < hi))
                        ++lo;
                if (hi != lo)
                {
                        list[hi] = list[lo];
                        --hi;
                }

        }
        list[hi] = pivot;
        pivot_point = hi;
}
```

Right-to-left scan until
smaller value found here

pivot = 12

| 12 | 8 | 7 | 6 | 14 | 20 | 30 | 5 | 19 | 13 | 15 | hi = 7 |
| 0 | 1 | 2 | 3 | 4 | 5 | 6 | 7 | 8 | 9 | 10 | |

Left-to-right scan until
larger value found here

pivot = 12

| 5 | 8 | 7 | 6 | 14 | 20 | 30 | 5 | 19 | 13 | 15 | lo = 4 |
| 0 | 1 | 2 | 3 | 4 | 5 | 6 | 7 | 8 | 9 | 10 | |

Right-to-left scan looking for
smaller value on next iteration

| 5 | 8 | 7 | 6 | 14 | 20 | 30 | 14 | 19 | 13 | 15 | lo = hi |
| 0 | 1 | 2 | 3 | 4 | 5 | 6 | 7 | 8 | 9 | 10 | |

meeting point between lo and hi

| 5 | 8 | 7 | 6 | 12 | 20 | 30 | 14 | 19 | 13 | 15 | hi = lo = 4 |
| 0 | 1 | 2 | 3 | 4 | 5 | 6 | 7 | 8 | 9 | 10 | a[4] = pivot |

Algorithm recursively
called for this
segment

And then for
this segment

Given the previous **partition** function, **quick_sort** itself must call on **partition** and then use the returned value of **pivot_point** to decide whether or not recursive calls are necessary to perform more refined partitioning of the segments to the left and right of **pivot_point**. The recursive logic for this decision is given in the following function **quick_sort**:

```
void quick_sort(list_type list, int lower, int upper)
{
        int pivot_point;

        partition(list, lower, upper, pivot_point);
        if (lower < pivot_point)
            quick_sort(list, lower, pivot_point - 1);
        if (upper > pivot_point)
            quick_sort(list, pivot_point + 1, upper);
}
```

For instance, after the first call to **quick_sort** for a partitioning pass on the data in Table 8.1, we would then recursively call on **quick_sort** with **lower** = 1 and **upper** = 4. This would trigger deeper level recursive calls from which we would ultimately return, knowing that the segment of the array between indices 1 and 5 is now sorted. This return would be followed by a recursive call to **quick_sort** with **lower** = 6 and **upper** = 10.

The run-time trace diagram of recursive calls to **quick_sort** for the data of Table 8.1 is given in Figure 8.1. You should verify this call-return pattern by walking through the preceding function.

◆ FIGURE 8.1

Run-time trace diagram of (recursive) calls to **quick_sort** data in Table 8.1

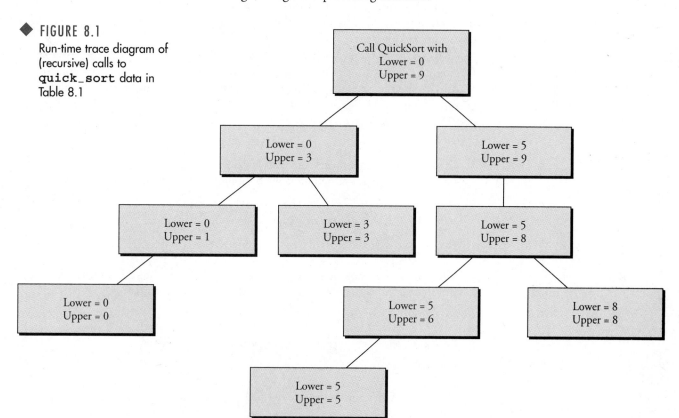

## Efficiency of the Quick Sort

As mentioned earlier, the average run-time efficiency of the quick sort is $O(n \log_2 n)$, which is the best that has been achieved for a large array of size $n$. In the best case, it is quite easy to provide a rationale for this $O(n \log_2 n)$ figure. This best case occurs when each array segment recursively passed to **quick_sort** partitions at its midpoint; that is, the appropriate location for each pivotal value in the series of recursive calls is the midpoint of the segment being partitioned. In this case,

1 call to **quick_sort** (the first) is made with a segment of size $n$. ⎫
2 calls to **quick_sort** are made with segments of size $n/2$. ⎪
4 calls to **quick_sort** are made with segments of size $n/4$. ⎬ Overall $\log_2 n$ levels
8 calls to **quick_sort** are made with segments of size $n/8$. ⎪
                                                                ⎭
.
.
.

$n$ calls to **quick_sort** are made with segments of size 1.

Since each call with a segment of size $m$ requires $O(m)$ comparisons, it is clear that $k$ calls with segments of size $n/k$ will require $O(n)$ comparisons. Hence, the total number of comparisons resulting from the preceding sequence of calls will be $O(n \log_2 n)$.

If segments partition away from the midpoint, the efficiency of quick sort begins to deteriorate. In the worst case situation, when the array is already sorted, the efficiency of the quick sort may drop down to $O(n^2)$ due to the continuous right-to-left scan all the way to the last left boundary. In the exercises at the end of the section, you will explore how the worst case situation is affected by your choice of the pivotal element.

You may wonder how large a stack is needed to sort an array of size $n$. (Remember that this stack is implicitly created even when you use recursion.) Knuth has mathematically estimated that the size of the stack will generally not exceed $O(\log_2 n)$. However, in the worst case, it will be $O(n)$. (See D. E. Knuth's text, *Searching and Sorting*, cited in Section 8.1.)

**EXERCISES 8.2**

1. Consider the **quick_sort** function given in this section. Suppose we were to insert the following tracer output at the beginning of this function:

```
cout << lower << " " << upper << endl;
for (k = lower; k <= upper; ++k)
        cout << a[k];
cout << endl;
```

What would we see as output from these tracers if we were to call on **quick_sort** with the key array initially containing the following seven entries?:

60 12 90 30 64 8 6

2. Repeat Exercise 1 for a six-element array that initially contains

1 8 2 7 3 6

3. When is a bubble sort better than a quick sort? Explain your answer in a written statement.

## A NOTE OF INTEREST

### Privacy Issues Kill Lotus Database

The August 1989 issue of *Communications of the ACM* (Volume 32, No. 8) was dedicated to the role played by ethics in the education and career of a computer scientist. What are the social responsibilities that go along with state-of-the art capabilities to sort and search through gigabytes of information? A recent incident involving Lotus Development Corporation of Cambridge, Massachusetts, illustrated the importance of a social conscience in computing.

In late 1990, Lotus had planned the release of a product called MarketPlace. Designed for use on a personal computer equipped with CD-ROM storage, the so-called "household" version of MarketPlace supposedly contained information on 120 million Americans and 80 million households. This information included data on personal income, lifestyle, purchasing patterns, geographic location, and marital status. These data were compiled for Lotus by Equifax, the nation's largest credit reporting agency. Lotus foresaw a great demand for MarketPlace coming from a wide variety of large and small businesses. According to Michael W. Miller in the article "MarketPlace," which appeared in the November 13, 1990, issue of the *Wall Street Journal:*

> Advances in computers are making it easier to gather and piece together minutely detailed portraits of households, and marketers are gobbling these up to help choose targets for direct-mail and telephone campaigns.

One of the early Lotus press releases for MarketPlace began with the headline "We Found You . . . And Quite Frankly, It Really Wasn't That Hard."

What Lotus had not properly anticipated was the storm of protest that would arise from consumer advocacy groups and individual consumers concerning MarketPlace's apparent insensitivity to privacy issues. Miller's *Wall Street Journal* article described these concerns: "Privacy advocates' chief objection to MarketPlace was that it wouldn't be easy enough for consumers to delete their data, or correct any inaccuracies."

Lotus demonstrated its sensitivity to the ethical issues that had been raised by MarketPlace. In January 1991, James Manzi, Lotus's chairman, announced that Lotus was canceling the MarketPlace project. Manzi stated, "What drove our decision was the volume and tenor of the concerns that were being raised by consumers all over the U.S." Though Lotus may have exercised poor judgment in the original conception of MarketPlace, their decision to pull the plug after a sizable investment in the enterprise illustrates a high degree of social responsibility. Such ethical dilemmas are likely to play an increasing role in the careers of many computing professionals.

4. Under what circumstances would you not use a quick sort? Explain your answer in a written statement.

5. How does the choice of the pivotal value affect the efficiency of the quick sort algorithm? Suppose that the middle value or the last value in a segment to be partitioned was chosen as the pivotal value. How would this alter the nature of best case and worst case data sets? Give examples to illustrate your answer.

6. Develop run-time trace diagrams of function calls to **quick_sort** for a variety of test data sets (analogous to what was done in Figure 8.1). Use these diagrams to analyze the efficiency of **quick_sort.** What types of data sets yield $O(n \log_2 n)$ efficiency? What types yield $O(n^2)$ efficiency?

7. In Chapter 11, **pointer_sort** used an index of pointers to sort data logically without rearranging it. Adapt the pointer sort function to the quick sort algorithm.

8. Implement **quick_sort** in a nonrecursive fashion.

9. Implement a variation on the quick sort algorithm presented in this section, in which the pivot is chosen to be the median of the three values:

```
a[lo], a[(lo + hi) / 2], a[hi]
```

In a carefully written statement, explain why this variation should be more efficient than the version that chooses the pivot to be **a[lo]**.

## 8.3  The Heap Sort Algorithm

The *heap sort* is a sorting algorithm that is roughly equivalent to the quick sort; its average efficiency is $O(n \log_2 n)$ for an array of size $n$. The method, originally described by R. W. Floyd, has two phases. In the first phase, the array containing the $n$ data items is viewed as equivalent to a full binary tree. That is, the array to be sorted is viewed as the linear representation of a full binary tree containing $n$ items (see Chapter 7). (If you want to read Floyd's description of this method, see his article, entitled "Algorithm 245: Tree Sort 3" found in *Communications of the ACM* Volume 7, 1964: 701.) As an example, suppose we wish to sort the following array:

11 1 5 7 6 12 17 8 4 10 2

The tree now appears as shown in Figure 8.2.

The goal of phase 1 is to sort the data elements along each path from leaf node level to the root node. If we wish to sort in ascending order, then the numbers along any path from leaf node to root should be in increasing order. Eventually, after phase 1, the tree will be a heap as described in Chapter 7. That is, the data item at each node will be greater than or equal to both of its children. To achieve this, we take the following steps:

1. Process the node that is the parent of the rightmost node on the lowest level as follows: If its value is less than the value of its largest child, swap these values; otherwise do nothing.
2. Move left on the same level. Compare the value of the parent node with the values of the children. If the parent is smaller than the largest child, swap them.
3. When the left end of this level is reached, move up a level, and, beginning with the rightmost parent node, repeat step 2. Continue swapping the original parent with the larger of its children until it is larger than its children. In effect, the original parent is being walked down the tree in a fashion that ensures all numbers will be in increasing order along the path.
4. Repeat step 3 until the root node has been processed.

Figure 8.3 shows these steps applied to Figure 8.2.

Phase 2 of the heap sort finds the node with the largest value in the tree and cuts it from the tree. This is then repeated to find the second largest value, which is also removed from the tree. The process continues until only two nodes are left

◆ **FIGURE 8.2**
Full binary tree corresponding to array

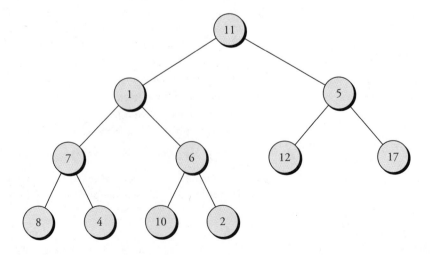

◆ FIGURE 8.3
Phase 1 of heap sort applied
to the binary tree in Figure
8.2

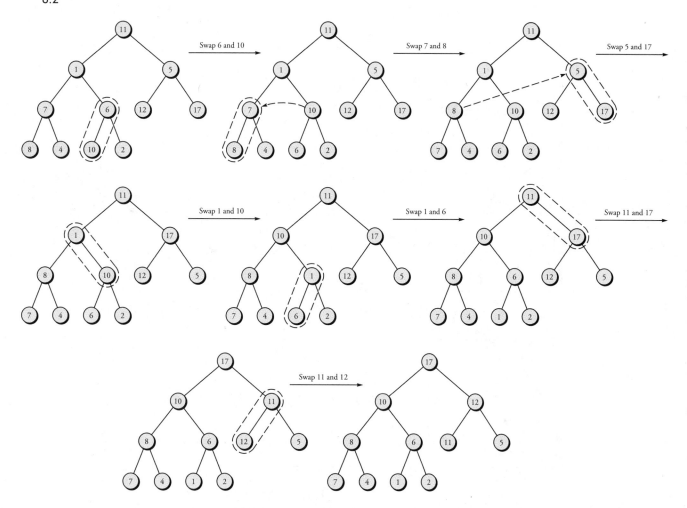

in the tree; they are then exchanged if necessary. The precise steps for phase 2 are as follows:

**1.** Swap the root node with the bottom rightmost child, and sever this new bottom rightmost child from the tree. This is the largest value.

**2.** Continue swapping the new root value with the larger of its children until it is not exceeded by either child. In effect, this new root value is now being walked down a path in the tree to ensure that all paths retain values arranged in ascending order from leaf node to root node. That is, the tree is being restored to a heap.

**3.** Repeat steps 1 and 2 until only one element is left.

Phase 2 of the heap sort begun in Figure 8.3 is shown in Figure 8.4 for the three highest values.

Both phase 1 and phase 2 use the same strategy of walking a parent down a path of the tree via a series of swaps with its children. The following function **walk_down**, isolates this crucial subordinate algorithm. In the linear representa-

◆ FIGURE 8.4
Phase 2 of heap sort for
three values

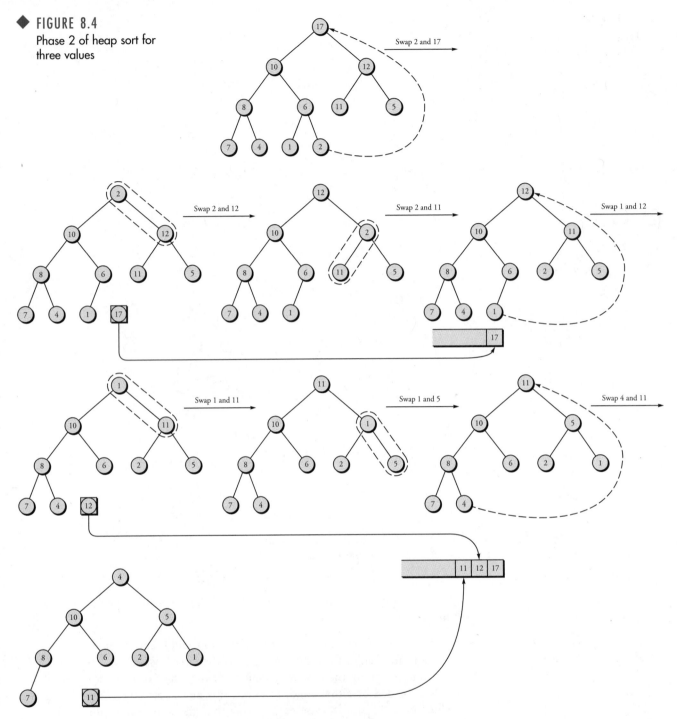

tion of a tree assumed by **walk_down**, the assignment statement $k = 2 * i$ will
make $k$ reference the left child of the node indicated by $i$. That is, this statement
will allow us to descend a level deeper into the tree.

```
// Function: walk_down
// Repeatedly exchange this parent with child of
// greatest value until the original parent is
// greater than both of its children
//
```

```
// Inputs: Array to be viewed as full binary tree.
// n, the number of entires in the array.
// j, the index of a parent node within the tree.
// Outputs: Tree array, as altered by this task.

void walk_down(list_type list, int j, int n)
{
    int i, k;
    element ref;
    boolean found_spot = FALSE;

    i = j;
    ref = list[i];

    // list[i] will move along the appropriate path
    // in the tree

    k = 2 * i + 1;

    // Initially k references left child of list[i]

    while ((k < n) && ! found_spot)
    {
        if (k < n - 1)
            // Have k reference largest child
            if (list[k + 1] > list[k])
                ++k;
        if (list[k] > ref)
            // Child must move up
        {
            list[i] = list[k];
            i = k;
            k = 2 * i + 1;
        }
        else
            // Appropriate spot has been found
            found_spot = TRUE;
    }
    list[i] = ref;
}
```

ref →

list[k]
larger
of

if list[k] > ref
k moves up

With the essential **walk_down** logic isolated in a separate function, phases 1 and 2 of **heap_sort** may now be developed easily. The loop for phase 1 repeatedly calls on **walk_down** to form the tree into a heap. Then a loop for phase 2 repeatedly swaps the root of the tree with the last child and calls on **walk_down** to allow this new root to find an appropriate position in the heap.

```cpp
void heap_sort(list_type list, int n)
{
    int y;
    element temp;

    // First phase arranges the tree into a heap

    y = n / 2 - 1;    // y starts at last node to have child
    while (y >= 0)
    {
        walk_down(list, y, n);
        --y;
    }
```

Swap these two, and then remove leaf node from further consideration.

```cpp
    // End of first phase; y is now used to point at the
    // current last array slot.

    y = n;
    while (y > 0)
    {
    // Interchange root with bottom right leaf node
        temp = list[0];
        list[0] = list[y - 1];
        list[y - 1] = temp;
        --y;
        walk_down(list, 0, y);
    }
}
```

## Efficiency of the Heap Sort

It is relatively easy to deduce that the heap sort requires $O(n \log_2 n)$ comparisons. To see this, note that the phase 1 loop in the preceding C++ function will execute $n/2$ times. Inside this loop we call **walk_down**, which in turn has a loop that will execute at most $\log_2 n$ times (because it merely follows a path down a full binary tree). Hence phase 1 requires at most

$$(n/2) * \log_2 n$$

iterations at its deepest level. Phase 2 may be similarly analyzed. The phase 2 loop iterates $n$ times. Within each iteration, **walk_down** is called, again resulting in at most $\log_2 n$ operations. Thus, phase 2 requires at most $n * \log_2 n$ iterations at its deepest level. Overall, we get

$$1.5n * \log_2 n$$

as an upper bound for the number of iterations required by the combination of phases 1 and 2. Thus, both quick sort and heap sort yield $O(n \log_2 n)$ efficiencies. In *Searching and Sorting*, referenced in Sections 8.1 and 8.2, Knuth has shown that, on the average, quick sort will be slightly faster since its big-O constant of proportionality will be smaller than that for heap sort. However, heap sort offers the advantage of guaranteeing an $O(n \log_2 n)$ efficiency regardless of the data being sorted. As we have already noted for quick sort, worst case data can cause its performance to deteriorate to $O(n^2)$.

### EXERCISES 8.3

1. Consider the **heap_sort** function given in this section. Note that **walk_down** is called at two points in the function: once in phase 1 and again in phase 2. Suppose that we were to trace the contents of the array being sorted after each call to **walk_down**. What would we see as output if we called **heap_sort** with an array that initially contained the following?:

   60 12 90 30 64 8 6

2. Repeat Exercise 1 for a six-element array that initially contains

   1 8 2 7 3 6

3. Where did the heap sort get its name?

4. What is a heap?

5. Is a heap sort always better than a quick sort? When is it? When isn't it? Explain your answer in a written essay.

6. What is the worst case and average case efficiency of the heap sort?

7. Give examples of arrays that generate the best and worst performances, respectively, for the heap sort algorithm. Explain why these arrays generate the best and worst performances.

8. In Chapter 1, **pointer_sort** used an index of pointers to sort data logically without rearranging it. Adapt the pointer sort function to the heap sort algorithm.

---

## 8.4 The Merge Sort Algorithm

### OBJECTIVES

- to understand the logic behind the merge sort algorithm

- to understand merge sort's reliance on a sub-algorithm that merges two sorted lists

- to develop a C++ function to perform the merge sort

- to analyze the efficiency of the merge sort

The essential idea behind *merge sort* is to make repeated use of a function that merges two lists, each already in ascending order, into a third list, also arranged in ascending order. The merge function itself only requires sequential access to the lists. Its logic is similar to the method you would use if you were merging two sorted piles of index cards into a third pile. That is, start with the first card from each pile. Compare them to see which one comes first, transfer that one over to the third pile, and advance to the next card in that pile. Repeat the comparison, transfer, and advance operations until one of the piles runs out of cards. At that point, merely move what is left of the remaining pile over to the third merged pile.

This logic is reflected in the generalized merge function that follows. For reasons that will become apparent when we incorporate it into a full sorting function, this version of merge begins with the two sorted lists stored in one array. The first list runs from subscript **lower** to **middle** of array **source**. The second runs from subscript **middle + 1** to **upper** of the same array. The merged result of the two lists is stored in a second array **destination**.

```
// Function: merge
// Merge the two ordered segments of source into
// one list arranged in ascending order.
//
// Inputs: Array source arranged in ascending order
// between indices lower..middle and middle + 1..upper, respectively.
// Outputs: The complete ordered list in destination.

void merge(list_type source, list_type destination, int lower,
    int middle, int upper)
{
    int s1 = lower;
    int s2 = middle + 1;
    int d = lower;

    // Repeat comparison of current item from each list.

    do
    {
        if (source[s1] < source[s2])
        {
            destination[d] = source[s1];
            ++s1;
        }
        else
        {
            destination[d] = source[s2];
            ++s2;
        }
        ++d;
    } while ((s1 <= middle) && (s2 <= upper));

    // Move what is left of remaining list.

    if (s1 > middle)
        do
        {
            destination[d] = source[s2];
            ++s2;
            ++d;
        } while (s2 <= upper);
    else
        do
        {
            destination[d] = source[s1];
            ++s1;
            ++d;
        } while (s1 <= middle);
}
```

Clearly **merge** is an $O(n)$ algorithm where $n$ is the number of items in the two lists to be merged. A question remains: How can **merge** be used to actually sort an entire array? To answer this, we need another function called **order** that will take the values in indices **lower** through **upper** of an array source and arrange them in ascending order in subscripts **lower** through **upper** of another array called **destination**. Notice that **order** is itself almost a sorting function except that it produces a sorted list in a second array instead of actually transforming the array it originally receives. Our use of **order** will be to obtain two sorted half-length sequences from our original array.

Then we will use the **merge** function we have already developed to merge the two sorted half-length sequences back into the original array. Of course, this merely defers our original question of how to use **merge** to sort because now we are faced with the question of how **order** will be able to produce two sorted half-length sequences. Here is where recursion enters the picture. To produce a sorted half-length sequence, we use **order** to produce two sorted quarter-length sequences and apply **merge** to the results. Similarly, the quarter-length sequences are produced by calling on **order** to produce sorted eighth-length sequences and applying **merge** to the results. The recursive termination condition for this descent into shorter and shorter ordered sequences occurs when **order** receives a sequence of length 1.

Given the crucial **order** function, the **merge_sort** function itself is almost trivial. It need merely create a copy of the array to be sorted and then call on **order** to sort the elements of the copy into the original. Note that, because **order** continually calls on **merge** and **merge** cannot do its work within one array, the need to create a copy of the original array is unavoidable. Complete C++ versions of **merge_sort** and **order** follow:

```
void merge_sort(list_type list, int n)
{
        list_type list_copy;

        for (int k = 0; k < n; ++k)              // Make copy for call to order.
                list_copy[k] = list[k];
        order(list_copy, list, 0, n - 1);
}


// Function: order
// Transfer source in ascending order to destination,
// between indices lower...upper.
//
// Inputs: source and destination, two arrays that are
// initially identical between indices lower...upper.
// Outputs: destination arranged in order between lower and upper.

void order(list_type source, list_type destination, int lower, int upper)
{
        int middle;

        if (lower != upper)
        {
```

```
       middle = (lower + upper) / 2;
       order(destination, source, lower, middle);
       order(destination, source, middle + 1, upper);
       merge(source, destination, lower, middle, upper);
     }
}
```

Recursively call order to get two sorted segments in source, which are then merged into destination. This requires destination originally to be a copy of source.

The run-time trace diagram of function calls in Figure 8.5 highlights the interaction between **order** and **merge** triggered by calling **merge_sort** with a sample array of size **n** = 11. The leaf nodes in this trace diagram represent the recursive termination condition reached when **lower = upper**.

## Analysis of the Merge Sort

From a run-time trace of function calls such as that appearing in Figure 8.5, it is quite easy to deduce that merge sort requires $O(n \log_2 n)$ comparisons. The reasoning required for this deduction is as follows. All the merge operations across any given level of the trace diagram will require $O(n)$ comparisons. There are $O(\log_2 n)$ levels to the trace diagram. Hence, the overall efficiency is the product $O(n \log_2 n)$. Notice that, like the heap sort, the merge sort can guarantee this efficiency regardless of the original data. That is, there is no worst case that can cause its efficiency to deteriorate (as there is for quick sort).

The price paid for using merge sort is in the memory space it requires. Of course, there is the stack space associated with recursion. More important, however, is the need for a duplicate copy of the array being sorted. In applications where the original array barely fits in memory, this space requirement will make merge sort totally impractical.

As steep as the memory price is, there is an added benefit to merge sort that makes it the only possible choice for certain applications: Merge sort may be written in a way that necessitates only sequential access to the lists being manipulated. As we have presented it here, random access is required at only one point in the algorithm, namely, in the **merge** function to access the second list beginning at subscript (**middle + 1**) of **source**. The need for this could have

◆ FIGURE 8.5
Run-time trace of function
calls to `order` and
`merge`

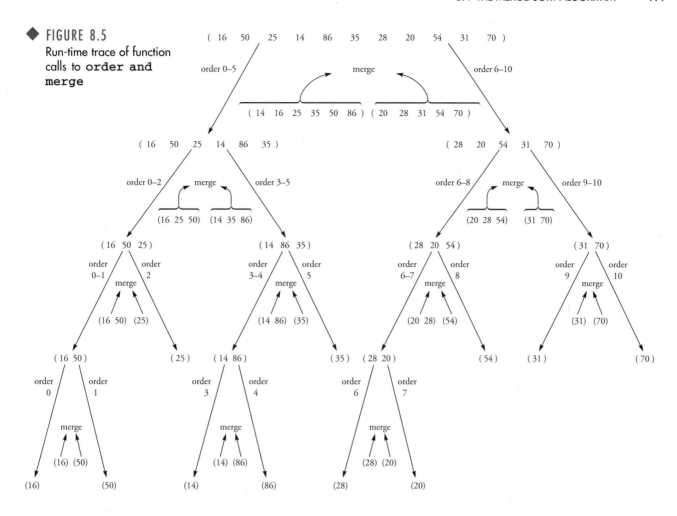

been eliminated by having **merge** work with two separate source arrays. That is, we would merge ordered arrays **source1** and **source2** into **destination**. This would be very costly with arrays since it would necessitate using three arrays to sort one array. However, it is less costly when the lists being manipulated are being implemented not by arrays but rather by dynamically allocated linked lists or sequential files. In both of these latter situations, the need to use sequential access would make the merge sort strategy the only appropriate sorting method. In the exercises at the end of the section and the programming problems at the end of the chapter, you will be asked to adapt **merge_sort** to such sequential implementations of a list. In particular, when the list exists in a file instead of main memory, the sorting method employed is said to be an *external sort* (as opposed to the *internal sorts* we have studied in this chapter).

EXERCISES 8.4

1. Consider the **merge_sort** function given in this section. Note that this function contains a subordinate function called **order.** Suppose that we were to insert the following tracer output at the beginning of the **order** function.

```
cout << lower << " " << upper << endl;
for (int k = lower; k < upper; ++k)
        cout << source[k] << " ";
cout << endl;
```

What would we see as output from these tracers if we were to call on **merge_sort** with an array that initially contained the following?:

60 12 90 30 64 8 6

2. Repeat Exercise 1 for a six-element array that initially contains

1 8 2 7 3 6

3. Implement **merge_sort** in a nonrecursive fashion.

4. In Chapter 11, **pointer_sort** used an index of pointers to sort data logically without rearranging it. Adapt the pointer sort function to the merge sort algorithm.

5. Identify and give an example of best case and worst case data sets for the merge sort algorithm. Explain why your data sets generate best and worst case performance.

6. A sorting method is said to be stable if two data items of matching value are guaranteed not to be rearranged with respect to each other as the algorithm progresses. For example, in the four-element array

60 $42_1$ 80 $42_2$

a stable sorting method would guarantee a final ordering of

$42_1$ $42_2$ 60 80

Classify each of the sorting algorithms studied in this chapter and in Chapter 1 as to their stability. (To see why stability may be important, consider Programming Problems 5 and 9 at the end of this chapter.)

7. You are to sort an array in a program in which the following considerations are to be taken into account. First, there is a large amount of data to be sorted. The amount of data to be sorted is so large that frequent $O(n^2)$ run times will prove unsatisfactory. The amount of data will also make it impossible for your program to use a large amount of overhead data (for example, stack space) to make the sort efficient in its run time. This is because the space required by the overhead data would potentially take up space needed by the array to be sorted. Second, you are told that the array to be sorted is often nearly in order to start with. For each of the seven sorting methods indicated, specify whether or not that method would be appropriate for this application and, in a brief statement, explain why your answer is correct.

   **a.** bubble sort

   **b.** insertion sort

   **c.** selection sort

   **d.** shell sort

   **e.** quick sort

   **f.** heap sort

   **g.** merge sort

---

**FOCUS ON PROGRAM DESIGN**

We have stressed repeatedly that analysis of algorithms combines formal mathematical techniques with experimental methodology. Certainly, nowhere is this better illustrated than in the analysis of sorting algorithms. For instance, among the four algorithms studied in this chapter, only two—heap sort and merge sort—can be placed with certainty in the $O(n \log_2 n)$ category by purely mathematical analysis. The other two—shell sort and qick sort—are apparently much more dependent on the original arrangement of the data being sorted.

## A NOTE OF INTEREST

### Public-Key Cryptography

The manner in which computers can sort through and in other ways manipulate information gives rise to concern over the security of electronic information. Cryptography is the science of encoding information to protect it from being viewed by unauthorized parties. Today, as an increasing amount of sensitive information is being transmitted in electronic and magnetic form, cryptography is becoming an increasingly important field.

A conventional encryption system works much like a mailbox with a combination lock. Anyone knowing the combination can open the box to leave a message or to read any of the messages in the box. In computerized information systems, the "combination" to the mailbox is a digital key; that is, a particular bit pattern that is applied to an electronic message to encode or decode it. In conventional systems, anyone knowing the digital key has access to the information in the electronic mailbox. Hence such systems are best suited to a small number of users and not to the networking of information among many computer installations that is possible with today's technology.

An interesting development in cryptography occurred in the early 1970s with the development of a theory for public-key encryption systems. Such systems work on two different digital keys: one for writing information into the electronic mailbox and the other to read encoded information that has been left in the mailbox. As a user of such an encryption system, you could freely give out the write key to your mailbox (the public key), allowing anyone to send you an encoded letter. However, you would keep the read key (the decoding key) secret so that only you would be able to make sense out of your mail.

The best known public-key encryption scheme is known as the RSA algorithm (after Rivest, Shamir, and Adleman,

the mathematicians who developed it). This algorithm is based on the difficulty of factoring large numbers that are the product of two prime numbers. For instance, the number $51 = 3 \times 17$ would satisfy this criterion except that it is not nearly large enough.

In the RSA system, the product of the two prime factors would be linked to your public key. However, this public key would include only the product, not the prime factors that comprise the product. Your private key would include each of the individual prime factors. Why should such numbers be large? The answer to this question lies in the present limitations of the area of mathematics known as number theory. It turns out that, given the product of two such prime factors without being told the factors themselves, number theory provides no known way of factoring the number into its prime factors in a reasonable amount of time, even using the most advanced supercomputers. From a security perspective, this means that your code could not be broken by outside agencies, even if they were using a computer to assist them.

The role of public-key cryptography in electronic data systems will no doubt become increasingly important in the future. For an excellent discussion of the method and some of the social concerns arising from it, you may want to read the article "Encryption: Technology, Privacy, and National Security," by Tom Athanasiou in *Technology Review* (August/September 1986):57–66. A very readable description of the RSA and other encryption algorithms is presented in "Cloak and Dagger" by Rick Grehan in the June 1990 issue of *Byte* magazine (Volume 15, No. 6: 311–324).

In this section, we present components of a program whose structure facilitates experimentation with a sorting algorithm. In particular, our program will be useful in the exploration of the shell sort algorithm. However, the underlying structure of the program makes it easy to incorporate other sorting algorithms. All that must be altered is the function that implements the particular sorting algorithm being studied. This function must not only do the sorting, but also profile the algorithm in the sense described in Chapter 1. All the other modules in the program are geared toward construction of an environment in which you can experiment with the sorting algorithm. These modules remain the same regardless of which sorting algorithm is chosen.

Input to the program is the list of integers to be sorted. This input may be provided in one of three forms:

**1.** A randomly generated permutation of the integers from `1, 2, 3, . . . size – 1, size` where `size` is the logical size of the list being sorted.

Recall that a permutation is an arrangement of the integers in which no repetitions occur.

**2.** A list of integers entered interactively, allowing input of particular data sets for which you want to profile the sorting algorithm.

**3.** A list of integers read one per line from a text file.

This final form of input, coupled with the program's ability to save a particular data set in a text file format that can later be read, allows you to fine-tune the sorting algorithm for data sets that prove particularly interesting from an efficiency perspective. That is, if you encounter a randomly generated or interactively input data set for which the efficiency of the sort algorithm seems to deteriorate, you can save that data set in a text file. Then you can adjust the sort algorithm to allow for the characteristics of that data set and rerun the program, loading the saved data set to see if your adjustments made a substantial improvement. This mode of experimental use of the program is illustrated in the following sample runs:

First run:

```
      1 - Load a random array
      2 - Interactively load an array
      3 - Load array from previous round

      Enter 1, 2, or 3 —>1

      Enter the number of values —>10
      Do you want to see the array? (Y/N) —>y
```

```
ARRAY[0] =      1
ARRAY[1] =      3
ARRAY[2] =      2
ARRAY[3] =      4
ARRAY[4] =      5
ARRAY[5] =      8
ARRAY[6] =      6
ARRAY[7] =      9
ARRAY[8] =      7
ARRAY[9] =      10
```

```
Sort required 51 loop iteration(s).
Sort required 4 swap(s) of data.
Sort required 78 comparison(s).

Do you want to see the array after sorting? (Y/N) —>y
```

```
ARRAY[0] = 1
ARRAY[1] = 2
ARRAY[2] = 3
ARRAY[3] = 4
ARRAY[4] = 5
ARRAY[5] = 6
ARRAY[6] = 7
ARRAY[7] = 8
ARRAY[8] = 9
ARRAY[9] = 10
```

```
Save this list for another run? (Y/N) ->y
Name for save file ->test.dat
Another Shell Sort? (Y/N) ->n
```

Then fine-tune the program to improve efficiency, and run again.

Second run:

```
        1 - Load a random array
        2 - Interactively load an array
        3 - Load array from previous round

        Enter 1, 2, or 3 ->3

        Enter the name of the file ->test.dat
        Do you want to see the array? (Y/N) ->y
```

```
ARRAY[0] =    1
ARRAY[1] =    3
ARRAY[2] =    2
ARRAY[3] =    4
ARRAY[4] =    5
ARRAY[5] =    8
ARRAY[6] =    6
ARRAY[7] =    9
ARRAY[8] =    7
ARRAY[9] =    10


Sort required 42 loop iteration(s).
Sort required 4 swap(s) of data.
Sort required 61 comparisons(s).


Do you want to see the array after sorting? (Y/N) ->n
Save this list for another run? (Y/N) ->n
Another Shell Sort? (Y/N) ->n
```

Notice how the profiling output gives evidence of the improved efficiency of the second run.

The modular structure chart for our program is given in Figure 8.6. Modular specifications and a partial program listing follow. In the programming problems at the end of the chapter, you will be asked to complete the program and then use it in various forms of exploration with the shell sort. You will also be asked to incorporate the design of the program into a vehicle for exploring other sorting algorithms.

A first-level pseudocode development for the main program is

Initialize the random number generator (if necessary—see Appendix 6)
Do
          Initialize the global profiling counters.
          Load the array by user-chosen method. Also return a duplicate copy of the array for potential saving in a file.
          Print the array if user wants to see it.
          Apply shell sort to the array.
          Output the global profiling counters.
          Print the sorted array if the user wants to see it.

◆ FIGURE 8.6
Modular structure chart for
Shell experimentation pro-
gram

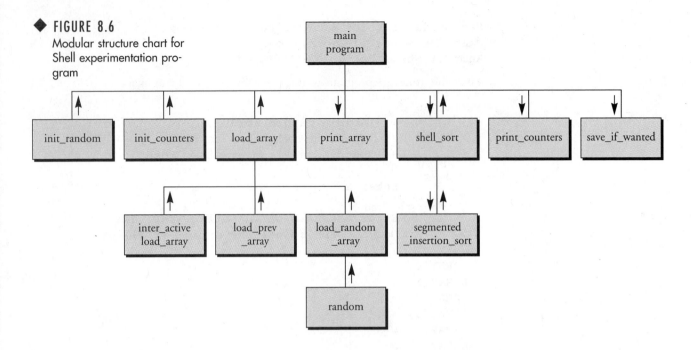

Save the copy of the original array if the user wants to.
Inquire if the user wants to shell sort another array.
While user indicates more sorts.

Modular specifications corresponding to the modular structure chart of Figure 8.6 are as follows:

**Module:** init_random
**Task:** Initialize the random number generator as described in Appendix 6. May be unnecessary if your version of C++ provides a random number generator.

**Module:** init_counters
**Task:** Obvious.
**Inputs:** Profiling counters as global variables—for number of comparisons, number of swaps, and number of loop iterations.
**Outputs:** Profiling counters set to zero.

**Module:** load_array
**Task:** Inquire about method for loading and then call on one of interactive-_load_array, load_prev_array, or load_random_array.
**Outputs:** The array to be sorted, a copy of that array for potential saving, number of values in array, integer indicating user choice for loading array: 1 for random permutation, 2 for interactive, 3 for file.

**Module:** interactive_load_array
**Task:** Inquire as to number of values. Then iterate through interactive input of that many values.
**Outputs:** Number of values in array, array to sort, and copy of that array for potential saving in file.

**Module:** load_prev_array
**Task:** Inquire as to name of file where array is stored. Then use while not eof loop to read data from file into array.

**Outputs:** Number of values in array, array to sort, and copy of that array for potential saving in file.

**Module:** random_load_array

**Task:** Inquire as to size of array. Generate a random permutation of the values 1, 2, . . ., size. There are several algorithms to do this. We leave it for you to discover one in the programming problems.

**Outputs:** Number of values in array, array to sort, and copy of that array for potential saving in file.

**Module:** random

**Task:** Use algorithm in Appendix 6 or random number generator provided with your version of C++.

**Outputs:** Randomly generated value.

**Module:** print_array

**Task:** Iterate through output of each array value.

**Inputs:** Array and its logical size.

**Modules:** shell_sort and segmented_insertion_sort

**Task:** See Section 8.1.

**Inputs:** Array of values and its logical size.

**Outputs:** Array sorted in ascending order.

**Module:** print_counters

**Task:** Print profiling counters to report on efficiency of algorithm for data set just sorted.

**Inputs:** Global profiling counters.

**Module:** save_if_wanted

**Task:** Inquire if user wants to save this list for further exploration. If user wants to save and list not originally loaded from file, write array to file in form compatible with load_prev_array module.

**Inputs:** Copy of original array, logical size of that array, integer indicating how user loaded array.

A partial program listing follows:

```
// Program file: focus.cpp

// This program allows the user to experiment with the shell_sort
// algorithm on a variety of different arrays of data.  The sort
// algorithm has been augmented to keep track of the number of
// swaps, comparisons, and loop iterations necessary to sort the
// current array. These can be used as a measure of comparison
// among various initial data arrays or among different sorting
// methods.  This method of measuring the amount of work required
// to sort the array is used because standard C++ has no built-in
// method of timing program execution.

// The data file created by the program when an array is saved is
// simply a text file with one element of the array per line of the
// file. Similarly, the program expects any file from which it is to
// read an array to have this format.

#include <iostream.h>
#include <fstream.h>
```

```cpp
#include "strlib.h"
#include "random.h"
#include "boolean.h"

const int MAX_LIST_SIZE = 500;

typedef int element;
typedef element list_type[MAX_LIST_SIZE];

// File streams for loading and saving array contents to files.

ifstream input_file;
ofstream output_file;

// Global counters for measuring work required to sort data in array.

int num_iterations;
int num_swaps;
int num_comparisons;

// Function: save_if_wanted
// Write the array out to a file if the user indicates
// that he wants to save it for future runs.  The file
// handling may require modification on some systems.
//
// Inputs: Array to save, size of array, type of load performed.

void save_if_wanted(list_type list, int length, int choice_of_load);

// Function: load_array
// Determine which method the user wants to use to
// load the array of data and call the appropriate function.
//
// Outputs: Both arrays, the size of the arrays, and the
// user's selection of type of load to be performed.

void load_array(list_type list, list_type list_copy, int &length,
     int &choice_of_load);

// Function: load_prev_array
// Open the file containing the previous array the
// user desires to use, read the data into the
// array, and make a copy of the array.  The file
// handling may require modification on some systems.
//
// Outputs: Both arrays along with their size.

void load_prev_array(list_type list, list_type list_copy, int &length);

// Function: interactive_load_array
// Prompt user to input data for the array, read it in, and make a copy of it.
//
// Outputs: both arrays along with their size.
```

```
void interactive_load_array(list_type list, list_type list_copy, int &length);

// Function: load_random_array
// Fill the array with a randomly generated permutation of the integers
// between 1...length, and then make a copy of the array.
//
// Outputs: both arrays along with their size.

void load_random_array(list_type list, list_type list_copy, int &length);

// Function: print_array
// Print the contents of the specified range of the array to the terminal.
//
// Inputs: Array of data, low and high ends of the range of indices of the array
// to be printed.

void print_array(list_type list, int low, int high);

void init_counters();

void print_counters();

void shell_sort(list_type list, int n);

void segmented_insertion_sort(list_type list, int n, int k);

int main()
{
    list_type list, list_copy;      // Lists of data
    int length;                     // Logical size of list
    char query;                     // User's response
    int choice_of_load;             // User's choice for loading array
    random_generator generator;     // Set up random number generator

    do
    {
        init_counters();
        load_array(list, list_copy, length, choice_of_load);
        cout << "Do you want to see the array? (Y/N) -> ";
        cin >> query;
        if ((query == 'Y') || (query == 'y'))
                print_array(list, 0, length);
            shell_sort(list, length);
            print_counters();
            cout << "Do you want to see the array after sorting? (Y/N) -> ";
            cin >> query;
            if ((query == 'Y') || (query == 'y'))
                    print_array(list, 0, length);
            save_if_wanted(list_copy, length, choice_of_load);
            cout << "Another Shell Sort? (Y/N) -> ";
            cin >> query;
    } while ((query == 'Y') || (query == 'y'));
        return 0;
}
```

```
void save_if_wanted(list_type list, int length, int choice_of_load)
{
}

void load_array(list_type list, list_type list_copy, int &length, int &choice_of_load)
{
        boolean valid;

        do
        {
                cout << endl << endl << endl;
                cout << " 1 - Load a random array" << endl;
                cout << " 2 - Interactively load an array" << endl;
                cout << " 3 - Load array from previous round" << endl;
                cout << endl;
                cout << " Enter 1, 2, or 3 -> ";
                cin >> choice_of_load;
                valid = (choice_of_load > 0) && (choice_of_load < 4);
                if (valid)
                        switch (choice_of_load)
                        {
                                case 1:    load_random_array(list, list_copy, length);
                                           break;
                                case 2:    interactive_load_array(list, list_copy,
                                           length); break;
                                case 3:    load_prev_array(list, list_copy, length);
                                           break;
                                default:   cout << choice_of_load << " is not a valid "
                                                << "response - try again" << endl;
                        }
        } while (! valid);
}

void load_prev_array(list_type list, list_type list_copy, int &length)
{
}

void print_array(list_type list, int low, int high)
{
}

void init_counters()
{
        num_iterations = 0;
        num_swaps = 0;
        num_comparisons = 0;
}

void print_counters()
{
```

```
                cout << endl;
                cout << "Sort required " << num_iterations << " loop iteration(s)." << endl;
                cout << "Sort required " << num_swaps << " swap(s) of data." << endl;
                cout << "Sort required " << num_comparisons << " comparison(s)." << endl;
                cout << endl;
        }

void shell_sort(list_type list, int n)
{
        int k = n / 2;

        ++num_comparisons;                                      // Efficiency stats
        while (k > 0)
        {
                ++num_iterations;                               // Efficiency stats
                segmented_insertion_sort(list, n, k);
                k = k / 2;
                ++num_comparisons;                              // Efficiency stats
        }
}

void segmented_insertion_sort(list_type list, int n, int k)
{
        int j;
        element item_to_insert;
        boolean still_looking;
        for (int i = k; i < n; ++i)
        {
                ++num_iterations;                               // Efficiency stats
                item_to_insert = list[i];
                j = i - k;
                still_looking = TRUE;
                ++num_comparisons;                              // Efficiency stats
                while ((j >= 0) && still_looking)
                {
                        ++num_iterations;                       // Efficiency stats
                        ++num_comparisons;
                        if (item_to_insert < list[j])
                        {
                                list[j + k] = list[j];
                                ++num_swaps;                    // Efficiency stats
                                j = j - k;
                        }
                        else
                                still_looking = FALSE;
                        ++num_comparisons;                      // Efficiency stats
                }
                list[j + k] = item_to_insert;
        }
}
```

**RUNNING, DEBUGGING AND TESTING HINTS**

1. To describe and understand the more complex sort algorithms, it is helpful to present them via subordinate algorithms and stepwise refinement. To this end, we have found it convenient initially to focus on subalgorithms (`segmented_insertion_sort` for `shell_sort`, `partition` for `quick_sort`, `walk_down` for `heap_sort`, and `merge` for `merge_sort`). Our method is illustrative of the stepwise refinement approach to problem solving: Break a complex problem down into smaller problems, solve these smaller problems, and then tie their solutions together to solve the original large problem.

2. Describing and understanding algorithms is a separate issue from their actual implementation in a specific programming language and on a real machine. One implication of this separation of algorithm description and algorithm implementation is the run-time cost associated with a function call. We must consider the hidden costs of making a function call and how deeply embedded the function call is in the iterative structure of the calling module.

3. Depending on the machine you are using, calling a function instead of directly inserting the code necessary may mean that your program spends more run-time handling the hidden cost of function calls than it does actually interchanging data items. If large data sets are being sorted and if run-time efficiency is of primary importance, then we should implement our algorithm without actually calling on a function.

4. Keep in mind the distinction between algorithm description and algorithm implementation when making decisions about whether or not to proceduralize a given sequence of instructions. What may be appropriately isolated as a trivial subalgorithm at the time when a designer is concerned with describing an algorithm may carry with it a steep price if implemented as a trivial function that is called on many times when the resulting program is put into use.

5. In making the decision whether to use functions or in-line code when implementing an algorithm, carefully weigh run-time considerations with respect to the clarity and readability of code. A useful rule of thumb is that only in exceptional circumstances should the code associated with a module exceed one printed page in length. This guideline allows in-line insertion of code for simple algorithmic units and assures that the overall software system does not become unwieldy.

**SUMMARY**

### Key Terms

diminishing increment sort
external sort
heap sort
internal sort

merge sort
partition
pivot

quick sort
relatively prime
shell sort

### Key Concepts

◆ This chapter has added four sorting algorithms to those already presented in Chapter 1. This gives us a large variety of tools from which to choose when we need to perform a sorting job.

◆ The following comparison table summarizes the pros and cons of each sorting method we've covered.

| Sorting Method | Chapter | Number of Comparisons in Terms of the Number of Data Items Being Sorted (n) | Space Requirement | Additional Comments |
|---|---|---|---|---|
| Binary tree | 16 | Between $O(n^2)$ and $O(n \log_2 n)$ depending on original data and whether tree height-balanced | Pointers for tree and possible stack space for recursive traversals | |
| Bubble | 10 | $O(n2)$ | No additional overhead | Loop check allows early exit as soon as array is ordered. |
| Heap | 17 | $O(n \log_2 n)$ | No additional overhead | |
| Insertion | 10 | $O(n^2)$ | No additional overhead | Loop check allows early exit as soon as item is correctly placed. |
| Merge | 17 | $O(n \log_2 n)$ | Requires duplicate array and stack space for recursion | Since only requires sequential access, can be used for linked lists and sequential files. |
| Pointer | 10 | Depends on method with which it is combined | Required list of pointers to maintain logical order | Can be combined with any method to substantially reduce size of data items being interchanged. |
| Quick | 17 | $O(n \log_2 n)$ on the average but $O(n^2)$ for worst cases | Stack space for recursion | |
| Radix | 10, 13 | $O(n)$ | Space for bins | Though $O(n)$, large constant of proportionality. Not generalizable to all types of data, for example, real numbers. |
| Selection | 10 | $O(n^2)$ | No additional overhead | |
| Shell | 17 | Between $O[n(\log_2 n)^2]$ and $O(n^{1.5})$ depending on increments used | No additional overhead | |

**PROGRAMMING PROBLEMS AND PROJECTS**

1. Complete the partial program presented in this chapter's Focus on Program Design section. Then use the completed program to explore empirically the shell sort algorithm. In particular, experiment with different sequences of diminishing increments.

   Write a report on your exploration. In your report you should compare various sequences of diminishing increments and rate them as to their performance on a variety of data sets.

2. Modify the shell sort so that it employs bubble sort logic on segments instead of insertion sort. Incorporate this change into the program presented in this chapter's Focus on Program Design section. Compare the observed efficiency of this new version of shell sort with the original on a variety of data sets. Which performs better? Explain your answer in a carefully written statement.

3. Modify the program presented in this chapter's Focus on Program Design section so that it becomes an experimental tool for quick sort, heap sort, or merge sort. Then

use the modified program to conduct an experiment similar to the one you did for shell sort in Problem 1. For instance, for Quick Sort, you could experiment with the selection of a pivot element or try invoking insertion sort when the size of the array segment to be partitioned becomes sufficiently small. Whatever experimentation you choose to do, write a report on your exploration. In your report, draw conclusions about the efficiencies of various strategies. Support your conclusions with empirical data obtained from your exploratory runs.

4. Given a sequential file containing an unordered list of passengers and their flight numbers for Wing-and-a-Prayer Airlines (Problem 2, Chapter 4; Problems 3 and 12, Chapter 7), produce a listing arranged in flight-number order. Passengers on the same flight should be ordered by last name. The easy version of this program assumes that all information will fit in memory, allowing the use of an internal sort. For an added challenge, write the program using an external sort algorithm. (*Hint:* Adapt **merge_sort** along the lines discussed in the text.)

5. The Bay Area Brawlers professional football team (Problem 4, Chapter 4; Problem 5, Chapter 7) has stored the records of all the players who have played on the team during the history of the team. One player's record consists of

Name

Total points scored

Number of touchdowns

Number of field goals

Number of safeties

Number of extra points

Write a program that lists players in order from the highest scores in the team's history down to the lowest. Those players who have scored the same number of points should then be arranged in alphabetical order.

6. Take *n* randomly generated integers. Now apply a bubble sort, a shell sort, a quick sort, a heap sort, and a merge sort. Observe, compare, and plot their execution time for *n* = 100; *n* = 1,000; *n* = 10,000; *n* = 100,000, . . . .

7. Put some hypothetical data in an external file and apply a modified merge sort to them.

8. Write a C++ program to complete the following steps:

- Artificially create a file with a large number of randomly chosen names.
- Read into an array all names that begin with *A* through some letter, say, *G*, chosen so that all the names will fit in the array.
- Sort this array with one of the sorting algorithms from this chapter and store this sorted array into another file.
- Now read into the array all those names from the file which begin with *H* through another appropriate letter.
- Sort the array and append it to the end of the new file.

Repeat this process until all names from the original file have been processed. The new file will be the sorted version of the original. Observe the execution time of your program. Analyze its efficiency in big-O terms.

9. Consider a list of records, each containing four fields:

Name

Month of birth

Day of birth

Year of birth

Write a program to sort this list in oldest-to-youngest order. People with the same birth date should be arranged alphabetically. One strategy you could employ would be to concatenate strategically the four fields into one, and then sort just that one field. Another strategy would be to sort the list four times, each time by a different field. (Think carefully about which field to sort first.) Which of the strategies would require that you choose a stable sorting algorithm? (See Exercise 7 in Section 8.4.)

**10.** Modify `merge_sort` so that it will sort a linked list instead of an array.

# 9 More Powerful Search Methods

*I do not search, I find.*
Pablo Picasso

In earlier chapters, we analyzed three methods of searching for items within a list: sequential search, binary search, and binary search tree. The sequential search, though easy to implement and applicable to short lists, is limited in many practical situations by its $O(n)$ search efficiency. The binary search offers a much faster $O(\log_2 n)$ search efficiency but also has limitations. Foremost among these limitations are the need to maintain the list in physically contiguous order and the need to maintain a count of the number of records in the list. Both of these limitations are particularly restrictive for volatile lists; that is, lists in which insertions and deletions are frequently made. In Chapter 7, a binary search tree emerged as offering the best of both worlds. Insertions and deletions can be done on a binary search tree by merely manipulating pointers instead of moving data, and an $O(\log_2 n)$ search efficiency can be achieved if the tree remains close to full. Unfortunately, to guarantee that the tree remains nearly full and hence ensure the $O(\log_2 n)$ efficiency, a sophisticated technique known as height balancing (see Chapter 7) is required. The complications involved in implementing this technique frequently dictate that it not be used. Essentially, you must weigh the significant cost in development time to implement a height-balanced tree against the risk that the order in which data arrive for insertion may cause search efficiency to deteriorate from $O(\log_2 n)$ to $O(n)$. If data items arrive in a relatively random order, then taking that risk may well be the prudent choice.

The efficiency of all three of these techniques is dependent on the number of items in the list being searched. In this chapter, we shall study another alternative, called *hashing*. Its efficiency is measurable in terms of the amount of storage you are willing to waste. In this sense, hashing can achieve phenomenally fast search times regardless of how much data you have, provided that you can afford to keep a relatively large amount of unused list space available.

We shall also explore some of the special considerations that enter into searching for data stored in a disk file instead of main memory. These considerations lead to a variety of search schemes, all of which employ some variation of a data structure known as an *index*.

In an ideal data processing world, all identifying keys such as product codes, Social Security numbers, and so on, would start at 0 and follow in sequence thereafter. Then, in any given list, we would merely store the key and its associated data at the position that matched the key. The search efficiency for any key in such a list would be one access to the list, and all data processors could live happily ever after! Unfortunately, in the real world, users (not being concerned with the happiness of data processing personnel) desire keys that consist of more meaningful characters, such as names, addresses, region codes, and so on. For instance, it may be that in a given inventory-control application, product codes are numbered in sequence beginning with 10,000 instead of 0. A moment's reflection should indicate that this is still a highly desirable situation since, given a key, we need merely locate the key at position

```
key_value - 10000
```

in the list, and we still have a search efficiency of 1. What we have done here is to define what is known as a *key-to-address transformation,* or *hashing function.* The idea behind a hashing function is that it acts on a given key in such a way as to return the relative position in the list where we expect to find the key.

Most hashing functions are not as straightforward as the preceding one and present some additional complications that we can quickly illustrate. Suppose we use the following hashing function:

```
hash(key_value) = key_value % 4
```

Then the set of keys 3, 5, 8, and 10 will be scattered as illustrated here.

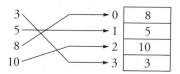

However, if we happen to have 3, 4, 8, and 10 as keys instead of 3, 5, 8, and 10, a problem arises: 4 and 8 hash to the same position. They are said to be *synonyms,* and the result is termed a *collision.* This situation, here a collision at position 0, is shown in the following illustration.

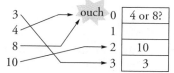

Clearly, one of the goals of the hashing functions we develop should be to reduce the number of collisions as much as possible.

## The Construction of Hashing Functions

The business of developing hashing functions can be quite intriguing. The essential idea is to build a mathematical black box that will take a key value as input and issue as output the position in the list where that key value should be located. The position emitted should have a minimal probability of colliding with the position that would be produced for a different key. In addition, the black box we create must ensure that a given key will always produce the same position as output. You should begin to note a similarity between some of the properties possessed by a good hashing function and a good random number generator such as that used in our simulation case study in Chapter 5. Indeed, list access via a hashing function is sometimes called *randomized storage,* and the first type of hashing function we discuss makes direct use of a random number generator.

**Method 1: Use of a Random Number Generator.** Many high-level languages provide a random number generator to produce random sequences of real values between 0 and 1. If one is not provided, you may easily write one using a method such as that described in Appendix 6. (For readable discussions of other methods of random number generation, see Chapter 7 of *Numerical Recipes* by William H. Press, Brian P. Flannery, Saul A. Teukolsky, and William T. Vetterling, Cambridge, England: Cambridge University Press, 1986.) Typically, all of these methods rely on having a global seed to start the process of generating random numbers. Computations done on this seed produce the random number. At the same time, the computations alter the value of the seed so that the next time the random number generator is called, a different random number will almost surely be produced.

In typical applications of random number generation, you need merely initialize the seed to some arbitrary value to start the random sequence. Once the seed is supplied, the random sequence is completely determined. If you have access to a system function that returns the current time, day, month, and year, this can be called to initialize the seed in a fashion that ensures there is only a very small likelihood of generating the same random sequence twice.

How does all of this relate to hashing? For a hashing application, we must slightly alter the definition of our random number generator so that the seed is supplied as a value parameter. Then we supply the values of search keys as the seeds. The nature of the random number algorithm ensures that

- Each time the same key is passed to the function, the same random value will be returned.
- It is unlikely that two different keys will yield the same random value.

The random number between 0 and 1 that is correspondingly produced can then be appropriately multiplied, truncated, and shifted to produce a hash value within the range of valid positions.

**Method 2: Folding.** In situations where the key to be positioned is not a pure integer, some preliminary work may be required to translate it into a usable form. Take, for instance, the case of a Social Security number such as

387- 58 -1505

Viewed as one integer, this would cause overflow on many machines. By a method known as *shift folding,* this Social Security number would be viewed as three separate numbers to be added

387

58

+ 1505

producing the result 1950. This result could either be regarded as the hash position itself or, more likely, as a pure integer that now could be further acted on by method 1 or 4 to produce a final hash position in the desired range.

Another often-used folding technique is called *boundary folding*. The idea behind boundary folding is that, at the boundaries between the numbers making up the key under consideration, every other number is reversed before being added to the accumulated total. Applying this method to our Social Security number example, we would have

387

85 (this number reversed)

+1505

yielding a result of 1977. Clearly, the two methods do not differ by much, and a choice between them must often be made on the basis of some experimentation to determine which will produce more scattered results for a given application.

Regardless of whether shift or boundary folding is used, one of the great advantages of the folding method is its ability to transform noninteger keys into an integer suitable for further hashing action. For keys such as names that contain alphabetic characters, the type of folding just illustrated may be done by translating characters into their ASCII (or other appropriate) codes.

**Method 3: Digit or Character Extraction.** In certain situations, a given key value may contain specific characters that are likely to bias any hash value arising from the key. The idea in *digit* or *character extraction* is to remove such digits or characters before using the result as a final hash value or passing it on to be further transformed by another method. For instance, a company may choose to identify the various products it manufactures by using a nine-character code that always contains either an A or B in the first position and either a 1 or 0 in the fourth position. The rest of the characters in the code tend to occur in less predictable fashion. Character extraction would remove the biased first and fourth characters, leaving a seven-character result to pass on to further processing.

**Method 4: Division-Remainder Technique.** All hashing presupposes a given range of positions that can be valid outputs of the hash function. In the remainder of this section, we assume the existence of a global constant **RECORD_SPACE,** which represents the upper limit of our hashing function. That is, the function should produce values between 0 and **RECORD_SPACE -1**. It should than be evident that

```
hash(key_value) = key_value % RECORD_SPACE
```

is a valid hashing function for integer **key_value**.

To begin examining criteria for choosing an appropriate **RECORD_SPACE**, let us load the keys 41, 58, 12, 92, 50, and 91 into a list with **RECORD_SPACE = 15**. Figure 9.1 shows the results. In this array, zeros are used to denote empty positions. However, if we keep **RECORD_SPACE** the same and try to load the keys 10, 20, 30, 40, 50, 60, and 70, we have many collisions, as shown in Figure 9.2.

Hence a different set of keys can cause disastrous results even though the list seemingly has plenty of room available. On the other hand, if we choose **RECORD_SPACE** to be 11, we have a list with considerably less room but no collisions. Figure 9.3 indicates the hashing positions when the same set of keys is acted on by 11 instead of by 15.

Although these examples of the *division-remainder technique* are far from conclusive, they suggest that choosing a prime number for **RECORD_SPACE** may produce a more desirable hashing function. The exercises at the end of this section

◆ FIGURE 9.1

Array with RECORD_SPACE = 15 loaded using a division-remainder hashing function

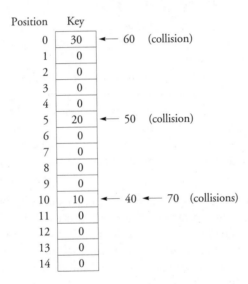

| Position | Key |
|---|---|
| 0 | 0 |
| 1 | 91 |
| 2 | 92 |
| 3 | 0 |
| 4 | 0 |
| 5 | 50 |
| 6 | 0 |
| 7 | 0 |
| 8 | 0 |
| 9 | 0 |
| 10 | 0 |
| 11 | 41 |
| 12 | 12 |
| 13 | 58 |
| 14 | 0 |

◆ FIGURE 9.2

Array from Figure 9.1, loaded differently, with several collisions

| Position | Key | |
|---|---|---|
| 0 | 30 | ◄— 60   (collision) |
| 1 | 0 | |
| 2 | 0 | |
| 3 | 0 | |
| 4 | 0 | |
| 5 | 20 | ◄— 50   (collision) |
| 6 | 0 | |
| 7 | 0 | |
| 8 | 0 | |
| 9 | 0 | |
| 10 | 10 | ◄— 40 ◄— 70   (collisions) |
| 11 | 0 | |
| 12 | 0 | |
| 13 | 0 | |
| 14 | 0 | |

have you explore this question more deeply. Apart from considerations of whether or not **RECORD_SPACE** should be prime, it is clear that the nature of a particular application may dictate against the choice of certain **RECORD_SPACE** values. For instance, in a situation where the rightmost digits of key values happen to follow certain recurring patterns, it would be unwise to choose a power of 10 for **RECORD_SPACE**. (Why?)

Despite such considerations, a hashing function usually cannot rule out the possibility of collisions; it can only make them less likely. You should quickly be able to imagine a key value that will produce a collision for the hashing function used in determining the list of Figure 9.3. Notice that, as the list becomes more full, the probability that collisions will occur increases. Hence, when using hashing as a search strategy, one must be willing to waste some positions in the list; otherwise search efficiency will drastically deteriorate. How much space to waste is an interesting question that we will soon discuss. Further, since hashing functions

◆ FIGURE 9.3

◆ FIGURE 9.3

Array with same keys as
Figure 9.2, but with
`RECORD_SPACE = 11:`
no collision results

| Position | Key |
|----------|-----|
| 0 | 0 |
| 1 | 0 |
| 2 | 0 |
| 3 | 0 |
| 4 | 70 |
| 5 | 60 |
| 6 | 50 |
| 7 | 40 |
| 8 | 30 |
| 9 | 20 |
| 10 | 10 |

generally cannot eliminate collisions, we must be prepared to handle them when they occur.

## Collision Processing

The essential problem in collision processing is to develop an algorithm that will position a key in a list when the position dictated by the hashing function itself is already occupied. Ideally, this algorithm should minimize the possibility of future collisions; that is, the problem key should be located at a position that is not likely to be the hashed position of a future key.

However, the nature of hashing makes this latter criterion difficult to meet with any degree of certainty, since a good hashing function does not allow prediction of where future keys are likely to be placed. We will discuss five methods of collision processing: linear, quadratic, rehashing, linked, and bucket. In all of the methods, it will be necessary to detect when a given list position is not occupied. To signify this, we use a global constant **EMPTY** to distinguish unoccupied positions. As you read, give some thought to the question of how deletions could be processed from a list accessed via one of these hashing methods. In particular, will the **EMPTY** flag suffice to denote positions that have never been occupied *and* positions previously occupied but now vacant? This question is explored in the exercises and in the programming problems at the end of this chapter.

## Linear Collision Processing

The linear method of resolving collisions is the simplest to implement (and, unfortunately, the least efficient). *Linear collision processing* requires that, when a collision occurs, we proceed down the list in sequential order until a vacant position is found. The key causing the collision is then placed at this first vacant position. If we come to the physical end of our list in the attempt to place the problem key, we merely wrap around to the top of the list and continue looking for a vacant position. For instance, suppose we use a hashing function of

```
hash(key_value) = key_value % RECORD_SPACE
```

with **RECORD_SPACE** equal to 6. We then attempt to insert the keys 18, 31, 67, 36, 19, and 34. The sequence of lists in Figure 9.4 shows the results of these insertions. When a collision occurs at the third insert, it is processed by the linear method; 67 is thus loaded into position 5.

◆ FIGURE 9.4
Insertion with linear collision
processing

| | First insert hash(18) = 4 | | Second insert hash(31) = 3 | | Third insert hash(67) = 4 | | Fourth insert hash(36) = 1 | | Fifth insert hash(19) = 5 | | Sixth insert hash(34) = 6 |
|---|---|---|---|---|---|---|---|---|---|---|---|
| 0 | 0 | 0 | 0 | 0 | 0 | 0 | 0 | 0 | 0 | 0 | 34 |
| 1 | 0 | 1 | 0 | 1 | 0 | 1 | 36 | 1 | 36 | 1 | 36 |
| 2 | 0 | 2 | 0 | 2 | 0 | 2 | 0 | 2 | 0 | 2 | 0 |
| 3 | 0 | 3 | 31 | 3 | 31 | 3 | 31 | 3 | 31 | 3 | 31 |
| 4 | 18 | 4 | 18 | 4 | 18 | 4 | 18 | 4 | 18 | 4 | 18 |
| 5 | 0 | 5 | 0 | 5 | 67 | 5 | 67 | 5 | 67 | 5 | 67 |
| 6 | 0 | 6 | 0 | 6 | 0 | 6 | 0 | 6 | 19 | 6 | 19 |

---

EXAMPLE 9.1    Suppose that an array has been loaded with data using the linear collision processing strategy illustrated in Figure 9.4. Write a C++ algorithm to seek a target key in this array.

```cpp
// Function: linear_hash
// Use linear hashing algorithm to search for target.
//
// Inputs: List of objects loaded by linear
// hashing method.
// target, the key of an object to be found.
// Outputs: If key matching target is found,
// return TRUE and the index at the key;
// otherwise; return FALSE.

boolean linear_hash(list_type list, key_type target,
    element &item)
{
    int k = hash(target);
    int j = k;
    boolean traversed = FALSE;
    boolean found = FALSE;

    while (! list[j].empty() && ! (found || traversed))
        if (target == list[j].get_key())
        {
            item = list[j].get_value();
            found = TRUE;
        }
        else
```

```
        {
            j = j % RECORD_SPACE;
            traversed = j == k;
        }
    return found;
}
```

| | | |
|---|---|---|
| 0 | 419 | target = 419 |
| | | hash(419) = RECORD_SPACE – 3 |
| . | . | |
| . | . | |
| . | . | |
| RECORD_SPACE – 3 | 511 | Repeated applications of |
| RECORD_SPACE – 2 | 312 | **else** clause ensure eventual |
| RECORD_SPACE – 1 | 705 | wraparound to first slot. |

Several remarks are in order concerning the function in Example 9.1. First, note that the function as it stands would not handle list processing that requires deletions to be processed. In such a situation, an additional flagging value would be needed to indicate a list position that had once been occupied and is now vacant because of a deletion. Without this distinction, we would not know whether or not to exit the search loop upon encountering an empty slot. You will explore the problem of deletions from a list maintained by hashing in greater detail in the exercises and programming problems. Second, note that the linear method is not without its flaws. In particular, it is prone to a problem known as *clustering*. Clustering occurs when a collision processing strategy relocates keys that have a collision at the same initial hashing position to the same region (known as a cluster) within the storage space. This usually leads to further collisions with other relocated values until everything is resolved. With linear collision processing, the clustering problem is compounded because, as one cluster expands, it can run into another cluster, immediately creating a larger cluster. This one large cluster ultimately causes collision resolutions to be drawn out longer than they would otherwise be. Hence, linear hashing is more likely to result in the clustering phenomenon pictured in Figure 9.5 than the other methods we discuss.

**Efficiency Considerations for Linear Hashing.** A final point to note about the linear hashing method is its search efficiency. Knuth has shown that the average number of list accesses for a successful search using the linear method is

$$(1/2) * [1 + 1/(1 - D)]$$

where

```
D = (number of currently active records)/RECORD_SPACE
```

(See Donald E. Knuth, *Searching and Sorting*, Volume 3 of *The Art of Computer Programming*, Menlo Park, Calif.: Addison-Wesley, 1973.) An interesting fact about this search efficiency is that it is not solely dependent on the number of records in the list but rather on the density ratio of the number of records currently in the list

◆ FIGURE 9.5

Clustering due to biased
hashing function and linear
processing

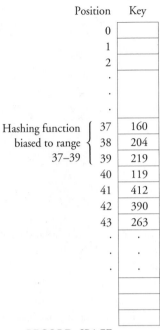

Position    Key

0
1
2
·
·
·

Hashing function    37 | 160
biased to range    38 | 204
37–39    39 | 219
40 | 119
41 | 412
42 | 390
43 | 263
·    ·
·    ·
·    ·

RECORD_SPACE

Suppose keys 160, 204, 219, 119, 412, 390, and 263 are located with

$$\text{hash}(160) = 37$$
$$\text{hash}(204) = 37$$
$$\text{hash}(219) = 37$$
$$\text{hash}(119) = 38$$
$$\text{hash}(412) = 38$$
$$\text{hash}(390) = 38$$
$$\text{hash}(263) = 39$$

If a linear method were not used, these keys would not necessarily cluster in positions 37– 43.

divided by the total record space available. In other words, no matter how many records there are, a highly efficient result can be obtained if one is willing to waste enough vacant records. This is what is meant by a *density-dependent search technique*. In the case of searching for a key that cannot be found, Knuth's results indicate that the average search efficiency will be

$$(1/2) * [1 + 1/(1 - D)^2]$$

Table 9.1 illustrates the effectiveness of linear collision resolution by showing the computed efficiencies for a few strategic values of $D$.

## Quadratic and Rehashing Methods of Collision Processing

Both the *quadratic* and *rehashing collision processing methods* attempt to correct the problem of clustering. They force the problem-causing key to immediately move a considerable distance from the initial collision. By the rehashing method, an entire sequence of hashing functions may be applied to a given key. If a collision results

◇ TABLE 9.1

Average search efficiency
for linear collision
processing

| $D$ | Efficiency for Successful Search (number of accesses) | Efficiency for Unsuccessful Search (number of accesses) |
|---|---|---|
| 0.10 | 1.06 | 1.18 |
| 0.50 | 1.50 | 2.50 |
| 0.75 | 2.50 | 8.50 |
| 0.90 | 5.50 | 50.50 |

from the first hashing function, a second is applied, then a third, and so on, until the key can be successfully placed.

The quadratic method has the advantage of not requiring numerous hashing functions for its implementation. Suppose that a key value initially hashes to position $k$ and a collision results. Then, on its first attempt to resolve the collision, the quadratic algorithm attempts to place the key at position

$$k + 1^2$$

Then, if a second attempt is necessary to resolve the collision, position

$$k + 2^2$$

is probed. In general, the $r$th attempt to resolve the collision probes position

$$k + r^2$$

(with wraparound taken into account). Figure 9.6 highlights this scattering pattern. At this point you should verify that, if the hashing function

```
hash(key_value) = key_value % RECORD_SPACE
```

is used with RECORD_SPACE equal to 7, the keys 17, 73, 32, and 80 will be located in positions 3, 4, 5, and 0 respectively.

**Efficiency Considerations for the Quadratic and Rehashing Methods.** Knuth's results (see *Searching and Sorting,* cited earlier in this section) demonstrate the effectiveness of the rehashing and quadratic methods versus the linear method. For the quadratic method, average search efficiencies improve to

$$1 - \log_e(1 - D) - (D/2)$$

◆ FIGURE 9.6

Quadratic collision processing

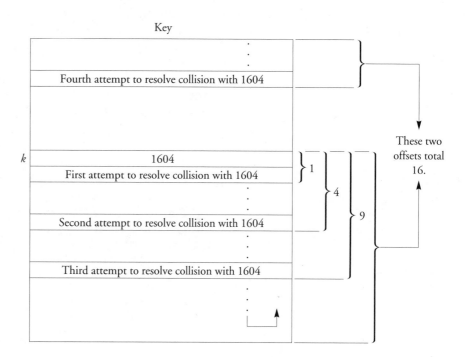

for the successful case and

$$1/(1 - D) - D - \log_e(1 - D)$$

for an unsuccessful search, where $D$ is density ratio as defined earlier in this section and $e$ is the base for the natural logarithm function.

Rehashing with a completely random sequence of rehashing locations for each key slightly improves the efficiencies of the quadratic method to

$$-(1/D) * \log_e(1 - D)$$

for the successful case and

$$1/(1 - D)$$

for an unsuccessful search. Compare the numbers presented in Table 9.2 for quadratic collision processing and (ideal) random rehashing to those in Table 9.1 for linear collision processing.

You may have surmised that the increased efficiency of the quadratic method entails at least some drawbacks. First, the computation of a position to be probed when a collision occurs is somewhat more obscure than it was with the linear method. We leave it for you to verify that the position for the $r$th probe after an initial unsuccessful hash to position $k$ is given by

```
(k + r² - 1) % RECORD_SPACE
```

A more significant problem, however, is that the quadratic method seemingly offers no guarantee that we will try every position in the list before concluding that a given key cannot be inserted. With the linear method, as the list became relatively dense when keys and insertions were attempted, the only way that the insertion could fail would be for every position in the list to be occupied. The linear nature of the search, although inefficient, ensured that every position would be checked. However, with the quadratic method applied to the **RECORD_SPACE** of Figure 9.7, you can confirm that an initial hash to position 3 will lead to future probing of positions 3, 4, and 7 only; it will never check positions 0, 1, 2, 5, or 6.

A satisfactory answer to the question of what portion of a list will be probed by the quadratic algorithm was fortunately provided by Radke for values of **RECORD_SPACE** that are prime numbers which satisfy certain conditions. Radke's results and their application to the quadratic algorithm are explored in the exercises at the end of the section. (If you wish to read Radke's results, see C. E. Radke, "The

◇ **TABLE 9.2**

Average search efficiency for quadratic and rehashing collision processing

| D | Efficiency for Successful Search (number of accesses) | | Efficiency for Unsuccessful Search (number of accesses) | |
|---|---|---|---|---|
| | Quadratic | Rehashing | Quadratic | Rehashing |
| 0.10 | 1.05 | 1.05 | 1.11 | 1.11 |
| 0.50 | 1.44 | 1.39 | 2.19 | 2.00 |
| 0.75 | 2.01 | 1.84 | 4.64 | 4.00 |
| 0.90 | 2.85 | 2.56 | 11.40 | 10.00 |

◆ FIGURE 9.7
Quadratic probing after
initial hash to 3

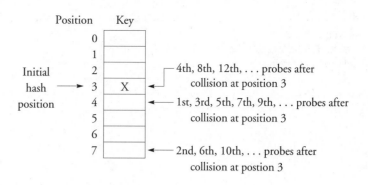

◆ FIGURE 9.8
Storage allocation for linked
collision processing

Use of Quadratic Residue Research," *Communications of the ACM,* Volume 13, No. 2 (February 1970):103–105.)

## Linked Method of Collision Processing

The logic of *linked collision processing* completely eliminates the possibility that one collision begets another. It requires a storage area divided into two regions: a *prime hash area* and an *overflow area.* Each record requires a link field in addition to the **key** and **other_data** fields. The global constant **RECORD_SPACE** is applicable to the prime hash area only. This storage concept is illustrated in Figure 9.8.

Initially, the hashing translates function keys into the prime hashing area. If a collision occurs, the key is inserted into a linked list with its initial node in the prime area and all following nodes in the overflow area. Figure 9.9 shows how this method would load the keys 22, 31, 67, 36, 29, and 60 for a **RECORD_SPACE** equal to 7 and hashing function

```
hash(key_value) = key_value % RECORD_SPACE
```

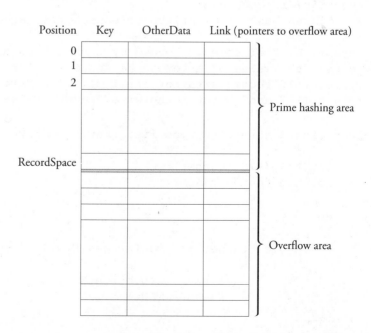

◆ FIGURE 9.9

Loading keys with
`key_value % RECORD_SPACE`
and linked collision processing

| Position | Key | Link |
|----------|-----|------|
| 0 | 0 | NULL |
| 1 | 22 | 7 |
| 2 | 0 | NULL |
| 3 | 31 | NULL |
| 4 | 67 | 9 |
| 5 | 0 | NULL |
| 6 | 0 | NULL |
| 7 | 36 | 8 |
| 8 | 29 | NULL |
| 9 | 60 | NULL |
| 10 | 0 | NULL |
| 11 | 0 | NULL |
| 12 | 0 | NULL |
| 13 | 0 | NULL |
| 14 | 0 | NULL |
| 15 | 0 | NULL |
| 16 | 0 | NULL |

---

**EXAMPLE 9.2**

Suppose that an array has been loaded with data using the linked collision processing strategy illustrated in Figures 9.8 and 9.9. Write a C++ function to find a target key in this array.

We have made the **link** fields integer pointers to other array locations instead of C++ dynamic memory pointers to facilitate using the algorithm with a random access file. As written, the function assumes that all key locations in the prime area have had their corresponding key and link fields initialized to appropriate constant flags for **EMPTY** and **NULL**, respectively. The assumption is also made that no keys will be deleted.

```
// Function: linked_hash
// Use linked hashing algorithm to search for target.
//
// Inputs: List of objects loaded by linked hashing method.
// target, the value of a key to be found in list.
// Outputs: If record with key field matching target is found,
// return TRUE and object; otherwise, return False

boolean linked_hash(list_type list, key_type target element & item)
{
        int k = hash (target);
        boolean found = FALSE;

        do
        {
                if (target == list[k].get_key())
                {
                        item = list[k].get_value();
                        found = TRUE;
                }
```

```
        else
                k = list[k].link();
    } while ((! found && (k != NULL));
    return found;

}
```

**Efficiency Considerations for Linked Hashing.** Knuth's efficiency results for the linked hashing method depend on a density factor $D$, which is computed using the `RECORD_SPACE` in the prime hashing area only. Hence, unlike the other hashing methods we have discussed, the linked method allows a density factor greater than 1. For example, if the `RECORD_SPACE` for the primary hash area were 200 and the overflow area contained space for 300 additional records, then 400 active records would yield a density factor of 2. Given this variation, average search efficiencies for the successful and unsuccessful cases are $1 + D/2$ and $D$, respectively. Table 9.3 shows computations of this search efficiency for selected values of $D$, and should be compared to the corresponding results for the linear and quadratic methods, which were presented in Tables 9.1 and 9.2, respectively.

## Bucket Hashing

In the bucket hashing strategy of collision processing, the hashing function transforms a given key to a physically contiguous region of locations within the list to be searched. This contiguous region is called a *bucket*. Thus, instead of hashing to the $k$th location, a key would hash to the $k$th bucket of locations. The number of locations contained in this bucket would depend on the bucket size. (We assume

◇ **TABLE 9.3**
Average search efficiencies
for the linked method

| $D$ | Efficiency for Successful Search (number of accesses) | Efficiency for Unsuccessful Search (number of accesses) |
|---|---|---|
| 2 | 2 | 2 |
| 5 | 3.5 | 5 |
| 10 | 6 | 10 |
| 20 | 11 | 20 |

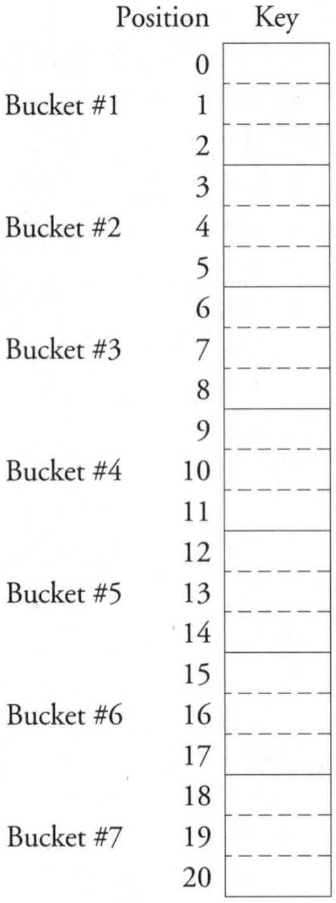

◆ FIGURE 9.10

Storage allocation for bucket
hashing

|  | Position | Key |
|---|---|---|
|  | 0 |  |
| Bucket #1 | 1 |  |
|  | 2 |  |
|  | 3 |  |
| Bucket #2 | 4 |  |
|  | 5 |  |
|  | 6 |  |
| Bucket #3 | 7 |  |
|  | 8 |  |
|  | 9 |  |
| Bucket #4 | 10 |  |
|  | 11 |  |
|  | 12 |  |
| Bucket #5 | 13 |  |
|  | 14 |  |
|  | 15 |  |
| Bucket #6 | 16 |  |
|  | 17 |  |
|  | 18 |  |
| Bucket #7 | 19 |  |
|  | 20 |  |

that all buckets in a given list are the same size.) Figure 9.10 illustrates this concept for a list with seven buckets and a bucket size of 3.

Having hashed to a bucket, the target must then be compared in sequential order to all of the keys in that bucket. On the surface, it would seem that this strategy could do no better than duplicate the efficiency of the linked hash method discussed earlier. Indeed, because a sequential search is conducted in both cases after the initial hash is made, the average number of list accesses for a successful or unsuccessful search cannot be improved by using buckets. Moreover, provisions for linking to some sort of overflow area must still be made in case a series of collisions consumes all of the space in a given bucket.

What then could be a possible advantage of using buckets? If the list to be searched resides entirely in main memory, there is no advantage. However, if the list resides in a disk file, the bucket method will allow us to take advantage of some of the physical characteristics of the storage medium itself. To see this, we must realize that a one-surface disk is divided into concentric *tracks* and pie-shaped *sectors* as indicated in Figure 9.11.

There are two ways in which the bucket hashing strategy may take advantage of the organization of the data on a disk. First, when records in a contiguous random access file are stored on a disk, they are generally located in relative record number order along one track, then along an adjacent track, and so on. The movement of the read/write head between tracks is generally the cause of the most significant delays in obtaining data from a disk. The farther the movement, the greater the delay. Hence, if our knowledge of the machine in question allows us to make a bucket coincide with a track on the disk, then hashing to the beginning of a bucket and proceeding from there using a sequential

◆ FIGURE 9.11
One-surface disk

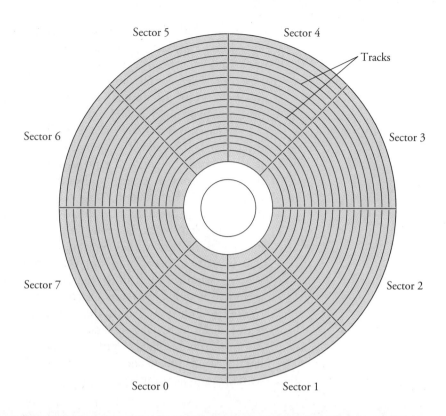

Sector 5    Sector 4

Tracks

Sector 6    Sector 3

Sector 7    Sector 2

Sector 0    Sector 1

---

## A NOTE OF INTEREST

### Machine Translation

When the search algorithms discussed in this chapter were first discovered, they sparked a flurry of activity in an area known as machine translation. Programs in this area attempt to translate text from one natural language to another, for example, English to German. Early attempts at machine translation tended to view the process as essentially the searching of a large dictionary. Hence, to translate the English sentence

*The sun is yellow*

the program would simply find each of the words in a disk-based version of an English-to-German dictionary and arrive at the German sentence

*Die Sonne ist gelb.*

However, machine translation activity was soon slowed by the complexities of syntax (grammar) and semantics (meanings) in natural language. The translation of some sentences by these early systems produced some rather humorous results. According to computer folklore cited in the article "Computers Gain as Language Translators Even Though Perfect Not They Always" by William M. Bulkeley (*Wall Street Journal*, February 6, 1985, p. 25), the follow-

ing translations occurred in an early English-to-Russian system.

| English Phrase | Russian Translation |
|---|---|
| The spirit is willing but the flesh is weak. | The vodka is good but the meat is rotten. |
| Out of sight, out of mind. | Invisible maniac. |

Results such as these caused a government panel to declare, in 1966, that computerized translation would never be practical. Today, as linguists have more successfully formalized rules of syntax and semantics, machine translation is making somewhat of a comeback. In restricted domains, such as the translation of language specific to technology and business, products are being developed as time-saving aids to human translators.

Two issues of the *Communications of the ACM*—Volume 33, No. 5 (May 1990) and Volume 33, No. 8 (August 1990)—contain a variety of articles describing progress that has been made in processing natural languages. These articles provide an excellent starting point for you to explore this topic more thoroughly.

search within the bucket (that is, the track) will greatly reduce head movement. A linked hashing strategy, on the other hand, could cause considerable movement of the read/write head between tracks on the disk, thereby slowing program execution. This consideration is an excellent example of how one must examine more than just the number of list accesses when measuring the efficiency of a program involving disk files.

A second advantage of the bucket hashing algorithm when disk files are being searched is related to the way in which records are transferred between the disk and main memory. Frequently, programming languages create the illusion that each record accessed requires a separate disk access. However, records are frequently blocked, that is, positioned in contiguous regions on a track of the disk, so that a fixed number of them are brought into main memory when a record in that block is requested. This means that, if the record requested happens to be part of the block presently in main memory, a program statement that requests a record may not even require a disk access but only a different viewing window applied to the block already in main memory. Since main memory manipulations are orders of magnitude faster than the rate of data transfer to and from a disk, this means that positioning our buckets to coincide with a disk block will necessitate only one disk access each time an entire bucket is sequentially searched. Here again, the more scattered nature of a purely linked hashing algorithm would not allow this disk-oriented efficiency consideration to be taken into account.

**EXERCISES 9.1**

1. Assume a hashing function has the following characteristics:

   Keys 459 and 333 hash to 0.

   Key 632 hashes to 1.

   Key 1090 hashes to 2.

   Keys 1982, 379, 238, and 3411 hash to 9.

   Assume that insertions into a hashed file are performed in the order 1982, 3411, 333, 632, 1090, 459, 379, and 238.

   **a.** Indicate the position of the keys if the linear method is used to resolve collisions.

|  Record No. | Key |
|-------------|-----|
| 0 |  |
| 1 |  |
| 2 |  |
| 3 |  |
| 4 |  |
| 5 |  |
| 6 |  |
| 7 |  |
| 8 |  |
| 9 |  |
| 10 |  |

**b.** Indicate the position of the keys if the quadratic method is used to resolve collisions.

| Record No. | Key |
|:----------:|:---:|
| 0 | |
| 1 | |
| 2 | |
| 3 | |
| 4 | |
| 5 | |
| 6 | |
| 7 | |
| 8 | |
| 9 | |
| 10 | |

**c.** Indicate the position of the keys and the contents of the link fields if the chaining (that is, linked) method is used to resolve collisions. Use zeros to represent NULL links and assume that the first record used in the overflow area is 11, then 12, then 13, and so on.

| Record No. | Key | Link |
|:----------:|:---:|:----:|
| 0 | | |
| 1 | | |
| 2 | | |
| 3 | | |
| 4 | | |
| 5 | | |
| 6 | | |
| 7 | | |
| 8 | | |
| 9 | | |
| 10 | | |

Prime Area

| Record No. | Key | Link |
|:----------:|:---:|:----:|
| 11 | | |
| 12 | | |
| 13 | | |
| 14 | | |
| 15 | | |
| 16 | | |
| 17 | | |
| 18 | | |
| 19 | | |
| 20 | | |
| 21 | | |

Overflow Area

**2.** Repeat Exercise 1 with the order of insertion of keys reversed.

**3.** We have covered binary search, linked lists, binary trees, and hashing as methods of implementing a one-key table ADT. Choose the method you would use to implement the data list involved for each of the following three real-world applications. In each case you should choose the most appropriate implementation technique. "Most appropriate" refers here to efficient handling of all of the required operations while not being too powerful; that is, not doing something that should be easy in an overly complicated way. Then provide a written rationale as to why yours would be the appropriate method.

**a.** The list to be maintained is the card catalog of a library. Frequent additions to and deletions from this catalog are made by the library. Additionally, users are frequently searching for the data associated with a given book's key. However, the library rarely prints out an ordered list of all its holdings. Hence ordering the list is not to be considered a high priority.

**b.** You are writing a program that maintains the lists of passengers on flights for an airline company. Passengers are frequently added to these lists. Moreover, quite often passengers cancel flight plans and must be removed from a list. You are also told that the airline frequently wants alphabetized listings of the passengers on a given flight and often needs to search for a particular passenger by name when inquiries are received from individuals.

**c.** You are writing a program to access a large customer database and build up counts for the numbers of customers from each of the 50 states plus the District of Columbia. To do this you will use a list of records consisting of the two-character state abbreviation and an integer representing the count of customers from that state. For each customer you read in from the database, you must find the customer's home state in your list and increase the corresponding count field. At the end, print out the counts in order alphabetized by the two-character state abbreviation.

**4.** Write functions to insert a key into a list to be searched by
   **a.** linear hashing
   **b.** quadratic hashing
   **c.** linked hashing
   **d.** bucket hashing

**5.** Write functions to search for a key via
   **a.** quadratic hashing
   **b.** bucket hashing

**6.** Devise strategies to delete keys from a list being maintained by each of the four hashing strategies in Exercise 4. Write C++ versions for each of these algorithms. Given your deletion strategy, describe in detail the modifications (if any) that must be made in the various search and insertion functions of Exercises 4 and 5.

**7.** In Section 9.1 we mentioned a result by Radke that answered the question of how many array slots would be probed by the quadratic hashing algorithm for certain values of **RECORD_SPACE**. In particular, Radke showed that if **RECORD_SPACE** is a prime number of the form $4m + 3$ for some integer $m$, then half of the array slots would be probed by the sequence of probes

$$k, k + 1^2, k + 2^2, k + 3^2, \ldots$$

where $k$ is the original hash position. Radke also showed that the other half would be probed by the sequence

$$k - 1^2, k - 2^2, k - 3^2, \ldots$$

Rewrite your insertion and search functions for the quadratic method in Exercises 4 and 5 to take into account Radke's result.

**8. a.** Given the arrival of integer keys in the order 67, 19, 4, 58, 38, 55, 86 and **RECORD_SPACE = 9** with

```
hash(key_value) = key_value % RECORD_SPACE
```

trace the insertion steps of linearly processing collisions.

| Index | key_value | |
|---|---|---|
| 0 | 0 | (0 indicates empty position) |
| 1 | 0 | |
| 2 | 0 | |
| 3 | 0 | |
| 4 | 0 | |
| 5 | 0 | |
| 6 | 0 | |
| 7 | 0 | |
| 8 | 0 | |

**b.** Given the arrival of integer keys in the order 32, 62, 34, 77, 6, 46, 107 and `RECORD_SPACE = 15` with

`hash(key_value) = key_value % RECORD_SPACE`

trace the insertion steps of quadratically processing collisions.

| Index | key_Value | |
|---|---|---|
| 0 | 0 | (0 indicates empty position) |
| 1 | 0 | |
| 2 | 0 | |
| 3 | 0 | |
| 4 | 0 | |
| 5 | 0 | |
| 6 | 0 | |
| 7 | 0 | |
| 8 | 0 | |
| 9 | 0 | |
| 10 | 0 | |
| 11 | 0 | |
| 12 | 0 | |
| 13 | 0 | |
| 14 | 0 | |

**c.** Given the arrival of integer keys in the order 5, 3, 16, 27, 14, 25, 4 and `RECORD_SPACE = 11` with initial hashing function

`hash1(key_value) = key_value % RECORD_SPACE`

trace the insertion steps of the rehashing collision processing method where the secondary hashing function is

`hash2(key_value) = 5 * key_value % RECORD_SPACE`

Assume that if the secondary hashing function is not successful in locating a position for the key, then linear collision processing is used from the address indicated by the secondary hashing function.

| Index | key_value | |
|---|---|---|
| 0 | 0 | (0 indicates empty position) |
| 1 | 0 | |
| 2 | 0 | |
| 3 | 0 | |
| 4 | 0 | |
| 5 | 0 | |
| 6 | 0 | |
| 7 | 0 | |
| 8 | 0 | |
| 9 | 0 | |
| 10 | 0 | |

Comment on the effectiveness of rehashing with this particular secondary hashing function. Can you think of a better one? Explain why yours is better.

**9.** In a written statement explain how hashing could be used to search for keys that were not unique. For instance, you might have several people identified by the same name.

---

## 9.2   Two Abstract Data Types Revisited

### OBJECTIVES

- to discuss how hashing could be used to implement the one-key table ADT

- to evaluate the efficiency of hashing as an implementation strategy for the one-key table ADT

- to discuss how hashing could be used to implement the two-key table ADT

We can analyze hashing from a pragmatic perspective by considering how it might be used to implement two ADTs introduced in Chapter 2: the one-key table and the two-key table. You will then be asked to carry out these implementations in the exercises and in the programming problems at the end of the chapter.

### The One-Key Table ADT Implemented by Hashing

In this context, hashing emerges as yet another list maintenance strategy to be evaluated and compared to those strategies we have already discussed: array with binary search, linked list, and binary tree. Hence we must examine its performance with respect to the same **insert, retrieve, remove,** and **traverse** operations that were introduced in Chapter 2 and then used to evaluate these other one-key table implementation techniques. Assuming the existence of an appropriate hashing function to act on the key and a willingness to waste enough storage to allow for fast searching, hashing will clearly perform very well in all of these areas with the exception of ordering data. Here is where we have to pay a price for the scattered storage of records that are located via a hashing function.

Nonetheless, there are strategies that can be used to allow hashing and ordering of data to coexist. One such strategy would simply be to use a pointer sort algorithm (see Chapter 1) to sort the data logically when an ordered list is needed. This strategy has the drawback of not maintaining the list in order but actually performing a potentially costly sort algorithm each time an ordering is requested. Clearly, this strategy would not be wise if such an ordering were requested frequently and unpredictably.

In situations where requests for ordering would come frequently enough to make maintaining the list in order (as opposed to sorting) a necessity, we could follow a strategy that would combine the search speed of hashing with the ordered list advantages offered by a linked list implementation. This combination would have us use hashing to search for an individual record but would add link fields to each record so that a linked list for each desired ordering could be woven through the collection of hashed records. Implementing this combination of hashing and linked lists would entail the following considerations with respect to the one-key table operations:

- **insert**: In effect, the hashing/collision processing algorithm would provide us with an available node to store data. Each linked list involved would then have to be traversed to link the node into each ordering in the appropriate logical location.
- **retrieve**: There is no problem here because the hash algorithm should find the desired record quickly.
- **remove**: This is similar to the **retrieve** operation. Use hashing to find the record to be deleted, then adjust the link field appropriately. A doubly linked list could prove to be particularly valuable here. (Why?)
- **traverse**: There is no problem here because the linked lists constantly maintain the appropriate orderings.

## The Two-Key Table ADT Implemented by Hashing

We have already suggested two implementation strategies for two-key tables.

1. In Section 2.4 we described a strategy that would simply create a list of the rows and columns corresponding to nontrivial values in the table. Thus, determining the value of the data at a conceptual row/column location is simply a matter of searching this list.
2. In Chapter 4, we described a strategy that would form a linked list of the nontrivial columns in each row. Here, determining the value of the data at a conceptual row/column location is reduced to the problem of sequentially searching a relatively small linked list.

At the time we explored these two strategies, the first one appeared to be less attractive. Because the data in the list of row/column coordinates corresponding to nontrivial values are likely to be volatile, physically ordering the data for a binary search would not be practical. Yet, without a binary search, requests to inspect the value at any given location are met with the $O(n)$ response time of a sequential search. Hashing allows us to search for a row/column coordinate in the list of the first strategy in a very efficient fashion, probably faster than the sequential search along the linked list representing a given row required by the second strategy. Moreover, since the order of the data in the list is not important for this application, the scattered nature of hashed storage does not present any obstacle at all.

The considerations we have discussed with respect to these two ADTs make it evident that hashing is a very attractive table implementation technique. It will be extremely efficient in regard to the **insert, retrieve,** and **remove** table operations if we are willing to pay the price of wasting enough storage to get a reasonably low density ratio. The only other drawback to hashing, in addition to this wasted storage, is the price that must be paid if various orderings of the data are frequently needed.

**EXERCISES 9.2**

1. Suppose that we combine hashing with a linked list in the fashion described in Section 9.2 so that all one-key table operations can be efficiently performed. Which of the variations on a linked list structure would be most effective in this context? Ex-

plain why in a carefully worded statement. (*Hint:* Think about the **retrieve** and **delete** operations.)

**2.** Give an example of an application where the hashing implementation of a two-dimensional table described in this section would be less efficient (overall) than the linked list implementation described in Chapter 4. Explain why in a carefully worded statement.

**3.** Provide implementations of all one-key table operations using the hashing strategy described in this section. Provide alternative implementations of the traverse operations: One should invoke a pointer sort and another should combine hashing with a linked list.

**4.** Provide implementations of all two-key table operations defined in Chapter 2 using the hashing strategy described in this section.

---

## 9.3 Indexed Search Techniques (Optional)

### OBJECTIVES

- to understand the differences between searching in main memory and in random access disk storage

- to understand how an index may be used to advantage when searching for data in a random access file

- to study how the indexed sequential search methodology is implemented

- to discuss the efficiency of the indexed sequential search strategy

- to understand how the B-tree data structure may be used to implement an index for a random access file

- to discuss the efficiency of B-trees

- to understand how the trie data structure may be used to implement the index for a random access file keyed by strings of variable length

- to discuss the efficiency of tries

All of the search strategies we have studied up to this point could be applied to lists implemented in main memory or on a random access disk. However, with the exception of bucket hashing, none of the methods we have studied actually takes into account physical characteristics of disk storage in an attempt to enhance their efficiency. In practice, because retrieval of data from a disk file is orders of magnitude slower than retrieval from main memory, we often cannot afford to ignore these special characteristics of disk files if we want reasonable response time for our searching efforts. The indexing schemes that we are about to discuss in this section are primarily directed toward file-oriented applications and thus will take into account the operational properties of this storage medium. We encourage you to reread the discussion of bucket hashing at the end of Section 9.1 for a summary analysis of file storage considerations.

The idea behind the use of an index is analogous to the way in which we routinely use an address book to find a person whom we are seeking. That is, if we are looking for a person, we do not knock on the doors of numerous houses until we find the one where that person lives. Instead, we apply a search strategy to an address book. There we use the name of the person as a key to find a pointer—that is, an address—which swiftly leads us to where the person can be found. Only one actual "house access" must be made, although our search strategy may require numerous accesses into the address book index.

In a computer system, records (or more precisely blocks) could play the role of houses in the search scenario just described. Data records on disk are (when compared to main memory) terribly slow and awkward creatures to access. One of the reasons for this is that there is often so much data that must be moved from disk to main memory every time a record is accessed. Because of this, the conceptual picture for the general setup of an indexed search must be revised. The list of keys is no longer parallel to the actual data with which they are logically associated, rather it is parallel to a list of pointers, which will lead us to the actual data. The revised picture is presented in Figure 9.12.

The general strategy of an indexed search is to use the key to search the index efficiently, find the relative record position of the associated data, and from there make only one access into the actual data. Because the parallel lists of keys and relative record positions require much less storage than the data, frequently the entire index can be loaded and permanently held in main memory, necessitating only one disk access for each record being sought. For larger indices, it still remains

◆ FIGURE 9.12

General setup for an indexed search

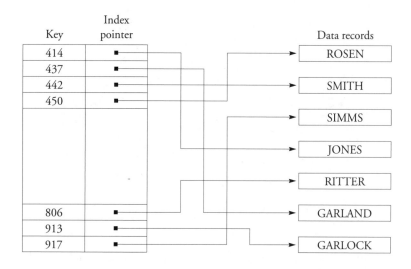

true that large blocks of keys and associated pointers may be manipulated in main memory, thereby greatly enhancing search efficiency.

## Indexed Sequential Search Technique

The *indexed sequential search* technique is also commonly recognized by the acronym *ISAM,* which stands for *indexed sequential access method.* Essentially it involves carefully weighing the disk-dependent factors of blocking and track size to build a partial index. The partial index, unlike some other index structures we will study, does not reduce to one the number of probes that must be made into the actual data.

To continue the analogy between searching for data and searching for a person, the indexed sequential strategy is somewhat like an address book that would lead us to the street on which a person lives but leave it to us to check each of the houses on that street. The ISAM method correspondingly leads us to an appropriate region (often a track or a cylinder containing multiple tracks within a disk pack) and then leaves it to us to search sequentially within that region.

As an example, let us suppose that we can conveniently fit the partial index, or directory, pictured in Figure 9.13 into main memory and that the organization of our disk file allows six records per track. This directory is formed by choosing the highest key value in each six-record track along with a pointer indicating where that track begins. Here our pointers are simply relative record numbers; in practice they could well be a more disk-dependent locator. The strategy to conduct an indexed sequential search follows:

**1.** Search the main memory directory for a key that is greater than or equal to the target.
**2.** Then follow the corresponding pointer out to the disk and there search sequentially until we find a match (success) or the key that the directory maintains as the high key within that particular region (failure).

For the data given in Figure 9.13, this technique would mean that the 36-record file would require no more than six main memory index accesses plus six disk accesses, all of which are located in the same track.

For larger files, it may be advantageous to have more than one level of these directory structures. Consider, for instance, the two-level directory structure for a

◆ FIGURE 9.13

One-level indexed sequential
file

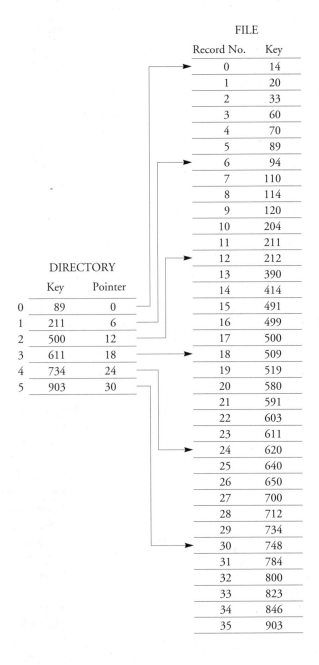

FILE

| Record No. | Key |
|---|---|
| 0 | 14 |
| 1 | 20 |
| 2 | 33 |
| 3 | 60 |
| 4 | 70 |
| 5 | 89 |
| 6 | 94 |
| 7 | 110 |
| 8 | 114 |
| 9 | 120 |
| 10 | 204 |
| 11 | 211 |
| 12 | 212 |
| 13 | 390 |
| 14 | 414 |
| 15 | 491 |
| 16 | 499 |
| 17 | 500 |
| 18 | 509 |
| 19 | 519 |
| 20 | 580 |
| 21 | 591 |
| 22 | 603 |
| 23 | 611 |
| 24 | 620 |
| 25 | 640 |
| 26 | 650 |
| 27 | 700 |
| 28 | 712 |
| 29 | 734 |
| 30 | 748 |
| 31 | 784 |
| 32 | 800 |
| 33 | 823 |
| 34 | 846 |
| 35 | 903 |

DIRECTORY

| | Key | Pointer |
|---|---|---|
| 0 | 89 | 0 |
| 1 | 211 | 6 |
| 2 | 500 | 12 |
| 3 | 611 | 18 |
| 4 | 734 | 24 |
| 5 | 903 | 30 |

file with 216 records given in Figure 9.14. Here we might suppose that storage restrictions allow the entire primary directory to be kept in main memory, the secondary directory to be brought in from a disk file in blocks of six key–pointer pairs each, and the actual data records to be stored six per track. The primary directory divides the file into regions of 36 records each. The key in the primary directory represents the highest valued key in a given 36-record region, but the pointer leads us into the subdirectory instead of the actual file. So, we search the primary directory for a key greater than or equal to the target we are seeking. Once this is done, we follow the primary directory pointer into the secondary directory. Beginning at the position indicated by the primary directory's pointer, we again

◆ FIGURE 9.14
Two-level directory structure

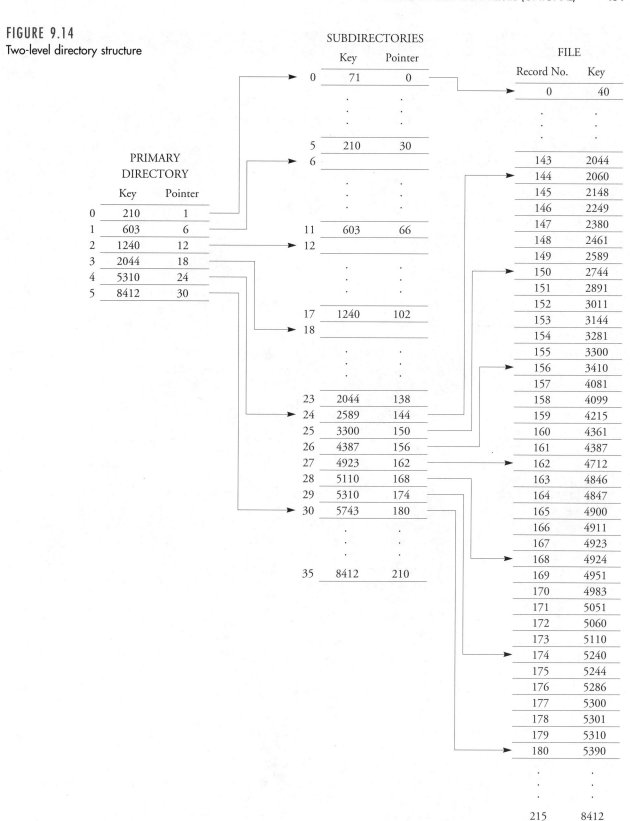

## A NOTE OF INTEREST

### Data Integrity, Concurrent Updates, and Deadlock

The problems of finding and allowing a user to access a particular record in a file are complicated somewhat in a system that allows several users to access that file simultaneously. To see why this is so, it is important to recall that when you actually manipulate a record or part of an index from a file, you really have a copy of that portion of the file in your main memory area. Now suppose that two users are not only accessing the same file simultaneously but also the same record in that file simultaneously. A scenario such as the following could emerge:

The solution used in many systems is that of a *record lock facility*. With such a facility, the user who has a file record in main memory for updating is considered the owner of that record to the exclusion of any other users accessing that record. That lock on the record exists until the user writes the (perhaps altered) record back to the disk file. Hence, in our scenario, User 2 would not have been able immediately to obtain the record for key XYZ. Instead, that user would sit idle in a wait state until the record became available.

Memory Area for User 1                     Memory Area for User 2

XYZ Record          Disk file          XYZ Record

User 1 requests record associated with key XYZ.
User 2 requests record associated with key XYZ.
User 1 updates address field of that record.
User 2 updates inventory field of that record.
User 1 makes change in the file by writing that record to disk.
User 2 makes changes in the file by writing that record to disk.

What will be wrong with the new record that exists in the disk file? Clearly, the address change made by User 1 will have been destroyed when User 2's copy of the record is written back to the disk. We have what is known as a *data integrity* problem caused by the *concurrent updating* of the same record by two users. The situation can become much worse than merely losing an address change. Imagine the havoc created if one of the users deleted the record while the other was processing it or if the portion of the file being simultaneously updated by two users was not a data record but instead part of the file index.

The concurrent update problem must be avoided in any multiuser system if data integrity is to be ensured.

Although the record-locking approach guarantees data integrity, it is not without its own set of problems. For instance, consider the following scenario:

User 1 requests and gets record for key XYZ.
User 2 requests and gets record for key ABC.
To process record XYZ, User 1 needs data associated with record ABC.
Because record is owned by User 2, User 1 must wait in idle state.
To process record ABC, User 2 needs data associated with record XYZ.
Because record is owned by User 1, User 2 must wait in idle state.

Though data integrity has been maintained, we now have two users in an infinite wait state known as a *deadlock* or, more glamorously, *fatal embrace*. The avoidance and/or detection of deadlock situations in a multiuser environment is a nontrivial problem. If you are interested in exploring it more deeply, see Harvey M. Deitel's *An Introduction to Operating Systems*, 2nd ed. (Reading, Mass.: Addison-Wesley, 1990).

search for a key greater than or equal to the target. Notice that fetching one block of six key–pointer pairs from the subdirectory has necessitated one disk access in our hypothetical situation. In return for this single disk access, we are able to subdivide the 36-record region determined by the primary directory into six 6-record regions, each of which will lie entirely on one track by the time we get out to the actual disk file. Following the subdirectory's pointer to the file, we end up with a relatively short sequential search on the storage medium itself. In this example, the maximum number of disk accesses required to find any record would be seven, and six of those would be isolated on one track of the disk.

**Efficiency Considerations for the Indexed Sequential Search.** It should be clear from the preceding discussion that the search efficiency of the indexed sequential technique depends on a variety of factors. Included among them are the following:

- To what degree the directory structures are able to subdivide the actual file
- To what degree the directory structures are able to reside in main memory
- The relationship of data records to physical characteristics of the disk such as blocking factors, track size, cylinder size, and so on.

It should also be clear that the indexed sequential method may not be ideal for a highly volatile file. This is because, as implicitly indicated in Figures 9.13 and 9.14, the actual data records must be physically stored in increasing (or decreasing) key order. The requirement for physical ordering is obviously not conducive to frequent insertions and deletions. In practice, the solution to this problem is that each file subregion, which is ultimately the subject of a sequential search, is equipped with a pointer to an overflow area. Insertions are located in this overflow area and linked to the main sequential search area. As the overflow area builds up, the search efficiency tends to deteriorate. In some applications, this deterioration can be so severe that data processing personnel have been known to refer to the ISAM technique as the intrinsically slow access method.

The way to avoid deterioration is to reorganize the file periodically into a new file with no overflow. However, such reorganization cannot be done dynamically. It requires going through the file in key sequential order and copying it into a new one. Along the way, the indices must be rebuilt, of course. These types of maintenance problems involved with the ISAM structure have led to the development of several more dynamic indexing schemes.

## Binary Search Tree Indexing

The concept of a binary search tree was covered in Chapter 6. The only twist added when the binary tree plays the role of an index is that each node of the tree contains a key and a pointer to the record associated with that key in some larger data aggregate. The advantages of using a binary search tree as an index structure include:

- A search efficiency potentially proportional to $\log_2 n$
- The ability to traverse the list indexed by the tree in key order
- Dynamic insertion and deletion capabilities.

These qualities make the binary search tree the ideal index structure for situations in which the entire tree can fit in main memory. However, if the data collection is so large that the tree index must itself be stored on disk, the efficiency of the structure is less than optimal. This is because each node of the index may lie in a disk block separate from the other nodes and hence require a separate disk access. Using an example of 50,000 keys, a search of a *binary tree index* could require 16 disk accesses. To solve this problem, we would like to cluster those nodes along a given search path into one, or at least relatively few, disk blocks. The *B-tree* index structure is a variation on the tree index that accomplishes this goal.

## B-Tree Indexing

We begin this discussion of B-trees by reminding you that one index entry requires nothing more than a key and a pointer. Moreover, we have assumed that both the key and the pointer are integers, and we continue to operate under this assumption during our discussion of B-trees. We emphasize this point here because, in a B-tree, a given tree node will in fact contain many such key–pointer pairs. This is because a given B-tree node will in fact coincide with one disk block. The idea behind a B-tree is that we will somehow group key–pointer pairs that are related in the search algorithm into a few strategic B-tree nodes, that is, disk blocks. At this point, we make a formal definition; later, we'll clarify this definition via some examples.

**B-tree of order *n*:** A B-tree of order *n* is a structure with the following properties:

1. Every node in the B-tree has sufficient room to store $n - 1$ key–pointer pairs.
2. Additionally, every node has room for $n$ pointers to other nodes in the B-tree (as distinguished from the pointers within key–pointer pairs, which point to the position of a key in the file).
3. Every node except the root must have at least $(n - 1) / 2$ key–pointer pairs stored in it.
4. All terminal nodes are on the same level.
5. If a nonterminal node has $m$ key–pointer pairs stored in it, then it must contain $m + 1$ non-null pointers to other B-tree nodes.
6. For each B-tree node, we require that the key value in key–pointer pair $KP_{i-1}$ be less than the key value in key–pointer pair $KP_i$, that all key–pointer pairs in the node pointed to by $P_{i-1}$ contain keys that are less than the key in $KP_i$, and that all key–pointer pairs in the node pointed to by $P_i$ contain key values that are greater than the key in $KP_i$.

According to property 5 of the definition, we can think of a B-tree node as a list

$$P_0, KP_1, P_1, KP_2, P_2, KP_3, \ldots, P_{m-1}, KP_m, P_m$$

where $P_i$ represents the *i*th pointer to another B-tree node and $KP_i$ represents the *i*th key–pointer pair. Note that a B-tree node will always contain one more pointer to another B-tree node than it does key–pointer pairs. With this picture in mind, the sixth and final property of our definition makes sense. Figure 9.15 illustrates how this rather involved definition applies to a B-tree node with three key–pointer pairs.

◆ FIGURE 9.15

Example of a B-tree node
with three key–pointer pairs

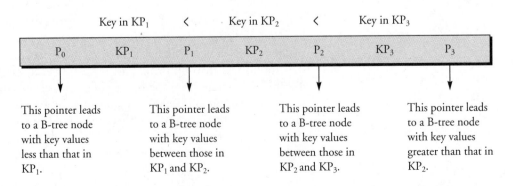

As a further illustration of this definition, a complete B-tree of order 6 serving as an index structure for the 36-record file of Figure 9.13 appears in Figure 9.16. (In this figure, the slash between numbers denotes a key–pointer pair; | denotes a null pointer.) Carefully verify that all six defining properties are satisfied.

◆ **FIGURE 9.16**
B-tree index of order 6 for file in Figure 9.13

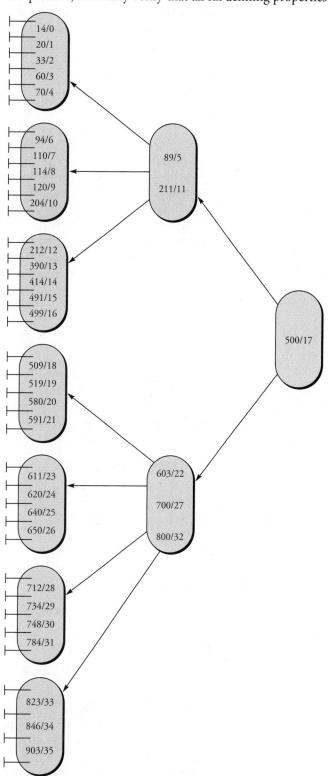

The choice of order 6 for Figure 9.16 was made only for the purposes of making the figure fit on a page of text. In practice, the order chosen would be the maximum number of B-tree pointers and key–pointer pairs that we could fit into one disk block. That is, the choice should be made to force a disk block to coincide with a B-tree node. It is also worth noting that B-trees of order 3 have special application as a data structure apart from indexing considerations. This application is covered in the programming problems at the end of the chapter.

### Efficiency Considerations for B-Tree Indexing.

Let us now consider what is involved in searching a B-tree for a given key. Within the current node (starting at the root), we must search sequentially through the key values in the node until we come to a match, a key value that is greater than the one being sought, or the end of the key values in that particular node. If a match is not made within a particular B-tree node, we have a pointer to follow to an appropriate follow-up node. Again, you should verify this algorithm for several of the keys appearing at various levels of Figure 9.16. The sequential search on keys within a given node may at first seem unappealing. However, the important fact to remember here is that each B-tree node is a disk block that is loaded entirely into main memory. Hence, it may be possible to search sequentially on hundreds of keys within a node in the time it would take to load one new node from disk. Our main concern is to minimize disk accesses, and here we have achieved a worst case search for our 36-entry file in three disk accesses.

What in general is the search efficiency for a B-tree index? It should be clear from the nature of the structure that the maximum number of disk accesses for any particular key will simply be the number of levels in the tree. So the efficiency question really amounts to knowing the maximum number of levels that the six defining criteria would allow for a B-tree containing $n$ key–pointer pairs. That is, this number would be the worst case search efficiency. To determine this number, we use the minimum number of nodes that must be present on any given level. Let $l$ be the smallest integer greater than or equal to $k/2$ where $k$ is the order of the B-tree in question. Then

Level 0 contains at least 1 node.
Level 1 contains at least 2 nodes.
Level 2 contains at least $2l$ nodes.
Level 3 contains at least $2l^2$ nodes.

.
.
.

Level $m$ contains at least $2l^{m-1}$ nodes.

An argument based on Knuth's research (see *Searching and Sorting*, cited in Section 9.1) uses this progression to show that the maximum number of levels (and thus the worst case search efficiency) for $n$ key–pointer pairs is

$$\log_k[(n+1)/2]$$

Thus, a B-tree search has an $O(\log_k n)$ efficiency where $n$ is the number of records and $k$ is the order of the B-tree. Note that this can be considerably better than an $O(\log_2 n)$ search efficiency. As an example, the index for a file of 50,000 records, which would require on the order of 16 disk accesses using a binary tree structure, could be searched with 3 disk accesses using a B-tree of order 250. Note that, given typical block sizes for files, the choice of order 250 for this example is not at all unrealistic.

Unlike ISAM, the B-tree index can dynamically handle insertions and deletions without a resulting deterioration in search efficiency. We next discuss how B-tree insertions are handled; making deletions is left for an exercise. The essential idea behind a B-tree insertion is that we must first determine which bottom-level node should contain the key–pointer pair to be inserted. For instance, suppose that we want to insert the key 742 into the B-tree of Figure 9.16. By allowing this key to walk down the B-tree from the root to the bottom level, we could quickly determine that this key belongs in the node presently containing

```
712/28
734/29
748/30
784/31
```

Since, by the definition of a B-tree of order 6, this node is not presently full, no further disk accesses would be necessary to perform the insertion. We would merely need to determine the next available record space in the actual data file (36 in this case) and then add the key–pointer pair 742/36 to this terminal node, resulting in

```
712/28
734/29
742/36
748/30
784/31
```

A slightly more difficult situation arises when we find that the key–pointer pair we wish to add should be inserted into a bottom-level node that is already full. For instance, this would occur if we attempted to add the key 112 to the B-tree of Figure 9.16. We would load the actual data for this key into file position 37 (given the addition already made in the preceding paragraph) and then determine that the key–pointer pair 112/37 belongs in the bottom-level node

```
94/6
110/7
114/8
120/9
204/10
```

The stipulation that any B-tree node except the root have at least $(n - 1) / 2 = 2$ key–pointer pairs allows us to split this node, creating one new node with two key–pointer pairs and one with three key–pointer pairs. We also have to move one of the key–pointer pairs up to the parent of the present node. The resulting B-tree is given in Figure 9.17.

Although it does not happen in this particular example, note that it would be entirely possible that the movement of a key–pointer pair up to a parent node that is already full would necessitate a split of this parent node, using the same function. Indeed it is possible that key–pointer pairs could be passed all the way up to the root and cause a split of the root. This is in fact how a new level of the tree would be introduced. A split of the root would force the creation of a new root, which would only have one key–pointer pair and two pointers to other B-tree nodes. However, at the root level this is still a sufficient number of pointers to retain the B-tree structure. Because the insertion algorithm for a B-tree requires checking

◆ FIGURE 9.17
B-tree of Figure 9.16 after
insertion of 112/37 and
742/36

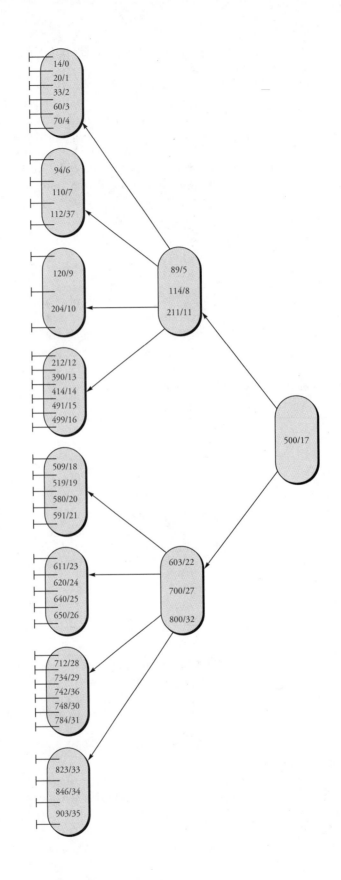

whether a given node is full and potentially moving back up to a parent node, it is convenient to allow space within a node to store both of the following:

- A count of the number of key–pointer pairs in the node
- A back pointer to the node's parent.

## Trie Indexing

In all of the indexing applications we have discussed so far, the keys involved have been integers. In practice, however, we must be prepared to deal with keys of different types. Perhaps the worst case is that of keys that are variable-length character strings. *Trie indexing* has developed as a means of retrieving keys in this worst case. (The term itself is derived from the four middle letters of "retrieve," though it is usually pronounced "try.")

Let us suppose that the strings in the following list represent a set of keys. Each string may be thought of as a last name followed by initials and a delimiting $.

```
ADAMS BT$

COOPER CC$

COOPER PJ$

COWANS DC$

MAGUIRE WH$

MCGUIRE AL$

MEMINGER DD$

SEFTON SD$

SPAN KD$

SPAN LA$

SPANNER DW$

ZARDA JM$

ZARDA PW$
```

An individual node in a trie structure for these keys follows:

$ A B C D E F G H I J K L M N O P Q R S T U V W X Y Z

trie node

It is essentially a fixed-length array of 28 pointers: one for each letter of the alphabet, one for a blank, and one for the delimiter. Each pointer within one of these nodes can lead to one of two entities—either another node within the trie or the actual data record for a given key. Hence it may be convenient to embed a

Boolean flag in each pointer indicating the type of entity to which it is pointing. The trie structure for the preceding list of keys is given in Figure 9.18. In this figure, pointers to nodes labeled as data records lead us outside of the trie structure itself.

The logic behind a trie structure may best be seen by tracing through an example. This search algorithm involves examining the target key on a character-by-character basis. Let us begin by considering the easy case of finding the data record for ADAMS BT$. In this case, we look at A, the first character in the key, and follow the A pointer in the root node to its destination. From what we have previously said, we know that its destination will be either another node within the trie structure or an actual data record. If it were a node within the trie, it would be a node on the search path for all keys that begin with A. In this case, there is only one key in our list that begins with A, so the A pointer in the root node leads us directly to the actual data record for ADAMS BT$.

◆ FIGURE 9.18
Trie index structure

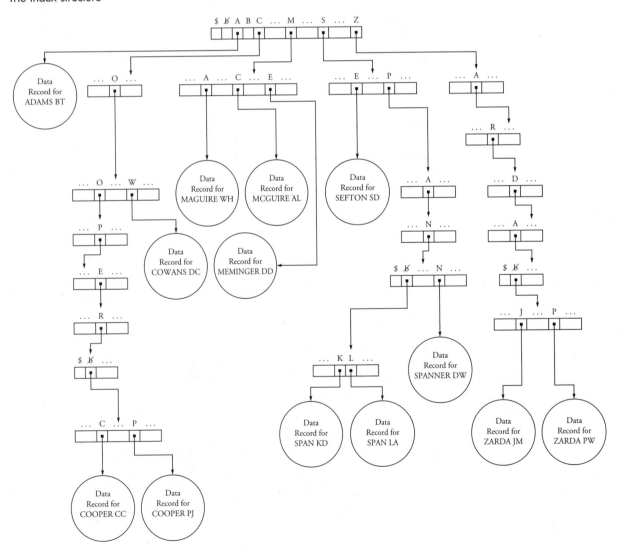

On the other hand, the search path to find the key COOPER CC$ in the trie is somewhat longer. We follow the C pointer from the root node down a level to a node shared by all keys starting with C. From there, the O pointer is followed to a trie node shared by all keys that start with CO. The process continues down level by level, following the O pointer to a trie node shared by all keys starting with COO, then the P pointer to a node for all keys starting with COOP, the E pointer to a node for all keys starting with COOPE, the R pointer to a node for all keys starting with COOPER, and the blank pointer to a node shared by all keys starting with COOPER followed by a blank. Notice that, as each character is read in, we must continue following these pointers from trie node to trie node (instead of from trie node to actual data record) until we finally reach a point where the next character to be read will uniquely define the key. At this point, the key in question need no longer share its pointer with other keys that match it on an initial substring. Hence the pointer may now lead to an actual data record. This is what happens in our example when we read in the next C to form the uniquely defined substring COOPER C.

**Efficiency Considerations for Trie Indexing.** The search efficiency for the trie index is quite easily determined. The worst case occurs when a key is not uniquely defined until its last character is read. In this case, we may have as many disk accesses as there are characters in the key before we finally locate the actual data record. You may have observed, however, that there is another efficiency consideration to take into account when using the trie method. This is the amount of wasted storage in the trie nodes. In our example using a short list of keys, only a small percentage of the available pointers are ever used. In practice, however, a trie would only be used for an extremely large file, such as the list represented by a phone book with names as keys. In such a situation, a much larger number of character combinations occurs and the resulting trie structure is correspondingly much less sparse.

A final point to consider relative to trie indexes is their ability to handle insertions and deletions dynamically. Here, we discuss insertions; deletions are left as an exercise. Insertions may be broken down into two cases. For both we must begin by reading the key to be inserted, character by character, and following the appropriate search path in the trie until

- we come to a trie node which has a vacant pointer in the character position corresponding to the current character of the insertion key.

or

- we come to an actual data record for a key different from the one that is being inserted.

The first case is illustrated by trying to insert the key COLLINS RT$ into the trie of Figure 9.18. We would follow the search path pointers until we came to the trie node shared by all keys starting with CO. At this point, the L pointer is null. The insertion is completed by merely aiming the presently null L pointer to a data record for the key COLLINS RT$. The second case is illustrated by trying to insert the key COOPER PA$ into the trie of Figure 9.18. Here, following the search path of the trie would eventually lead us to the data record for the key COOPER PJ$. The dynamic solution is to get a new trie node, aim the P pointer presently leading to the data record for COOPER PJ$ to this new trie node, and use the A and J pointers in the new trie node to lead us to data records for COOPER PA$

◆ **FIGURE 9.19**
Trie of Figure 9.18 after
inserting COLLINS RT$ and
COOPER PA$

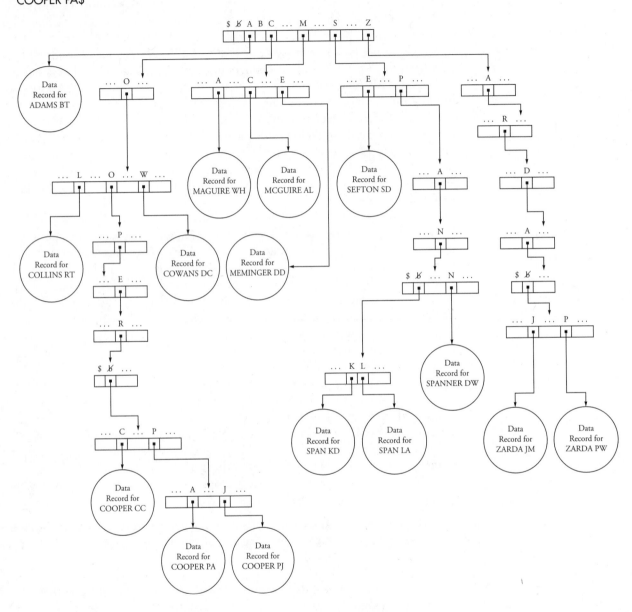

and COOPER PJ$, respectively. Both the COLLINS RT$ and COOPER PA$
insertions are shown with the resulting trie in Figure 9.19.

**EXERCISES 9.3**

**1. a.** Suppose that the records associated with keys 810, 430, 602, 946, 289, 106,
and 732 are stored in positions 0, 1, 2, 3, 4, 5, and 6 respectively of a file.
Draw a B-tree index of order 8 for this file.

**b.** Suppose the key 538 then arrives for insertion in position 8. Redraw your B-tree
of order 8 after this insertion.

2. Suppose that the following strings arrive for insertion into a trie index:

CARTER
HERNANDEZ
HERMAN
HERMANSKI
HERSCHEL
HALL
CARSON
CARSWELL
CARSEN

   **a.** Draw the trie index.

   **b.** Draw the index after CARSWELL and HERMANSKI have been deleted.

3. Discuss the key deletion strategy for B-trees. Write a function to implement your strategy.

4. Discuss a key deletion strategy for trie indexes. Write a function to implement your strategy.

5. Carefully read your system reference material concerning the specifics of how disk file records are blocked. Then explain how this knowledge would influence your decisions in the construction of

   **a.** a B-tree index structure

   **b.** a trie index structure

   **c.** a bucket hashing structure

   **d.** an ISAM index structure

6. All of the search strategies we have discussed assume a key that is uniquely valued. That is, no two records have the same value for their key field. In practice, this will not always be the case. We may have duplicate keys. For instance, a list of personnel records may contain two records for different people with the same name. In a carefully worded statement, discuss how each of the search strategies we have covered would have to be modified to perform a duplicate key search. What effect would these modifications have on the performance of the algorithm?

7. Develop a function to search a list via ISAM. Initially assume just one directory. Then alter the function so that it would work with one subdirectory.

8. Devise functions to handle insertions into and deletions from a list maintained by the indexed sequential method. Do the strategies reflected by these functions require any modifications in your answers to Exercise 7? If so, explain the nature of these modifications.

9. Write the algorithm to insert a key into a B-tree.

10. Write an algorithm to insert a key and its data record into a trie.

---

**FOCUS ON PROGRAM DESIGN**

A theme of the Focus on Program Design section in the two previous chapters has been the development of programs that allow us to experiment with algorithms. Such programs are extremely useful for algorithms whose analysis defies purely mathematical techniques. Certainly the strategy of hashing, presented in Section 9.1, falls into this category of algorithms. The efficiency of hashing is dependent on a variety of factors: the randomness with which your hashing function scatters keys into the record space, the amount of space you are willing to sacrifice to empty storage locations, and the effectiveness of your collision-processing strategy in reducing clustering.

Because of hashing's dependency on these factors, an experimental tool for testing various hashing strategies can be very valuable in predicting how effective hashing will be for a particular application. In this section, we discuss the design of such an experimental program for situations in which we wish to study the effectiveness of hashing on keys that are strings.

As with the previous chapter's Focus on Program Design program, we want to choose between three forms of input for our experimentation:

1. A sequence of randomly generated string keys
2. A sequence of string keys that we enter interactively, so that we can enter specific data sets particularly relevant to our experimentation
3. A sequence of string keys read one per line from a file.

From last chapter's program, we will also borrow the facility to save a particularly interesting data set in a text file form that can later be read by the program. This will allow you to fine-tune the algorithm by altering the hashing function or selecting a different collision-processing method and then testing the new program with the same set of data. An example of such experimental runs with the program follows.

## First Run: Hash Table with Record Space for 40, 30 Slots Filled with Random Strings.

```
How large is record space for hash table? 40
Choose method for loading hash table:

        1 - Load table with random strings
        2 - Interactively load the table
        3 - Load the table from a file

Enter 1, 2 or 3 → 1

Enter number of values in table → 30
Print the table? (Y/N) → y
NONEMPTY SLOTS OF THE TABLE:

        ARRAY[ 2] = \TUFqY]Y-tlLcTIxGRnPHUjikDzoxy
        ARRAY[ 3] = UVo{texGxxYSbwNMqI\UoGKR-YYdDe
        ARRAY[ 4] = Qrfh[oDFXECsJOdcotqoXaoD{paxhN
        ARRAY[ 5] = OTSK{onLIBZ^U'VfDwdKrmOhqbSjBx
        ARRAY[ 6] = MID\argowZc-Z[vMF[hZzBxkJiohi
        ARRAY[ 7] = Pr]Rncs{CXOREpjkyYRtmmFRaXHbWv
        ARRAY[10] = 'kgPl^[lJrmTsSfbw\JBXrVOVDTose
        ARRAY[14] = O'S'[SL^sVJn'Pdw'aJ^votElbqLFZ
        ARRAY[15] = J[lsvd{LwcRvQyiF{SPPKLDyrIIpGl
        ARRAY[16] = LkYsfFhnyvdKPnPe'Niiup{xXHMxGj
        ARRAY[18] = pKiWMJzLLNfho-jYGcPxJzVsDRDiqE
        ARRAY[19] = YC's^ZPOXZEnHe{BnbI'Xp'uEvOgr\
        ARRAY[20] = bT{bZGcKmhwGfdFxH]IOPrIbHQJ]oS
        ARRAY[21] = NILYPSQnhr-H'u{CuDnErrunYr[kif
        ARRAY[22] = \]kmBdbnLhSQBN{ncqjtwe\II\WFPe
        ARRAY[23] = fByLV{fqOhOLSfotfZYZReHYTn{Wp\
        ARRAY[24] = ^NSsPsYp\{kSKOUw[ISOWOjnzHbIVU
```

```
ARRAY[25] = eLWstIC'ZLPsUwHXgvhk\jzWpsHwlx
ARRAY[26] = IxV'GzjKFeq[IXptTukEjhdbuQ-wSQ
ARRAY[27] = HPyGpLkGZINJEh-pnVghemjPgZlJxx
ARRAY[28] = XPDHfZTwyCzkGCMokZNEv]dCllXN
ARRAY[29] = GvpO^bWgPubRY]\jEsI[OddGCRzM^]
ARRAY[30] = EZzxgV'ih'nLJ-nCLsdnqISzHvyMJl
ARRAY[31] = qwbs{HblUTCIwEzfox-nB^iHfRbPmu
ARRAY[32] = KWQcS[WdJSyZl]FeJbpl\HMVjiTCzs
ARRAY[35] = RUhjdEgb{x]d''NWPXx\OGjZaMcpOP
ARRAY[36] = ysb[z-gCgghfDskqOiqKRiFOPZ'bM^
ARRAY[37] = PngO'I\efYtwfJykbvnc-PWE'mqkiz
ARRAY[38] = KB]Uiq]kLxmylwUdXUTLMmlSOkh-cq
ARRAY[39] = iJtgsTbicsFueT]{uRqZdRKZGwdc\m
```

```
Average length for successful search 2.13
Average length for unsuccessful search 4.87


Save the input values for this table? (Y/N)→ y
Name for save file → test.dat
Another table? (Y/N) → n
```

## Second Run: Now Adjust Hashing Function and/or Collision Processing, and Run Again

```
How large is record space for hash table? 40
Choose method for loading hash table:


        1 - Load table with random strings
        2 - Interactively load the table
        3 - Load the table from a file


Enter 1, 2 or 3 → 3


Enter the name of the file → test.dat
Print the table? (Y/N) → n
Average length for successful search 1.92
Average length for unsuccessful search 4.76


Save the input values for this table? (Y/N) → n
Another table? (Y/N) → n
```

Note the slight improvement in efficiency for the second run.

A modular structure chart for the program appears in Figure 9.20. Notice from the modular structure chart that a package of queue modules is used in the program. As a sequence of string keys is loaded into the hash table by the program, the keys are also placed on the queue. Then, after the hash table has been loaded, these keys are removed from the queue. As each key is removed from the queue, we search the hash table for it, accumulating a profiling counter as the search for the key is performed. The key is then returned to the tail of the queue. If the user chooses to save the sequence of string keys to a text file, we merely proceed through the queue, writing each key to the file as it is removed from the queue.

To accumulate the statistics for the average unsuccessful search, the program generates a fixed number of additional random keys—assuming that the probability

◆ FIGURE 9.20

Modular structure chart for hashing experimentation program

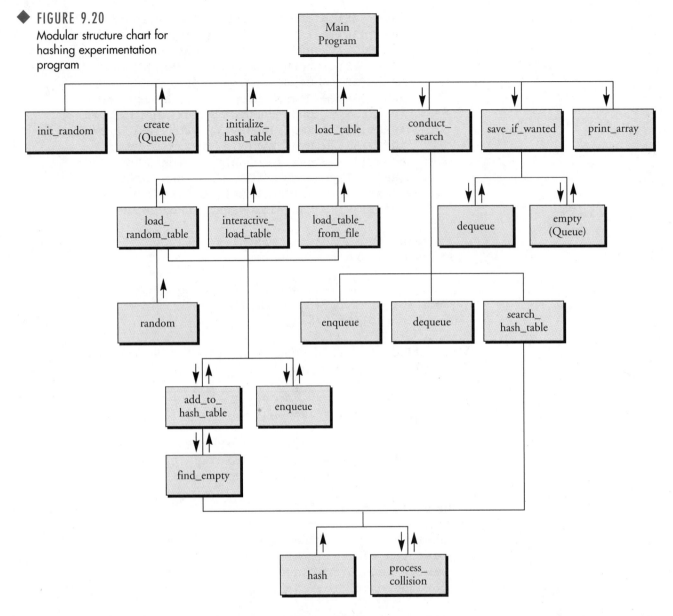

of any such key matching one already in the table is virtually zero. The program is exercised by sending each of these randomly generated keys through the search algorithm. A profiling accumulator for unsuccessful searches is maintained as these keys are processed.

A first-level pseudocode development for the main program is given by:

Initialize the random number generator (see Appendix 6)
Create the queue used to store a copy of keys in order of generation
Initialize the value used to flag an empty slot
Do
        Initialize hash table to all empty slots
        Load the table of a specified logical record space with
            number of keys specified by user, also returning a queue
            containing the sequence of keys generated

If the user wants, print the hash table
Conduct searches: accumulate and print profiling counters
　　for successful and unsuccessful searches
Save the sequence of keys from queue to a file if the user
　　wants
Inquire if the user wants to load another table
While user indicates no more tables to load

Refinement of this pseudocode into C++ yields the following main program:

```cpp
// Program file: focus.cpp

// This program allows users to experiment with hashing on
// an array implementation of a list of strings. A hashing
// function is provided, but users are encouraged to
// try their own hashing functions. The current implementation
// makes use of the linear collision processing strategy, but
// is written in such a way that other strategies can be substituted easily.

// The program is designed to create the list of strings
// in one of three ways: allow a user to interactively
// specify the contents of the list, generate a random list,
// or read a previously saved list in from a file. The
// program will also save the contents of the list for later
// reuse if desired.

// The data file created by the program when a table is saved is
// simply a text file with one element of the table per line of
// the file. Similarly, the program expects any file from which
// it is to read a table to have this format. Internally, the
// program uses a queue to store the incoming table elements
// in the order they arrive so that they can be saved to the
// file in that same order.

#include <iostream.h>
#include <fstream.h>

#include "strlib.h"
#include "queue.h"
#include "random.h"

const int MAX_HASH_TABLE_SIZE = 2000;

float average_search_length;                    // Global statistic
random_generator generator;                     // Random number generator

#include "hash.h"

int main()
{
    string empty_slot("");                      // String for empty hash table entry
    hash_table<string> table(empty_slot);       // Hash table
```

```
    queue<string> copies;              // Copies of keys generated
    char query;                        // User's response
    ifstream input_file;               // Input file stream
    ofstream output_file;              // Output file stream

    do
    {
            load_table(table, choice_of_load, copies, input_file);
            cout << "Print the table? (Y/N) → ";
            cin >> query;
            if ((query == 'Y') || (query == 'y'))
                    print_table(table, 1);
            conduct_search(table);
            save_if_wanted(copies, choice_of_load, output_file);
            cout << "Another table? (Y/N) → ";
            cin >> query;
    } while ((query == 'Y') || (query == 'y'));
    return 0;
}
```

Specifications for individual modules in the program follow. You will implement these specifications in the programming problems, thereby providing yourself with a means of exploring the effectiveness of a variety of hashing functions and collision-processing methods.

**Module:** load_table

**Task:** Determine logical size of record space in table and choice for loading. Dispatch to load_random_table, interactive_load_table, or load_table_from_file, respectively.

**Inputs:** table, an empty hash table, and copies, an empty queue.

**Outputs:** An integer indicating the user's choice for loading the hash table: 1 for randomly generated strings, 2 for interactively loaded strings, 3 for strings read from file. Table is returned loaded with strings generated by chosen method. Copies contains sequence of strings generated by chosen method.

**Module:** load_random_table

**Task:** Inquire as to number of strings to generate.
  For each string,
    Fill it with randomly generated characters.
    Call on add_to_hash_table to load string into table.
    Call on enqueue operation to add string to copies queue.

**Outputs:** Hash table loaded with randomly generated strings and a queue copies, which contains each of the strings in the order of their generation.

**Module:** interactive_load_table

**Task:** Inquire as to number of strings that will be entered.
  For each string,
    Allow user to enter it interactively.
    Call on add_to_hash_table to load string into table.
    Call on enqueue operation to add string to copies queue.

**Outputs:** Hash table loaded with strings entered interactively by user and a queue copies, which contains each of the strings in the order they were entered.

**Module:** load_table_from_file

**Task:** Inquire as to name of file to load.

    while not end of input file

        Read string from file.

        Call on add_to_hash_table to load string into table.

        Call on enqueue operation to add string to copies queue.

**Outputs:** Hash table loaded with strings read from file and a queue copies, which contains each of the strings in the order they were read.

**Module:** conduct_search

**Task:** Perform empirical testing on hashing method for this particular data.

    For each queue in copies queue.

        Dequeue that key.

        Call on search_hash_table to find that key, accumulating a profiling count of number of probes into table that are required to find the key.

        Enqueue that key back into copies queue.

    Report on average length for successful searches conducted in first step

    For a fixed number of unsuccessful searches

        Randomly generate a key not in table.

        Call on search_hash_table to attempt to find that key, accumulating a profiling count of the number of probes into table that are required to determine that the key cannot be located.

    Report profiling information for unsuccessful searches.

**Inputs:** Hash table. Copies queue containing string keys in order generated by load_table module.

**Module:** save_if_wanted

**Task:** Inquire if user wants to save this data set for further exploration. If user wants to save and data set was not originally loaded from file write copies queue to file in form compatible with load_table_from_file module.

**Inputs:** Copy queue containing keys in order originally generated.

**Module:** print_table

**Task:** Iterate through table from low to high, printing nonempty slots.

**Inputs:** Hash table. Low and high: indices of table between which nonempty table positions are to be printed.

**RUNNING, DEBUGGING AND TESTING HINTS**

1. When using hashing as a search strategy, provide yourself with a means of experimenting with your hashing function and collision-processing strategy. This will allow you to tailor your program to the particular kind of keys that are stored in the hash table.

2. Searching for data in a random access file involves different criteria than searching for data in main memory. Programs that search for data in random access files should minimize file accesses at the expense of main memory accesses. Indexed searches provide ways of doing this.

3. If a search program has to handle duplicate keys, that is, different records associated with the same key value, the search algorithm will have to be adjusted appropriately. Be sure you know and decide in advance whether this added complexity is necessary.

## SUMMARY

### Key Terms

boundary folding
buckets
clustering
collision
density-dependent search
   techniques
digit/character extraction
division-remainder technique
folding

hashing
hashing function
index
key-to-address transformation
linear collision processing
linked collision processing
overflow area
prime hash area

quadratic collision processing
randomized storage
rehashing collision processing
sectors
shift folding
synonyms
tracks

### Key Terms (Optional)

binary tree index
B-tree
concurrent updating
data integrity

deadlock
fatal embrace
indexed sequential access
   method (ISAM)

indexed sequential search
record lock facility
trie indexing

### Key Concepts

◆ The following table gives a concise synopsis of the search strategies that have been discussed in this and earlier chapters. Additional comments emphasize particular strengths or weaknesses of the strategy in terms of the one-key table operations we have considered throughout the text.

| Method | Efficiency ($n$ = number of records) | Other Components Regarding One-Key Table Operations |
| --- | --- | --- |
| Binary | $O(\log_2 n)$ | Data must be maintained in physical order, hence making insertions and deletions inefficient. |
| Binary tree index | $O(\log_2 n)$ index probes, 1 file probe | Guaranteeing this efficiency requires height balancing. |
| B-tree index order $k$ | Worst case requires $1 + \log_k[(n + 1)/2]$ disk accesses for index | Choose $k$ so that index node coincides with disk block. |
| Indexed sequential | $O$(size of index) index probes, $O[n/(\text{size of index})]$ file probes | Index and file require physical ordering to maintain efficiency. |
| Linear hashing | Average successful: $(1/2) * [1 + 1/(1 - D)]$ <br> Average unsuccessful: $(1/2) * [1 + 1/(1 - D)^2]$ <br> where density $D = n/\mathtt{RECORD\_SPACE}$ | Data not maintained in any order. |
| Linked hashing | Average successful: $1 + D/2$ <br> Average unsuccessful: $D$ (where $\mathtt{RECORD\_SPACE}$ used in computation of $D$ is that in primary hash area) | Data not maintained in any order. |
| Quadratic hashing | Average successful: $1 - \log_e(1 - D) - (D/2)$ <br> Average unsuccessful: $1/(1 - D) - D - \log_e(1 - D)$ | Data not maintained in any order. |
| Rehashing | Average successful: $-(1/D) * \log_e(1 - D)$ <br> Average unsuccessful: $1/(1 - D)$ | Data not maintained in any order. |
| Sequential | $O(n)$ | |
| Trie index | $O$(number of characters in target) | Specifically suited for character strings. |

◆ In addition to hashing, other search strategies specifically oriented toward file structures include indexed sequential search, B-trees, and tries.

◆ As an implementation strategy for one-key tables, hashing fares very well in all of the operations except ordering. It thus represents a very viable addition to the list implementation strategies discussed in earlier chapters: array or random files with binary search, linked lists, and binary trees.

## PROGRAMMING PROBLEMS AND PROJECTS

1. Complete the program designed in this chapter's Focus on Program Design section. Then use the program as a means of conducting experiments on hashing. In your experiments, you should try a variety of hashing functions and collision-processing strategies. You might also try to adjust the generation of random strings so that, although still random, the strings conform to rules for particular kinds of data. That is, if the data consist of names of the form

   **COOPER, J. C.**

   the random generation of characters could be modified based on the probabilities of certain letters being used and on the average length of last names. Write up a report in which you analyze each of the hashing functions and collision-processing strategies you use. Back up your analysis with empirical profiling data obtained from the **conduct_search** module of your program.

2. Implement the registrar's system described in Example 3.1 using hashing as a list maintenance technique. Be sure that you devise an appropriate strategy to output the ordered listings that the registrar must have.

3. Implement the Wing-and-a-Prayer flight/pilot database (Focus on Program Design, Chapter 2) using the implementation technique described in Section 9.2. For an added challenge, assume that the rows of the flight/pilot table are indexed by pilot name instead of pilot number. How could this complication be handled in a way that minimizes the memory needed to store the implementation of a two-key table?

4. A B-tree of order 3 is often called a 2–3 tree since each node has 2 or 3 children. Because of its low order, a 2–3 tree is not particularly applicable as a file index. However, if we store up to two actual data records in each node instead of up to two key–pointer pairs, then a 2–3 tree becomes an alternative to an ordered binary tree for implementing a list. Develop search, insertion, and deletion algorithms for such a 2–3 tree structure. Compare its performance characteristics with those of an ordered binary tree.

5. Implement the registrar's system of Problem 2 using a 2–3 tree representation of a list (see Problem 4.)

6. Wing-and-a-Prayer Airlines has the records of all its customers stored in the following form:
   - Last name
   - First name
   - Address
   - Arbitrarily long list of flights on which reservations have been booked.

   Using a trie index, write a search-and-retrieval program that will allow input of a customer's last name (and, if necessary, the first name and address to resolve conflicts created by matching last names) and then output all flights on which that customer has booked reservations.

7. SuperScout Inc. is a nationwide scouting service for college football talent to which the Bay Area Brawlers professional team subscribes. As the pool of college talent increases in size, SuperScout has found that its old record-keeping system has dete-

riorated considerably in its ability to quickly locate the scouting record associated with a given player in its file. Rewrite their scouting record system using a trie to look up the record location of the data associated with a given player's name.

8. Using a large collection of randomly generated keys, write a series of programs that will test various hashing functions you develop. In particular, your programs should report statistics on the number of collisions generated by each hashing function. This information could be valuable in guiding future decisions about which hashing functions and techniques are most effective for your particular system.

9. Consider a student data record that consists of

   - Student identification number
   - Student name
   - State of residence
   - Sex.

   Choose an index structure to process a file of such records. Then write a program to maintain such a file as a one-key table.

10. Suppose that data records for a phone book file consist of a key field containing both name and address, and a field containing the phone number for that key. Devise an appropriate index for such a file. Then write a program which calls for input of

    a. A complete key.
    b. If a complete key is not available, as much of the initial portion of a key as the inquirer is able to provide.

    In the case of part a, your program should output the phone number corresponding to the unique key. In the case of part b, have your program output all keys (and their phone numbers) that match the provided initial portion.

11. Consider the following problem faced in the development of a compiler. The source program contains many character-string symbols such as variable names, function names, and so on. Each of these character-string symbols has associated with it various attributes such as memory location, data type, and so on. However, it would be too time consuming and awkward for a compiler to actually manipulate character strings. Instead, each string should be identified with an integer that is viewed as being equivalent to the string for the purpose of compiler manipulation. In addition to serving as a compact equivalent form of a string symbol within the source program, this integer can also serve as a direct pointer into a table of attributes for that symbol. Devise such a transformation that associates a string with an integer, and which in turn serves as a pointer into a table of attributes. Test the structure(s) you develop by using them in a program that scans a source program written in a language such as C++. You will in effect have written the symbol table modules for a compiler.

12. Write a spelling checker program. Such a program must scan a file of text, looking up each word it finds in a dictionary of correctly spelled words. When a word cannot be found in the dictionary, the spelling checker should convey this fact to its user, giving the user the opportunity to take one of the following steps:

    a. Skip the word.
    b. Change the spelling of the word in the text file.
    c. Add the word to the dictionary so it will not be reported as incorrectly spelled in the future.

    Since the dictionary for such a program will be searched frequently and is likely to become quite large, an efficient search algorithm is an absolute necessity. One possibility in this regard is to use a trie index with pointers into a large string workspace instead of the pointers to data records described in Section 9.3. Test your program with a text file and dictionary large enough to handle all of the possibilities your algorithm and data structure may encounter.

**13.** If you solved one of the problems from Chapter 2 that involved maintaining a one-key table, redo that problem using hashing combined with linked lists as an implementation technique. When finished, write a report in which you empirically compare the performance of your two implementations.

**14.** If you solved one of the problems from Chapter 2 that involved maintaining a two-key table, redo that problem using hashing of row and column indices as an implementation technique. When finished, write a report in which you empirically compare the performance of your two implementations.

# Appendixes

# Appendix 1
# Reserved Words

The following words have predefined meanings in C++ and cannot be changed. The words in bolface are discussed in the text. The other words are discussed in Stanley B. Lippman, *C++ Primer,* 2nd edition, Reading, MA: Addison-Wesley Publishing Company, 1993.

| | | | | | |
|---|---|---|---|---|---|
| asm | continue | **float** | **new** | **signed** | try |
| auto | **default** | **for** | **operator** | sizeof | **typedef** |
| **break** | **delete** | **friend** | **private** | static | union |
| **case** | **do** | goto | **protected** | **struct** | **unsigned** |
| catch | **double** | **if** | **public** | **switch** | virtual |
| **char** | **else** | inline | register | template | **void** |
| **class** | **enum** | **int** | **return** | **this** | volatile |
| **const** | extern | **long** | **short** | throw | **while** |

# Appendix 2
# Some Useful Library Functions

Some of the most commonly used library functions in the first course in computer science come from the libraries **math, ctype,** and **string**. Descriptions of the most important functions in each of these libraries is presented in the following five tables.

math

| Function Declaration | Purpose |
| --- | --- |
| double acos(double x); | Returns arc cosine for $x$ in range -1 to +1 |
| double asin(double x); | Returns arc sine for $x$ in range -1 to +1 |
| double atan(double x); | Returns arc tangent of $x$ |
| double atan2(double y, double x); | Returns arc tangent of $y/x$ |
| double ceil(double x); | Rounds $x$ up to next highest integer |
| double cos(double x); | Returns cosine of $x$ |
| double cosh(double x); | Returns hyberbolic cosine of $x$ |
| double exp(double x); | Returns $e$ to the $x$th power |
| double exp(double x); | Returns absolute value of $x$ |
| double floor(double x); | Rounds $x$ down to next lowest integer |
| double fmod(double x, double y); | Returns remainder of $x/y$ |
| double ldexp(double x, double exp); | Returns $x$ times 2 to the power of exp |
| double log(double x); | Returns natural logarithm of $x$ |
| double log10(double x); | Returns base 10 logarithm of $x$ |
| double pow(double x, double y); | Returns $x$ raised to power of $y$ |
| double sin(double x); | Returns sine of $x$ |
| double sinh(double x); | Returns hyberbolic sine of $x$ |
| double sqrt(double x); | Returns square root of $x$ |
| double tan(double x); | Returns tangent of $x$, in radians |
| double tanh(double x); | Returns hyperbolic tangent of $x$ |

`ctype`

| Function Declaration | Purpose |
| --- | --- |
| `int isalnum(int ch);` | ch is letter or digit |
| `int isalpha(int ch);` | ch is letter |
| `int iscntrl(int ch);` | ch is control character |
| `int isdigit(int ch);` | ch is digit (0-9) |
| `int isgraph(int ch);` | ch is printable but not ' ' |
| `int islower(int ch);` | ch is lowercase letter |
| `int isprint(int ch);` | ch is printable |
| `int ispunct(int ch);` | ch is printable but not ' ' or alpha |
| `int isspace(int ch);` | ch is a whitespace character |
| `int isupper(int ch);` | ch is uppercase letter |
| `int isxdigit(int ch);` | ch is hexadecimal digit |
| `int tolower(int ch);` | Returns lowercase of ch |
| `int toupper(int ch);` | Returns uppercase of ch |

`string`

| Function declaration | Purpose |
| --- | --- |
| `int *strcat(int *s1, const int *s2);` | Appends copy of s2 to end of s1 |
| `int strcmp(const int *s1,`<br>`    const int *s2);` | Compares s1 and s2 |
| `int *strcpy(int *s1, const int *s2);` | Copies s2 to s1, including '\0' |
| `int strlen(const int *s);` | Returns length of s, not including '\0' |

# Appendix 3
# Syntax Diagrams

The following syntax diagrams correspond to the syntax forms used to describe the features of C++ discussed in the text. Two points of caution are in order. First, the diagrams in this appendix by no means represent an exhaustive description of C++. Second, many of the features discussed in this text have more than one syntactically correct construction (for example, **main** can be preceded by either **int** or **void**, but the C++ programming community prefers **int**). By confining your attention to preferred ways of using a small subset of features, we hope to place your focus on concepts rather than syntax. Students wanting to learn more features of C++ or other ways of expressing them are referred to Stanley B. Lippman, *C++ Primer,* 2nd edition, Reading, MA: Addison-Wesley Publishing Company, 1993.

The terms enclosed in ovals in the diagrams refer to program components that literally appear in programs, such as operator symbols and reserved words. The terms enclosed in boxes refer to program components that require further definition, either by another diagram or by reference to the text. The syntax of terms for which there are no diagrams, such as **identifier**, **number**, **string**, and **character**, should be familiar to anyone who has read this text.

**Main program module**

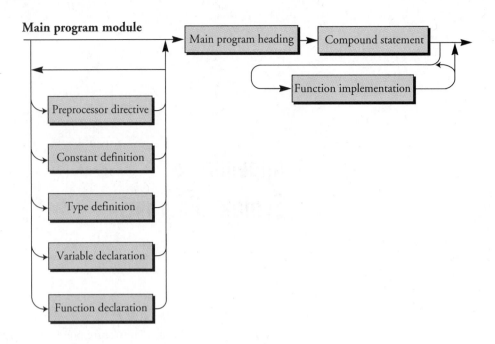

**Preprocessor directive**

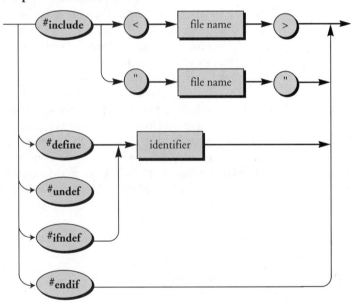

**Constant definition**

## Type definition

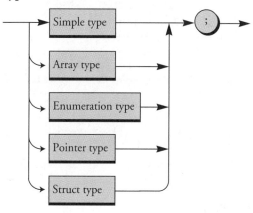

## Simple type

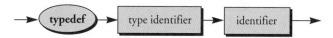

## Array type

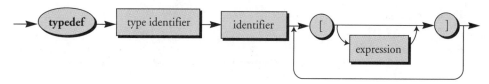

## Enumeration type

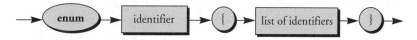

## Pointer type

## Struct type

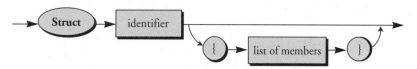

## List of members

**Variable declaration**

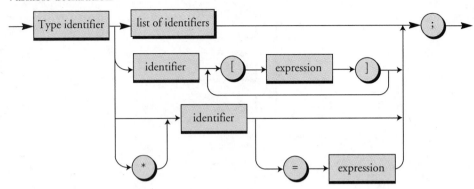

**List of identifiers**

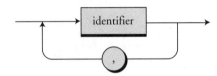

**Function declaration**

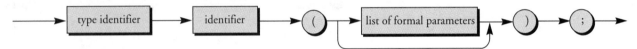

**Main program heading**

**Compound statement**

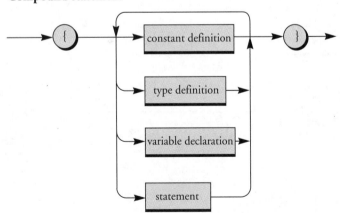

**Statement**

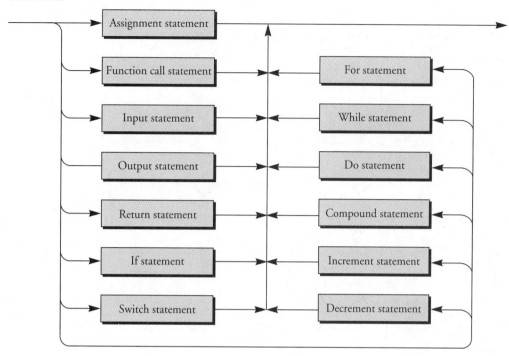

**Assignment statement**

**Function call statement**

**Input statement**

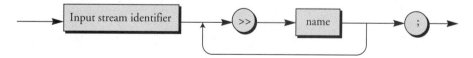

**Output statement**

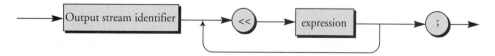

**Return statement**

**If statement**

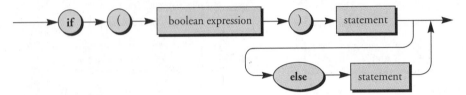

**Switch statement**

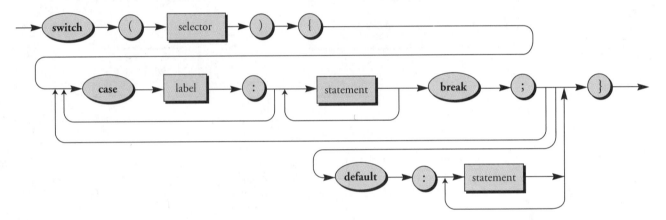

**For statement**

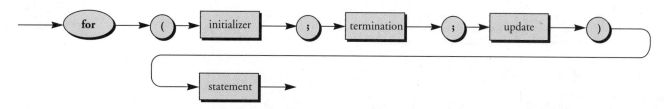

**While statement**

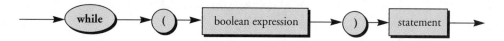

**Do statement**

**Increment statement**

**Decrement statement**

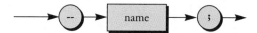

**Function implementation**

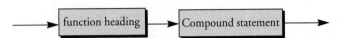

**Function heading**

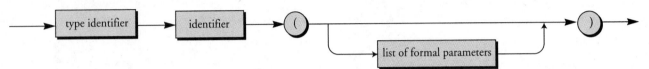

**List of formal parameters**

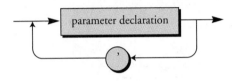

**Parameter declaration**

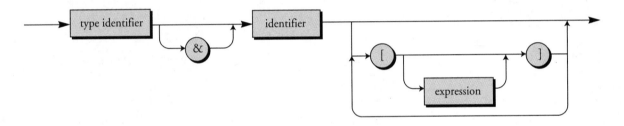

**Expression**

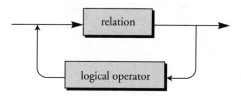

**Relation**

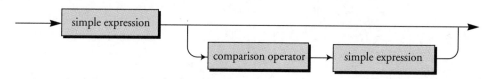

**Simple expression**

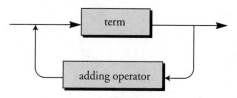

**Term**

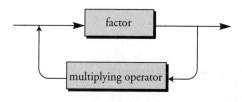

**Factor**

**Primary**

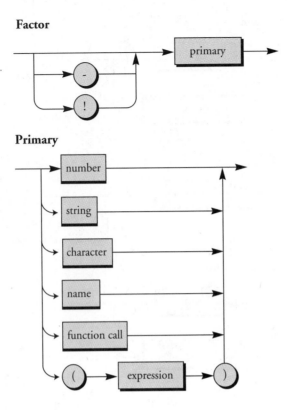

**Name**

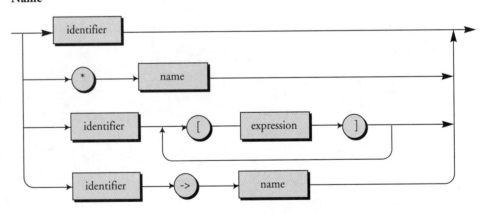

**Function call**

**List of actual parameters**

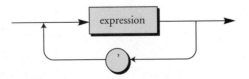

**Logical operator**

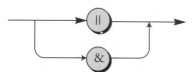

**Adding operator**

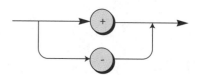

**Comparison operator**

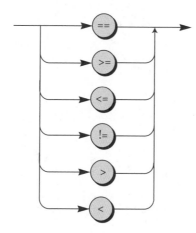

**Multiplying operator**

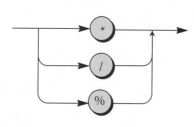

**Class declaration module**

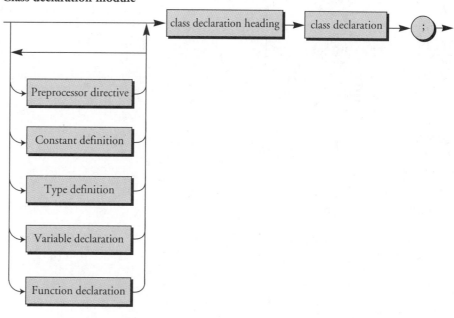

**Class declaration heading**

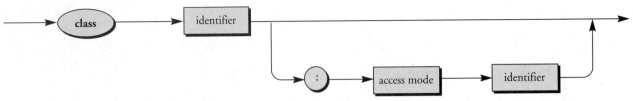

**Class declaration**

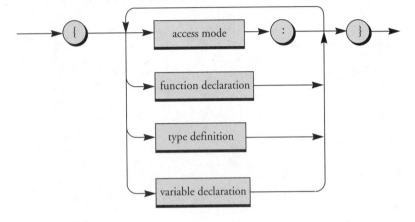

**Access mode**

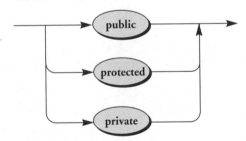

# Appendix 4
# The ASCII Character Set

The table included here shows the ordering of the ASCII character set. Note only printable characters are shown. Ordinals without character representations either do not have standard representation or are associated with unprintable control characters. The blank is denoted by " ♭ ".

The American Standard Code for Information Interchange (ASCII)

| Left Digit(s) | Right Digit | | | | | | | | | |
|---|---|---|---|---|---|---|---|---|---|---|
| | 0 | 1 | 2 | 3 | 4 | 5 | 6 | 7 | 8 | 9 |
| 3 | | | ♭ | ! | " | # | $ | % | & | ' |
| 4 | ( | ) | * | + | , | – | . | / | 0 | 1 |
| 5 | 2 | 3 | 4 | 5 | 6 | 7 | 8 | 9 | : | ; |
| 6 | < | = | > | ? | @ | A | B | C | D | E |
| 7 | F | G | H | I | J | K | L | M | N | O |
| 8 | P | Q | R | S | T | U | V | W | X | Y |
| 9 | Z | [ | \ | ] | ^ | — | ` | a | b | c |
| 10 | d | e | f | g | h | i | j | k | l | m |
| 11 | n | o | p | q | r | s | t | u | v | w |
| 12 | x | y | z | { | \| | } | ~ | | | |

*Codes < 32 or > 126 are nonprintable.

# Appendix 5
# Some Useful Format Flags

The use of the manipulators **setw, setprecision, fixed,** and **showpoint** to format output occurs in several places in the text. Because the use of **fixed** and **showpoint** in C++ has not been standardized, the statement

```
cout << fixed << showpoint;
```

may not have the desired effect of displaying real numbers in fixed point format with trailing zeros in some implementations of C++. However, the following way of specifying the same kind of format is standard, though not as simple:

```
cout << setiosflags (ios::fixed | ios::showpoint);
```

The **setiosflags** manipulator takes a list of flags as a parameter. The general form for using **setiosflags** is

setiosflags($<flag_1>$ | $<flag_2>$ | ... | $<flag_n>$)

**setiosflags** also works with output file streams, as in the following statement:

```
output_file << setiosflags(ios::fixed | ios::showpoint);
```

Some useful flags are listed in the following table:

| Flag Name | Meaning |
| --- | --- |
| ios::showpoint | Display decimal point with trailing zeros |
| ios::fixed | Display real numbers in fixed point notation |
| ios::scientific | Display real numbers in floating point notation |
| ios::right | Display values right justified |

# Appendix 6
# A Random Number Generator

Most programming languages currently in widespread use provide a function for generating random numbers. C++ provides a library function, `rand()`, that returns an integer between 0 and the compiler-dependent constant **RAND_MAX**, inclusive. Both the function and the constant are declared in the library header file `stdlib.h`. Unfortunately, the numbers generated by `rand` are not as random as we would like. The reason for this is that the number returned by `rand` depends on an initial value, called a *seed*, that is the same for each run of a program. Thus, the sequence of random numbers generated by a program that uses this method will be exactly the same on each run of the program.

To help solve this problem, another function, **srand(seed)**, also declared in `stdlib.h`, allows an application to specify the initial value used by `rand` at program start up. Using this method, two runs of a program that use different values for **seed** will thus receive different sequences of random numbers. The problem then becomes one of providing an arbitrary seed value. Rather than force a user to enter this value interactively, most applications obtain it by reading the current time from the computer's internal clock. The C++ function `clock()`, declared in the **time.h** library header file, returns the current time on the computer's clock. When converted to an integer, this value can serve as a fairly arbitrary seed for a random number generator in most programs.

To summarize the discussion so far, the following lines of code would display 10 random numbers between 0 and **RAND_MAX**, depending on the current time on the computer's clock at program start up:

```
#include <iostream.h>
#include <stdlib.h>
#include <time.h>

int  main()
{
    srand(int(clock));
    for (int i = 1; i <= 10; ++i)
        cout << rand() << endl;
    return 0;
}
```

Particular clients of a random number generator might desire a narrower or a wider range of numbers than **rand** provides. Ideally, a client would specify the range by passing integer values representing the lower and upper bounds of the desired range to a function. To see how we might use **rand** to implement this feature, first consider how to generate a number between 0 and an arbitrary upper bound, **high**, inclusive. For any two integers, *a* and *b*, *a* % *b* is between 0 and *b* – 1, inclusive. Thus, the expression **rand() % high + 1** would generate a random number between 0 and **high**, inclusive, where **high** is less than or equal to **RAND_MAX**. To place a lower bound other than 0 on the result, we can generate a random number between 0 and **high – low + 1**, and then add **low** to the result. Thus, the complete expression for computing a random number between a lower bound and an upper bound would be **rand() % (high – low + 1) + low**.

Now that we have settled the details of the system tools and arithmetic operations necessary for generating random numbers, we can specify a random number generator as a server or class in C++. The abstract operations are the following:

---

**Create operation**

Preconditions:    Receiver is an arbitrary random number generator in an unpredictable state.

Postconditions:   Receiver is seeded from the internal clock of the computer.

**next_number operation**

Preconditions:    Receiver is a random number generator. **low** and **high** are integer values such that **low < high <= RAND_MAX**.

Postconditions:   An integer representing a random number between **low** and **high**, inclusive, is returned.

**Reset operation**

Preconditions:    Receiver is a random number generator.

Postconditions:   The receiver is reinitialized with a new seed from the internal clock of the computer.

---

Note that we do not provide a **create** operation with a user-specified seed. This could easily be added. The class declaration and implementation modules follow:

```
// Class declaration file: random.h

#ifndef RANDOM_H

class  random_generator
{

    public:

    // Class constructor

    random_generator();

    // Member functions

    int next_number(int low, int high);
    void reset();

};
```

```
#define RANDOM_H
#endif

// Class implementation file: random.cpp

#include <stdlib.h>
#include <time.h>
#include <assert.h>
#include "random.h"

random_generator::random_generator()
{
    srand(int(clock()));
}

int random_generator::next_number(int low, int high)
{
    assert((low < high) && (high < RAND_MAX));
    return rand() % (high - low + 1) + low;
}

void random_generator::reset()
{
    srand(int(clock())));
}
```

The following short program uses an instance of the random generator class to output 10 random numbers in the range from –50 to 50:

```
#include <iostream.h>
#include "random.h"

int main()
{
    random_generator numbers;

    for (int i = 1; i <= 10; ++i)
        cout << numbers.next_random(-50, 50) << endl;
    return 0;
}
```

# Glossary

**abstract data type (ADT)**  A form of abstraction that arises from the use of defined types. An ADT consists of a class of objects, a defined set of properties of those objects, and a set of operations for processing the objects.

**abstraction**  The description of data structures at a conceptual level, apart from their implementation using a particular technique and language.

**abstract syntax tree**  *See* **parse tree.**

**access adjustment**  A method of changing the access mode of an inherited member from within a derived class. For example, a derived class may inherit all members from a base class in protected mode, and then make some members public by means of access adjustments. *See also* **access mode, base class, derived class,** and **inheritance.**

**access mode**  A symbol (**public, protected,** or **private**) that specifies the kind of access that clients have to a server's data members and member functions. *See also* **private member, protected member,** and **public member.**

**accumulator**  A variable used for the purpose of summing successive values of some other variable.

**actual parameter**  A variable or expression contained in a function call and passed to that function. *See also* **formal parameter.**

**address**  Often called address of a memory location, this is an integer value that the computer can use to reference a location. *See also* **value.**

**ADT**  *See* **abstract data type.**

**ADT generality rule**  An abstract data type should not be limited by the types of its components. Wherever possible, users should be able to specify the component types of a generic abstract data type.

**ADT implementation rule**  An implementation of an ADT must provide an interface that is entirely consistent with the operations specified in the ADT's definition.

**ADT layering rule**  Existing abstract data types should be used to implement new abstract data types, unless direct control over the underlying data structures and operations of the programming language is a critical factor. A well-designed implementation consists of layers of ADTs.

**ADT use rule**  An algorithm that uses an ADT should access variables of that abstract data type only through the operations provided in the ADT definition.

**algorithm**  A finite sequence of effective statements that, when applied to the problem, will solve it.

**alias**  A situation in which two or more identifiers in a program come to refer to the same memory location. An alias can become the cause of subtle side effects.

**analysis phase**  The first phase of the software system life cycle in which the systems analyst determines the user's needs and develops formal specifications describing the proposed system and its requirements.

**ancestor**  A tree node that is hierarchically related to another tree node at a lower level in the tree.

**application software**  Programs designed for a specific use.

**argument**  A value or expression passed in a function call.

**arithmetic/logic unit (ALU)**  The part of the central processing unit (CPU) that performs arithmetic operations and evaluates expressions.

**array**  A data structure whose elements are accessed by means of index positions.

**array index**  The relative position of the components of an array.

**artificial intelligence (AI)**    The field of computer science in which the goal is to program the computer to mimic intelligent human behavior.

**ASCII collating sequence**    The American Standard Code for Information Interchange ordering for a character set.

**assembly language**    A computer language that allows words and symbols to be used in an unsophisticated manner to accomplish simple tasks.

**assertion**    Special comments used with selection and repetition that state what you expect to happen and when certain conditions will hold.

**assignment statement**    A method of putting values into memory locations.

**association**    A data structure whose two parts are a key and a value.

**association list**    A data structure consisting of a set of associations. *See also* **association.**

**attribute**    A property that a computational object models, such as the balance in a bank account.

**automatic program synthesis**    A process whereby one computer program can be given the specifications for another computer program, generate the code to satisfy those specifications, and then prove the correctness of that code.

**Backus-Naur grammar**    A standard form for defining the formal syntax of a language.

**base class**    The class from which a derived class inherits attributes and behavior. *See also* **derived class** and **inheritance.**

**behavior**    The set of actions that a class of objects supports.

**best case**    The arrangement of data items prior to the start of a sort function to finish in the least amount of time for that particular set of items. *See also* **worst case.**

**big-O analysis**    A technique for estimating the time and space requirements of an algorithm in terms of order of magnitude.

**big-O notation**    Saying that an algorithm is O(*f(n)*) indicates that the function *f(n)* may be useful in characterizing how efficiently the algorithm performs for large *n*. For such *n*, we are assured that the operations required by the algorithm will be bounded by the product of a constant and *f(n)*.

**bin sort**    *See* **radix sort.**

**binary digit**    A digit, either 0 or 1, in the binary number system. Program instructions are stored in memory using a sequence of binary digits. Binary digits are called bits.

**binary search**    The process of examining a middle value of a sorted array to see which half contains the value in question and halving until the value is located.

**binary search tree**    A binary tree with the ordering property.

**binary tree**    A tree such that each node can point to at most two children.

**binary tree search**    A search algorithm driven by the hierarchical relationships of data items in a tree with the ordering property.

**binding time**    The time at which a program variable is bound to a particular value. This can occur either at compile time or at run time.

**bit**    *See* **binary digit.**

**black box testing**    The method of testing a module whereby the tester is aware of only what the module is supposed to do, not the method of implementation or the internal logic. *See also* **white box testing.**

**block**    The area of program text within a compound statement, containing statements and optional data declarations.

**blocked queue**    In an operating system, the queue of processes that have requested a resource currently owned by another process.

**Boolean expression**    An expression whose value is either true or false. *See also* **compound Boolean expression** and **simple Boolean expression.**

**bottom-up testing**    Independent testing of modules.

**boundary conditions**    Values that separate two logical possibilities. These are important cases to check when testing a module.

**boundary folding**    A variation on shift folding: in boundary folding, the digits of every other numeric section are reversed before the addition is performed.

**branch**    In a tree, a link between a parent and its child node.

**breadth-first traversal**    A visiting of all nodes in a graph; it proceeds from each node by first visiting all nodes adjacent to that node.

**B-tree**    An efficient, flexible index structure often used in database management systems.

**bubble sort**    Rearranges elements of an array until they are in either ascending or descending order. Consecutive elements are compared to move (bubble) the elements to the top or bottom accordingly on each pass. *See also* **heap sort, insertion sort, merge sort, quick sort, radix sort, selection sort,** and **shell sort.**

**bucket**    In bucket hashing, a contiguous region of storage locations.

**bucket hashing**    Method of handling collisions whereby the hashing function sends the key to a bucket of locations rather than a single location. The key is then placed by performing a sequential search within the bucket.

**bus**    A group of wires imprinted on a circuit board to facilitate communication between components of a computer.

**byte** A sequence of bits used to encode a character in memory. *See also* **word.**

**call** Any reference to a subprogram by an executable statement. Also referred to as invoke.

**central processing unit (CPU)** A major hardware component that consists of the arithmetic/logic unit (ALU) and the control unit.

**character set** The list of characters available for data and program statements. *See also* **collating sequence.**

**child node** A node that descends from another node in a tree.

**children** Nodes pointed to by a node in a tree.

**circular linked list** A linked list whose last node points to the first or head node in the list.

**class** A description of the attributes and behavior of a set of computational objects.

**class constructor** A member function used to create and initialize an instance of a class.

**class declaration module** An area of a program used to declare the data members and member functions of a class.

**class destructor** A member function defined by the programmer and automatically used by the computer to return dynamic memory used by an object to the heap when the program exits the scope of the object. *See also* **dynamic memory.**

**class implementation module** An area of a program used to implement the member functions of a class.

**class template** A special kind of class definition that allows clients to specify the component types of objects of that class.

**client** A computational object that receives a service from another computational object.

**clustering** Occurs when a hashing function is biased toward the placement of keys in a given region of the storage space.

**code (writing)** The process of writing executable statements that are part of a program to solve a problem.

**cohesive subprogram** A subprogram designed to accomplish a single task.

**collating sequence** The particular order sequence for a character set used by a machine. *See also* **ASCII collating sequence** and **EBCDIC collating sequence.**

**collision** Condition in which more than one key hashes to the same position with a given hashing function.

**column-major order** A means of traversing a two-dimensional array whereby all of the data in one column are accessed before the data in the next column. *See also* **row-major order.**

**comment** A nonexecutable statement used to make a program more readable.

**compatible type** Expressions that have the same base type. A parameter and its argument must be of compat-

ible type, and the operands of an assignment statement must be of compatible type.

**compilation error** An error detected when the program is being compiled. *See also* **design error, logic error, run-time error,** and **syntax error.**

**compiler** A computer program that automatically converts instructions in a high-level language to machine language.

**compound Boolean expression** Refers to the complete expression when logical connectives and negation are used to generate Boolean values. *See also* **Boolean expression** and **simple Boolean expression.**

**compound statement** Uses the symbols { and } to make several simple statements into a single compound statement.

**conditional statement** *See* **selection statement.**

**constant** A symbol whose value cannot be changed in the body of the program.

**constant definition section** The section where program constants are defined for subsequent use.

**constant parameter** A method of declaring a formal array parameter so that the value of an actual array parameter will not change in a function.

**constant reference** A method of declaring a formal parameter so that the actual parameter is passed by reference but will not change in a function.

**control structure** A structure that controls the flow of execution of program statements.

**control unit** The part of the central processing unit that controls the operation of the rest of the computer.

**copy constructor** A member function defined by the programmer and automatically used by the computer to copy the values of objects when they are passed by value to functions.

**counter** A variable used to count the number of times some process is completed.

**coupling** The amount of interaction between a pair of modules.

**cubic algorithm** A polynomial algorithm in which the highest nonzero term is $n^3$.

**data** The particular characters that are used to represent information in a form suitable for storage, processing, and communication.

**data abstraction** The separation between the conceptual definition of a data structure and its eventual implementation.

**data flow diagram** A graphic tool used by systems analysts to represent data flow and transformations as a conceptual process. Also referred to as a bubble diagram.

**data member** A data object declared within a class declaration module.

**data type**    A formal description of the set of values that a variable can have.

**data validation**    The process of examining data prior to its use in a program.

**deadlock**    An infinite wait state in which two processes each own system resources the other needs and will not release until they have obtained the remaining resources they need. Also referred to as fatal embrace.

**debugging**    The process of eliminating errors or "bugs" from a program.

**declaration sections**    The sections used to declare (name) symbolic constants, data types, variables, and subprograms that are necessary to the program.

**decrement**    To decrease the value of a variable.

**density**    The number of storage locations used divided by the total number of storage locations available.

**density-dependent search technique**    A Search technique whose efficiency is determined solely by the density of the data.

**depth-first traversal**    A visiting of all nodes in a graph, proceeding from each node by probing as deeply as possible along one path leading from that node.

**dereference**    The operation by which a program uses a pointer to access the contents of dynamic memory. *See also* **dynamic memory** and **pointer variable.**

**derived class**    A class that inherits attributes and behavior from other classes. *See also* **base class** and **inheritance.**

**design error**    An error such that a program runs, but unexpected results are produced. Also referred to as a logic error. *See also* **compilation error, run-time error,** and **syntax error.**

**design phase**    The second phase of the software system life cycle. In this phase, a relatively detailed design plan is created from the formal specifications of the system produced in the analysis phase.

**dictionary**    A data structure consisting of a set of associations. *See also* **association.**

**digit/character extraction**    In creating a hashing function, the process of removing from a key those digits of characters that may bias the results of the function.

**digraph**    A graph having some edges that point in only one direction.

**diminishing increment sort**    A sort in which the number of segments in any one pass decreases with each successive pass. *See also* **shell sort.**

**directional graph**    *See* **digraph.**

**divide-and-conquer algorithms**    A class of algorithms that solves problems by repeatedly dividing them into simpler problems. *See also* **recursion.**

**division-remainder technique**    A hashing technique that ensures that the result will be a valid output. It uses the modulus operation to scale the value into the proper range.

**dominant term**    The highest power of $n$ in a polynomial. For large $n$, the behavior of the entire polynomial will approach the behavior of a polynomial that contains only that term.

**doubly linked list**    A linked list in which each node has two pointers instead of one. One of these points to the previous node in the list and the other points to the next node in the list.

**do . . . while loop**    A post-test loop examining a Boolean expression after causing a statement to be executed. *See also* **for loop, loops,** and **while loop.**

**dynamic memory**    Memory allocated under program control from the heap and accessed by means of pointers. *See also* **heap** and **pointer variable.**

**dynamic structure**    A data structure that may expand or contract during execution of a program. *See also* **dynamic memory.**

**EBCDIC collating sequence**    The Extended Binary Coded Decimal Interchange Code ordering for a character set.

**echo checking**    A debugging technique in which values of variables and input data are displayed during program execution.

**edge**    A direct connection between two nodes in a graph.

**effective statement**    A clear, unambiguous instruction that can be carried out.

**empty statement**    A semicolon used to indicate that no action is to be taken. Also referred to as a null statement.

**encapsulation**    The process of hiding implementation details of a data structure.

**end-of-file marker**    A special marker inserted by the machine to indicate the end of the data file.

**end-of-line character**    A special character ('\0') used to indicate the end of a line of characters in a string or a file stream.

**entrance-controlled loop**    *See* **pretest loop.**

**enumerated data type**    A set of symbolic constants defined by the programmer.

**equivalence classes**    A partitioning of all the logical possibilities that can be checked when testing a module. All test cases within a single equivalence class are identical from the standpoint of the logic of the module.

**error**    *See* **compilation error, design error, logic error, run-time error,** and **syntax error.**

**executable section**    Contains the statements that cause the computer to do something.

**executable statement**    The basic unit of grammar in C++ consisting of valid identifiers, standard identifiers, reserved words, numbers, and/or characters, together with appropriate punctuation.

**execute**    To carry out the instructions of a program.

**exit-controlled loop**   *See* **post-test loop.**

**expert system**   A program able to reason as an expert in a limited domain.

**exponential algorithm**   An algorithm whose efficiency is dominated by a term of the form $k^n$.

**exponential form**   *See* **floating point.**

**extended if statement**   Nested selection where additional **if . . . else** statements are used in the else option. *See also* **nested if statement.**

**factorial**   The product of the first N positive integers (denoted as N!).

**fatal embrace**   *See* **deadlock.**

**field width**   The phrase used to describe the number of columns used for various output. *See also* **formatting.**

**FIFO**   *See* **queue.**

**file stream**   A data structure that consists of a sequence of components that are accessed by input or output operations.

**finite state automata**   Algorithms driven by a table indexed by the possible states that can exist and the possible categories of input symbols are called finite state algorithms. Machines running such algorithms are finite state automata.

**first-in, first-out (FIFO)**   *See* **queue.**

**fixed-repetition loop**   A loop used when it is known in advance the number of times a segment of code needs to be repeated.

**fixed point**   A method of writing decimal numbers where the decimal is placed where it belongs in the number. *See also* **floating point.**

**floating point**   A method for writing numbers in scientific notation to accommodate numbers that may have very large or very small values. *See also* **fixed point.**

**folding**   A method of hashing in cases where the key is not an integer value.. The nonnumeric characters are removed and the remaining digits are combined to produce an integer value.

**for loop**   A structured loop consisting of an initializer expression, a termination expression, an update expression, and a statement.

**formal parameter**   A name, declared and used in a function declaration, that is replaced by an actual parameter when the function is called.

**formal verification**   The use of logic to produce a proof of the correctness of an algorithm.

**formatting**   Designating the desired field width when printing integers, reals, and character strings. *See also* **field width.**

**free store**   *See* **heap.**

**friend of a class**   The process of making the data members of one class available to another class.

**front pointer**   The pointer to the front of a queue.

**function**   *See* **library function** and **user-defined function.**

**function member**   A function declared within a class declaration module.

**functional abstraction**   The process of considering only what a function is to do rather than details of the function.

**generic abstract data type**   An abstract data type whose component types are specified as parameters. For example, a generic stack ADT could be used to create stacks of integers as well as stacks of characters.

**general list**   A collection of data items that are related by their relative position in the collection.

**general tree**   A set of nodes that is either empty or has a designated node (called the root) from which descend zero or more subtrees.

**generalized nested loops**   Loops whose nesting depth is determined at run time using recursive logic.

**global identifier**   An identifier that can be used by the main program and all subprograms in a program.

**global variable**   *See* **global identifier.**

**graph**   A set of data elements called nodes and the paths between them called edges.

**halting problem**   A problem concerned with determining whether or not a given program will terminate or loop indefinitely when provided with a given set of input data.

**hardware**   The actual computing machine and its support devices.

**has-a relation**   The property of one class having an object of another class as a data member. *See also* **is-a relation.**

**hashing**   A density-dependent search technique whereby the key for a given data item is transformed using a function to produce the address where that item is stored in memory.

**head pointer**   A pointer to the first item in a list.

**header file**   A C++ file that provides data and function declarations in a library to client modules.

**heap**   An area of computer memory where storage for dynamic data is available.

**heap**   A binary tree with the heap property.

**heap property**   A binary tree has the heap property when the data at any given node are greater or equal to the data in its left and right subtrees.

**heap sort**   A sort in which the array is treated like an array implementation of a binary tree. The items are repeatedly manipulated to create a heap from which the root is removed and added to the sorted portion of the array. *See also* **bubble sort, insertion sort, merge sort, quick sort, radix sort, selection sort,** and **shell sort.**

**height balancing**   A technique for ensuring that an ordered binary tree remains as full as possible in form.

**heuristics**  Rules of thumb that cut down on the number of possible choices to examine. They often lead to quick solutions but do not guarantee a solution the way an algorithm does.

**hierarchy**  A relation between nodes whereby one is viewed as above or prior to another.

**high-level language**  Any programming language that uses words and symbols to make it relatively easy to read and write a program. *See also* **assembly language** and **machine language.**

**identifiers**  Words that must be created according to a well-defined set of rules but can have any meaning subject to these rules. *See also* **library identifiers.**

**implementation file**  A C++ file that provides the implementations of data and functions declared in a header file.

**index**  *See* **array index** or **loop index.**

**indexed sequential access method (ISAM)**  The most common method of indexed sequential search.

**indexed sequential search**  Use of a partial index based on disk-dependent factors to find the proper portion of the disk for sequential searching for a key.

**index sort**  Sorting an array by ordering the indices of the components rather than exchanging the components.

**inductive assertion**  A method of formally proving the correctness of an algorithm by using an inductive proof.

**infinite loop**  A loop in which the controlling condition is not changed in such a manner to allow the loop to terminate.

**infix**  Algebraic notation in which the operator appears between the two operands to which it will be applied.

**infix priority**  A function that ranks the algebraic operators in terms of their precedence.

**information hiding**  The process of suppressing the implementation details of a function or data structure so as to simplify its use in programming.

**inheritance**  The process by which a derived class can reuse attributes and behavior defined in a base class. *See also* **base class** and **derived class.**

**inorder predecessor**  The node preceding a given node in an inorder traversal.

**inorder successor**  The node following a given node in an inorder traversal.

**inorder threads**  Pointers to the inorder predecessor and successor of a node.

**inorder traversal**  A binary tree traversal in which a node's left subtree is visited first, then that node is processed, and finally the node's right subtree is visited.

**input**  Data obtained by a program during its execution.

**input assertion**  A precondition for a loop.

**input device**  A device that provides information to the computer. Typical devices are keyboards, disk drives,

card readers, and tape drives. *See also* **I/O device** and **output device.**

**insertion rule**  For binary trees, a rule whereby a new item is placed in the left subtree of an item greater than it or in the right subtree of an item less than it.

**insertion sort**  Sorts an array of elements that starts with an empty array and inserts elements one at a time in their proper order. *See also* **bubble sort, heap sort, merge sort, quick sort, radix sort, selection sort,** and **shell sort.**

**instance**  A computational object bearing the attributes and behavior specified by a class.

**integer arithmetic operations**  Operations allowed on data of type **int.** This includes the operations of addition, subtraction, multiplication, division, and modulus to produce integer answers.

**interface**  A formal statement of how communication occurs between subprograms, the main driver, and other subprograms.

**invariant expression**  An assertion that is true before the loop and after each iteration of the loop.

**invoke**  *See* **call.**

**I/O device**  Any device that allows information to be transmitted to or from a computer. *See also* **input device** and **output device.**

**is-a relation**  The property of one class being a derived class of another class. *See also* **has-a relation, derived class,** and **base class.**

**iteration**  *See* **loops.**

**key**  A field in a data structure that is used to access an element in that structure.

**key-to-address transformation**  A transformation in which the key of a data item maps to the address at which the data are stored.

**keywords**  Either reserved words or library identifiers.

**last-in, first-out (LIFO)**  *See* **stack.**

**leaf**  In a tree, a node that has no children.

**level**  All nodes in a tree with a path of the same length from the root node.

**lexical analysis**  The task of recognizing valid words or tokens in an input stream of characters.

**l-value**  A computational object capable of being the target of an assignment statement.

**library constant**  A constant with a standard meaning, such as **NULL** or **INT_MAX**, available in most versions of C++.

**library function**  A function available in most versions of C++. A list of useful C++ library functions is set forth in Appendix 2.

**library identifiers**  Words defined in standard C++ libraries. *See also* **identifiers.**

**LIFO**  *See* **stack.**

**linear algorithm**  A polynomial algorithm in which the highest nonzero term is $n$.

**linear collision processing**  Method of handling a collision in which the storage space is searched sequentially from the location of the collision for an available location where the new key can be placed.

**linear ordering**  Any ordering of data in which there is an identifiable first element, second element, and so forth.

**linear representation (of binary tree)**  An implementation of a binary tree in an array. For a given node stored at index position $K$, that node's left child is at position $2K$, and the right child is at position $2K + 1$.

**linear search**  *See* **sequential search.**

**linked collision processing**  Method of handling a collision in which the second key is stored in a linked list located in an overflow area.

**linked list**  A list of data items where each item is linked to the next one by means of a pointer.

**linked representation**  An implementation of a binary tree in which pointer fields are used to reference the right and left child of a node in the tree (as opposed to the linear representation of a binary tree).

**LISP (LISt Processor)**  A highly-recursive computer programming language used heavily in artificial intelligence (AI).

**list traversal**  The process of sequentially visiting each node in a list.

**local identifier**  An identifier that is restricted to use within a subblock of a program.

**local variable**  *See* **local identifier.**

**logarithmic algorithm**  An algorithm whose efficiency is dominated by a term of the form $\log n$.

**logic error**  *See* **design error.**

**logical operator**  Either logical connective (&, ||) or negation (!).

**logical size**  The number of data items actually available in a data structure at a given time. *See also* **physical size.**

**logical order**  An ordering of data items according to some defined criterion such as alphabetic, increasing numeric, and so forth. That logical order of the data may or may not be the physical order of the data as stored in the computer.

**logically sorted**  Data have been logically sorted when pointers to the data have been sorted, even though the data itself have not been touched. Hence, items that the sort places consecutively need not be physically adjacent.

**$\log_2 n$ search algorithm**  A search algorithm whose efficiency is dominated by a term of the form $\log_2 n$.

**loop index**  Variable used for control values in a loop.

**loop invariant**  An assertion that expresses a relationship between variables that remains constant throughout all iterations of the loop.

**loop variant**  An assertion whose truth changes between the first and final execution of the loop.

**loop verification**  The process of guaranteeing that a loop performs its intended task.

**loops**  Program statements that cause a process to be repeated. *See also* **for loop, do . . . while** loop, and **while loop.**

**low-level language**  *See* **assembly language.**

**machine language**  The language used directly by the computer in all its calculations and processing.

**main block**  The main part of a program.

**main driver**  The main program when subprograms are used to accomplish specific tasks. *See also* **executable section.**

**main (primary) memory**  Memory contained in the computer. *See also* **memory** and **secondary memory.**

**main unit**  A computer's main unit contains the central processing unit (CPU) and the main (primary) memory; it is hooked to an input device and an output device.

**mainframe**  Large computers typically used by major companies and universities. *See also* **microcomputer** and **minicomputer.**

**maintenance phase**  The fifth phase of the software system life cycle. In this phase, changes must be made in the original program either to fix errors discovered by the users of the program or to meet new user needs.

**manifest interface**  The property of a function such that, when the function is called, the reader of the code can tell clearly what information is being transmitted to it and what information is being returned from it.

**mapping function**  A function that transforms row-column array coordinates to the linear address of that array entry.

**memory**  The ordered sequence of storage cells that can be accessed by address. Instructions and variables of an executing program are temporarily held here. *See also* **main memory** and **secondary memory.**

**memory location**  A storage cell that can be accessed by address. *See also* **memory.**

**merge**  The process of combining lists. Typically refers to files or arrays.

**merge sort**  Sort in which the array is repeatedly split in half and then these pieces are merged together. *See also* **bubble sort, heap sort, insertion sort, quick sort, radix sort, selection sort,** and **shell sort.**

**message**  In object-oriented programming, a signal to perform an operation on an object.

**message-passing**  In object-oriented programming, one object's telling another object to perform an operation that is part of its encapsulation.

**method of inductive assertions**  Method of formally verifying the correctness of an algorithm by identifying the input assertions, output assertions, and loop invariants of the algorithm and constructing a verification proof by mathematical induction.

**microcomputer** A computer capable of fitting on a laptop or desktop, generally used by one person at a time. *See also* **mainframe** and **minicomputer.**

**minicomputer** A small version of a mainframe computer. It is usually used by several people at once. *See also* **mainframe** and **microcomputer.**

**mixed-mode** Expressions containing data of different types; the values of these expressions will be of either type, depending on the rules for evaluating them.

**modular development** The process of developing an algorithm using modules. *See also* **module.**

**modularity** The property possessed by a program that is written using modules.

**module** An independent unit that is part of a larger development. Can be a function or a class (set of functions and related data). *See also* **modular development.**

**module specifications** In the case of a function, a description of data received, information returned, and task performed by a module. In the case of a class, a description of the attributes and behavior.

**modular structure chart** A graphic tool used by software designers to display the hierarchical relationships among the modules of the software system.

**modular testing** A method of testing in which each module is tested immediately after it has been completed rather than when the entire system has been completed.

**multilinked list** A linked list in which each node has two or more link fields.

**natural language** A language by which humans normally communicate (such as English), as opposed to a formal programming language (such as C++).

**negation** The use of the logical operator ! to negate the Boolean value of an expression.

**nested if statement** A selection statement used within another selection statement. *See also* **extended if statement.**

**nested loop** A loop as one of the statements in the body of another loop.

**nested selection** Any combination of selection statements within selection statements. *See also* **selection statement.**

**network** A graph in which the edges have weight values associated with them.

**node** One data item in a linked list.

**null character** The special character ('\0') used to mark the end of a string in C++.

**null statement** *See* **empty statement.**

**numerical analysis** A field concerned with obtaining numerical answers to mathematical problems which involve much computation.

**object code** *See* **object program.**

**object-oriented programming** A programming paradigm in which a data object is viewed as the owner of operations, as opposed to procedural programming in which an operation is passed data objects as actual parameters. Object-oriented programming emphasizes the ADT approach and allows the users of an ADT to extend the operations of an ADT library in a convenient and efficient fashion.

**object program** The machine code version of the source program.

**one-key table** A set of values each of which is accessed by specifying a unique key value, where the key values are ordered.

**opened for reading** Positions an input stream pointer at the beginning of a file for the purpose of reading from the file.

**opened for writing** Positions an output stream pointer at the beginning of a file for the purpose of writing to the file.

**opening a file** Positions a pointer at the beginning of a file. *See also* **opened for reading** and **opened for writing.**

**operating system** A large program that allows the user to communicate with the hardware and performs various management tasks.

**ordered collection** A data structure that supports indexing for retrieval or change of data items, the detection of the logical size of the structure, and addition or removal of data items from the logical end of the structure.

**order of magnitude** Power of ten. Two numbers have the same order of magnitude if their representations in scientific notation have identical exponents to designate the power of ten.

**ordering** A means of arranging the elements in a list.

**ordering property** In a binary tree, the data in each node of the tree are greater than or equal to all of the data in that node's left subtree and less than or equal to all of the data in its right subtree.

**ordinal data type** A data type ordered in some association with the integers; each integer is the ordinal of its associated character.

**output** Information that is produced by a program.

**output assertion** A postcondition for a loop.

**output device** A device that allows you to see the results of a program. Typically it is a monitor or printer. *See also* **input device** and **I/O device.**

**overflow** In arithmetic operations, a value may be too large for the computer's memory location. A meaningless value may be assigned or an error message may result. *See also* **underflow.**

**overloading** The process of using the same operator symbol or identifier to refer to many different functions. *See also* **polymorphism.**

**parallel arrays** Arrays of the same length but with different component data types.

**parallel processing** The use of more than one processor to execute parts of a program concurrently. The effect is that these parts are completed in parallel rather than in sequence.

**parameter** *See* **argument.**

**parameter list** A list of parameters. An actual parameter list is contained in the function call. A formal parameter list is contained in the function declaration and heading.

**parent** In a tree, the node that is pointing to its children.

**parse tree** Tree representation of the syntactic structure of a source program produced by a compiler. Also referred to as abstract syntax tree.

**parser** A program that checks the syntax of an expression and represents that expression in a unique form.

**parser generator** A program that can take the input grammar for a language and produce the parser for that language.

**parsing** The procedure of checking the syntax of an expression and representing it in one unique form.

**partition** In quick sort, the process of moving the pivot to the location where it belongs in the sorted array and arranging the remaining data items to the left of the pivot if they are less than or equal to the pivot and to the right if they are greater than the pivot.

**passed by reference** When the address of the actual parameter is passed to a subprogram.

**passed by value** When a copy of the value of the actual parameter is passed to a subprogram.

**path** A sequence of edges which connect two nodes in a graph or network.

**peripheral memory** *See* **secondary memory** and **memory.**

**permutation** An ordered arrangement of the first $n$ positive integers in which each integer appears exactly once.

**physical size** The number of memory units available for storing data items in a data structure. *See also* **logical size.**

**pivot** Item used to direct the partitioning in quick sort.

**pointer** A memory location containing the location of another data item.

**pointer sort** A sort in which pointers to the data are manipulated rather than the data itself.

**pointer variable** Frequently designated as `ptr`, a pointer variable is a variable that contains the address of a memory location. *See also* **address** and **dynamic memory.**

**polymorphism** The property of one operator symbol or function identifier having many meanings. *See also* **overloading.**

**polynomial algorithm** An algorithm whose efficiency can be expressed in terms of a polynomial.

**postcondition** An assertion written after a segment of code.

**postfix** Unambiguous algebraic notation in which the arithmetic operator appears after the two operands upon which it is to be applied.

**postorder traversal** A binary tree traversal in which at any node, that node's left subtree is visited first, then that node's right subtree is visited, and finally that node is processed.

**post-test loop** A loop where the control condition is tested after the loop is executed. `do . . . while` loop is a post-test loop. Also referred to as an exit-controlled loop.

**precondition** An assertion written before a particular statement.

**prefix** Unambiguous algebraic notation in which the arithmetic operator appears before the two operands upon which it is to be applied.

**preorder traversal** A binary tree traversal in which at any node, that node is first processed, then that node's left subtree is visited, and finally that node's right subtree is visited.

**pretest condition** A condition that controls whether the body of the loop is executed before going through the loop.

**pretest loop** A loop where the control condition is tested before the loop is executed. A `while` loop is a pretest loop. Also referred to as an entrance-controlled loop.

**primary memory** *See* **main memory** and **memory.**

**prime hash area** In linked collision processing, the main storage area in which keys are placed if no collision occurs.

**priority queue** A queue in which the entries on the queue are ranked into groups according to priority. Such a queue requires a rear pointer for each different possible priority value.

**private member** A data member or member function that is accessible only within the scope of a class declaration.

**profile an algorithm** A means of empirically measuring the execution of an algorithm by inserting counters to keep track of the number of times certain instructions are executed during a run of the program.

**program** A set of instructions that tells the machine (the hardware) what to do.

**program heading** The heading of the main block of any C++ program; it must contain the identifier `main`.

**program proof** An analysis of a program that attempts to verify the correctness of program results.

**program protection** A method of using selection statements to guard against unexpected results.

**program walk-through** The process of carefully following, using pencil and paper, steps the computer uses to solve the problem given in a program. Also referred to as a trace.

**programming language**    Formal language that computer scientists use to give instructions to the computer.

**prompt**    A message or marker on the terminal screen that requests input data.

**proportional**    Term applied to two algebraic functions whose quotient is a constant.

**protected member**    A data member or member function that is accessible only within the scope of a class declaration or within the class declaration of a derived class.

**protection**    *See* **program protection**.

**pseudocode**    A stylized half-English, half-code language written in English but suggesting C++ code.

**public member**    A data member or member function that is accessible to any program component that uses the class.

**quadratic algorithm**    A polynomial algorithm in which the highest nonzero term is $n^2$.

**quadratic collision processing**    Method of handling a collision in which the storage space is searched in the $k^2$ place, for successive integer values of $k$ starting at the location of the collision, until an available spot is found.

**queue**    A dynamic data structure where elements are entered at one end and removed from the other end. Referred to as a FIFO (first-in, first-out) structure.

**quick sort**    A relatively fast sorting technique that uses recursion. *See also* **bubble sort, heap sort, insertion sort, merge sort, radix sort, selection sort,** and **shell sort.**

**r-value**    A computational object capable of being assigned to a variable.

**radix sort**    Sorts integer data by repeatedly placing the items into bins and then collecting the bins, starting with the least significant digit for the first pass and finishing with the most significant digit. Also referred to as bin sort. *See also* **bubble sort, heap sort, insertion sort, merge sort, quick sort, selection sort,** and **shell sort.**

**random access**    Ability to access any elements in a list without first accessing all preceding elements.

**random access file**    A file whose components can be accessed using random access.

**random number generator**    A function that returns a number in a given range each time it is called. The numbers it returns are statistically random in that after repeated calls to the function, the sequence of numbers returned is evenly distributed over the interval yet each one is completely unpredictable.

**randomized storage**    A name given to list access via a hashing function.

**range bound error**    The situation that occurs when an attempt is made to use an array index value that is less than 0 or greater than or equal to the size of the array.

**reading from a file**    Retrieving data from a file.

**ready queue**    In an operating system, the queue of processes with cleared access to all the resources the processes require to run.

**real arithmetic operations**    Operations allowed on data of type `float`. This includes addition, subtraction, multiplication, and division.

**rear pointer**    The pointer to the rear of a queue.

**receiver object**    A computational object to which a request is sent for a service.

**recursion**    The process of a subprogram calling itself. A clearly defined stopping state must exist. Any recursive subprogram can be rewritten using iteration.

**recursive step**    A step in recursive process that solves a similar problem of smaller size and eventually leads to a termination of the process.

**recursive subprogram**    *See* **recursion**.

**reference parameter**    A formal parameter that requires the address of the actual parameter to be passed to a subprogram. The value of the actual parameter can be changed within the subprogram.

**rehashing**    Method of handling a collision in which a sequence of new hashing functions is applied to the key that caused the collision until an available location for that key is found.

**rehashing collision processing**    Resolving a collision by invoking a sequence of hashing functions on a key.

**relational operator**    An operator used for comparison of data items of the same type.

**relative ordering**    Ordering imposed on the entries in a list by their relative positions in that list.

**relatively prime**    Two numbers are relatively prime if and only if their only common factor is 1.

**repetition**    *See* **loops**.

**reserved words**    Words that have predefined meanings that cannot be changed. They are highlighted in text by capital boldface print; a list of C++ reserved words is given in Appendix 1.

**return type**    The type of value returned by a function.

**robust**    The state in which a program is protected against most possible crashes from bad data and unexpected values.

**root**    The first or top node in a tree.

**row-major order**    A means of traversing a two-dimensional array whereby all of the data in one row are accessed before the data in the next row. *See also* **column-major order.**

**run-time error**    Error detected when, after compilation is completed, an error message results instead of the correct output. *See also* **compilation error, design error, logic error,** and **syntax error.**

**scope of identifier**    The largest block in which the identifier is available.

**secondary memory**    An auxiliary device for memory, usually a disk or magnetic tape. *See also* **main memory** and **memory.**

**sector**    A particular portion of a magnetic disk used at the machine language level in addressing information stored on the disk.

**seed**    A global number used as the basis for generating random numbers in random number generating function.

**selection sort**    A sorting algorithm that sorts the components of an array in either ascending or descending order. This process puts the smallest or largest element in the top position and repeats the process on the remaining array components. *See also* **bubble sort, heap sort, insertion sort, merge sort, quick sort, radix sort,** and **shell sort.**

**selection statement**    A control statement that selects some particular logical path based on the value of an expression. Also referred to as a *conditional statement.*

**self-documenting code**    Code that is written using descriptive identifiers.

**semantics**    The semantics of an algorithmic statement is the action dictated by that statement.

**semaphore**    In an operating system, special flags that regulate the addition and removal of processes to and from the blocked and ready queues.

**sender**    A computational object that requests a service from another computational object.

**sentinel value**    A special value that indicates the end of a set of data or of a process.

**sequential access**    Requirement that elements of a list must be accessed according to the list's ordering so that before a particular element can be accessed, all preceding elements must be accessed first.

**sequential access file**    A file whose components must be accessed using sequential access.

**sequential algorithm**    *See* **straight-line algorithm.**

**sequential search**    The process of searching a list by examining the first component and then examining successive components in the order in which they occur. Also referred to as linear search.

**server**    A computational object that provides a service to another computational object.

**shaker sort**    A variation on the bubble sort in which each pass through the data positions the (current) largest element in the (current) last array index *and* the (current) smallest element in the (current) first array index.

**shell sort**    Sort that works by dividing the array into smaller, noncontiguous segments. These segments are separately sorted using the insertion sort algorithm. The number of these segments is repeatedly reduced on each successive pass until the entire array has been sorted. *See also* **bubble sort, heap sort, insertion sort, merge sort, quick sort, radix sort,** and **selection sort.**

**shift folding**    A variation on folding in which each numeric part of the key is treated as a separate number, and these numbers are added to form an integer value. *See also* boundary folding.

**short-circuit evaluation**    The process whereby a compound Boolean expression halts evaluation and returns the value of the first subexpression that evaluates to TRUE, in the case of ||, or FALSE, in the case of &&.

**siblings**    The child nodes of a given node.

**side effect**    A change in a variable, which is the result of some action taken in a program, usually from within a function.

**sieve of Eratosthenes**    A technique devised by the Greek mathematician Eratosthenes for finding all prime numbers greater than 2 and less than or equal to a given number.

**simple Boolean expression**    An expression where two numbers or variable values are compared using a single relational operator. *See also* **Boolean expression** and **compound Boolean expression.**

**simulation**    A computer model of a real-life situation.

**simulation of system stack**    Technique used to eliminate recursion by making a program explicitly perform the duties of the system stack.

**software**    Programs that make the machine (the hardware) do something, such as word processing, database management, or games.

**software engineering**    The process of developing and maintaining large software systems.

**software reuse**    The process of building and maintaining software systems out of existing software components.

**software system life cycle**    The process of development, maintenance, and demise of a software system. Phases include analysis, design, coding, testing/verification, maintenance, and obsolescence.

**sort-merge**    The process of repeatedly subdividing a long list, sorting shorter lists, and then merging to obtain a single sorted list.

**sorted collection**    A derived class of ordered collection, in which the data items are maintained in ascending or descending order. *See also* **ordered collection.**

**source program**    A program written by a programmer. *See also* **system program.**

**sparse table**    A table in which a high percentage of data storage locations will be of one uniform value.

**stack**    A dynamic data structure where access can be made from only one end. Referred to as a LIFO (last-in, first-out) structure.

**stack priority**  Function to hierarchically rank algebraic operators in order of precedence.

**standard simple types**  Predefined data types such as `int`, `float`, and `char`.

**state space**  The space of all possible states which can be generated in the solution to a given problem.

**state-transition diagram**  A diagram used to model the logic of a finite state machine.

**stepwise refinement**  The process of repeatedly subdividing tasks into subtasks until each subtask is easily accomplished. *See also* **structured programming** and **top-down design.**

**stopping state**  The well-defined termination of a recursive process.

**straight-line algorithm**  Also called *sequential algorithm,* this algorithm consists of a sequence of simple tasks.

**string**  An abbreviated name for a string literal.

**string literal**  One or more characters, enclosed in double quotes, used as a constant in a program.

**string data type**  A data type that permits a sequence of characters. In C++, this can be implemented using an array of characters.

**structure chart**  A graphic method of indicating the relationship between modules when designing the solution to a problem.

**structured design**  A method of designing software by specifying modules and the flow of data among them.

**structured programming**  Programming that parallels a solution to a problem achieved by top-down design. *See also* **stepwise refinement** and **top-down design.**

**stub programming**  The process of using incomplete functions to test data transmission among them.

**subblock**  A block structure for a subprogram. *See also* **block.**

**subprogram**  A program within a program. Functions are subprograms.

**subscript**  *See* **array index** or **loop index.**

**subtree**  A subset of a tree that is itself a tree.

**symbol table**  A list of identifiers maintained by a compiler as it parses a source program.

**synonyms**  Two keys that hash to the same position and therefore cause a collision.

**syntax**  The formal rules governing construction of valid statements.

**syntax diagramming**  A method to formally describe the legal syntax of language structures; syntax diagrams are set forth in Appendix 3.

**syntax error**  An error in spelling, punctuation, or placement of certain key symbols in a program. *See also* **compilation error, design error, logic error,** and **run-time error.**

**system software**  The programs that allow users to write and execute other programs, including operating systems such as DOS.

**system testing**  Exercising the interfaces between modules instead of the logic of a particular module.

**systems analyst**  The person responsible for analyzing the needs of the users and then formally specifying the system and its requirements to meet those needs.

**tail-recursive**  The property that a recursive algorithm has of performing no work after each recursive step. *See also* **recursion.**

**test cases**  Collection of sets of test data that will exercise all the logical possibilities the module will encounter. Each test case has a corresponding expected result called the test oracle.

**test oracle**  The expected result for a particular test case when a module is being tested.

**testing phase**  The fourth phase of the software system life cycle. In this phase, the program code is thoroughly tested in an effort to discover errors both in the design of the program and in the code itself.

**test program**  A short program written to provide an answer to a specific question.

**thread**  A pointer contained in a tree node which leads to the predecessor or successor of the node relative to a specified traversal.

**threaded tree**  A tree in which threading is used.

**threading**  A technique of avoiding recursion in tree traversal algorithms whereby the pointers unused in tree formation are turned into pointers to the inorder predecessor and inorder successor of that node.

**time/space trade-off**  The maxim that an attempt to make a program more efficient in terms of time will only come as a result of a corresponding decrease in efficiency in terms of space, and vice versa.

**token**  A language symbol comprised of one or more characters in an incoming stream of characters. The basic unit in lexical analysis.

**top-down design**  A design methodology for solving a problem whereby you first state the problem and then proceed to subdivide the main task into major subtasks. Each subtask is then subdivided into smaller subtasks. This process is repeated until each remaining subtask is easily solved. *See also* **stepwise refinement** and **structured programming.**

**trace**  *See* **program walk-through.**

**track**  A particular portion of a magnetic disk used at the machine language level in addressing information stored on the disk.

**tree**  *See* **general tree.**

**tree of recursive calls**  *See* **run-time trace diagram.**

**tree traversal**   A means of processing every node in the tree.

**trial-and-error backtracking**   Recursion in which more recursive calls may be made after the first return operation occurs.

**trie index**   A type of indexing used when the keys are variable-length character strings. Although taken from the word *retrieve,* trie is pronounced "try."

**Turing machine**   A hypothetical computing machine which consists of input and output units, and infinite memory in the form of a sequentially organized tape to store characters from a finite alphabet, a finite collection of states in which the machine could exist in at any given time, and a control unit capable of checking and potentially modifying the contents of any memory cell.

**two-dimensional array**   An array in which each element is accessed by a reference to a pair of indices.

**two-key table**   A set of values each of which is accessed by two keys, where the set of primary keys is ordered and the set of secondary keys for each primary key is also ordered.

**two-way merge**   The process of merging two sorted lists.

**type**   *See* data type.

**undecidable proposition**   A statement within an axiomatic system such that neither that statement nor its negation can be proven by reasoning within the system itself.

**underflow**   If a value is too small to be represented by a computer, the value is automatically replaced by zero. *See also* **overflow.**

**user-defined data type**   A new data type introduced and defined by the programmer.

**user-defined function**   A new function introduced and defined by the programmer.

**user-friendly**   A phrase used to describe an interactive program with clear, easy-to-follow messages for the user.

**value**   Often called value of a memory location. Refers to the value of the contents of a memory location. *See also* **address.**

**value parameter**   A formal parameter that is local to a subprogram. Values of these parameters are not returned to the calling program.

**variable**   A memory location, referenced by an identifier, whose value can be changed during a program.

**variable condition loop**   A repetition statement in which the loop control condition changes within the body of the loop.

**variable declaration section**   The section of the declaration section where program variables are declared for subsequent use.

**vertex**   A data object (or node) in a graph.

**volatile list**   A list that undergoes frequent insertions and deletions.

**weight**   The numeric value associated with an edge in a network.

**while loop**   A pretest loop examining a Boolean expression before causing a statement to be executed.

**white box testing**   The method of testing a module in which the tester is aware of the method of implementation and internal logic of that module. *See also* black box testing.

**word**   A unit of memory consisting of one or more bytes. Words can be addressed.

**worst case**   The arrangement of data items prior to the beginning of the sort procedure which causes that procedure to take the longest amount of time for that particular set of items. *See also* **best case.**

**writing to a file**   The process of entering data to a file.

# Answers to Selected Exercises

## CHAPTER 1

### Section 1.2

1. Insertion sort provides for a possible early exit from its inner loop. This early exit can potentially reduce the number of comparisons necessary, especially for data that are "almost" in order.

3. Selection sort does not provide for an early exit from either the outer or the inner loop; however, it does guarantee that only $n$ data exchanges will be made—fewer than either insertion or selection sort can guarantee (both require $n^2$ data exchanges on average).

5.

| | K=1 | K=2 | K=3 | K=4 | K=5 | K=6 |
|---|---|---|---|---|---|---|
| 43 | 12 | 12 | 12 | 12 | 12 | 12 |
| 40 | 40 | 18 | 18 | 18 | 18 | 18 |
| 18 | 18 | 40 | 24 | 24 | 24 | 24 |
| 24 | 24 | 24 | 40 | 39 | 39 | 39 |
| 39 | 39 | 39 | 39 | 40 | 40 | 40 |
| 60 | 60 | 60 | 60 | 60 | 60 | 43 |
| 12 | 43 | 43 | 43 | 43 | 43 | 60 |

7. This sort algorithm resembles a bubble sort, but is different in that small array entries "bubble up" instead of having large array entries "bubble down" on each successive pass. That is, in the bubble sort we can guarantee that after the $k$th pass, the *largest k* array entries are in their rightful place; whereas, in this sort algorithm, we can guarantee that after the $k$th pass, the *smallest k* entries are in their rightful place.

| Original | k=1 | k=2 | k=3 | k=4 | k=5 | k=6 |
|---|---|---|---|---|---|---|
| 43 | 12 | 12 | 12 | 12 | 12 | 12 |
| 40 | 43 | 18 | 18 | 18 | 18 | 18 |
| 18 | 40 | 43 | 24 | 24 | 24 | 24 |
| 24 | 18 | 40 | 43 | 39 | 39 | 39 |
| 39 | 24 | 24 | 40 | 43 | 40 | 40 |
| 60 | 39 | 39 | 39 | 40 | 43 | 43 |
| 12 | 60 | 60 | 60 | 60 | 60 | 60 |

9. This sort algorithm resembles insertion sort in that it, too, positions the $k$th element in its rightful place among $k - 1$ entries already in order. The difference between the two sorts lies in the section of the array each has sorted with each successive iteration. In insertion sort, the *first* $k + 1$ entries are in order after the $k$th pass; in this sort, the *last* $k$ entries are in order after the $k$th pass.

| Original | k=1 | k=2 | k=3 | k=4 | k=5 | k=6 |
|---|---|---|---|---|---|---|
| 43 | 43 | 43 | 43 | 43 | 43 | 12 |
| 40 | 40 | 40 | 40 | 40 | 12 | 18 |
| 18 | 18 | 18 | 18 | 12 | 18 | 24 |
| 24 | 24 | 24 | 12 | 18 | 24 | 39 |
| 39 | 39 | 12 | 24 | 24 | 39 | 40 |
| 60 | 12 | 39 | 39 | 39 | 40 | 43 |
| 12 | 60 | 60 | 60 | 60 | 60 | 60 |

**11.** The integers

| |
|---|
| 20 |
| 30 |
| 40 |
| 50 |
| 10 |

or any such arithmetically or alphabetically ordered data cause the bubble sort to make comparisons, but no data are interchanged until the 10 is "bubbled up" to the top. For the insertion sort, the inner loop is shut off after a single comparison, until the final 10 is reached. Then the 10 is inserted at the top.

**13.**
```
// Same inputs, outputs, and task as insertion sort.
// New logic: move element only after all comparisons
// per loop are finished.
void modified_insertion_sort(list_type list, int n)
{
    int i, j, k, remember;
    boolean done;

    for (k = 1; k < n; ++k)
    {
        j = k;
        remember = j;
        done = FALSE;
        while ((j >= 1) && ! done)
            if  (list[remember].get_key() <
                    list[j - 1].get_key())
                    --j;
            else
                    done = TRUE;
        if (j != remember)
        {
            for (k = remember; k >= j + 1; --k)
                    list[k] = list[k - 1];
            list[j] = list[remember];
        }
    }
}
```

Section 1.3

**1. a.** Inner loop: $m - 6$ repetitions. Outer loop: $n$ repetitions. For each outer loop repetition, the inner loop is traversed $m - 6$ times. Therefore, $(m - 6) \times n$ overall repetitions are performed. This is $O(n^2)$.
   **b.** The inner loop will be executed $\log_2 n$ times and the outer loop will be executed $n$ times. Thus the loops are $O(n\log_2 n)$.
   **c.** The inner **do...while** is executed $n/2$ times for each execution of the outer loop. The outer **do...while** is executed $n$ times. Thus there are $n \times (n/2)$ repetitions. Thus the loops are $O(n^2)$.

**3.** The efficiency of the algorithm in question is constant—32 operations—for all input. Remembering that in big-O analysis, we are concerned primarily with the order of magnitude of the algorithm's efficiency, we write this algorithm's efficiency as $O(1) * 32$. And recalling that constants bear no importance except in comparing algorithms with the same big-O, we drop the constant 32 to arrive at the big-O that most accurately characterizes the algorithm—$O(1)$.

**5. a.** The $n^3\log_2 n$ term dominates and this is $O(n^3\log_2 n)$.
   **b.** The $4^n$ exponential term will (eventually) dominate any polynomial terms. Thus this is $O(4^n)$.
   **c.** The $2^n$ exponential term will (eventually) dominate any polynomial terms. Thus this is $O(2^n)$.

**7.** For this small set of integers, the trace of the insertion sort is

| | | | | | | | | | |
|---|---|---|---|---|---|---|---|---|---|
| 20 | | 20 | | 20 | | 20 | | 10 |
| 30 | | 30* | | 30 | | 30 | | 20 |
| 40 | | 40 | | 40* | | 40 | | 30 |
| 50 | | 50 | | 50 | | 50* | | 40 |
| 10 | | 10 | | 10 | | 10 | | 50 |

The inner loop of the insertion sort is "shut off" after one comparison for each value of K, until the "bottom" 10 is reached. At that point, four swaps are required to move it into the "top" position. For this almost ordered data, the insertion sort is $O(n)$.

**9.** Since $n^2$ dominates $n^2 + \log_2 n$, $O(n^2 + \log_2 n)$ is the same as $O(n^2)$. Hence, we have the following answers for a—d.

**a.** You are both correct for any algorithm whose performance is dominated by a term such as $n^k$ for $k \geq 2$ or $a^n$ for any base a > 1.

**b.** You are both wrong for any linear or logarithmic algorithm.

**c.** No.

**d.** No.

Section 1.4

**1.**

|     | K=1 J=1 | K=1 J=2 | K=1 J=3 | K=1 J=4 | K=1 J=5 | K=1 J=6 |
|-----|---------|---------|---------|---------|---------|---------|
| 1   | 2       | 2       | 2       | 2       | 2       | 2       |
| 2   | 1       | 3       | 3       | 3       | 3       | 3       |
| 3   | 3       | 1       | 4       | 4       | 4       | 4       |
| 4   | 4       | 4       | 1       | 5       | 5       | 5       |
| 5   | 5       | 5       | 5       | 1       | 6       | 6       |
| 6   | 6       | 6       | 6       | 6       | 1       | 7       |
| 7   | 7       | 7       | 7       | 7       | 7       | 1       |

| K=2 J=1 | K=2 J=2 | K=2 J=3 | K=2 J=4 | K=2 J=5 |
|---------|---------|---------|---------|---------|
| 3       | 3       | 3       | 3       | 3       |
| 2       | 2       | 2       | 2       | 2       |
| 4       | 4       | 5       | 5       | 5       |
| 5       | 5       | 4       | 6       | 6       |
| 6       | 6       | 6       | 4       | 7       |
| 7       | 7       | 7       | 7       | 4       |
| 1       | 1       | 1       | 1       | 1       |

| K=3 J=1 | K=3 J=2 | K=3 J=3 | K=3 J=4 |
|---------|---------|---------|---------|
| 3       | 3       | 3       | 3       |
| 2       | 5       | 5       | 5       |
| 5       | 2       | 2       | 2       |
| 6       | 6       | 6       | 7       |
| 7       | 7       | 7       | 6       |
| 4       | 4       | 4       | 4       |
| 1       | 1       | 1       | 1       |

| K=4 J=1 | K=4 J=2 | K=4 J=3 |
|---------|---------|---------|
| 3       | 3       | 3       |
| 5       | 5       | 5       |
| 2       | 2       | 7       |
| 7       | 7       | 2       |
| 6       | 6       | 6       |
| 4       | 4       | 4       |
| 1       | 1       | 1       |

| K=5 J=1 | K=5 J=2 |
|---------|---------|
| 3       | 3       |
| 5       | 7       |
| 7       | 5       |
| 2       | 2       |
| 6       | 6       |
| 4       | 4       |
| 1       | 1       |

| K=6 J=1 |
|---------|
| 7       |
| 3       |
| 5       |
| 2       |
| 6       |
| 4       |
| 1       |

3. Ten passes would be made through the outer **while** loop of the radix sort algorithm because the length of the longest data it em is ten characters. It is assumed that strings are padded with space beyond their last alphabetical character.

**Pass 0:**
List: CHOCOLATE VANILLA CARAMEL PEACH STRAWBERRY CHERRY

**Pass 1:**
Bins: Space: CHOCOLATE VANILLA CARAMEL PEACH CHERRY
   Y: STRAWBERRY
List: CHOCOLATE VANILLA CARAMEL PEACH CHERRY STRAWBERRY

**Pass 2:**
Bins: Space: VANILLA CARAMEL PEACH CHERRY
   E: CHOCOLATE
   R: STRAWBERRY
List: VANILLA CARAMEL PEACH CHERRY CHOCOLATE STRAWBERRY

**Pass 3:**
Bins: Space: VANILLA CARAMEL PEACH CHERRY
   R: STRAWBERRY
   T: CHOCOLATE
List: VANILLA CARAMEL PEACH CHERRY STRAWBERRY CHOCOLATE

**Pass 4:**
Bins: Space: PEACH CHERRY
   A: VANILLA CHOCOLATE
   E: STRAWBERRY
   L: CARAMEL
List: PEACH CHERRY VANILLA CHOCOLATE STRAWBERRY CARAMEL

**Pass 5:**
Bins: Space: PEACH
   B: STRAWBERRY
   E: CARAMEL
   L: VANILLA CHOCOLATE
   Y: CHERRY
List: PEACH STRAWBERRY CARAMEL VANILLA CHOCOLATE CHERRY

**Pass 6:**
Bins: H: PEACH
   L: VANILLA
   M: CARAMEL
   O: CHOCOLATE
   R: CHERRY
   W: STRAWBERRY
List: PEACH VANILLA CARAMEL CHOCOLATE CHERRY STRAWBERRY

**Pass 7:**
Bins: A: CARAMEL STRAWBERRY
   C: PEACH CHOCOLATE
   I: VANILLA
   R: CHERRY
List: CARAMEL STRAWBERRY PEACH CHOCOLATE VANILLA CHERRY

**Pass 8:**
Bins: A: PEACH
   E: CHERRY
   N: VANILLA
   O: CHOCOLATE
   R: CARAMEL STRAWBERRY
List: PEACH CHERRY VANILLA CHOCOLATE CARAMEL STRAWBERRY

**Pass 9:**
Bins: A: VANILLA CARAMEL
    E: PEACH
    H: CHERRY CHOCOLATE
    T: STRAWBERRY
List: VANILLA CARAMEL PEACH CHERRY CHOCOLATE STRAWBERRY

**Pass 10:**
Bins: C: CARAMEL CHERRY CHOCOLATE
    P: PEACH
    S: STRAWBERRY
    V: VANILLA
List: CARAMEL CHERRY CHOCOLATE PEACH STRAWBERRY VANILLA

5. An application in which the array of data items consumed all available memory would not have the space necessary to store the array of pointers.

7. Although the introduction of pointers into the bubble sort routine will not improve its $O(n^2)$ nature, there will most likely be an increase in run-time efficiency. This is because physical swapping of data is drastically reduced. If the data to be swapped were records with numerous fields of records themselves, many machine operations would be involved. But with pointers, only integers need be swapped, involving many fewer machine operations.

9. The pointer strategy would have the least effect on selection sort, because it guarantees a fewer number of data exchanges (only one per outer loop iteration) than either of the other sorts. Since the pointer sort affects the efficiency of data exchanges, and since fewer swaps are made with selection sort, less overall time is saved with selection sort than with the other two sorting algorithms; these sorting algorithms swap more often, and would therefore benefit more significantly from improved swapping efficiency.

11.
```
// Function: pointer_selection_sort
// Selection sort logic using pointers
//
// Inputs: a list of data values, a list of pointers,
//         and n, the logical size of the list
// Output: the list of pointers pointing to sorted data
void pointer_selection_sort(list_type list,
    int_array pointers, int n)
{
    int min_position, temp;

    for (int k = 0; k < n - 2; ++k)
    {
        min_position = pointer[k];
        for (int j = k + 1; j < n - 1; ++j)
            if (list[pointer[j]].get_key() <
                list[min_position].get_key())
                min_position = pointer[j];
        temp = pointer[k];
        pointer[k] = pointer[min_position];
        pointer[mid_position] = temp;
    }
}
```

13.
```
// Function: digit
// Determine the kth digit of a number
//
// Inputs: integers number and k
// Output: the kth digit of number
int digit(int number, int k)
{
    int p = pow(10, k);
    int q = pow(10, k - 1);
    return (number - p * (number / p)) / q;
}
```

**Section 1.5**

1. Initial array with **low, high,** and **middle = (high + low) / 2. target** is 43. **found** is FALSE to begin.

| Low | | | | Mid | | | | High | |
|---|---|---|---|---|---|---|---|---|---|
| 0 | 1 | 2 | 3 | 4 | 5 | 6 | 7 | 8 | 9 |
| 18 | 40 | 46 | 50 | 52 | 58 | 63 | 70 | 77 | 90 |

| Low | Mid | | High | | | | | | |
|---|---|---|---|---|---|---|---|---|---|
| 0 | 1 | 2 | 3 | 4 | 5 | 6 | 7 | 8 | 9 |
| 18 | 40 | 46 | 50 | 52 | 58 | 63 | 70 | 77 | 90 |

| | | Mid | | | | | | | |
|---|---|---|---|---|---|---|---|---|---|
| | | Low | High | | | | | | |
| 0 | 1 | 2 | 3 | 4 | 5 | 6 | 7 | 8 | 9 |
| 18 | 40 | 46 | 50 | 52 | 58 | 63 | 70 | 77 | 90 |

Since 43 < 52, **high** points to 3.
Since 43 > 40, **low** points to 2.
Since 43 < 46, **high** points to 1 and the search ends with **found = FALSE.**

3. A symbol table is a list of the identifiers that have been declared in a program and which the compiler continually searches as the program is compiled. Since the sequential search is O($n$), the continual searching of the symbol table uses up too much time to be practical.

5. 21 or fewer times.

7. This version of the binary search will work correctly provided the variable **n** never comes in as 0 (indicating an empty list). In this situation, **middle** will be computed to be 0, which will generate an array index out-of-range error.

11. Although still O($n$) in its efficiency, the code for this version of the algorithm can reduce the number of comparisons by a factor of 2. This is because we need not test for the sentinel and the target data each time through the loop.

## CHAPTER 2

Section 2.1

1. Characteristics of the software engineering approach to system development are

   - Analysis of the situation (interviews, observations, research, and so on).
   - Design of a solution (beginning with a completely abstract non-physical design).
   - Construction of a model (to anticipate various construction problems).
   - Construction of actual solution.
   - Maintenance.

**3.**

```
                          MEMORANDUM
    TO: Recalcitrant Team Member
  FROM: Dedicated Software Engineer
    RE: Tactful note defending software engineering
        principles


As a dedicated team member whose paycheck depends on
''getting it done'' on time, I am as committed as you to
meeting the deadlines set forth for this project. At the
same time, I do not care to fall prey to the unreliable,
inelegant methods of our predecessors in this company,
whose lack of planning often resulted in software
products with serious flaws—flaws that ended up costing
this company dearly. Let me offer two sound reasons why
delving into the details of Pascal code without a
conceptual model, as you have suggested, would spell
disaster. First, without a conceptual model, our team
would not be able to work as a team. With potentially
differing ideas of the system design, individual members
would inevitably waste time writing pieces of the system
that did not fit together. Moreover, since team members
would not have laid out the system beforehand, they would
not be cognizant of what basic tasks are done frequently
throughout the system. Hence, many lines of redundant
code would be written, thus wasting time as well as
space. Second, what if the final system we've coded
turned out not to work? Flaws that we could have detected
with a conceptual model would not have been discovered
until the system was up and running. And by that time,
all of our hours of coding would have been wasted. In
short, if it is your interest to implement a reliable,
working system—and to do so on time—creating a conceptual
design simply cannot be avoided. Although it may seem
like a waste of time initially, it will more than pay for
itself in the end by ensuring that our final system has
the best design possible, and is reliable enough to
deserve the trust our company will need to place in it.
Our team will meet at 9:00 a.m. tomorrow morning to begin
carving out a conceptual design. We hope to see you
there.
```

Section 2.2

**3.** Because the keys are physically ordered in the array, we can do a binary search for the position where we should insert the new key. The search process will thus be logarithmic. However, the data movement required to make room for the new value in the array will still be linear, so the overall behavior of the algorithm will still be linear.

**5.** The answer to this problem is the same as the answer to Exercise 3.

Section 2.3

**3.** The formal specification of the operations for an ordered collection follows:

---

**Create operation**

Preconditions: The ordered collection is in an unpredictable state.

Postconditions: Memory is reserved for an ordered collection object capable of storing **MAX_ARRAY_SIZE** data elements, and length is set to 0.

**Length operation**

Preconditions: The receiver is an ordered collection object, appropriately initialized.

Postconditions: The value of length is returned.

**Subscript operation**

Preconditions: The receiver is an ordered collection object, appropriately initialized, length must be greater than 0, and the index parameter is an integer value in the range $0 <=$ **index < length**.

Postconditions: The location of the data element, which can be used either to reference or to store a value, is returned.

**Assignment operation**

Preconditions: The receiver is an ordered collection object in an unpredictable state. The parameter is an ordered collection object, appropriately initialized.

Postconditions: The contents of the parameter object, from position 0 to position **length – 1**, are copied into the receiver object, and the receiver's length is set to the parameter's length.

**Equality operation**

Preconditions: The receiver is an ordered collection object, appropriately initialized. The parameter is an ordered collection object, appropriately initialized. Objects in the ordered collection can be compared using a standard equality operation.

Postconditions: Returns TRUE if the two collections are the same length and each pair of objects in the two collections are equal, and FALSE otherwise.

**Add last operation**

Preconditions: The receiver is an ordered collection object, appropriately initialized, the parameter is an **element** object, and **length < MAX_ARRAY_SIZE**.

Postconditions: **length** is incremented by one, and the parameter element is placed in the last position in the ordered collection.

**Remove last operation**

Preconditions: The receiver is an ordered collection object, appropriately initialized, and **length > 0**.

Postconditions: **length** is decremented by one, and the last data element in the ordered collection is returned.

**Add first operation**

Preconditions: The receiver is an ordered collection object, appropriately initialized, the parameter is an **element** object, and **length < MAX_ARRAY_SIZE**.

Postconditions: **length** is incremented by one, the data elements in the ordered collection are shifted up by one index position, and the parameter element is placed in the first position in the ordered collection.

**Remove first operation**

Preconditions: The receiver is an ordered collection object, appropriately initialized, and **length > 0**.

Postconditions: **length** is decremented by one, the data elements in the ordered collection that come after the first element are shifted down by one index position, and the first element in the ordered collection is returned.

**Remove operation**

Preconditions: The receiver is an ordered collection object, appropriately initialized, the parameter is the data element to be removed, the parameter must equal an element currently in the list, and **length** is greater than zero.

Postconditions: **length** is decremented by one, and the data elements in the ordered collection that come after the parameter element are shifted down by one index position.

**Section 2.4**

**3.** The abstract specification of operations on a three-key table is

---

**Create operation**
Preconditions:    Receiver is an arbitrary three-key table in an unpredictable state.
Postconditions:    Receiver is initialized to an empty table.

**Empty operation**
Precondition:    Receiver is a three-key table.
Postcondition:    If receiver contains no objects, the Boolean value TRUE is returned; otherwise, the Boolean value FALSE is returned.

**Store operation**
Preconditions:    Receiver is a three-key table. **key1** is the key1 value. **key2** is the key2 value. **key3** is the key3 value. **item** is an object to be inserted in receiver. If **key1, key2**, and **key3** do not specify an item already in the table, there is memory available to store **item**.
Postconditions:    If an object is already associated with **key1, key2**, and **key3** in the table, it is replaced by item. Otherwise, the table has **item** inserted and associated with the key1, key2, and key3 values.

**Remove operation**
Preconditions:    Receiver is a two-key table. **key1, key2**, and **key3** are the key values associated with an object to be removed from the table.
Postconditions:    If the object with the key values **key1, key2**, and **key3** can be found in the table, it is removed from the table, **item** contains the object associated with the key values **key1, key2**, and **key3**, and the operation returns TRUE. Otherwise, the operation returns FALSE, **item's** contents are undefined, and the table is left unchanged.

**Retrieve operation**
Preconditions:    Receiver is a two-key table. **key1, key2**, and **key3** are the key values associated with an object to be found in the table.
Postconditions:    If the pairing of **key1, key2**, and **key3** can be found in table, then item contains the object associated with **key1, key2**, and **key3** and the operation returns TRUE. Otherwise, the operation returns FALSE, and item's contents are undefined. In either case, the table is left unchanged.

---

# CHAPTER 3

**Section 3.1**

**3.** Here is one possible way to depict the flow of information:

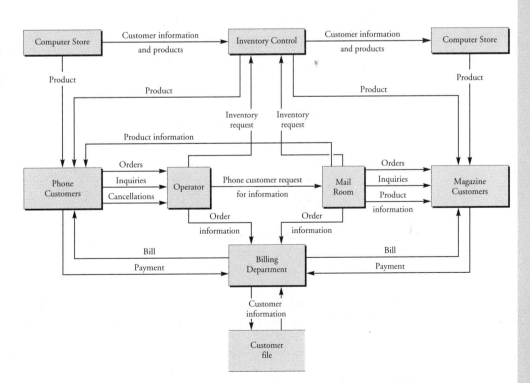

**Section 3.2**

1. A module that is functionally cohesive performs exactly one predefined task and does it without unexpected outcomes.
3. Since one of the modules performs two tasks, the system is not functionally cohesive. A better design would be

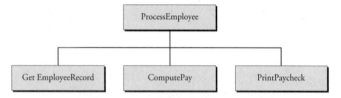

5. Using global variables is a poor strategy from a data coupling perspective because one function might corrupt the data needed by other functions.
7. Data flow diagrams and modular structure charts are similar in that both are used as devices to partition the system logically in to a set of subcomponents, each with a well-defined, specific task. The fundamental difference between these two modeling tools lies in the way in which each depicts the interaction among system subcomponents. Data flow diagrams present the system's subcomponents as a (more or less) linear sequence of modules through which system data flow and by which they are processed; modular structure charts present the system as a hierarchy depicting relationships among high-level (boss) and low-level (worker) modules. Thus, modular structure charts more accurately represent how the system will be designed in a computer language; they constitute the next logical refinement of the system in its evolution from abstraction to implementation.

Section 3.3

1. In the analysis phase, the system analyst, through interviews, inspections, observations, and so on reports what the user's needs are. In the design phase, the designer studies the analyst's report and designs a solution for the user. In the coding phase, the programmer codes the design provided by the design phase. In the testing phase, the system is checked for performance under varying conditions, especially boundary conditions in the data being used. In the maintenance phase, the system is modified and updated to meet changing user needs and/or to correct errors in the system.
3. A robust module is one that does not "bomb" when it receives invalid data. If every module in a system were completely robust, the system would most likely be too slow to be of practical use: too much time would be consumed by each module in checking to make certain that the data it received were valid.
7. Test data for **read_real** could be as follows. (Note that a space is indicated by "_".)

| Val | Rationale | Expected Results |
|---|---|---|
| _00.000 | a form of 0 | valid |
| 0.0 | a form of 0 | valid |
| –0.0 | a form of 0 | valid |
| +0 | a form of 0 | valid |
| 5.356 | "conventional" number | valid |
| 0.002 | "conventional" number | valid |
| _.05 | nothing left of decimal | valid |
| 0_5_.703 | spaces between digits | invalid |
| 56 | no decimal | valid |
| 75. | unguarded decimal | valid |
| . | decimal only | invalid |
| –7 | – without decimal | valid |
| –.5 | unguarded decimal | valid |
| +7 | + without decimal | valid |
| Hi.there | test a string | invalid |
| –. | test no digit case | invalid |
| +. | test no digit case | invalid |
| –_5.7 | test space trailing sign | valid |

Note that the current algorithm would accept "–.", ".", and "+." all of which would be invalid numbers.

**11.** Note that this finite state machine accepts digits only in the string before the '.'; in the extension, only letters and the underscore are acceptable (including the '_' immediately following the '.'). The associated function follows:

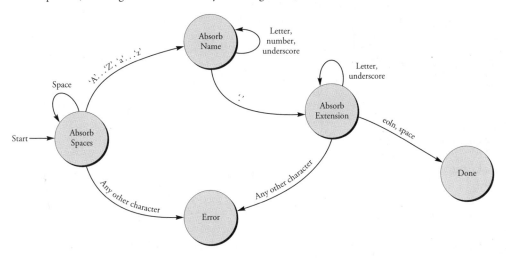

Section 3.4

**3.** It could. Proofs of correctness do not take into account the limitations of a particular machine. Factors such as rounding errors in arithmetic computation, faulty user input, and exceeding the overflow and underflow cutoffs for numeric storage can all cause a "proven" algorithm to fail.

## CHAPTER 4

Section 4.1

**1.** The array involved in the pointer sort of Chapter 1 is not a linked list because its cells do not store links (to other array cells) that indicate the order in which the cells are to be traversed (the pointer array is always traversed sequentially). Instead, the pointers stored in the pointer array serve as indices to cells in a separate array (which contains the real data of interest).

**3.** With respect to search efficiency, both the linked list and unordered array implementations provide $O(n)$ access to list nodes; both require a sequential search. However, whereas both implementations require $O(n)$ comparisons to find a node, the linked list strategy requires only $O(1)$ data exchanges actually to delete the node. Compare this to the $O(n)$ exchanges needed by the array implementation. With respect to add efficiency, the linked list implementation strategy is at a disadvantage, requiring $O(n)$ operations to find a node's rightful place in the list, and $O(1)$ operations actually to insert it. The unordered array, on the other hand, provides $O(1)$ add efficiency, since nodes are always added to the end of the array. With respect to sort efficiency, the linked list is maintained in sequential order, so no sort is required to traverse it sequentially. In contrast, the unordered array requires an $O(n^2)$ pointer sort before it can be traversed sequentially. Here, the linked list strategy is at an advantage.

**5.**
```
void print_sqrt(int &x)
{
    cout << sqrt(x);
}
```

**7.**
```
int position_of_first_zero(linked_list<int> &list)
{
    int data, position;
    boolean found = FALSE;

    if (list.empty())
        return 0;
    else
    {
        list.first();
        position = 1;
        while (! found && (position <= list.length()))
```

```
        {
            list.retrieve(data);
            if (data == 0)
                found = TRUE;
            else
            {
                ++position;
                list.next();
            }
        }
        if (found)
            return position;
        else
            return 0;
    }
}
9. int sum(linked_list<int> &list)
{
    int total, data;
    boolean found;
    total = 0;
    list.first();
    found = list.retrieve(data);
    while (found)
    {
        total = total + data;
        list.next();
        found = list.retrieve(data);
    }
    return total;
}
11. template <class E>
    void append(linked_list<E> &a,
        linked_list<E> &b)
    {
        int data;
        boolean found;

        a.first();
        while (! a.at_end())
            a.next();
        a.next();
        b.first();
        found = b.remove(data);
        while (found)
        {
            a.insert(data);
            a.next();
            found = b.remove(data);
        }
    }
```

Section 4.2

1. **a.**, **d.**, and **f.** are syntactically correct.
   **b.** Incorrect—cannot assign an integer to a pointer variable.
   **c.** Incorrect—cannot use a type name to refer to a member of a structure.
   **e.** Incorrect—cannot delete an integer.

3. `a->next->next = b;`
   effects the deletion of the second node.

5. `a->next->next->next->next = a;`
   `a = a->next;`
   `a->next->next->next->next = NULL;`

Section 4.4

1. The traverse operation uses a pointer sort, which is $O(n^2)$, to prepare the list of pointers for the traversal. The traversal itself is then $O(n)$. Thus, the overall efficiency of the operation is $O(n^2)$.

# CHAPTER 5

Section 5.1

1.

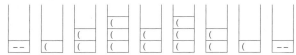

| S | S<br>Push(S,4) | S<br>Push(S,10) | S<br>Push(S,12) | S<br>Pop(S,Item) | S<br>Push(S,3∗Item) | S<br>Item := Ontop(S) | S<br>Push(S,3∗Item) |

5. The stack would grow and shrink as follows:

9. Because the new stack declaration contains a linked list as a data member, the copy constructor, assignment operation, and destructor will be considerably simplified. Specifically, the copy constructor and the assignment operation merely use the assignment operator to copy the values of the data members from the parameter object to the receiver object. No destructor is in fact necessary, because the destructor for the linked list data member will be run automatically when a stack object goes out of scope. In short, using a linked list as a data member entirely relieves the implementer of the stack class of the need to access the implementation details of the linked list class.

Section 5.2

**1.** Infix: A+B*C-D/P-R
Postfix: ABCD-PR-/*+
Prefix: +A*B/-CD-PD

**3.**

| Ch | OpStack | Postfix | Commentary |
|----|---------|---------|------------|
| # |  |  | Push # |
| P |  |  | Read Ch |
|  |  | P | Append Ch to Postfix |
| + |  |  | Read Ch |
|  | +<br># |  | Push Ch |
| ( |  |  | Read Ch |
|  | +<br>(<br># |  | Push Ch |
| Q |  |  | Read Ch |
|  |  | PQ | Append Ch to Postfix |
| – |  |  | Read Ch |
|  | –<br>(<br>+<br># |  | Push Ch |
| F |  |  | Read Ch |
|  |  | PQF | Append Ch |
| ) |  | Read Ch |  |
|  | +<br># | PQF– | Pop and Append |
| / |  |  | Read Ch |
|  | /<br>+<br># |  | Push Ch |
| Y |  |  | Read Ch |
|  |  | PQF–Y | Append Ch |
| # |  |  | Read Ch |
|  |  | PQF–Y/+# | Pop and Append rest of stack |

**9.** If operand 'A' has a stack priority that is greater than or equal to the infix priority of operand 'B,' then 'A' has equal or greater operator precedence; therefore, it is appended to the postfix string before B, and will be applied before B. Such precedence, however, can be overridden by parentheses, which force the operators between them to be unconditionally appended to the postfix string, regardless of their stack priority. In summary, the order in which operators are appended to the postfix string is dictated by stack priority relative to infix priority; equal or greater stack priority indicates either higher operator precedence (if the two operators being compared are different) or left-associativity, if the two operators being compared are the same. Hence, if we want to make the 'operator' right associative, we merely make its infix priority greater than its stack priority. Our infix and stack priority functions would then appear as follows:

| Priority: | * | / | + | – | ( | ) | ^ | # |
|-----------|---|---|---|---|---|---|---|---|
| Infix | 2 | 2 | 1 | 1 | 5 | 0 | 4 | 0 |
| Stack | 2 | 2 | 1 | 1 | 0 | undefined | 3 | 0 |

The adjusted infix and stack priorities reflect both the fact that exponentiation has the highest operator precedence, and the fact that all operators except exponentiation are left-associative.

Section 5.3

**3. a.** Introduce an integer variable **minutes_idle**, which is initialized to 0 before entering the **for** loop. We then add the following **ELSE** clause to the **IF ((time_left_on_car == 0) && car_queue.empty())** clause:

```
else if ((time_left_on_car == 0) && car_queue.empty())
    //This minute is idle
    ++minutes_idle;
```

**b.** To make this count, we merely dequeue the **car_queue** until it is empty after we have exited the **for** loop. In C++, this amounts to introducing an integer variable **cars_remaining**, which we initialize to zero before dequeuing begins:

```
int cars_remaining = 0;
```

Now we are prepared to execute a **while** loop:

```
while (! car_queue.empty())
{
    minute = car_queue.dequeue();
    ++cars_remaining;
}
```

## CHAPTER 6

Section 6.1

**3. a.** 92
6
14
**b.** 14
6
92

Note, however, that because this function neglects to test **list** for being NULL before referencing **list**, the program may behave mysteriously at run time.

**c.** 14
6

Note that because this function neglects to test **list** itself for being NULL before it references **list->next**, the program may behave mysteriously at run time when the empty list is passed in for **list**.

**5.** Program (a) will achieve the original intent presented. Its output is

**MADAM**

Program (b) will fail because it globally declares the characters being read so the recursive calls do not result in copies of the characters being pushed onto the system stack. Consequently, only the last character read is remembered and written when the recursion unwinds. Its output is

**MMMMM**

**7.** This function computes the smallest value in **number_array** within the subrange 1 .. *n*, where *n* is the value originally passed in.

Section 6.2

**5.** The output is as follows:

```
1 16
9 16
9 11
9 16
```

7. The stack frames for this function should contain three pieces of information: The current value of M, the current value of N, and the point in the program to which to return.

|                |
|----------------|
| m=1, n=3, RP 1 |

(1)

|                |
|----------------|
| m=1, n=3, RP 3 |
| m=1, n=3, RP 1 |

(2)

|                |
|----------------|
| m=1, n=2, RP 3 |
| m=1, n=3, RP 3 |
| m=1, n=3, RP 1 |

(3)

|                |
|----------------|
| m=1, n=1, RP 3 |
| m=1, n=2, RP 3 |
| m=1, n=3, RP 3 |
| m=1, n=3, RP 1 |

(4)

|                |
|----------------|
| m=1, n=1, RP 2 |
| m=1, n=1, RP 3 |
| m=1, n=2, RP 3 |
| m=1, n=3, RP 3 |
| m=1, n=3, RP 1 |

(5)

|                |
|----------------|
| m=1, n=1, RP 4 |
| m=1, n=2, RP 3 |
| m=1, n=3, RP 3 |
| m=1, n=3, RP 2 |

(6)

|                |
|----------------|
| m=1, n=2, RP 4 |
| m=1, n=3, RP 3 |
| m=1, n=3, RP 2 |

(7)

|                |
|----------------|
| m=1, n=2, RP 4 |
| m=1, n=3, RP 2 |

(8)

|       |
|-------|
| EMPTY |

(9)

The output is as follows:

```
1 3
1 2
1 1
1 0
0 1
0 2
0 3
0 4
5
```

11. *Hint:* Consider the number of ways that M can be broken down into quarters and dimes plus the number of ways that (M = 50 cents) can be broken down into half dollars, quarters, and dimes. The total of these two provide the answer in terms of quantities that are (recursively) easier to compute.

Section 6.3

5. The output is as follows:

```
12  1  2  3  4  3  3  4
 4  3  4  2  2  3  4  3
 3  4  4  3  4  3  2  3
 4  3  3  4  4  3  4  4
 2  3  4  3  3  4  4  3
 4
```

# CHAPTER 7

Section 7.1

1.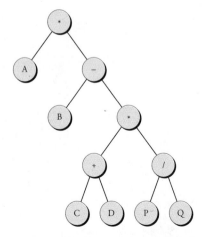

**3.** A tree is a hierarchically ordered data structure consisting of nodes and links to nodes. A tree is accessed by a node called the root.

**5. a.** and **c.** are binary trees with the heap property.

   **b.** is not, because the node containing 35 is a subtree of the node containing 19. Similar situation for the node containing 39.

**9. a.**

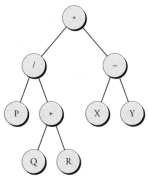

   **c.**

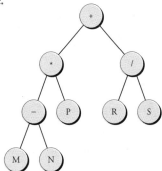

## Section 7.2

**17.** As each node is visited during the traversal, its data contents are placed at the logical end of the structure (an array or file, perhaps) or device (output on a terminal screen, perhaps). At the end of the traversal, the data will appear in sorted order in the destination structure or on the destination device.

## Section 7.3

**1. a.** is full.

   **b.** and **c.** are not full.

**5. b.**

## Section 7.4

**1.**

| Item | 1 | 2 | 3 | 4 | 5 | 6 | 7 | 8 | 9 | 10 |
|------|-----|-----|-----|-----|-----|-----|-----|-----|-----|-----|
| 10 | 10 | | | | | | | | | |

| Item | 1 | 2 | 3 | 4 | 5 | 6 | 7 | 8 | 9 | 10 |
|------|-----|-----|-----|-----|-----|-----|-----|-----|-----|-----|
| 20 | 20 | 10 | | | | | | | | |

| Item | 1 | 2 | 3 | 4 | 5 | 6 | 7 | 8 | 9 | 10 |
|------|-----|-----|-----|-----|-----|-----|-----|-----|-----|-----|
| 30 | 30 | 10 | 20 | | | | | | | |

| Item | 1 | 2 | 3 | 4 | 5 | 6 | 7 | 8 | 9 | 10 |
|------|-----|-----|-----|-----|-----|-----|-----|-----|-----|-----|
| 40 | 40 | 30 | 20 | 10 | | | | | | |

| Item | 1 | 2 | 3 | 4 | 5 | 6 | 7 | 8 | 9 | 10 |
|------|-----|-----|-----|-----|-----|-----|-----|-----|-----|-----|
| 50 | 50 | 40 | 20 | 10 | 30 | | | | | |

| Item | 1 | 2 | 3 | 4 | 5 | 6 | 7 | 8 | 9 | 10 |
|------|-----|-----|-----|-----|-----|-----|-----|-----|-----|-----|
| 60 | 60 | 40 | 50 | 10 | 30 | 20 | | | | |

| Item | 1 | 2 | 3 | 4 | 5 | 6 | 7 | 8 | 9 | 10 |
|------|-----|-----|-----|-----|-----|-----|-----|-----|-----|-----|
| 70 | 70 | 40 | 60 | 10 | 30 | 20 | 50 | | | |

| Item | 1 | 2 | 3 | 4 | 5 | 6 | 7 | 8 | 9 | 10 |
|------|-----|-----|-----|-----|-----|-----|-----|-----|-----|-----|
| 80 | 80 | 70 | 60 | 40 | 30 | 20 | 50 | 10 | | |

| Item | 1 | 2 | 3 | 4 | 5 | 6 | 7 | 8 | 9 | 10 |
|------|-----|-----|-----|-----|-----|-----|-----|-----|-----|-----|
| 90 | 90 | 80 | 60 | 70 | 30 | 20 | 50 | 10 | 40 | |

| Item | 1 | 2 | 3 | 4 | 5 | 6 | 7 | 8 | 9 | 10 |
|------|-----|-----|-----|-----|-----|-----|-----|-----|-----|-----|
| 100 | 100 | 90 | 60 | 70 | 80 | 20 | 50 | 10 | 40 | 30 |

Section 7.5

**1.** The indentation can be obtained by increasing the indentation before traversing the left (child) subtree and decreasing the indentation again before traversing the right (sibling) subtree.

**3.** Preorder traversal

```
P Q T U V C D E
M N O W A G B H
I J X K L
```

Section 7.6

**1.** The order of the nodes would be Seattle, Chicago, Miami, New Orleans, Dallas, New York, Washington, Milwaukee, Phoenix, San Francisco, Los Angeles, Las Vegas, Minneapolis, Oklahoma City.

**3.** One way the cities could be visited is as follows: Seattle, Chicago, San Francisco, Miami, New Orleans, Las Vegas, Milwaukee, Los Angeles, Dallas, Washington, Phoenix, Minneapolis, New York City, Oklahoma City.

**9.** Eliminating the requirement that **node** be a subrange of an ordinal type would mean that there would not be a convenient way to index the nodes in the graph, making the normal operations more difficult to perform. One strategy to overcome that problem would be to build an indexing scheme that would make use of a two-key table.

# CHAPTER 8

Section 8.1

**1.** 60   12   90   20   64    8    6 8   12    6   20   64   90   60 6   12
     8   20   60   90   64 6    8   12   20   60   64   90

**3.** The shell sort is named after its inventor D. L. Shell.

**5.** Relatively prime values of the increments are better because they insure distinct increments that will not divide evenly into each other so that data that have been compared to each other are less likely to be compared again.

**7.** The best case for the shell sort algorithm presented in this section would be a data set with the data already in order: each segment would be in order and no data would be swapped. The worst case would be a data set arranged in descending order because every data element would be out of order and there would be a maximum number of data swaps.

Section 8.2

**1.** The output would be as follows:
```
1    7
60 12 90 30 64 8 6

  1  4
  6 12 8 30

  2  4
12 8 30

  2  2
  8

  4  4
30

  6  7
64 90

  7  7
90
```

**3.** The bubble sort is better than the quick sort when the data are already in order. The bubble sort can safely conclude that the data are in order after the first pass through the data; the quick sort must perform the entire sort even if the data are already in order.

5. The choice of the pivotal point will not change the overall efficiency of the quick sort; however, it does dramatically change the best and worst data sets.

9. All of the quick sort function would remain the same as in the book. One line in the partition function would change from

```
pivot := key[low];
```

to

```
// Assume that median gives the median of three values.
pivot := median(key[low], key[low + high] / 2,
    key[high]);
```

This variation should be more efficient because the pivot value is more likely to split the array being sorted more evenly. Quick sort is most efficient when the array is split at the midpoint.

Section 8.3

1. 
```
60  12  90  30  64   8   6
60  12  90  30  64   8   6
60  64  90  30  12   8   6
 6  64  60  30  12   8  90
 8  30  60   6  12  64  90
12  30   8   6  60  64  90
 6  12   8  30  60  64  90
 8   6  12  30  60  64  90
 6   8  12  30  60  64  90
```

3. The sort derives its name from the heap structure that it uses in sorting the data.

5. The heap sort is not always as efficient as the quick sort. On average, the quick sort is slightly better than the heap sort because its big-O constant of proportionality will be smaller. However, the heap sort handles data already sorted much faster than the quick sort.

Section 8.4

1. The output for **merge_sort** would be
```
  1   7
60  12  90  30  64  8  6

  1   4
60  12  90  30

  1   2
60  12

  1  1
60

  2   2
60  12

  2   2
60  12
```
and so on . . .

# CHAPTER 9

Section 9.1

**1. a.** Record No.   Key

| Record No. | Key |
|---|---|
| 0 | 333 |
| 1 | 632 |
| 2 | 1090 |
| 3 | 459 |
| 4 | 379 |
| 5 | 238 |
| 6 | |
| 7 | |
| 8 | |
| 9 | 1982 |
| 10 | 3411 |

The keys would have the following positions:

**c.** With the chaining method, the keys and links would be

| Record No. | Key | Link | | Record No. | Key | Link |
|---|---|---|---|---|---|---|
| 0 | 333 | 13 | | 11 | 3411 | 13 |
| 1 | 632 | 0 | | 12 | 459 | 0 |
| 2 | 1090 | 0 | | 13 | 379 | 14 |
| 3 | | | | 14 | 238 | 0 |
| 4 | | | | 15 | | |
| 5 | | | | 16 | | |
| 6 | | | | 17 | | |
| 7 | | | | 18 | | |
| 8 | | | | 19 | | |
| 9 | 1982 | 12 | | 20 | | |
| 10 | | | | 21 | | |

**3. a.** The best method to implement the card catalog in this situation would be hashing. Hashing allows for very quick searches and is fairly good at handling additions and deletions. Since the library rarely prints out an ordered list of books, the time it takes to sort the list doesn't really matter.

**c.** The best method to implement the data base would be the binary search. The states are kept in order by two-letter code. All the program need do is access the record quickly, increment a field, and be able to print the list out in order. All these are handled very well by a binary search.

Section 9.2

**1.** As suggested in the text, the doubly linked list is the best choice for implementing linked lists with hashing. When the order of the list is disturbed during a change of a key field or during a deletion of an item in the list, the linked list must be rebuilt. If a doubly linked list is not used, the list would have to be traversed to find the predecessor node in the linked list. The doubly linked list makes rebuilding lists more efficient.

Section 9.3

**1. a.**

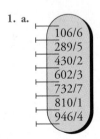

106/6
289/5
430/2
602/3
732/7
810/1
946/4

**5. a.** For the ISAM index, this knowledge will enable us to set the index so that the subsequent search on the disk will be more efficient.

**c.** The trie is constructed the same no matter what the disk structure may be.

# Index